John Newton Harman, Sen.

ANNALS

OF

Tazewell County, Virginia

From 1800 to 1922

IN TWO VOLUMES

By

JOHN NEWTON HARMAN, Sr.

Tazewell, Virginia

Member Virginia Historical Society

VOLUME I—IN TWO PARTS

PART 1

Containing Records of Courts, etc., from 1800 to 1852

PART 2

Containing a Republication of Bickley's History of the "Settlement and Indian Wars of Tazewell County," published 1852

Southern Historical Press, Inc.
Greenville, South Carolina

This volume was reproduced from
An 1922 edition located in the
Publisher's private Library

All rights reserved. No part of this publication may be reproduced,
stored in a retrieval system, transmitted in any form, posted
on to the web in any form or by any means without
the prior written permission of the publisher.

Please direct all correspondence and orders to:

www.southernhistoricalpress.com
or
SOUTHERN HISTORICAL PRESS, Inc.
PO Box 1267
375 West Broad Street
Greenville, SC   29601
southernhistoricalpress@gmail.com

Originally published: Richmond, Virginia, 1922
New material Copyright 2020 by LaBruce Lucas
ISBN #0-89308-955-9
All rights Reserved.
Printed in the United States of America

DEDICATED

To the Memory of the Pioneer Families of Tazewell County, Virginia

They felled the forests; built their cabins; protected their homes from savages; fostered education; believed in, and lived the Christian Religion, thereby leaving to us, their descendants, this priceless heritage.

Preface to Volume One and Announcement of Volume Two

During several years we have been gathering information for the purpose of publishing a Genealogy of the Harman family of Southwest Virginia, and of related families. In pursuance of this purpose, we made inspection of records of the Land Office and the Public Library at Richmond; of the County Court Records of Frederick, Shenandoah, Rockingham, Augusta, Montgomery, Wythe, Smythe, Washington, Giles, Russell and Tazewell Counties.

Later it occurred to us that a similar genealogy of other pioneer families of Tazewell County would be as interesting to their descendants as that of the Harmans and related families is to us. This led us to undertake the publication of the "ANNALS OF TAZEWELL COUNTY" from 1800 to 1922.

We now present to the reader Volume One of the ANNALS OF TAZEWELL COUNTY from 1800 to 1852, which contains extracts from the court records during that period of general public interest and which are of special interest to the descendants of the pioneer families of the county.

During the period covered by Volume One the County of Tazewell embraced the territory now composing the County of Buchanan and parts of Giles and Bland Counties in Virginia, and the County of McDowell and parts of Mercer and Logan Counties in West Virginia.

Volume One, Part 1, contains extracts from court records pertaining to court orders, wills and deeds; the names of all civil and military officers of the county; all lawyers admitted to the bar; all preachers licensed to celebrate the rites of matrimony, and an exact copy of the marriage registers from 1800 to 1852; every deed made to churches of all denominations from 1800 to 1922; the names of all the representatives in the General Assembly of Virginia from 1800 to 1852; the Governors of the State, and a list of Revolutionary pensioners, and various other records in the clerk's office of general interest.

Part 2 of Volume One is a republication of Bickley's History of the "SETTLEMENT AND INDIAN WARS OF TAZEWELL COUNTY," published in 1852. This first history of Tazewell, by Dr. Bickley, is a most valuable volume.

ANNOUNCEMENT.

Volume Two, which will contain an extension of nearly all the features of Volume One, will also embrace, in addition thereto, a list of Confederate soldiers, and a complete roll of the soldiers in the World War who went from Tazewell County. All these records will be brought down to 1922.

A special feature of Volume Two will be a genealogy of old Tazewell families, together with biographical sketches of many who have achieved official professional or industrial distinction in the county; also a list of the incorporated towns in the county, together with the names of the mayors, town sergeants and present population.

Another important feature of Volume Two will be a short history of the beginning and progress of the different religious denominations in the county, provided representatives of the several churches will prepare and furnish these historical sketches.

We have not written a history of Tazewell. We have simply presented history as already officially written in the public records of the county. We have not copied all the records of general public interest, but have selected those most intimately connected with the pioneer families of the county.

J. NEWTON HARMAN, Senior.

Tazewell, Virginia, December, 1922.

Before the Gates of the Wilderness Road

THE SETTLEMENT OF SOUTHWESTERN VIRGINIA.
By Judge Lyman Chalkley

Taken from the Virginia Historical Magazine with permission of the Author.

In speaking of the conditions existing in Virginia and North Carolina immediately preceding the trip of Boone, when he is supposed to have blazed a trail through the mountains to Kentucky, which, after his time, came to be called "The Wilderness Road," Speed, in his history of that road, describes somewhat carefully a thoroughfare and highway from Philadelphia through Winchester, Staunton and other points in the Shenandoah Valley, extending "to an important station at the waters of New River which run to the west. At that point another road which led out from Richmond through the central parts of Virginia intersected the one just described. Thus were brought together two tides of immigrants. Near the forks of the road stood Fort Chissel, a rude blockhouse built in 1758, by Colonel Bird immediately after the British and Americans captured Fort Duquesne from the French." And the same authority says further: "Beside the road which passed along the Valley of Virginia, and the one which ran out from Richmond to the intersection at New River, there were other traveled ways or traces which led up to Cumberland Gap from the Carolinas and through the mountains of East Tennessee." He concludes: "Thus it appears that all the roads from the Atlantic States converged upon the points, Fort Pitt and Cumberland Gap." Of Fort Chissel (Chiswell) he says: "It is a point of great interest in studying the Kentucky immigration. It was there the immigrants reached the borders of the great wilderness. The wild, rough, dangerous part of the journey commenced when New River was crossed at Inglis' Ferry, and the travelers turned squarely toward the setting sun."

Monette tells us, as of the year 1762, "the people from the sources of James were crossing the dividing ridges and descending upon the Greenbrier, New River and other tributaries of Kenhawa. Others from Roanoke and North Carolina were advancing westward upon the sources of the Stanton, Dan, Yadkin, Cataba and Broad, along the eastern base of the Blue Mountains, with wistful eyes upon the beautiful country of the Cherokees." And again Monette says, as of 1767: "Settlements were now advancing rapidly from the eastern portions of Pennsylvania, Maryland and Virginia, and emigrants were pressing forward upon the upper tributaries of the Monongahela and upon the great branches of Cheat River. On the south, the frontier counties of Virginia and North Carolina were pouring forth their hardy pioneers who were still advancing and already settling the fertile regions upon the headwaters of New River, as well as upon the sources of Greenbrier. Others full of enterprise and western adventure were exploiting the country drained by the great branches of Clinch River, and were forming remote, isolated settlements in Powell's Valley, still further north and west, and also upon the waters of the North Fork of Holston, in the regions near the present towns of Abingdon and Wytheville.

"The counties of Rockbridge, Augusta, Greenbrier and Frederick were frontier regions, occupied by a sparse population, exposed to the dangers of savage massacre; the towns of Staunton, Lexington, and Winchester were remote frontier trading posts, inhabited by a few persons, who formed a connecting link between the Indians and the eastern people of Virginia."

So far, the references have been to that portion of the territory which lies within the present borders of the State of Virginia. To the south of the present Virginia-Tennessee line lay a narrow strip running northeast and southwest, mountain and valley, watered by the Holston, Clinch and Powell rivers. This is a continuation of the same fertile valleys and rugged mountains of the Virginia side, where all these rivers have their rise. This district north (that is, west) of the Holston was at first believed to be within the boundaries of Virginia, and settlers acted accordingly. They pre-empted their lands under Virginia laws and protection. They formed the

Watauga Association, according to Phelan, in 1772. He tells us: "But a still more serious trouble was impending over the infant communities. About 1769 Colonel Donelson had made a treaty with the Indians by which Virginia bought what was called the western frontiers. By this treaty, it was supposed that the Watauga region went to that colony. Believing themselves in Virginia, the Watauga people supposed themselves governed by Virginia laws, and looked to that State or colony for protection against Indian aggressions and the raids of horse thieves. North Carolina, herself, took no steps looking to the exercise of any authority over the settlements, many of which had been made in violation of the treaty with the Cherokees at Lochaber in 1770. It had everything to lose and nothing to gain by recognizing them as being on North Carolina territory, which recognition would carry with it the obligation of protecting them against the inroads of the Indians."

These extracts from familiar authorities have been quoted in the hope that through their means would be recalled most readily that portion of the sources of the Ohio which lies in the extreme southwestern corner of the present State of Virginia and the extreme northeastern corner of Tennessee contiguous. This section had been known to the white, and a path marked out by travel certainly fifteen years prior to the earliest date that has been mentioned. It also appears that there was an established traffic over this district between the whites of the eastern settlements and the Cherokees as early as 1740. Heyward is authority for it that: "A Mr. Vaughan, of Amelia County, Virginia, went, in 1740, as a packman with traders to the Cherokees. He found the country west of Amelia sparsely inhabited, the last hunter's cabin he saw was on Otter River, a branch of Stanton (Roanoke) now in Bedford County (which lies east of the Blue Ridge). He described the trading path from Virginia, crossing New River, English's Ferry, Seven Mile Ford on the Holston, Grassy Springs, Nolichucky and the French Broad." In 1741, John Smith, Zachariah Lewis, William Waller, Benjamin Waller, Robert Green and James Patton were granted an order of Council of Virginia for one hundred thousand acres on James River and Roanoke, and extending to and including waters of the Indian or New River. Patton was manager and employed Smith, who was the Colonel John Smith who was captured by Indians and had many experiences which are familiar. These two were occupied in inducing immigration until 1751. Patton eventually bought out all the patentees except Smith and Lewis. These were the worthies of the land in their generation, and many incidents in their careers might be detailed. They were of the Scotch-Irish settlers in the Shenandoah, the centers of which was Augusta County, from whose records the data here presented will be mainly taken. This county was formed in 1745 and until 1769 included all the territory that has been mentioned. The records of the District and Superior Courts having jurisdiction over practically the same territory until nearly 1800 are also there. Prior to 1745 there are perhaps additional data of record in Orange County and at Richmond which have not been carefully examined, but the writer had not had access to them. Perhaps, also, much could be gathered from the files of the courts of Fincastle, Botetourt and Washington counties, which were all erected early from the territory of Augusta, but they are not readily accessible. No doubt, the papers of Lunenburg and other counties adjacent on the east, on the other slope of the Blue Ridge, would contain material and incident. The investigator is confined for the present to the movement of that body already mentioned, who migrated in mass from Pennsylvania into the Shenandoah Valley, blazing the way, settling and cultivating the soil, driving out the Indians, establishing churches and schools and a distinctive civilization, making clear and safe the avenue right up to the very entrance of the wilderness. These hardy, courageous, prudent, foresighted people were fortified and prepared by long tradition of migration and colonization, of coveting the land and driving out the Canaanites. The conditions were somewhat analogous in America and in Ireland. Their historian in Kentucky says: "After the subjugation of Ulster, in the reign of James I, the semi-barbarous natives were replaced by a colony of tenants from Great Britian, attracted thither by liberal grants of land." Smythe says of them: "The more decidedly a man is Presbyterian the more decidedly is he a Republican." Davidson says: "The Presbyterians of Virginia, like the rest of their brethern were marked by an inextinguishable love of liberty, and during the Revolution were staunch Republicans to a man. At the very first meeting of the Presbytery of Hanover after the Declaration of Independence, they sent a memorial to the House of Delegates identifying themselves with the common cause. They presented others in 1777 and 1784, protesting against a general assessment for the support of religion. And still another petition in 1785, signed by 10,000 persons, was argued before the House of Delegates for three days. The main object of all these petitions was to complain of the partial and peculiar privileges still continued to the Episcopal, late the established church and its vestrymen."

The Synod of Philadelphia, before the erection of the Virginia and Transylvania Synods (the Transylvania Synod included the churches and communities in Kentucky) had these worthy people under its immediate charge. The ecclesiastical patriarch of the flock was the Rev. John Craig. He has left a name and character of honor and a memory of worthy service. At an early time he was sent to visit the brethern on New River and Holston. On his return, he reported such a surprisingly large list of elders whom he had ordained in that sparsely settled region, that the Synod remonstrated and asked questions. He defended himself by saying, "Where I cudna get hewn stones, I tuk dornaks." Wherever they established a church they established a school. In 1774 those of the faith established two academies, one Hampden-Sidney, in the eastern, and Liberty Hall (now Washington and Lee University) in the western part of the State, giving each a name indicative of their desire to be free.

The authorities of the colony of Virginia, in looking to the protection of its western frontier, had erected a series of forts on the "Western Waters," as this district was called. There were local stockades were the people gathered in time of peril, at various places. Indeed, nearly every early settlement seems to have been at some time looked upon as the fort of its own immediate vicinity. But they were not continuously occupied for any considerable period by royal troops. Of these, the most prominent was Fort Lewis, a few miles east of the present town of Salem, in Roanoke County. At the time of Colonel Bird's (Byrd's) expedition against the southwestern Indians, this was the frontier settlement of Virginia. In August, 1760, Colonel John Smith, of the Virginia regiment under Byrd, sent out against the Cherokees, was in command at Fort Lewis. Captain John Blagg, commanded a company under Smith. Joseph Ray was contractor and commisary for the army. In 1763, colonization had progressed so far that it was necessary to build a road between New River by Fort Chiswell to Fort Lewis. Notwithstanding the statement from Heyward that this was the frontier settlement in 1759, we should not take it that the country had not been settled before that time; for, in the records of the vestry of Augusta Parish, we find that William Bryan and Jas. Neilley were appointed processioners in 1747 for the country contiguous to the fort.

Vaux's Fort lay on the Roanoke, higher up. In 1756 it had been devastated by Indians and twenty-seven people were killed or taken prisoners. Heyward says that after this massacre there were left no settlers west of the Blue Ridge except a few men who worked at the lead mines. Shortly after Colonel Byrd's expeditions, however, that is in 1763, John Smyth, William Grymes, James Nealey and Israel Christian were appointed to view the roads that led from Vaux's over the New River on the lands of John Buchanan and likewise by Ingles' Ferry to the lead mines. And in 1767 James Neeley, Philip Love, William Christian and William Bryan were appointed viewers of a road from Vaux's by Ingles' Ferry to Peak Creek on the north side of New River. The petitioners were all men of note in the development of the country: Frederick Stern, Isaac Job, Thomas Grayson, John Bell, Henry Skaggs, Joseph Hix, John Draper, George Baker, Joseph Hord, Levy Smith, Erasmus Noble, Samuel Peffer, James Coudon, Edward Vansell, Humphrey Baker, Anthony Bledsoe, James Newell and Alexander Page.

Colonel Byrd, in 1758, built two forts at the command of the Colonial Government, Fort Chiswell, near the forks of the roads from Pennsylvania, and from Richmond, on the waters of New River, and the fort at Long Island, on Holston River, in the present County of Sullivan, Tennessee. Monette states that this was the first fort established on the Holston. The year before, that is in 1757, Fort Loudoun was established by Andrew Lewis on the Tennessee River at the mouth of Tellico. It was afterwards known as Watauga. The next year, in 1758, 200 settlers went there in a body. Phelan states: "Fort Loudoun was garrisoned by royal troops, and the Cherokees, regarding it as a protection against the vengeance of the French offered donations of land to artisans as an inducement to come there. The warfare between the English and the French which raged in all parts of the world, was too far from the region of East Tennessee to affect it, otherwise than indirectly." It was the scene of a terrible massacre immediately after the reduction of Duquesne, the Cherokees captured it and all in the fort were destroyed. This fort has the distinction of having been manned by twelve cannon, which will testify to its importance. It was near the present city of Knoxville, the center of a district tacitly under the protection of the colony of Virginia, although none of the county governments exercised jurisdiction.

The most northerly limits of the section lying before Cumberland Gap and the entrance to the Wilderness Road are along the divide which separates the waters of the James and Roanoke (or Stanton) rivers, both of which take their rise west of the Blue Ridge Mountains and break through that range, flowing east and southeast; the sources of the Shenandoah and New Rivers (or Woods River) flowing north and northwest, and the Holston and its tributaries flowing south and southwest. The tide of migration had been steady from the beginning southwards from the Shenandoah Scotch-Irish settlements of Augusta. There was here the usual course of settlements following the streams and valleys. The leaders of this migration had kept in close touch with the authorities at Williamsburg, with which place communication was open and constant. Its general course seems to have been directed from the capital with decision, promptness and wisdom. Indeed, these leaders were men of large caliber and great force, and had a motive sufficiently exciting to keep them active. It must be admitted that the main object of the leaders was self-aggrandizement. A bureaucracy and cabal were in complete control and there was the opportunity to establish families and fortune through grants of large tracts of land, which were no sooner marked out than they were taken under the military protection of the colony. The grant to Jas. Patton, Smith and Lewis, and others of 100,000 acres in 1741 has already been mentioned. This lay upon the headwaters of the Roanoke and James, and Monette says: "In none of the provinces had the infatuation for western lands been carried to a greater extent than in Virginia. Blair reported in 1757 to the Executive Council of Virginia that the quantity of lands then entered to companies and individuals amounted to three millions of acres, a large portion of which had been granted as early as 1754." The most important of these grants within the borders of the section now under consideration was that to the Loyal Company on the 12th of July, 1749. It was 800,000 acres beginning on the North Carolina (Tennessee) line and running westward on condition that it should be divided into plats and surveys made and returned to the secretary's office within four years. It was not completed in four years, and in June, 1753, the Council granted four years' further time. This was interrupted by the French and Indian War, and at the close the Council was restrained by the British Government. Afterwards, the officers and soldiers entitled to lands under the proclamation of 1763, began to make settlements, and the agents and settlers under the company petitioned the Council that they might hold of the company and soldiers might be restrained from interfering with them; and in 1773, the Council allowed the settlers to make surveys and return them to the office. In 1753, a survey was made under this grant for Timothy Cole, of 190 acres in Washington County, in Rich Valley, on the waters of the North Fork of Holston River. The company gave titles upon payment of surveyor's fees and £3 for every one hundred acres. Dr. Thomas Walker had the management of the affairs of the company, as well as being a member, and he appointed William English his agent. Cole abandoned his land, and then in 1768 Joseph Scott and Stephen Trigg paid the fees on the same tract and they conveyed to David Ross in 1775. The affairs of the Loyal Company were before the Supreme Court of Virginia and, in 1783, the title of the company to all lands surveyed under it prior to 1776 was established. In 1803, action was brought by Edmund Pendleton and Nicholas Lewis, surviving partners of the Loyal Company, against one of the earliest settlers, John Crunk.

Among the very early settlers under the Loyal Company, were members of the Harman family. The general course of business under that company and the trials of settlers may be gathered from depositions relating to their early settlement. In 1751, Henry Harman and his uncle Valentine Harman, were on a hunting expedition when they camped on Sinking Creek of New River, in the present Giles County, and Valentine made what was called an improvement by killing trees. In 1754 he procured a survey under the Loyal Company. In the same year Valentine made a contract with a Dunker, George Hoopaugh, who, it was alleged was poor and lived on Valentine's charity, that George should go and live on the place as tenant. In 1757 Valentine was killed by Indians, in the presence of his nephew, Daniel Harman, and Daniel was taken prisoner, but escaped. No one but George Hoopaugh (Hoopack) lived on Sinking Creek at the time. He continued living there until 1775, when he moved off because of fear of the Indians. He returned, however, when he claimed the land as by settlement and made a conveyance of it. Although the grantees of the large tracts were speculators on a large scale, yet the same was not generally true of the settlers. While they were, no doubt, influenced by the prospect of rich lands at a small price, yet as a rule they were looking for a place for bona fide settlement, to make their abiding place, establish their households and pursue their fortunes. They were following upon the footsteps of numerous traders, hunters and trappers who had traversed the wilderness, back and forth, named its hills and streams and acted as prospectors and guides, but their mission was ended with the coming of population. The land speculator was not popular. The titles were but badly recorded and became matter of dispute as the lands became more valuable. These troubles became frequent about 1800, when nearly every piece of land was subject of controversy in the courts in some form. One of the most frequent causes of complaint was that officers and soldiers had located bounty warrants for service in the French and Indian wars so as to conflict with the prior rights of actual settlers. In 1770 James Anderson made a settlement on Cove Creek of North Fork of Holston in Washington County. The next year Samuel Lammie (Lamie, Lamme, Lamb) settled and improved near him and then bought out Anderson. He continued to live there until 1774, when he was killed by Indians, whereupon his brother, Andrew Lamie, took possession and lived there until 1805, when action was brought against Arthur Campbell, who set up a claim. Arthur Campbell claimed that Andrew made no lawful settlement because he had no family, and claimed that in 1770 Andrew and Samuel Lemmie settled three or four miles higher up Cove Creek. In 1774 Samuel was captured by Indians and carried to Canada. Previous to that time the belief prevailed in the new settlement that single men, by what was called "taking up land," might hold the same, and this taking up was commonly designated by marking trees with the initial letters of the claimant's name, making a few brush heaps near the center of the land, and sometimes a log pen or small cabin. Andrew Lammie continued on the place, according to Campbell, during the Revolution, and was an avowed adherent to the enemies of the country and spurned the offers of the Commonwealth. After the Revolution Andrew moved to the place his brother had claimed and settled on it. Arthur Campbell says further: "The law itself that gave occupants a privilege to obtain donation lands was extorted from the legislature by the representations of a numerous band of emigrants which the affairs of America at the time made it good policy to concilate, although not a few of them were deserters from the danger their eastern brethren were then involved in." Of Arthur, himself, it was said that he was "land mungering," for it was reported that he "was a surveyor himself and had white and black persons chain carriers with a chain, part made of rope and part of leather wood bark, and running as he pleased through other persons' claims, making corners and measuring lines at will, that a number of his marks were about the land in controversy." The land involved in this suit is that locally known as "Campbell's Choice."

It was customary for the large proprietors to give distinctive names to their own lands. James Patton named his "Smithfield." Dr. Thomas Walker gave the name "Wolf Hills", which is the site of the present town of Abingdon. "Burke's Garden" was the seat of James Thompson in the present county of Tazewell. It had been originally that of Thomas and John Ingles, who settled there in 1749.

One of the difficulties of determining accurately the dates and circumstances of the first settlement of any of these regions is that frequently a whole district in which a community established itself would be entirely depopulated by an incursion of the Indians, those of the settlers who were not killed, abandoning their improvements, which were then relocated by those who came in after the Indians had retired. These later claimed by their own, a new right, all trace of the former being wiped out. It was characteristic of the people that after each Indian attack, not only fresh adventurers came and occupied the land but in larger numbers than before. But at times there would be several years before the recovery. That there were settlers in considerable numbers before the grant to Patton and others in 1741, and the Loyal Company, south and west of that, in 1749, is sufficiently evident from many sources; but they were frequently and disastrously driven back. In 1753 and 1754 all the settlements were disturbed, but there was a return tide immediately after. After Pontiac's war and the treaty with France, there was a very large migration.

Among the very early settlers on Roanoke (or Stanton) River was John Robinson, who came in 1743. He was killed by the Indians in 1756. His brother, Thomas Robinson lost his life at the Big Defeated Camps on the west of the Cumberland Mountain, and all his family were destroyed. In 1753 he qualified as captain of a company of foot, which would indicate that his section was fairly well settled in that year. He was the son of James Robinson, of Pennsylvania, and was sent by his father to purchase land upon Roanoke as a settlement for the children of James, who followed John, and they together with their friends and relatives, the Crocketts, the Loyes, the Pattersons, the Calhouns, the Pattons and the Montgomeries, were prime agents in the establishment of civilization. As is usual in such communities the neighbors were very apt to fall out and say unkind things about each other, but fortunately, these people took their troubles into court, which became a clearing house of bad feeling. James Patton, who was president of the County Court, vestryman, member of the General Assembly, coroner, sheriff, county lieutenant, and a captain of cavalry in the militia service, all at the same time, could give and take hard knocks. In 1746 he haled into court all the Calhouns—Hames, Ezekiel, William and Patrick, on the charge that they were divulgers of false news, to the great detriment of the inhabitants. Apparently the Calhouns were in the habit of "crying worlf." In 1750 James Calhoun started the "news" that Colonel Patton had made over all his estate to his children to defraud his creditors, and that Patton could give no good title to purchasers. Patton instituted proceedings immediately against Calhoun for slander, which hung fire by reason of hung juries in the county court until 1754, when a mandamus was issued by the General Court to dismiss the cause. In the same year, 1750, James Calhoun contracted with Patton for two surveys of land, but before they were made out and signed by the governor the law was changed so as to give the governor a fee of one pistole for signing each patent. This Patton charged to Calhoun, but Calhoun refused to pay. Suit was brought by Patton in 1752 and a trial had. The jury, having been four days in retirement, asked to be discharged, but Patton's attorneys objected and they were ordered to consider further and if they could not agree, to return next court. In March 1753, the same jury was called and John Smith, being absent was fined. Defendant's attorney moved the court to dismiss

Har—2

the jury and impanel a new one, but patton in person objected and the court was of opinion that the cause be continued and the same jury try the issue. The cause of John Smith's absence was that when the jury were called by the sheriff to take their places in the box, John jumped out of the back window of the courthouse and escaped At the succeeding court none of the jurors appeared, and an order was entered to summon them to the next court, and at the next court, August, 1753, a mandamus was received from the General Court to dismiss the jury, which was done, and the case continued. Shortly afterwards the matter was submitted by parties to arbitration and the finding was that each party pay one pistole, which was entered by the court as its judgment in August, 1754.

By November, 1746, the settlements southwest of the Roanoke had become so important that on the 19th of that month four roads were ordered to be built leading from the Roanoke settlements. The first was run from Reed Creek to Eagle Bottom and thence to the top of the ridge that parts the waters of New River and those of the South Fork of the Roanoke, and these settlers were ordered to work it. George, Ezekiel, William and Patrick Calhoun, Bryant White, William Hanlow, Peter Rentfro and his two sons, George and Tinker, Jacob Woolman and two sons, John Black, Simon Hart, Michael Claine, John Stroud, Samuel Stalkner and all the Dunkers. James Calhoun and Charles Hart were to be overseers. The second road was ordered from Adam Harmon's on the new River, to the north branch of Roanoke, with these workers: George Draper, Israel Lorton and son, George Harmon, Thomas Looney, Jacob Harman and three sons, Jacob Castle, John Lane, Valentine Harmon, Adren Moser, Humberston Lyon, James Skaggs, Humphrey Baker, John Davis, Frederick Sterling and his two sons. The third road was ordered to run from the ridge above Tobias Bright's that parts the waters of New River from the branches of Roanoke to the lower ford of Catawba Creek, with these workers: William English and two sons, Thomas English and son, Jacob Brown, George Bright, Benjamin Ogle, Paul Garrison, Elisha Isaac, John Donahy, Philip Smith, Mathew English and others to be nominated by George Robinson and James Montgomery. The fourth road extended from the ridge dividing the waters of New River from the waters of South Branch of Roanoke to end in a road that leads over the Blue Ridge, which was the state highway to Richmond, James

Campbell and Mark Evans were the overseers, with these workers: Old Mr. Robinson and his sons, Thomas Wilson and his two sons, William Beus and his brother, all the Ledfords, Admuel and Henry Brown, Samuel Niely, James Burk, James Bean, Francis Estham, Ephraim Voss and servants, Francis Summerfield, John Mason, Tasker and Thomas Tosh, John and Peter Dill, Uriah Evans' sons, Methyselah Griffiths and sons, John Thomas, Peter Kinder. These names belong among those of the fathers, whose homely virtues and faithful manhood were the foundation of a free and virtuous people. Peace to their ashes.

In 1747 Valentine Sevier petitioned for license to keep an ordinary at his own house, alleging that "he is very much infested with travelers." He was probably living at that time to the north, on the waters of the Shenandoah. In 1746 his lands were processioned in that section. 1747 he was indicted for swearing six oaths, and at the same time appointed inspector of pork and beef. In 1747 he was arrested for raising a riot in the court yard, whereupon he begged fitting pardon and was discharged. He owned about 1600 acres in the present counties of Rockingham and Shenandoah.

On the third of September, 1747, Captain James Campbell and Erwin Patterson were appointed processsioners of lands on the waters of Roanoke. These were the most southern bounds for which processioners were appointed, so that it must be taken that there were few settlers actually living upon New River, Holston, Clinch and Powell on that date. In July, 1748, Michael and Augustine Price purchased land on New River from Israel Lorton. In 1749, Thomas and John Ingles settled at Burke's Garden, now in Tazewell County. At that time Samuel Akerling owned lands in Dunker Bottom on New River, and in 1750 sold to Garrett Zinn, who moved almost immediately to Carolina to escape massacre at the hands of the Indians. In the same year Adam Harman entered four hundred acres on New River, six miles above Wolf's Creek. The population must have been there, however scattered, as there was a justice of the peace, Thomas Ingles and a constable, William Ingles. In the same year, 1750, a road was ordered from Ezekiel Calhoun's to Woods (New) River, John McFarland and Joseph Crockett were to be surveyors and the following were the workers: Henry Batton, Mordecai Early, Jacob Goldman, John Downing, John Goldman, Charles Sinclair, Nathaniel Wilshire, William Sayers, William

Hamilton, Humbertson Lyon, Frederick Carloch, Robert Norris, James Miller, James Cove, Samuel Montgomery, Steven Lyon, John Conley, Andrew Linam, James Willkey, Samuel Stanlick, James Maies, Robert McFarlin, James Harris, John Vance, John Stride, Robert Miller, Alexander Sayers, John Miller, Jacob Castle, Robety Alcorn, John Forman, William Miller.

In 1752 Samuel Stalnaker, after whom a fort was named qualified as a captain in the militia. William Richey and John Vance were living on Reed Creek. The same year, Obadiah Garwood and two sons, Noah and Samuel (or Samuel Garwood and two sons, Noah and Obadiah) made a settlement on Clinch River in the present Tazewell County. Shortly afterward they returned to the north to bring their families; but the Indian war broke out and the country became untenable. Jeremiah Pate helped the Garwoods improve their land.

In 1753, William Leeper was appointed constable on New River in the place of Adam Harman, who had already served one year, so that during this troublous period the government was kept in operation nominally even if the reign was not tight. This Adam Harman had qualified as a captain of foot in 1747; had been the accuser in proceedings against Jacob Castle in 1749, charged with threatening to aid the French, and in 1752 had qualified as captain of a troop of horse. In the same year, 1753, a road was ordered from Samuel Stalnaker's on Holston River, to James Davis', with these workers: James Davis and his sons, Frederic Garlock, David, George and Conrad Carlock, Frederick Stern, Jacob and Adam Stalnaker, Jacob and Henry Goldman, Isaiah Hamilton, Hamilton Shoemaker, Timothy Cole, Humphrey Baker and son, George Stalnaker, Adam Andrews, Mathias Larch, Michael Hook, Martin Counce and Jacob Mires.

In March, 1754, a road was ordered on Reed Creek, on Holston River and on Craig's Creek. Immediately after the clouds burst and the Indians committed frightful massacres in all the settlements, in some cases destroying all the inhabitants. The Holston River community was almost annihilated. James Patton was killed; members of the Draper and English families were murdered or taken prisoners. Fort Vause was taken. Valentine Harmon was killed. The list through 1745, 1755, 1756, 1757, 1758, is well known. In 1755 Court process was returned "not executed by reason of the murder done on New River by the Indians." But there was returned to the court in 1755 the valuation of the improvements on the "naked farm" on Roanoke, the property of Peter Evans, which is quite interesting. The improvements consisted of 18 acres cleared and well fenced, under corn and rye, and ten acres of clear meadow; 100 fruit trees value at £1; one hay house, 15 x 10, £1.10; one corn crib, fifteen by four feet, £0.10; one spring house, 18 feet by 12 feet, £0.15; five head of horses and one breeding sow, £40.15; one wagon and gears, one axe and grubbing hoe and two plows and gears, £33. During the years 1756, 1757, 1758, 1759, there is not a single entry in the current orders of the court relating to these settlements.

In 1760, Captain John Blagg commanded a company of the Virginia Regiment under Col. John Smith and Colonel Byrd at Dunkard Bottom on New River. Among the soldiers were Lieutenants, Hansley, John Smith, John Lukis, Samp Evans, Richard Dodd, Richard Newport, Thomas Deigs, John Contrel, Captain Blagg commanded at Long Island in 1761. James Huston was armorer, and Frederick Elphistone was purveyor to the army at Reed Creek, Stalnaker's and Long Island. In the same year effort was made to serve judical process, but without success.

On November 19, 1762, John Wiltshire, Alexander Sayers and Jacob Castle were appointed to view and report as to the valuation of the improvements made by John Staunton on New River, and three days afterwards John Thompson, Henry Ferguson and Hugh Mills were appointed to view the nearest and best way from the Stone House to the Bedford line. In the same year, James Robinson, whose relations had been, some taken prisoners, some killed and some dispersed, returned to the Roanoke country from Pennsylvania.

In 1763, the country had been freed of the enemy and settlers began to return. In March, William Beard was there. In April, William Grymes, Jas. Neilly and William Robinson were appointed road overseers from Grymes' clearing to Madison's; John Craig, thence to New River, on the lands of John Buchanan; Alexander and William Sayers, thence to Fort Chiswell; William Preston, to apportion the tithables as far as Fort Lewis and William Thompson, thence to Fort Lewis. In November, John Smith, William Grymes, James Neally, Israel Christian were appointed to view the roads that lead from Vause's over the New River on the lands of John

Buchanan and likewise by Ingles' Ferry to the lead mines. In this year Michael Kimberling's father made a settlement on Walker's Creek in the present county of Tazewell, and was there killed by the Indians.

In 1764 the most southern district for which processioners were appointed was Roanoke.

In 1765 William Robinson, James Neeley, William Bryans were appointed to view a road from Vause's by Ingles' Ferry to Peake Creek. William Bell was living at Colonel Chiswell's mines. Andrew Baker settled on land in the present county of Grayson, within the grant to the Loyal Company. It was originally surveyed in 1753 for Peter Jefferson, Thomas and David Meriwether and Thomas Walker. It was the Peach Bottom tract. John Cox settled there the same year. George Collins and George Reeves settled there in 1767.

In March of that year Samuel Moody, Thomas Goodson, John Richards, William Ward, Hugh Crockett, Jacob Kent, Robert Crockett, Philip Love, Joseph Crockett petitioned for a road from Vause's to Samuel Woods'. In May, John Buchanan appealed to the General Court against the establishment of the road from Vause's to Peak Creek on the ground that it is on the land of the western waters and it is contrary to His Majesty's proclamation to grant any order for clearing any road thereon. In November, Joseph McMurtry and George McAfee reported that there were not enough tithables to make a wagon road from McMurtry's Mill through McAfee's Gap to the wagon road; and it was only practicable to clear it for carrying loads on horseback until the country is better settled. In that year Anthony Bledsoe built a mill at Fort Chiswell.

But by 1768 the settlers were beginning to petition the County Court of Augusta to assume jurisdiction over the territory which had been disputed land and by treaties recognized as belonging to the Indians. In that year the inhabitants of Reed Creek, of Holston, filed their petition: "That whereas we, your petitioners, for some time past, have been debarred settling and improving and cultivating our patent lands on the western waters, the reason whereof is best known to our legislators, but by virtue of the late treaty held to the northward, we hope we may, without offense, petition your worships to give orders that there may be alterations and amendments made on the old road leading from Captain Ingles' Ferry to James Davis' on the head of the Holston River, and appoint such surveyors as you in your wisdom shall think fit, and your petitioners, as in duty bound will pray. Joseph Black, James Holice, John Montgomery, Robert Montgomery, James Montgomery, George Breckinridge, Alexander Breckinridge, Robert Breckinridge, Robert Campbell, Robert Doack, William Doack, William Sayers, Arthur Campbell, William Davis, James Hayes, Samuel Hopes, William Leftwich, Jasper Gender, George Gender, Jacob Kinder, William Phips, John Houncal, Barnet Small, John Smith, John Bets, Robert Buchanan, Robert Davis, Samuel McAdam, James Davis, Nicholas Buchanan, Alexander Buchanan.

John Campbell, on his way to the Holston, in 1768, overtook a number of persons, who informed him they were coming to settle on a tract owned by Dr. Thomas Walker, known as the Wolf Hill Tract. In 1768, Robert Doack sowed turnips on Reed Creek, but made no settlement. In the same year constables were appointed on New River. In that year Michael Hoofacre settled in Rich Valley, a north fork of Holstein. When he came there was no improvement nor anything like an improvement except a hunter's cabin.

In 1769 the whole section embracing the head waters and sources of the New River, Clinch, Holston and Powell Rivers was erected into a separate county, and the surveyor was ordered to run the dividing line between Augusta and Botetourt as far as the western waters. Robert Doack was Dr. Thomas Walker's agent for the Wolf Hill Tract, and Thomas Armstrong was one of the earliest settlers. In the same year, John Smith, John Morgan and a large party settled on Moccasin Creek. Daniel smith and Josiah Gamble succeeded Doack as agent for the Wolf Hill Tract. Daniel Smith was the school teacher of the community.

In 1770, William Herbert settled on Cubb Creek, in the present Washington County. The first settlement on the land had been by James McCarthy. Patrick Porter moved to Clinch in 1770. In the same year Jacob Young, who had settled on Reed Creek in the present county of Wythe, soon moved to Holstein. William McGhee (McGaughey) made a settlement in 1771 in Turkey Cove of Powell's Valley in the present Lee County. Peter Cloud and Thomas Lovelady had been living there some time before. McGee moved in from Holsten River, where he had been living. In the same year Valentine Harman improved a piece of land on Clinch in the present Tazewell County. Samuel Walker came at the same time, and William Wynne was then living there. In 1771 Colonel James Dysart and Joseph Ray made a tour of nine months through Kentucky and of evelen months in 1772. In 1769 they made a similar tour of six months. Isaac Blangy (or Ballinger) had settled in App's (Abb's) Valley prior to 1771. It has borne that name since 1760. Robert Poage bought land there in the fall of 1771. Colonel James Maxwell and James Peerey settled on Clinch in 1772 and the same year John Stutler and Uriah Stone came. Maxwell lived there until 1784, and during that time two of his daughters were killed by Indians. The same land had been improved in 1760 and was called Ingles' Crabb Orchard, settled by John Ingles. In this year, 1772, Francis Fugate settled on Big Moccasin Creek. John Montgomery had gone there in 1771 with his father, Alexander Montgomery. The same year, John Tate settled. Francis Cooper settled there in 1770. Big Moccasin, about this time, became totally vacated for fear of Indians, and remained so about one year. In 1771 there was not a family on the north (west) side of Clinch Mountain for a distance of ten miles. Henry Dougherty made a stttlement on Laurel Fork of Holston River in 1773. Mrs. Nancy Tate, Robert Fowler and James Crabtree followed soon after.

The Indians became troublesome in 1774 and continued so for several years. William McAfee settled on Sinking Creek of New River in 1774. In the same year Andrew Cowan settled on the North Fork of Clinch, which was called Stim's Creek. Hugh Gullion had a settlement on Walker's Creek in 1774. He was killed at Point Pleasant. In 1775, William Fitzgerel made a crop of corn at Martin's Station in Powell's Valley and made an improvement near Cumberland Gap on a creek called Station Creek. William Herbert was living on Reed Creek in 1776.

The Indians attacked the settlement on Cubb Creek in 1776 and killed some people. They were very troublesome in Washington County from 1776 to 1779. Titus and John Benton were killed in Rye Cove in 1777. Charles Carter had settled there in 1775. This settlement was broken up by the Indians for several years. Felty Hoover and his sons, John and Abraham, settled on Black Water at the Flat Lick, a north branch of Clinch, in 1777. Thomas Rodgers was living on the land in 1765, when he was driven off by the

Indians. The land lies in Lee County near Cumberland Gap, it had been originally improved by John Wallen about 1760. In 1778 Joseph Drake, who had moved from Sinking Creek to New River, on account of the Indians, moved to Kentucky, where he was killed by the Indians.

In the spring of 1781 all the settlers in Turkey Cove, in Powell's Valley, moved out because of Indians.

And thus the tide again receded. But when it returned, the breach in the barrier had been accomplished, the channel was open, the floods flowed in whirling and swirling and seething to the vortex from north, east, southeast; hordes of Presbyterian Irish, of Welsh and Dutch, of English Baptists and Episcopalians, of Carolina refugees, seeking surcease from persecution and convention in the land of freedom and fatness—Kentucky.

The Wilderness Road

Fort Chiswell is designated in the preceding article, by Judge Chalkley, as the point "where the imigrants reached the borders of the great wilderness." The road which connected Fort Chiswell with Long Island and the Blockhouse on the Holston was an important link in this great "primary highway system" connecting southwest Virginia and Kentucky. Crossing New River at Ingles' Ferry at Radford, the road passed southwest through the present towns of Pulaski, Max Meadows, Wytheville, Marion and Abingdon to the Blockhouse, the Virginia end of the Wilderness Road, which road followed "Boone's Path" from the Blockhouse to Boonesborough Kentucky.

William Allen Pusey, A. M., M. D., in his recent book, published 1921, entitled "The Wilderness Road to Kentucky," says: "The Wilderness Road proper began at the Blockhouse. The roads from the north and the south brought the traveler to this point. The Blockhouse was the last station before Moccasin Gap or Big Moccasin Gap, the gate to the Indian country, and about the same distance from the important western rendezvous of the Holston pioneers, Long Island, in the South Fork of the Holston River. It was, of course, for these reasons that the early travelers to Kentucky were used to gather at the Blockhouse in order to form parties for the trip to Kentucky."

"The Blockhouse was established about 1777, perhaps even in 1775, when Boone's party went out, by Captain John Anderson who lived in it from that time until his death. It was located in Carter's Valley at a point where the hills open out into a valley half a mile wide and a mile long. This little valley is today a meadow surrounded by wooded hills. . . . ."

"The old road to the Blockhouse from Long Island, to the mouth of Reedy Creek still exists. This is the road which Boone Followed on his journey of 1775."

"From the Blockhouse the present road through Moccasin Gap, Gate City, Speer's Ferry, Clinchport, Duffield to Kane's Gap in

Powell Mountain is in practically the exact location of the "Wilderness Road. . . . ."

"The road passes down Wallen Creek to Stickleyville. . . . Beyond the present Stickleyville the road passed over Wallen Ridge and reached Powell Valley on Station Creek. . . . Five miles down Station Creek Valley from Wallen Ridge was situated Valley Station. . . . From Station Creek the old road followed directly west to Jonesville along a direct but now little used road. . . . On the retaining wall of the yard of the courthouse at Jonesville is one of the Boone markers. From Jonesville to within a few miles of Cumberland Gap the old road is preserved practically in the present direct road between these points which is now a State road. From Boone's Path to Cumberland Gap a modern graded road has been built which, for the most part, is in the location of the old road. . . . Half a mile east of the village of Rose Hill, the road crossed Martins Creek. Martin's Station was located a mile south of this point. Martin's Station was the important station on the road between the Blockhouse and Crab Orchard. It was the station of Captain Joseph Martin, who was Virginia Agent for Indians Affairs. . . . Martin was living at this station when Boone and Henderson made their journeys in 1775. . . . Beyond Martin's Station the road passed into the valley of Indian Creek and followed down this valley almost to Cumberland Gap."

We will not follow the location of the "Wilderness Road" beyond Cumberland Gap. The distance from the Blockhouse to Boonesborough, Kentucky, is a little over two hundred miles.

Based on the account given by H. Addington Bruce in his "Daniel Boone and the Wilderness Road" we give the following abridged account of the doings at the "Seat of government" which Boone founded. The "Wilderness Road" to Kentucky was begun at the Blockhouse, on the Holston, March 10, 1775, by thirty men, under the direction of Colonel Daniel Boone, and within fifteen days they had completed the road to within fifteen miles of Boonesborough, Kentucky.

Boone and his party were employed by Richard Henderson of North Carolina, to blaze this trail, cut the brush and logs, making it wide enough for horses laden with goods, wares and merchandise fastened to packsaddles. Henderson, having purchased that section of Kentucky from the Cherokees formed a company called the

Transylvania Company for the purpose of colonizing same. Boone's instructions from Henderson were as follows: "To cleave a road through the wilderness and select a seat of government for the proposed colony."

Soon after Boone and his party of road cleavers reached their destination, Henderson with a party of about fifty joined them and they proceeded to lay the foundation of the new government. Elections were held about May 20, 1775, and three days after, the delegates gathered at Boonesborough where they met under a giant elm. The Boonesborough delegation was composed of Daniel and Squire Boone, William Cocke, Richard Callaway, William Moore, and Samuel Henderson. The delegation from Harrodstown: Thomas Slaughter, Dr. John Lythe, Valentine Harman and James Douglas. The Boiling Spring delegation: James Harrod, Nathan Hammond, Azariah Davis and Isaac Hite. St. Asaph delegation: John Todd, Samuel Wood and Alexander Spottswood Dandridge. The proceedings were opened by prayer by Dr. Lythe, who was a clergyman of the Church of England. Thomas Slaughter was elected presiding officer. The three proprietors—Henderson, Hart and Luttrell—were then notified that the "Transylvania House of Delegates" was duly organized and would be pleased to hear any suggestions they might have to make.

"In 1776 the Legislature of Virginia passed an act organizing Kentucky County, which included within its boundaries the splendid section of country which Henderson had bought from the Cherokees. With this Act, Transylvania became only a memory and the ambitious project of the Transylvania partners was ended forever."

CHAPTER I.

ORGANIZATION OF THE MILITIA; ORIGIN AND HISTORY OF JUSTICES OF THE PEACE; EXTRACTS FROM THE CONSTITUTIONS OF 1776, 1830 AND 1851; GENERAL ASSEMBLY; QUALIFICATIONS FOR MEMBERSHIP THEREIN, AND QUALIFICATIONS FOR VOTING AND HOLDING OFFICE.

MILITIA.

On March 9, 1819, the following Act of the General Assembly was passed (see Revised Code of 1819, page 93).

Whereas a well regulated Militia constitutes the great defence of a free people, and it is expedient to carry into effect the laws of the Congress of the United States, providing for the national defence by establishing an Uniform Militia throughout the United States:

1. "Be it therefore enacted that the counties of Washington, Russell, Lee, Scott, Grayson and Tazewell shall compose one Brigade. . . .

2. "The several counties and corporations within this commonwealth, shall constitute the battalion, portion of Battalion, Regiment, or portions of Regiment, as now established: Provided, that it shall be lawful for the executive to divide or alter the regimental districts in the several counties, as circumstances may require," etc. . . .

3. "And every Battalion shall, if convenient, be formed into five companies; each company to consist of not less than sixty men, including non-commissioned officers, musicians and privates, nor more than one hundred and eight, officers included," etc. . . .

4. "There shall be a Adjutant General for the Militia of the state, a Major General to each Division, and a Brigadier General to each Brigade, to be appointed by the joint ballot of both houses of the General Assembly, who shall reside within the limits of their respective commands; and there shall be a Colonel, Lieutenant-Colonel, and Major to each Regiment, and a Captain, Lieutenant

and Ensign to each Company, who shall be appointed and commissioned agreeable to the constitution and laws of this Commonwealth," etc. . . .

44. "There shall be a muster of each troop of Cavalry and company of Artillery in the months of April and October in every year, at such places as a majority of the members constituting the said troop or company, shall, from time to time, fix upon; and it shall be the duty of the commanding officer of any such troop or company, and he is hereby required, at each and every muster, to call his roll, examine every person belonging thereto, and note down all delinquiencies occuring therein, and make return thereof, to the Commanding Officer of the Batallion," etc. . . .

45. "There shall be a muster in each company of Militia, including the light companies, in the months of April and October in every year. . . . And there shall be a muster of each Batallion in the month of October or November in every year, etc. . . .

48. "It shall be the duty of every Commanding Officer of a Regiment, Batallion or Company, at their respective musters, to keep their respective corps under arms for a period of at least two hours, and to cause them to be trained and exercised, agreeably to the moode of discipline prescribed by congress," etc. . . .

JUSTICES OF THE PEACE.

During the period—from 1800 to 1852—covered by Volume One of the ANNALS OF TAZEWELL COUNTY, the most important institution in the Government of the County was the County Court, which was composed of Justices of the Peace. Inasmuch as this volume contains many orders entered by the County Court at its monthly and quarterly terms, it will be interesting to a large number of our readers to know something of the history of the Justices of the Peace.

From "Henning's Justice," 3d Edition, 1820, beginning at page 417, we quote as follows:

"The term 'Justices of the Peace,' though familiar in England long before the settlement of Virginia, was not introduced into the laws of the colony until the year 1661. From the earliest period of our settlement (in 1607) to the year 1629, 'commanders of plantations' are alone mentioned in our laws, as persons authorized to exercise civil jurisdiction. They also possessed the supreme military command of the settlement. A commission expressing their powers and jurisdiction, may be seen in the 1st vol. of the Statutes at Large, page 181. In the year 1629, 'commissioners of monthly courts' were appointed by commission from the governor, and had jurisdiction in civil cases and petty offences only. In 1632, similar commissions issued to different parts of the colony, styling the persons appointed 'commissioners,' for the places to which they were assigned; and after specifying their jurisdiction, in matters civil and criminal, they were moreover empowered 'to do and execute whatever a justice of the peace or two or more justices of the peace might do,' according to the laws of England. The term 'commissioners' was, however, generally used in our ancient statutes, till by degrees that of 'Justices of the Peace' was adopted."

By the fifteenth article of the Constitution of Virginia, June, 1776, it was provided: "The governor, with the advice of the privy council, shall appoint justices of the peace for the counties; and in case of vacancies, or a necessity of increasing the number hereafter, such appointments to be made upon the recommendation of the respective county courts.'

The judges of the supreme courts, as well as the justices of the peace, are expressly declared by statute, to be "conservators of the peace."

Extracts from the First Constitution of Virginia, Adoped June 29, 1776.

"The Legislative shall be formed of two distinct branches, who, together, shall be a complete Legislature. They shall meet once or oftener, every year, and shall be called the General Assembly of Virginia.

"One of these shall be called the House of Delegates, and consist of two Representatives to be chosen for each county, and for the district of West Augusta, annually, of such men as actually reside in and are freeholders of the same, or duly qualified according to law, and also one Delegate or Representative to be chosen annually for the city of Williamsburg, and one for the borough of Norfolk, and a Representative for each of such other cities and boroughs as may hereafter be allowed particular representation by the Legislature." . . .

"The other shall be called the Senate, and consist of twenty-four members, of whom thirteen shall constitute a House to proceed on business, for whose election the different counties shall be divided into twenty-four districts; and each county of the respective district, at the time of the election of its Delegates, shall vote for one Senator, who is actually a resident and free-holder within the district, or duly qualified according to law, and is upwards of twenty-five years of age." . . .

"A Governor, or Chief Magistrate, shall be chosen annually, by joint ballot of both houses." . . .

"A Privy Council or Council of State, consisting of eight members, shall be chosen by joint ballot of both Houses of Assembly, either from their own members or the people at large, to assist in the administration of government. They shall annually choose out of their own members a President, who in case of the death, inability, or necessary absence of the Governor from the government, shall act as Lieutenant Governor."

Qualification of Voters. Act Passed 1785.

"Every white male citizen, aged twenty-one years, being possessed of twenty-five acres of land with a house, the superficial content of the foundation whereof is twelve feet square, or equal to that quantity, and a plantation thereon, or fifty acres of unimproved land, or a lot or part of a lot of land in a City or Town with a house thereon," . . . .

"Any Elector qualified according to this Act, failing to attend any annual election of Delegates or of a Senator, and if a poll be taken, to give or offer to give his vote, shall pay one-fourth of his portion of all such levies and taxes as shall be assessed and levied in his County the ensuing year;" . . . .

An Amended Constitution or form of Government for Virginia. Adopted 1830.

"The House of Delegates shall consist of one hundred and thirty-four members, to be chosen annually for and by the several counties. The twenty-six counties lying west of the Alleghany mountains to have 31 delegates;" Tazewell County being entitled to one delegate.

"The other house of the general assembly shall be called the senate, and shall consist of thirty-two members, of whom thirteen shall be chosen for and by counties lying west of the Blue Ridge of mountains," . . . .

"The counties of Tazewell, Wythe and Grayson shall form a district.'" . . . .

Members of the house of delegates must have attained the age of twenty-five years, and members of the senate, thirty years.

Ministers of the gospel and priests of every denomination shall be incapable of being elected members of either house of assembly.

Qualification of Voters. 1830.

The voter must be possessed of freehold in land of the value of twenty-five dollars, the evidence of title to which must have been recorded two months before he shall offer to vote, and every such citizen who shall own and be himself in actual occupation of a leasehold estate, with the evidence of title recorded two months before he shall offer to vote. The term of the leasehold must not be less than five years, and the annual value or rent of twenty dollars; and must be a housekeeper and head of a family within the county or election district, and shall have been assessed and paid taxes within the preceding year.

In all elections the vote shall be given openly and not by ballot.

The Governor is to be elected by the joint vote of the two houses of the general assembly. He shall hold office for a term of three years and shall be ineligible to that office, for three years next after his term of service shall have expired.

There shall be a council of state, to consist of three members, any one or more of whom may act. They shall be elected by joint vote of both houses of the general assembly, and remain in office three years. The governor shall, before he exercises any discretionary power conferred on him by the constitution and laws, require the advice of the council of state, which advice shall be registered in books for that purpose, signed by the members present and consenting thereto, and laid before the general assembly when called for by them. . . . The senior councillor shall be lieutenant governor, and in case of the death, resignation, inability or absence of the governor from the seat of government, shall act as governor."

Extracts from the Amended Constitution of Virginia, 1851.

"Every white male citizen of the commonwealth of the age of twenty-one years, who has been a resident of the state for two years, and of the county, city or town where he offers to vote for twelve months next preceding an election—and no other person—shall be qualified to vote for members of the general assembly and all officers elective by the people;" . . . . There is excluded, however, from this provision of universal male suffrage, the pauper, those of unsound mind and those who have been convicted of bribery in an election, or of any infamous offense."

Under this constitution, the House of Delegates consisted of one hundred and fifty-two members, to be chosen biennially for and by the several counties, cities and towns of the commonwealth.

"At the first general election, the county of Russell shall elect two delegates, and the county of Tazewell shall elect one delegate; at the second general election, the county of Tazewell shall elect two delegates, and the county of Russell shall elect one delegate; and so on, alternately, at succeeding general elections. . . .

"The Senate shall consist of fifty members to be elected for a term of four years."

The counties of Mercer, Monroe, Giles and Tazewell form the Fortieth Senatorial District.

Members of the House of Delegates must be twenty-one years of age; and members of the Senate must be twenty-five years of age.

"The governor shall be elected by the voters, at the times and places of choosing members of the general assembly. . . .

"A lieutenant governor shall be elected at the same time and places, and for the same term as the governor. . . .

"In case of the removal of the governor, or of his death, resignation or inability etc. . . ., the duties of the governor shall devolve upon the lieutenant governor; . . . . The lieutenant governor shall be president of the Senate."

County Courts.

"There shall be in each county of the commonwealth a county court, which shall be held monthly, but not less than three nor more than five justices, except when the law shall require the presence of a greater number.

The jurisdiction of the said court shall be the same as that of the existing county courts, except so far as it is modified by this constitution, or may be changed by law.

Each county shall be laid off into districts, as nearly equal as may be in territory and population. In each district there shall be elected, by the voters thereof, four justices of the peace, who shall be commissioned by the governor, reside in their respective districts, and hold their offices for the term of four years. The justices so elected shall choose one of their own body, who shall be the presiding justice of the county court, and whose duty it shall be to attend each term of said court. The other justices shall be classified by law for the performance of their duties in court.

The justices shall receive for their services in court a per diem compensation, to be ascertained by law, and paid out of the county treasury; and shall not receive any fee or emolument for other judicial services.

The power and jurisdiction of justices of the peace within their respective counties shall be prescribed by law.

County Officers.

The voters of each county shall elect a clerk of the county court, a surveyor, an attorney for the commonwealth, a sheriff, and so many commissioners of the revenue as may be authorized by law, who shall hold their respective offices as follows: The clerk and the surveyor for the term of six years; the attorney for the term of four years; the sheriff and the commissioners for the term of two years. Constables and overseers of the poor shall be elected by the voters as may be prescribed by law.

The officers mentioned in the preceding section, except the attorneys, shall reside in the counties or districts for which they were respectively elected. No person elected for two successive terms to the office of sheriff, shall be re-eligible to the same office for the next succeeding term; nor shall he during his term of service, or within one year hereafter, be eligible to any political office.

The justices of the peace, sheriffs, attorneys for the commonwealth, clerks of the circuit and county courts, and all other county officers, shall be subject to indictment for malfeasance, misfeasance or neglect of official duty; and upon conviction thereof, their offices shall become vacant."

"Done in convention in the city of Richmond, on the first day of August, in the year of our Lord one thousand eight hundred and fifty-one, and in the seventy-sixth year of the commonwealth of Virginia.

JOHN Y. MASON,
President of the Convention.

S. D. WHITTLE,
Secretary of the Convention."

CHAPTER II.

GOVERNORS, MEMBERS OF CONSTITUTIONAL CONVENTIONS AND MEMBERS OF THE GENERAL ASSEMBLY OF VIRGINIA FROM 1800 TO 1852.

This chapter is taken from "A Register of the General Assembly of Virginia, 1776 to 1918, and of the Constitutional Conventions", by Earls G. Swem, Assistant State Librarian, and John W. Williams, Clerk of the House of Delegates.

GOVERNORS.

PATRICK HENRY. July 5, 1776—June 1, 1779.

THOMAS JEFFERSON. June 1, 1779—June 12, 1781.

THOMAS NELSON. June 12, 1781—November 30, 1781 (resigned).

BENJAMIN HARRRISON. November 30, 1781—November 30, 1784.

PATRICK HENRY. November 30, 1784—November 30, 1786.

EDMOND RANDOLPH. November 30, 1786—November 12, 1788 (resigned).

BEVERLEY RANDOLPH. November 12, 1788—December 1, 1791.

HENRY LEE. December 1, 1791—December 1, 1794.

ROBERT BROOKE. December 1, 1794—November 30, 1796.

JAMES WOOD. November 30, 1796—December 6, 1799.

JAMES MONROE. December 19, 1799—December 29, 1802.

JOHN PAGE. December 29, 1802—December 11, 1805.

WILLIAM H. CABELL. December 11, 1805—December 12, 1808.

JOHN TYLER, SR. December 12, 1808—January 15, 1811.

JAMES MONROE. January 19, 1811—April 3, 1811 (resigned to become Secretary of State).

GEORGE WILLIAM SMITH. April 3, 1811—December 26, 1811 (lost his life in the burning of the Richmond theater).

PEYTON RANDOLPH. December 26, 1811—January 4, 1812.

JAMES BARBOUR. January 4, 1812—December 11, 1814.

WILSON CARY NICHOLAS. December 11, 1814—December 11, 1816.
JAMES P. PRESTON. December 11, 1816—December 11, 1819.
THOMAS MANN RANDOLPH. December 11, 1819—December 11, 1822.
JAMES PLEASANTS. December 11, 1822—December 11, 1825.
JOHN TYLER, JR. December 11, 1825—March 4, 1827.
WILLIAM B. GILES. March 4, 1827—March 4, 1830.
JOHN FLOYD. March 4, 1830—March 31, 1834.
LITTLETON WALLER TAZEWELL. March 31, 1834—March 30, 1836.
WYNDHAM ROBERTSON. March 30, 1836—March 31, 1837.
DAVID CAMPBELL. March 31, 1837—March 31, 1840.
THOMAS WALKER GILMER. March 31, 1840—March 20, 1841.
JOHN MERCER PATTON. March 20, 1841—March 31, 1841.
JOHN RUTHERFORD. March 31, 1841—March 31, 1842.
JOHN MUNFORD GREGORY. March 31, 1842—January 5, 1843.
JAMES MCDOWELL. January 5, 1843—January 1, 1846.
WILLIAM SMITH. January 1, 1846—January 1, 1849.
JOHN BUCHANAN FLOYD. January 1, 1849—January 1, 1852.
JOSEPH JOHNSON. January 1, 1852—January 1, 1856.

CONSTITUTIONAL CONVENTIONS.

MEMBERS REPRESENTING TAZEWELL COUNTY.

1776—Convention met May 6, 1776, and adjourned July 5, 1776.
   Fincastle County: Arthur Campbell and William Russell.
1788—Convention met June 2, 1788, and adjurned June 27, 1788. This Convention was called to consider the Federal Constitution. Montgomery County: Walter Crockett and Abraham Trigg. Russell County: Thomas Carter and Henry Dickerson.
1829-30—Convention met October 5, 1829, and adjourned January 15, 1830.
   Washington, Lee, Scott, Russell and TAZEWELL: *John B. George, Andrew McMillan, Edward Campbell and William Byars.*

1850-51—Convention met October 14, 1850, and adjourned August 1, 1951.

Mercer, Giles, TAZEWELL and Monroe Counties: Augustus A. Chapman, Allen T. Caperton and Albert G. Pendleton.

MEMBERS WHO REPRESENTED TAZEWELL COUNTY IN THE GENERAL ASSEMBLY OF VIRGINIA FROM 1801 TO 1852.

Session: December 7, 1801—February 2, 1802.
House of Delegates: Thomas Witten and David Ward.
Senate: James P. Preston. At this time the Senatorial District was composed of the counties of Botetourt, Greenbrier, Kanawha, Montgomery, Monroe, Lee, Grayson, TAZEWELL, Russell, Washington and Wythe.

Session: December 6, 1802—January 29, 1803.
House of Delegates: David Ward and Thomas Witten.
Senate: James P. Preston.

Session: December 5, 1803—February 3, 1804.
House of Delegates: John Grills and Henry Bowen.
Senate: James P. Preston.

Session: December 3, 1804—February 1, 1805.
House of Delegates: Henry Bowen and James Thompson.
Senate: Daniel Sheffey.

Session: December 2, 1805—February 6, 1806.
House of Delegates: William Neal and James Thompson.
Senate: Daniel Sheffey.

Session: December 1, 1806—January 22, 1807.
House of Delegates: James Thompson and Andrew Peery.
Senate: Daniel Sheffey.

Session: December 7, 1807—February 10, 1808.
House of Delegates: James Thompson and Andrew Peery.
Senate: Daniel Sheffey.

Session: December 5, 1808—February 18, 1809.
House of Delegates: James Thompson and John Cecil.
Senate: Francis Smith.

Session: December 4, 1809—February 9, 1810.
House of Delegates: James Thompson and David Ward.
Senate: Francis Smith.

Session: December 3, 1810—February 14, 1811.
House of Delegates: David Ward and John Cecil.
Senate: Francis Smith.

Session: December 2, 1811—February 21, 1812.
House of Delegates: James Thompson and John Cecil.
Senate: Francis Smith.

Session: November 30, 1812—February 23, 1813.
House of Delegates: John Ward and James Thompson.
Senate: Henley Chapman.

Session: May 17-26, 1813; December 6, 1813—February 16, 1814.
House of Delegates: John Ward and Joseph D. Peery.
Senate: Henley Chapman.

Session: October 10, 1814—January 19, 1815.
House of Delegates: James Thompson and John Ward.
Senate: Henley Chapman.

Session: December 4, 1815—February 28, 1816.
House of Delegates: James Thompson and Rees B. Thompson.
Senate: Henley Chapman.

Session: November 11, 1816—February 22, 1817.
House of Delegates: James Thompson and Rees B. Thompson.
Senate: Francis Preston.

Session: December 1, 1817—February 26, 1818.
House of Delegates: John B. George and Rees B. Thompson.
Senate: Francis Preston.

Session: December 7, 1818—March 13, 1819.
House of Delegates: Thomas Harrison and John B. George.
Senate: Francis Preston.

Session: December 6, 1819—February 25, 1820.
House of Delegates: John B. George and Thomas Peery.
Senate: Francis Preston.

Session: December 4, 1820—March 5, 1821.
House of Delegates: Henry P. George and William Gillespie.
Senate: David Campbell. Senatorial District now composed of the counties of Washington, Lee, Scott, Russell and TAZEWELL.

Session: December 3, 1821—March 4, 1822.
House of Delegates: Henry P. George and James C. Davidson.
Senate: David Campbell.

Session: December 2, 1822—February 25, 1823.
House of Delegates: John B. George and William Thompson.
Senate: David Campbell.

Session: December 1, 1823—March 10, 1824.
House of Delegates: John B. George and Thomas Peery.
Senate: David Campbell.

Session: November 29, 1824—February 18, 1825.
House of Delegates: John B. George and William Shannon.
Senate: John D. Sharp.

Session: December 5, 1825—March 9, 1826.
House of Delegates: John B. George and John Ward.
Senate: John D. Sharp.

Session: December 4, 1826—March 9, 1827.
House of Delegates: John B. George and William Shannon.
Senate: John D. Sharp.

Session: December 3, 1827—March 1, 1828.
House of Delegates: John B. George and Hervey Deskins.
Senate: John D. Sharp.

Session: December 1, 1828—February 17, 1829.
House of Delegates: Thomas J. George and Hervey Deskins.
Senate: John H. Fulton.

Session: December 7, 1829—February 23, 1830.
House of Delegates: Thomas J. George and William Barns.
Senate: John H. Fulton.

Session: December 6, 1830—April 19, 1831.
House of Delegates: Robert Gillespie.
Senate: David McComas. Senatorial District now composed of TAZEWELL, Wythe and Grayson counties.

Session: December 5, 1831—March 21, 1832.
House of Delegates: Robert Gillespie.
Senate: David McComas.

Session: December 3, 1832—March 9, 1833.
House of Delegates: Hervey George.
Senate: David McComas.

Session: December 2, 1833—March 14, 1834.
House of Delegates: Hervey George.
Senate: David McComas.

Session: December 1, 1834—March 12, 1835.
House of Delegates: James W. M. Witten.
Senate: David McComas.

Session: December 7, 1835—March 24, 1836.
House of Delegates: Robert Gillespie.
Senate: David McComas.

Session: December 5, 1836—March 31, 1837.
House of Delegates: Robert Gillespie.
Senate: Samuel McCamant.

Session: January 1—April 9, 1838.
House of Delegates: James W. M. Witten.
Senate: Samuel McCamant.

Session: January 7—April 10, 1839.
House of Delegates: Addison Crockett.
Senate: Samuel McCamant.

Session: December 2, 1839—March 19, 1840.
House of Delegates: James C. Spotts.
Senate: Samuel McCamant.

Session: December 1, 1840—March 22, 1841.
House of Delegates: James C. Spotts.
Senate: James H. Piper. Senatorial District now composed of TAZEWELL, Wythe, Grayson, Smythe and part of Pulaski.

Session: December 6, 1841—March 26, 1842.
House of Delegates: Henry Bowen.
Senate: James H. Piper.

Session: December 5, 1842—March 28, 1843.
House of Delegates: James C. Spotts.
Senate: James H. Piper.

Session: December 4, 1843—February 15, 1844.
House of Delegates: Alexander Harrison.
Senate: James H. Piper.

Session: December 2, 1844—February 22, 1845.
House of Delegates: Harvey G. Peery.
Senate: James H. Piper.

Session: December 1, 1845—March 6, 1846.
House of Delegates: Samuel Laird.
Senate: James H. Piper.

Session: December 7, 1846—March 23, 1847.
House of Delegates: Thomas H. Gillespie.
Senate: John W. Johnston.

Session: December 6 1847—April 5, 1848.
House of Delegates: Thomas H. Gillespie.
Senate: John W. Johnston.

Sessions: December 4, 1848—March 19, 1849; May 28—June 4, 1849; June 11—August 17, 1849.
House of Delegates: Harvey George.
Senate: Thomas M. Tate. Senatorial District now composed of TAZEWELL, Wythe, Grayson, Smythe, Carroll and Pulaski.

Session: December 3, 1849—March 22, 1850.
House of Delegates: Hervey George.
Senate: Thomas M. Tate.

Session: December 2, 1850—March 31, 1851.
House of Delegates: James W. M. Witten.
Senate: Thomas M. Tate.

Sessions: January 12—June 7, 1852. November 22, 1852—April 11, 1853.
House of Delegates: James W. M. Witten.
Senate: Charles H. Greever. Senatorial District now composed of TAZEWELL, Mercer, Monroe, and Giles

CHAPTER III.

Act Creating, and Fixing the Boundary Lines of Tazewell County, and Subsequent Changes Made of Such Lines.

The original Act of the General Assembly of Virginia, authorizing the formation of Tazewell County and fixing the boundaries thereof, was passed at the session of 1799, on December 19th. The boundaries designated therein are as follows: "Beginning on the Kanawha line, which divides Montgomery and Wythe Counties, thence to where said line crosses the top of Brushy Mountain, thence along the top of said mountain to its junction with Garden Mountain, thence along the top of said mountain to the Clinch Mountain, thence along the top of said mountain to the head of Cove Creek, a branch of the Maiden Spring Fork of Clinch River, thence a straight line to Mann's Gap in Kent's Ridge, thence North 45° West to the line which divides Kentucky from Virginia, thence along said line to the Kanawha line, and with said line to the place of Beginning."

For a full and complete record of "The Origin and Descent of Tazewell County", the reader is referred to Chapter VI, Pendleton's History of Tazewell County, beginning on page 547. Extracts from said chapter:

"On the 19th of December, 1799, the General Assembly passed an act creating the county of Tazewell to be formed from a part of Wythe, and a part of Russell. From the foregoing synopsis of the processes by which Tazewell County came into existence it is easy to trace its civil descent from the first colony planted at James town. The following is the line of descent:

"The Grand Assemblie Holden at James City the 21st of August, 1633," passed an act that divided the Virginia Colony into eight shires, which were to be governed as the shires of England, and named as follows:

"James City, Henrico, Warwick River, Warroskuyoak, Charles City, Elizabeth City, Charles River and Accawmack."

"The Grand Assemblie, holden at James Citty the 2nd of March, 1642-3" passed an act which declared in part: "It is likewise enacted and confirmed that Charles River shall be distinguished by this name (County of York)." This meant that Charles River Shire, created by the act of August 21st, 1633, should thereafter be known as York County, and in this manner York County was created in 1643.

New Kent County was formed from York County in 1654.

King and Queen County was formed from New Kent in 1691, the third year of the reign of William and Mary.

Essex County was formed from a part of (old) Rappahannock in 1692. "Old Rappahannock" having previously been a part of York County.

Thus it is seen that the two counties, King and Queen and Essex, were directly descended from Charles River Shire.

King William County was formed from King and Queen County in 1701.

Spottsylvania was formed from Essex, King and Queen, and King William in 1720.

Orange County was formed from Spottsylvania in 1724.

Augusta County was formed from Orange in 1738.

Botetourt County was formed from Augusta in 1769.

Fincastle County was formed from Botetourt in 1772.

Washington County and Montgomery County were formed from Fincastle in 1776.

Russell County was formed from Washington in 1786.

Wythe County was formed from Montgomery in 1789.

Tazewell County was formed from Wythe and Russell in 1799.

By and through the foregoing detailed processes, covering a period of one hundred and ninety-two years, the great county of Tazewell was generated from the first permanent English settlement made upon the North American Continent".

The boundary lines of the county were changed by subsequent Acts as follows:

An Act, forming Giles County, Acts, 1805-6, p. 49.

An Act, changing Russell County line, Acts 1806-7, p. 3.

An Act, forming Logan County from part of Tazewell, 1823-24, p. 16.

An Act, adding part of County to Wythe and Russell, 1825-26, p. 8.

An Act, adding part of Tazewell to Giles County, 1825-26, p. 14.

An Act, running dividing line between Giles and Tazewell, 1827-28, p. 29.

An Act, adding part of Tazewell to Logan County, 1833-34, p. 85.

An Act, adding part of Tazewell to Giles County, 1835-36 p. 64.

An Act, forming Mercer County from part of Tazewell, 1836-37, p. 41.

An Act, forming Buchanan County from part of Tazewell, 1857-58, p. 49.

An Act, forming McDowell County from part of Tazewell, 1857-58, p. 67.

An Act, forming Bland County from part of Tazewell, 1861, p. 141.

CHAPTER IV.

Laws Concerning Marriage; Copy of Marriage Records From 1800 to 1852-3.

Under the law governing marriages existing in 1800 and for many years thereafter, the contracting parties not only had to obtain the license from the Clerk of the County, but the prospective husband was required to execute bond with security, before obtaining marriage license. A copy of such proceedings is here given:

"Sir

You please to grant Solomon Milam Licens to marry my daughter Nancy Harman and in so doing you will oblidge your friend
To Mr. Joseph Moore ———— Daniel Harman
Dpt. Clerk under John Ward of Tazewell County November 29th 1804.

      Sworn to before me this 29th of November 1804
test   J. MOORE
ADAM HARMAN
HENRY HARMAN."   *Bond.*

"Know all men by these presents that we Solomon Milam and Adam Harman are held and firmly bound unto John Page Esqr. Governor of Virginia and his successors in the sum of one hundred & fifty Dollars payment whereof well and truly to be made to the said Governor and his successors we bind ourselves our Heirs & c Jointly and severally firmly by these presents sealed with our Seals and dated the 29th day of November 1804.

The condition of the above obligation is such that whereas the above bound Solomon Milam hath this day obtained License for his marriage with Nancy Harman, if therefore there is no legal cause to prevent the marriage for which the said license was given, then the above obligation to be void, otherwise to remain and be in force.

Teste   SOLOMON MILAM (Seal)
Moore, D. C.   ADAM HARMAN (Seal)"

The originals of the above proceedings are on file in our office.

An Exact Copy of Marriage Records From 1800 to 1852-3 as Shown by Marriage Registers Numbers One and Two.

"A Return of Marriages executed by John Tollett
    Dec. 30th 1802, Thomas Cartmill & Nancy Compton
    Jany 4th 1803, John Burgess and Janey Shannan
    March 11th —— Moses Justice and Susanna Stump
    March 17th —— Bird Lockerd and Nancy Mcentosh
    April 24th David Young & Janey Bollen
    May 10th John Stafford & Nancy Runyon
    May 25th Stephen Deskins & Anne Mctosh
    June 17th John Shields & Lizabeth Coburn
    Augt 29th Samuel Young & Rebecca Danel
    Sept 1st John Pruett and Polly McBroom
    Sept 15th James *Mor* and Nancy Shannan
    January 5th 1804 Samuel Lusk & Sarah Bailey
    January 10th William Suter & Rebecca Dills
    January 10 Thomas Gison and Polly Peery

                                    JOHN TOLLETT

A memorandum of Marriages in the year 1801
    Adam Milam and Mary Stokes Apl. 28th
    Paul Whitley & Nancy Maxfeel June 10
    Samuel Whitten & Susanna Grenup July 30
    William Whitten & Nancy Hall November 5th

The Year 1802
    George Justice & Martha Mcfarlon January 20
    John Shively & Pheby Lewis January 18
    David Shredar and Rhoda Nuckles March 2
    James Peery and Pheby Pickens March 16
    Hesecia Harman and Polly Brown Apl. 6
    John Crockett & Polly Peery April 20
    Thomas Harrison & Rebecka Peery May 8
    Thomas Ferguson & Mary Jones June 28th
    Samuel McCoy & Elizabeth Davis Augt. 12
    Moses Wortmon and Elizabeth Muncy June 17th

                                    JOHN TOLLETT

Marriages solemnized by D. Ward

  15th May 1801 Joseph Harrisson Rachel Lockart
  10th Feby 1803 John Graham Rebecka Witten
  18th June 1802 Wm. Wingo—Mary McGuire
  2nd Nov. 1801 Robert Doak—Rachel Thompson
  19th Oct. 1802 Nathl. Young—Sally Deskins
  6th Augt. 1802 Rees Gillespie—Levicie Bowen
  5th Nov. 1801 Robert Pritchett—Charity Lockart
  23rd Nov. 1803 Steph. Blankenship—Jane Peterson
  4th Feby 1804 Wm. Gent Peggy Robertson
  25th Apl. 1804 Wm. Maxwell—Mary Witten
  24th Jany. 1804 Presly Davis—Sally Cochrall
  8th July 1805 Danl. Lockart Polly Ward
  Augt. 1805 James Lockhart Polly Bowland
  20th Augt 1805 Mark Gent—Polly Robertson
  —— Samuel C. Sellars Nancy Daniel
  1803 Wm. McGuire—Margaret Brown
  ——Joshua Cecil—Jane Cummins
  1805 Wm. Newton—Betsey Todd
  —— Isaac Brown—Polly Thompson
  Feby 1805 Mathew Stephenson Betsey Brooks
  1804 Benjn. Oney—Sally Allen

  I do certify that the above named persons have been lawfully joined together in Matrimony by me since the time I was authorized to marry in Tazewell County   DAVID WARD

                                Sep 24th 1805

  Agreeable to License legally obtained, I have solemnized the Rites of matrimony between John Brown & Phebe Claypool the 26th of June 1800   EDWARD KELLY

  Benjamin Ramy and Nancy Oney the 26th of June 1800
  Abel Griffith & Zilpha Bruster the 9th of Sept 1800
  Embly Millard & Sara Roark the 7th of October 1800

  I do hereby certify that I have joined Thomas Morgan & Rachel Blankenship in the State of matrimony according to law. Given under my hand this 21st day of October 1801

                                  ALEXR. ROSS

Agreeable to License legally obtained I have solemnized the matrimony between Ralph Steel and Mary Griffitt the 3rd day of February 1803   EDWARD KELLY

This is to certify to the Clerk of Tazewell County that Isaac Adkins & Elizabeth Hager was lawfully joined in holy matrimony on the 6th day of May 1804, according to Law, by viirtue of License bearing date February 16th 1804. This given under my hand this 6th day of May 1804   NEH. BONHAM
Teste:
PETER DILLS
MARY DILLS

I do hereby certify that according to the Act of the General Assembly, I have solemnized the holy ordance of matrimony between David Bishop & Elizabeth Wolford, February 20th 1801
                    by JAMES HOBBS

A List of Licensed Marriages Selabrated as followeth,
    Daniel Day & Christena Milam Marid Sepr. 11th 1805
    George Davidson and Elizabeth Cartmill Marrid Sepr. 26th 1805
    Thomas Workman & Sarah Deskins Married October 24th 1805
    Benjamin Pruet & Mary Maloney Married January 7th 1806
    William Maxwell & Elizabeth Maxwell Married Jany 23 1806
                    By me HENRY HARMAN

These are to certify that on the Blank day of August 1804 was William Berry & Patty Knot Joined in Holy wedlock by me Nehemiah Bonham By virtue of Publication. N. B. I having lost the papers of this marriage renders me unable to give the day of the Month

This is to make known to all whom it concerns that on the 11 day of February 1804 was Joined in holy Matrimony Elias Kid and Margaret Bagley by virtue of License from the County Court of Tazewell By me   NEHE. BONHAM

Marriages Solemnized by Henry Harman
    James Conley & Rachel Stobough 22nd May 1806
    Ambrus Hall & Peggy Peery June 3d 1806
Solomon Peery & Sally Cartmill Feby 7th 1806
    William Taylor & Sally Taylor Nov. 27th 1806
    Samuel Morgan & Phebey Stuart June 3th 1806

Thomas Stratton & Nancy Morgan March 27th 1806
William Luster and Molley Blankenship Dec. 18th 1806
Henry Harman & Martha Bailey Jany 1 1807
William Lusk & Charity Runyan Dec 25th 1806
Benjaman Runyan & Polly Lusk Jany 6th 1807
John Maxwell & Jean Maxwell Jany 8 1807
Samuel Witten & Pheby Winne Jany 8th 1807
Thomas Mitchell & Polly Harman — 8th 1807
Samuel Dailey & Catey Peery June 17th 1806

HENRY HARMAN

Marriages Solemnized by David Ward between the 24th of Sept 1805 & the 28th day of May 1807
David Belshe & Nelly Asberry
William K. Higginbotham & Elizabeth Boling
William Boling & Levina Asberry
Peter Gollehen & Priscella Fulks
Joseph Oney & Susannah Witten
George Todd & Sarah Brooks
James Vandike & Susannah Moore
George Shortridge & Dicey Elkins
John Smith & Peggey Belche

DAVID WARD

A List of Marriages Selebrated
Married William Dills & Rebeca Day January 27th 1807
Frederick Cook & Jinny Neele Feby 10th 1807
John Compton & Polly Walls March 5th 1807
James Slater & Caty Davis August 6th 1807
John Bartrum & Polley Davis August 2th 1807
James Starr & Jenny Doak Nov 5 1807
Thomas Peery & Polley Peery Feby 4th 1808

By me HENRY HARMAN

The following marriages were solemnized by the Subscriber
1st David Peery & Eleanor Harman Dec 18th A. D. 1806
2nd John Jones & Ruthy Luster Dec 21st A. D. 1806
3th William Davidson & Phebe Harmon A D 1806
4th James Scaggs & Kenah Witten A D 1807
5th Phillip Vincel & Eleanor Davis A D 1807
6th Hugh Currin Peggy Wynne A D 1807

7th William Price & Betsey Cecil A D 1807
8th James Gillaspey and Polly Greenup A D 1807.

JOAB WATSON

I hereby certify that Mr. John Greenup was married to the amiable Miss Linny Cecill of Montgomery on March 13th A. D. 1808 Sunday evening.   JOAB WATSON

I do certify that the following is a true List of the names of persons joined together in the state of matrimony by me since my last return

August 4th 1807 Joseph Smith Taba Asberry
Octo 28th 1807 William Asberry Polly Smith
Sep 24th 1807 John Prater Margret Griffits
Nov. 7th 1807 James Harrisson, Polley Gillaspey
Dec 31st 1807 Drury Young Sophia Henkle
Dec 31st 1807 Jas. Husk Rebeckah Whitt
Jany 15th 1808 Charles Bates Sally Bruster

DAVID WARD
March 22nd 1808

I do Certify that I have celebrated the rights of Matrimoney between Ralph Fulk and Mary Clark they applying with a licens from the Clerk of Tazewell County this 16th day of July 1807

RICHD. BROWNING

Agreeable to Licence legally obtained *am* have Solemnised the rights of Matrimony between Peter Day and Jane fannan Febuary the 18th 1808   EDWARD KELLY

Agreeable to License legally obtained I have solemnized the right of Matrimoney Between Robert Shortridge and Rebecah Brown this 31st day of December 1807   EDWARD KELLEY

Thise are *saddisfy* all whome it may concern that on the 10th day of Julye 1808, was William Richardson and Rhoda Hicks Joined in Matrimoney By Virtue of Licence from the County Clerk of Tazewell County bearing Date July 5th 1808

By me NEHE. BONHAM

Tazewell County to wit

Robert Wiley and Mary Mason came before me and were joined together in the holey State of Matrimoney 15th day of July 1809

ISAAC QUINN

Tazewell County towit

This is to certify that That William Clark and Ann Asberry came before me and ware Joined togeather in the Holy State of Matrimoney August 29th 1809   ISAAC QUINN

I also certify to you that on the 25th day of August 1809 Thomas Little Eunice Allen was Joined in matrimoney together according to Law by Licence from Joseph Moore by me
                                    JOHN PERRY

I also certify to you that on the 12th Day of October 1809 Isam Tomblinson and Polly Peery was Joined in matrimoney together according to Law by me   NEHEMIAH BONHAM

I also certify to you that on the 15th day of October 1809, John Shannon and Jenny Cartmill was Joined Joined in matrimoney together according to Law, by me   JOHN PERRY

I Certify to you that on the 29th Day of October 1809 James Milam and Peggy Davidson were Joine in matrimony togehter according to Law, by me   JOHN PERRY

I Certify to you that on the 7th day of November 1809 Zachariah Toler and Lucy Blankenship were Joined in matrimoney together according to Law, by me   JOHN PERRY

Nov. 25th 1808 William Bailey & Elly Shannon
Dec. 28th 1808 Wm. Blankenship & Avey Williams
Febe 3d 1809 Danl. Deskins & Peggy Francisco
March 30 Do Howard Havins & Mattey Davidson
March 16th Do. Wm. Jones & Nancy Todd
July 26th Do. Robt. Maxwell & Rebeah Maxwell
Octo. 22nd Do George Cummings & Polly Brumfield
July 5th Do. George Peery & Jenney Thompson

I do certify that the above is a true list of persons names Joined together in the State of Matrimoney by me since the last Return
                                    DAVID WARD
                                    Octo 23d 1809

This to Sertify that I jined these persons toGether in the Holley Estate of Matrimony

Lennel Clyburn and Nancy Brooks on December 12 Day 1809

Henry Bolin and Mary Higginbotham on December 19th Day 1809

William Thompson and Leuece Gelaspy on January 25th Day 1801

William Garrisson and fanny Higginbotham on July 3 Day 1801

James Griffitt and Sinthy Nelson on August 2 Day 1801

Jined toGether by me   DAVID YOUNG

This is to Certify that I joined together John Asberry and Polly Ratliff on the 17 day of Janary 1811

And I also Joined together Thomas Chafin and Polly Asbury on the 8th day of May 1811

And I also Joined together John Gillespie and Roda Harman on the 31st day of January 1811

And I also Joined together Charles Higginbotham and Milly Blankenship on the 21st day of May 1811

These are Joined by   DAVID YOUNG

This is to certify that I joined William Curl and Rebecca Oney on the 6th day of June 1811

Thomas Cecil & Jinney Stratton on the 28th day of August 1811

John Smith & Polly Vincel on the 29th day of August 1811

Jonathan Williams & Betsy Blankenship on the 19th day of Sep. 1811

These are Jined together By me   DAVID YOUNG

This to certify that on the 8th day of November 1811 I joined together John Cecil and Linny Witten in holey matrimoney

    DAVID YOUNG

This is to Certify to John Crockett Clerk of T C that on the 15th Day of November 1809 Eli Blankenship and Polly Smith were married together by licene from under Joseph Moore hand by me

    JOHN PERRY

I also certify to you on the 30th day of November 1809 James P. Carrel & Patsey Peery was Joined together according to law, by me   JOHN PERRY

I also certify to you that on the 1st Day of Feby 1810 Henry Runyan and Hannah Collins was Joined together according to Law, by me   JOHN PERRY

I also certify to you that on the 14th day of June 1810 Larkin S. Kidd and Elizabeth Jones was Joined together according to law by me   JOHN PERRY

I also certify to you that on the 1st Day of Nov. 1810 George Perry and Nancy Bruster was Joined together according to law, by me   JOHN PERRY

I also certify to you that on the 25th day of Decemb. 1810 John Wynne and Olivy Peery was Joined together according to Law by me   JOHN PERRY

I Certify to you that on the 22nd Day of July 1810 Rober Neel and Rebeckah Waggoner was Joined together according to Law by me   JOHN PERRY

I Certify to John Crockett C T C that on the 26 day of December 1810 James Marrs & Sally Workmon was Joined together according to law by me   JOHN PERRY

I Certify to you that on the 11th day of April 1811 Fielding Burton & Thursza Hager was Joined together according to Law by me   JOHN PERRY

I Certify to you that on the 26th Day of May 1811 Adom Waterford and Betsey Day people of Colour was Joined together according to Law by me   JOHN PERRY

I Certify to you that on the 20th Day of June 1811 Charles Lusk and Anne Runyan was Joined together according to Law by me   JOHN PERRY

Tazewell County

These are to certify that on the 9 day of June 1812 Hickman Cumpton & Elizabeth Justice was Joined in Holy matrimoney By Virtue of Licence bearing date May 29th 1812 This given under my hand this day & year above written   NEHEM. BONHAM

I Certify to the Clerk of Tazewell County Towit, That on the 9th day of July 1811 Absolum Godfrey and Polley Bailey was Joined in the holey *Esta*te of Matrimoney by Licence Dated July the 6th 1811 me   JOHN PERRY

I Do Certify to the Clerk of Tazewell County that on the 11th Day of July 1811 Elijah Kidd & Tilly Neel was Joined Together in the holey estate of Matrimoney by publication of the Banns by me   JOHN PERRY

I Certify to the Clerk of Tazewell County that on the 29th day of August 1811 Archibald Peery and Nancy Peery was Joined together in the holy estate of matrimoney by licence dated the 28th of August 1811 by me   JOHN PERRY

I Certify to the Clerk of Tazewell County on the 15th Day of September 1811 Hervy Stump & Milly Cecil was Joined together in the holey estate of matrimoney by Licence Dated the 10th day of Sept. 1811 by me   JOHN PERRY

I also cerify to the Clerk of Tazewell that on the 24 Day of December 1811 Hiram Peery & Ruth Lasley was Joined together in the holey estate of Matrimoney by licence Joseph Moore by me
JOHN PERRY

I also certify to the Cilerk of Tazewell that on the 2d Day of March 1812 Charles Pleasant & Betsey Blackwell was Joined together in holy wedlock by license by J. Moore by me
JOHN PERRY

I also certify to the Clerk of Tazewell that on the 12th day of March 1812 *Ziba* Mitchum & Vena Smith That on the 22d of March 1812 Richard Lambert & Frankey Stowers was Joined together in the holey estate of wedlock by Publishing the Baons by me
JOHN PERRY

I also certify to the Clerk of Tazewell County that on the 23d of April 1812 Dodrigge Baily & Phebe Belcher was Joined together by licence the 6th day of June

Abraham Harris & Rachel Williams was Joined together by publication of Baans by me   JOHN PERRY

I certify to the Clerk of Tazewell, that on the 21 Day of August 1812 John Lambert and Rebeckah Power was Joined by licence Also on the 1st day of Sept 1812 Robert Wynne & Peggy Russell was Joined by licence John Carter & Betsey Carver on the 10th Day of Octo 1812 was Joined by publication of the *Baans* by
JOHN PERRY

October 26th day 1812

This is to Sertify that I have Joined these persons in holy wedlock

Joined Jacob Butcher & Hannah Beverly on the 2 day of Jany 1812

Joined Charles Young and Polly Trent on the 12 day of March 1812

Joined Witt Asberry & Betsey Chafin on the 25 day of March 1812

Joined Daniel Young & Mary Johnston on the 11 day of June 1812

Joined James Asberry & Caty Francisco on the 25 day of June 1812

Joined William Griffiitts & Leathea Ratliff on the 15 day of October 1812

These Joined together in the holy state of matrimoney by me

DAVID YOUNG

Tazewell County towit

I David Young do Certify that the following List contains all the marriages Celebrated by me within the preceeding year

Archabald Elkins & Hannah Stephenson on the 5 day of January 1815

James Charles & Anne Wynn on the 19th day of January 1815

Buse Harmon & Nancy Cecil on the 19th day of April 1815

Neely Johnston & Caty Davis on the 8 day of June 1815

William Bevers & Rebeccah Mitchel on the 11 day of June 1815

William Davis & Levina Totten on the 15th day June 1815

Thomas Brown & Rachel Mentosh on 22 day of June 1815

Abednego White & Nancy Blackwell 27 day of July 1815

Hezekiah Blankenship & Nancy Boling on the 14th day of Sept 1815

Leonard Harper & Pattey Follen on the 14 day of Sept. 1815

John Mitchel & Sally Hankins on the 5 day of October 1815

These are Joined together by me in the year 1815

DAVID YOUNG

A return of marriages

I Do certify to John Crockett Clerk of Tazewell County that John Crow & Sally Lambert was Joined together in the holy estate of Matrimoney the 30th Day of December 1813

Ephriam Dumbar & Elizabeth Harman on the 20th day of Jany 1814

Jameson Richard Billips & Nancy Wright on the 13th day of March 1814

Richard Lambert & Nancy Fortner on the 28th day of April 1814

John Shannon & Rebecah Cumpton on the 7th day of Augst. 1814

Philip Solsberry & Betsey Bailey on the 22nd day of Jany 1815

William Carter & Catherine Williams 22nd day of Jany 1815

John Gilbert & Sally Taber on the 16th day of April 1815

John Belcher & Jincey Nuckles on the 5th day of May 1815

JOHN PERRY

Tazewell County towit

I David Young do Certify that the following List contains all the marrid*ges* Celebrated by me within preceeding Year

I Joined together Joseph Pruett and Susannah Clevinger on 2nd day of Jany 1814

    Joseph Hankins & Nancy Mitchel on the 2 day of January 1814
    David Allin & Margret Dailey on the 24th of February 1814
    John Deskins & Polly Totten on the 4 day of April 1814
    Joseph Welle & Polly Henkel on the 20th of April 1814
    Andrew Edmonson & Jean C. Bowen on the 10th day of November 1814
    Thomas Dailey & Sally MCantosh 28th day of September 1814
    These are Joined together by me in the year 1814

                                            DAVID YOUNG

Wm. Oney and Sarah Brown married March 22th 1812
John Richa and Elizabeth MCKintosh married July 14th 1813
Wm. Green and Sarah Bostick married October 3th 1814

                                            WILLIAM LAZEWEL

Tazewell County towit

This is to certify that I Joined the following persons in holey wedlock in the year 1813

    James Prater and Phebe Griffitts on the 14th day of January 1813
    Hiram Witten and Jinney Lard on the 15th day of February 1813
    Isaac Quinn and Cinthea Witten on the 6th day of October 1813
    Samuel Young & Sarah Folling on the 18th day of October 1813

                                            DAVID YOUNG

I do hereby certify to the Clerk of Tazewell County that on the 27 Day of December 1812 Cornelias Brown *Alias Stump and Betsey Cotton* was Joined together in Matrimoney by Publication of the Banns by me   JOHN PERRY

    Robert Wynn & Levina Hix on the 4th day of Feby 1813
    Robert Ward & Jinney Peery 9th day of Feb 1813
    Jesse Belcher & Sophia McKinsey on the 16th day of April 1813
    William Hearn & Busannah Hix 3th day of June 1813
    James Toler & Nancy Wall on the 5th day of August 1813
    James MCNeely & Milly Wall on the 5th day of August 1813
    John Milam & Barbara Shrader on the 26th day of August 1813

Samuel Wynn & Sally Hix on the 2nd day Sept. 1813

Jedediah Mitcham & Joana Smith on the 13th day of Sept 1813

John Crow (or Cron) & Sally Lambert on the 30th day of December 1813

Ephram Dunbarr & Elizabeth Harman on the 20th day of Jany 1814   JOHN PERRY

Tazewell County December 25th 1815

This certifies that I solemnised the marage Contract between Adam Vincel and Sally Lockhart

Joseph Moore D.CC.   ISAAC QUINN

This is to certify that on the ninth day of April last I celebrated the rights of matrimoney between W. Muncey & Sally Dailey according to Law

Given under my hand as above

1816 August 27th   GEORGE EAKINS

Tazewell County towit

I David Young do certify that the following List contains all the Marriages Celebrated by me within the preceeding year

I Joined Balam Boling and fanny Higginbotham together on the fifteenth day of february 1816

I also Joined Charles Dayley and Hannah Bruster together on the Sixth day of June 1816

I also Joined thomas Bruster and Rebecah MCantosh together on the 19th day of Sept

These are joined together by me   DAVID YOUNG

Sir

I transmit to your office By your authority on the twenty ninth of September 1815 Joined together John Cummings and Polly Right

    JAMES CHARLES

I do hereby certify that on the 3rd of September 1816 I celebrated the nuptal Rites between Henry Hennegar and Peggy Corbit according to Law   GEORGE EAKINS

I do hereby certify that on the 5th of April 1812 I Celebrated the nuptial rites between Adam Harman & Lavisa Harman according to Law   SAML. H. THOMPSON

I Do certify to John Crockett Clerk of Tazewell County that on the 16th day Apl. 1815 John Gibbit & Sally Taber was Joined togetheer in the holy Estate of matrimoney by licence by me

    JOHN PERRY

I also Certify to the Celrk of T County that on the 29th Day of April 1815 John Belcher and Jenney Nuckles was joined together in the holy estate of Matrimoney by licence by me

JOHN PERRY

I do certify to John Crockett Clerk of sd. County that on the 6th Day of August 1815 Joshua Peery and Nancey Power was Joined together in the holy estate of matrimoney by licence by me

I do certify to John Crockett Clerk of sd. County that on the 29th Day of february 1816 Larkin Stowers and Nancy Lambert was Joined together in the holy estate of matrimoney by licence by me

JOHN PERRY

I do Certify to the Clerk of said County that on the 6th day of June 1816 Henry Epperheart and Christena Day was joined together in the holy estate of matrimoney by licence by me

JOHN PERRY

I Do Certify to the Clerk of Tazewell County that on the 2nd day of July 1816 Gideon Wright and Elonor Waggoner

Also James Power and Raches Cecel the 11th day of sid. month & date was Joined together in the holy estate of matrimony by licence by me

JOHN PERRY

I do certify to the Clerk of Tazewell County that on the 21st day of November 1816 Christopher Dillion & Rhoda Bailey was Joined together in the hold estate of matrimoney by licence by me

JOHN PERRY

I also certify to John Crockett Clerk of Tazewell County that on the 3th Day of December 1816 David Steel and Matty Perry was Joined together in the holy estate of Matrimoney by Licence by me

JOHN PERRY

Oct 31st 1816

This day I solemnised the Marriage Contract between John Dawson and Betsey White Tazewell Cy Virginia

ISAAC QUINN

This certifies that the marage Contract has been Duly solemnised between William Gibson and Permilia Peery March 10th 1817

ISAAC QUINN

This certifies that the Marage Contract has been Legaly Solemnised between George Webb and Betsey Perdew March 10th 1817

ISAAC QUINN

This Certifies that the Marage Contract has been duly solemnised between James Coldwell and Sally Cecil March 20th 1817

          ISAAC QUINN

Tazewell County towit

I David Young do hereby Certify that the following list contains all the marrages Celebrated by me within the preceeding year

Absolum Young and Sally Brumfield on the 12 day December 1816

George MCantosh and Isbel Bruster on the 19 day December 1816

Randle Henkle & Charlotte Young on the 19th day December 1816

Joseph Higgenbotham & Milly Young on the 6th day February 1817

Squire Oney and Hannah Scaggs on the 22nd day May 1817

Alexander Ward and Jenney Thompson on the 19 day June 1817

John W. Johnston Levise S. Bowen on the 7 day October 1817

Rubin Pruett & Nancy Vandikes on the 30th Day of October 1817

Henry Blankenship and Sally Vandikes 30 day of October 1817

Joshua MGuire & Polly MGuire on the 6th day November 1817

These are executed by me   DAVID YOUNG

I Do hereby certify to John Crockett Clerk of Tazewell County that on the time registered on this list the following Couples was Joined together by me John Perry to wit,

Daniel Clark & Mary Mattingley May 28th 1817 by Licence

Also Rolin Dillion and Betsey Clark August the 21 by licence 1817

Joseph Claypole & Rebeckah Sanders August 31:1817 by publication of Banes

Also Hiram Compton & Jenny Shannon September the 23th 1817 by licence

Also Eli Lusk & Elizabeth Bailey on November the 23d 1817 by licence

Also Absolum Lusk and Dilly Bailey on November 27th 1817 by licence

Also Henry Stump and Sally Pruit March 26th 1818 by publications of Banes, All being Joined together in holy matrimony according to the rites and ceremonies of the Church to which they belong by me   JOHN PERRY

April the 10th 1818

These Certify that the Marriage Contract has been solemnised between James Witten and Rebecca Peery   ISAAC QUINN

May the 10th 1818

These Certify that the Marriage Contract has been solemnised between Thomas Peery and Anne Gose   ISAAC QUINN

November the 4th 1817

These Certify that the marriage Contract has been duly solemnised between John Vincell and and Nancy Barrett
                                   ISAAC QUINN

November the 8th 1817

These Certify that the marriage Contract has been Duly Solemnised between William Sayers and Lettay Laird
                                   ISAAC QUINN

Married by me according to Law

John Davidson & Tabitha Witten December 25th 1817 Tazewell County Virginia and

Samuel Dillion & Polly Rinehart March 29th 1818 Tazewell County Va.   JAMES PORTER A E

June 23th 1818

Sir I transmit to your office By your authority on the 15th July 1817 Joined together Peter Gose and Isabella Kimbrough in holy state of matrimony,

Also Robert Waddle and Polly Johnston on the 17 October 1817

Likewise on the 3 day of March 1818 James Hall & Magdalen Wynn   JAMES CHARLES

Tazewell County towit

I David Young do certify that the following list contains all the Marriages Celebrated by me within the preceeding year

I Joined Samuel Cecil and Rebeca Smith together according to Law on the 18 day of November 1817

I Joined George Asburry and Polly Chaffin together according to Law on the 22nd day of April 1818

I Joined John Barns and Lilley Heldrith together according to law on the 8th day of October 1818

I Joined Stephen Low & Susannah Griffitts together according to law on the 17th day of Sept 1818

I Joined Milton Ward and Matty D. Thompson together according to Law on the 15th day of Octo 1818

I Joined Tolbert Blankenship and Jane Bostick together according to Law on the 20th day of October 1818

I Joined David Stephenson and Phebe Belcha together according to Law on the 5th day of November 1818

These are Joined together By me   DAVID YOUNG
October the 21st 1818

This certify that the marriage contract has been duly solemnised between Philip Greever and Mary Workman

                                            ISAAC QUINN

Sept. 25th 1818

These certify that the marriage contract has been duely solemnised between Alexander Harrison and Malvina Harman

                                            ISAAC QUINN

October the 12th 1818

These certify that the marriage contract has been duely solemnised between Henry Harman and Polly Day

                                            ISAAC QUINN

November the 19th 1819

I do hereby certify to John Crockett Clerk of Tazewell County that the under named Persons were joined together by me on the day and month and year annexed to their names in the holy state of Matrimony Viz.

    Philip Cecil and Elizabeth Tomlinson on December the 3rd 1818
    Jesse Belcher and Elizabeth Dillion December the 25th 1818
    Joseph Hix and Rebekah Dills February the 16 1819
    Low Brown and Elenor Compton February the 25 1819
    Hampton Foster and Jemima Waggoner June the 17th 1819
    Jonathan Pauley and Susannah Boyd July the 15 1819
    Joshua Hervy and Nancy Walls August the 17 1819
    Phillip Harless and Caty Hager September the 16 1819
    William Bailey and Susanna Lusk November the 11 1819
    Thomas Cassaday and Elizabeth Neel November the 25 1819.
    Certifyed by me   JOHN PERRY

N. B. These were all Married by licence

Tazewell County to wit

I David Young do certify that the following list contains all the marriages celebrated by me within the preceeding year.

I Joined Robart Gillespie and Jane Ward on the 31 day of December 1818

I Joined Rees Ward and Elizabeth Bowen on the 29 day of January 1819

I Joined Jeames Bruster and Rachel Lockhart on the 7 day of January 1819

I Joined Moses Beavers and Phebe Harman on the 9 day of February 1819

I Joined George Wolford and Poley Green on the 11 day of Febury 1819

I Joined Maxwell Mars and Jane Brooks on the 18 day of March 1819

I Joined Squire Johnston and Polly Luster on the 1 day of June 1819

I Joined Oliver Crafford Catherine Griffitts on the 20 day of June 1819

I Joined Fedrick Clark and Polly Kindrick on the 10 day June 1819

I Joined Thomas Bruster and Polly Deskins the 25t day July 1819

I Joined Moses Christian and Polly Beevers on the 29 day of July 1819

I Join'd Archable Barnet and Nancy Beevers on the 29 day July 1819

I Joined James Witten and Levicy Thompson on the 4 day November 1819

I Joined Robert Allen and Betsey Kesky on the 18 day November 1819

These are executed by me   DAVID YOUNG
Tazewell County December the 28 1819

Performed the Matrimonial Rites. Wm. Boils & Anny Vincell January 22 1819

Alexander Cook & Elenor Stump Sept. 16 1819

John C. Lusk & Polly Corder 21 October 1819

Wm. Wilson & Jenny Maxwell June the 3 1819

John Gipson & Cynthie Peery March the 18 1819

Cornelius Shannon & Anne McGrannahan December the 11, 1819 August the 23rd 1819.   JAMES CHARLES

These are certify that the marriage contract has been duly solemnised between Henry Vincell and Elizabeth Doake
    ISAAC QUINN

October the 2nd 1819.
   These are to certify that the marriage contract has been duly solemnised between Martain Peery & Ruth ODonald
                              ISAAC QUINN

December the 3rd 1819.
   These are to certify that the marriage contract has been duly solemnised between Charles Tiffany and Maria Crockett
                              ISAAC QUINN

August the 10th 1820
   These are to certify that the marriage contract has been duely solemnised between Henry P. George and Polly A. Williams
                              ISAAC QUINN

May 24th 1820
   These are to certify that the marriage contract has been duely solemnised between Joseph McGuire & Chloe Trent
                              ISAAC QUINN

March the 30th 1820
   These are to certify that the marriage contract has been duely solemnised between Joseph Peery and Peggy Gose
                              ISAAC QUINN

February the 10th 1820
   These are to certify that the marriage contract has been duely solemnised between Thomas Rutledge & Attillia Peery
                              ISAAC QUINN

January the 20th 1820.
   These are to certify that the marriage contract has been duely solemnised between John Nunneley and Permilla Mitchel
                              ISAAC QUINN

January the 21st 1820
   These are to certify that the marriage contract has been duely solemnized between James Peery and Nancy Harman
                              ISAAC QUINN

Tazwell County to wit
   I David Young do certify that the following List contains all the marriages celebrated by me within the preceding year.
   I Joined Adam Harman and Ruth Christian on the 20 day of August 1819
   I Joined Jacob McLaughlin and Elizabeth Clark on the 17 day of Febury 1820

I Joined Harvey Steel and Jean Asbery on the 21 day of September 1820

I Joined Thomas Asbery and Levicy Brooks on the 23 day of March 1820

I Joined George Green and Anne Bostick on the 10 day of March 1820

I Joined James Brooks and Polly Asbery on the 24 day of August 1820

I Joined Rees B. Duff and Lilly Bowen on the 3d day of October 1820

I Joined William Smith and Polly Green on the 30 day of July 1820

I Joined Robert Young and Nancy White on the 25 day of May 1820

I Joined William Barns and Levisa Ward on the 11 day of January 1821

I Joined Elihu McMeans and Nancy Griffitts on the 22 day of February 1821

I Joined Archibald Thompson and Polly Thompson on the 22 day of Febury 1821

Executed by me   DAVID YOUNG

I do hereby certify to John Crockett Clerk of Tazewell County that in the year 1819 on the 15th day of July Jonathan Pauley and Susanna Boyd were joined together in the holey estate of Matrimony by me   JOHN PERRY

That on the 17 day of Augt 1819 Joshua Hervey and Nancy Walls were joined together in the holy estate of matrimony by me
            JOHN PERRY

That on the 16 day of September 1819 Phillip Harless and Caty Hager was joined together in the holy estate of Matrimony by me
            JOHN PERRY

That on the 11th day of November 1819 William Bayley and Susannah Lusk were joined together in the holy estate of matrimony by   JOHN PERRY

That on the 16 day of March 1820 Richard Lambert and Sally Runyon were joined together in the holy estate of matrimony by me
            JOHN PERRY

That on the 6 day of September 1820 Archibald Bailey & Elizabeth Lusk were joined together in the holy estate of matrimony by me
JOHN PERRY

That on the 7th day of September 1820 James MComas and Rebekah Bailey were joined together in the holy estate of matrimony by me
JOHN PERRY

That on the 23d day of November 1820 Charles Scisn and Sally Perry were joined together in the holy state of Matrimony by me
JOHN PERRY

That on the 4th day of January 1821 Reuben Q. Andrews Jenny Knuckles were joined together in the holy estate of matrimony by me
JOHN PERRY

That on the 18th day of January 1821 William Knuckles and Lucy Slauter were joined together in the state of matrimony by me
JOHN PERRY

Tazewell County January 13th 1821.

Sir I transmit to your office by your authority on the third of March 1820 celebrated the matrimonal rights of Benjamin C. Robbins and Juliett Hall

Likewise on the 27th of July 1820 that of Jonathan Peery and Elizabeth Peery.

On the Eleventh day of July 1820 that of Moses Workman and Sarah Mars

On the fourth day of January 1821 that of James Wilson and Pamela Peery

Return made in the year and date above written
JAMES CHARLES

Tazewell County to wit

I David Young do certify that the following list contains all the marriages celebrated by me within the preceding year

I Joined William Brown and Jean Kindrick on the 9th day of March 1821.

I Joined Moses Davis and Nelly Ratcliff on the 29th day of March 1821

I joined William Deskins and Caty Brown on the 17th day of May 1821

I joined John Brooks and Mary Ann Asberry on the 31st day of May 1821

I joined Jeames McGuire and Betsey Brown on the 2 day of August 1821.

I joined Henry W. Cisil and Rebecca Claypole on the 2 day of August 1821

I joined Lynsa Boland and Levicie Brooks on the 11th day of October 1821

I joined Edley MGuire and Susanna Arnhart on the 25th day of October 1821

I joind Samuel Calwell and Ann Eliza Cisel on the 22 day of November 1821

Executed by me   DAVID YOUNG

Tazewell County to wit

I do hereby certify to John Crockett Clerk of said County that in the month of June 1821 James Pendleton and Patsey Millar also John Coleman and Milly Nuckles and George Rinehart and Patsey Nuckles were all joined together in the holy estate of matrimony by me but I have misplaced the licence I do not recolect the day of the month perhaps they are returned and entered already.

I also certify to sd. Clerk that on the 14th of August 1821 William Witton and Jenny Ward was joined together in the holy estate of matrimony by me

I certify to said Clerk that on the 20th day of September 1821 Thomas Ward and Elizabeth Sanders were joined together in the holy estate of matrimony by me

I also certify to said Clerk that on the 22nd of November 1821 Joseph Brown and Nancy Griffey also Benjamin Prince and Nancy Belsher were joined in the holy estate of matrimony by me

I certify to said Clerk that on the 2nd Day of December 1821 William W. Compton & Sarah Compton were joined together in the holy state of matrimony by me

I also certify to the said Clerk that on the 12th day of Jany. 1822 Caleb Davidson and Lockey Jones were joined together in the holy estate of matrimony by me   JOHN PERRY

I do hereby certify to John Crockett Clk of Tazewell County that on the 14th of February 1822 Benjamin Ball and Temperance Fortner was joined together in the holy estate of matrimony by me
                                                JOHN PERRY

I also certify to said Clerk that on the 21st day of Feby 1822 John Corder and Ruth Lusk were joined together in the holey estate of matrimony by me   JOHN PERRY

N. B. All the Couples were joined together by licence from said Clerk except James Pendleton and Patsey Miller which was joined together by publication of the *Banes*   JOHN PERRY

I certify to John Crockett C. T. C. that on the 30th of March 1820 Jubal Jones and Jane Suter were joined together in the holy estate of matrimony by me   SAMUEL NEWBERRY

These are to certify that the marriage contracts have been duely solemnised between the following persons

   Richard and Rebecca Whitt November 18th 1820
   John Beavers and Polly Dillion September 25th 1821
   Woodward South and Dama Moore April 4th 1321
   Lewis Horton and Ruth Davis November 30th 1820
   John Wiley and Eleanor Wilson May 31st 1821
   Richard Bailey and Betsey Rinehart Nov. 28th 1820
   John C. Williams and Eleanor Peery October 20th 1820
   Samuel D. Sayers and Jinney Higginbotham September 16th 1820
   John Sayers and Betsey Goodwin August the 15th 1820
                                                       ISAAC QUINN

I certify that in pursurance of a licence from the Clerk of the County Court of Tazewell I have on the 29' day of March 1822 solemnized the rites of matrimony agreeable to the forms and customs of the Methodist Episcopal Church between James Adams and Levisey Milam

Given under my hand this 10th day of August 1822
                                     ANCIL RICHARDSON, Deacon

These certify that the marriage contracts has been duly solemnised between the following couples in 1822

   Ancil Richardson and Jane G. Davidson
   James Wilson and Eleanor Crockett
   Campbell Maxwell and Jane Whitley
   Israel Vandyke and Polly Beavers
   Nathaniel Pratt and Peggy Laird
   John Crockett and Polly Boyl
   Abraham Still and Patsey P. Moore
   John Boyl and Jane Taylor
   David Christian and Linney Trent   ISAAC QUINN

December the 30th 1822

A List of Marriages celibrated by William Lanwell in the Year of our Lord 1822 in Tazewell County Va

Masteon Christian and Jane McVeinster September 1st

Daniel Jonson Haner Shepley Feby 2

April the 15th 1823

Sir I return to your office on the 6th day of July 1822 Joined together in the Holy Estate of Matrimony Acles Fannon & Eleanor Workman

On the 24th day of October 1822 Jene Bainey & Mary Cook

On the 5th day of December 1822 James Wynn & Sophia Peery

On the 2 Day of January 1823 Phillip Greever and Nancy Ritter

Yours &c   JAMES CHARLES

I hereby certify that on September 19th 1822 I joined together Chrispy Anos Walker and Eleanor C. Whitten as man and wife by virtue of a licence obtaind from the Clerk of Tazewell County Court Given under my hand May 5th 1823

LANDON DUNCAN M. N. T.

Tazewell County to wit

I David Young do certify that the following list contains all the marriages celebrated by me within the preceeding year

Robert Belcher and Nancy on March 21

William Jackson & Jean Matinglee on June 20

Hiram Bolen & Lucy Goodwin April 25

John M. Lockheart & Sally McGuire May 2

Henry Gillespie & Ruth Chaffin April 14

John Stephenson & Lizabeth harkrider Febry. 12

John Augustus Cook & polly Oney Sep 19

Samuel Cerril & Lizabeth Belcher Des 22

Hugh Young and Levicy Bowen January 16

John Steel and Peggy Shufflebarger Jun 24

George Higginbotham & Patsey Chaffin Jun 21

Evans Griffitts & Polly Ratliff Jun 11

William Blankenship & Bersheba Ratliff Jun 28

These are Executed by me   DAVID YOUNG

(1823)

I do hereby certify to John Crockett Clerk of Tazewell County that on the 17th day of October 1822 William Blankenship and

Sally Bailey was joined together in the holy estate of matrimony by licence from you by me John Peery

I do hereby certify to sd. Clerk of said County that on the 31st day of December 1822 James Hager & Susanna Reader was joined together in the holy estate of matrimony by licence from you, by me
JOHN PERRY

I do hereby certify to sd. Clerk of sd. County that on the 17th day of June 1823 Thomas S. Walker & Christiana Waggoner was joined together in the Holy estate of Matrimony by publication of Bans By me   JOHN PERRY
October 6th 1823

Tazewell County from a licence from your office I transmit the following marriage to wit James Bruce and Elizabeth Justice Solemnized by me on the 18th of September 1823
JOSHUAY BRUCE

These certify that the marrage Contracts have been duly Solemnised between the following Couples in 1823

Mathias Harman and Polley Barnett
Harvey G. Peery and Rebea Williams
Ephram Marrisson & Sophea Harman
William Thompson and Matilda Witten
Charles C. Gibson and Derinda Cecill
Robert Barrett and Peggy Maxwell
John Boiles and Jane Taylor
Isaac Dailey and Elizabeth Cecell
Henry Patterson and Polley Bandy
Wm. M. P. Quinn and Eliza Witten
Zachariah Cecill and Abigail Quinn   ISAAC QUINN
Tazewell County Virginia

This certifyeth that on the 13th of February last I solemnized the right of matrimoney between Rees B. Gillespie and Mary Ann Tiffaney according to Licence granted from your office
ANCEL RICHARDSON
Feby 14th 1824

I do hereby certify that on the 9th day of March 1824 was Jacob Wagoner and Harriot Williams Joined in Holy Mattrimoney according to Law, by me Nehemiah Bonham By Virtue of Lawfull publication this given under my hand this 24th day of March

The day and Year above written

To the Clerk of Tazewell County

I do hereby certify that I have joined the following persons in the state of matrimony according to law to wit

John Baily and Polly G. Witten January 2nd 1822

Joseph McKinney and Martha Dillion Sept 26th 1822

John Belsher and Sally Brown October 8th 1822 and

Archibald Melony & Rachel Hankins Sept 5th 1823

Given under my hand this 22nd day of Sept 1823

WILLIAM SHANNON

Tazewell County to Wit march 11th 1824

This solemnised the right of matrimoney between Randolph Scott & Isabella Kendrick by authority of licence from this Court

W. S. KENDRICK

Tazewell County Sct To John Crockett Clerk of Tazewell County

I do hereby certify that on the sevrel dates under written I joined together in the holy state of matrimony the several Couples underneath named To wit,

Clay Bailey & Rebeca atkins December 10th 1823 by licence from under your hand by S. M. Stilwell D C

Also Alem Hager & Elizabeth Bailey December the 11th 1823 by Licence from under your hand by S. M. Stilwell D. C.

Also John I Woodridge & Sarah Srader January the 8th 1824 by licence from under your hand by S. M. Stilwell D C

Also John Grills & Addeline Yoct January 29th 1824 by licence from under your hand John Crockett D S C

Also Milam Fletcher & Jane Coleman June 27th 1824 by licence from under your hand John Crockett C S C

Also Benjamin Tickle & Martha Neel July the 8th 1824 by licence from under your hand By S M Stilwell D C Eche (?) of which being Joined according to the rules & ceremoneys of the Church to which I Belong Given under my hand

JOHN PEERY

Tazewell County August 22 1824

This is to Certify that I have Celebrated the Rights of Matrimoney agreable to the Proper authority between Joshua McGuire and Susan Harman Given under my hand

ABRAHAM STILL

Tazewell County to wit

I David Young do Certify that the following List Containg all the marriages Celebrated by me within the preceding year.

I Join James Griffy and Alethia Griffitts on the 9 July 1822

James Robertson and Lucy Baird on April 4 1823

Deskins Green and   Ratliff on the 5th Day of February 1823

Elijah Norwd and Jinney matney on 12th day February 1823

John Christian and Cathan McKenster August 4th 1823

Robert Horton and Nancy Steel February 24th day 1824

Larkin Bishop and Ester Mcguire October 7 1824

Burdine H Correl and lydia Doke october 23 1824

Asa Harper and Elender Jackson December 23d 1824

Isaac Robins and Betsy Asbury January 30th 1825

Ebenezer C. Hatch and Betsy Sawyers Febuary 1 1825

James Seatt and Elizabeth Kindrick February 14th 1825

These are Executed by me   DAVID YOUNG

The Marriag of Robert Davidson an Polly Harman was solemnized By me Feb 3d 1825   ACIL RICHARDSON

December the 30th 1824 Tazewell Cy

These Certify that Marriage Contracts have been duly solemnised between the following within this year

Evan D. Williams an Isabella kendrick

James Quinn and Elenor Witten

James Barnet and Abigal Hedrick   ISAAC QUINN

To they Clerk of Tazewell County Return to your office for 1824 Celebrated the matrimonial Right

July the 8th William Day Elizabeth Thompson

August the 5th Isaac King Rebecca Dills

17th october Thomas Owens Hannah Crockett

23rd December William Dickeson Betsey Martain

11th November William Peters Sally Peery S. M. Stilwell.

January 15th 1825   JAMES CHARLES

March 23d 1825

Solemnised the rights of matrimoney between Cornelius McGuire and Margaret Steel both of this County by licence from this office

         W. P. KENDRICK T. E.

Tazewell County to wit

I do hereby certify to John Crockett Clerk of Tazewell County that on the 26th day of August 1824 John Lambert and Grayilla Suiter was joined together in the holy estate of matrimoney by licence from under your hand by me   JOHN PERRY

I also certify to said Clerk of said County that on the 17th day of November 1824 James White and Polly Bailey was joined together in the holy estate of matrimoney by licence from under your hand by me   JOHN PERRY

I also certify to said Clerk of sais County that on the 25 day of November 1824 William Payne and Peggy Lusk was joined together in the holy estate of matrimoney by licence from under your hand by me   JOHN PERRY

I also certify to John Crockett Clerk of said County that on the 17th day of December 1824 Isaac Adkins batchelor and Polly Lusk was joined together in the holy estate of matrimony by licence from under your hand by me   JOHN PERRY

I also certify to said Clerk of said County that on the 25th day of January 1825 Isaac ODonnell and Rebecca Swader was joined together in the holy estate of matrimony by licence from under your hand by me   JOHN PERRY

I also certify to said Clerk of Tazewell County that on the 15th day of February 1825 Robin Carver and Sally Fortner was joined together in the holy estate of matrimony by licence from your office by me   JOHN PERRY

I also Certify to said Clerk of Tazewell County that on the 24th day of March 1825 Reuben Steel & Clarissa Peery was joined together in the holy estate of matrimony by licence from your office by me   JOHN PERRY

I Edward T. Peery minister of the Gospel and duly authorised by law to perform the rights of matrimoney—have Joined the following persons in the holy estate of matrimoney within the County of Tazewell in pursuance to licens issd from the office of said County Jocab Griffitts to Nancy McFarlane on the 19th April 1825
     EDWARD T. PEERY

Solemnised the right of matrimoney between John M. Powell and Polly Lusk the 22nd of December 1825 by me
     ANCIL RICHARDSON L D.

Tazewell County towit

From a licence obtained from your office to cilebrate the rites of marage between Josiah Bruce and Sally Justice I have celebrated the same on the 15th day of September 1825

        SAMUEL NEWBERRY

 Beturn to your office for 1825
 Celebrated the rights of matrimoney of
 24th February Michael Stump & Polly Crockett
 4th August Edward Hannon & Jane Maxwell
 6th September Milton Haws & Laodician Franklin
 13th September Allen Justice & Elleanor Flummer
 6 October Thomas Franklin & Margaret Stump

This 29th December of the above date   JAS. CHARLES

This is to certify that I celebrated the rites of matrimoney between Bery Humphreys and Susan Moore on the 17th day December 1825. Given under my hand   JOSIAH B. DAUGHTRY

Tazewell County towit

I David Young do certify that the following list contains all the marriages celebrated by me within the preceeding year.

I joined Isaac Nelson & Susanah Young on the 8th day of March 1825

I joined John Montgomery & Jane McMillen on the 14th day of March 1825

I joined William Lyon & Lucinda Medows on the 7th day of April 1825

I joined John Brooks & Rebecca Marrs on the 4th day of June 1825

I joined Peter Gose and Nancy Smith on the 23rd day of July 1825

I joined Joseph Moore & Hannah Elkins on the 4th day of October 1825

I joined John Dougherty & Nancy Ward on the 6th day October 1825

I joined Archibald Asbury & Eliza Davis on the 28th day of October 1825

I joined George Steel & Elizabeth Steel on the 22nd December 1825   DAVID YOUNG

This is to certify that I solemnised matrimony Between *E*lexander Beavers & Elizabeth Hankins Sept 22nd 1825

JONATHAN QUICKSALL

I certify that I solemnised the marriage between John Harkrider & Nancy Francisco October 23rd 1825

JONATHAN QUICKSALL

This is to Certify that I solemnised marriage between Patrick McGlachlin & Rachel Pucket Sept 15th 1825

JONATHAN QUICKSALL

I Certify that I solemnised the marriage between Andrew McGuire & A*miab*le Beavers November 24 1825

JONATHAN QUICKSALL

This to Certify that I solemnised marriage Between John Howell and Rebeccah Hankins July 10th 1825

JONATHAN QUICKSALL

Celebrated the rights of matrimoney between Peter Fox and Polly Hall on the 24th November 1825 agreeable to a licens issued from Tazewell County Clerks Office

JAMES CHARLES

This is to certify that I celebrated the rights of matrimoney between Berry Umphres and Susan Moore on the 17th day of December 1825
J. B. DOUGHERTY

This is to certify that the marriage contract has been duly solemnised between William Gillespie and Jane Crockett

Simon Davis and Rebecca Bayan

Edmon Harrisson and lilly Deskins

Addison Crockett and Lettisia Harman in 1825

ISAAC QUINN

Celebrated the right of matrimoney Between James P. McGranahan and Cynthia Brown. Solemnised on the 7th Sept 1826 by me
ANCIL RICHARDSON

Local deacon of the Methodist Episcopal Church

Solemnised the rights of matrimony Between Fransis Crockett & Martha C. George this 12th October 1826

ANCIL RICHARDSON

Local Deacon of the Methodist Episcopal Church Return to your office

On the 7th day of July 1826 Joined together John Wilson and Catherine Henneger
JAMES CHARLES

To the Clerk of Tazewell County
  October 23d 1826
  I do hereby Certify to the Clerk of Tazewell County that on the 18th Day of August 1825 David Pane and Betsey Cassiday was Joined together in the holey State of Matrimoney by me
By licence from under your hand
  I do also certify to John Crockett said Clerk of said County that Isaac French and Rhoda Day was Joined together in the holy estate of matrimoney on the 20th day of October 1825 by licence from under your hand by me   JOHN PERRY
  I also certify to said Clerk of said County that on the 1st Day of December 1825 Robert Neel and Nancey Waggoner was Joined together in the holey Estate of matrimoney by licence from under your hand by me
  I do hereby certify to said Clerk of said County that on the 28th Day of January 1826 Samuel Haywood and Patsey Tiller was Joined together in the holey estate of matrimoney by Publication of Banes by me   JOHN PERRY
To John Crockett Clerk of Tazewell County
Return to your office for 1825 Celebrated the matrimonial rights of
 24th February Michael Stump & Polly Crockett
 4th August Edward Hannon & Jane Maxwell
 6th September Allen Justice & Elenor Flummer
 6th October Thomas Franklin & Margret Stump
This 29th December of the above date   JAMES CHARLES
  Mr. John Crockett CLK (on margin of this page is written "This is recorded 6 pages back")
  To the Clerk of the County Court of Tazewell I certify that I celebrated the rights of matrimoney between William Johnston & Nancy Prater the 5th of febuary 1826
   WILLIAM MCGUIRE Ordained Preacher
  To the Clerk of the County Court of Tazewell I certify that I celebrated the rites of matrimoney between Aaron Asbury & Rebecca bishop the 23d of febuary 1826
   WILLIAM MCGUIRE Ordaind Preacher
  To the Clerk of the County Court of Tazewell I certify that I cilibrated the rites of matrimony between Moses Asbury and Patsey luster the 26 of february 1826
   WILLIAM MCGUIRE Ordaind Preacher

To the Clerk of the County Court of Tazewell I certify that I cilibrated the rites of matrimony between Harvey Lester and Catherine bishop June 1st 1826

WILLIAM MCGUIRE ordained Preacher

To the Clerk of the County Court of tazewell I certify that I cilibrated the rites of matrimoney between John Blankenship and Elizabeth Johnston the 7th day of May 1826

WILLIAM MCGUIRE ordaind Preacher

To the Clerk of the County Court of tazewell I certify that I cilibrated the rites of matrimony between Charles Matenler and Hannah Miller the 12 day of July 1826

WILLIAM MCGUIRE ordaind Preacher

To the Clerk of the County Court of tazewell I certify that I celabrated the rites of matrimoney between Joseph Brown and Elizabeth Steel the 12th day of September 1826

WILLIAM MCGUIRE ordaind Preacher

To the Clerk of the County Court of tazewell I certify that I cilabrated the rites of matrimony between Larkin bishop and Polly Clevenger the 1st day of December 1826

WILLIAM MCGUIRE ordaind Preacher

The foregoing list of marriages I have solemnised according to the rules and ceremonies of the Church to which I belong and by licens obtained from the Clerk of the County Court

WILLIAM MCGUIRE L. P.

I do certify that I solemnized the rite of matrimoney betwen the following persons Tazewell County Virginia Syms Thompson & Nancy Witten December 19th 1826

Charles French & Rebecca Carter December 8th 1826
ANCIL RICHARDSON Local Deacon in the Methodist Episcopal Church

This to Certify that I Joined Jonathan Whitt and Polly Eearnhart together after the order of our Church June 28th 1824

This is to certify that I Joined Milburn Whit and Haley Hankins together after the order of our Church. Jany 30th 1824

JONATHAN QUICKSALL

This is to certify that I Joined Jesse Baunnon and Polly Webb after the Order of our Church June 30th 1824

JONATHAN QUICKSALL

This is to certify I Joined Richard Whitt and Ellin Miller together as man and wife after the Order of our Church after publishing the bans three times in two weaks at three Different places December 5th 1824   JONATHAN QUICKSALL

Sir from a license obtained from your office to celebrate the rites of marriage between William Flemmer and Nancy pr*estice* celebrated by me on the 8th october 1826 Given under my hand 4th August 1827   JOSHUA BRUCE

These are to certify that on the 10th day of June 1827 Hiram Pennington & Nancy Lusk was Joined in the holy matrimoney by virtue of License from the County Clerk of Tazewell celebrated by
NEHEMIAH BONHAM

Tazewell County towit

I David Young do certify that the following list contains all the marriages celebrated by me within the preceeding year

I joined Peter Naler & Margaret Brooks on the 10th day of May 1827

I joined James Wilson Margaret Gillespie on the 11th day of September 1827

I joined Rees Bowen and Lusinda Blankenship on the 25th day of Sept 1827

I joined Colenius MGuire and Theressa Gose on the 1st day of November 1827

I joined Joshua Corell and Jane Wynn on the 13th day of December 1827

Executed and Returned by David Young on the 21 J. 1828
Tazewell County to wit

I David Young do certify that the following list contains all the marriages celebrated by me within the preceding year

I joined John Thompson & Lydia Ward on the 29th day of December 1825

I joined George S*tph*eson an Jemima Jent on the 16th day of July 1826

I joined William Williams and Margaret Gillespie on the 28th day of Sept 1826

I joined George Asberry and Nancy Brooks on the 10th day of April 1826

I joined Charles Higginbotham and Rebecca Ballard on the 26th day of Decr 1826

I joined Tyre D. Thompson and Nancy Williams on the 25th day of November 1826

I joined Robert McMullen & Nancy Sayers on the 27th day of April 1826

I joined John Allen and Esther Neel on the 14th day of September 1826

I Joined Skillen McGuire and Mary Drake on the 4th day of January 1826

I Joined Richard Belshe and Peggy Goodwin on the 2d day of February 1826

I Joined Robert Sayers and Martha McMillen on the 11th day of February 1827

I Joined James Rutledge and Nancy Thompson on the 1st day of February 1827

I Joined George Grubb and Jane Ward on the 1st day of March 1827

I joined Smith Ward and Polly Belsher on the 21st day of March 1827

These are all executed by me   DAVID YOUNG

A List of Marriages Celebrated by John Peery in the year 1827

Daniel Burress & Rebecca Peery on the 11th day of January 1827

William Tabor and Elizabeth Peery on the 2nd day of August 1827

Isaac Lambert & Rebecca Suter 20th day of Sepr 1827

On the 6th day of November 1827 Larkin Atkins and Legcy Atkins

Hardy Fortner and Polly Carter was Joined together on the 1st day of January 1828

George Kidd and Evalina Dills Suten on the 12th day of Febuary 1828

Squire Hager and Elizabeth Jones on the 28th day of February 1828   JOHN PEERY

On the 18th January 1827 Joined together John Whitmon & Mayanna Peery

On the 14th June Abram Baugh and Delany Tomlinson

On the 7th June John Lewis & Polly Henneger

December 22nd 1827   JAMES CHARLES

Published according to Law and Joined together on the 27th May Nelson Greeen & Elizabeth Hanshea

On the 15th July James Green and Lucinda Sprinkle Dec. 22nd 1827
JAMES CHARLES

I do certify that I celebrated the bans of matrimony between John Thompson and Mary A. George on the 5th of June 1827
JONATHAN QUICKSALL

I do certify that I celebrated the bans of matrimony between Philip Vincill and Polly Meadows on the 13th July 1828
JONATHAN QUICKSALL

I do certify that I celebrated the bans of matrimony between William Harrisson and Shorne Whitt on the 11th September 1827
JONATHAN QUICKSALL

I do certify that I united William Beavers and Nancy Harrisson in the holy estate of matrimony on the 23th day of October 1828
JONATHAN QUICKSALL

December 22nd 1827

I do certify that the following are the names of all the persons that I have solemnized the rite of matrimony between in this year

1 James Srader & Mary Day the 1st day of February 1827

2 Baldwin L. Sisson & Sarah Ann Eliza Parris the 22nd March 1827

3 Thomas Harvey Mitchell & Larrissa Brown the 12th April 1827

4 Jesse Taber & Susanna Turner on the 24 of October 1827

5 Daniel Fletcher & Ann Coleman on the 13th December 1827

Given under my hand

ANCIL RICHARDSON Local Deacon of the Methodist Episcopal Church

To the Clerk of the County of Tazewell County

I do certify that I did celebrate the rites of matrimony between Thomas Steel and Jernacy Remine on the 30th of October 1828 By license obtained from the Clerk office at said County
WILLIAM MCGUIRE L P

To the Clerk of the County Court of Tazewell

I Certify that I celebrated the rites of matrimony between Thomas Davas and Mary Leard november the 26th 1827 according to the rites and seremonies of the Church to which I belong

To the Clerk of the County Court of Tazewell

I certify that I celebrated the rites of matrimony between Elijah Ratlef and Mary Burchet January the 31st 1828 according to the rules of the Church to which I belong

To the Clerk of the County Court of Tazewell

I certyfy that I celebrated the rites of matrimony between Shadrach Ratlef and Elizabeth Matenee March the 6th 1828 according to the rules of the church to which I belong.

The above marriges was sollemnized by licens from the Clerk of the County Court of Tazewell

By me WILLIAM MCGUIRE Ordained Precher

This certify that the marrage contract has been legally solemnised between the following persons to wit

Thomas Crabtree and Susannah Mitchell in Sept 1826
James G. Guthrie and Elizabeth Deskins in Sept 1827
James Q. Kendrick and Elizabeth Dills in July 1827
George W. Messick and Lydia Kendrick in Sept 1827
Elijah Sprinkle and Patsy Stobough in April 1828
Jesse Dillion and Cintha Perdue in Feby 1827

ISAAC QUINN

A Return of marriages to the Clerk of Tazewell County

James Jackson & Any Taber Feby 19th 1824
Josiah Smyth & Elizabeth Fletcher June 24th 1824
Isaac Bell & Nancy Sanders Sept 21st 1824
Robit Tomblin & Elizabeth Waldern July 8th 1825
Francis Taber & Mary Sanders Octo 20th 1825
Henry Bailey & Polley Bailey Nov. 8th 1825
Archibald Bruster & Elizabeth Lockhart Jany 5th 1826
Reuben Garratson & Omy Bailey Jany 10th 1826
Christian Peters & Polly F Bailey July 6th 1826
Isom Belsher & Rebeckah Bailey Octo 20th 1826
Isaac Holbrook & Malvina Williams Octo 26th 1826
John Bailey & Jane Rinehart Nov 22nd 1827
Thomas ODaniel & Nancy Martin March 13th 1828
Samuel Lambert & Rebeckah Lambert Apl 16th 1829
Elkenah Wolf & Frances Becklehimer Apl 23rd 1829
Richard Taber & Mildred Shrader Augst 27th 1829
Ezekiel French & Charerie Carter Sep 3 1829

William Whitley & Polley B. Moore Nov 12th 1829

Alexander Tomblinson & Polley Workman Nov 16th 1829

I do hereby certify that I have solemnized the above marriages according to law Certified under my hand this 2nd day of December 1829   WILLIAM SHANNON

Tazewell County towit

I David Young do Certify that the following List Contains all the marriages celebrated by me within the present year

I Joined John H. Gose and Rachel Higginbotham on the 17th day of April 1828

I Joined William Nutter and Jane Miller on the 8 day of October 1828

I Joined Harvey Ward and Lina Payne on the 14th day of August 1828

I Joined Christopher Gose and Polley H. Boland on the 14th day of August 1828

I Joined Emanuel Lockhart and Elizabeth Corel on the first day of Jany 1829

I Joined Gilbert R. Rogers and Senia Doak on the 5 day of January 1829

These are all Executed by me   DAVID YOUNG

I do hereby Certify to John Crockett Clerk of Tazewell County and State of Virginia Gent. That on the 30th Day of March 1828 David Bayley and Elizabeth Lusk was Joined together By publication of Bands in the Holey Estate of Matrimoney by me
                               JOHN PERRY

I do also Certify to said Clerk of sd. County that on the 8th Day of July 1828 John Simpson and Caty Gross was Joined together by Publication of Bands in the holey estate of matrimoney by me   JOHN PERRY

I Do hereby Certify to sd. Clerk of Sd. County that on the 5th Day of August 1828 Obadiah Workman and Rebeccah Lambert was Joined together by Publication of Bands In the Holey estate of Matrimoney By me   JOHN PERRY

I Do hereby Certify to sd. Clerk of Sd. County that on the 7th day of August 1828 Chrisley Foglesong and Rhoda Jones was Joined together in the Holey Estate of Matrimoney by license from sd Clerk by me   JOHN PERRY

I Do Certify to said Clerk of sd. County that on the 25th Day of December 1828 Andrew Stowers and Polley Terry was Joined together in the Holey Estate of Matrimoney by License from sd Clerk of sd County by me JOHN PERRY

I Do Certify to said Clerk of Tazewell County that on the 18th Day of January 1829 Tazewell Stump and Jemima Lambert was Joined together in the Holy Estate of Matrimoney by Publication of Bands by me JOHN PERRY

I Do hereby Certify to sd. Clerk of sd County that on the 5th Day of February 1829 Elisha Kidd and Peggy Peery was Joined together in the Holy Estate of Matrimony by License and all the above according to Law by me JOHN PERRY

I do certify that on the 3rd day of July 1828, I solemnized the rite of matrimony between Erastus Granger Harman and Sally Bane, given under my hand this 5th day of March 1829
ANCEL RICHARDSON
L D of the M E Church

I do hereby certify that I solemnized the rites of matrimony between George Cecill and Elizabeth Linsen taffy September 6th and

William T. Moore & Matilda Peery September 10th and

James P. Nelson & Mary Myers October 29th all in the year 1829 in the County of Tazewell State of Virginia Given under my hand & Seal this 11th day of Decembere 1829
JOYCE N T BURUM

I James Charles do hereby certify that the following is a correct list of marriages celebrated by me since my last return

Jacob Sinsentaffy and Nancy Hellemdollar on the 18 day of January 1828

William Patterson and Elizabeth Day on the 28th day of May 1828

Charles Taylor and Elizabeth Harrisson on the 8th day of May 1828

Alexander Suiter and Catherine Gose on the 13th day of November 1828

Aron Wilson & Sally Maxwell on the 6th day of September 1828
JAMES CHARLES

Tazewell County Virginia

To the Clerk of the Court

I certify that this is a true list of the marriages solemnized by me in the year 1829

  2st. between John M Neal & Martha Harman
  1st. between George B. Clark & Elizabeth Flummer
  3rd Do David Whitley & Matilda Haven
  4th Do William Shannon & Polly B. Moore
  5th. Do John J. Barrum & Cosby Peery

Dec. 31st 1829   ANCEL RICHARDSON

Return to the Clerks office of Tazewell County for 1829

On the 5th of February Joined together Michael Stump & Anna Barnet

On the 21st July Joined together Thomas Gillespie and Maria Peery

On the 6th of August Joined together Samul Lane & Christen Harman

On the 24th of December Joined together Daniel Bowman & Christener Owens

January 11th 1830   JAMES CHARLES

Mr. John Crockett C L K

December 23rd 1829

I do certify to the Clerk of the County Court of Tazewell that the following list of Marrages was celebrated by me William McGuire since the first day of January 1829 Viz,

  february 5th Charles Matenlee and Abigail Brown
  March 10th Flemmon Childers and Charity Matinlee
  March the 19th Edward Bileter and Ann brown
  April the 9th Squire Wingo and Mary Shipler
  June the 11th Mathias Keen and Therssa Skins
  June the 18th Thomas Christian and Mary Alizer
  June 21st Moses Pruett and Jane Wingo
  July 21st Joseph Vandike & Abigale Matenlee
  July 23rd William Peery and Elizabeth Creswell
  September the third Smith Jackson & Margret Matenlee and William Brown and Isabella Williams same date
  November the 3 William Matenler and Nancy Vandike

Tazewell County towit

I certify that the following list contains all the marriages celebrated by me David Young, within the preceding year

I Joined David Cawan and Rebeckah Bowan on the 19th day of May 1829

I Joined George D. Brown and May H. Kindle on the 5 day of March 1829

I Joined Thompson Daugherty and Lydia Dills on the 1 day of April 1829

I Joined Robert F. Rutledge and Lydia Thompson on the 8 day of October 1829

I Joined Thomas Crabtree and Peggy Chafin on the 1 day of October 1829

I Joined Thomas Powell and Anna Neel on the 19th day of October 1829

I Joined Jarrat Boland *I* and Nancy Vinsant on the 1 day of December 1829

I Joined Henry Vincell and Polly Wolford on the 14th day of January 1830

I Joined Thomas Higginbotham and Gracey Goodwin on the 17 day January 1830

These are Joined together by me   DAVID YOUNG

A List of Ma*rr*idges

John Stinson and rachel Drake January 28th 1830

James Ha*r*son and Caty B*e*nours May 25th 1829

Henry Wilson and Mahala Woosley August 19th 1829

John *b*ishop *p*olly Asberry January 1st 1830

Samuel Steel and R*eB*ecca Ratliff March 25th 1830

Also published and Joined together

*f*ielden *p*oston and Nancy *g*enea*n*s May 10th 1829

James Kneel and Caty Kneel august 16th 1829

these are all the ma*r*ridges cilebrated By Me in the *following yeare* to John Crockett Cl   WILLIAM HENKLE

Tazewell County towit

To John Crockett Clk of said County I Do certify to John Crockett said Clerk that

Larkin K. Neel and Rinda Kidd was Joined together in Holy matrimony on the 24th Day of March 1829 by Publication of Banns by me   JOHN PERRY

I Certify to said Clerk that on the 14th of April 1829 Reuben Bailey and Polly Adkins was Joined in holy matrimony by license by me   JOHN PERRY

I also Certify to said Clerk that on the 20th day of Febuary 1830 Jeremiah Hager and Rhoda Stump was Joined together in in holy matrimony by me   JOHN PERRY

I also Certify to said Clerk also that on the 25th Day of Feby 1830 Jeremiah Hager and Rhoda Stump was Joined together in Holy matrimony by license by me   JOHN PERRY

I Certify to said Clerk of said County that on the 8th Day of April 1830 Henry Yost & Temperance Benham was joined in Holy matrimony by me   JOHN PERRY

I hereby certify that celebrated the Rites of matrimony between Josh Earnheart and Mary Quicksall the 15th May 1828
    J. QUICKSALL

I hereby certify that I celebrated the Rites of matrimony between William Srader and Susanna Webb July 18th 1830
    JONATHAN QUICKSALL

I hereby Certify that I celebrated the Rites of matrimony between Wade Hoofman Ester *gene bened* May 27, 1830
    JONATHAN QUICKSALL

I hereby Certify that I celebrated the Rites of matrimony between William Dolton and Mariah Srader April 27th 1830
    JONATHAN QUICKSALL

I do certify that I solemnized the rites of Matrimoney between William Gillespie & Margret Peery the 25th day of March 1830 both of the County of Tazewell

Given under my hand August 18th 1830   JOHN I. BURUM Tazewell County Va.

I Certify that I have solemnized the rite of Matrimony between persons this year

1st David Mills & Nancy Bailey the 4th of Feby 1830
2d Daniel C. Harman & Margret Gillespie the 11th March 1830
3 James Harris & Jane Harmon 18th March 1830
4 Benjamin Lusk & Anna Compton the 2nd of Sept 1830
This the 4th day of November 1830
    ANCIL RICHARDSON L. E.
    In the M. E. Church

I do certify that I solemnized the rites of Matrimony Between Austin Patton & Marinda Thorn the 18th day of May 1830 in the County of Tazewell

Also between Thomas G. Witten & Rebecca T. Ward August 19th 1830 both of the County of Tazewell

Given under my hand this 25th day of August 1830

WILLIAM C. CUMMINGS

Mr. Crockett

You will incert the following Couples on your record of Marriages Celebrated by me   DUGALD MCINTYRE

Samuel Sayers & Elizabeth Gose

The above Couple was married on the 12 of January 1830 December 24th 1830   Your &C

DUGALD MCINTYRE

I Certify to the Clerk of County Court of Tazewell that the following marriages was Celebrated by me WM MCQUIRE since the first day of January 1830 Viz,

James Davis & Margret Shannon March 4th 1830

John Reed & Nancy Christian June 13th 1830

Given under my hand this 24th day of December 1830

WM. MCGUIRE

I do hereby certify to the Clerk of Tazewell County that I have solemnized the following marriages according to law, towit,

James French & Peggy Day Dec. 31 1829

Reuben Bailey & Milley Belsher May 4th 1830

William Coleman & Patsey Rinehart Sept. 16th 1830

Ancel Richardson & Elizabeth Milam Sept 21st 1830

William Pane & Judy Belsher October 28th 1830

WILLIAM SHANNON

October 29th 1830

For 1830 Sir I return to your office January the 7th I Joined together Robert Wynne & Sally Fox

On the 1st day of April Joined together Wm. Cannen and Oliva Perry

January the 23d 1831   JAMES CHARLES

Mr. John Crockett C. L. K. Tazewell County to wit

I, David Young do Certify that the following List contains all marriages celebrated by me within the preceding year

I joined William Deskins and Rebecca Deskins in holey wedlock on the 27th day of January 1831

I joined Robert Smith and Jane Belsher together in holy wedlock on the 3d day of December 1830

I joined James Bostick and Margret Smith in holey wedlock on the 23d day of March 1830

I joined John Wilson and Polly Whitt in holey wedlock on the 26 day of August 1830

I joined William Brooks and Rebecah Corll in the holy wedlock on the 2nd day of February 1830

I joined Heny Ward & Juley Wilson in holey wedlock on the 28 day of March 1830

I Joined John Young and Jane Smith in the holey wedlock on the 23 day of September 1830

I joined Anderson Smith and Lisey Gillespie in the holey wedlock on the 23 September 1830

I Joined William Montgomery and Jane Smith in Holey wedlock on the 28th Jany 1830

I joined Richard Belshe and Nancy McMillen in Holey wedlock on the 8 day August 1830

I joined Daniel Lockhart and Alamanda Ginings in holey wedlock on the 3 day of March 1831

Executed by me   DAVID YOUNG

Tazewell County, towit,

I do certify to John Crockett Clerk of Tazewell County, that on the 20th day of Feby 1830, Constance Adams and Nancy Flummer was joined together in the holy estate of Matrimony by license from under your hand by me   JOHN PERRY

I do certify to said Clerk of said County that on the 23rd day of September 1830 Joseph H. Totten and Polly Suitor was joined together in the holy estate of matrimony by licence from under your hand by me   JOHN PERRY

I do certify to said Clerk of said County that on the 25th day of November 1830 Elisha Compton and Rebecca Shannon was joined together in the holy estate of matrimony by licence from under your hand by me   JOHN PERRY

I also certify to said Clerk of said County that on the 3rd day of February 1831 Alexander Prewett and Martha Day was joined together in the holy Estate of Matrimony by licence from under your hand by me   JOHN PERRY

I do certify to said Clerk of said county that on the 10th day of February 1831 Randle Holebrook and Polly H. Waggoner was joined together in the holy Estate of Matrimony by a licence from under your hand by me   JOHN PERRY

I do certify to John Crockett Clerk of Tazewell County that on the 2nd day of June 1831 Barkley Stump and Polly Yose was joined together in the holy Estate of Matrimony by publication of Banns by me   JOHN PERRY

I do certify to the Clerk of the County Court of Tazewell that the following marriages was celibrated by me William McGuyer since the first of January 1831 given under my hand this sixteenth day of December 1831 viz,

    Daniel Christian and Hannah Harrison April the 23
    Reuben S. Fudge and Nancy Harman June the first
    Jacob White and Latisha Prewett August the 18
    John McGuyer and Jennsy Shrader September 28

I James Charles do hereby certify that the following is a true list of the marriages celebrated by me for the year 1831 and also two that I celebrated in 1830, which was mislaid and not returned, viz.

    Robert Wynne and Sally Fox January 7th 1830
    Wm. G.W. Carrane and Olivia Peery April 1st 1830
    Joseph Barnett & Barbara Hedrick June 15th 1831
    James G. Hatch & Christenor Peery 15th Feby. 1831
    Harman Wynn & Hanah Thompson 6th Feby 1831
    George Owry & Catherina Myars 23rd June 1831
    Jacob Burton and Catherine Stump 25th August 1831
    William Snider & Barbara Hanchos 29th Dec. 1831
    I also celebrated the following marriage in 1832
    Preston Edmonds to Rejina Jones Jany 5th 1832
                                             JAMES CHARLES

A return of Marriages Executed by William Shannon to the Clerk of Tazewell

    Joel Davis and Polly Mullins Feby. 17, 1831
    Henry Sluss and Betsey Coleman May 22, 1831
    Veincon Carter and Sarah Havens June 20, 1831
    Joseph A. Moore & Martha P. Moore Augt 30, 1831

Jesse Kindle & Jane Brown Sept. 1st 1831

Masten Dillion and Margaret Neely Sept 19, 1831

Edley Maxwell and Sally Bailey Oct 6th 1831

Harden Nuckels & Edy Nuckels Oct 15, 1831

James M. Peery & Nancy Bane Oct 20th 1831

Henry Thomas & Eleanor Jane Smith Jany. 10 1831

Tazewell County viz,

I Do certify to John Crockett Clerk of Tazewell County that on the 10th day of February 1831 Randle Holebrook and Polly H. Waggoner was joined together in the Holy Estate of matrimony according to the rites and ceremonys of the church to which I belong by licence from under your hand by me   JOHN PERRY

I Do certify to John Crockett Clerk of Tazewell County that on the 3rd day of Febry 1831 Alexander Prewett and Martha Day was joined together in the Holy Estate of Matrimony according to the rules and ceremonies of the Church to which I belong by licence under your hand by me   JOHN PERRY

I Do hereby Certify to John Crockett Clerk of Tazewell County that on the 13th day of September 1831 William Stump and Polly Hager was joined together in the Holy Estate of matrimony according to the rules and ceremonies of the Church to which I belong by Publication of Baans by me   JOHN PERRY

I Do Certify to John Crockett Clerk of Tazewell County that on the 18th day of October 1831 Jeremiah Lambert Junior and Eleanor Waggoner was joined together in the Holy Estate of Matrimony according to the Rules and ceremonies of the Church to which I belong by license from under your hand by me
  JOHN PERRY

I Do Certify to John Crockett Clerk of Tazewell County that on the 25th day of December 1831, Solomon Lambert and Betsey Carter was joined together in the Holy Estate of matrimony according to the rules and ceremonys of the Church to which I belong by licence from under James C. Spotts D. C. hand by me
  JOHN PERRY

I John J. Buren Decon in the Methodist E. Church do hereby certify that I solemnized the rites of matrimony between the following persons (viz)

William T. Moore & Matilda Peery 10th Sept. 1829

George Cecil & Elizabeth Sincentaffy 6th Sept. 1829

James P. Nelson & Mary Myers 29 Oct 1829
Given under my hand this Decm 25 1829

JOHN J. BUREN

A return to the Clerks Office of Tazewell County for 1832
Joined together William M. Maxwell & Elizabeth Taffer on the 17th day of May

July 19th Joined together Jacob Brown & Jane Helmandollar

August 28th Joined together Howard Havins & Sally Carter
Written January 16th 1833   JAMES CHARLES

Tazewell County towit

I David Young do certify that the following list containing all the marriages celebrated by me with the preceeding year

I joined Daniel Horton and Susanah H. Kindle together in Holy wedlock on the 23d June 1831.

I joined William E. Higginbotham and Louisa Ward in Holy wedlock on the 8th day September 1831

I joined Garland Hurt and Rebecca Dailey in Holy wedlock on the 1st day of November 1831

I joined William A. Young and Martha Young in Holy Wedlock on the 23th day of December 1831

I joined James McNeil and Margaret Vincel in Holy wedlock on the 17th day of July 1832

I joined Peter E. Wynn and Mary Correll in Holy wedlock on the 25th day of May 1832.

I joined William Young and Polly Whitt in Holy wedlock on the 19th day of June 1832

I joined William Young and Nancy W. Molloy in Holy Wedlock on the 27th Sept 1832

I Joined together James Buchannon & Nancy Buchannon in Holy Wedlock on the 27th day of September 1832

I joined Jared W. Bolen and Fanny Young in Holy wedlock on the 23rd day of August 1832.

These executed by me   DAVID YOUNG

1832

I also joined James Neil and Delila Kirk in Holy wedlock on the 17th day of January 1833   DAVID YOUNG

A List of marriages. I do hereby sertify on the 22nd Novm. 1831 I joined Jefferson Deskins and Polly Gent together in matrimony

    Timothy Whitt and Nancy Hinkle January 19 1832
    Marcus A. P. Whitt and Nancy Kendrick March 8th 1832
    William Brewster and Rebecca Dolton January 14th 1832
    William Stephenston and Elizabeth Jones February 14 1832
    John Prewet & Peggy Cecil June 7, 1832
                                                  WILLIAM HENKLE

A return of marriages to the Clerk of Tazewell County executed by William Shannon:

    Lewis Belsher & Rebecca Dillion February 9 1832.
    William R. Bane & Nancy Havens April 12th 1832
    Micajah Bailey and Mahaley Blankenship 7th 1832
    Certified under my hand this 11th day of June 1832
                                                 WILLIAM SHANNON

I do hereby certify that the following persons have been joined together into the holy state of matrimony according to law, to wit,

    On the 11th day of March 1830, Andrew Baldwin with Katherine Fox both of Tazewell County Va.

    On the 28th day of Oct. 1830, John Sprecker with Elizabeth Rudy, both of Tazewell County Va.

    Given from my hand Feb 12th 1831   JACOB SHERER,
                                                 Minister of the Gospel

    On the 24th of Feb 1831, Dav. Rudy with Barbara Sprecker both of Tazewell County Va.   JACOB SHERER
                                               Minister of the Gospel

A return of marriages to the Clerk of Tazewell executed by William Shannon Sen.

    Micajah Bailey & Mahala Blankenship June 7th 1832
    Henry W. Dills & Julia Ann Davidson June 26, 1832
    Wesley Fields & Rebecca Billips July 3rd 1832
    Skidmore Pauley & Elizabeth Stowers Aug. 16th 1832
    James H. Moore & Jane S. Moore Sept 11th 1832
    Squire M. Compton & Hannah Coleman Sept 25th 1832
    James Matheny & Nancy Havens Nov. 1st 1832
                                        WILLIAM SHANNON Sen.
                                                      Dec. 9th 1832

I doo certify to the Clerk of the County Corte of Tazewell that the following marriages was selebrated by me William McGuire sesce the first of January 1832. Given under my hand this 24th day of December 1832 Viz:

Elijah McGuire & Elizabeth Claypool January the 5 1832
James McCrery & Mary Cothan February the 3 1832
Shadcrick Steel & Christener Deskins Sept 2nd 1832
John McGuire & Rebecca Cecil December 25
A list of Marriages
William Lester & Ruth Bishop Sept 6, 1832
Jonathan Whitt & Polly Harnan the 5 day of October 1832
Thomas Lester & Margaret Drake December the 24 1832
Hezekiah Woosley & Margaret Husk June the 25, 1833
Richard Ratcliff & Lydia Ratliff July the 12th 1833

WILLIAM HINKEL

To the Clerk of the County Coart of Tazwell, I do certify that the following Mariages was celibrated by me sence the first of January 1833. Viz:

Isaac Johnston & Patse Asbury January 29th
William Moore & Mary Brown March 5th
John Vandike & Nancy Mitchel Apriel 11th
William Steele & Polly Brown November 11th
Archabald Pruet & Elizabeth Brewster December 3d
William Harper & Nancy Ratliff December 3d

Given under my hand this seventh day of January in the year of our Lord 1834   WILLIAM MCGUIRE L. P.

To the Clerk of Tazdwell County, I hereby return the following certificate of Marriage to wit on 25 Day of November 1833, I joined together in the holy state of matrimony Andrew Hartwell and Jane Blankenship by virtue of a license from the Clerk of Tazdwell County.   WILLIAM GARRETSON

I do hereby certify that I celebrated the rites of matrimony between James ONeil & Louisa Totten May 9th according as the law directs. Given under my hand and seal this 23 day July 1833.

I do hereby certify that I celebrated the rites of matrimony between James M. Whitley Hester An Totten 17th May according as the law directs. given under my hand 23 day of July 1833.

I do hereby certify that I celebrated the rites of matrimony between Samuel Waldon & Sally Bailley July 4th according as the law directs. Given under my hand 23 day of July 1833.

WILLIAM SHANNON

March the 16th 1833. Tazewell County to wit:

I do hereby certify to John Crockett Clerk of Tazewell County, that on the 28th of June 1832, Thomas Terry & Adaline Carter was joined together in the holy Estate of Matrimony by a license from under your hand by me JOHN PERRY

I also certify to you that on the 21st day of August 1832 Joseph Compton & Nancy Shannon was joined together in the Holy Estate of Matrimony by a licence from under your hand by me

JOHN PERRY

I do also certify to said Clerk that on the 25 day of September 1832 Owry Steel & Elizabeth Cook was joined together in the holy estate of matrimony by a license from under your hand by me

JOHN PERRY

I also certify to said Clerk that on the 30th day of October 1832 William Adams & Nancy Neel was joined together in the holy estate of matrimony by a license from under your hand by me

JOHN PERRY

I also certify to said Clerk that on the 25th day of November 1832 Jacob Stump & Widow Polly Stump was joined together in the holy Estate of Matrimony by a licence from under your hand by me JOHN PERRY

Marriages celebrated by me in Tazewell Co Virginia
William Burke & Peggy Stobough September 2d 1831
John Ourey & Marinda Workman July 7th 1832
Elijah Havens & Peggy Conally February 26th 1833
The above marriages were celebrated by me

DUGALD MCINTYRE

July 24th 1833

Tazewell County to wit,

I David Young do certify that the following list contains all the marriages celebrated by me within the preceding year ending on the last of Dec 1833

I joined Elexander Scott & Margaret Young in Holy Wedlock on the 24th day of January 1833

I joined Giles Dougherty & Polly Doke in holy wedlock on the 22nd day of January 1833

I joined Samuel Drake & Lilly Higginbotham in Holy Wedlock on the 7th day of Febuay 1833

I joined Elijah Elett & Margaret Dills in holy wedlock on the 2 day of April 1833

I joined Henry Gillespie & Elender Gillespie in Holy Wedlock on the 23d day of Aprile 1833.

I joined Nathaniel Alsop & Lucy Young in Holy Wedlock on the 28 day of Aprile 1833

I joined Elisha McGuire & Nancy White in Holy wedlock on the 3 day of September 1833

I joined Moses Higginbotham & Elender B. Smith in Holy Wedlock on the 15 day of October 1833

I joined Smith Deskins & Polly Deskins in Holy Wedlock on the 31 day of October 1833

I joined Miles Ginnings & Lincy Kneel in holy wedlock on the 5 day of November 1833

I joined Thomas Gillespie & Mary Rader in Holy Wedlock on the 24th of December 1833

These are executed and returned by me   DAVID YOUNG
Tazewell County towit,

I David Young do certify the following list contains all the marriages celebrated by me during the preceding year

DAVID YOUNG

I joined William Smith & Elizabeth Lee in holy wedlock on the 2d day of January 1834.

I joined Solomon Stratton & Nancy McGuire in holy wedlock on the 14th day of February 1834

I joined Alexandria G. Thompson & Sally D. Allen in holy Widlock on the 25th day of February 1834

I joined Bird Lockhart & Charlotte Asbury in holy wedlock on the 30 day of March 1834

I joined Samuel W. Young & Nancy Young in Holy widlock on the 24 day of Aprile 1834

I joined James Malory & Jane Asbury in Holy wedlock on the 27 day of Aprile 1834

I joined Robert Belsher & Jane Higginbotham in holy wedlock on the 19 day of June 1834

I joined William Chiddic and Nancy Lowder in Holy wedlock on the 19 day of June 1834

I joined Richard Young & Mary E. Smith in holy wedlock on the 25 day of November 1834

I joined Charles Mitchel & Sally Barrett in holy wedlock on the 2 day of December 1834

These are celebrated within the preceeding year and returned by me on the 19 day of January 1835   DAVID YOUNG

A List of Rights celebrated in the year 1834

    On the 28th day of January, William I Watts & Sarah Peery

    On the 2d day of March John Carter & Dicey Hawes

    On the 27 day of March Jacob Snider & Layer Conley

    On the 23d December Council Walker & Nancy Bailey

    On the 3d April Henry H. Gillespie & Nancy B. Harman

    On the 22d day of May:

    On the 14th January Henry Bartlett & Nancy Peery

    On the 30th day of October, William Taber & Charity Runion

This 28th day of January and year above   JAMES CHARLES

A List of Marriages

    Low Brown to Mary Tabor, November the 14th 1833

    John S. Moore & Margaret Whitley December 19 1833

    Hugh T. Rineheart & Julina Godfrey November 21st 1833

    Colby Holbrook & Nancy Milam December 19 1833

    William Dills & Nancy Harman December 26 1833

    James Day & Easter Prewatt Mar 4, 1834

    Joshua S. Mooney & Peggy Bailey January 15 1834

    Henry Belcher & Mary Ann Belcher January 28 1834

    Andrew L. French & Rebecca Day May 15 1834

I do certify that I have celebrated the rights of matrimony between the above named persons of 1833 & 1834   Given from under my hand this 14th day of June 1834

                        WILLIAM SHANNON Sen

List of Marriages celebrated in the County of Tazewell by the subscriber

    Rawley Blankenship & Leah Payne on the 21st July 1833

    Elijah Blankenship & Betsy Blankenship on the 9 November 1833

    George Drake & Peggy Potters on the 24th of March 1834

    Joel Gibson & Rachel Diel on the 5th March 1834

    Given under my hand this 12th June 1834   DAVID PAYNE

I do certify to the Clerk of the County Court of Tazewell that the following marriages was celebrated by me William McGuire since the first of Janury 1834. Given under my hand this 25th November 1834 Viz:

George Grifeths & Margaret Grifeth married February the 14th 1834

Samuel Steele & Charlotte Steel maried Feb 17 1834

Christopher Q Crawford & Clarissa Higginbotham maried Aprile the 3, 1834

John W. Steele & Mary Webb maried September 4th 1834

James Bostick & Sally Gent married September the 18 1834

Aheart Simmerman and Elizabeth Hatch maried October the 23 1834

Jackson Johnson and Susannah Cordill maried November 6 1834

Thomas Brooks & Polly McGuire Maried November 20th 1834

George Prater & Sally Pruet maried December 9 1834

        WILLIAM MCGUIRE

A List of Marriages

John Baly Permilia Swarder May 1834

Robeurt Hankins & Nancy Beavers Sept 1834

James Luster & Jerusa Asbury Sept 1834

Enis Ratliff Anny McMeanes October 1834

John Stpenson & Sarh VanDike Febury 1835

John VanDike & Lena Whitt March 1835

James M. Whitt & Rebecca Day 1835

Henry H. Bolen & Elender G. Blankenship. they wear published and joined togeather in matrimony March 1835

I Do hereby certify that all the above namd persons are joind in matrimony   WILLIAM HINKLE

This is to certify that I have celebrated the rites of matrimony between Jesse Davis and Peggy S. Godfrey according to Law on the 8th day of January last. Given under my hand this 30th day of September 1835   HUGH JOHNSTON

John Cline & Polly his wife wedded on the 20th Octo 1835

        DAVID PAIN

December 19th 1835

I do certify to the Clerk of the County Court of Tazewell that the following mariages was cilibrated by me cence the first of January 1835 Viz:

Deskins Green & Rachel Grifitts married January the 13th 1835

Marke T. Lockhart & Nancy Deskins Maried February the 25th 1835

Thomas Asberry and Mariah Brown maried March the 24 1835

James Stephenson & Mary Oney maried May the 21st 1835

Milton Lockheart & Rebecca Brewster married July the 9 1835

William Wilson & Rach Steel Maried October the 29th 1835

Quinton Persell and Sarah Prater maried November the 17th 1835

Given under my hand this nineteenth day of December 1835

    WILLIAM MCGUIRE L P

        Tazewell Va

Sir, I return to your office for the year 1835 by your athority this 26th day of January as followeth,

On the 6th day of January Joined together Robert Harman & Rhoda Harman

On the 13th Jan. Rees T. Bowen & Maria Louisa Peery

June the 4 day James Bailey & Martha Blankenship

On the 15th July Edley C Maxwell & Mary Sincen Taffy

August 18th John Cecil & Peggy Harman

September the 3rd I Nelson & Nancy Chapel

October the 29th George W Thompson & Polly Buchanon

On the 3d November Henry Hedrick & Nancy Whitley

Celebrated by me   JAMES CHARLES

Capt. John Crockett

 Jeffersonville

I do hereby certify to the Clerk of Tazewell that I have joined the following persons in the State of Matrimony according to law, to wit

Henry Swader & Edy Day Aug 6th 1835

John Bailey & Polly Bailey Apl 14th 1835

Harden Nuckles & Elizabeth K. Runyon Apl 16th 1835

Elijah Nuckles & Polly Carter Apl 21st 1835

John Matheny & Mary Havens Sept 21st 1835

James Dills & Polly Davidson Octo 22, 1835

Certified under my hand this 30th of Octo 1835

      WILLIAM SHANNON

Mr. Shannon has also returned to this Office the license Authorising the marriage of Henry Louthen & Cosby T. Brown with the following endorsement "Executed the 14 Jany"

Also he has returned to this Office the license authorising the the marriage of Ransom Kennedy & Lucinda Day with the following endorsement "Executed 15th Dec 1835"

The licence issued from this Office authorizing the marriage of John Louther & Eliza Jane Meek has been returned here with the following certificate thereon written "Solemnized on the ninth of Sept 1834 by JN T. WATT".

I do hereby certify that the following persons have been joined into the holy estate of Matrimony according to Law, to wit:

On the 10th of April 1834 Jacob Sprecker with Lucretia Ritter both *both* of Tazewell County Va

Given under my hand this 9 day of March 1836

JACOB SHERER
Minister of the Gospel

Tazewell County to wit:

I David Young, do certify that the following list contains all the marriages celebrated by me within the preceding year:

I Joined John H Suthers and Mary Ann Forgerson together in holy wedlock on the 12 day January 1835

I Joined James Thompson and Levisa Harrisson in holy wedlock on the 15 day of Febuary 1835

I Joined Abel Maloy and Hanah Asberry in holy wedlock on the 26 day of February 1835

I Joined James Lockhart and Elizabeth Jennings in holy wedlock on the 25th day of Aprile 1835

I joined Isaac Oney and Linney Boling in holy wedlock on the 8 day of August 1835

I joined Richard Brooks and Ellemsa Sipers in holy wedlock on the 2 day of September 1835

I joined William Mares and Sally Brooks in holy wedlock on the 26 day of September 1835

I joined James D. Thompson & Lydia Mitchell in holy wedlock on the 6 day of November 1835

I joined George Chapple and Rebecha Lockhart in holly wedlock on the 14 day of December 1835

Executed by me DAVID YOUNG on the 25 dy of January 1836.

Tazewell County Va A list of Marriags
  I do hearby certify that I joind in matrimmony
  Abel Hankins and Polly Henkel—December—1835
  Michal Hickman and Pelina Pruett—October—1836
  William Anderson & Arminda Jones—Novmber—1836
  Henry Whitt & Elenda Davis—December—1836
                    WILLIAM HENKEL

I Hereby certify that I celebrated the rites of matrimony between Charle Caffee & Nancy Bailey in Tazewell County Va on the 24 day of March 1836.

Given under my hand this 24 day of March 1836
                    MOSES E. KERR M. of G.

Edmond Harrisson and Cleary Payne wase marred on the 24 day of Aprile 1836

Ellie Bally and Hannah Lurster wase Marrid on the 21 of Aprile 1836

Alexander Gipson and Mily Carver wase marrid on the 14 day of Jenerary 1836

Natten Gipson and Polly Sinney waste marrid on the 14 day of Jennary

Henry Darrset and Silby Stacy was Marridg on the 14 day of Jenuary   DAVID PAYNE.

  Marriages celebrated in Tazewell County by Dugald McIntyre
  Joseph Pendleton & Mary Wynn August 15 1833
  Jacob Romans & Eliza Snider September 25 1833
  The above celebrated by me   DUGALD MCINTYRE
  April 19th 1836
Tazewell County To wit November the 19th 1836.

I do certify to John Crockett Clerk of Tazewell Co That on the 29th day of April 1836 Harvy Totton of Smith County was married to Sally Sutor of this county by a licence from your office by me
                    JOHN PERRY

I do certify also to said clerk of Tazewell County that on the 15th day of November 1836 Jonathan Pauley and Martha Lambert was joined together in the holy Estate of Matrimony by licence from your office by me   JOHN PERRY

This is to certify that the rites of Matrimony was celebrated by me between Wm. G. Davidson & Elizabeth Allen on the 28th of July 1836   A. PATTON

This is to certify that the rites of Matrimony was celebrated by me between James Thornton & Matilda Rinehart on the 8th day of September 1836   A. PATTON

Marriages celebrated by the Subscriber

Thomas Christian and Anna Altizer wer joined in matrimony by me Oct 23d 1836.

Richard Deal & Susan Barns were joined in matrimony by me on the same day   DAVID PAYNE

December 16th 1836 I do certify to the Clerk of the county court of Tazewell that the following marriages was celibrated by me sense the 28th of december in the year 1835 Viz:

Milton Vandyke and Judgeza Muncy married December 31 1835

William McGuire and Rachel Wingo married January 4th 1836

Patton Harper and Nancy Harkrider maried December 15th 1836.

Given under my hand this seventeenth of December in the year 1836   WILLIAM MCGUIRE L. P.

A list of marriages celebrated by the subscriber during the year 1836

Nov. 13 William G. Williams & Elizabeth Rader

Dec. 8 Bartley Belcher and Sally Taber

Dec. 17 Moses Belcher and Nancy Taber

           JAMES CHARLES

This is to certify that the rites of matrimony were lawfully celibrated by me between the following persons,

Stephen Thompson & Minerva Thompson July 21 1836

George W. G. Browne & Sarah Ann Gillespie October 24 1836

           DAVID YOUNG

           December 28 1836

A return to the Clerks office of Jeffersonville for the year 1837 as followeth,

Joind together April 20 John Litts and Clarissa T. Watts

July 18 Joined together Mastin Bailey & Rebecca Harman

August the 8 Joind together James S. Vail & Margaret Harrison

October the 14 joind together John Spratt & Ann C. Buchanan

January 6 Joind together William Clay & Malvina Harman

To the Clerk of Tazewell County January 30 1837

           JAMES CHARLES

I do hereby certify to the clerk of Tazewell County that I have joined the following persons in the state of matrimony, to wit:

Henry Swrader & Edy Day Aug 6th 1835
Vertin Holbrook & Phebe Taylor Feby 18 1836
Felex Williams & Nancy Bailey March 1 1836
Randal Collins & Violet Fortner April 14 1836
John H. Hoge & Elizabeth Moore Dec 1 1836
James Taber Jr. & Sally Brown Jany 12 1837
Lewis Milam & Elizabeth Gates Apl 13 1837
Henry Puckett & Amy Taber April 20 1837

Certified under my hand this 26 of May 1837

WILLIAM SHANNON

I do hereby certify that I have celebrated the rites of matrimony on the fourth of October 1836 between Alexander Harrison & Letitia S. Taylor.

Given under my hand April 25 1837   HUGH JOHNSTON

I do hereby certify that I have celebrated the rites of matrimony on the first day of June 1836 between John Hagey and Sussanah Hedric

Given under my hand April 25 1837   HUGH JOHNSTON

I certify that I have celebrated the rites of matrimony between the following persons

James Harper and Mary Stephenson on the 21 day of May 1837
Uriah Estess and Lucinda Estess on the 30 day of April 1837

DAVID PAYNE

May 24 1837

This is to certify that I Jacob McDaniel a regular licensed and ordained minister in the Methodist E. P. Church, have on this the 18th day of August 1837 celebrated the rites of matrimony between Raleigh Gross and Wilmarth Terry, according to the rights and ceremonies of our church   J. McDANIEL

To the Clerk of the Court for Tazewell Co Va.

A list of marriages. I do hereby certify that on the 7 of February 1837 I joined in Matrimony William Hankins and Polly Michell

Also Thomas H. Asbury and Charlotte Hankins in February the 22nd 1837

Also Allen Dalton and Nancy Bruster May the second 1837
Also David Bishop and Sarah Johnston March the 16 1837

Also George Harson and Lucy Hankins May the 7 1837
Also Silas Chappell and Nancy Lockhart May the 7 1836
Also John Mars and Sally Prewett June 20 1837
Given under my hand   WILLIAM HENKEL

These are to certify to the Clerk of the Court of Tazewell County that agreeable to the license presented me I have solemnized the rites of matrimony between John Y. Cresswell and Cinthy Whitt on the 15 day of Oct 1837   JOHN WALLIS JR

I certify that I celebrated on the 10 Oct 183 the rites of matrimony between Charles H. Greever and Eliza Harrison
                                    HUGH JOHNSON

To the Clerk of Tazewell

This is to certify that the rites of matrimony ware celebrated by me between the following persons within the year 1837

Howard Bane & Martha Haven January 12 1837
Thos. S. King & Matilda P. Davidson April 11 1837
Silas Eagle & Martha Sincentafee March 28 1837
John M. Witten & Catherine Peery Sept 19 1837
                                    ARNOLD PATTON

Tazewell County to wit. I David Young do certify that the following list contains all the marriages celebrated by me within the preceding year

I Joined James Chappell & Margaret Hall in holy wedlock on the 10 January 1837

I joined Jacob Asbury & Polly E. Higginbotham in holy wedlock on the 18th April 1837

I joined Jacob Farrar & Sally Sipirs in holy wedlock on the 1 day of May 1837

I joined Jordan E. Boland & Margaret Higginbotham in holy wedlock on the 19 June 1837

I joined James Asbury & Jane G. Bolland in holy wedlock on the 17 Oct 1837

I joined Dabney C. Maloy & Sintha Young in holy wedlock on the 30 November 1837

I joined Adam Ritter & Nancy T. Ward in holy wedlock on the 16 November 1837

I joined Andrew P. Gipson & Rebeckah B. Ward in holy wedlock on the 14 December 1837   D. YOUNG
                                    December 25 1837

A List of Marriages for the year 1837 viz,
Edmond Steel and Phebe McMeans married February the 9 1837
Reuben Ratliff and Sarah Johnson married March the 28 1837
David Goodwin and Louisa M. Cecil married June the 25 1837
John Christian and Katy Alltizer married July 27 1837
Hugh a Compton and Elizabeth Wingo married September the 29 1837
Charles Biliter and Mary Green married October the 5 1837
James Oney and Rhoda Day married December the 17 1837
I do certify to the clerk of the County Court of Tazewell that the above marriages was celebrated by me sence the first of January 1837 Given under my hand this 26 day of December 1837
　　　　　　　　　　　WILLIAM MCGUIRE L. P.

Georden Bayley and Bresey Lester was joind together in the holy state of matrymoney on the 5 day of Dec 1837

Also Hezekiah Blankenship & Elizabeth Stasy on the 19th day of Dec. 1837

Also Abram Steward & Easter tainey on the 3d day of January 1838 by me　　　　　　　　　　DAVID PAYNE

I do hereby certify to the Clerk of the County Court of Tazewell, that I have joind the following persons together in the estate of matrimony according to law viz:

Andrew Stowers and Elizabeth Trillaman Nov 30 1837
Andrew Payne & Elizabeth Billips Dec 6 1837
John D. Havens & Peggy Ann Harman Dec. 14 1837
John Louthian and Lydia Annis Brown Jany 4 1838
William Belcher and Polly Milam Jany 25 1838
Given under my hand this 26 day of January 1838
　　　　　　　　　　　　WILLIAM SHANNON

This is to certify that the rites of matrimony were celebrated by me between William P. Wynn & Margaret H. Bane on the 7th of March 1838

Also between David Staley & Jane W. Maxwell on the 8th of March 1838　　　　　　　　　　　　A. PATTON

A list of marriages. I do hereby certify that I joined in the holy estate of matrimony Muncy Deskins and Rachel Ratliff the first day of August 1837 and William Pruett and Nancy Marrs December the 26 day 1837

also Robert Hankins and Susan Hankins March 27 1838
　　　　　　　　　　　　WILLIAM HENKEL

Tazewell County towit: I do hereby certify to the Clerk of said County that on the 26 day of December 1837

Thomas Dunn Folio and Anne Burton boathe of Tazewell County were joind together in the holy estate of matrimony by me

JOHN PERRY

Also William Clerk and Nancy Cook were joined together in the holy estate of matrimony on the 19th day of April 1838 by me

JOHN PERRY

This is to certify that on the 16th of this instant I married Polly Fletcher and Addison Robinett by publication

Given under my hand the 16th of September 1838

DAVID PAIN

Presby Blankenship and Rutha Jones married October the 4 1838 and

also James White and Nelly Barnet the 7th of the same

DAVID PAYNE

I do hereby certify to the clerk of the County Court of Tazewell that the following marriages was celebrated by me sense the first of January 1838 viz:

Stephen Fuller and Elnor Daly married the 4 January

Samuel M. Higginbotham and Dorind C. Cecil married the 9th of January

Davidson Adkins and Delile Tury married the 11th of January

Miles Claypole and Sarah Gose married the 1st of March

William S. Cecil and Nancy S. Anderson married the 8th of March

Hiram Stephenson and Lucinda Arenheart married the 29th of April

Henery Curle and Nancy Matenle maried the 2d of August

Asa Helton and Mary Vance maried the 8 of November

Campbell Hurst and Ann Eliza Stephenson married the 2 of December

All within the present year of 1838. Given under my hand this 22d day of December 1838   WILLIAM MCGUIRE

Tazewell County to wit, I David Young do certify that the following list contains all the marriages celebrated by me within the preceding year

I joined Edward Wilson & Sally Goodwin in holy wedlock on the 28th day of December 1837

I joined Wesley Gibson and Catherine T. Curen in holy wedlock on the 4 of January 1838

I joined Thomas Gibson & Rachel Ward in holy wedlock on the 4th day January 1838

I joined George T. Thompson and Margaret Thompson in holy wedlock the 12 July 1838

I joined John Crockeett (Jnr) and Margaret Gillespie in holy wedlock on the 6th day of June 1838

I joined William Griffites & Cornelia Mitchell in holy wedlock on the 17th day August 1838

I joined Samuel T. Gipson & Margaret Wood in holy wedlock on the 28th day September 1838

I joined Harviley Cook & Usale Reed in holy wedlock on the 18 day October 1838

I joined Elihu Lester & Malinda Asbury in holy wedlock on the 4th day of November 1838

These are executed by me
December 31 1838   DAVID YOUNG

The 6 day of January 1839 John A Ruhar and Jenny Swader was married   DAVID PAYNE

This is to certify that pursuant to a license issued in the Clerks office for Tazewell May 15th 1838 there was marriage solemnized between D. T Fox and Martha Crabtree on the 24 of May

Given under my hand this 12 day of January 1839
           JOHN FORESTER

Tazewell County to wit: Return to the Clerks Office in Jeffersonville of the matrimonial rites celebrated in the year 1838 as followeth.

On the 18th day of Janury Sanders Steward and Nancy B. Harman

On the 5th day of February William Thompson & Marinda Jane Harman

27th February William G. White & Matilda Harman

12th day of December Addison A. Spotts and Harriet T. Peery

20th December John Henshaw & Elecy Crow

10th day of March William A. Peery & Eleanor T Witten

29th day of March James H. Buchanan & Nancy Doak

12th day of April David B. Gruan & Nancy Thompson

10th day of May Zachariah S. Witten & Mary T. Tiffany

14th day of June Amos Totton & Rebecca Wright
24th July Rufus K. Crockett & Jane Peery
23d day of August William I Watts & Ellen Peery
1st day of November John C. Bandy & Elizabeth H. Peery
By me JAMES CHARLES Local Elder of the Methodist Episcopal Church 15th January 1839

MR. GEORGE W. G. BROWNE

A list of Marriages Tazewell County Va.

I do hereby certify that on the 15th day of August 1838 I joined together in the holy estate of matrimony

Joseph H. Dosson and Susan Barnett

Also Calvin Low and Letitia Pruett October the 7th 1838

Also Charles Philips and Jane Patten 15 day of January 1839 and

William Elswick and Lucinda Deskins the 8 day of May 1839

WILLIAM HENKEL

I certify that I have joined together in the holy state of matrimony according to the form and ceremony of the Methodist Episcopal Church

Joshua Deal and Ruth Blankenship on the 14 day of February and

Thomas Birk and Polly Tailer on the 18th day of June

Thomas Luster and Polly Richards on the 15 day of August by publication in the County of Tazewell in the year A. D. 1839

JOHN BOGLE
Methodist preacher

I certify to the Clerk of Tazewell that on the 30th May 1839 I joined in the holy state of matrimony Isaac Bailey and Martha Belcher   WILLIAM SHANNON

To the Clerk of Tazewell County Court I do hereby certify that I joined Henry Gipson and Sinthy Deal in the banns of matrimony on the 26th day of August 1838 by publication

I also joined Jesse Wit and Polly Jones in the banns of matrimony on the 20th day of June 1839 by publication

JOSEPH LOONY

I hereby certify that I have joined together in the holy estate of matrimony according to the forms and customs of the Methodist

E. Church in Tazewell Co. Va. in the year 1839, the following persons Viz:

Waddy T. Curren & Martha Wynn Feby 5

Ira Tiller & Nancy Carter Sept. 4

Oct 23d 1839   J. I. WEAVER

Virga: Tazewell County Vigt. I do hereby certify to the Clerk of the County of Tazewell that I have joind the following persons in the estate of matrimony to wit

Beza Scott & Marinda Carter Feby 5 1839

Cornelius Compton & Jane Patterson Feby 10 1839

John R. McClaa & Oliva Marrs March 10 1839

Henry Belsher & Rachel Nely Dec. 6 1838

March 25 1839   WILLIAM SHANNON SEN

I do certify to the Clerk of County Court of Tazewell, that I have joined together in the holy state of matrimony according to the forms and cerimones of the Methodist Episcopal Church by licens issued from the Clerk and by publication the following marriages viz:

Edward Blankenship and Mahala Johnson married January the 1 1839

Meshark Steel and Nancy Wolford married January the 9th 1839.

William Alltizar and Loves Harmon married by publication January the 20 1839

Thomas W. Sayers and Margaret Muncy maried January the 24 1839

John Deskins and Polly Luster maried March 20 1839

Daniel Harman and Mary Jane Bishop maried April the 10 1839

Washington Deskins and Olivia Whitt married June the 12 1839

James Deskins and Sally Maxwell maried June the 13th 1839

Isaac Luster and Nancy Blankenship married July the 2d 1839

William Elswick and Mary Vincel maried Sept the 27 1839

James Bostic and Sarah Luster maried October the 24 1839

Aaron Quicksel and Elizabeth Prater maried December the 18 1839

James Hankins and Elizabeth Quicksel Maried December the 24th 1839

The above marriages was celibrated by me sence the first day of January 1839. Given under my hand this 29th day of December 1839   WILLIAM MCGUIRE

110   ANNALS OF TAZEWELL COUNTY, VIRGINIA.

I David Young do certify that the following list contains all the marriages celebrated by me within the preceeding year

I joined Jonathan Smith and Rebecca Young in holy wedlock on the 24 day of January 1839

I joined John Six and Jane Young in holy wedlock on the 15 day of January 1839

I joined James Higginbotham and Levisa Turley in holy wedlock on the 11th day of April 1839

I joined John Gillespie and Nancy Thomas in holy wedlock on the 27th day of May 1839

I joined Jarred Boling and Isabella Goodwin in the holy wedlock on the 27th day of June 1839

I joined John C. Harrison and Elizabeth I. Duff in holy wedlock on the 4th day of July 1839

I joined Robert Brooks and Sarah An Vincill in holy wedlock on the 12th day of September 1839

I joined Thomas Davis and Jane Marrs in holy wedlock on the 21st day of November 1839

Return of marriages December 31st 1839

These was executed by me   DAVID YOUNG

The license issued from this office dated Dec 4, 1839 authorizing the marriage of David Gose and Rebecca Jane Witten was returned here on the 11 of Jany 1840, with the following certificate written "Sillerated the 12th of this by me"

"WILLIAM SHANNON"

Sir I return a list of Marriages to your office in Jeffersonville for the year 1839 as followeth:

March 14th Alexander Ward & Martha Peery
April 2d Gordon McDonald & Recca Hall
May 1st Lewis E. McDonald & Sally B. Taylor
June 7th Peter Teel & Rebecca Compton
Aug. 29 Retsey N. Harris & Louisa Peery
October 11 John Odle & Polly Gates
November 4th Tilman Franklin & Jane Cummings
December 16 James Owens & Margaret Peery

February 22d Published according to law I joined together James M. Gillespie & Matilda Buenty both of this County by me

JAMES CHARLES
Local Elder of the Methodist Episcopal Church

March 30 1840   Mr. George W. G. Browne Clerk

I do hereby certify that the following persons have been joined into the holy state of matrimony according to law, to wit,

On the 2d day of April 1840 Rev John Griever to Margarett Peery both of Tazewell Co. Va

Given from under my hand, this 8 day of Feb 1840
               JACOB SCHERER Minister of the Gospel

To the Clerk of Tazewell County Court, I do hereby certify that I joined Benjamin Cox and Betsey Carter in the Banns of matrimony on the 18th day April 1840 by licens
                              JOSEPH LOONY

Mr. George W. G. Browne Sir Mister Benjamin Belcher and Susanna Lester was married on the 4th of June 1840 by me

Tazewell County to wit: I certify to Geo. W. G. Browne Clerk of Tazewell County that on the 13th day of October 1839 John Yost was married to Elizabeth Stump by license from under your hand by me   JOHN PERRY

I also certify to said clerk of said County that on the 19th day of September 1839 James Hawry was married to Margaret Hictenridge by license from under your hand by me   JOHN PERRY

I also certify to said Clerk of said County that on the 20th day of February 1839 Hickman Stowers was married to Sally Burton in the holy estate of matrimony by me   JOHN PERRY

I also certify to said Clerk of said County that on the 8th day of October 1840 Isaac Holbrook was married to Ann Stump, according to the rules & ceremonies to which I belong of the Methodist Episcopal Church by license from under your hand by me
                              JOHN PERRY

These are to certify to the Clerk of the Court of Tazewell County that agreeable to the licens presented me I have solemnized the rites of matrimony between Stephen Compton and Ann Eliza Vencill on the 22d of Octo 1840

Given under my hand   JOHN WALLIS Jr

A list of marriages, I do hereby certify that on the 26th day of June 1839 I joined Joseph Harson and Patty Hankins in matrimony

Philip H. Vincel and Rebecca Pruett October the 27 1839

John Puckett and Mary Cassell August the 19 day 1839

Richard Ratliff and Mary McGlothlin October the 10 1839

Harrison I. Hueff and Elizabeth Phipps December the 25 1839

George Deskins and Catherine Deskins March the 2d day 1840
Luther Low and Lavisa Christian the 6th day of May 1840
Rees Davis and Nicy Henkel the 5th day of March 1840
William Grose and Nancy Landenhavn April 15 1840

WILLIAM HENKEL

November the 17th 1840

Mr. George W. G. Brown Sir I married Thomas Deel and Tilda Gipson on the 5 of November 1840   DAVID PAYNE

November 17 1840

Mr. George W. G. Brown Sir I married David Payne and Louisey Lambert on the 12 of November 1840   DAVID PAYNE

Tazewell County to wit. I David Young do certify that the following list contains all the marriages celebrated by me within the preceding year

I joined William B. Smith and Maria Gillespie in holy matrimony on the 24 day of February 1840

I joined Tim Sprinkle and Elizabeth Young in holy matrimony on the 10th day of September 1840

I joined Charles C. Taylor and Ellen E. Bowen in holy matrimony on the 22d of September 1840

I joined Henry Files and Elizabeth Lowder in holy matrimony on the 22d of July 1840

I joined Linsey Luster and Margret Gillespie in holy matrimony on the 24th December 1840

The rights of these are celebrated by me this 30 day of December 1840   DAVID YOUNG

I return to the Clerks office of Jeffersonville of matrimonial rites celebrated in the year 1840 as followeth,

1st day of January James M. Crawford & Ellen Bandy
February the 3d Hiram Robinett & Ruth Odell
February the 14th Pleasant Franklin and Elizabeth Helmindollar
February 24th Hervey Wilson and Polly Hagy
February 30 Henry Harman and Nancy Harman
March the 5 Adam Hedrick and Elizabeth Whitley
June 2d James P. Whitman & Elizabeth P. Bean
29th July John Jones & Christena
April 16 Augustus Cole & Margaret P. Harman
December 24th John H. Suthers and Jane R. Vencil

October 27d Larkin Meadows and Jane Thompson
December the 4 Rees Crabtree & Jemima Spracher
Joined together by me JAMES CHARLES local Elder of the Methodist Episcopal Church April 16th 1841
December 28th 1840

To the Clerk of the County Court of Tazewell, I do certify that the following marriages was celibrated by me sense the first of January 1840 viz:

Harvey Claypool and Nancy Brown Maried April the 9 1840

George W. Lockhart and Elizabeth Brown maried April the 14 1840

Daniel Quicksel and Malinda Oney maried June 18 1840

John M. Brown and Elenor Brown maried September the 17 1840

Daniel W. Horton and Elenor Muncy maried October the 4th 1840

Robert McGlothlin and Rebecca An Croel married October the 29th 1840

The above mriages was solemnized by me sence the first of January 1840. Given under my hand this 28th day of December 1840   WILLIAM MCGUIRE

A list of marriages of 1840 and 1841

I do hereby certify that on the 16th day of July 1840 I joined in the holy estate of matrunony

William White and Elizabeth Prewett

Berdine Deskins and Margaret Maxwell July 16 1840

Richard Gates and Lilly Altizer 6th of September 1840

John Prewett and Nancy Howell July 11 1840

Wilkinson Colins Margaret Jones Nov 12 1840

Moses Davis Catherine Griffitts Nov. 8 1840

James Francisco and Elizabeth Lindimoed November 22d 1840

Milton Hankins and Elizabeth Webb Nov. 22 1840

Adam Bedners and Rachel Whitt Jany 6 1841

James Stephenson Elener D. McGuire Jany 14 1841

           ELDER WM. HENKEL

To the Clerk of Tazewell County Court I certify that by license from you I celebrated the rites of matrimony between Hamilton R. Bogle and Sarah Ann Cecil on the 9th day of February 1841

           WM. I C ROGERS

To the Clerk of Tazewell County Court I do hereby certify that I joined Hiram Yates & Cintha Lester in the State of matrimony on the 17 day of December 1840

I also joined James Yates & Perlina Shortridge in the state of matrimony on the 11th day of February 1841

JOSEPH LOONY

Mr. George W. G. Brown, Sir

I married William Lester and Sally Blankenship on the 9th of May 1841   DAVID PAYNE

To the Clerk of the County Court of Tazewell, I do certify that the following marriages was celebrated by me William McGuire viz:

John A. Brown and Nancy Lockhart married December the 30 1840

Joseph Rudd and Martha Rudd married January the 12, 1841

Joseph Blankenship and Eleanor Blankenship married February the 26 1841

John M. Crismond and Elizabeth Shannon married June the 1 1841

John Ratliff & Matilda Ratliff married August the 19 1841

James Compton and Amy Claypool maried August the 19 1841

George Bishop & Elizabeth Rose married August 19 1841

Peter Ratliff and Mary Ann Young married September 2d 1841

Samuel Cecil & Nancy Curde maried September 30 1841

James M. Rud and Sarah Rud married November 4 1841

I do certify that the within marriages was celebrated by me according to the forms and ceremonies of the Methodist Episcopal Church. Given under my hand this 22nd of December 1841

WILLIAM MCGUIRE....

To Mr. George W. G. Browne

Tazewell County to wit: I David Young do certify that the following list contains all the marriages celebrated by me within the preceeding year   D. YOUNG

I joined together Shadrach Comb and Elizabeth Bolland in holly wedlock the 2d day of April 1841

I joined together Henry W. Miller and Mary Ann Helms in holly wedlock on the 8th April 1841

I joined together David Turlay and Jane Bolland in holy wedlock on the 25 May 1841

I joined together Andrew Beavers and Helen Dawson in holly wedlock on the 29th August 1841

I joined together Rees B. Gillespie Jr and Emmerine V. Gillespie in holy wedlock on the 23rd of December 1841

These are joined together by me within the preceeding year

DAVID YOUNG

I do certify to the Clerk of the County Court of Tazewell, that I have joined the following in the state of matrimony, to wit

Harrisson Taber & Nancy Runion Dec 3 1840
Lewis Belsher & Martha Runion Dec 3 1840
Solomon W. Day and Jane Billips Octo 27, 1840
Samuel Carter & Matilda Carter Dec 22 1840
Andrew P. Moore & Nancy Cummings Jany 28, 1841
Floyd P. Shannon & Elizabeth Roark March 4th 1841
Henry Milam & Marinda Totten March 11, 1841
Thomas S. Gillespie & Nancy Shannon April 15th 1841
Andrew Milam & Jane Milam July 22nd 1841
Elkanah Champ & Nancy Carter Sept 30th 1841
Gustavus A. Beemer & Mary Jane McDonald Octo 27, 1841
Joshua Day & Adeline Harry Feby 22nd 1842
Joseph Looney & Lavinia Day March 3rd 1842

WILLIAM SHANNON
March 12th 1842

Tazewell County, to wit,

These are to license and permit you to join together in the holy state of Matrimony, Francis Michum and Christina Milam, according to the forms and customs of your Church, and for so doing this shall be your sufficient warrant, Given under my hand this 30th day of March 1842   GEO. W. G. BROWNE, C.

To any minister legally authorized to celebrate

Executed 31st March 1842

WM. SHANNON

To the clerk of Tazewell County Court,

I do hereby certify that I joined Shadrach Stacy and Julian Smith in the state of matrimony on the 8th day of August 1841

I also joined Daniel Blankenship and Sophia Luster in the state of Matrimony on the 2nd day January 1842

JOSEPH LOONEY

Mr. George W. G. Browne, Clerk of Tazewell County

On the 12th day of March 1842 George W. Payne and Armendy Beavers was married   DAVID PAYNE.

Mr. George W. G. Browen Clerke of Tazewell County

On the 20th day of Marche 1842 Simaen Payne and Marian Barnes was married   DAVID PAYNE

A list of Marriages

I do hereby certify that in July the 16 1841 I joined together in the holy state of matrimony John Altiser and Sally Beavers

Also Elias Harman and Sally McGuire August 17th 1841

Also James Clear and Tabith Rose October the 20, 1841

Also Reuben A. Whitt & Lydia Pruett March the 30, 1842

Also Joshua Puckett and Margaret Curl November the 26 1842

Also William Puckett and Luvicey Curl December 18th 1842

Also John Bunyan Whitt and Katharine Beavers April the 14th 1842

Also Noah Whitt and Matilda McGuire May the 3, 1842

           WM. HENKEL

Mr. George Brown, Charles Painter and Matilda Barns was married on the 10th day of July 1842   DAVID PAYNE

I do certify that I joined together in Holy wedlock James Q. Kendrick and Rebecca W. Witten on the 21st day of July 1842

           GEO. W. G. BROWNE, L. P.

I certify that on the 4th day of August 1842 I joined together in wedlock James M. Freeman and Sarah Williams Given under my hand Aug 5, 1842   GEO. W. G. BROWNE L. P.

June 14th 1842

I return to your Office in Jeffersonville Tazewell County a list of marriages for the year 1841

On the 30th day of January, joined together Daniel Hagy and Euphinia Yost

March the 11th John Helmandollar and Elizabeth Susan Martin

March 30th Anderson Cook and Jane Hall

April 4th William Seabolt and Lydia Beavers

April 4th William Hicks and Catherine Straton

June 1st Gordon C. Thorn and Agnes C. Shannon

June 1st Robert R. Montague and Grizilda Gose

October 28th Mark Hendrickson and Sally Scoto
October 26th Jefferson I. Myers and Malinda Whitley
By me JAMES CHARLES

Geo. W. G. Brown Clerk

Mr. George W. G. Brown. Sir, On the 1st of September I ma*rid* Benjamin Spense and Catharne Deel
October the 1st 1842.

Mr. George W. G. Brown, Sir, I ma*rid* William Mullins Ha*n*ah Os*bun* on the 1st of September   DAVID PAYNE

Tazewell County to wit, Having found a licence that has been misplaced, I now certify to Geo W. G. Browne Clk of sd. County, that on the 13th day of October 1839, John Yost and Elizabeth Stump was joined together in the holy estate of Matrimony by me
JOHN PERRY

Also I certify to said Clerk that on the 13th day of October 1842, Anderson Atkins and Annaliza Atkins was joined together in the holy estate of matrimony by me   JOHN PERRY

I do certify to the Clerk of the County Court of Tazewell that the following marriages was celebrated by me William McGuire according to the forms and seremonies of the Methodist Episcopal Church, and by licens obtained from the clerk of said Court viz,

James Burk & Louisa S. McGuire Married February the 10th 1842.

Benjamin W. Compton and Margaret Cecil married february the 24, 1842.

Leonard Harper and Louisa *A*renhart married february the 27 1842

John M. Hurt and Louisa M. McGuire married Aprile 10, 1842

Thomas Bandy and Sally Woolridge married July the 16 1842

Timothy Lester and Charlote Blankenship married August the 4, 1842

William W. Stephenson and Scynthia Lockheart married September the 15, 1842

James Reed and Dorcas Deal married November the 3, 1842

William Blankenship and Rinda Johnson married November the 24, 1842

The above marriages was *s*elebrated by me sinc the first of January 1842. Given under my hand this the 27th day of December 1842   WILLIAM MCGUIRE

Kiah Blankenship and Rachel Sanders was married on the 6th day of November 1842

Also Mikel Cline and Mart*hrew* Lambert on the 10th of November 1842
            DAVID PAYNE

Tazewell County to wit:

I David Young do certify that the following list contains all the mariages celebrated by me within the preceding year

I join together in holy wedlock James M. Lewis & Margaret Wil*l*son on the 26th January 1842

I join together in holy wedlock Harvey P. Wit*e*n & Polly Peery on the 3d day March 1842

I join together in holy wedlock Lewis Cooper & Eliza Asbury on the 2d day Feb*u*ary 1842

I join together in holy wedlock Jesse Kinder & Letitia Stump first day March 1842

I join together in holy wedlock William B. Young & Nancy Giluspie on 5 day of May 1842

I join together in holy wedlock Thomas Peery Jr. & Rebecca G. Whi*t*en on the 16th June 1842

I join together in holy wedlock Samuel K. Whitten & Nancy H. Peery on 7th of July 1842.

I join together in holy wedlock Colvin F. Dyer & Tabitha Asbury on the 27th of Oct. 1842.

The Ma*r*rages wa*r*e celebrated by me within the preceding year
            DAVID YOUNG
              December 18 1842.

I do certify that pursuant to license to me directed I celebrated the following marriages in the County of Tazewell during the year ending 31st Dec. 1842. viz:

Thomas K. Lambert & Charlotte Stowers Jan 18th 1842 and
James M. Compton & Lucinda Hix April 26th 1842
            A. N. HARRIS

Tazewell County the 21st 1845. I return a list to your Office of matrimoni*el* Rig*h*ts cellibrated as followeth—

1842 Granville H. B. Myers & Bathsheba Brown Dec 21, 1842
   Samuel Graham and Cozbi Harrisson November the 8, 1842
   Chapman A. Spotts & Elizabeth P. Whitman Spt 3*1* 1842.
   Benjamin Layne and Margaret E. Crockett Jan. 4, 1842
   Samuel McCormick & Mariah Harman August 25, 1842

1843 Thomas H. Franklin and Abigail Havens February 14, 1843
William W. Compton and Nancy Compton Dec 28, 1843
Mitchell Cline & Nancy Whitley May 4th 1843
John B. Gillespie and Martha Cross July 27th 1842
1844 James W. Shannon and Nancy Cumpton February 15 1844

By me JAMES CHARLES Local Elder of the Methodist Episcopal Church   Date Above

Clerk Geo W. G. Brown

I do hereby certify that on the 5th day of January 1843, I joined together Andrew Jackson Bully and Elizabeth M. Witten in lawful wedlock. Given under my hand this 6th day of January 1843.   GEO. W. G. BROWNE, L. P.
                                    M. E. Church

To the Clerk of Tazewell County Court

I do hereby certify that I joined Peter Coleman and Mahala Stiltener in the state of matrimony on the 20th day of December 1842

I also joined Christopher Stiltener and Mary Ann Whitaker in the state of matrimony on the 31st day of January 1843.

I also joined Elias Stiltener and Nancy Matney in the state of matrimony on the 9th day of March 1843   JOSEPH LOONEY

To the Clerk of Tazewell County Court

I do hereby certify that I joined William Stacy and Rebeccah Blankenship in state of matrimony on the 9th day of May 1843
                        JOSEPH LOONEY

I do hereby certify that on the 18th day of May 1843 I united in holy wedlock Rawley W. Witten and Julian Ann V. Harrisson. Given under my hand this 20th day of May 1843
            GEO. W. G. BROWNE L. P.
                        Methodist Esp. Church

On the 31st day of May 1843, I joined Isaiah Roberts and Melinda Miller in holy wedlock   GEORGE EKIN M. E.C.

This is to certify that on the 6th June 1843, the undersigned, a minister of the Methodist Protestant Church, celebrated the rites of matrimony between James V. Logan and Eleanor H. Vincil, agreeably to a license issued from the Clerk's Office of Tazewell County, Virginia   GEORGE R. BARR
                            June 7th 1843

On the 6th day of July 1843, I joined John S. Dougherty and Hannah Peery in lawful wedlock

Given under my hand this 6th July 1843

GEO. W. G. BROWNE L. P.

M. E. Church

I do hereby certify that on the 24th day of August 1843, I joined David G. Yost and Hannah Wolf in lawful wedlock

GEO. W. G. BROWNE

May the 25th 1843

Mr. George W. G. Browne, Sir on the 4th day of May I mared Philip Lambert and Elizabeth Russell   DAVID PAYNE

May the 25th 1843

Mr. George W. G. Brown Sir On the 14th of May I mared Allen Mileum and Martha Lester   DAVID PAYNE

May the 25th 1843

Mr. George W. G. Brown Sir: On the 19 of May I mared Amos Totton and *Susy* Mitchum (or *Sary*)   DAVID PAYNE

I do certify to the Clerk of the County Court of Tazewell that the following marriages was celebrated by me since the first day of January 1843, viz:

Green Ball and Sarah Steel was married April the 13, 1843

John Vance and Rhody Griffitts was married April the 18th 1843

William King and Dorcas Prater was married May the 7th 1843

James H. Remines and Ruth Hickman was married August the 20th 1843

William McGuire and Virginia Linn was married October the 11th 1843

The above marriages was celebrated by me according to the forms and ceremonies of the Methodist Episcopal Church since the first of January 1843

Given under my hand this the 28th of December 1843

WILLIAM MCGUIRE

Tazewell County, to wit:

I David Young do certify that the following list contains all the marriages celebrated by me, D. Young, within the preceeding year.

I joined together in holy wedlock on the 27 of Aprile 1843, Jacob Deskins and Rachel Harper

I joind in holy wedlock, John Spratt and Jane Peery on the 18th of May 1843

I joind in holy wedlock David Bolin and Louisa J. B. Anderson on the first of June 1843

I joind in holey wedlock Walter W. Thompson and Narcissa Thompson on the 24th of August 1843

I joind in holey wedlock Henry Deskins and Marissa Harper on the 12th of October 1843.

I joind in holey wedlock George W. Bolen and Delilah S. Stanley on the 30 of November 1843

I joined in holey wedlock Jonathan E. Blankenship and Frances Smith on the 28th of Desember 1843

These are joined together by me this 25th of December 1843

DAVID YOUNG

Pursuant to a license issued from the Clerks Office of the County Court of Tazewell County on the 12th day of November, I joined together in holy matrimony, Robert J. Stephenson and Elizabeth Ann Crabtree

Given under my hand this 13th February 1844

R. C. ROBERTS

To the Clerk of Tazewell County Court, I do hereby certify that I joined Robert Stewart and Martha Jane Davis in the state of matrimony on the 9th day of October 1843. by license

Also I joined Ruel Osbourne and Syndesty Breeden in the state of matrimony on the 10th day of December 1843—by publication

Also I joined Mathew Stiltner and Polly Lester in the state of matrimony on the 28th day of March 1844—by publication.

JOSEPH LOONEY

I do hereby certify that I joined Asa Alley and Angeline Hedrick in lawful wedlock on the 11th day of January 1844

GEO. W. G. BROWNE, L. P.

A list of marriages.

I do heareby certify that on the 30th day of June 1843 I joined together in matrimony Jeremiah Whitt and Nelinda McGuire

William Whitt and Sarh Ann Lockhart 12 day of July 1843

and Alexander Pruett and Sarah Ann Harrison July 14 1843

and Thomas Whitt and Polly Bruster Stpt the 12 1843

and John McCenville and Elizabeth Pruett November the 22 day 1843 and Carter Hankins and Nancy Hankins on the 9th day of February 1844

and Martian Sowers and Sally Gilfin Aprile the 21 1844

WILLIAM HENKEL

Charter Mitchel and Elizabeth Payne was marid on 24 day of April 1844   DAVID PAYNE

George Brown

George W. Payne

I do hereby certify that on the 4th day of April 1844 I joined Francillo M. Moors & Polly Ananda Peery in lawufl wedlock

GEO. W. G. BOWNE

I do hereby certify that on the 29th day of May 1844 I joined Jacob Cameron and Margaret Fox in lawful wedlock

GEO. W. G. BOWNE

I do hereby Certify that on the 4th day of June 1844 I joined William Allen and Sally Oney in lawful wedlock

GEO. W. G. BOWNE

June this the 25th day 1844

Mr. George W. G. Browne .. John Spense and Elisabeth Deel was marred on the 16 day of June 1844   DAVID PAYNE

August the 13 .. 1844

Mr. George W. G. Brown.. Si.. On th.. 27th of June 1844 I mared Elijah Mitchum an.. Tilda Squitner and also

On the 21st of July 1844, Benjamin Mullins and Nebba Hall was marred   DAVID PAYNE

Mr. George Brown.. Sir:

Abner H. Vester and Poley Tomson was marred on the 15th day of Sepember 1844 and

Maston Tesen an Dicy Roberts was maridon the 29th day of September 1844   DAVID PAYNE

Mr. George W. Brown: Sir,

James Payne and Elizabeth Sisemore was married on the 21 day November 1844   DAVID PAYNE

I certify that on the 12th day of September 1844 I Joined John B. Marrs and Priscilla Ray in lawful wedlock

GEO. W. G. BROWNE

I certify that on the 12th day of September 1844 I joined William T. Moore & Mary B. Barns in lawful wedlock

GEO. W. G. BROWNE

I certify that on the 16th day of September 1844 I joined Augustus Neel & Frances Taylor in lawful wedlock
GEO. W. G. BROWNE

I certify that on the 19th day of September 1844 I joined John Harkrider & Elizabeth Grills in lawful wedlock
GEO. W. G. BROWNE

I certify that on the 26th day of September 1844 I joined Isaac Repass and Phebe Clara Hedrick in lawful wedlock
GEO. W. G. BROWNE

I certify that on the 24th day of October 1844 I joined Jefferson Matney and Julia A. Crockett in lawful wedlock
GEO. W. G. BROWNE

I certify that on the 5th day of December 1844 I joined James C. Thompson and Martha G. Rader in lawful wedlock
GEO. W. G. BROWNE

Tazewell County, to wit:

I David Young do certify that the following list contains all the marriages celebrated by me D. Young within the preceding year

I joined in holey wedlock William Brooks and Jane Boland on 13 of February 1844

I joined in holey wedlock Daniel C. Wilson and Eleaner Boland on the 15th of February 1844

I joind in Holey wedlock Henry Buchanan and Nancy Wilson on the 16th of May 1844

I joind in holey wedlock John C. Hopkins and Levisa B. Gillespie on the 20th of June 1844

I jined in holey wedlock George W. Deskins and Wyrinda Rader on the 11th of July 1844

I joind in holey wedlock William O. George and Eleanor W. Witten on the 8th of August 1844

I joind in holey wedlock William Asbury and Sarah Ann Gillespie on the 27th day of August 1844

I joind in holey wedlock Moses S. Sayers and Darcey Asbury on the 16th of September 1844

I joined in holey wedlock Floyd G. Meadows and Cosby J. Ceral on the 12 of Desember 1844

Executed by me
DAVID YOUNG

I do certify to the Clerk of the County Court of Tazewell that the following marriages was celebrated by me william McGuire, Viz:

John McGuire and Mary Bishop marrid Febuary the 7

Thomas Barrott and Nancy Whitt marrid March the 12

Richard Steel and Celia Drake marrid May the 28th

James Moore an Debbe Cooper .. published and marrid accordin.. to law May the 2.

Ebeneser Bruster and Hana Whitt marrid March the 14th

James Wilson and Rebecca M. Barrott maried August the 22.

Augustus B. Sayers and Jane A. Brown married September the 17

Daniel Harman and Susan Hatch maried September 19th

Moses Michel and Nancy Asbery maried October the 17th

John Pruet and Alce Spence maried December the 26th

The above marriages was celebrated by me according to the forms and ceremmes of the Methodist Episcopal Church since the first day of January 1844.

Given under my hand this the 31 day of December 1844

WILLIAM MCGUIRE

To the Clerk of Tazewell County Court

I do hereby certify that I joined Ashville H. Smyth and Matilda Stacy in the state of matrimony on the 8th day of July 1844

Also, I joined John Yates and Martha Shortridge in the state of matrimony on the 14th day of November 1844

Also, I joined Boon Shortridge and Nancy Elswick in the state of matrimoney on the 14th day of November 1844

Also, I joined Eli Thomis and Elender Hobbs in the state of matrimoney on the 25th day of December 1844.

JOSEPH LOONEY

By virtue of a marriage license issued from the Clerk's Office of the County County Court of Tazewell County Va. I hereby certify that on the 13th day of December 1844—I joined together in holy wedlock Benjamin Lusk & Cynthia B. Shannon.

MOSES E. KERR M. G.

A list of Marriages

I do hereby sertifye that I joined in the holey state of matrimoney Bennyon Low & Roddy Whitt on the 2nd day of July 1844

Also Harvey H. Patterson & Jane Patterson on the 24th of October 1844

Also James Deskins & Marget Hickman on the 25th of March 1845.

Given under my hand this 18th of June 1845

WILLIAM HENKELL

To Mr. George W. G. Browne Sir: This is to certify that on the 4th day of November last I joined together in the holy state of matrymoney Simpson Casey & Marry Barnet

Allso on the 23d of the same instant, Moses Workman & Mary Blankenship

Given under my hand this 8th day of December 1845

DAVID PAYNE

"END OF REGISTER No. 1"

In pursuance to an order of April Court to us directed we have examined the Clerks Office of this County and find the Wills recorded & the Deeds Recorded to March Court and the Marrige Certificates nearly Recorded, and the estrays are also Recorded and the other Papers appeared to be in as good order as the situation of the office would admit of as far as we knew. Given under our hands this 14th day of May 1846   WILLIAM GEORGE
HENRY HARMAN

Note by Author:

The second half of Register No. 2, is so badly written that several words could not be read at all. 'I' and 'J' are written alike; 'S.' 'L.' and 'T.' are usually written alike. When any of these five letters appears as an initial, one cannot determine which letter is intended. With the aid of County Clerk and County Treasurer in deciphering the badly written words and letters, we feel that a minimum of errors will be found.

MARRIAGE REGISTER NUMBER 2.

1844 to 1852-3

I certify that on the 31st day of December 1844, I joined Crockett Stump and Mary Doak in lawful wedlock

GEO. W. G. BROWNE L. P.

I certify that I joined Edmond Holley and Levisey Stump in the bonds of wedlock on the 14th day of March 1844

GEO. W. G. BROWNE

I certify that I joined William Odle and Louisa Myers in the bonds of wedlock on the 16th day of January 1845

GEO. W. G. BROWNE

I certify that I joined Anderson Belsher and Letitia Ann Carter in lawful wedlock on the 22nd day of January 1845.

GEO. W. G. BROWNE

I certify that I joined John Billups and Francina Odle in lawful wedlock on the 6th day of February 1845.

GEO. W. G. BROWNE

I certify that Audley H. Wilson & Cynthia Whitley in lawful wedlock on the 18th day of February 1845

GEO. W. G. BROWNE

I certify that I joined George Shannon and Virginia Shannon in lawful wedlock on the 27th day of February 1845.

GEO. W. G. BROWNE

I certify that I joined Robert C Graham and Elizabeth P. Witten in lawful wedlock on the 6th day of March 1845

GEO. W. G. BROWNE

I certify that I joined Tobias Belsher and Margaret Milam in lawful wedlock on the 15th day of March 1845

GEO. W. G. BROWNE

This the 15th day of March 1845. Mr. George W. Brown: Sir, David Pain and Catheraner Charles *was* marid February the 20 day

DAVID PAIN

This the 15th day of March 1845 .. Mr. George W. Brown, Sir, Jacob Smith an... Elizabeth Smith was marride the 2nd day of March 1845

DAVID PAIN

I certify that on the 15th July 1845, I joined William Taber and Nancy Totten in holy wedlock   GEO. W. G. BROWNE L P

M. E. Church

I certify that on the 9th day of August 1845, I joined Harman Lewis and Dorcas King in holy wedlock

GEO. W. G. BROWNE L P

Meth. E. Church

I certify that on the 3d day of July 1845, I joined Starling F. Watts and Jane M. George in holy wedlock.

GEO. W. G. BROWNE

I certify that on the 21st day of August 1845, I joined Zachariah Walden and Irene Danoy in lawful wedlock

GEO. W. G. BROWNE

April 23 day 1845. Mr. George N. Broun Sir. Samson Estept and Mahala Osben was marred on the 23d of March.

DAVID PAYNE.

and William Odear and Abigail Jones was marred on 27 day of March 1845

DAVID PAYNE.

Mr. George W. G. Brown Sir:

Nathn Blankship and Saly Wilds was marred on 28th day of July 1845

DAVID PAYNE

Mr. George W. G. Brown Sir:

Slrantle Workman and Srilda Weeb was marred on the 2nd day of August 1845

DAVID PAYNE

On the 22d May 1845, I joined William Prince & Martha L. Taber in holy wedlock

GEO. W. G. BROWNE

On the 30th day of May 1845, I joined Hezekiah Billups and Nancy Davidson in holy wedlock

GEO. W. G. BROWNE

On the 13th day of June 1845, I joined Peter Atkins & Rhoda Belsher in holy wedlock

GEO. W. G. BROWNE

This is certify that on the 22d February 1845. I joined John G. Carr and Martha J. Witten in holly wedlock

December 18, 1845   C. CAMPBELL T. E. M. E. C.

I do hereby certify that on the 3rd day of November 1845, I joined William O. Yost & Elizabeth Jane Whitman together in holy wedlock. Given under my hand this 18th Dec. 1845

COLEMAN CAMPBELL, T. E. M. E. Church

On the license issued for the marriage of Thomas Marrs and Milly Ann Runnien, the following endorsement is made "Executed the 6th day of November 1845 by   WM. SHANNON"

December the 30th 1845

I do certify to the Clerk of the County Court of Tazewell, that the following marriages were celebrated by me in the term of the present year.

1st. Viz: Brooks Martin and Nancy Vandike married January the 9th by publication.

2nd Jeremiah W. Steel and Martha Lockhart, married March the 11th 1845.

3rd. William Patton Oney and Sar*ey* Elswick, married February the 5th 1845.

4th John M. Stephenson and Emma Whitt, married April the 15th 1845

5th William Estep and Sary Lane, married by publication April 23rd 1845.

6th Shadrach Steel and Martha Blankenship, married June the 5th 1845.

7th John W. Eslwick and Nancy Oney married July the 2nd 1845

8th John Horton and Sara.. Brown married September 10th 1845

9th William D. Hurt and Elizabeth McGuire, married October the 22nd 1845

10th Jacob Johnson and Elizabeth Bishop, married December the 24th 1845.

The above marriages were celebrated by me since the 1st of January 1845. Given under my hand this the 30th of December 1845.   WILLIAM MCGUIRE

I certify that on the 9th day of September 1845, I joined Hervey Wise & Eliza Havens in lawful wedlock GEO. W. G. BROWNE

I certify that on the 30th day of October 1845, I joined Samuel W. Austin & Christina Harman in lawful wedlock.

GEO. W. G. BROWNE

I certify that on the 24th day of December 1845, I joined Iredell Burcham & Margery McMeans in lawful wedlock.

GEO. W. G. BROWNE.

I certify that on the 15th day of January 1846, I joined Alexander H. Thompson and Polly Day in lawful wedlock

GEO. W. G. BROWNE.

To the Clerk of Tazewell County Court

I do hereby certify that I joined Michael Luster and Melinda Stiltner in the state of matrimony on the 2nd day of October 1845.

Also I joined Silas Ratliffe and Sally Looney in the state of matrimony on the 23rd day of October 1845

Also I joined Walter Matney and Elizabeth Looney in the state of matrimon*ey* on the 29th day of January 1846

Also I joined Sparrel Ratliff and Nancy Ratliff in the state of matrimon*ey* on the 10th day of February 1846.

Also I joined Abednego Ratliff and Mary Ann Childers in the state of matrimoney on the 12th day of February 1846.

Also I joined William H. Vance and Sarah Ratliff in the state of matrimoney on the 24th day of March 1846.

Also I joined Dickson Carter and Charlotte Coleman in the state of matrimoney on the 8th day of April 1846.

JOSEPH LOONEY.

A list of Mar*iedgs* 1845

I do hereby sertify that I joind Harvey Grose and Matilda Martin in mat*termoney* on the 12th day of January 1845.

Also Harvey Deskins & Jane Jent on the 15th of August 1845.

Also Joseph Jones & Catherine Vandike on the 20th August 1845.

Also George T. Harrisson & Dicy Henkell on the 11th June 1845.

Also William Christian & Sally Altizer 10th Sept. 1845

WILLIAM HENKEL

Tazewell County Sct

I do hereby certify to the Clerk of the County Court of Tazewell, that on the 11th of Dec. 1845, I joined William P. Maxwell and Matilda B. Whitley in the holy state of matrimony.

WILLIAM SHANNON
11th Dec. 1845

This is to certify that I, David Young, joined together in hol*l*y wedlock William H. Buchanan and Jane Thompson on the 3rd July 1845. DAVID YOUNG.

I do certify to the Clerk of the County Court of Tazewell that the following mar*a*ges was celebrated by me in the year 1846, Viz:

John Green and Peggy Vincell, married January the 29th day 1846.

Danial Johnson and T*ishe* Gross maried Aprile the 24th day 1846.

John G. Cipers and Malinda Stephenson maried May the 12 day 1846

John T. Sayers and Polly Wingo maried September the 3rd day 1846

Thomas Quicksell and Rebecca Harckrider maried September the 3d day 1846.

William Oney and Catherine Barnett maried September 27th day 1846

Thomas M. Scott and Martha J. Repass married Oct 8th 1846

William M. Harman and Hariet Browning maried November the 19 day 1846

James Allen and Caroline Helms maried November 19th day 1846.

Given under my hand this the 29 day of December 1846

WILLIAM MCGUIRE.

To the Clerk of Tazewell County Virginia,

I hereby certify that I did unite in holy matrimony James Brown and Nancy Wolf on the 18 of August 1846.

And that I did also unite in holy matrimony William Cooper and Mary Lambert on the 17 of September 1846.

And that I did also unite in holy matrimony Conrod P. Hale and Margaret M. Witten on the 22nd of Oct. 1846

All of them by virtue of Marriage licence from your office

JAMES CALFEE.

Tazewell County, to wit:

I David Young do certify that the following list contains all the marriages celebrated by me within the two last years.

I joined Henry P. Bowling & Nancy Anderson in holy wedlock on the 13th March 1845.

I joined James Harrisson & Nancy W. Barns in holy wedlock on the 19th August 1845.

I joined Wilson Carter & Polly Blankenship in holy wedlock on the 29 October 1845.

I joined Hiram H. Hyden & Patient Rudd in holy wedlock on the 11th June 1846.

I joined Calvin Gillespie & Catherine Boling in holy wedlock on the 7th July 1846.

I joined Joseph Gill & Elizabeth Payne in holy wedlock on the 28 July 1846.

I joined James Steel & Nancy Jane Cecil in holly wedlock on the 2nd July 1846.

I joined Jesse Bates & Elizabeth H. Asbury in holy wedlock on the 28th December 1846.

The above were celebrated by me   DAVID YOUNG
                                     Decemeber 28, 1846.

I do hereby certify that on the 27th day of January 1846 I joined Daniel H. Wright and Martha P. Harman in holy wedlock. Given under my hand   GEO. W. G. BROWNE L. P.

I do hereby certify that on the 26th day of March 1846 I joined Jacob Myers and Eliza Thompson in lawful wedlock
                        GEO. W. G. BROWNE L. P.

I do hereby certify that on the 2nd day of June 1846 I joined William Patterson and Nancy Patterson in Lawful wedlock
                        GEO. W. G. BROWNE L. P.

I do hereby certify that on the 16th day of June 1846, I joined John Sexton and Julia Ann Witten in lawful wedlock
                        GEO. W. G. BROWNE L. P.

A list of Marridges. September the 4th 1846.

I do hereby sertify that I joind togeather in the holey estate of Matrimoney, Burrell Ratliff & Mary Puckett on the 29th of January 1846

Also James Smith & Saley Puckett on the 2nd day of Aprile 1846

Also Smith Carter & Jane Cuppenheffer on the 14th day of June 1846
                        WILLIAM HENKEL.

A list of Marriages by J. J. Greever.

joined together in wedlock in Oct. 1841, John W. Johnston and Nicketti B. Floyd.

Isaac Goodman and Ann Spracher in February 1842
Joseph Goodman and Martha Spence in June 1842
Stephen Rhudy and Cynthia Ann Mahood in April 1844
Rufus G. Newlane an Jane Day in September 1844
Peter Ritter and Margaret Spracher in July 1845
George Spracher and Phebe Ritter in August 1845
Jesse Peery and Angeline Mahood in January 1845
Chapman Duncan and Lorthy Jones in March 1846
                        J. J. GREEVER.

I do hereby certify that on the 12th of September 1845 I jined Archable Pruet and Martha Mitchel in holy wedlock. Given under my hand this 12 day   JOHN SIZEMORE

I do hereby certify that on the 10th day of October 1845 I jind William Vaun and Luisa Combs in holy wedlock. Given under my hand this day   JOHN SIZEMORE

I do hereby certify that on the 26th day of November 1845 I jined John Pruet and Lydia Beavers in holy wedlock. Given under my hand this day   JOHN SIZEMORE.

I do hereby that on the 10th December, I joind Andrew More and Nancy Mitchem in holy wedlock. Given under my hand this day   JOHN SIZEMORE.

I do hereby certify that on the 5th day of May 1846 I jiond James Mitchel and Anna Webb in holy wedlock. Given under my hand this day   JOHN SIZEMORE.

I do hereby certify that on the 8th day of February 1846 I jined Garret P. Lambert and Martha Rusel in holy wedlock. Given under my hand this day   JOHN SIZEMORE.

I do hereby certify that on the 2nd day of Septem. 1846 I joind Bird Bruster and Elizabeth Whitt in holy wedlock. Given under my hand this day   JOHN SIZEMORE.

August the 2nd day 1846.
Mr. George W. G. Brown, Sir,

I have marrey Ize Jacson and Rebeccey Gipson on the 29th day of may.   DAVID PAYNE

October the 22d 1846.

Mr. George W. Brown Sir: I marred Daniel Jewel and Minurvey Patric on the 28th of August 1846.   DAVID PAYNE.

Mr. Geor W. G. Brown Sir: I marred Obadiah Blankenship and Nancy Patric on the 1st of September 1846.   DAVID PAYNE

Mr. Geor. W. G. Brown Sir, I mared Isaac Roberts and Dorcas Mullins on the 5th of October 1846.   DAVID PAYNE.

I do hereby certify that on the 10th day of December 1846 I joined William W. Harman and Polly Taylor together in holy wedlock

To the Clerk of Tazewell County Court   SAMUEL A. MILLER
To the Clerk of Tazewell County Court.

I do hereby certify that I joined Samuel Fields and Nancy Stiltner in the state of matrimoney on the 29th day of October 1846

Also I joined Conley Deel and Sarah Gibson in the state of Matrimony on the 31st day of October 1846.

Also I joined Morgan Davis and Martha Lester in the state of Matrimony on the 10th day of June 1847   JOSEPH LOONEY

I do hereby certify that on the 21st day of July 1846, I joined William B. Harman and Rynda Hatch in lawful wedlock
GEO. W. G. BROWNE

I do hereby certify that on the 13th day of August 1846, I joined Witten Cecil and Angeline B. Peery in lawful wedlock
GEO. W. G. BROWNE.

February th.. 23th 1847

Solemnize.. the writes of matrimoney between Andrew J. Honaker & Eleanor Neel Dec. the 22d 1846.

Solemnized the writes of matrimony between Elias Burton & Sarah Stowers Feb. 26th 1846

Solemnize the writes of matrimony betwen John Burge & Sariah Rakes Febr. the 7th 1847.

Solemnize the writes of matrimony betwen James McNeel & Rebecca M. Robnett Aug the 27 1846.

Sollemnize the writes of marimoney between William Kidd & Malinda Gose March the 12th 1846.

Sollemnize the writes of marimony between Russell Hager and Sariah Stump January th.. 21 1847.

Sollemnize the writes of matrimony between Simms Stowers and Jane T. Evans Sept the 10th 1846.

Sollemnize the writes of matrimony between John Steel and Elen Compton July 30th 1846.   WM. E. NEEL

I do hereby certify that on the 11th day of March 1847, I joined John Thompson and Sophrinia Burrass in holy wedlock.
JOHN B. LOGAN.

I do hereby certify that on the 8th day of April 1847, I joined together in holy wedlock, John Odair and Elizabeth Payne
DAVID PAYNE

On the license issued for the marriage of John N French and Eliza Jane Honaker, the following endorsement is made "I do hereby certify that the within parties were united together as man & wife May the 6th 1847, by me
WILLIAM ROBESON Min of the M. E. C. S."

This is to certify that on the 24th Aug. 1847, I did joine together in matrimony, William A. Young and Melinda Bolling.
Witness my hand Aug 27th 1847.   JOHN B. LOGAN

I certify that on the 23d day of September 1847, I joined James T. Dailey and Bernetta Emily Belchy in lawful wedlock.
JOHN B. LOGAN

I do hereby certify that on the 9th day of November 1847, I joined William Asberry and Lavila Mitchel.. in holy wedlock. Given under my hand this 9th Nov. JOHN SIZEMORE

I do hereby certify that on the 13th day of November 1847, I joined William Stump and Rachel Pruett in holy wedlock. Given under my hand this 13th day Nov. JOHN SIZEMORE

I do hereby certify that on the 23rd day of November, 1847 I joined Elijah Pruett and Sary Pruett in holy wedlock. Given under my hand this 28th November JOHN SIZEMORE

I do hereby certify that on the 31st day of March 1847 I joined Edward S. Rose and Nancy Reed in holy wedlock. Given under my hand this 31st day of March JOHN SIZEMORE

I do hereby certify that on the 1 day of Aprial 1847 I joind Tobias Sizemore and Lydia Mitchel in holy wedlock. Given under my hand this 1 day of Aprial JOHN SIZEMORE

I do hereby certify that on the 23d day of March 1847 I joined William Hankins and Haner Asberry in holy wedlock. Given under my hand this 23rd day of March JOHN SIZEMORE

I do hereby certify that on the 9th day of Aprial 1847 I joined Thomas P. Patterson and Deliah Rose in holy wedlock. Given under my hand this 9th day of Aprial JOHN SIZEMORE

I do certify that on the 9th day of Aprial 1847 I joined Riley Altizer and Jane Stevenson in holey wedlock. Given under my hand this 9th Aprial JOHN SIZEMORE

I do hereby certify that on the 12th day of August 1847 I joined Matthias H. Beavers and Anna Stevenson in holy wedlock. Given under my hand this 19th day of August JOHN SIZEMORE

I do hereby certify that on the 7th day of September 1847 I joined Pleasant M. Lawson and Matilda Lawson in holy wedlock. Given under my hand this 7th day of Se.. JOHN SIZEMORE

I do hereby certify that on the 18th day of April 1847 I joined Owen Sizemore and Nancy Lambert in holy wedlock. Given under my hand this 18th Aprial JOHN SIZEMORE

I certify that on the 21st of Oct 1847, I did join together in lawful wedlock James McBrown & Margaret Higginbotham
JOHN B. LOGAN

Mr. George W. G. Browne, Sir

I marred Thomas Mitchem and Mary Wolf on the 26th of September 1847.   DAVID PAYNE

Mr. George W. G. Brown.. Sir

I marred Henry A. Harman & Christiner Harman on the 26 of August 1847.   DAVID PAYNE

Mr. George W. G. Brown.. Sir

I marred James C. Lester an.. Elizebeth Blanknship on the 29th of August 1847   DAVID PAYNE.

Mr. George W. G. Browne, Sir,

I marred John M. Blankenship and Beca Blankenship on the 29th of August 1847   DAVID PAYNE

I certify that on the 18th November 1847 I did joine together in lawful wedlock, Armstrong Rose & Susan Williams

    JOHN B. LOGAN

Tazewell County, to wit:

I, David Young do certify that the following list contains all the marriages celebrated by me within the preceeding year

I joind James Q. Smith and Rebecah P. Thompson in holly wedlock on the 20th Aprile 1847

I joined Charles G. Higginbotham and Amanda M. More in holly wedlock on the 10th June 1847.

I joined Bird Lockhard and Sally Brooks in holly wedlock on the 2nd September 1847.

I joined James E. Hayter and Louisa B. Thompson in holly wedlock on the 7th October 1847

These are celebrated by me   DAVID YOUNG

I do certify to the Clerk of the County Court of Tazewell that the following marriages has been celebrated by me viz:

John Stevenson and Katharine Oney married January the 10th day 1847.

Jeremiah Brown and Mary Hinkle was married January the 20th day 1847.

John W. Claypool and Mary Lockhart was married January the 28th day 1847.

Abner Spence and Phebe Gent married February the 24th day 1847

Samuel C. Daile and Virginia B. Minter was married April the 1 day 1847

Hiram C. Compton and L*ou*rinda McGuire was married April the 1 day 1847

Henry M. Harman and *Sausaniah* Christian was marṛied Augus.. the 10th day 1847.

John H. Gates and Louisey Christian was married June the 10th day 1847

John Pucket.. and Ruth Burcham was married March the 24 day 1847

John Steele and Elizabeth Nicewonder was married March the 25th day 1847

The above marriages was celebrated by me, according to the forms and Seremonies of the Methodist Episcopal Church since the first day of January 1847. Given under my hand this the 28th day of December 1847   WILLIAM MCGUIRE

I certify that on the 14 July 1846, I joined Thomas S. Carnahan and Letitia Peery in lawful wedlock
GEO. W. G. BROWNE, V D M

I certify that on the 27th Jan. 1847, I joined George Thompson & Rebecca King in lawful wedlock   GEO. W. G. BROWNE.

I certify that on the 28th January 1847, I joined John C. Gillespie and Mary E. Kendrick in lawful wedlock
GEO. W. G. BROWNE

I certify that on the 3d day of June 1847 I joined Calvin Waldron and Nancy Wright in l awful wedlock
GEO. W. G. BROWNE

I certify that on the 20th day of October 1847 I joined Henry May and Rhoda Harman in lawful wedlock
GEO. W. G. BROWNE

I certify that on the 21st day of October 1847 I joined William Cornwell and Mary Spence in lawful wedlock
GEO. W. G. BROWNE

I certify that on the 9th day of November 1847, I joined Thompson S. Crockett and Rachel L. Cecil in lawful wedlock
GEO. W. G. BROWNE

November 25th 1847. Celebrated the rites of matrimony betwixt Samuel Thompson & Matilda Harman by licence

December 16th 1847—Celebrated the rites of matrimony betwixt Howard Havens & Sarilda Harmon by licence

December the 28th 1847—Selebrated the rites of matrimony betwixt Daniel Harman, Rebecca Dillion by licence

WM. V. SHANNON.

I do hearby certify on the 24 day of February I joined in holy wedlock Thomas Christian and Polly Barnett

WILLIAM HENKEL.

January 3, 1848. celebrated the rites of matrimony betwixt James Parker & Mary Martin by license

January 20th 1848. Celebrated the rites of matrimony betwixt Benjamin McMullin & Celia Carter by licence

January 27, 1848. Celebrated the rites of matrimony betwixt John Henry Burchfield & Martha Billups by licence

WM. V. SHANNON

I do hereby certify that on the 11th day of January 1848, I joined William T. Lambert & Mary Barnett in lawful wedlock

GEO. W. G. BROWNE

I do hereby certify that on the 1st day of February 1848 I joined Solomon Rose and Nancy Pike in lawful wedlock

GEO. W. G. BROWNE

I do hereby certify that on the 17th Feb. 1848 I joined Isaac Q. Runnion and Rachel Blankenship in lawful wedlock

GEO. W. G. BROWNE

Mr. George W. Brone. Moses Muncy Rachel Jones was married on the 16th day of August 1848   DAVID PAYNE

I certify that on the 28th December 1848 I united Harvey Belsher and Julia Prince in Lawful wellock

GEO. W. G. BROWNE

I certify that on the 4th day of January 1849 I united William L. Graham and Louisa Thompson in lawful wedlock

GEO. W. G. BROWNE

Solemnize the rites of Matrimony between Mathias Fox and Sarah Ann Lowder June the 31st 1848.

Solemnize the rites of Matrimony between Edward A. Bowles and Margaret Kinnaman August 26th 1848

Solemnize the rites of Matrimony between Russell Alford and Julia Kidd Dec. the 10th 1848

Given under my hand this the 28th of February 1849.

WM. E. NEEL

To the Clerk of Tazewell County Court

I do hereby certify that I joined Suel Stacy and Priscilla Breeding in the state of Matrimony on the 4th day of July 1847

Also I joined Frederick Stiltner and Louisa Collins in the State of Matrimony on the 9th day of September 1847

Also I joined Willis Blankenship and Mary Jane Smith in the State of Matrimony on the 5th day of December 1847.

JOSEPH LOONEY

To the Clerk of Tazewell County Court

I do hereby certify that I joined Joshua Deel and Prudence Gibson in the state of Matrimony on the 27th day of July 1848.

Also I joined Alfred H. Breeding and Stacy in the state of Matrimony on the 8th day of March 1847

Also I joined William Presley and Sarah Stiltner in the state of Matrimony on the 22d day of March 1849

Also I joined Alexander MClannahan and Abigail Ratliff in the state of matrimony on the 3rd day of May 1849

JOSEPH LOONEY

I certify that on the 24th day of August 1848 I joined James Shepherd and Elizabeth M. Wilson in lawful wedlock

GEO. W. G. BROWNE.

I do hereby certify that on the 8th of October 1848, I joined John D. Peery and Mary C. Gregory in lawful wedlock.

GEO. W. G. BROWNE

I do hereby certify that on the 9th day November 1848, I joined Henry D. Harman and Elizabeth Hale in lawful wedlock.

GEO. W. G. BROWNE

I do certify that on the 5th day of October 1848 I joined Rufus K. Harrisson and Louisa Gillespie in lawful wedlock.

GEO. W. G. BROWNE.

Mr. Georg.. W. G. *Brown*.. John Rose and Char*itoty* Burch*fied* was married on the 20th day of Oct 1848   DAVID PAYNE

Tazewell County to wit

I David Young do certify that the following list contains all the marriages celebrated by me within the preceeding year

I joined James Marshal and Lavica Boland in Hol*ly* wedlock on the 20th day of Feb. 1848

I joined Jordan W. Boling and Elizabeth Jane Cecil in holy wedlock on the 30th day of March 1848

I joined Robert Steel and Julia Ann Cecil in holy wedlock on the 13th day of April 1848

I joined Moses Pruett and Susan Arms in holy wedlock on the 17th day of August 1848.

I joined Henry Stephenson and Catherine Deskins in holy wedlock on the 8th day of August 1848.

I joined James B. Boland and Elizabeth Jane Brooks in holy wedlock on the 10th October 1848

I joined Samuel W. Cecil and Elizabeth Goodwin in holy wedlock on the 12th day of October 1848.

I joined Lindsay B. Boling and Mary Jane Deskins in holy wedlock on the 2nd day of November 1848.

I joined Robert C. Boyd and Rebecca Eveline Young in holy wedlock on the 28th day of November 1848.

DAVID YOUNG
December 28 1848

December 25th 1848

To the Clerk of the County Court of Tazewell

I do certify that the following marriages was *cli*brated by me Viz:

James Burk & Margaret Griffitts married December the 30 1847

Edward Prophet and Sarah Keen married January 6th 1848

Isam S. Cordele & Elizabeth Hickman married January 13th 1848

Robert M. Drake & Jemima L. McGuire married February 10 1848

Isaac Johnson & Elizabeth Vencil married March 16th 1848

Christopher Richison and *Manda* Mal*v*inia Samples married March 16th 1848.

George W. Steel and Mary Ann Steel married March 30 1848

John R. Brown & Rachael Wilson married March 30 1848

John Keen and Elizabeth Keen married June 26 1848

Christopher Deskins and Sarah Oney maried June 29 1848.

Eli Steel & Virginia McGuire maried October 26th 1848

George W. Hurst and Mary Stephenson married October 25 1848

Herivy H. Pruett and Susan Barnett married December 7th 1848

The above marriages was celebrated by me according to the forms and ceremonies of the Methodist Church and all except the first since the first day of January 1848. Given under my hand this 25th day of December 1848   WILLIAM MCGUIRE

I hereby certify that on the 2nd day of February 1848 I have joined together in matrimony Alexander Christian and Catherine Vandike. Given under my hand this 17th of December 1848.

JOHN SIZEMORE

This is to certify that on the 23d of March 1848 I have joined together in matrimony Anthony Christian and Nancy Vandike. Given under my hand 17th of December 1848

JOHN SIZEMORE

February the 24th 1848

Celebrated the rites of matrimony by licence between Andrew L. Brown and Eliza McMullen   by WM. V. SHANNON

March the 1st 1848.

Celebrated the rites of matrimony by license between David Bell & Charlotie Shrader   by WM. V. SHANNON

April 27th 1848

Celebrated the rites of Matrimony by license between Andrew Owens and Rhodicen Havens   by WM. V. SHANNON

Septembeer 8th 1848.

Celebrated the rites of Matrimony by license Between Elias Hale and Rhoda Moore   by WM. V. SHANNON

September 28th 1848.

Celebrated the rites of Matrimony by license between Isaac A. Moore and Elizabeth C. Tabor   by WM. V. SHANNON

September the 7th 1848

Celebrated the rites of matrimony by license between Stephen Glandon & Catherine Stump   by WM. V. SHANNON

December 19th 1848

Celebrated the rites of matrimony by license between Joseph Gillenwater and Mary An.. Glandon   by WM. V. SHANNON

I do hereby certify that on the 9th day of January 1849 I joined William Howry and Rhoda J. Morton in lawful wedlock

GEO. W. G. BROWNE

I do hereby certify that on the 18th day of January 1849 I joined Gustavus R. Crockett and Zerilda Gillespie in lawful wedlock

GEO. W. G. BROWNE

I do hereby certify that on the 18th day of January 1849, I joined Robert Winston and Mary A. Gillespie in lawful wedlock.

GEO. W. G. BROWNE

I do hereby certify that on the 25th day of January 1849, I joined William L. D. Gillespie and Lydia J. Kendrick in lawful wedlock   GEO. W. G. BROWNE

I do hereby certify that on the 29th day of January 1849, I joined Benjamin Tate and Jane Die in lawful wedlock
                                 GEO. W. G. BROWNE

do hereby certify that on the 13th day of February 1849, I joined Anthony Myers and Polly Perry in lawful wedlock
                                 GEO. W. G. BROWNE

I do hereby certify that on the 1st day of March 1849, I joined William Holly and Mary Ann Susan Goff in lawful wedlock
                                 GEO. W. G. BROWNE

Mr. George W. *Bown* Sir

Thomas Aldric (Alias Aldridge) and Jane Beavers was marryed on the 4th day of Jeny 1849   DAVID PAYNE

Mr. George W. G. Browne Sir

William Bruster and Rebecca Harman was married on the 23d February 1849

Geor. W. G. Browne Sir

Thomas Muncy and Clerica Harrisson was marred on the 7th day of December 1848   DAVID PAYNE

These are to certify the Clerk of the Court of Tazewell County, that agreeable to the license presented me I have solemnized the rites of Matrimony between James Griffitts and Louisa Martin on the 24 day of May 1849. Given under my hand this 24th day of May 1849   JOHN WALLACE

To the Clerk of Tazewell County Virginia.

I hereby certify that I joined in holy wedlock on Wednesday the fifteenth day of August 1849 Mr. Peter H. Dills and Miss Nancy Jane Harman according to the forms and usages of the Methodist Episcopal Church South. Given under my hand this 20th August 1849   RICHARD. A. CLAUGHTON
                     Minister of the M. E. C. South

To the Clerk of Tazewell County at the Court house

This is to certify that I joined togeather Condly Blankenship and Polly Justice in the holy estate of Matrimony on March the 15th 1849 And under my hand & *siel*   THOMAS M. MULLINS

To the Clerk of Tazewell County at the Courthouse

This is to certify that I joind togeather David Jesse Osbourne and Rhoda Keen in the holy estate of matrimony on the 18h day of August 1849   THOS. M. MULLINS

To the Clerk of Tazewell County at the Court House

This is to certify that I join.. togeather William Collins and Levicy Johnson in the holy estate of matrimony Given under my hand on the 24th of August 1848   THOS. M. MULLINS

To the Clerk of Tazewell County at the Court House

This is to certify that I join.. togeather Isham Hall Elizy Marcum in holy matrimony on the 6th day of Sept 1848. Given under my hand & siel   THOS. M. MULLINS

To the Clark of Tazewell County at the Courthouse

This is to sirtfy that I joind togeather William W. Justice and Peggy Blankenship on the 16th day of August 1849. Given under my hand & siel   THOS. M. MULLINS

This is to certify that on the 9th day of August 1849 I joined together William Waddle and Eady Watson. August 21st 1849
    JOHN B. LOGAN

I do hereby certify that on the 27 day of June 1849, I joined Robert T. Atkins and Jane Harman in lawful wedlock
    GEO. W. G. BROWNE

I certify that on the 23rd day of August 1849, I joined Daniel H. Gillespie & Margaret L. Harman in lawful wedlock.
    GEO. W. G. BROWNE

I certify that on the 16th day of August 1849, I joined James A. Cliborne and Angeline Brooks in lawful wedlock
    GEO. W. G. BROWNE

This is to certify that on the 25th Oct 1849, I joined together in the holy estate of matrimony John Smith & Margaret J. Griffith of Tazewell Co. Virginia   JOHN B. LOGAN

Oct 29 1849

To the Clerk of Tazewell County Cort

I do hereby certify that I joined Clinton Stacy and Sally Yates in the state of matrimony on the 19th Day of July 1849

Also Hiram Blankenship and Eveline Blankenship on the 23rd Day of July 1849.

Allso James Paign and Nancy Breeding on the 2nd day of September, 1849.   GEORGE GIBSON

I do hereby certify that on this day I joined together Isaac Belsher and Martha Milam in holy wedlock. Given under my hand this the 19th of May 1849   JOHN SIZEMORE

I do hereby certify that on this day I joined together Aner H. Luster and Marir Wolf in holy wedlock. Given under my hand this the 9th of May 1850   JOHN SIZEMORE

Joseph Short and Mary Ann Corpley was married on the 25th day of October 1849   DAVID PAYNE

Mr. George W. Brown Sir

William Lester and Milley Lockhart was maryied on the 9th day of December 1849.   DAVID PAYNE

I certify that on the 24th day of August 1849, I joined in wedlock William C. Johnson and Sophia Robnett
        R. A. CLAUGHTON

Celebrated the rite of matrimony by authority of license between Aaron Graham & Barbary Ann Martin on the 1st day of March 1849 by me   WILLIAM V. SHANNON

Celebrated the rite of matrimony by authority of license between John Bogle & Elizabeth Furgison on the 19th of November 1849 by me   WILLIAM V. SHANNON

Celebrated the rite of matrimony by authority of license between William W. Brown Malvina Jane Laird on the 25th day of December 1849 by me   WILLIAM V. SHANNON

This is to certify that on the 30th day of October 1849 I joined together in the holy state of matrimony George W. Johnson & Elizabeth Bateman of Tazewell Co. Va.   JOHN B. LOGAN

To the Clerk of Tazewell County Court

I do hereby certify that I joined Henderson Elswick and Catherine Looney in the state of matrimony on the 1st day of November 1849

Also I joined Charles Stiltner and Elizabeth Presley in the state of matrimony on the 9th day of May 1850

Also I joined Robert Shortridge and Ruth Luster in the state of matrimony on the 4th day of June 1850
        JOSEPH LOONEY

I do certify to the Clerk of the County Court of Tazewell that the following marriages were celebrated by me during the present year viz:

Joseph Bishop & Jane Stephenson married February the 1st 1849

Reese Davis & Sarah Vance married March the 15th 1849

*A*dison Christian & Rebecca Christian married March the 30th 1849

Jeremiah Cecil & Fanny Greene married April the 14th 1849

Joseph Cordell & Mary Vess married April the 21st 1849

Patton J. Lockhart & Caroline S. McGuire married July the 17th 1849

Daniel Christian & Lurany Pruett married August the 12th 1849

Robert H. Barrett & Margaret Bruster married August the 14th 1849

Granville G. Cecil & Linney S. McGuire married August the 16th 1849....

Bird L. Bruster & Elizabeth M. Barrett married September the 11th 1849

Lewis Rose & Margaret Rose married November 14th 1849

The above marriages were celebrated by me according to the forms & ceremonies of the Methodist Episcopal Church since the first of January 1849. Given under my hand this 29th of December 1849
         WILLIAM MCGUIRE

I do hereby certify that on the 26th day of September 1849 I joined Madison Dailey and Margaret Bogle in lawful wedlock
         GEO. W. G. BROWNE

I do hereby certify that on the 27th day of September 1849 I joined John H. Barnett & Larissa J. Barnett in lawful wedlock
         GEO. W. G. BROWNE

I do hereby certify that on the 4th day of October 1849 I joined John G. Baylor and Julia A. W. Brown in lawful wedlock
         GEO. W. G. BROWNE

I do hereby certify that on the 17th day of Ooctober 1849, I joined Archibald T. Buchanan and Rebecca P. Thompson in lawful wedlock
         GEO. W. G. BROWNE

I do hereby certify that on the 9th day of November 1849 I joined George Poff and Martha Fields in lawful wedlock
         GEO. W. G. BROWNE

I do hereby certify that on the 14th day of February 1850, I joined Samuel W. Cecil and Adelia M. C. Sanfley in lawful wedlock
         GEO. W. G. BROWNE

I do hereby certify that on the 20th day of February 1850 I joined Joseph Stras and Eleanor Letitia Higginbotham in lawful wedlock
         GEO. W. G. BROWNE

I do certify that on the 8th day of March 1850, I joined Thomas Mathews & Anna Rose in lawful wedlock

GEO. W. G. BROWNE

Tazewell County to wit

I David Young do certify that the following List contains all the marriages celebrated by me within the preceeding year December 1849

I joined Thomas J. Brooks and Catherine Spence in holy wedlock on the 25th day of January 1849

I joined Wesley McGuire and Margaret Deskins together in holy wedlock on the 15th day March 1849

I joined Joseph Pruett and Malinda Mitchell together in holy wedlock on the 3rd of May 1849

I joined Elijah Harris and Mary Bishop together in Holy wedlock on the 3rd day June 1849

I joined Elijah Lockhart and Jicy Boland together in Holy wedlock on the 4th September 1849

I joined David T. Humphrey and Salina J. Higginbotham together in Holy wedlock on the 15th day November 1849

I do certify the above list to be correct

DAVID YOUNG

To the Clerk of the County Court of Tazewell

I hereby certify that on the 8th day of November 1849 I did unite in matrimony John W. Bailey with Amy McDonald by virtue of a Licence from your office   JAMES CALFEE

I do hereby certify that on the 16th day of January 1851 I joined Thomas R. Gillespie and Mary S. Thompson in lawful wedlock   GEO. W. G. BROWNE

Tazewell County towit

I David Young do certify that the following list contains all the marriages celebrated by me within the preceeding year

I joined James Asbury and Nancy Elizabeth Wilson in Holy wedlock on the 29th January 1850

I joined Allen Dolton and Nancy Rudd in Holy wedlock on the 13th June 1850

I joined Rees B. Green and Louisa Higginbotham in Holy wedlock on the 7th November 1850

I joined Amos Cowden and Sarah Bowling in Holy wedlock on the 26th November 1850

I joined William B. Gillespie and Elizabeth Stratton in Holy wedlock on the 26th December 1850   DAVID YOUNG
Dec 31st 1850

This is .... Certify that on the 10th day of March 1850 I joined togather in Holy state of Matrimony Guy T. Harrisson & Nancy Bruster   DAVID PAYNE

This is to certify that on the 28th Feb. 1850 I joined together in the Holy state of matrimony Robert Conley and Tabitha Stratton of Tazewell Co. Va.   JOHN B. LOGAN

This is to certify that on the 21st Feb 1850 I joined together in the Holy state of Matrimony Henry Green and Eleanor Green of Tazewell County Va.   JOHN B. LOGAN

This is to certify that on the 24th January 1850 I joined together in the Holy state of Matrimony Isaac Young & Ellen Johnson of Tazewell Co. Va.   JOHN B. LOGAN
Jany 24th 1850   M. P. Church

Celebrated the rites of matrimony by Wm. V. Shannon on the 27of January 1850 Randolph Carter and Marieta Hedrick

Celebrated the rites of matrimony by Wm. V. Shannon on the 28th Febuary 1850 James H. McMullin and Elizabeth Boil

Celebrated the rites of matrimony by Wm. V. Shannon on the 8th of January 1850 Daniel Shrader and Jane Brooks

Celebrated the rites of matrimony by Wm. V. Shannon on the 26th February 1850 Leonard Myars and Polly Leindamood

Celebrated the rites of matrimony by Wm. V. Shannon on the 17th of March 1850 Isaac Emshwiler and Matilda Carter

Celebrated the rites of matrimony by Wm. V. Shannon on the 25th of April 1850 James A. Martin Mary Jane Smith

Celebrated the rites of matrimony by Wm. V. Shannon on the 12th of August 1850 Henry T. Peery Nancy W. Gillespie

Celebrated the rites of matrimony by Wm. V. Shannon on the 12th of December 1850 Granville H. Hedrick Polly B. Whitley

Celebrated the rites of matrimony by Wm. V. Shannon on the 18th of December 1850 John W. Johnston Margaret D. Nash

Celebrated the rites of matrimony by Wm. V. Shannon on the 7th of January 1851 Daniel Carter Elizabeth Owens

Celebrated the rites of matrimony by Wm. V. Shannon on the 5th day of February 1851 Greenville Fergerson Eliza Wright

To the Clerk of the County Court of Tazewell I doo certify that the following marriages was celebrated by me Viz:

Meshack Ratliff Lucinda Ratliff married January the 31st 1850

James Hasbury and Levica Christian maried February 6th 1850

Gilbert M. Peery and Susan Sayers married february 21st 1850

John Vincel and Catharine Lester married Aprile the 4th 1850

Joshua W. Sparks and Cynthia Hankins married April 23rd 1850

James W. Bevers and Elizabeth Whitt married May 8th 1850

John Blankenship and Lille Deskins married May 8th 1850

James G. Whitt and Nancy Webb married September the 4th 1850

Thomas Beavers and Nancy Christian married October the 2nd 1850

Henry Vincel and Elizabeth Steward married October the 24th 1850

The above marriages was Celebrated by me according to the forms and seremonies of the Methodist Church since the first of January 1850 Given under my hand this 31st day of December 1850

WILLIAM MCGUIRE

Mr. George G. Brown Sir

Danel Christan and Sarah Monuts was married on the 20th day August 1850   DAVID PAYNE

This is to certify to the Clerk of Tazewell County that on the 15th day of Aug 1850 that I join together in the Holy state of Matrimony Andrew Baker and Harriet Smith

Allso on the 13th day of Sept 1850 I joined together in the holy state of matrimony Walter Matney and Elizabeth Fields

Allso on the 8th of Sept 1850 I joined together in the holy state of matrimony Squire Davis and Lairsinda Blankenship

GEORGE GIBSON

I do hereby certify that on the 31st May 1850 I joined Greenville Pack & Susan Parr in lawful wedlock

GEO. W. G. BROWNE

I do hereby certify that on the 6th day of June 1850, I joined James S. French and Laura J. George in lawful wedlock

GEO. W. G. BROWNE

I do hereby certify that on the 31st July 1850 I joined Thomas Stephenson & Rhoda Brown in lawful wedlock

GEO. W. G. BROWNE

I do hereby certify that on the 4th day of December 1850 I joined James B. Thompson & Mary Thompson in lawful wedlock

GEO. W. G. BROWNE

I do hereby certify that on the 8th day of January 1851 I joined William P. Dills and Melinda Kinder in lawful wedlock

GEO. W. G. BROWNE

These are to certify the clerk of the court of Tazewell county that agreeable to the Licence presented me I have solemnized the rites of matrimony between William Speres & Elizabeth Coldwell on the 17th day of Sept 1850   JOHN WALLIS

I do hereby certify that I Solemnized the rites of matrimony between Crockett P. Gillespie and Sarah Ann Crabtree Oct the 16th 1850   WM. E. NEEL

I do hereby certify that on the 7th November 1850 I solemnized the rites of matrimony between Mr. James A. Repass and Miss Lucinda J. Suiter in Tazewell Co.   JAS. A. BROWN

Feb 6th 1851

November the 5th day 1850

Mr. G. W. Brown Sir

Richard Wilee was married and Elizabeth Davis on the 5th day of November 1850   DAVID PAYNE

I do hereby certify that on the 1st day of January 1851 I joined John D. Vencil & Julia A. Peery in holy wedlock

L. W. CROUCH

I do hereby certify that on the 8th day of January 1851 I joined Witten A. Cecil & Nancy C. Wynn in holy wedlock

L. W. CROUCH

I do hereby certify that on the 9th day of January 1851 I joined Stephen G Samples & Louisa M. Goodwin in holy wedlock

L. W. CROUCH

I do hereby certify that on the 21st day of February 1851 I joined Henry P. Neel and Lydia Taylor in lawful wedlock

GEO. W. G. BROWNE

I do hereby certify that on the 27th day of February 1851 I joined Rice Waldron & Rebecca Beavers in lawful wedlock

GEO. W. G. BROWNE

I hereby certify that on the 4th day of March 1851 I joined Archibald Barnett (son of James) and Julia Ann E. Ritter in lawful wedlock   GEO. W. G. BROWNE

I hereby certify that on the 26th day of March 1851 I joined James C. Dickenson & Lucinda M. Kindrick in lawful wedlock
Mr. George W. G. Browne Sir

Wm. Harman and Melinda Bruster was marred on the third day of August 1851   DAVID PAYNE Senior

April 29th 1851
Mr. George W. Brown

These are to certify that on the tenth day of April 1851 that I did solemnize the rites of matrimony between Floyd Lusk Clarassa Lambert of your County by virtue of marage licens from your office in Tazewell County   WM. WALKER BILLE

I do certify that by virtue of a license joined by the Clerk of the court of Tazewell County I celebrated the rite of matrimony during the quarter ending March 31st 1851 between Stephen Lambert & Elizabeth Jane Grills March 15th. Given under my hand this 31st day of March 1851   S. RHUDY
        Min of the Ev. L. Church

To the Clerk of the County Court of Tazewell

I certify that on the 8th day of May 1851 I united in marriage Charles Tabor with Harriett Harvey and

Also on the 18th day of June I united in marriage Wilbur Slade with Margaret Tabor

Given under my hand this June 22d 1851
      JAMES CALFEE, JR.

Virginia Tazewell County to wit

This is to sertify to the Clerk of .... County Court that on the 30th day of September 1851 I celebrated the rights matrimony between Joab Justice .... Polly Blankenship

Also on the 17th day of February 1851 I selebrated the rights of matrimony between William R. Justice and Elizabeth Davis this 25th 1851   GEORGE GIBSON

I doo hereBy certify that on this day I joined together in holy wedlock Joseph Rose & Drusilla Totten March 16th 1851
      JOHN SIZEMORE

I do herby certify that I solemnized the rites of matrimony between Peter Ball & Mary Cecil Jan the 8 1851

Also between David L. Neel & Polly Hopkins April the 3rd 1851

Also between Joshua Spence & Dilla Burgot May the 8th 1851

Also between Benjamin S. Walker and Elizabeth Steel the day 1851

Also between Wm. Cook and Mary M. Lambert the 1st day of July 1851

WM. E. NEEL

July the 1st 1851

I do hereby certify that on the 3rd day of April 1851 I joined Franklin Kindser and Polly A. Brown in lawful wedlock

GEO. W. G. BROWNE

I do hereby certify that on the 2nd day of April 1851 I joined Obadiah Belsher and Visy Stump in lawful wedlock

GEO. W. G. BROWNE

I do hereby certify that on the 9th day of April 1851 I joined William R. Harman and Virginia Crockett in lawful wedlock

GEO. W. G. BROWNE

I do hereby certify that on the 3d day of June 1851 I joined Patterson Bowers and Maria Letitia Crockett in lawful wedlock

GEO. W. G. BROWNE

I certify that on the 26th June 1851 I joined Harden Pack & Nancy E. Dean in lawful wedlock   GEO. W. G. BROWNE

This is to *sirtify* that I joined together in the holy state of matrimony Manville Daniels and Sara Keen according to li*sene ishue*d from the Clerks Office By James M. Brown

Also Josiah Lam.. and Mary Bowen
Also Lewis Riff and Margaret Collins
Also David Jesey oshlym and Rhody Keen
Also Conly Blankenship and Polly Justice
Also William W. Justice and Peggy Blankenship
Also George W. Hurst and Ruthy Christian
Also George Daniels and Elizabeth Gibson
Also Noah Byrchfield and ....

Given under my hand this 9th June the Lord day 1851

THOMAS MULLINS

Mr. G. W. G. Browne Sir

G. W. Charles and Elis Payne was married on the 3 day of August 1851

Marte Charste and *Marget Robnet* was marred on the 13th day of August 1851   DAVID PAYNE

I do hereby cirtify that on the 6th day of September 1849 I joind Herenten Cline and Sarah Lambert in lawful wedlock

THOMAS K. LAMBERT

I do hereby certify that on the 31st day of October 1850 I joined William Marshal and Martha Belcher in lawful wedlock

THOMAS K. LAMBERT

To the Clerk of Tazewell County Court

I do hereby certify that I joined John Nuckles and Lucinda Jackson in the state of matrimony on the 15th day of August 1850

Also I joined John V. Lester and Rachel Stiltner in the state of Matrimony on the 22 day of October 1850

Also I joined Levi Clevinger and Pricey Matney in the state of matrimony on the 5th day of December 1850

Also I joined William Ward and Mary Keen in the state of Matrimony on the 4th day of Jane 1851   JOSEPH LOONEY

I do hearby cirtify that on the 7th of Febuary 1850 I joined Thomas Gross and Elizabeth Belcher in lawful wedlock

THOMAS K. LAMBERT

I do hearby cirtify that on the 10th day of October 1850 I joined Andrew Belcher and Mary Gross in lawful wedlock

THOMAS K. LAMBERT

I do certify to the Clerk of the County Court of Tazewell that the following marriages was celebrated by me viz:

Montiville Steele and Susannah Maxwell married January 23d 1851

Robert Beavers and Lydia Mitchell married January 28th 1851
John McGuire and Sarah Wills married 6th March 1851
Owen Mitchell and Elizabeth Vandike married 10th April 1851
Basil Elswick and Julia F. Steel married June 15th 1851
Samuel Woltz and Nancy Blankenship married July 17th 1851
Alexander Beavers and Rachel Barnett married July 30th 1851
Thomas Altizer and Rebecca Beavers married July 31st 1851
Jonas Sparks and Polly Hankins married 19th Aug 1851
David Prince and Elizabeth Creed married 4th Sept 1851
William B. Brown and M. I. Brown married 4th Dec 1851
William Stinson and Sabina Claypool married 9 Decr. 1851
William T. Morton and Analiza McGuire married 23d Dec. 1851

The above marriages was celebrated by me according to the ceremonies of the M. E. Church since the 1st of January 1851.

Given under my hand this 30th December 1851

WILLIAM MCGUIRE

Tazewell County to wit

I David Young do certify that the following list contains all the marriages celebrated by me within the preceeding year

I joined Archibald Rudd & Mary Jane Lawson in holy wedlock on the 15th of April 1851

I joined James R. Spence & Diana Sayers in holy wedlock on the 5th day of May 1851

I joined Isaac K. Dougherty and Nancy A. Hoops in holy wedlock on the 13th day of August 1851

I joined Daniel A. Mollery and Nancy Belsher in holy wedlock on the 23d of September 1851

I joined William Hoops and Charlotte Asberry in holy wedlock on the 13th November 1851

I joined Nathaniel Young & Fanny Chalmers in holy wedlock on the 11th day of December 1851

I joined Wesley Gibson & Rebecca Jane Ward in holy wedlock on the 23d day of December 1851

Given under my hand this 30th December 1851

DAVID YOUNG

I certify that on the 26th day of August 1851 I joined Jesse Underwood and Eliza Belsher in lawful wedlock

GEO. W. G. BROWNE

I certify that on the 16th day of October 1851 I joined George G. Hickman and Maria T. Baker in lawful wedlock

GEO. W. G. BROWNE

I certify that on the 5th day of November 1851 I joined William W. Dunn and Emily Gillespie in lawful wedlock

GEO. W. G. BROWNE

I certify that on the 9th day of December 1851 I joined William E. Peery and Catherine M. Cecil in lawful wedlock

GEO. W. G. BROWNE

I certify that on the 22nd day of January 1852 I joined Henry H. Marrs & Lucinda Shrader in lawful wedlock

GEO. W. G. BROWNE

I do hearby cirtify that on the 3rd day of April 1851 I joined James Bell and July A. Stowers in lawful wedlock
                    THOMAS K. LAMBERT

I do hearby cirtify that on the 5th day of June 1851 I joined Samuel W. Dilion and Tempy Dilion in lawful wedlock
                    THOMAS K. LAMBERT

Mr. G. W. G. Brown Sir

I marred Alexander Beavers and Mary Rose on the 2nd day of August 1851   DAVID PAYNE

To Geo. W. G. Browne CLK

This is to certify that on the 25th day of October 1851 I joined together in holy wedlock Audley Whitt and Hannah Smith
                    DAVID PAYNE Senr.
                              Decr. 12th 1851

Tazewell Co. Va.

This is to certify to the Clerk of this County that I married within the bounds of said County on the 3rd July 1851 Samuel A. Claytor & Margaret Six and

On the 23rd December 1851 George Thompson & Mary E. Claytor   ISAAC N. NAFF
                              Jany. 10th 1852

The license issued from this office dated June 16th 1851 authorizing the marriage of John H. Hoilman and Eliza Jane Neel was returned here on the .... day of .... 1851 with the following certificate thereon written "The within executed by me July 10th 1851"   "J. H. HOGE"

I do certify that on the 2d day of May 1852 I joined Peter White & Jane Ellen Rutherford in lawful wedlock
                    THOMAS MULLINS

I do hearby certify that on the first Day of January 1852 I joined together Samuel Bell and Charity Milam in Lawful wedlock
                    THOMAS K. LAMBERT

I do hereby certify that on the 25th day of March 1852, I joined together Samuel Marrs and Martha Odanold in Lawful wedlock
                    THOMAS K. LAMBERT

I certify that on the 14th day of February 1850 I joined William T. Kendrick & Maria T. Gillespie in lawful wedlock
                    GEO. W. G. BROWNE

Mr. George W. G. Browne Sir

I marrid Shorter Smith and Elizabeth Robinett on the 27th day of February 1852   DAVID PAYNE

I hereby certify to the Clerk of the County Court of Tazewell County Va. that on the 7th day of this inst I married Haynes Thomas and Louisa Thompson agreeable to the laws of Virginia and the rules of our church Given under my hand this 8th day of March 1852.   SAML. ROGERS

I do hereby certify that I solemnized the rites of matrimony between J. W. Neel & Caroline Steel

Also between Wm. Deavor and Martha Repass.

Also between John Kittz and Lucinda Stump February the 26th 1852   WM. E. NEEL

I do hereby certify that I solemnized the rites of matrimony between R. H. Hicks and Elizabeth Jane Maxwell April the 27th 1852

Also between Isaac N. Stratton and Rhoda Fletcher June the 17th 1852

Also between Maddison A. Neel and Barbara Gose July the 6th 1852

Also between between Hiram D. Lambert & Christina Stowers July 19th 1852   WM. E. NEEL

Mr. Geo. W. G. Browne Sir,

I, married William Luster & Polly Lester on the 4th day of April 1852   DAVID PAYNE Sen.

To the Clerk of the County Court of Tazewell

I hereby certify that I did unite in holy matrimony John Taber & Elizabeth Crockett on the 30th day of Oct 1851 by virtue of a license from your office. Given under my hand

            JAMES CALFEE
               Elder Christian Church

Mr. Samuel L. Graham, Clerk of Tazewell County

This is to certify that on the 18th day of November 1852 I joined together Henry Harrisson & Rebaka J. Brewster in the holy state of matrimony. Given under my hand this 30th Nov. 1852.

            DAVID PAYNE

Mr. Graham, Clerk Tazewell County Sir,

I married Archibald Minar & Lidey Charles on the 22nd day of September 1852   Yours & c.

            DAVID PAYNE Sen

I do hereby certify that on the 2nd day of April 1851 I joined Obadiah Belsher and Vicy Stump in lawful wedlock
GEO. W. G. BROWNE

I do hereby certify that on the 9th day of April 1851 I joined William R. Harman and Virginia Crockett in lawful wedlock
GEO. W. G. BROWNE

I do hereby certify that on the 3rd day of June 1851 I joined Patterson Bowers and Maria Letitia Crockett in lawful wedlock
GEO. W. G. BROWNE

I certify that on the 26 June 1851 I joined Hardin Pack & Nancy E. Dean in lawful wedlock   GEO. W. G. BROWNE

Virginia Tazewell County to wit

This is to certify to the Clerk of County Court that on the 30th day of September 1850 I *selebrated* the *rights* of matrimony between Joabb Justice Polly Blankenship

Also on the 17th day of February 1851 I *selebrated* the *rights* of matrimony between William R. Justice and Elizabeth Davis This 25th 1851   GEORGE GIBSON

This is to certify that I joined together in the holy estate of matrimony Manville Daniels and Sarah Keen according to license *ishued* from the Clerks Office by   JAMES W. BROWN

   Also Josiah *lam an* Mary Bowen
   Also Lewis Rife and Margret Collins
   Also James M. Hurst an.. Ruthy Christian
   Also George Daniels and Elizabeth Gibson
   Also Noah Birchfield and ....
Given under my hand this June the ..cond day 1851
THOS. MULLINS

Celebrated the rites of matrimony between William Franklin and Jane Gibson on the 2nd day of Febuary 1852 by
WM. V. SHANNON

Celebrated the rites of matrimony between Rufus Totten and Jane .... on the 1 of July 1852 By
WM. V. SHANNON

This is to certify that I J. J. Greever a minister of the Evangelical Lutheran Church being authorized by the Clerk of the County Court of Tazewell County Va. Solemnized the rites of matrimony between the following persons Viz:

Thomas W. Witten Eleanor Harrisson the 15th of September 1846

Also Joseph D. Grubb and Julia Ann Rhudy on the 20th of Sept 1848

Also between John P. Harman and Louisa Harman on the 12th of Oct 1848

Also between William Hedrick Zilla Murphy on the 2nd of Nov. 1848

Also between William L. Clark and Elizabeth S. Litz on the 1st of February 1849

Also between Jacob Burket and Catherine Rhudy on the 16th of March 1848

Also between George W. Buchanan & Martha Thompson on the 27th of June 1848

Also between Jacob Rhudy and Catherine W. Spracher on the 25th of Nov. 1847

Also between William Gilpin and Elizabeth Brown on the 23rd of Decem. 1847

Also between Robert G. Crockett and Mary Crockett on the 9th of Nov. 1847

Also between George S. Ritter & Elizabeth M. Hedrick on the 8th of July 1847

Also between Michael Bough and Sally Ritter on the 14th of Oct. 1847

Also between David Lowder and Matilda Henigar on the 11th of March 1849

Also between John Young and Susannah Newton on the 11th of July 1849

Also between Rees Heninger and Francis Louthan on the 2nd of April 1850.   J. J. GREEVER

Virginia Tazewell County to wit

This is to sertify to the Clerk of Tazel Court on 11th day of December I did celebrate the rights of matrimony between Clinton Blankenship and *paluy* lester in the year 1851 also on the 14th day of December I did *silibrate Rights* of *matrioney* of William Davis..

Virginia Tazewell County to-wit:

These are to license and permit you to join together in the holy state of matrimony according to the forms and ceremonies to which you belong George Kelly and Mary Jane Bowen and for so doing this shall be your sufficient warrant. Given under my hand as Clerk of the said county the 21st day of July 1852.

To any Minister of the Gospel S. L. Graham C legally authorized to celebrate the rites of matrimony. The parties named within were married by me the 8th of Aug. 1852.

R. V. WHEELAN.
Bp of Whlg.

Celebrated the rites of matrimony between John E. Hale and Mary R. Moore on the 2nd of June 1852 by

WM. V. SHANNON

Celebrated the rites of matrimony between Abraham Smith and Polly Runnion the 2nd of September 1852 by

WM. V. SHANNON

Celebrated the rites of matrimony between Ruben Richardson and Harriet Billips on the 9th of September 1852 by

WM. V. SHANNON.

Celebrated the rites of matrimony between Cyrus McDonald and Lavena W. Moore on the 14th of September 1852 by

WM. V. SHANNON.

Celebrated the rites of matrimony between John Murphy and Maria Shannon on the 16th of November 1852

WM. V. SHANNON.

Celebrated the rites of matrimony between David N. Waggoner and Maria E. Deaton on the 25th of November 1852

WM. V. SHANNON.

State of Virginia Tazewell Co S. S:

This certifies that on the 21st day of October A D 1851 Isaiah J Burke and Mary E Thompson were legally joined in marriage by me

WM M BALDWIN.

I do hereby certify that I solemnize the rites of matrimony between Peter Ball and Mary Cecil Jan the 8 1851.

Also between David S. Neel and Polly Hopkins, April"3 1851

Also between Joshua & Dolly Bengot May the 8th 1851

Also between Benjamin S Walker and Elizabeth Steel the .... day 1851

Also between Wm. Cook & Mary M. Lambert the 1st day of July 1850

WM. E. NEEL
July the 1st 1851.

Also on the 26 December 1851 I did *silibrate brate* the *Rights* of matrim*oney* be*tw*en William Y*ats* Kissy Davis

Also on the 1 day of April 1852 I did silibrate the Rights of matriony betwen William Ratliff Caroline Ward

Also on the 6 day of April 1852 I did silibrate the Rights of matermony betwen Conley Blankenship and Elizabeth Charles

GEORGE GIBSON

To the Clerk of Tazewell County Court

I do hereby certify that I joined John P. Keen and Narcisa Baker in the state of matrimony on the 9th day of January 1853

Also I joined James Clevenger and Mary Looney in the state of matrimony on the 13th day of October 1853.

JOSEPH LOONEY

This to sertify that I joined togeather in the holy estate of matrimony Thos Church and Margaret Mullins on the 21 day of December 1853   THOS. MULLINS

Tazewell County to wit:

I certify that on the 15 day of Dec 1853 at the house of Mark R. Bogle in said County I solemnized the rites of m*arimony* between Edward Ma*eeil* & Rachel Ann Bogle both single the sd. Ma*eeils* age is 16 years old, and the .... Rachel is 18 years old, the sd. Edwar M*aeel* was born in Giles County his residence in Tazewell County on Wolf Creek at the time of his marriage the sd. Rachel Ann Bogle was born in Tazewell, residence on Wolf Creek.

I also certify that the 25 of Jan 1854 at the house of John Le*wises* in Tazewell County I solemnized the rites of matrimony between John G. Bruce .... Louisa Lewis the sd. Bruce was a widow he is 25 years old and born in Wythe County his residence at the time of his marriage was in Tazewell County occupation working about, the sd. Louisa Lewis was single aged 26, born in Tazewell County.

Given under my hand this the 31 day of January 1854.

WM. E. NEEL

To the Clerk of Tazewell County Court:

I hereby certify that on the 11th day of February 1852 I joined James T. Myers and Mary B. Stump in lawful wedlock:

On the 17th day February 1852 I joined Binjamin Bruster and Louisa Jane Marrs in lawful wedlock

On the 10th day of March 1852 I joined Thomas Whitaker and Elizabeth Taylor in lawful wedlock

On .... of March 1852 I joined Ebenezar S. Howard and Susannah R. Witten in lawful wedlock

On 23 day of March 1852 I joined Thomas Tubley and Martha T. Gregory in lawful wedlock

On the 8th day of April 1852 I joined Tilman Fields and Paulina Byles in lawful wedlock

On the 29th day of April 1852 I joined Moses Preston and Jane H Perry in lawful wedlock   On the 9th day of June 1852 I joined Rees T. Kinder and Teely Kinder in lawful wedlock

On the 10th day of June 1852 I joined Mathias H. Peery and Mary F. Gillespie in lawful wedlock

On the 16th day of June 1852 I joined William summers and Martha L. Bane in lawful wedlock

On 15th day of July 1852 I joined Edward McMeans and Julia Yost in lawful wedlock

On the 27 day July 1852 I joined Asas Thompson & Christena Grills in lawful wedlock

On 15th day of September 1852 I joined David Kinser and Amanda E. Brison in lawful wedlock

On 16th september 1852 I joined Thominas Bruster and Elizabeth Marrs in lawful wedlock

On 28th day of October 1852 I joined Abraham Jenkins & Livy Helmandollar in lawful wedlock

On 23 day of Dec 1852 I joined Archibald Rudd & Mary Marshall in lawful wedlock   GEO. W. G. BROWNE

Those are to certify the Clerk of the court of Tazewell County that agreeable to the licens presented me I have soelemnised the rits of matrimony between James H. Vance and Eliza J. Elswick on the 10th day of February 1853

Given under my hand this 12 day of February 1853
                                               JOHN WALLICE

To the Clerk of Tazewell County Court

I hereby certify that I did unite in holy matrimony Steven Tabour and Eleaner Havins on the 18th day of January 1853. Given under my hand   JAMES CALFEE

To the Clerk of the County Court of Tazewell Cty. Va.

 This is to certify that on the 20th of Sept 1853 the rites of matrimony were duly solemnised by me between Rufus Brittain & Sarah Elizabeth Peery   ISAAC N. NAFF
Tazewell Ch Va.
Sept 28th 1853

 I hereby certfy that I solemnised the rits of matrimony between John T. Nash & Elizabeth Shannon on the 18 day of January 1853
         GEORGE STEWARD

Mr. Samuel L. Graham Sir

 On the 22nd day of Sept 1853 I joined together holy state of matrimony John Cline of Henry Martha Lambert
         GEORGE W. PAYNE

To Clerk of Tazewell County Court

 I hereby certify that I did unite in marriage Isaac P. Taber and Nancy Prince on the 22 day of July 1852, By virtue of a license from your office. Given under my hand   JAMES CALFEE

To Clerk of County Court of Tazewell I hereby certify that I did unite in Holy matrimony on the 3d day of August 1852 Isaac Feraby with Elizabeth Lirm by virtue of a licens from your office. Given under my hand   JAMES CALFEE

 I certify to Clerk of the County Court of Tazewell that I on the 13th day of Feb 1854 at the house of John Elswick in Tazewell Cty. I solemnised the rits of matrimony between John Loony & Lusy Elswick the said John Looney is 20 years old was born in this county lives in this county is a farmer his parents name are John Loony & Syntha Loony. The said Lucy Elswick is 16 years of age single at the time came in this county lives in this county her parents names are John Elswick Winny Given under my hand this 1st day of March 1854   GEORGE GIBSON
Tazewell Cty To wit

 I David Young do certify that the following list contains all marriages celebrated by me within the preceeding year

 I joined Benjamin Wilson and Lear Lucinda Wilson in holy wedlock on 1st Jan 1852

 I joined John B. Brooks and Mary Jane Johnson in holy wedlock on the 9th day March 1852

 I joined James H. Claytor and Mary Ann Corell in Holy wedlock on the 25th March 1852

I joined John Buchanan and Mary Jane Thompson in holy wedlock on the 29th day of April 1852

I joined Joseph J. Valt and Mary M. Young in holy wedlock on 5th August 1852

I joined John Starling and Martha Asbury in holy wedlock on 30th March 1852

I joined Martin Griffits and Polly Ann Wallis in holy wedlock on 25th August 1852

I joined Wm. Stratten and Polly Barnett in holy wedlock on 4th November 1852

I joined Ransom Gent and Virginia Ward in holy wedlock on 18th Nov. 1852

I joined Wm. H. Daugherty and Louisa M. Hurt in holy wedlock on 8th Dec 1852

I joined Wm. Spence and Elizabeth Spence in holy wedlock on 30th Dec. 1852   DAVID YOUNG

To the Clerk of the Court of Tazewell Cty.

I certify that I Joined Addison Robinett and Matilda Wolfe in holy matrimony on 15th Dec 1852   DAVID PAYNE

I do hereby certify that on 10th day March 1853 I joined together Jonas Keen and Judith A Keen in lawful wedlock
ELIJAH VANCE

I do hereby certify that on 25th day of March 1853 I joined together James Coleman and Jane Jackson in lawful wedlock
ELIJAH VANCE

I do hereby certify that on the 6th day of Jan 1853 I joined Charles F. Tiffany and Jane Moore in lawful wedlock
GEO. W. G. BROWNE

I do hereby certify that on the 27th day of June 1853 I joined Robert Crockett and Eliza Jane Moore in lawful wedlock
GEO. W. G. BROWNE

I do hereby certify that on the 11th day of August 1853 I joined together Frederick Stiltner and Polly Stiltner in lawful wedlock
ELIJAH VANCE

To the Clerk of the Court of Tazewell

I hereby certify that on the 28th of July 1853 I solemnized the marriage of Thomas Bandy Lilly Christain. Given under my hand
DAVID PAYNE

("Void" written on margin of Register)

To the Clerk of the Court of Tazewell Cty Va

This is to certify that I joined in holy wedlock on 25th Day of Dec 1853 Miss Louisa Hoolbrook & Jas. Bruster

G. W. PAYNE

("Void" written on margin of Register)

To the Clerk of the Court of Tazewell

I do hereby certify that I joined Wm. Ratliff and Patsey Ratcliff in the state of matrimony on the 22nd day of July 1852

JOSEPH LOONEY

To the Clerk of the County Court of Tazewell I hereby certify that I joined in holy wedlock John M. Ratcliff and Eleaner Ward this 25th day of July 1852   JOSEPH LOONEY

I hereby certify that I celebrated the rites of matrimony Madison Allen and Emily Carpenter June 5th 1853. Given under my hand this 6th June 1853   J. H. HOGE

To the Clerk of the Court of Tazewell Cty. Va. I do certify that the following marriages were celebrated by me Viz:

Joseph Harrisson and Margaret Gillespie married February 10th 1852

John Patten and Susannah Hinkle married January 14 1852

Smith Asbury Syndia Christian married Jan 22, 1852. Robert Martin & Sarah Painter married February 18th 1852

Wm. P. Lincus and Mary B. Cecil married April 8th 1852

Josiah Elswick and Elizabeth Compton married June 10th 1852

Elijah McMeans and Elizabeth Bishop married June 25th 1852

John M. Brown and Dorinda Davis married Dec 2nd 1852

Harvey W. McGuire and Rosinda Steel married Dec 14th 1852

Albert P. Asbury and Elizabeth C. Stephenson married Dec 23rd 1852

Paris Robinett and Elizabeth Martin married Dec 23d 1852

The above marriages were celebrated by me since the 1st of January 1852, according to the forms and ceremonies of the Methodist Episcopal Church. Given under my hand this 25th day of Dec. 1852   WM. MCGUIRE

To the Clerk of the Court of Tazewell Cty. Va.

I hereby certify that I joined in holy wedlock Jackson Reed and Charlotte Moron Sep 9th 1852

("Void" written on margin of Register)

Wm. Mullens & Rachel Canada married on Sep 10th 1852 ("Void" written on margin of Register)

Wm. Collins and Nancy Lambert June 1852

Jesse Bane and Nancy Reed August 1st 1853. Given under my hand Dec. 5th 1853

("Void" written on margin of Register)

THOMAS MULLINS

I do hereby certify that I solemnised the rits of matrimony between James Witten and Matilda J. Davidson March 30th 1853 ("Void" written on margin of Register)

Also between W. Stowers and Rachel *Felt*cher

Also between Wm. T. Holmes and Julia Cundiff

Also between James Carver & Maryam Repass. Given under my hand this 30th March 1853   WM. E. NEEL

A list of marriages solemnised by Bird Lockhart in the year 1853

Married February 3d 1853 Andrew Bruster and Sarah M. Marrs

Married February 13th Bird W. P. Lochard Susanah E. Barnett

Married Aseby Lochard and Rebecca Bruster April 5th

April 14th Married James Stevenson and Susanah Christian

April 27th married Samuel Robinett and Selah Lambert

July 7th married Bartlett Spence and Sarah Mreed

July 10th married Elisha Ony and Elizabeth Whitt

Sep 8th married Milton Lochart & Rebecca Brown

Sep 28th married Robert Beavers & Lydia E. Brown

Oct 6th married James J. Lewis and Cosby J. McGuire

Nov 2nd married Wesley Baldwin and Elizabeth Quicksel Tazewell County Va.   BIRD LOCHART

To the Clerk of the County Court Va.

This is to certify that on this 14th July 1852 William Stevenson and Frances Repass were legally married by the authority of license issued on 10th July 1852 by S. L. Graham

Respectfully   ISAAC N. NAFF

Tazewell Cty. to wit

I David Young do certify that the following list contains all the marriages celebrated by me within the preseding year

I joined James Mars and Jane E. Harper in holy wedlock on the 9th day February 1853

I joined Jacob F. Saulyers & Martha Jane Puckett in holy wedlock on 3 day March 1853.

I joined Wm. Griffits and Nancy Green in holy wedlock on 10th day March 1853

I joined George Harper and Marinda Steel in holy wedlock on 12th day April 1853

I joined James Spence and Orlena Sawyers in holy wedlock on the 25th of May 1853

I joined Samuel Meadows & Eleanor Brooks in holy wedlock on 31st May 1853

I joined Levi F. Fulcher and Mary H. Turley in holy wedlock on 30th Oct 1853

I joined John Sawyers & Delila Carter in holy wedlock on 17th Nov. 1853 DAVID YOUNG

Dec 27th 1853
To the Clerks office Tazewell Cty Va.

I hereby certify that I joined Franklin Smith & Purlina Blankenship in holy wedlock on 20th Jan 1853
("Void" written on margin of Register)

I celebrated the rits of matrimony between Henry Loony and Elizabeth Loony

Given under my hand 20th Jan 1853 GEORGE GIBSON
Virginia Tazewell Co.

I do certify that I solemnized the rits of matrimony on 15th day Nov 1853 at the house of Wm. Stump in said county between Jeremiah Hagar and Emely Myers the said Jeremiah Hager was a widower and the said Emely Myers was single and also the said Hager is a smith By trade and the Miss Myers knows how to spin & Weav and dow other House work the said Hager is forty two & the said Miss Myers is thirty the 7th day of June 1853.

Given under my hand this Nov 30 1853 WM. E. NEEL

This is to certify to the Clerk of the County Court of Tazewell that on the 25th day of Nov 1852 I celebrated the rites of matrimony between James R. Patterson & Polly C. Mahood

Also between John Elliot & Elizabeth Newton on 22d Dec 1853

Given under my hand this 20th day July 1854

Feb 28th 1853 J. J. GREEVER
To the Clerk of the Court of Tazewell Cty. Va.

I do certify that the following marriage was celebrated by me Viz Isaac Elswick and Sarah J. Griffits Married February 17th 1853.

The above marriages was celebrated by me since the first Jan 1853. Given under my hand this 28th day of February
WM. MCGUIRE

("Void" written on margin of Register)
To S. L. Graham Clerk of Court of Tazewell County Va
This is to certify that on 31st of August 1853 I united in holy matrimony Wm. R. King and hannah Weimer agreable to a license issued by you.
Given under my hand this 21st day Oct 1853
J. D. VINCEL

July 28 1853
Mr. Samuel L. Graham Sir,
Thomas Bandy and Lilly Christian was married the day and date above written   DAVID PAYNE

Mr. S. L. Graham
This is to certify that I married on the 25th day of December 1853 Miss Louisa Holbrooks and James Brewster
G. W. PAYNE

This is to certify that I joined together in the holy estate of matrimony Jackson Reed and Charlotte Moran a Bout Sept the 9th day 1852

And also William Mullins and Rachel Canada about the 10th of Sept 1852

And also William Collins and Nancy Lambert some time in June 1852

And also Jessey Been and Nancy Reed about the first of August 1853

Given under my hand this December the 5 day 1853
THOMAS MULLINS

Va. Tazewell County
I do hereby certify that I solemnized the rites of matrimony between James R. Witten & Matilda S. Davidson
Also between John W. Stowers & Rachel Fletcher
Also between William T. Holmes & Julia Cundiff
Also between James Carver & Mary Ann (?)
Also between Thomas Burrass & Mary Ann Repass.
Given under my hand this the 30 day of March 1853
WILLIAM E. NEEL

Virginia Tazewell County to wit

This is to certify to the Clerk of our Court that on 2 day of January 1853 I did celibrate the Right of matrimony between Franklin Smythe and Purlina Blankenship

Also I did on the 20 day of January 1853 celibrate the Rights of matrimony between Henry Looney Elizabeth Looney

To S. L. Graham C of Tazewell Co   GEORGE GIBSON

This is to certify that 31st of August 1853 I united in holy matrimony William R. King and Hannah Weimer agreeable to a licens issued by you. Given under my hand this 21st day of Oct 1853   JN O. D. VINCEL

This is to certify that on the 28th of Sept I united in holy matrimony James Albert & Eliza Ann Calvert all of this county

Given under my hand 21st day of Sept 1853

    JOHN D. VINCIL

This is to certify that I joined together Simeon Payne and Jane Moncy in the holy state of matrimony on the 14th day of February 1853.   THOMAS MULLINS.

I hereby certify to the clerk of the County court of Tazewell, Va. that on the 6th day of November 1853 by virtue of license from under your hand I solemnized the rites of matrimony between Howard Shortridge & Tabitha A Russell.

Also on the 18th day of *sep*tember 1853 I solemnized the rites of marriage between Abram Beckelheimer & Milenda J. Russell. Given under my hand.   HERNDON MURPHY.

Celebrated the rites of matrimony between Boyd Owens and Cyrena Osborne on the 20th of January 1853 by Wm. V. Shannon.

Celebrated the rites of matrimony between George W Riley and Virginia Bowman on the 27th of January 1853 by

    WM. V. SHANNON.

Celebrated the rites of matrimony beteween June Sluss and Clarinda Gooldy on the 27th of January 1853 by

    WM. V. SHANNON.

Celebrated the rites of matrimony between John Richardson and Elizabeth French on the 6th day of April 1853 by

    WM. V. SHANNON.

Celebrated the rites of matrimon between William H. Gates and Polly Harper on the 4th of August 1853 by

    WM. V. SHANNON.

Celebrated the rites of matrimony between John S. Moore and Emely Shannon on the 3 of October 1853

by WM. V. SHANNON.

Celebrated the rites of matrimony between John W. Neel and Eliza Harman on the first of November 1853 by

WM. V. SHANNON.

Celebrated the rites of matrimony between Wesley P. Whitley & Margaret R. Peery on the 2 of November 1853 by

WM. V. SHANNON.

Celebrated the rites of matrimony between Wesley W. Mars and Salatha A. Tabor on the 12 of November 1853 by

WM. V. SHANNON.

I certify that on the 25th day of Oct 1853 I celebrated the rites of marriage between Jefferson Keen & Maragaret Honaker.

THOMAS MULLINS.

I certify to the Clerk of the county court of Tazewell that on the 14 day of Feb. 1853 I celebrated the rites of marriage between Simeon Payne & Jane Muncy   THOMAS MULLINS.

I certify to the clerk of the county court of Tazewell that on the 8th day of Sept 1851 I celebrated the rites of marriage between Isaac W. Lambert and Lucinda Collins   THOS. MULLINS.

I do hereby certify that on the 14th day of April 1853, I joined James Spence and Lucinda Kinder in lawful wedlock

GEO. W. G. BROWNE.

I do hereby certify that on the 14th day of April 1853, I joined Powell Shannon and Mary J. Peery in lawful wedlock

GEO. W. G. BROWNE.

To Clerk County court of Tazewell County va.

I certify that I entered in Holy matrimony William F. Stowers farmer son Andrew Stowers with Mahala Shilling on the 28th day Sept.

Alexander Bailey farmer son of Jesse Bailey with Matilda McDowell daughter of Henry P. McDowell on the 29th Sept 1853.

Given under my hand this Nov 1 day 1853.

JAMES CALFEE.

Note by Author:
The incorrect spelling and other mistakes shown in the foregoing copy of the marriage registers, should be charged jointly to those who celebrated the rites, and to the Clerks and deputy Clerks who recorded same. The tooth of time which has gnawed into these old records must also share this responsibility.

CHAPTER V.

COUNTY COURT LAW ORDERS, FROM JUNE 1800 TO MAY 1810.
ORDER BOOK No. 1.

The first Court for Tazewell County was held June, 1800, at the residence of Henry Harman, Jr., about three miles northeast of the present Court House, pursuant to the Act of 1799. The Harman farm is now owned by Wm. F. Harman, whose present residence stands practically on the site of the log house in which the first court was held. A former owner of this property tore the old house down and used the logs therein to construct a barn, which barn is now standing a short distance north of the former site of the said house in which the first term of the Court was held.

The names of the Justices, noted at the first term of this Court for Tazewell County, are as follows:

David Ward, Samuel Walker, Robert Wallace, Henry Bowen and David Hanson. James Maxwell qualified as Sheriff and John Ward was appointed Clerk.

The July Term shows the following Justices: David Ward, George Peery, Robert Walker, William Neel, Samuel Walker, Henry Bowen and David Hanson.

The November term shows Justices present: David Ward, George Peery, Samuel Walker, John Peery, John Thompson, Thomas Witten, Hezekiah Harman, Hezekiah Whitt, Thomas Gillespiee, William Neel and Joseph Davidson; and new Justices who qualified at this term, viz: William Hall, James Thompson and James Brown.

Several pages of the first part of the County Court Law Order Book are missing. However, beginning with the first word of the said book as it now exists, all that remains of the record for the *June Term, 1800,* is as follows:

"Hezekiah Harman being appointed yesterday to lay off the land offered by William Peery & Sam'l Ferguson for the use of the County made report that he had laid off twenty three acres and twentyeight square poles ten acres and twenty eight square poles being of Fergusons land thirteen acres of Wm. Peerys land whereupon the Court were unanimously of opinion that the public buildings should be erected on the land so laid off and that William George James Witten and John Crockette do lay off and circumscribe two acres for the purpose of building the public Buildings for this county and the balance of the land remain for (the) benefit of the County only saving and reserving to the said Peery four quarter acre lots out of the land he (this) day conveyed to the County and reserving to the said Ferguson two quarter acre lots where out of the land he this day conveyed to the (co).

Joseph Moore came into Court and profered to lay off the lots for a town where the public buildings are to be erected in quarter acre lots for the price of 33 1-3 cents each and it is ordered that William George, James Witton and John Crockett do attend as Commissioners and direct the surveying of the lots to Morrow.

Absent: David Ward, Robert Wallace & Saml Walker.

Ordered that David Ward and Samuel Walker be commissioners to contract for the building of a Jail for this County and that they do advertise the same in the most public place to be let to the lowes bidder at next Court.

Present: David Ward & Samuel Walker Gent.

Absent: Henry Bowen & David Hanson Gent.

Ordered that Henry Bowen & David Hanson be commissioners to attend the running of the line between this County & Russell and that they notify the Court of Russell of their appointment.

Ordered that Court adjourn until Court in Course and that they will meet next Court at the place appointed for erecting the public buildings for this county DAVID WARD."

In the short time intervening between the adjournment of the June term and the beginning of the July term a temporary structure of buck-eye logs was built in a day by an assembly of citizens from all parts of the county, who brought their axes, broad axes, etc. It is said that the cost to the county of this temporary temple of justice was ten dollars.

"*At a Court held for Tazewell County July the 1st 1800* in the new Court House according to adjournment of the last Court

Present David Ward, George Peery Robert Wallace William Neel Samuel Walker Henry Bowen Thomas Witten and David Hanson Gent"

The County Road established from Henry Marrs' Mill to the top of the Valley Rigde & from the way that an old path formerly went to James Cecil's thence down the Baptist Valley on the side of said Valley next to the head of Sandy to Joseph Bolands, and that Isaac Dailey be surveyor of said road."

A road is ordered to be cut from the old County line to the top of Clinch Mountain, and that Henry Bowen, Gent, is assigned to furnish William Garrisson, Surveyor of said Road, with a list of tithables.

A road is ordered to be cut from the mouth of Aps Valley up said Valley to the head and from thence to William Peery's. And George Peery is to be Surveyor of the road to the top of Stony Ridge. William Taylor is appointed Surveyor of the road from the top of the Stony Ridge to where it intersects with the Bluestone road.

"John Peery, upon application for building a water grist mill upon his own land, it is ordered that a writ of Adquaddamnum directed to the Sheriff of this County be granted, commanding said Sheriff to summon twelve good and lawful freeholders of this County to meet on the lands of said John Peery, on the twelfth day of this month on oath according to law, and make report of their proceeding to this Court."

Thomas Gillespie appointed Guardian of Levisa Bowen, infant of John Bowen, deceased.

Orders signed by Samuel Walker.

August Term: "On the motion of Hezekiah Harman, Surveyor of the County of Tazewell, he is permitted to lay off and circumscribe the Town lots out of the lands offered by William Peery and Samuel Ferguson for the use of the County to be sold for the benefit of the County."

James Stokes asked leave of the Court to build a water grist mill on his own land and a writ of adquaddamnum was awarded.

Ordered that Isaac Bristow be Surveyor of the road from the County line to the lower fork of the Whetstone Run and that Henry Bowen Gent is assigned to furnish him with a list of tithables.

"The Court having taken in consideration the propriety of building a Court House, ordered that David Ward, Samuel Walker James Thompson and George Peery Gent be appointed commisioners to set up publickly on 1st day of November Ct. next and let the building thereof go to the person who will build it cheapest, and that they the commissioners give public notice hereof in writing in the County of Russell, Wythe, Washington and Tazewell. an The said Court House to be finished on or before the first day of May, 1802."

"Ordered that John Grills, William Hall, Josiah Wynne and Henry Harman, Gent, do view and work out the nearest and best way for a wagon road leading from William Hall's in Burk's Garden to this Ct. house" etc.

Orders signed by David Ward.

September Term. "Thomas Gillespie, William Garrison, Obadiah Gent and Robert Barns, being appointed to view and mark out the nearest and best way for a road from the Court House into the River road between Henry Marrs and John Greenups made their report. Ordered that the same be cut accordingly."

"Ordered that John Peery have leave to build his mill and dam agreeable to the verdict returned by the jury on his making good the highway that will be injured by the said dam and making a slope for the passage of fish." Orders signed G. Peery.

October Term. "John Peery, Joseph Davidson, Thomas Witten, William George, John Thompson, Hezekiah Whitt, Thomas Gillespy, Hezekiah Harman and John Tollet produced a commission from his Excellency the Governor appoint them Justices of the peace in and for the County of Tazewell and there upon they took the necessary Oaths of Office and took their seats accordingly."

"Ordered that John Powers be Constable in this County."

"Ordered that a County levy of twenty-five cents be collected from each tithable in the County." Orders signed by David Ward.

November Term. The first Grand Jury is empanneled, which is composed of the following persons: Andrew Thompson, foreman, James Witten, William Brooks, Edley Maxwell, James Sloan, Thomas Brewster, William Witten, William Wynne, James Moore, James Cecil, William Cecil, George Asberry, Timothy Roark, John Young, James Lockhart, John McIntosh, William Kidd and John Peery, Gent.

William Hall, James Thompson and James Brown, qualified as Justices of the Peace.

William George, granted license to keep an ordinary at Tazewell Court House for the term of one year.

William Neel and Henry Harman were appointed Commissioners to meet with the Commissioners of Wythe County for the purpose of running the dividing line between the Counties of Tazewell and Wythe.

Orders signed by G. Peery.

At a quarterly session of said Court, held on the 5th day of November, 1800, for the trial of cases, the following order was entered:

"Ordered that Francis Smith be allowed one fourth part of the allowance to be made to James M. Campbell as Attorney for the Commonwealth for the services of said Smith in favor of the Commonwealth at November Term, 1800."

Orders signed by David Ward.

December Term. Thomas Peery granted leave to keep an ordinary at his house.

1801

January Term. William George and William Peery qualified as Coroners of the County under a Commission of the Governor dated September 13, 1800.

"Ordered that the following persons be recommended to the Governor as fit and capable persons to be appointed to fill the following offices: Joseph Davidson, to act as Colonel Commandant for the 112th Regiment; John Thompson, Major of the 1st Batallion of said Regiment; John Ward, Major in the 2nd Battalion of the 112th Regiment; Archibald Thompson, Hezekiah Harman and Andrew Davidson, to act as Captains in the 1st Battalion of said Regiment; John Davidson, Ambrose Hall and John Maxwell, to act as Lieutenants in the 1st Battalion of said Regiment; Elias Harman, John Cartmill and James Peery, to act as Ensigns in said Battalion; George Davidson, to act as Captain of a Company of Light Infantry of the 1st Battalion of said Regiment; and William Peery, Jr. for Lieutenant and William Williams Ensign of the 1st Battalion; Thomas Ferguson, James Witten and Thomas Greenup, to act Captains in the 2nd Battalion of the 112th. Regiment; Rees Bowen Abraham Eheart and William Smith, Lieutenants in 2nd Battalion of said Regiment; Hugh Wilson, John Cecil and Samuel Belshey, Ensigns in 2nd Battalion of said Regiment; Samuel Witten, Captain of a Company of Light Infantry in the 2nd Battalion of said Regiment and William Witten Jr. Lieutenant, and Rees Gillespie Ensign, in said Battalion."

Orders signed by David Ward.

At a Quarter-Session, held *March 3,* 1801, the second Grand Jury was empanneled, to-wit: Archibald Thompson, foreman, John Compton, Andrew Davidson, Henry McBroom, Shadrack White, Robert Higginbotham, Samuel Ferguson, Thomas Greenup, William Dills, Jeremiah Witten, Ebenezer Brewster, Henry Asberry, Elijah King, William Smith, Smith Deskins, John Peery and Timothy Roark.

David Ward and John Tollett qualified to celebrate the rites of matrimony.

Andrew Thompson's Certificate of Qualification as Commissioner of the Revenue of this County, for the year of 1801.

May Term. Daniel Sheffey qualified to practice law.

The Third Grand Jury empanneled, is composed of the following persons, to-wit: Henry Harman, foreman, Edley Maxwell, James Lockheart, Richard Pemberton, Abraham Davis, Daniel Harman, William Wynne, John Peery, William Davis, Richard Oney, William Brooks, Jeremiah Witten, Thomas Greenup, William Cecil, James Witten and Larkin Kidd.

Orders signed by David Ward.

June Term. James Thompson qualified to practice law.

July Term. "Ordered that the Tavern rates for this County be as follows to wit

For a Dinner 25 Cents, a breakfast 17 cents, Lodging in clean sheets 8 cents, Whiskey by the half pint 8 cents, Rum French Brandy or wine by the half pt 25 cents, Cider beer or Mathagalum by the quart 8 cents, Peech or apple Brandy by the half pint $12\frac{1}{2}$ cents. Corn Oats or barley by the gallon 8 cents, Stalage with hay or fodder for 12 hours $12\frac{1}{2}$ cents, Pasturage for 12 hours $12\frac{1}{2}$ cents."

Orders signed by David Hanson.

September Term. John Cecil appointed Commissioner for 1802.

John Ward mentioned as Clerk of the County.

Joseph Moore appointed as Deputy Clerk.

Orders signed by David Ward.

September Term. "This Court proceeds to make up in their minutes an account of all expenses incurred by the Court under the authority of the Law, in that case made & provided the following are Claimants of the County towit

The Clerk of this County for exofficio services for the year 1800 & 1801 $50.00 The same for examining the Commissioners Books for the year 1801 $10.00 To the State atto for the year 1800 $60.00 To the States Atto for the year 1801 30.00 To the Sheriff fo exofficio services for the year 1800 & 1801 $50.00

The claims allowed last Sept Court $12.50 William Wall for one old wolf $2.08 Henry Harman Senr for three old wolves $6.25 Archd. Thompson for two old Ditto $4.16 Same one Ditto 2.08 Joseph Hicks two old Ditto 4.16 John Davidson one old Ditto 2.08 Jacob Hager Same 2.08 John Hamilton Same 2.08 Archd. Bailey Same 2.08 George Webb Same 2.08 Henry Harman Senr for his Services as Commissioner for running the County line between Wythe & Tazewell 15½ days at $2 31.00 Joseph Moore for laying off the lots in Jeffersonville 12.00 Hezekiah Harman for furnishing a book to record the Land Warrants in his office 3.00 David Ward Saml. Walker & George Peery Commissioners appointed for letting out and contracting for the building of a Court House 20.00 Samuel Walker & David Ward commissioners for letting & contracting the building of a jail 6.00 John Pruitt for one old wolf head 2.08 William W Brown two old Ditto 4.16 Same One Ditto 2.08 Christopher Marrs for erecting a line posts at the forks of a Road 1.00 James Peery Senr for one old wolf head 2.08 Thomas Peery allowed for making benches for the court to set on 2.00 William George for Brandy at letting out the building of the Court house 1.50 Thomas Harrison for rum & Brandy at selling the Front & back lotts 4.16 William Williams for building a Court house for this County 938.00 William Smythe for building a jail for this County 220.00 William Williams for making certain repairs to the Courthouse which is to be completed agt next Court 15.00 Hezekiah Harman for surveying the public land 5.25. John Crockett for furnishing stampt paper 4.34 William George John Crockett James Witten and Thomas Harrisson Commissioners to attend the laying off the Town lotts 16.00 Henry Harman for trouble sustained in holding the first Court at his house 2.00 (Total) 1481.94."

Orders signed by David Ward.

October Term. John Campbell qualified to practice law.

James Maxwell Sheriff of the County.

Dec. T. Joshua Day appointed Constable in Captain Hezekiah Harman's Company

1802

January Term. Henly Chapman qualified to practice law in this Court.

Mar. T. "Ordered that Rees Bowen be recommended to his Excellency the Governor as a fit and proper person to act as Captain in the 2nd Batallion of the 112th Regiment, in the room of Thomas Ferguson who was heretofore recommended and has resigned his claim thereto; and that Hugh Wilson be recommended to the Governor as a fit and capable person to act as Lieutenant in the 2nd Battalion of the 112th Regiment in the room of Reese Bowen, promoted. Ordered that Brittain Smith be recommended as a fit and proper person to act as Ensign in 2nd Batallion of 112th Regiment."

William McBroom qualified as Constable in this County.

Hezekiah Harman, Surveyor, had his brothers Elias and Henry Harman appointed his deputies.

June Term. Robert Barns is noted as deceased, at this term.

George Peery Esq. qualified as Sheriff of this County, having been appointed as such by James Monroe, Esqr., Governor of Virginia.

Andrew Peery qualified as Deputy Sheriff.

July T. "George Peery, Robert Wallace and William Neel are recommended to the Executive as proper and fit persons to act as Sheriff of this County for the year 1803."

Aug. T. "John Cecill Commissioner of the Revenue.

"Ordered that Thomas Harrisson have leave to keep an ordinary at his house in Jeffersonville for the term of one year, on his giving bond and security in the Clerk's Office, according to law."

Sept. T. "Ordered that David Peery be appointed Commissioser of the Revenue for the year 1803."

Isaac Brown qualified as Deputy Surveyor of the County.

Oct. T. Peter Dills and Elijah King appointed Constablees.

Tyron Gibson presented for "Profane cursing on the 29th day of May last at Bowen's race ground" and also present said Gibson for "challenging Charles Young to fight at same time and place."

John Ratcliff and Peter Dills fined $8.00 each for failing to attend as Grand Jurors.

(Noted that James Maxwell was Sheriff at Dec. T. 1801.)

Nov. T. John Goodwin appointed Constable.

1803

Jan. T. On motion of Phebe Harman, widow of Daniel Harman, deceased, leave is granted her to administration on his estate.

Mar. T. "The Court having taken into consideration the propriety of carrying into effect the law concerning poor Schools have considered that it would not be proper in this County".

May T. "Ordered that William Ferguson be fined 83 cts. for profane swearing in the presence of the Court."

June T. The Court appointed the following Constables: John Stobaugh, John Powers, Jesse Wilson, William Clark, John Lard, John Davis and John Goodwin.

On the resignation of John Ward, who was Major in the 2nd Batallion of the 112th Regiment, the Court recommended Hezekiah Harman Gent as a fit person to fill the said Office.

Ambrose Hall recommended to the Governor as a fit person to act as Captain in the 1st Batallion in the 112th Regiment in the Room of Hezekiah Harman, promoted; and that Elias Harman be recommended as Lieutenant in the room of Ambrose Hall, promoted.

John Day recommended to act as Ensign in the room of Elias Harman, promoted.

Richard Brooks appointed Constable.

July T. "Ordered that James Thompson be appointed Attorney for the Commonwealth in the room of James M. Campbell."

"Ordered that David Waggoner and Abraham Davis be fined for raising a riot and for swearing two oaths in the presence of the Court."

"Ordered that Robert Wallace, William Neel and Samuel Walker be recommended to act as Sheriff for this County for the year 1803."

Aug. T. John Stobaugh presented by the Grand Jury for a breach of the peace, "by insulting and choaking John Odare on the 9th day of this inst. at the dwelling house of William Walls, by the information of John Odare yeoman."

William Ferguson and Edward McDonald presented for fighting on last Court day at Jeffersonville.

Then follow several indictments of Overseers of the roads for failure to keep roads in repair.

Samuel Lusk presented for assaulting and beating William Jefferey.

John Laird and John Laughry presented for fighting.

Also same against George Davidson and William Smith.

These are sample entries of the character of indictments.

Felony indictments are not very frequent. It seems that most of the fighting is of the more harmless variety, with no other weapons than those furnished by nature.

Sept. T. "David Peery produced an account of his services as Comr. of the Revenue, and the Court have considered that fifty six days were requisite for the said Commissioner to perform the services aforesaid, ordered that it be certified to the Auditor of Public accounts."

Ordered that Samuel Witten be appointed Comr. of the Revenue for the year 1804.

Oct. T. Alexander Walker qualified to practice law in this Court.
Nov. T. Enos Moore appointed Constable. John Langhry appointed Constable.

1804

March T. Thomas Harrison and William George licensed to keep Ordinaries in their respective homes in Jeffersonville.

"Ordered that the following persons be recommended to his Excellency, the Governor and the honorable privy council as proper and fit persons to fill the offices to their several names annexed: Andrew Peery Captain in the 1st Batallion of the 112th Regiment in the room of Andrew Davidson, resigned; Thomas Cartmill Lieutenant, in the room of John Davidson, George Davidson, Jr. Ensign in the room of John Cartmill, Elias Harman Captain, Jeremiah Lambert, Lieutenant; and Stephen Lambert, Ensign in said Harman's Company; John Day, Lieutenant in the room of Elias Harman & Elijah Kidd, Ensign in the room of John Day; David Peery, Ensign in the room of James Peery; Jonathan Davis, Ensign in the Rifle Company, in the room of William Williams Hugh Wilson, Captain in the 2nd Batallion of the 112th Regiment, in the room of Rees Bowen, resigned; James Lockhart, Lieutenant in the room of

Hugh Wilson, promoted; Charles Young, Ensign, William Smith, Captain in the room of Thomas Greenup resigned, Thomas Bruster, Ensign.

Dec. T. Henry Harman qualified a Justice of the Peace.

Certificates of the qualification of the following officers were filed, viz: Hez Harman, as Major for the 2nd Batallion of the 112th Regiment etc. Ambrose Hall, Captain in the 1st Batallion of said Regiment; Elias Harman, Lieutenant in 1st Batallion.

1805

May T. William Clark qualified as Costable.

June T. "Ordered that the same Commissioners that were appointed to let out the building of stocks for this County, be appointed to have a pillory and whipping post added to the same and give a plan thereof to the undertakers."

Ambrose Hall appointed deputy for Robert Wallace, Sheriff.

Richard Brooks appointed a Constable.

Ordered that William Neel, Samuel Walker and Henry Bowen be recommended as fit persons to act as Sheriff of Tazewell County for the year 1806.

July T. Elias Harman recommended as a fit person to act as Captain in the 1st Batallion of the 112th Regiment, to take command of part of the Company formerly commanded by Hezekiah Harman who has been promoted.

Augt. T. Henry Harman appointed to celebrate the rites of matrimony in this county in the room of John Tollett, resigned.

"John Ward came into Court and resigned his office as Clerk, whereupon the Court proceeded to the appoinment of another, and John Crockett was appointed Clerk."

Joseph Moore was appointed Deputy Clerk.

Sept. T. John Powers appointed Constable.

Oct. T. James Jones appointed Constable.

Samuel Witten appointed Commissioner of the Revenue for the year 1806.

Nov. T. John Belcher appointed Constable.

Thirty-six wolf heads allowed and paid for at $2.08 each.

Rev. John McClure, a minister of the Methodist Episcopal Church, authorized to celebrate the rites of matrimony

1806

June T. Jeptha F. Moore and William Thompson qualified to practice law in this Court.

Frederick Cook qualified as Constable.

William Neel qualified as Sheriff of the County, and John Cecil and Samuel Cecil' qualified as deputies.

The following persons recommended to the Governor as officers, viz: "Jeremiah Lambert and David Peery for Lieutenants John Justice, James Conley, Adam Harman and William Shannon as Ensigns, all for the 1st Batallion, 112th Regiment; and John Cecil as Captain of 2nd Batallion, William Gillespie, Captain of said Batallion; James Peery, John Ratliff and John Smith as Lieutenants in said Batallion of 112th Regiment; Joseph Oney, Rees Thompson, Hezekiah Oney and William Higginbotham as Ensigns in 2nd Batallion.

Ordered that the following Militia Officers be recommended viz: "John Thompson for Colonel of 112th Regiment in the room of Joseph Davidson, resigned; Hezekiah Harman to Command the 1st Batallion instead of the 2nd; Archibald Thompson to command the 2nd Batallion; David Peery as Captain in the room of Archibald Thompson, promoted; Adam Harman, Lieutenant in the place of John Maxwell, resigned."

Ambrose Hall qualified as deputy Sheriff.

"Ordered that William Neel, Samuel Walker and Henry Bowen be recommended as fit persons to act as Sheriff for the year 1807."

Thomas Burriss recommended to act as Ensign in the room of David Peery, promoted.

Augt. T. George Rinehart appointed Constable.

Sept. T. Samuel Witten recommended as Captain in the room of James Witten resigned and Jeremiah Lambert to act as Lieutenant in the room of Elias Harman, promoted, and John Day as Lieutenant in the room of Ambrose Hall, promoted.

George Davidson, William Taylor, Elias Harman, John Laird, James Peery, John Lesley, James Witten, William Williams, Adam Harman, William Ward and Thomas Harrisson were recommended as fit persons to be added to the Commission of the Peace for this County.

Oct. T. William Harman appointed Commissioner of the Revenue for 1807.

Nov. T. John Chapman qualified to practice law in this Court. Grand Jury, at this term, found no indictments.

1807

Jan. T. John Wilson appointed Constable.

June T. John Davis (little) appointed Constable.

The following persons recommended for appointment, viz: "Samuel Lusk, Lieutenant in Captain Andrew Peery's Company, George Rinehart, Ensign in said Company; William Shannon, Lieutenant in Captain George Davidson's Company; William Brown, Ensign in said Company, Daniel Horton, Ensign in Captain William Smith's Company; James P. Thompson (Burke's Garden), Captain in a Company of Cavalry; Isaac Brown, First Lieutenant in said Company; George Peery (William's Son), 2nd Lieutenant in said Company; John Wynne, Cornet in said Company; George Steel, Lieutenant in Captain John Cecil's Company; David Fannon, Junr. Ensign in said Company; William Higginbotham, Lieutenant in Captain Wm. Gillespie's Company; William Asberry, Ensign in said Company."

At this Court a number of chancery causes were heard and determined.

Samuel Walker, Henry Bowen and David Hanson were recommended as fit persons to be appointed Sheriff for the year 1808.

July T. George Steel appointed Constable.

Sept. T. Fleming Trigg qualified to practice law in this Court. Several persons were fined $.83 each for profane swearing.

Thomas Peery (George's Son) appointed Commissioner of the Revenue for the year 1808.

Oct. T. Allowances made to pay for thirty-six wolf heads at $2.08 each, which were killed during the year 1807.

Nov. T. John Davis and Geo. Steal qualified as Constables.

"It is Ordered to be certified to the Register of the Land Office that Polley Dials is the youngest child of Andrew Dials, decd & that the same Polly is now 21 years of age and that the said Andrew Dials was killed by the Indians in 1787"

John Belcher and John Wilson qualified as Constables.

1808

March T. Richard Brooks appointed Constable.

April T. Henry Smith appointed deputy Surveyor of the County.

John Cecil appointed Captain of the Light Infantry of the 112th Regiment.

Samuel Lusk appointed Lieutenant, same Regiment.

John Hall appointed Constable.

(May Term, 1808, missing)

June T. "David Young exhibited in Court a license to preach, and took the oaths required by law, whereupon he is exempted from Militia duty."

Henry Bowen qualified as Sheriff of the County under a commission from the Governor.

William Gillespie appointed Deputy Sheriff.

Thomas Peery qualified as Commissioner of the Revenue for the County.

July T. George Rinehart qualified as Constable.

Sept. T. Thomas Chambers qualified to practice law in this Court.

William Day qualified as Constable.

1809

April T. "Ordered that the following persons be recommended to the Governor and honorable privey council to be appointed to fill the following offices: William Shannon, Captain; William Brown, Lieutenant; James Harrisson, Ensign; James Peery (son of Thomas), Captain; Rees Thompson, Lieutenant; Richard Brooks, Ensign; John Ratliff, Captain; Daniel Horton, Lieutenant; James Vandike, Ensign"—all in the 112th Regiment.

"Ordered that John Cecil, John Laird, John Wynne, Isaac Brown and William Taylor be recommended to his Excellency the Governor and honorable privey counsel as fit and proper persons to be added to the commission of the Peace in this County."

"Ordered that John Peery Esqr be appointed to solemnize the rights of matrimony in the room of Henry Harman decd."

May T. "Orderd that John Cecil be paid $6.00 for keeping this Court house clean for the year 1807."

Claims for killing 35 wolves at $2.08 each were allowed by the Court.

"Ordered that a levy of 50 cents each be laid on each tithable for the county levy and 12½ cents be laid for the Poor rates."

James Peery, son of Thomas, appointed Commissioner of the Revenue of the County for the year 1810.

June T. Daniel Horton and William Smith were appointed Constables in the 2nd Batallion.

"Ordered that James Thompson, Prosecuting Attorney in this Court be allowed the sum of $60.00 per annum for his services to this time and the sum of $100.00 be allowed him for 20 months services prior thereto."

David Hanson, George Peery and William Neel are recommended to the Governor and Honorable Privy Council as fit and proper persons to execute the office of Sheriff in the County of Tazewell for the year 1810.

Allowance made, at $2.08 each, for killing of fourteen wolves.

"Henry Bowen, John Thompson and John Ward appointed Commissioners to meet three commissioners of the County Court of Washington on the top of Clinch Mountain at the gap formerly called Cookseys gap on the 1st day of July next to agree on the manner and condition of opening a wagon road from Tazewell Court house to the Salt Works in Washington County."

Augt. T. John Day appointed Constable in the 112th Regiment.

Sept. T. "Ordered that the following persons be recommended to his Excellency the Governor and Honorable Privy Council as fit and proper persons to be appointed to the following offices in the 112th Regiment, viz: Hezekiah Harman, Colonel; Archibald Thompson, Major in 1st Batallion and Ambrus Hall in the 2nd Batallion; John Day Captain in 2nd Batallion; James Conley, Lieutenant; Peter Gose, Ensign; Isaac Brown, Captain of the Cavalry; George Peery, 1st Lieutenant; John, Wynne, 2nd Lieut. Elias H. Neel as Cornett in said Company of Cavalry."

Oct. T. James Jones appointed Constable.

Nov. T. John Cecil, John Laird, Isaac Brown Qualified as Justices of the Peace.

Hezekiah Harman qualified as Colonel of the 112th Regiment of the Militia of this Commonwealth and Ambrus Hall qualified as Major in said Regiment, under commissions issued by John Tyler, Esqr, Governor of Virginia.

David Young having proven to the satisfaction of the Court that he is a legal licensed preacher he was authorized to solemnize the rites of matrimony in this County.

Dec. T. William Taylor qualified as Justice of the Peace.

1810

Jan. T. John Wynne qualified as a Justice of the Peace.

Henry Bowen appointed Constable in the 1st Bat., 112 Regt.

Feb. T. John Belcher appointed Constable for one year in the 2nd Batallion.

David young is authorized to celebrate the rites of matrimony, as a local preacher.

Mar. T. Peter Gose qualified as Ensign in the 112th Regiment.

Apr. T. "It is Ordered by the Court that George Peery and David Hanson Esqr be appointed commissioners to superintend an election for Overseers of the Poor instanter."

This is the first election for local officers noted in the records.

Thomas ONeel qualified to practice law in this Court.

"Ordered that the following persons be recommended to his Excellency, the Governor and Honorable privy council as fit and proper persons to be appointed as the following officers in the 112th Regiment, Viz: Samuel Lusk, Captain; George Rinehart Lieutenant; John Shannon, Ensign; Thomas Burriss, Lieutenant, in the room of Adam Harman, resigned; Daniel Harman, Ensign; John Lambert, Lieutenant.

May T. William Gillespie appointed Commissioner of the Revenue for the County for the year 1811.

CHAPTER VI.

LAW ORDER RECORDS COUNTY COURT, BOOK NUMBER 2, FROM JUNE TERM, 1810 TO MAY TERM, 1817

1810

June T. "At a Court of quarter Session held for the County of Tazewell, the 26th day of June 1810. Present David Hanson, Thomas Gillespie, William Neel, John Laird & William Taylor Gent."

"William Brooks senr. foreman, Peter Dills, Joshua Day Henry Harman Junr. Howard Bane, Henry Shrader, William Maxwell, Stephen Deskins, John Davis (little) Henry Asberry, William Griffitts, Charles Young, Sam Young, William Garrison, John Power, David Peery, Jeremiah Witten, Alexander Sawyers, David Young and Richard Ony were sworn a Grand Jury to make inquest for the body of this County, who having received their charge withdrew from the bar to consider of their presentments."

"Absent William Neel Gent, Present David Ward Absent D. Hanson Gent."

"A Power of Attorney from William Fletcher, Joshua Day, Edward Milam, James Milam, Henry Pruett and Aron Fletcher to Lewis Milam, was acknowledged in Court by the said Joshua Day, Edward Milam, Aron Fletcher and Henry Pruett, and proven as to the acknowledgment of Williams Fletcher by the oath of Henry Pruett, Aron Fletcher and Edward Milam, and ordered to be recorded as to them."

"A List of Insolvents for the year 1809 was exhibited in court by the Sheriff and allowed and Ordered to be certified to the Auditor of public accounts."

"Absent D. Ward Gent. Present John Wynne Gent."

"Ordered that Peter Dills be appointed Overseer of the Road in the room of John Compton Senr. and that with the usual hands he keep the same in repair."

"Present Wm. Neel Gent."

"An appraisement of the Estate of Henry Harman dec'd was returned to Court and ordered to be recorded."

"Present David Ward Gent."

"David Hanson exhibited in Court a Commission from his Excellency John Tyler esq. Governor of this Commonwealth appointing him Sheriff for this County, whereupon he with William Neel, Thomas Witten, Henry Bowen and John Cecil entered into the bond required by law, and took the oaths required by law"

John Powers, John Wilson and Lawrence Murry appointed Constables of the County to act in the 1st Batallion, for a period of two years.

Adam Harman appointed Constable of the County to act in the Second Batallion for a term of two years.

July T. William Patton qualified as deputy Sheriff.

1811

April T. "It is ordered by the Court that the jailer of this County be allowed twenty-five cents per day for dieting of Debtors confined in the jail of this County."

May T. Wm. Smith Gentleman, qualified to practice law in this court.

"Ordered that William Gillespie Comr. of the Revenue in this County be allowed Eighty five Dollars for his Services . . . . for the present year."

"Ordered that William Witten be appointed Comr. of the Revenue for this County. . ."

June T. John George qualified as deputy Sheriff; William Peery and Daniel Horton appointed Constables to act in the second Batallion, 112 Regiment."

"Ordered that Thomas Harrisson and Jenny George be licensed to Keep Ordinaries in their houses in Jeffersonville"

"Ordered that John Belcher, William Smith and John Wilson be appointed Constables to act in the second Batallion of the 112 Regiment, and that William Day be appointed act. Constable in the Second Batallion in the 112 Regiment."

William Hall, John Peery and Joseph Davidson were recommended to the Governor as proper persons to be appointed Sheriff of this County for the year 1812.

Nov. T. Lewis Amiss qualified to practice law in this Court.

"Ordered that William Brown be recommended to the Governor as a fit and proper person to be appointed Captain in the room of William Shannon resigned, in the infantry & 112 regiment, and

Henry Harman Lieutenant in the room of William Brown promoted, and Daniel Justice Jnr Ensign in the said Company, and Henry Davidson Ensign in room of John Shannon, and Philip Lambert Ensign in the room of John Justice resigned."

1812

Jan. T. "ordered that Thomas Witten, William Taylor and John Laird, Gent. be appointed Commissioners to settle with David Hanson, Sheriff of this County for the collection of the County levy for the year 1810 and 1811, and return the statement thereof"

"Ordered that Henry Davidson be appointed Constable in the first Battallion. . . ."

May T. John Williams qualified to practice law in this court.

Joseph D. Peery appointed Comr of the Revenue for one year.

June T. Thomas Cassidy and John Powers appointed constables in the first Battalion for a term of two years.

"Ordered that William Witten Comr of the Rev. be allowed $100 for his services for the present year."

"Ordered that Henry Bowen be recommended to his Excellency the Governor and honorable privy Council as a fit person to be appointed Major in the second Batallion & 112 Regiment in the room of Archibald Thompson, resigned, and that Hiram Witten be recommended as a fit person to be appointed Ensign in the Second Battalion 112 Regiment in Captain Cecil's rifle Company".

"William Hall exhibited in Court a Commission from George Wm. Smith (Gov. of Va. bearing date the 11th of July last past appointing him Sheriff of the County of Tazewell. . ." and he qualified as such. John B. George, on motion of said Sheriff, was appointed by the Court as his deputy.

"Ordered that Ambrose Hall, Elias Harman, Samuel C. Witten, Archibald Thompson and John Lasley be recommended to his Excellency the Governor, and honorable privy Council as fit and proper persons to be added to the Commission of the peace in this County."

Ordered that James Milam be appointed Constable in the First Battalion & etc.

Thomas Peery and William Griffitts Jr., be recommended to be appointed Ensigns in the Second Battalion 112 Regiment of the Militia of Virginia.

"Ordered that Jeremiah Claypoole, Daniel Horton, William Gillespie, William Ward and Henry Bailey be recommended to his Excellency the Governor &c. as fit and proper persons to be added to the Commission of the Peace in this county."

"Ordered that William Hall, David Ward, and John Peery Gentlemen, be recommended to his Excellency & etc. as fit and proper persons to be appointed Sheriff for this county for the year 1813."

Oct. T. "Ordered that Isaac Brown and William Taylor Gent. be appointed as valuers of lands under the Act entitled "An act concerning Land".

Nov. T. Granville Henderson qualified to practice law in this Court.

1813

June T. John Wilson, Wm. Day, William Peery, William Smith and Daniel Horton appointed Constables &c.

July T. William Hall qualified as Sheriff of the County.

Sept. T. Daniel Horton recommended to the Governor as a fit person to be appointed Captain in the room of John Ratliff resigned, in the Second Battalion 112 Regiment, and Wm. Griffitts was recommended for Lieutenant in the room of Daniel Horton, promoted, Hiram Witten recommended for Lieutenant in the room of George Steele resigned; and John Witten recommended as Ensign in the room of Hiram Witten, promoted.

Daniel Horton and Peter Gose recommended to the Governor & etc. as proper persons to be added to the Commission of the Peace in this County.

"Ordered that William Thompson Junr. be appointed Commissioner of the Revenue for the year 1814."

Oct. T. John B. George qualified as deputy Sheriff.

Henry P. George appointed deputy Sheriff.

1814

May T. The following persons were ordered to be recommended to the Governor for appointment to the offices named, viz: Henry Davidson for Lieutenant in Samuel Lusk's Company in the room of George Rinehart resigned; John Shannon Ensign; Thomas Brown, Ensign in Daniel Horton's Company; Robert Peery Ensign in Isaac Brown's Light Horse Company in room of Elias H. Neel resigned;

Evans Peery Ensign in David Peery's Company in room of Daniel Harman resigned. Additional Commissioners of the Peace: Thomas Harrissson, Junr., James Peery, Senior, and Ambrose Hall.

June T. John Belcher, Travis Kendle, Henry Creswell, William Day, Thomas Cassiday, Lewis Milam, Cornelius Shannon, and Joshua Peery, appointed Constables for the term of two years.

John Gillespie recommended for Lieutenant in Capt. David Peery's Company. Wm. Davis recommended as Ensign.

Aug. T. Thomas Harrisson, James Peery Senr, and Ambrose Hall, qualified as Justices of the Peace.

Frederick Cook appointed Constable.

1815

Jan. T. "William Gillespie Comr. of the Revenue being called away in the service of his Country, his brother Robert Gillespie is appointed his assistant."

David Ward qualified as Sheriff of the County, having been appointed by the Governor on the 19th day of August, 1814.

"Ordered that Thomas Peery of Abbs Valley be appointed Lieutenant in Captain William Gillespie's Company now in service and that the same be certified to the Governor."

May T. Alexander Ward and John B. George appointed deputy Sheriffs.

June T. John Belcher and John Wilson, appointed Constables.

William Smith recommended for Justice of the Peace.

John Brown appointed a Constable.

Aug. T. Hiram Witten recommended for appointment as Captain of a rifle Company in the room of Captain John Cecil, resigned.

John Witten recommended for Lieutenant in the room of Hiram Witten promoted, and Thomas Brown, Ensign.

Sept. T. John B. George and William Smith recommended to be appointed Justices of the Peace.

Ordered that Robert Ward be appointed Comr. of the Revenue for the ensuing year.

Nov. T. Hiram Witten took the oath as required by law as Captain of a rifle Company etc.

Dec. T. Ordered that Thomas O Neel Gent prosecute in this Court on behalf of the Commonwealth until James Thompson returns from Richmond etc. or until his succeessor is appointed.

1816.

Jan. T. William Smith qualified as a Justice of the Peace.

Feb. T. John B. George qualified as a justice of the Peace.

May T. "On the motion of John Deskins who made satisfactory proof to the Court that his left Ear was bit off in a fight with John Jones by the said John Jones, it is therefore ordered that the same be Recorded."

June T. John B. George qualified as deputy Sheriff.

"Oredered that John Peery, Joseph Davidson and Thomas Witten be recommended to his Excellency the Governor as fit persons to Execute the office of Sheriff of this County for the ensuing year."

"It is ordered by the Court that the Sheriff collect of each tithe sum of forty four cents as a county levy to defray the Expenses of the County for the ensuing year."

"Ordered that John B. George be recommended to his Excellency, the Governor, to be first Lieutenant in a Company of Cavalry in the room of George Peery resigned; that John Barns be recommended for Lieutenant in Captain William Gillespie's of Malitia 2 Battalllion 112 Regiment, and Robert Gillespie Ensign in said Company."

"Ordered that Henry Criswell, Frederick Cook, Travis Kendle, William Day, and Thomas Cassiday be appointed Constables in the County for two years."

William Thompson recommended as a fit person to be appointed Second Lieutenant in a company of cavalry in the room of John Wynn resigned, and Harvey George Cornet in said Company in the room of Robert Peery resigned.

Sept. T. "Ordered that William Taylor be appointed Commissioner of the Revenue for the year 1817."

Oct. T. "Personally appeared in Court William Higginbotham a Lieutenant formerly in the service of the United States, in the State of Virginia for the defence of the Borough of Norfolk, and deposed on oath after being duly sworn, that Micajah A. Thorn a Sergeant in the Company to which he was attached, which Company belonged to the 7th Regiment, commanded by Col. David Sanders, and that the sd. Thorn departed this life at the sd. Borough on the 4th day of Dec. 1814 in the sd service leaving a widow Susanna Thorn and ten children which all are now residents of the County of

Tazewell in the State of Virginia, and the sd. Susanna still remains the widow of the sd. Thorn as was proven in Court by the oath of William Smith Esquire, who also deposed that the said widow and deceased were lawfully married."

"The said William Higginbotham further deposeth, that James Suter a soldier in the said Company, departed this life, in the Borough of Norfolk in December 1814 in the sd. service, leaving a widow Caty Suter and six children who are all residents of the County of Tazewell in the State aforesaid, and that the said Caty still remains the widow of the said James Suter, & Ellender Neel after being duly sworn deposeth that the said widow & the deceased was lawfully married."

"The said William Higginbotham further deposeth, that Henry Stump a soldier in said Company, departed this life in Borough of Norfolk, in December 1814 in the service of the United States leaving a Widow Ellender Stump and two children, who are all residents of the County of Tazewell in the State aforesaid, and that the said Ellender Stump remaines the widow of the sd. Henry Stump & John Wynn Esq. after being duly sworn deposeth that the said widow and the deceased were *was* lawfully married."

"Joseph M. Clark and Cornelius Johnston after being duly sworn deposeth that they were both soldiers and belonged to the sd. Company, and was in the service at Norfolk when the above recited persons, departed this life at Norfolk."

Ordered that Henry Davidson be recommended etc. as a fit person to be appointed Captain in a Company of Militia in the room of Samuel Lusk; and John Davidson Lieutenant in said Company in the room of Henry Davidson promoted.

John Crockett. Clerk of the Court was directed to give notice that at the next term a contract will be made to have a complete map of the County.

Nov. T. "Ordered that Thomas O'neel Gent be appointed prosecutor on behalf of the Commonwealth in this Court until James Thompson, the former prosecutor, returns."

"William Campbell, being the lowest bidder, was awarded the contract for making a map of the county at the price of $23.00"

1817

Jan. T. "On the motion of John Crockett (Clerk), William Gillespie qualified as his deputy.

Mar. T. "Adam Waterford, emancepated slave, made satisfactory proof of his being a man of extraordinary merit was granted permission to reside in the Commonwealth and within this County."

April T. James Campbell qualified to practice law in this Court.

William Gillespie and John Laird recommended to the Governor for Comr. and assistant Comr of the Revenue in pursuance of an Act of the General Assembly passed the 18th day of Feb. 1817.

May T. Harvey George Peery qualified as deputy Sheriff.

Hezekiah Harman Conl. of the Militia of this County resigned his appointment as Col. at last Court.

Henry Bowen recommended to be appointed Colonel in the place of Hez. Harman, resigned.

William Gillespie recommended to the Governor to be appointed Major in the room of Henry Bowen, promoted.

John Barnes recommended for appointment as Captain in the room of William Gillespie, promoted.

Robert Gillespie recommended to be Lieutenant in the Second Batalion 112 Regiment.

Alex. Ward recommended as Ensign in 2 Batallion and 112 Regiment in John Barns Company.

Robert Gillespie recommended to be appointed Lieutenant in 2nd Batallion & 112 Regiment.

William Davidson recommended for Ensign 1st Batallion 112 Regiment—Henry Davidson's Company.

Philip Lambert, Jr., recommended for Justice of the Peace.

CHAPTER VII.

LAW ORDER BOOK JUNE 1817 TO DECEMBER 1820.

1817

June Term.

"At a Court held for the County of Tazewell on Tuesday the 24th day of June, 1817.

Present Thomas Gillespie, William Taylor, James Peery, Thomas Harrison, John Laird and Peter Gose Gent."

Caty Suiter, administratrix of James Suiter, Decd. Surety William Cecil, Peter Gose and John Deskins, in the penalty of Seven Hundred Dollars.

John Wilson, John Brown, William Peery and John Shannon appointed Constables.

Ordered that the County levy on each tithable be fixed at fiifty-three cents for the present year.

"Edley Maxwell Pltff. ⎫
      Vs. ⎬ Case
Charles Stratton Deft. ⎭

"John Crockett comes into Court and undertakes for the defendant in case he should be cast in this suit, if he does not pay the condemnation of the court he will do it for him, or surrender his body in person in discharge thereof."

(This order is here inserted to show the form of order entered in this class of litigation in the early records)

Joseph P. Lambert appointed Constable for two years.

July T. "John Peery, Joseph Davidson and Thomas Witten are by the Court recommended to his Excellency, the Governor as fit persons to execute the office of Sheriff of this County, for the ensuing year."

Sept. T. "John Barns produced in Court a Commission from his Excellency, the Governor, dated the 16th of August, 1817 appointing him a Captain in the hundred and twelfth Regiment & 17th Brigade, third Division of the Melitia of this county and took the oath required by law."

Alexander Harrisson appointed Commissioner of the Revenue for the County for the ensuing year.

Nov. T. David McCommas qualified to practice law in this Court.

"On the petition of Brooks Mattingley for to have his stock mark recorded which is a crop of the left ear and an under Bit out of the right ear, which is ordered by the Court to be entered of record."

1818

Jan. T. Christopher Chaffin appointed a Constable in the 2nd Batallion in the room of John Belshe.

Mar. T. Charles C. Johnston qualified to practice law in this Court.

April T. Arthur M. Henderson qualified to practice law in this Court.

May T. Under Act of Assembly authorizing same, School commissioners were appointed by the Court as follows: Thomas Witten, Senior, John Laird, Thomas Gillespie, Ambrose Hall, Hezekiah Harman, Henry Bowen, Elias H. Neel, Wm. Taylor, John Davidson, John Cecil and Isaac Quinn.

June T. "Henry Bowen, Colonel of the Militia of this County, came into Court and entered his resignation as Colonel."

"Ordered that the following persons be recommended to his Excellency the Governor as Militia officers: Ambrose Hall, Colonel Commandant in the room of Henry Bowen resigned; William Gillespie, Lieutenant Colonel; David Peery, Major in the room of A. Hall promoted; John Gillespie, Captain in the room of David Peery promoted; Alexander Harrisson, Lieutenant; Henry Harman Ensign Peter Gose, Captain; Philip Lambert, Lieutenant; Stephen Gose, Ensign; George Thompson, Ensign in Capt. Peery's Company."

Elias H. Neel recommended for a Justice of the Peace.

Thomas Cassaday appointed Constable.

Thomas O Neel is added to committee of school Commissioners.

"Joseph Davidson, Thomas Witten and John Thompson are by the Court recommended to his Excellency the Governor as fit persons to execute the office of Sheriff of this County for the ensuing year."

"Shorter Smith a Citizen of Tazewell County Virginia Came into Court and declars on oath that he served in the Revolutionary

War in the Continental Service against the common Enemy, he states that he entered with Captain Henry Debais, in the State of New Yourk, he was marched from Poughkipsee in the said State of New Yourk to Senectedy & afterwards jointd the company of Captain Samuel F. Pell the Regiment, second New York of the New Yourk line on the Continental establishment, Commanded by Col. Philip Vancourt (?) and he was afterwards marched to John Town fourt and from thence to fourt Herkimer and from thence to fourt Stammix and was left a guard at Prinston as his Co dep to little York, where Corn Wallis was Captured, he thinks the time he enlisted was in the year 1781 after the Capture of Corn Wallis, he was marched to Jessey and from thence marched to Snake Hill; where he was discharged, he was discharged the 7th of June 1783, and cannot now furnish his discharge, he relinquishes all other Calaim to any other pention."

Ordered that all Counterfeit money held by any and all citizens of the county be deposited in the Clerk's Office etc.

——————————— is charged with "stealing a few Mulatto boys."

July T. William Williams, Patton George and Richard Oney were added to the Board of School Commissioners.

"Isaac Stratton, William Hall, George Cummings, John Evans and David Scrivener severally appeared in Court, and stated that they were Soldiers and served in the revolutionary war and each of them having given in riting a statement of the officers & C. who they served under. Which statements is ordered by the Court to be recorded and copiys thereof transmited to the secretary of War, they having severally taken the Oaths required by the act of Congress respecting pentioners."

"Agreeable to the Act of Congress passed at the last Session William Hall of Tazewell County & State of Virginia, comes into Court & prefers his Claim to a pension. He states that he served in the Revolutionary war as a soldier in the Continental line. He was enlisted by Capt John Shelton the Regiment Commanded by Colo. Stephens. He does not recollect his Christian name. He was marched from Williamsburg where he enlisted to the long bridge and was present at the Battle with the Brittish, under the command of Fordyce from the long bridge he was marched in pursuit of the Brittish to Norfolk, and saw the conflagration of that place by the British. After the British quit Norfolk, he was again marched to the long bridge where he wintered. He served between ten and eleven months. He was marched from the long bridge to Williamsburg from thence to Fauquier Court house where he was discharged by Capt John Shelton. He cannot furnish his discharge having no expectation of any remuneration from his Country any more than what he received he paid little attention to his discharge. He renounces all claim to any other pension. He is in indigent circumstances or is likely to be so. is a cripple in his right arm and needs the assistance of his Country. He cannot at present furnish any other evidence. He further states that he was in an affair with the British at Hampton. Thomas O Neile States that he heard William Hall more than once mention that He was at the Battle with Fordyce. John Evans states he has herd him say he was at the aforesaid Battle with Fordyce. The said Hall came into Court and made oath that the aforesaid statement is true. He was entered in the year 1775 or 1776."

"George Cummings comes into Court and States that he was enlisted by Captain Wm. Long in Rockbridge County in the State of Virginia in the second Virginia Regiment commanded by Colo. Brent. His Majors name was Lee. He was marched from Rockbridge to the warm Springs in Greenbrier County, he was then marched from Greenbrier to Williamsburg, & from thence to the Valley forge in Pensylvania He was marched from the valley forge to the State of Jersey and was present at the battle of Monmouth and was at Stony point at the taking of it, and was likewise present at the taking of a fort belonging to the British, at Paulus hook. He was enlisted for three years, he served faithfully untill he was discharged in Greenbrier by Capt Long. He states that he left his discharge with Colo. Meariweather in Richmond. He renounces all claim to any other pension, is in indigent cercumstances and needs the assistance of his Country. The aforesaid Cummings makes oath that the aforesaid statement made by him is true, John Laird Esquire Magistrate of Tazewell County States, that he heard the said Cummings frequently state before the passage of the Act of Congress, giving pensions to officers & Soldiers, that he served in the Continental Service of the United States & he believes his statement to be correct. He served under General Mulingburg, General of Brigade."

"John Evans states he served n the Continental Service in the Revolutionary War in the first Virginia State Regiment Commanded by Colo. Charles Dabney He further states that he served he thinks during the span of 10 months He was at the siege of little York & was present at the capture of Lord Cornwallis—his Captains Name Tabb he does not recollect his Christian name. He was employed after the siege of little York, in taking some Refugees who did not come under the terms of Capitulation. He was marched from little York to Portsmouth in Virginia in order to demolish some works made thair by the British, he took up winter Quarters at Portsmouth where he was enculated—He went from thence to Richmond and from there to Warwick. He was discharged at Richmond on the 22nd day of February 1782 by Capt Elija Christian of Amhurst County. Capt. Christian moved to Georgia and he has never seen *it* since. He renounces all claim to any other pension is in indigent cercumstances and needs the assistance of his Country. The said John Evans comes into Court and declares on oath that the aforesaid statement is true."

"David Scrivener came into Court and makes oath that he served in the Continental line of the United States. He enlisted by John Mober (?) a private in Capt. Charles Crays Company in the first pensylvania Regiment Commanded by Colo. Benjm. Chambers he serves he thinks about six years. He was at the Battle of Long Island and also at the Battle of the White Planes and was likewise at the Battle of Germantown. He was also at the Storming of Stony point, he was at the ski*rming* at Paoli and was also present at the taking of the Hessions at Trenton he was discharged in South Carolina by Capt Davis. He served likewise under Samel Craig His discharge he lost in Augustine in East Florida having fell out of a boat in crossing the River at Augustine. He renounces all claim to any other pension, is in indigent cercumstances and needs the assistance of his Country all which is humbly submitted. He forgot to state that he was wounded at the Battle of Germanton, He further states that he served Generally under General Waye."

1819

May T. Joseph Davidson having been appointed Sheriff of this County by the Governor on Oct. 8th last past qualified as such. James Doak and Hervey George qualified as his deputies.

An indictment was returned into Court charging the defendant with selling one quart of cider at the price of 12½ cents which is .04½ more than the price fixed by the Court.

June T. John Davidson, Adam Harman (Sandy) William McGuyer, Philip Lambert and Elias H. Neel (little) recommended unto his Excellency the Governor and the Honorable privy Council as fit persons to be added to the County Commissioners of the Peace in this County. (James C. Preston was Governor at this time)

Ordered that Robert Young, Bazel Tabor, James McCommas, William Peery, John Wilson and John Brown be appointed to act as Constables in this County.

Hezekiah Harman, John Crockett and John Witten appointed by the Court to make settlement and report to Court as follows: With the Treasurer of Jeffersonville; with James Thompson for money received by him for wolf scalps; with Wm. Hall and John Peery late Sheriffs of the County; and with the Overseers of the Poor.

July T. Certificates of the qualifications of Henry Harman as Ensign with the Militia of the Commonwealth, and of David Peery as Major in the 112 Regiment 17th Brigade and 3rd Division of the Militia of this Commonwealth.

Henry P. George qualified as deputy for Joseph Davidson, Sherif.

Aug. T. Adam Harman, Junr. Orphan of Daniel Harman dec'd came into Court and made choice of Thomas Harrisson for his guardian.

John Milam appointed Constable in the room of Bazel Tabor.

Sept T. Ordered that Isaac Quinn be appointed Comr. of the Revenue for the ensuing year.

Oct. T. William Gillespie produced in Court a Commission from the Governor dated the 11th day of May last appointing him Lieutenant Colonel of the 112 Regiment of the 17th Brigade and third Division of the Militia. Agreeable to the Act of the General Assembly directing School Commissioners to be elected at the October Court, the Court proceeded to nominate and appoint, Thomas Witten, John Laird, Thomas O Neill, Hezekiah Harman, William Taylor, William Williams, Richard Oney, Ambrose Hall and Thomas Harrisson.

Nov. T. John Senton qualified to practice law in this court.

1820

Feb. T. "A certificate of the qualification of Kiah Harman & Granger Harman as fit persons to survey land, by William Taylor Esq. was returned to Court and thereupon on motion of Hezekiah Harman, Surveyor of Tazewell County, it is ordered that the said Kiah Harman & Granger Harman be admitted his deputies."

May T. Philip Lambert recommended appointment as a Justice of the Peace.

Vacancies in the 112 Regiment. Recommendation of persons to fill same, viz: Thomas Brown, lieutenant in place of John Witten resigned in a company of Riflemen; Thomas Brewster Ensign in the same company in the place of Thomas Brown promoted; John B. George Captain of Company of Cavalry in place of Isaac Brown resigned; Wm. Thompson 1st Lieutenant in the same Company vice John B George promoted; Hervey George, 2nd Lieutenant; James C. Davidson cornet vice Hervey George promoted; Milton Ward Ensign in Capt Barns' Company of Infantry in the room of Alexander Ward who failed to qualify; George Thompson Lieutenant in Captain James Peery's Company of Infantry vice Rees B. Thompson; Archibald Thompson junr. Ensign in place of George Thompson promoted; James Wilson Ensign in Captain John B. Gillespies Company of Infantry, vice Henry Harman resigned.

June T. Joseph Davidson, Thomas Witten and John Thompson reecommended as fit person to be appointed Sheriff.

A levy of 1.75 upon each tithable ordered to pay claims against the county.

Recommended to the Governor and privy Council the following to be added to the Justices of the Peace for this County, viz: William Gillespie, Hervey George, William Thompson, John Davidson, William Williams and Thomas Peery.

Recommended to the Governor as fit persons to serve as Sheriff for the year 1821: Thomas Witten, John Thompson and Hezekiah Whitt.

Henry Gillespie, Frederick Cook, Thomas Brewster, Thos. I. George, James Day, Kiah Harman and George Brown are appointed Constables.

July T. William Neel Emancipated Dimon a Slave, a man of color. John M. Neel and Elias Harman made oath to the said writing.

Aug. T. Joseph Davidson qualified as sheriff, with James C. Davidson and Thomas I. George, his deputies.

"On the 23rd day of August 1820 before us Thomas Witten, William Taylor, John Wynn and James Peery; Justices of the peace of the County Court of Tazewell in the state of Virginia personally appeared David Scrivener age sixty three years, resident in the County of Tazewell aforesaid in the said district, who being by us first duly sworn, according to law doth on his oath make the following declaration, in order to obtain the provision made by the late act of Congress entitled "An act to provide for certain persons engaged in the land and naval service of the United States in the revolutionary War": That he, the said David Scrivener enlisted for the term of two years, on the 12th day of July in the year 1776 in Sawcon County in the State of Pennsylvania in the company commanded by Captain Charles Craig of the Regiment commanded by Colo. ———— Hand in the line of the State of Pennsylvania, and the continental Establishments, that he joined his Regiment at Long Island in the State of New York; that he continued to serve in said Corps for the space of twenty two months or thereabouts; that he then re-enlisted for and during the war in the State of New Jersey in the company commanded by Captain Samuel Craig of the Regiment of Infantry commanded by Colonel ———— Chambers in the line of the State of Pensylvania on the continental Establishment, that he continued to serve in the said Corps, or in the service of the United States until the year 1783, when he was discharged from service on Ashley river in the state of South Carolina from General Waynes Brigade, and as well as he recollects he then was commanded by Captain Davis; that he was in the battles of Long Island, White Plains, Germantown, Trenton, Stony point, and Paola; he further declares that he was taken prisoner in the state of New Jersey on second river commonly called at that day the English neighborhood by seven Tories, that he was taken to a prison ship and was detained upwards of one year, that he made his Escape from Lord Cornwallis's Army at Bollings Bridge between Petersburg in Virginia and Halifax in North Carolina, and joined his own Corps at the place where he was discharged; that he was wounded at the Battle of Germantown. And that he is in reduced circumstances, and stands in need of the assistance of his Country for support; and that he has no other evidence now in his prower of his said Services. Sworn to and declared before us the day and year aforesaid."

"We, Thomas Witten, William Taylor, John Wynn & James Peery Justices of the peace of the County Court of Tazewell in the state of Virginia as aforesaid do certify that it appears to our satisfaction that the said David Scrivener did serve in the revolutionary war, as stated in the preceding declaration, against the common enemy, for the term of nine months at one time, on the continental Establishment and we now transmit the proceedings and testimony taken and had before us, to the Secretary for the Department of war, pursuant to the directions of the aforementioned act of Congress. We are also satisfied that he needs the assistance of his Country for support. We further certify that he made his first declaration on the 28th day of July 1818. Given under our hands this 23rd day of August 1820. Signed Thomas Witten, Wm. Taylor, John Wynn & James Peery."

"The said David Scrivener exhibited in Court a schedule of his Estate as follows: two sows and some pigs of the value of $5; nothing more, who made oath that the said Schedule contains all the property in his possession or otherwise".

Sept T. Hervey George, Thomas Peery, William Gillespie, John Davidson and William Williams qualified as Justices of the Peace.

Hervey George appointed Comr. of the Revenue of the County for the ensuing year.

"A schedule of the Estate of Isaac Stratton a pensioner resident in the County of Tazewell in the State of Virginia was exhibited in Court and ordered to be recorded to wit: One sow and two pigs, one old horse nearly worn out & that he has not secreted nor embezzled anything whatever."

"This day Isaac Stratton personally appeared before us (in open Court) Hezekiah Harman, william Taylor, James Peery, William Williams, William Gillespie & Hervey George Justices of the peace in the County aforesaid and made Oath that the above schedule contains all the property he holds in his possession; that his family consists of a sickly wife and three daughters who are all of full age, which we hereby transmit to the Secretary for the Department of war. Given under our hands and seals this 27th day of September 1820: Hez. Harman (SEAL) W. Taylor (SEAL) James Peery (SEAL) William Williams (SEAL) William Gillespie (SEAL) Hervey George (SEAL)"

Oct. T. Recommended Philip Lambert, James C. Davidson, James S. Witten & William Barns for appointment as Justices of the Peace.

Nov. T. James E. Brown qualified to practice law in this court. William Thompson Jr. qualified as Justice of the Peace.

Requests the County Court of Wythe Co. to cooperate in making a better road between Tazewell Court House and Wythe County Court House so as to pass Robert Steel's and intersect with the Cove in Wythe County.

Dec. T. Philip Lambert and James C. Davis qualified as Justices of the peace.

CHAPTER VIII.

COUNTY COURT ORDERS FROM JANUARY 1821 TO JUNE 1825.

1821

Jan. T. James S. Witten and William Barns qualified as Justices of the Peace.

"On the 24th day of January 1821, personally appeared in open Court, being a Court of record established as such by the laws of Virginia which proceeds according to the Courts of common law, with a jurisdiction unlimited in point of amount, keeping a record of their proceedings and having the power of fine and imprisonment; James Robertson, aged 78 years resident in the County of Tazewell in the 13th Judicial Circuit in the said State who, being first duly sworn, according to law, doth on his oath declare that he served in the Revolutionary war as follows: That he enlisted in the army of the revolution on continental establishment at Little York in the State of Pennsylvania in the Company commanded by Capt. David Greer in the Regiment commanded by Col. ———— Erwin of the 6th Regiment of the Pennsylvania line for the term of one year unless sooner discharged and that he served the whole year out; that after the expiration of his first enlistment he re-enlisted in the Company commanded by Capt. Robert Hopes at little York aforesaid in the Regiment commanded by Col. Thomas Hartley (or Hastley) in the Pennsylvania line for and during the war and was discharged at the city of Philadelphia after returning from South Carolina some time after peace had been proclaimed and that he made his original declaration on the 26th day of May 1818 that he has been inscribed on the pension list, Roll of the Virginia Agency No. 6261; and made oath that he was a resident citizen of the United States, on the 18th day of March 1818, and that he has not, since that time, by gift, sale or in any manner disposed of my property, or any part thereof, with intent thereby so to diminish it as to bring myself within the provisions of an act of Congress, entitled "An act to provide for certain persons engaged in the Land and Naval Service of the

United States, in the revolutionary war." passed on the 18th day of March 1818; and that I have not, nor has any person in trust for me, any property or securities, contracts or Debts, due to me, nor have I any income other that what is contained in the Schedule hereto; as follows to wit: One mare $30, one cow $10 two sows 8 pigs & 1 barrow $8. . . . $48. He also declares that he has no trade, that his family consists of himself and his wife only, that his wife is upwards of 60 years of age and as to himself he has been unable to walk for upwards of ten years, without his crutches, that he is unable to ride on horseback, or go to any place unless hauled and entirely unable to do any kind of labor."

Feb. T. John Tevis, an ordained minister of the Methodist Episcopal Church, authorized to celebrate the rites of matrimony.

Joseph Draper Gentleman qualified to practice law in this court.

It is ordered that the following persons be recommended to the Governor etc. as fit persons to fill vacancies in the 112th Regiment, to-wit:

Robert Gillespie Captain, vice Capt John Barnes resigned,
Milton Ward Lieutenant, vice Robert Gillespie promoted,
Hugh Young Ensign, vice Milton Ward promoted,
Kiah Harman Lieutenant vice Alexander Harrisson resigned,
John Augustus Cook, a native of Great Brittain took the oath of allegiance.

May T. Following certificates of qualifications of Militia officers:

Robert Gillespie, Captain of a Company of Infantry; Hervey George 2nd Lieutenant of Cavalry; James Wilson Ensign of Infantry; Kiah Harman Lieutenant of Infantry; Thomas Brewster Ensign of Riflemen

June T. Thomas Witten Gentleman, produced in Court a Commission to be Sheriff of this County, and qualified as such.

James S. Witten and William McDonald qualified as his deputies.
John Wilson appointed Constable by the Court for the year 1823.

Henry Gillespie, John Brown, William Peery, Robert Young, Hervey Deskins, Frederick Cook, George Brown, James Day and Henry Pruett are by the Court appointed Constables in this County for the term of two years from the date hereof.

Sept. T. Henry Harman (Daniel's son), Surveyor of road from Bluestone road near George Peery Junior to Wm. Taylor)

Twenty one Justices present at this term of Court.

Rees B. Gillespie was elected by the Justices, Comr. of the Revenue.

It was ordered that Ephraim Dunbar be recommended to the Governor etc. as a fit person to be added to the Commissioners (Justices) of the Peace in this county. Thomas Mann Randolph was Governor of Virginia at that time.

Oct. T. "Watt" a slave held by the heirs of Dudley Young dec'd is authorized to sue for his freedom, and counsel was assigned him for this purpose.

Nov. T. (Joseph Hankins appointed overseer of the road from Stephen Deeskins to the Baptist Valley near John Hankins)

1822

Jan. T. "On the 22nd day of January 1822 personally appeared in open Court being a Court of record established as such by the laws of Virginia which proceeds according to the course of common law, with a Jurisdiction unlimited in point of amount, keeping a record of their proceedings and having the power of fine and imprisonment: Isaac Stratton aged sixty seven years as well as he recollects having no register of his age resident in the County of Tazewell in the 13th Judicial Circuit in the said State, who, being first duly sworn, according to law, doth on his oath declare that he served in the revolutionary war as follows:

That he enlisted in the army of the revolution on continental establishment in the County of Amherst in the State of Virginia under Doctor Wilcox who volunteered his services as a Captain and afterwards (having enlisted his full Company) refused to march, and he was then transferred to the company commanded by Captain John Overton in the 14th Virginia Regiment commanded by Colo. William Davis, his enlistment was in the year 1778 and was marched to Valley Forge in the State of Pennsylvania where he joined the Grand Army—he also states that he was at the battle of monmouth, at the storming of Paulus hook when and where three hundred men or upwards were taken prisoners by the American Army, this claimant also states that he was on the detachment at the storming of Paulus hook commanded by Major Lee, he was at the storming of Stony point after that he served four months under the command of Colo. Morgan and was generally on the Brittish lines, and after the expiration of four months under Colo. Morgan he joined his aforesaid 14th Virginia Regiment that he served about two years and six months from his first enlistment until he was discharged at Fredericksburg in the State of Virginia by the said Colo. Davis, and that he made his original declaration before the passing of the act of Congress providing for certain persons engaged in the land and Naval services of the United States, in the revolutionary war, passed on the 18th day of March 1818 That he has been inscribed on the Pension list Roll of the Virginia Agency No. 15310 and made oath that he was a resident citizen of the United States, on the 18th day of March 1818; and that he has not, since that time, by gift, sale or in any manner disposed of his property, or any part thereof, with intent thereby so to diminish it as to bring himself within the provisions of an act of Congress, entitled "An act to provide for certain persons engaged in the land and naval services of the United States, in the revolutionary war, passed on the 18th day of March 1818, and that he has not, nor has any person in trust for him, any property, or securities, contracts or Debts, due to him, nor has he any income other than what is contained in the Schedule hereto: as follows to wit: A Lot of wild Hogs. . . . $5.00 He declares that he has no trade except that of farming that he lives on rented land, and not able to plough without pain, being disabled by pain in his right leg and thigh, that his family consists of a sickly wife between 65 and 70 years of age that he has three daughters living with him and that they are all upwards of 21 years of age and out for themselves

his
ISAAC x STRATTON
mark

And it is the opinion of the said Court that the total amount in value in sd. schedule is $5. Sworn to, and declared on the 22nd day of January 1822 before the Court."

"On this 22nd day of January 1822 personlly appeared in open Court being a Court of Record, established as such by the laws of Virginia, which proceeds according to the course of common law, with a Jurisdiction unlimited in point of amount, keeping a record of their proceedings and having the power of fine and imprisonment; Archibald Maloney age 73 years to the best of his recollection resident in the County of Tazewell in the 13th Judicial circuit in the said State, who being first duly sworn according to Law, doth on his oath declare that he served in the revolutionary war as follows: That he enlisted in the Army of the revolution on continental establishment at Lancaster in the State of Pennsylvania in the Company commanded by Capt John Alexander in the 7th Pennsylvania Regiment commanded by Colo. Butler in the year 1778 or thereabouts and served three years, after which he re-enlisted under the same captain and served in the same Regiment during the war. He states that he was in the Battles of Paulus Hook, Staten Island, Elizabethstown point, at the storming of Fort Washington at York Island, White plains, Storming of Stony point & Monmouth, he was taken prisoner at York Island and confined in a prison ship nine months, that he served five years and nine months in the war of the revolution in the Militia & continental army. That he made his original declaration before the passage of the act of Congress of the 18th day of March 1818 that he has been inscribed on the pension list, Roll of the Virginia agency No. 15,304; and made Oath that he was a resident citizen of the United States on the 18th day of March 1818; and that he has not since that time by gift, sale or in any manner disposed of his property, or any part thereof, with intent thereby so to diminish it as to bring himself within the provisions of an act of Congress, entitled "An act to provide for certain persons engaged in the land and naval service the United States in the revolutionary war, passed on the 18th day of March 1818; and that he has not, nor has any person in Trust for him any property, or securities, contracts or Debts, due to him, nor has he any income other than what is contained in the Schedule hereto annexed as follows towit:

"A lease on 20 acres of poor land for life rated to be worth $5; a year rent One ax the value of $1.25 He states and declares that he has no trade, that he has always followed farming as long as he has been able, that he is incapable of laboring for a livelihood, that he has no family and is hardly able to wash his own clothes.

his
ARCHIBALD x MALONEY
mark

Sworn to and declared, on the 22nd day of January 1822 in presence of the Court and it is the opinion of the Court that the total amount in value of the property exhibited in the aforesaid Schedule is $1.25 and that the yearly rent of his land is of the value of $5: See declaration of March 1818

Feb. T. Thomas J. Michie qualified to practice law in this court.

Mar. T. William Smith Esq. qualified to practice law in this court.

Thomas Witten qualified as Sheriff of this county.

Ordered that the County be laid off into three districts for the election of Overseers of the Poor.

Apr. T. Harold Smythe qualified to practice law in this court.

Ephraim Dunbar qualified as a Justice of the Peace.

The election held on April 20th 1822 resulted in the choice of Overseers of the Poor as follows: John Ward and John Harrisson were elected in the Western district, John Wynn in the Central district and Peter Dills and Henry Bailey in the Eastern district.

May T. Thomas Witten Junior, is by Thomas Witten Gentleman, Sheriff of this County, appointed deputy.

June T. William McDonald qualified as deputy Sheriff.

July T. Edward B. Bailey qualified to practice law in this Court.

Citizens of Jeffersonville were allowed to build porches to their houses not more that 8 feet in width so as not to obstruct passengers & etc.

Aug. T. (Nancy Harman, orphan of Henry Harman, decd. who is over 14 years old chose John B. Gillespie as her Guardian for the purpose of obtaining marriage license)

Lewis Horton appointed Constable.

Sept. T. Seventeen Justices present.

John Peery Senr. (Clear Fork) is appointed to celebrate the rites of matrimony in the county.

1823

Jan. T. Silas M. Stilwell qualified as deputy Clerk.

Mar. T. John B. George Esqr. who has been commissioned by the Executive of this State Major of the fifth Regiment of Cavalry in the fifth Division of the Militia qualified as such.

May T. Erastus Granger Harman is nominated to his Excellency the Governor as a fit person to fill the place of Lieutenant in the Company commanded by Captain John Gillespie in the 112th

Regiment Thomas Shannon recommended to the Governor for Ensign in same Company.

James Davidson recommended for Lieutenant in the room of Philip Lambert promoted in the same Regiment.

John Thompson, Hezekiah Whitt and Thomas Gillespie are by the Court recommended as fit persons to fill the office of Sheriff for the present year.

Richard Roberts is recommended as a fit person to fill the place of Lieutenant in the Company commanded by Captain Gillespie, in the 112th Regiment. Levi Horton recommended etc. to filll the place of Ensign in Captain Robert Gillespie's Company.

June T. Having been elected by the respective Companies, the following persons are recommended to the Governor as fit persons to be appointed to the offices named, viz: Thomas Bowen, Captain of the Rifle Company formerly commanded by Captain Hiram Witten; Cornelius Johnston as Lieutenant; Moses Beavers as Ensign; Peter Gose for Captain of a new Rifel Company, consisting of seventy five men; James Meek Lieutenant; and Peter Litz, Ensign; Andrew Brown Ensign in Captain Henry Davidson's Company.

Philip Lambert Captain in room of Peter Gose appointed Captain of a new Rifle Company.

William Peery and Lewis Horton appointed constables. Also Hezekiah Bonham. Henry Gillespie, William Henneger, Joseph Clark, William Dills, Tilman Crockett, Evin D. Williams, Samuel Cecil, Edmond Harrison, and Henry Prewitt appointed Constables.

July T. Thomas Witten Gentleman, is continued in office of Sheriff, upon failure of his successor to qualify, and William McDonald qualified as his deputy.

Augt. T. George Thompson recommended to the Governor etc. to be appointed Captain in the room of James Peery promoted, and that Joshua Curel be appointed Ensign; that Archibald Thompson Junior be appointed Lieutenant, in the room of George Thompson promoted.

James Oney recommended for Major in 112 Regiment.

Thomas I. George qualified a Lieutenant in the Troop of Cavalry.

Sept. T. Harvey George Qualified a Captain of a Troop of Cavalry.

John Cecil appointed Comr of the Revenue for this year.

Oct. T. William Barnes appointed a Comr. of the Revenue.

John S. McFarlane qualified to practice law in this court.

Dec. T. Alexander Harrison appointed deputy Sheriff.

Cornelius Johnston qualified Lieutenant in a Rifle Company.

Jonathan Quicksall produced in Court credentials of his ordination and also of his being in regular communion with the Baptist Church of Christ and was authorized to celebrate the rites of Matrimony agreeable to the forms of said church.

Silas Moore Stilwell Gentleman given a certificate on which to apply for license to practice law.

1824

Mar. T. A deed of manumission from George Harman to Thomas Bell, a man of color was proven in Court by the oaths of Hezekiah Harman and Erastus G. Harman two of the witnesses thereto and ordered to be recorded.

June T. John Thompson Gentlemen qualified as Sheriff, and Hervey Deskins and Thomas I. George qualified as his deputies.

John Thompson, Hezekiah Whitt and Thomas Gillespie recommended for Sherriff.

John Laird gave bond in the penalty of $2,000 and qualified as Treasurer of the School Commissioners.

June T. William Vencil recommended to be Ensign in a company of Riflemen etc.

Philip Lambert recommended for appointment as Captain etc.

John Thompson qualified as Sheriff.

Sept. T. Henry P. George was appointed Commissioner of the Revenue.

John G. Gray Gentlemen, qualified to practice law in this court

Guy Harrisson appointed Constable.

Nov. T. Jubel Jones appointed a Constable in the first Batallion of the 112th Regiment. John Chapman qualified to practice law.

Nehemiah Bonham appointed Constable in same Batallion.

James C. Davidson and Addison Crockett recommended to be commissioned as Lieutenants in 112th and 105th Regiments respectively.

Andrew Brown and James Wilson recommended to be commissioned as Ensigns in Captain Henry Davidson's Company, and in Capt. Robert Gillespie's Company respectively.

Dec. T. Edward T. Peery a minister of the Methodist Church was authorized to celebrate the rites of matrimony.

1825

Feb T. Addison Crockett, on motion of John Crockett, Clerk of the Court, is admitted as his deputy.

April T. Andrew Brown qualified as Ensign in 112th Regiment.

May T. John Hutchenson qualified to practice law.

The following persons recommended to the Governor as officers in the Militia, viz: Archibald Thompson for Captain and Joshua Corel Lieutenant, and Thomas Davis, Ensign in Capt Thomas Brown's Company of Riflemen.

June T. John Wilson, William Peery, Nehemiah Bonham, Robert Gillespie, Jubel Jones, Lewis Horton, Joseph P. Lambert, Tillman Crockett, William Henniger, William Davidson, Samuel Cecil, E. D. Williams, Stephen Deskins and Guy T. Harrison, appointed Constables for the term of two years.

Harvey Deskins appointed Deputy Sheriff.

CHAPTER IX.

COUNTY COURT LAW ORDERS FROM JULY 1825 TO DECEMBER 1831.

1825

July T. "At a quarterly Session continued and held for the County of Tazewell at the Court House thereof on Friday the 28th day of July 1825.

Present John Cecil, William Williams, Harvey George and John Wynn Gentlemen, Justices"

(No orders of general nature at this term. Only litigated matters considered.)

Augt. T. "At a Court held for the County of Tazewell at the Court House on the 23rd day of August, 1825.

Present, Thomas Witten, Hez. Harman, Ambrose Hall, Peter Gose and John Davidson, Gentlemen, Justices.

(Moses Hankins appointed Administrator of John Hankins)

Sept. T. Present, Thomas Witten, John Wynn, Harvey George and Thomas Peery, Gentlemen, Justices. At a later day of the Sept Term, Thomas Gillespie, Joseph Davidson, John Laird, John Cecil, William Williams, Thomas Gillespie, William Thompson, Ephraim Dunbar, James C. Davidson, Philip Lambert, John Wynn, Hez. Harman and Ambrose Hall were present.

Erastus Granger Harman was elected by the Justices, Commissioner of the Revenue for the ensuing year. Said Harman resigned his office as Deputy Surveyor before his election as Comr. of the Revenue.

John Lambert recommended to be commissioned Ensign in Captain Philip Lambert's Company.

Oct. T. Present, Harvey George, John Cecil, Thomas Gillespie and William Smith Gentlemen, Justices.

Nov. T. Present, Henry Bowen, William Taylor, Peter Gose, John Davidson Joseph Davidson, John Wynn and Thomas Witten, Gentlemen, Justices.

The Court petitioned the General Assembly to pass an act validating the deeds made by the Court to lots out of the 23 acres & 28 poles of land conveyed for the public buildings of the County etc.

(Lettitia Harman, orphan of Henry Harman decd. chose John Gillespie for her Guardian)

William McGuire a minister of the Methodist Church was authorized to celebrate the rites of matrimony.

Lieutenant Colonel William Gillespie recommended for appointment as Colonel Commandant in the room of Ambrose Hall resigned Major James Peery is recommended to be Commissioned as Lieutenant Colonel in the 112th Regiment etc. and Captain Henry P. Davidson is recommended to be commissioned Major in said Regiment.

1826

Jan. T. "Present, Hez Harman, Ambrose Hall, Thomas Harrisson, Isaac Brown, and John Wynn, Gentlemen, Justices."

Andrew Brown recommended for Captain in the 1st Battalion 112th Regiment; and William W. Compton to be commissioned Lieutenant in same Company, and John Bailey (Henry's Son) to be Ensign.

Feb. T. "Present, John Laird, John Davidson, Hezekiah Whitt, William Williams, Thomas Peery, John Wynn and Peter Gose, Gentlemen, Justices.

Hezekiah Whitt qualified as Sheriff of the County.

Mar. T. "Present, Joseph Davidson, Ambrose Hall, Henry Bowen, Thomas Harrisson, and Harvey George, Gentlemen, Justices."

Thomas I. George qualified as Deputy Sheriff.

Ordered that the County be divided into three precincts for the purpose of electing Overseers of the Poor etc.

May T. "Present, Thomas Witten, John Wynn, William Williams, John Laird, John Davidson, Wm. Thompson, Jas. Witten and Hezekiah Harman, Gentlemen, Justices."

James Mayhood recommended for Ensign in 1st Batallion 112 Regt.

June T. "Present, Henry Bowen, William Taylor, John Wynn, Thomas Witten, William Barns, Harvey George, Thomas Peery, Isaac Brown, Peter Gose, James Witten, John Laird, William Williams, John Thompson, Thomas Harrisson, John B. George and Hez. Harman, Gentlemen, Justices."

We have given the names of the Justices who held the Courts during the last year. It is our purpose to do this occasionally so that the reader may get the names of the active majistrates during the year.

Hez. Whitt, Thomas Gillespie and Hez. Harman are by the Court recommended etc. as fit persons to execute the office of Sheriff of this county for the ensuing year

Thomas Davis recommended to be commissioned an Ensign in Captain Thomas Brown's Company.

Thomas Cassady appointed a Constable.

On the motion of James Devor and Margaret his wife the said Margaret being one of the heirs of Mary Dunn, dec'd. the following heirs were summoned to appear and show cause why 100 acres of land in Burks Garden should not be sold etc. viz: Daniel Robinett, James Waddle, and Ann his wife, Michael Robinett, Polly Harman, Thomas Fickle Mary Fickle, James Workman, Rachel his wife, heirs of Betsy Fickle, dec'd. James Steel and Ester his wife, John Dunn, Thomas Dunn and Mark Bogle, Allen Newberry and Betsy his wife, Polly Bogle & Dunn Bogle, heirs of Rachel Bogle dec'd etc.

An order of publication in the Wythe Gazette to be published for eight weeks as notice to said heirs.

Aug. T. Jeremiah Lambert, James Harrisson and Shadrach White appointed Constables etc.

Sept. T. John Davidson appointed Commissioner of the Revenue for the ensuing year.

Oct. T. Erastus G. Harman appointed as Deputy Surveyor.

Nov. T. John Foster Gentleman, qualified to practice law in this Court.

1827

Mar. T. Hezekiah Whitt who has been continued in the office of Sheriff for the ensuing year, qualified as such, and Thomas I George and Samuel P. Davidson qualified as his deputies.

Henry P. McDowell recommended to be commissioned a Captain in the 2nd Batallion of the 112 Regiment, and Lewis Horton a Lieutenant in same and David Steele, Ensign.

Ordered that John Crockett, Clerk of this Court provide a County Seal for the County Court.

June T. Charles Beckem qualified to practice law in this Court.

Thomas Gillespie, Hezekiah Harman and John Cecil recommended for appointment as Sheriff for ensuing year.

William Peery, Robert Gillespie, Lewis Horton, Stephen Deskins, Samuel Cecil and Guy Harrisson appointed Constables in the Second Battalion for the term of two years.

Charles E. Harrison qualified to practice law in this court.

July T. Thomas Cassady and William B. Thorn (?) appointed Constables in the First Battalion etc.

Oct. T. Samuel Laird commissioned by the Governor as Coroner of this county.

Dec. T. Hugh Johnston, a minister of the Methodist Episcopal Church was authorized to celebrate the rites of matrimony.

1828

Jan. T. William Gillespie, Junr. appointed constable.

March T. William M. Fulton, Gentlemen, qualified to practice law in this Court.

Robert Gillespie appointed Deputy Sheriff.

Certificate of residence and good character given to James P. Pendleton, on which to base examination for license to practice law.

Joseph Belche appointed deputy Sheriff.

June T. A bill emancipating sundry slaves by Jacob Waggoner, Senr. ordered to be recorded.

Henry P. Davidson appointed a Constable.

Henry P. Davidson recommended to be appointed Colonel in the 112 Regiment; John Gillespie recommended to be appointed Lieutenant-Colonel; Robert Gillespie recommended for Major; Erastus G. Harman recommended for Captain; James Mahood, Lieutenant and William Harman as Ensign.

Lewis Horton recommended for Captain; Lewis Kendle, Lieutenant; George Steel, Ensign; Hiram D. Ward, Ensign.

A Plat or Map of the division line between the Counties of Giles and Tazewell was returned into Court and ordered to be recorded.

Albert G. Pendleton, granted certificate to obtain license to practice law.

Sept. T. Thomas K. Catlet, a minister of the Methodist Episcopal Church, was granted authority to celebrate the rites of matrimony.

Nov. T. Albert G. Pendleton admitted to practice law in this Court.

John J. Burum, a minister of the M. E. Church granted authority to celebrate the rites of matrimony.

Dale Carter qualified to practice law in this Court.

1829

March T. Erastus G. Harman commissioned Captain in the 1st Battalion 112 Regiment.

Thomas Gillespie Commissioned Sheriff of the County until the next Quarterly Court; and Robert Gillespie and James McNeil appointed Deputy Sheriff.

Henry P. Davidson commissioned Colonel of the 112 Regiment.

April T. Act of General Assembly passed Jan. 17th, 1828, prescribing the mode of conducting Special Elections. See. Act.

Robert Gillespie commissioned Major of the 112 Regiment.

May T. The following persons recommended as Militia Officers in the 112th Regiment, viz: John B. Gillespie, Junr., Captain, Lorenzo D. Gillespie, Lieutenant, James Milam, Captain.

June T. It is ordered by the court that Eleanor, the slave of William Witten, and Polly, the slave of John B. George, be exempted from the payment of County levy and Poor rates.

Thomas I. George, William Whitman, Erastus G. Harman, John P. Bailey, Geo. W. Messick, James Meek, Archibald Thompson, Junr., William Cox and William Dills, Gentlemen, are by the Court recommended to the Governor, etc. as fit persons to be commissioned Justices of the Peace of this county.

Henry P. Davidson, James Harrison, Charles Taylor, Charles Greever, Wm. B. Thorn, Joshua Day, and Thomas Cassady are appointed Constables in the 1st Battalion of this County to serve for the term of two years.

William Peery, Samuel Cecil, William Gillespie, John C. Williams, Lewis Horton, and Guy T. Harrison are appointed Constables in the 2nd Battalion etc.

We have given the names of Constables which appear for the first thirty-one years of the County for the purpose of preserving their names as well as to show their official positions. After 1831 the names of Constables will be omitted for a few years.

"It is ordered that the Sheriff of this County collect from each tithable, seventy three cents to cover expenses of the County for last year and also the sum of twenty seven cents laid by the overseers of the Poor to cover the expenses of the Poor for the succeeding year."

"Abram, a man of Color, is granted permission to sue in this Court to obtain his freedom."

"John Laird is allowed $150.00 for his services as Comr. of the Revenue for the present year, and John Crockett, Clerk is allowed $20.00 for examining the Commr's Books."

Aug. T. James C. Spotts qualified to practice law in this Court.

Abram, the colored man slave won his suit for freedom and the Sheriff was directed to release him from custody.

Sept. T. William Anderson commissioned Lieutenant.

Nov. T. Recommended for officers in 1st Battalion, 112th Regiment; James Meck, Captain; Peter Litz, Lieutenant and David Gose, Ensign.

1830

Feb. T. James F. Pendleton granted certificate of residence and good character to obtain license to practice law.

Isaac Leftwick qualified to practice law in this Court.

David Fleming, a minister of the Methodist Episcopal Church, granted authority to celebrate the rites of matrimony.

March. T. Hezekiah Harman, under a commission by the Governor, qualified as Sheriff of the County, and Erastus G. Harman and Kiah Harman, were appointed his deputies, and John Litz, Jailer and Deputy Sheriff.

April. T. George W. Hopkins, Gentleman, qualified to practice law in this Court.

May. T. License to keep ordinaries granted to divers persons, who proved to the Court that they were persons of "Good character, not addicted to drunkness or gaming."

June T. Mathias Harman Senior, qualified as administrator of William Harman, dec'd., June 21st, 1830, and Buse Harman named as surety. Kiah Harman, William Taylor, James Mahood and Daniel Harman were appointed appraisors of William Harman's estate.

David Goodman appointed Constable.

Minor Wynn appointed School Commissioner in the room of William Williams, and Hervey George in the room of Hezekiah Harman.

June T. John Scaggs appointed Surveyor of road.

Joseph Stras qualified to practice law in this Court.

Campbell Harman appointed Surveyor of Road.

James F. Pendleton resigned as Deputy Clerk.

Aug. T. James F. Pendleton qualified to practice law in this Court.

Sept. T. Harvey G. Peery appointed Constable in the place of John C. Williams, resigned.

Nov. T. Hezekiah Harman, John Cecil and John Laird recommended by the Court for appointment as Sheriff of the County.

M. Chapman qualified to practice law in this Court.

Moses E. Kerr, minister of the M. E. Church was authorized to celebrate the rites of matrimony.

Frank S. Pendleton qualified as Deputy Clerk.

John B. Gillespie recommended as Colonel in the 112th Regiment and Robert Gillespie Lieutenant-Colonel. Harvey George qualified as Major.

1831

March T. Hezekiah Harman again qualified as Sheriff under a commission of the Governor.

Edward Boyd qualified to practice law in this Court.

John Laird's appraisers appointed.

June T. John Crockett received the votes of twenty-one magistrates present, and was re-elected Clerk of the Court.

Ordered that the County be divided into two districts, according to the Batallions of the County, whereupon the following persons were nominated: Constables elected for the Eastern District: Henry P. Davidson, Charles Taylor, Robert Harrison, Henry Dills and George Hall. For the Western District: Harvey G. Peery, William Peery, Louis Horton, David Gooden, Guy Harrison and James Wilson.

The following list of persons were recommended by the Court to the Governor for appointment as Justices of the Peace: William

Dills, William T. Moore, Samuel P. Davidson, Hugh Tiffany, Jr., William Cox, George W. Messick and Samuel Witten.

James C. Spotts qualified as Deputy Clerk.

Aug. T. Hezekiah Harman, late Sheriff of this County, was nominated for Surveyor of the County, and his nomination certified to the Governor. Said Harman having no opposition for the office.

Sept. T. Daniel Harman, orphan of Daniel Harman, Dec'd., chose Samuel Laird as his Guardian.

Oct. T. John P. Bailey appointed Commissioner of the Revenue.

Nov. T. Hezekiah Harman presented a Commission from the Governor appointing him Surveyor of the County for a term of seven years.

Dec. T. John Crockett, Clerk of the Court.

CHAPTER X.

County Court Law Orders, Feb. 1832 to Dec. 1841.

1832

Feb. T. John Crockett, Gentleman, qualified as Sheriff of the county until 1833.

Mar. T. William Gillespie, James W. M. Witten and Erastus G. Harman appointed deputies for John Crockett, Sheriff.

Apr. T. Hugh Tiffany, Jr., qualified as a Justice of the Peace.

May T. "The Freeholders and Householders having failed to elect overseers of the Poor, the Court doth appoint William Smith, John Wynn and Henry Bailey to hold said office until a new election."

June T. Albert G. Pendleton, Esquire, Attorney prosecuting for the Commonwealth in this county, allowed $60.00 for his services.

Edward Adkins, a Revolutionary soldier applied for a pension

"The following declaration & certificate was returned to Court and ordered to be entered in the minutes thereof, "Virginia, County of Tazewell, to wit, On the 14th day of April, 1832 personally appeared before the subscriber, a Justice of the County Court of Tazewell, being a Court of record, Edward Adkins, resident in said County, aged seventy-six years, who being first duly sworn according to law, doth on his oath make the following declaration, in order to obtain the provision made by the Acts of Congress of the 18th March 1818, & the first of May 1820: that he the said Edward Adkins enlisted & served for the term of three years & six months, on the —— day of ——————— at Nelsons Ferry, in the State of New York he believes, in the Company Commanded by Captain Smith, in the Regiment under General Green in the line of the State of New York; on the Continental establishment: that he continued to serve under General Green & Marion until the end of the war when he was discharged from the service in Winchester, which he thinks is in South Carolina: that he hereby relinquishes every claim whatever to a pension, except the present: that his name is not on the roll of any State except New York; and that the following are the reasons for not making earlier application for a pension; that since first informed of the law, which has been but a short time, he was ignorant in what manner or where to apply. And in pursuance of the Act of the 1st May 1820 I do solemnly swear that I was a resident citizen of the United States the 18th March 1818 & that I have not since that time, by gift, sale or in any manner disposed of my property, or any part thereof, with intent thereby, so to diminish it as to bring myself within the provisions of an Act of Congress, entitled an Act to provide for certain persons, engaged in the land & naval service of the United States in the revolutionary war, passed the 18th March 1818, and that I have not, nor has any person in trust for me any property, or securities contract or debts due to me, nor have I any income whatsoever being entirely destitute of, and maintained solely by the parish wherein I reside.

Sworn to and declared on the 14th day of April 1832

SAMUEL P. DAVIDSON, J. P.

I Samuel P. Davidson, a Justice of the Court of Tazewell, holden in the County of Tazewell where the declarant resides, do hereby certify that the above named Edward Adkins is from a disease called an inflamation or soreness of his leg with which I am relibly informed & believe he has been afflicted for the space of many years, unable to attend the Court of which I am a Justice, and I do not think from present appearances that he will be able to attend the Court above named at its next session. I have therefore in pursuance of the Act of Congress of the 1st March 1823, attended at his place of abode and administered the foregoing oath.

SAMUEL P. DAVIDSON, J. P."

July T. Adopted a plan and appointed James Meek, Thomas Fowler, William Cox, James C. Spotts, and David Wade to receive proposals for constructing a new Court House. The said court house to be completed by the 25th day of December, 1833.

Addison Crockett elected and qualified as constable.

Samuel Witten qualified as a Justice of the Peace.

Aug. T. Low Brown made declaration as a Revolutionary soldier;

"On the 21st day of August 1832 personally appeared before the Court of the County aforesaid, Low Brown, resident of the said County of Tazewell and State of Virginia aged seventy-six years, who being first sworn according to law, doth on his oath make the following declaration, in order to obtain the benefit of the provision made by the Act of Congress passed June 7th. 1832. That he enlisted in the Illinois regiment of the army of the United States in the year 1779 with Captain Jesse Evans and served in the Illinois regiment under the following named officers Colonel George Rogers Clark Lieutenant Col. John Montgomery Col., in the Company of Captain Jesse Evans; that he left the service the first day of August 1780 as appears from a discharge of that date, under the hand of Lieutenant Colonel John Montgomery certifying that his time of enlistment (which was eighteen months) had expired at that time that at the time of his enlistment he resided in the County of Montgomery State of Virginia, that he marched through the country at present the States of Tennessee and Kentucky by water from the mouth of big Creek which empties into Holstein to the mouth of Teennessee river, and then to Kaskaskia in Illinois by water. He hereby relinquishes his every claim whatever to a pension or any annuity except the present, and he declares that his name is not on the pension roll of any agency in any State—sworn to and subscribed the day and year aforesaid. LOW BROWN.

And the said Court do hereby declare their opinion that the above named applicant was a revolutionary soldier and served as he states."

Peter Gose elected, by the Justices present, as Commissioner of the Revenue for the ensuing year.

Joseph Stras appears frequently as Commissioner to settle accounts with Fiduciaries.

Oct. T. John Crockett, Clerk of the county.

Declaration of Thomas Witten, a Revolutionary soldier:

"On the 15th day of October 1832 personally appeared in open Court before the County Court of Tazewell County in the State of Virginia, now sitting, Thomas Witten a resident of Tazewell and State of Virginia, aged eighty years in the month of January next, who being first duty sworn according to law, doth on his oath make the following declaration in order to obtain the benefit of the Act of Congress passed June 7th 1832.

That he entered the service of the United States under the following named officers, and served as herein stated. That he was ensign regularly commissioned and belonged to the Company commanded by Captain Thomas Mastin, and Lieutenant James Maxwell when he first entered the service early in the month of June, 1776 and was attached to the State regiment Commanded by Col. William Preston and Major Walter Crockett who was afterwards promoted the appointment of Col. ——— That the duty which as ensign to the appointment of Col. ——— That the duty which as ensign aforesaid, during the remainder of the year 1776, which devolved upon the said Thomas Witten, and the Company to which he belonged, was to perform frequent scouting expeditions as Indian Spies to defend the western frontier of Virginia lying along the valley of Clinch river from the head waters of Bluestone river to the forks of Clinch river wihtin the now limits of Russell County in the State aforesaid from the massacres of the Indians by whom the whole western border was then infested That he resided in the now County of Tazewell in the State of Virginia, then perhaps Montgomery, That he does not now remember whether he was drafted or not, but he thinks that he was called out by an order of the Commanding officer Col. William Preston, That he was engaged in no general battle or engagement during his scouting expedition in the year 1776 but partook in several little skirmishes and was an eye witness of some of many instances of unhuman butchery and massacres committed upon the frontier families within the range of his marches, That none of the regular soldiers were quartered in the western frontier for the protection and defence of the settlers, but that the malitia were occassionally drafted and sent to the relief of the frontiers from the counties of Montgomery and Washington embracing all that section of country now comprised in the counties of Lee, Scott, Russell, Tazewell, Giles, Grayson Monroe etc. etc.

The said Thomas Witten further states that he continued to act as an ensign as aforesaid, until the close of the revolutionary war—that he thinks that he was engaged as an Indian Spy, as aforesaid fully six months in each year, and the ballance of each year were permitted by the commanding officers to return to their families and remain at home during the winters of each year from the year 1776 til the termination of the revolutionary war, when the Indians ceased to annoy and murder the settlers upon the said frontier. That he does not now know what has become of his commission as ensign, but thinks upon his resigning he surrendered it to his commanding officer, so that it is not now in his power to produce it. That he knows of three persons now living who can testify to his services aforesaid viz, William Cecil, Nancy Cecil and Joseph Oney. Hereby relinquishes any claim whatever to a pension or annuity except the present and declares that his name is not on the pension roll of the agency of any state. Sworn to and subscribed the day and year aforesaid. THOMAS WITTEN.

And on the 15th day of October, 1832 personally appeared in open Court before the same Court hereinbefore named now sitting William Cecil a witness in behalf of Thomas Witten herein, in open Court who being first duly sworn according to Law, deposeth and saith that he has been acquainted with Thomas Witten for many years and that he knows that the said Thomas Witten served as an Indian Spy in the war of the revolution and from the best of his recollection he believes that the foregoing declaration sworn to and subscribed by the said Thomas Witten contains a true and correct recital of the services of the said Thomas Witten, and that the said Thomas Witten was an ensign during the time of his services as aforesaid and that he was a private belonging to the Company in which the said Thomas Witten was ensign. Sworn to and subscribed in open Court the day and year aforesaid.

WILLIAM CECIL.

This day Nancy Cecil personally appeared in open Court, before the same Court herein before named, and after being first duly sworn according to Law deposeth and saith, that she was acquainted with Thomas Witten herein named in the time of the revolutionary war and that to her knowledge the said Thomas Witten served in the war of the revolution as an ensign in the Company commanded by Captain Thomas Mastin, and Lieutenant James Maxwell and that she believes the foregoing declaration sworn to and subscribed by the said Thomas Witten contains a true and correct statement of the services of the said Witten in the war of the revolution Sworn to and subscribed in open Court the day and year aforesaid.

NANCY CECIL.

This day Joseph Oney personally appeared before the County Court of Tazewell County in the State of Virginia, in open Court who after being first duly sworn according to Law, deposeth and saith that he has been acquainted with Thomas Witten for many years and that he was a private in the Company of Capt. Thomas Mastin and that the said Thomas Witten was an Ensign in the same Company in the war of the revolution and continued to serve as such until the close of the revolutionary war. That he believes the foregoing declaration sworn to and subscribed by the said Thomas Witten contains a true and correct statement of the services of the said Witten in the revolution. Sworn to and subscribed in oppen Court the day and year aforesaid. JOSEPH ONEY.

And the said Court do hereby declare their opinion, after hearing the testimony of William Cecil, Nancy Cecil and Joseph Oney that the above named applicant Thomas Witten was an Indian Spy in the revolutionary war, and served as he states. And the said Court doth further certify upon their own knowledge from a long acquaintance with the before named witnesses who have signed the preceding affidavits, are citizens of Tazewell County except Joseph Oney who is a resident of the County of Giles and credible persons, and that their statements are entitled to credit."

"State of Virginia Tazewell County, to wit,

On the 16th day of October 1832, personally appeared in open Court, before the County Court of Tazewell County in the State of Virginia now sitting William Cecil a resident of Tazewell County and State of Virginia aged about eighty-three years, who being first duly sworn, according to Law, doth on his oath make the following declaration, in order to obtain the benefit of the Act of Congress passed June 7th 1832. That he entered the service of the United States early in the year 1776 in the now County of Tazewell in the State of Virginia under Captain Thomas Mastin, Lieutenant James Maxwell and ensign Thomas Witten, and that the said Company belonged to the regiment of the Virginia State line, commanded by Col. William Preston and Major Walter Crockett, that at the time when he first entered the service as aforesaid he resided in the County of Tazewell then called Montgomery, where he has continued to reside ever since, That the company to which he belonged was never required by the commanding officers of the regiment to which it was attached, to perform any other duty in the war of the revolution, except as Indian Spies to defend the western frontier of Virginia. That he continued with his said Company to perform that duty fully six months in each year from 1776 till the final termination and close of the revolutionary war. The said William Cecil further states, that the Company to which he belonged, consisted of men mostly resident on the border country, and during the period aforesaid from 1776 till the close of the war, they were kept in continual readiness, and were never regularly discharged, or called out for any definite period of time, as the Malitia from the adjacent country who were drafted to perform regular routines of duty, and that they were permitted every year upon the approach of winter to return to their respective homes, subject to be called out against the Indians as fresh emergencies might require. That he was in no battle of any importance during the time of his services aforesaid except those little skirmishes common to the savage mode of warfare, that he was an eye witness to some of the many instances of unhuman butchery and massacre committed by the Indians upon the families of the frontier settlers. That he does not think the Company to which he belonged was drafted to perform tours of duty, but being composed chiefly of the frontier settlers where the Indians were more particularly troublesome, and which suffered mostly from their contiguity to the ruthless savage, with a sparce population and in a situation comparatively defenceless and unprotected, they were always kept in readiness and regarded by the officers of the said regiment as minute men; that the Company to which he belonged was chiefly engaged during the period aforesaid, in defending that part of the western frontier of Virginia, lying along the Valley of Clinch river from the head waters of Blue Stone river to the forks of Clinch river in the now County of Russell. The said William Cecil further states, that none of the continental Troops or officers of the regular army of the United States, were ever sent to the relief of that part of the western frontier to which he belonged, that he now remembers, nor was he acquainted with any of the officers of the regular army. That in the whole he served in the war of the revolution as an Indian Spy, aforesaid fully six months in each year from 1776 until the close of that war, and that he knows of three persons now living, who can testify to his service as herein stated, viz, Thomas Witten who was his ensign, Joseph Oney and Nancy Cecil. That being permitted to return to his home every winter to be recalled the ensuing spring, he never obtained a regular discharge in writing from his commanding officer, so that he cannot now produce that evidence of his services.

He hereby relinquished every claim whatever to a pension and declares that his name is not on the pension roll of any agency of any State. Sworn to and subscribed the day and year aforesaid.

WILLIAM CECIL.

This day Thomas Witten personally appeared before the County Court of Tazewell County in open Court now sitting, and being duly sworn according to law; doth on his oath say that he has been acquainted with William Cecil, the above named applicant, who has subscribed the foregoing declaration, and that the said William Cecil served as is stated in the said declaration in the war of the revolution, as an Indian Spy under Captain Thomas Mastin, Lieutenant James Maxwell and himself as ensign, and that the said Company formed part of the regiment of the Virginia State line commanded by Col. William Preston and Major Walter Crockett. Sworn to and subscribed in open Court the day and year aforesaid.

THOMAS WITTEN.

This day came Joseph Oney personally before the same Court in open Court now sitting, and after being duly sworn according to law, doth on his oath say, that he has been acquainted with William Cecil the above named applicant, who has subscribed the foregoing declaration, for many years, and was with the said Cecil as an Indian Spy in the war of the revolution, and that the foregoing declaration, subscribed as aforesaid by the said William Cecil, contains a correct recital of the services of the said Cecil as aforesaid in the war of the revolution, under Thomas Mastin, Lieutenant James Maxwell, and Ensign Thomas Witten, and that the said Company formed a part of the regiment of the Virginia State line, commanded by Col. William Preston and Major Walter Crockett. Sworn to and subscribed in open Court the day and year aforesaid.

JOSEPH ONEY.

And the said Court do hereby certify their opinion, after hearing the testimony of Thomas Witten and Joseph Oney who have sworn to and subscribed the foregoing affidavits that the above named applicant was an Indian Spy in the war of the revolution and served as he states. And the Court further certifies that it appears to them from a long personal acquaintance with, that Thomas Witten and Joseph Oney who have sworn to and subscribed the foregoing affidavits are credible persons and that their statements are entitled to full credit.

"State of Virginia, Tazewell County to wit

On this 16th day of October 1832 personally appeared in open Court before the County Court of Tazewell County now sitting, Joseph Oney a resident of Giles County in the State of Virginia, aged about seventy-nine years, who being first duly sworn according to law doth on his oath, make the following declaration in order to obtain the benefit of the Act of Congress passed June 7th 1832.

That he entered the services of the United States to the best of his present recollection in the spring of the year 1777, under Captain Thomas Mastin, Lieutenant James Maxwell and Ensign Thomas Witten, and that the said Company belonged to the Virginia State line Regiment commanded by Col. Williams Preston and Major Walter Crockett. That at the time he first entered the services aforesaid that he resided in the now County of Tazewell, then perhaps the County of Montgomery. That the Company to which he belonged was never called upon by the commanding officers of the Regiment to which it was attached, to perform any other services in the war of the revolution except as Indian Spies to defend the wesern frontier. That he continued with his said Company to perform that duty fully six months in each year for four years, when he left the neighborhood in which he then lived, and removed to Walkers Creek within the then County of Montgomery, but now County of Giles where he has resided ever since. The said Joseph Oney further states that the company to which he belonged consisted of men mostly resident upon the frontier, and that during the period of four years aforesaid they were kept in continual readiness, and never regularly discharged as the Militia from the adjacent County, who were drafted to perform regular tours or routine duty, but that they were permitted every year upon the approach of winter, to return to their homes, subject to be called out against the Indians as fresh emergencies might require. That he was in no general engagement during the time of his services as aforesaid, except those little skirmishes which characterize the savage mode of warfare. That he witnessed some among the many instances of indiscriminate ferocity and barbarism inflicted by the Savage enemy upon the families of the frontier settlers. That he does not think the company to which he belonged was drafted to perform tours of duty, but that it was composed of the resident men of the country in which the Indians were peculiarly troublesone, and which suffered most from their immediate exposure to the ruthless savage, that the population of the country was then sparse, and comparatively defenceless and that from their contiguity to the abodes of the Indians, were always regarded by superior and inferior officers of the Regiment as minute men always ready upon the shortest warning to assemble in defence of the frontier settlements, situated in the Valley of Clinch river from the head waters of Bluestone river, to the forks of Clinch river in the now County of Russell. He further states that none of the Continental troops were ever sent to the relief of that part of the western frontier to which he belonged, that he now remembers, nor was he acquainted with any of the officers of the regular army. That in the whole he served in the war of the revolution fully two years, that being six months in each year for four years.

That he knows of three persons now living in the county of Tazewell who can testify to his services as herein stated viz, William Cecil, Thomas Witten his old Ensign in the war aforesaid, and Nancy Cecil. The affidavits of the two former is herewith transmitted to the war Department. That being permitted to return to his home every winter to be called into service again the ensuing spring, he never obtained any regular discharge in writing from his commanding officers, so that he cannot now produce that evidence of his services.

He hereby relinquished every claim whatever to a pension or an annuity except the present, and declares that his name is not on the pension roll of any agency of any state.

Sworn to and subscribed the day and year aforesaid.

JOSEPH ONEY.

This day came William Cecil personally before the County Court of Tazewell County now sitting, and after being first duly sworn according to law, doth in open court depose and say, that he served with Joseph Oney who has subscribed the foregoing declaration in the war of the revolution in the Company of Captain Thomas Mastin, Lieutenant James Maxwell and Ensign Thomas Witten, and that the said Joseph Oney served in the said Company in the war of the revolution as an Indian Spy on the western frontier of Virginia as he has stated in his foregoing declaration, and that the said company to which the said Oney belonged was attached to the Regiment of the Virginia line, commanded by Col. William Preston and Major Walter Crockett. Sworn to and subscribed in open court the day and year aforesaid   WILLIAM CECIL.

This day came Thomas Witten personlly before the County Court of Tazewell County and after being first duly sworn according to law, doth in open court depose and say, that Joseph Oney who hath subscribed the foregoing declaration, served as is stated in the said declaration in the war of the revolution as an Indian Spy upon the western frontier of Virginia, and that the said Oney belonged during the whole period of his service in that war to the company commanded by Captain Thomas Mastin, Lieutenant James Maxwell and himself the said Thomas Witten as Ensign, and that the said company belonged to the State Regiment of the Virginia line commanded by Col. William Preston and Major Walter Crockett. Sworn to and subscribed in open court the day and year aforesaid.

THOMAS WITTEN.

And the said Court do hereby declare their opinion after hearing the testimony of Thomas Witten and William Cecil that the above named applicant was an Indian Spy in the war of the revolution, and served as he states. And the Court further certifies that Thomas Witten and William Cecil who have sworn to and subscribed the foregoing affidavits are credible persons, and that their statements are entitled to full credit."

Nov. T. "Hugh Tiffany Senr., a native of Ireland this day on oath declared his intention to become a citizen, and renounced allegiance to any foreign Prince, Potentate, State or Sovereignty whatever and particularly to William the 4th, King of Great Brittain & Ireland."

John Prewett's declaration as a Revolutionary Soldier:
"State of Virginia—Tazewell County to wit,

On the 20 day of November 1832 personally appeared in open Court before the Justices of the County Court of said County of Tazewell now sitting, John Prewett, resident of the said County and in the State of Virginia—aged 72 years, who being first duly sworn according to Law, doth on his oath make the following declaration in order to obtain the benefit of the Act of Congress the 7th June 1832. That he enlisted in the service of the United States about the latter part of May in the year 1775 under recruiting officer by the name of Edmanson, his first name not recollected the regiment and line to which he belonged he does not recollect, but well remembers that the campaign for which he was designed was called McIntosh Campaign Genl. McIntosh was the commander at the regiment to which he was to be attached, and Genl. Gray was an other field Officer Captain Michael Dougherty and Lieutenant Joseph Prion were the officers of his company. That he resided in the county of Washington and State of Virginia at the time he entered in the service. That he was marched to Anderson ferry on James River where the army to which he belonged remained for about three months, waiting for other companies which were expected to join them, from thence he was marched to the Light levels in the County of Greenbrier where his officers that saw proper to detain about a month longer, with the hope of being joined by the expected re-inforcements agreeable to their expectations they were joined by two other companies and he was then marched to the mouth of Elkhorn river where the army in consequence of the season it being in January or February, were compelled to encamp and remain there till the first of March 1776 as this applicant thinks it was. They were here joined Genl. Broadhead from the head quarters of McIntoshe's army as this applicant was informed, which was then some where in the Ohio State; Genl. Broadhead took charge of the provisions etc. and the army at this place and dispensed with the forces of Genl. Gray, and permitted him to march them back. On his return with his men Genl. Gray met with Captain James Thompson with a company of men who were on their way to join McIntosh at Col. Donalsons in the County of Greenbrier; that he and some other of his fellow soldiers not hearing, served out the time for which they enlisted, were forced to join Capt. Thompson's company & retrace their steps under his command to the mouth of Elkhorn, here he stopped to procure a supply of provisions & was delayed till about the first of May, about which time Capt. Thompson received orders that his services would not be demanded and that he might return home; That he was immediately marched back to the house of William Thompson in the County of Montgomery, where he and his fellow soldiers were dismissed, and told that they could get their regular discharge at any time that they would apply for it; that he never considered that it would be of any benefit to him and therefore never afterward applied for it; and that he had served out the full time for which he enlisted when he was dismissed by Captain Thompson, which was eighteen months, & that he knows of no person whose testimony he can procure that can testify to his service as stated. And that again in the year 1778, he was called out with many others of his countrymen under the command of Capt. Henry Patten, Lieutenant James Marrs, the other officers not recollected, to defend the frontier settlements from the depredation of the Indians, who had lately killed and carried off some persons in the settlements near the Clover bottoms; they pursued them to cole river but being unable to come up with them, they were marched back, and dismissed in the county of Montgomery, where they started from having been in the service this time about three weeks. And that again in the same year & about the month of May or first of April he was called out under the command of the same officers and Col. Cloyd as field officer to pursue the Indians who had killed and taken prisoners several families on New River when they arrived at the place where the Indians had committed their cruelties, they were informed that Capt. Wood with a company of men had pursued them, he was then marched back to Montgomery the place where he lived when he started on this expedition, and dismissed, having been in the service this tour about two weeks. Again in the fall of the year 1779, that he was stationed under Capt. Patton at the Lead Mines in the county of Wythe for one month to guard the mines from the tories. Again in the year 1779, and about ——— weeks after he was discharged from service at the lead mines and while still a resident of the County of Montgomery, he was called out in the Malitia, under the command of Col. Cloyd, Capt. Patterson, Lieutenant James Marrs and Ensign Daniel Howe to traverse the country about New River and part of North Carolina to rid it of the Tories who had become very troublesome about this time he was marched from Montgomery to the Moravaan Towns in North Carolina by the Mulberry fields to near the head of New River where our Company was met by Genl. William Campbell, who had been in pursuit of the same enemy from this place he was marched down New River to Montgomery and dismissed having been about four or five weeks in the service during this expedition and that again in the year 1781 and the month of February he was drafted to go out under the command of Gnl William Preston, Col. Cloyd the field officer and Capt. Patten Lieutenant Daniel Howe & John Day Ensign, the officers of the Company. These forces were intended as a reinforcement for the Southern army under the command of General Green, he was marched to North Carolina and on the night previous to the Battle of Whitsels Mills they joined Genl. Green and Pickens. He was in that engagement as well as another skirmish some days previous on the Alamans that after the engagement of Whitsels Mills from about the first of February 1781 until some time in March following, as will appear by the affidavit of Daniel Howe hereto annexed. He was marched about to different places in North Carolina and was discharged at Giford Court House a few days previous to the Battle at that place the time for which he was drafted having expired. He hereby relinquishes every claim whatever to a pension or annuity except the present and declares that his name is not in the pension roll of the agency of any State.

Sworn to and subscribed the day and year aforesaid.

his
John x Prewett."
mark

"State of Virginia Tazewell County.

On this 20th day of November in the year 1832 personally appeared in Open Court before the County Court of Tazewell County now sitting. John McLaughlin aged about seventy-six years, a witness for John Prewett, who after being duly sworn according to law, doth on his oath say and depose, that in the year 1778 he was in the service of the United States and that the regiment to which he belonged joined the Virginia Regiment to which John Prewett belonged, at a place in the State of North Carolina called the Balled Field but the said John McLaughlin does not now remember how long he then served with the said Prewett in the war of the revolution. He further deposes and says that he was also in the service aforesaid with the said Prewett, in the years 1779 and 1781 but how long he cannot now remember and the service rendered by the said Prewett whilst in the same army with the said John McLaughlin, were chiefly rendered in the State of North Carolina, but at one time they were together in the edge of South Carolina. That he then became personally acquainted with the said John Prewett who has sworn to and subscribed the foregoing declaration — and the said John McLaughlin further says on oath as aforesaid that he believes that declaration contains a true and correct recital of the services of the said John Prewett in the war of the revolution. Sworn to and subscribed the day and year aforesaid.

his
John x McLaughlin
mark

"John McLaughlin presented a declaration for a pension which was sworn to, examined and certified by the Court."

"Alexander Sayers presented a declaration to obtain the benefit of the pension law, passed on the 7th June 1832, which was sworn to examined by the Court and ordered to be certified

Dec. T. Present, Ambrose Hall, James C. Davidson, Philip Lambert, Hugh Tiffany, Peter Gose and Samuel Witten, Gentlemen Justices.

William and Phylis Wynn, orphans of Robert Wynn, choose Lavina Wynne as their guardian.

1833

Jan. T. Henry B. Harman was sworn in as Deputy Surveyor of the County.

Hezekiah Harman was appointed to survey and run off the lines of the town of Jeffersonville and that he place at each corner in said lines a stone of proper size, well fixed in the ground, and make report to court, accompanied with a plat of the town and certificates. And that John Crockett and Hugh Tiffany and Thomas Peery attend and superintend the execution of the said survey.

Feb. T. "David Lusk presented in court a declaration for a pension, which was sworn to, examined and ordered to be certified according to law."

Mar. T. John Cecil qualified as Sheriff of the County and James W. M. Witten, William M. Gillespie, and James McNeil qualified as his deputies.

Guy Harrison resigned his office as constable in the 2nd Battalion of the 112th Regiment of the Virginia Militia, and Daniel Christian was appointed to fill the vacancy; and Thomas Harrison and Guy Harrison became his sureties.

"Jane, Sally, Thomas and William Peery, orphans of James Peery, deceased, with the approbation of the Court, made choice of Martha Peery for their Guardian, and the Court doth appoint the said Martha Peery Guardian to Martha, Mary, Nancy, James, Elizabeth and Julia, other infant children of the said James Peery deceased; and thereupon the said Martha Peery with Robert Allen and William Brown her securety, entered into and acknowledged a bond in the penalty of $2,000 conditioned as the law directs."

May T. "It is ordered that William Hall and Daniel Harman (Sandy) be exempted from paying county levy and poor rates, in consequence of age and infirmity."

June T. The Justices on the bench proceeded to elect constables as follows: George P. Hall, Duncan Cameron, Henry Davidson, Addision Crockett for the Eastern District, and Hervey G. Peery James B. Wilson, Milton L. Lockhart and David Goodwin for the Western District.

"Ordered that Thomas P. Rader be allowed the sum of $3.00 for copying the draft of the New Court House, which is to be paid out of the years levy."

On motion of Moses Christian and others, it is ordered that a Bridleway from Sinking Waters to Rays Fork of Sandy be established.

Bird Lockhart and Cornelius White recommended for Justices of the Peace.

Elisha Mustard was presented by the Grand Jury for selling two bales of cotton in the county of Tazewell, without license, to Duncan Cameron on the 1st day of January, 1833.

Daniel Harman was presented by the Grand Jury for failing to keep the public road of which he is Surveyor, in legal repair. These are the only indictments found at this term of the Court

July T. David Payne authorized to celebrate the rites of matrimony "on the waters of Sandy" in this County.

Sept. T. Alexander Harrison and Samuel Witten were chosen by the votes of the Justices as Commissioners of the Revenue for the County.

1834

Jan T. John Wynne, Gentleman, presented his Commission and qualified as Sheriff.

Feb. T. Hiram Ingram a preacher of the Methodist Episcopal Church, took the oath of allegiance.

Mar. T. "Jared Bolin presented in Court a declaration for a pension, accompanied with the necessary certificates, which was sworn to and certified as the law required."

"Elisha McGuire, who has been commissioned a Lieutenant of Malitia in the first Batallion in this county, this day appeared in Court and took the oaths prescribed by law."

Francis R. Gregory and George W. Jones qualified to practice law.

May T. George W. G. Brown, Gentleman, qualified to practice law.

William Cox appointed a director to construct road from Price's Turnpike to Cumberland Gap.

Ordered Sheriff to summon the Justices to lay levy to build road from Price's Turnpike to Cumberland Gap, and to sue contractors for construction of the Court House.

"Ordered that the sum of $1.50 be levied upon each tithable in this county for the purpose of paying the claims against the county, and the poor rates for the present year."

June T. Resolutions of the Court on the death of Joseph Draper, Attorney at Law:

"Whereas information is given to this Court by George W. G. Browne, Esq. of the death of Joseph Draper, Esq. late a practising Attorney at this Bar, Resolved therefore, that this Court receives this intelligence with sincere sorrow: Resolved that this Court deeply sympathize with the Bar and with the connexions of the deceased in their grief for the loss of a man so distinguished in his profession and so valuable as a member of society. Resolved that in testimony of the regard in which this Court holds the memory of the deceased, the members Attorneys and Officers thereof will wear the usual badge of mourning for 30 days.

Resolved that copies of this order be transmitted to the parents and widow of the Deceased in token of the sympathy felt by this Court for their loss.

Resolved that these resolutions be published in the Western Virginia Argus and Virginia Republican."

Appointed Hervey George, Henry Bowen, James Meek, William Taylor and William Barns to meet with five delegates from each of the counties of Botetourt, Giles, Russell, Scott and Lee, at Jeffersonville, to decide on matter of building road from Price's Turnpike to Cumberland Gap.

July T. James C. Tate admitted to practice law in this Court.

Aug. T. John B. Floyd and Henry S. Kaine, attorneys, admitted to practice law in this Court.

Sept. T. John B. Gillespie and William Barnes were elected commissioners of the Revenue for the County, by a vote of the Justices, sitting as a court.

Oct. T. A deed of Emancipation for a slave by William Thompson, John Cecil and Thomas Witten, heirs of James Witten, deceased, admitted to record.

Charles Greever elected by the Justices, constable in the first Batallion, in place of George P. Hall, resigned.

John Justice appointed Constable to fill the vacancy occasioned by the resignation of Duncan Cameron in the First Batallion.

Nov. T. Elizabeth Quicksall and John Quicksall were appointed to administer on the estate of Jonathan Quicksall, deceased.

1835

Jan. T. Adam Harman and Lavicy, his wife, to William Harman deed admitted.

Feb. T. John Wynne re-appointed Sheriff of the County.

"Lee County having declined to accept the provisions of the Act of Assembly in respect to the construction of the road from Price's turnpike to Cumberland Gap. Joseph Stras and James C. Tate were designated to present to the authorities of Lee County the great advantages of said road and ask that said authorities reverse their former decision, and agree to cooperate."

Mar. T. John C. Price, Gentleman, admitted to practice law in this Court.

William P. Wynne and James McNeill appointed Deputy Sheriffs of this county.

July T. "William Witten Jr., Henry P. McDowell, John Justice, Charles H. Greever, Addison Crockett and Jeremiah Lambert, were declared duly appointed Constables, in the Eastern District of the County, to serve for two years, the Court being of opinion that they are men of honesty, probity and good demeanor".

"Harvey G. Peery, Lorenzo D. Gillespie, George Steele, Milton Lambert, and Robert Shortridge were declared duly appointed constables in the Western District of this county to serve for the term of two years, the Court being of opinion that they were men of honesty, probity and good demeanor."

"On motion of Jonathan Peery and James P. Harman, administrators of Mathias Harman, deceased, James C. Spotts, a Commissioner was appointed to settle said estate."

Sept T. Fifteen Justices on the bench. "Henry B. Harman having received a majority of the votes of the Justices present polled viva voce in open court (for the Eastern District) it is ordered that he be appointed Commissioner of the Revenue in the Eastern District of this county for the ensuing year".

Thomas H. Gillespie, having received a majority of votes on the final poll of the Justices present etc., was appointed Commissioner of the Revenue for the Western District of the county for the ensuing year.

Benjamin R. Floyd admitted to practice law.

The new Court House was ordered to be received as requested by Thomas J. George, one of the contractors.

October 28th *"At a Court of Quarterly Sessions* begun and held" etc.

"Samuel Laird being nominated, was unanimously elected to the office of Constable in the 2nd Batallion, in the place of Harvey G. Peery, retired."

"Samuel Laird, appointed Deputy Sheriff of the county, the Court being of opinion that the said Samuel Laird is a man of honesty, probity and good demeanor."

On same day, Samuel Laird resigned the office of Coroner of the County.

Dec. 31st. Jane Harman, John Harman and Mathias B. Harman, orphans of Mathias Harman, deceased, with the approbation of the Court, made choice of Buse Harman as their guardian, and therefore the said Buse Harman with Hezekiah Harman, his surety, gave bond in the penalty of 3,000.

Jan. T. William Taylor, Gentleman, qualified as Sheriff of the County and executed bond in the penalty of $30,000.

Kiah Harman recommended to the Executive for appointment as Escheator in the place of William Harman, resigned.

Minor Wynn qualified as coroner of the county during good behavior.

Mar. T. "On motion of John Crockett, Clerk of this Court, Geo. W. G. Browne is permitted to qualify as his deputy."

Charles Taylor, Robert G. Harrison and James Harrison appointed deputy Sheriffs of the County.

James W. Sheffey, an attorney at law, was admitted to practice law in this court.

Mathias Harman, Senior and Mathias Harman, Jr. et als. view a "bridleway from the back valley to the Reedy Spring on Dry Fork of Sandy, leaving the Back Valley at the gap on this side of Ebb Brewster's etc." As old Mathias Harman had previously died, the Mathias Senior here mentioned must have referred to his son, and Mathias Jr. to his grandson.

Apr. T. Charles H. Greever appointed a deputy for William Taylor, Sheriff of the county.

June T. "Ordered that the attorneys practicing in this court have leave at their own expense to make an alteration in the Bar of the Court room by removing the partition now standing therein and by closing the ends of the bar."

"Ordered that Peter Gose, William Cox, Erastus G. Harman, John Wynn and Samuel Witten be appointed Commissioners of Roads in this county in pursuance of the Act of March 3, 1835."

"Ordered that the sum of four dollars be allowed as the reward for killing a wolf above the age of six months and two dollars be the reward for killing a wolf under the age of six months; that one dollar be the reward for killing an old red fox, and fifty cents for killing a fox under the age of six months, to be paid out of the county levy."

"Ordered that a levy be laid on the lands and lots in this county equal to the amount of Revenue charged on the same by the existing laws, to be applied when collected, to the construction of the Cumberland Gap Road."

"Ordered that nine hours labor be taken as a day's labor, and that the value of a day's labor on said road be fixed at fifty cents".

"Hezekiah Harman, surveyor of this county and Henry Smith surveyor of Russell County, heretofore appointed to run the line between the two counties, in part, this day rendered a report which is ordered to be filed."

"Ordered that Hervey George and Thomas Peery be appointed to ascertain the expense of procuring a suitable tract of land and erecting a poor house; also the difference of expense of supporting the poor of this county in the present method and by means of a poor house."

Kiah Harman qualified as Escheator of the county of Tazewell

"Ordered that the following shall be the rate for keeping live stock taken in execution etc." For keeping a horse for one day, .04c; for cattle, .03c and for sheep .01½c.

July T. John W. C. Watson was admitted to practice law in this court.

Sept. T. Seventeen Justices on the bench.

Alexander Harrison was, by the votes of the Justices, chosen as Commissioner of the Revenue for the Eastern District and Chapman A. Spotts for the Western District of the county.

John Luster qualified as constable.

Dec. T. Henry B. Harman re-appointed Deputy Surveyor of the County.

Seventeen Justices on the bench.

Twenty-three Justices had been summoned for Dec. Term of the Court.

John Cook appointed as Constable in the Eastern District to fill the vacancy of John M. Compton, resigned.

John C. Harrison appointed Deputy Sheriff.

1837

Feb. T. Richard P. Mathews, Esq. qualified to practice law in this court.

John Young (of Charles) appointed a constable in the Eastern District of this county.

Occasionally insolvent debtors were confined in jail.

Mar. T. William Taylor qualified as Sheriff of the county and executed bond for $30,000.

James Harrison, Charles Taylor, John C. Harrison and Charles H. Greever appointed Deputy Sheriffs.

Christina Harman and Henry Harman dec'd. Appraisement of their estates ordered to be recorded.

Erastus G. Harman, Alexander Harrison, James C. Spotts, Thomas S. Carnahan and Hervey G. Peery qualified as Justices of the Peace.

Rates and prices to be paid at all ordinaries within this county: "Dinner, 25 cents; supper and breakfast, each, 18¾ cents; for ½ pint brandy or whiskey, 12½ cents; for ½ pint French brandy 25 cents; for ½ pint rum or wine 18¾ cents; lodging, 6¼ cents; for 1 gallon corn or oats, 12½ cents; for horse at hay 12 hours 8½ cents."

Kiah Harman appointed Deputy Surveyor of the county.

May T. Noted that William Cecil a Revolutionary soldier departed this life December 11th, 1836, leaving Nancy Cecil, his widow.

June T. Robert Gillespie authorized to procure a seal for this court.

Charles F. Tiffany was elected Overseer of the Poor in the place of John Davidson, who was taken from this county by the formation of the new county of Mercer.

Daniel Harman (D's Son) appointed Overseer of the Road.

David Hall, Jr., qualified to practice law in this court.

Frequent exemptions of men from payment of county taxes on account of old age and infirmity. Also exemption from working on public roads for same reason.

James Meek qualified as a Justice of the Peace, having been appointed by Wyndham Robertson, Lieutenant Governor and acting as Governor of the Commonwealth. Quite a number of appointments, etc. recently made by said Lieutenant Governor.

"Ordered that a levy be laid on all lands and lots, and that fifty cents be collected from each tithable, and applied to the construction of the Cumberland Gap Road. And that fifty cents be collected from each tithable to be applied to the construction of the road from the Cove across Clinch Mountain."

"Ordered that JOSHUA, a slave, belonging to the estate of the late Henry Harman, dec'd, be exempted from the payment of county levy and poor rates, on account of old age and infirmity."

"It appearing to the satisfaction of the Court by the testimony of respectable witnesses that William McGuire late of Tazewell County, State of Virginia, a revolutionary pensioner departed this life on the 5th day of March, 1837 leaving no widow, and that the said William McGuire left nine surviving children who are still living, to wit, Polly Wingo, wife of William Wingo, late Polly McGuire, Hannah Johnston, wife of Daniel Johnston, late Hannah McGuire, Nancy McGuire, Ellen Huckley, wife of Johua Huckley, late Ellen McGuire, Joshua McGuire, William McGuire, John McGuire and Priscilla Chrum, wife of Henry Crum and that these are the only children left by the said McGuire, Rachel Lewis, wife of Benjamin Lewis, one of the children of said William McGuire, having previously departed this life leaving ——————— her children and heirs. The Court orders these facts to be spread on the reecord."

"Ordered that the county be divided into two districts for constables by the Batallion line."

Twenty-four magistrates present and voting for constables.

Constables elected in the Eastern District: Addison Crockett, Jeremiah Lambert, Joseph H. Wynne, Charles H. Greever and Henry P. McDowell.

Constables elected for the Western District; Thomas H. Gillespie, Samuel Laird, Daniel Horton, Jr., Witten Cecil, John Young, Jacob Webb, Edward Harrison and Reese Crabtree.

William Cox allowed the sum of $24.00 for his services as Director of the Cumberland Gap and Price's Turnpike road on the part of this county.

Sept. T. George P. Thompson appointed constable in Eastern Dist. in the place of Addison Crockett, resigned.

Nov. T. Joseph Moore elected Commissioner of the Revenue for the Eastern District; and Bird Lockhart for the Western Dist.

"George W. G. Browne directed to transcribe the proceedings of this court from the 6th day of May, 1800 to Feb 11th, 1802, as contained in a paper book filed in the office; also records from March 14th, 1805 till 22nd May 1810; and also from the 21st day of March 1831 to 23rd November 1831; also Execution Book from August court 1800 to July 6th 1822." It appears from this Order that some kind of court proceedings were had in May, prior to the June term, which has previously been recorded wherein Henry Harman was "allowed $2.00 for trouble in holding the first court at his house" This does not change the fact that the first court was held at the home of Henry Harman, Jr. It only implies that some court preliminaries had been held there in May, as the Act fixes the first term to be held at said Harman's.

Dec. T. Christopher A. Tabler, Esq. qualified to practice law in this court.

Ordered an election for overseers of the Poor. Only freeholders and housekeepers are qualified to vote in said election.

1838

Jan. T. The right of Robert Morris in 75,000 acres of land was ordered to be conveyed.

The Justices having met for the purpose of electing a Clerk of the Court for a term of seven years, three candidates presented themselves, to wit: John Crockett, James C. Spotts and George W. G. Browne. On first ballot Crockett received twelve votes, Spotts ten and Browne ten. On second ballot Crockett received twelve, Spotts ten and Brown ten. On third ballot viva voce in open court the vote was unchanged. The court thereupon took a short recess, and on reassembling James C. Spotts withdrew his name and the following votes were cast: for Crockett thirteen, and Browne nineteen, William Gillespie declining to vote. Thereupon George W. G. Browne was declared duly elected for a term of seven years.

Erastus G. Harman was nominated for the office of assistant assessor for the Eastern District and William Barnes was nominated for Western District. Recommendations to the Governor for appointment of these two men.

July T. David P. Atkins appointed Constable in the Western District in the place of John Luster, resigned.

Thomas Davis appointed Deputy Surveyor of the county on motion of Hez Harman, Surveyor.

Thomas S. Gillespie was elected Commissioner of the Revenue for the Eastern District and William Thompson for the Western District.

Henry Bowen qualified as Sheriff of this county. William P. Wynne, David Gose, James McNeil and John Young, qualified as his deputies.

1839

Jan. T. Hezekiah Harman produced a Commission under the hand of the Governor, and with the seal of the Commonwealth thereto affixed, appointing him Surveyor of this county for the term of seven years from the date hereof.

Feb. T. Andrew S. Fulton admitted to practice law in this court. The compiler of these records was present in Bland County Court about 1867 or 1868 when Adrew S. Fulton, who was then Circuit Judge, announced his resignation because he refused to take the "Iron Clad Oath"

Henry Bowen qualified as Sheriff of the county for his second term.

William P. Wynne, David Gose, James McNeil and Davidson Atkins qualified as Deputy Sheriffs.

Joseph Stras appointed a Commissioner to state and settle various accounts etc.

March T. Edward Collins qualified as Justice of the Peace.

Certain Commissioners appointed to superintend the election at the following voting places: At the Court House, Shradrach White's, Charles Tiffany's and Mouth of Slate.

May T. Adam Beavers elected Constable in the Western District in place of Jacob Webb who has removed.

Joseph Looney qualified as Justice of the Peace.

William B. Young appointed constable instead of John Young, resigned.

Reuben C. Fudge recommended as Deputy Surveyor.

Hezekiah Harman and Henry B. Harman qualified as Deputy Surveyors of the County.

Appointed Commissioners to superintend the ensuing election at Peter Dills'

Charles H. Greever appointed Deputy Sheriff.

John W. Johnston qualified to practice law in this court.

June T. Robert Looney and Benjamin Cox qualified as Justices of the Peace.

At this Court there were thirty-two of the thirty-three Justices of the county present. James C. Spotts was the only one absent.

Ordered that James C. Spotts be appointed a Commissioner to borrow $2500 for the completion of the Cumberland Gap and Price's turnpike road.

Constables elected by the votes of the Justices present: Joseph H. Wynne, Jeremiah Lambert, Charles H. Greever, George P. Thompson, James T. Bane, Daniel C. Harman and John C. Harrison, for the Eastern District; and Milton Thompson, William B. Young, Thomas H. Gillespie, Daniel Horton, Jefferson Matney, Witten Cecil, John M. Lockhart, Samuel Laird, Mastin Christian and Elijah Vance for the Western District.

Elijah Vance qualified as Deputy Sheriff of this county.

Surveyors of highway in the Western District appointed and the boundaries fixed.

Aug. T. William Cecil qualified as Deputy Sheriff.

Election of Commissioners of the Revenue by the Justices for the ensuing year: William Witten was duly elected for the Eastern District, and Bird Lockhart for the Western District.

Oct. T. John B. Floyd qualified as Justice of the Peace.

Mastin Christian was elected constable for the Western District in the place of Adam Beavers, resigned..

Nov. T. "It appearing to be the duty of this court to recommend to the Executive a fit and proper person to filll the office of Surveyor of this county, Hez. Harman was recommended as such. Edward Collins recommended to be commissioned as a Justice of the Peace.

Waddy T. Currin is, by Henry Bowen, Sheriff of this County, appointed his deputy during pleasure.

1840

Jan. T. Reuben C. Fudge appointed a deputy Surveyor by Hezekiah Harman, Surveyor.

Feb. T. Thomas H. Gillespie and William B. Young are by Ambrose Hall, Sheriff of this County, admitted to be his deputies.

Mar. T. "It appearing to the satisfaction of the court, that Archibald Maloney, late a revolutionary pensioner in this County, departed this lifee on the 21st day of February, 1840, leaving his widow Rachel to whom he was legeally married 5th September, 1823, and two children to-wit, John Maloney and Mary, the wife of Benjamin Prewett, it is ordered that these facts be certified."

Elijah Vance, James Bane and Joseph H. Wynne qualified as deputies for Ambrose Hall, Sheriff.

William H. Witten appointed to be assistant Commissioner of the Revenue in the Eastern District.

Benjamin Cox resigned his commission as a Justice of the Peace.

May T. "Ordered that preachers of the various religious denominations have leave to preach in the Court House, provided their meetings do not interfere with the transaction of public business."

July T. Albert G. Pendleton allowed $100 as Prosecuting Attorney for the Commonwealth during the past year.

Elias G. W. Harman appointed deputy Surveyor of the county.

Sept. T. Thomas Hall qualified as deputy Sheriff.

John C. Harman, Constable in the Eastern District resigned and Charles Taylor was elected in his place.

John D. Peery was duly elected Commissioner of the Revenue in the Eastern District and Chapman A. Spotts in the Western District.

Oct. T. "Miner Wynn, School Commissioner, having removed from this county, Henry B. Harman is elected in his place by the vote of all the Justices present."

Dec. T. Daniel C. Harman and Jefferson Matney qualified as deputy Sheriffs.

1841

Jan. T. Charles H. Greever, constable in the Eastern District, having moved from the county, David B. Greever is appointed in his place.

Mar. T. Samuel Laird resigned as constable and John M. Witten was elected to fill the vacancy.

"Granville Lewis a free person of color having been registered by the Clerk of this Court, as the law requires, as follows to wit: The said Granville Lewis, who was registered on the 7th October, 1840 and numbered 2 is about 45 years of age, of a mulatto color, 5 feet 9 inches in stature, emancipated in Montgomery County in this State, and having the following marks, scars etc, to wit, Bushy hair, a mole on the left side of the bridge of the nose, the forefinger on the left hand crooked at the first joint, a scar on the nail of the little finger of the same hand, and one bone of the right leg broken above the ankle: whereupon the Court doth certify that said register has been truly made."

Charles Taylor and Joseph H. Wynn appointed deputies for Ambrose Hall, Sheriff of this county.

April T. "It appearing to the satisfaction of the court, from the oath of Hez. Harman and Erastus G. Harman, that Low Brown, late of Revolutionary pensioner, departed this life on the 28th day of January, 1841, it is ordered that the same be certified."

"It appearing to the satisfaction of the court, that William Brooks, late a Revolutionary pensioner, departed this life on the 24th day of January, 1841, it is ordered that the same be certified."

June T. George R. C. Floyd, James S. Vail and Charles H. Greever qualified as Justices of the Peace.

James T. Bane qualified as deputy for Ambrose Hall, Sheriff of the county.

Constables elected by vote of Justices present: Joseph H. Wynn, Jermiah Lambert, David B. Greever, James T. Bane, Charles Taylor, Geo. P. Thompson, and Daniel C. Harman for the Eastern District and Martin Gibson, Jefferson Matney, Mastin Christian, John M. Lochart, John M. Witten, William B. Young, Witten Cecil, Thos. H. Gillespie, George Steel and Milton Thompson, were elected for the Western District. "The court then determined to elect two additional constables; and Morgan Wynn and James Witten were elected."

"It appearing to the satisfaction of the Court, that William Brooks, deceased, was a Revolutionary pensioner, that he departed this life on the 24th day of January, 1841, leaving his widow, Anna Brooks, and the following being all his heirs and legal representatives, to-wit, John Brooks, William Brooks, Richard Brooks, Thomas Brooks, James Brooks, Margaret Kirk, Elizabeth Stephenson, Nancy Clyburn, Sally Todd, Polly Brooks and Louise Asberry, it is ordered that the same be certified."

"It appearing to the satisfaction of the Court, that Low Brown, dec'd, was a Revolutionary pensioner, that he departed this life on the 28th day of January, 1841, leaving no widow, and the following being all his heirs and legal representatives, to-wit, Polly Brown, the widow of Isaac Brown, dec'd, and ———————— heirs of said Isaac Brown, dec'd, Polly Harman, John Brown, Martha Peery, William Brown, Andrew D. Brown, Sally Belcher, George D. Brown, Joseph Brown, Low Brown, Jr., Cynthia McGranahan, Jane Kendall and Elizabeth Kendall, it is ordered that the same be certified."

July T. Appointed Isaac M. Benham a constable in the Eastern district.

Isaac M. Benham appointed deputy for Ambrose Hall, Sheriff of the county.

William P. Wynn qualified as Coroner for the county during good behavior.

Sept. T. "John J. Greever, this day produced credentials of his ordination and also of his being in regular communion with the Lutheran Church, took the oath of allegiance to this Commonwealth and with Thomas Peery, George Spracher and John B. Floyd, his securities, entered into and acknowledged a bond in the penalty of $1500.00 conditioned as the law directs: whereupon, on his motion, a testimonial is granted him in due form."

James Hankins appointed Surveyor of Highway upon precinct No. 9, Western district in the room of James Brewster etc. James H. Moore and William E. Higginbothan qualified as Justices of the Peace.

William G. Williams was elected Commissioner of the Revenue for the Eastern District and Reese B. Gillespie was elected for the Western District.

Oct. T. "Ordered that it be certified that it appears to this court from satisfactory evidence, that Thomas Witten was a pensioner of the United States at the rate of $250. per annum; was a resident of this county and died in this county on the 6th day of October, 1841; that he left no widow, but the following children, to-wit, Samuel C. Witten, Elizabeth Witten, William Witten, Rebecca Graham, Linney Witten, Tabitha Davidson, John Witten, Thomas Witten, James S. Witten and the children of Hiram Witten, dec'd, who was a son of said Thomas Witten, deceased."

Dec. T. Hervey George, administrator of Christina Harman, dec'd, presented reports of the heirs of the slaves belonging to said estate, for the years 1833, 1839 & 1840, which are ordered to be recorded."

Joseph H. Wynn resigned as constable in the Eastern dist. and Gorge Cook was appointed in his stead.

Joseph Wynn qualified as Justice of the Peace.

"Eliza Jane Harman, orphan of Daniel Harman, deceased, with the approbation of the Court made choice of John Crockett to be her guardian and the said John Crockett with Kiah Harman and John B. Floyd, his security, entered into and acknowledged a bond in the penalty of 1,000. conditioned according to law."

Hez. Harman, School Commissioner in this county, this day resigned; and therefore Addison Crockett is appointed School Commissioner in his stead."

John B. Harman was chosen constable of Eastern District in the place of James T. Bane resigned.

CHAPTER XI.

COUNTY COURT LAW ORDERS FROM JANUARY 1842 TO DECEMBER, 1852.

1842

Feb. Term. Thomas Davis elected Constable in the Western District, in the place of John Lockhart, resigned.

William H. Young was appointed Constable in the Western District in the place of James Witten resigned.

William G. Williams qualified as Commissioner of the Revenue for the Eastern District.

John B. George qualified as Sheriff of the county.

Mar. T. p. 78. Robert Latham and William P. Cecil qualified to practice law in this court. John B. George qualified as Sheriff. William M. Gillespie, Thomas H. Gillespie, George P. George appointed deputies for John B. George.

Jefferson Matney, Isaac Benham and Joseph N. Nash qualified as deputies for John B. George, sheriff of this county.

Aug. T. 140. William W. Harman qualified as deputy Surveyor of the County.

William H. Minter qualified as Deputy for George W. G. Brown, Clerk of the Court.

Sept. T. James S. Vail was elected Commissioner of the Revenue for the Eastern district and Thomas Witten for the Western District.

Nov. T. John Cecil, William Barns, Samuel Witten, William Thompson, Samuel Cecil, Chapman A. Spotts, Hervey George, James C. Spotts, Addison Crockett, Ambrose Hall, Gordon C. Thorn, Erastus G. Harman, Henry Harman and George R. C. Floyd appointed School Commissioners.

Samuel W. Higginbitham was elected a Constable in the Western district.

Thomas Witten was elected Commissioner of the Revenue.

1843

March T. Wade D. Strother admitted to practice law in this Court.

Hamilton R. Bogle elected a constable in the Eastern Dist. in the place of Henry W. Dills, resigned.

May T. "The office of Attorney for the Commonwealth in this court being vacant by the resignation of Albert G. Pendleton, Esquire, on the 20th April last, John W. Johnston is by the Court appointed Attorney for the Commonwealth by the votes of all the Justices present given viva voce in open Court, and therefore the said John W. Johnson took the several oaths prescribed by law."

June T. John A. Kelly, admitted to practice law in this court.

Constables elected at this term: Hamilton R. Bogle, John B. Harman, Charles Taylor, David B. Greever, Robert R. Montague, George Cook, Waddy T. Currin, Daniel C. Harman, Morgan Wynn, and William E. Neel, assigned to the Eastern District; and Milton W. Thompson, Samuel W. Higginbotham, William B. Young, George Steele, John M. Witten, Johny Creswell, Reese B. Gillespie, Jefferson Matney, George W. Deskins, Martin Gibson, and William Cecil, assigned to the Western District. And Gordon Lambert is assigned to the Western District.

Aug. T. Ordered that the county be divided into two districts for the election of overseers of the Poor, and that an election be held on the 22nd day of this month to consist of the freeholders and householders only, for the purpose of choosing three discreet and fit persons .... to serve for three years.

Peter Honaker was elected a constable in the Eastern district in the place of Wm. E. Neel, resigned.

Daniel H. Harman elected contable in place of John Y. Creswell, resigned.

Nov. T. Chapman A. Spotts elected Commissioner of the Revenue for the Western district, and Addison Crockett for the Eastern District.

Daniel H. Harman appointed deputy for John B. George, Sheriff of this county.

1844

Feb. T. John B. George, George P. George, Thomas H. Gillespie and Reese B. Gillespie are by William M. Gillespie Sheriff, appointed his deputies.

Mar T. Joseph Nash appointed deputy for William Gillespie, Sheriff.

May T. Declaration as Revolutionary soldiers to obtain the benefit of the Act of Congress passed June 7, 1832, made by Jessee Harper, John Thompson and Hezekiah Whitt.

Daniel Harman (of Adam) made surveyor of highway, precinct No. 15, Eastern District.

June T. "Ordered that the overseers of the Poor of this County, in contracting for the keeping of the poor of this county, be not governed entirely by the consideration of saving a few dollars and cents to the county, but that they ought to be governed by the feelings of humanity, and that they should contract, with such persons for their support, as are competent to provide for them in a decent and comfortable manner."

We trust that in the same spirit of humanity, of our present and future officers, in charge of this ministry, may continue to make the comfort of our unfortunate poor, their guide in administering this trust.

July T. Twenty-four members constituted a grand jury.

Aug. T. Daniel H. Harman appointed deputy for William Gillespie, Sheriff of the county.

Oct. T. James S. Vail elected Commissioner of the Revenue for Eeastern district and Thomas Witten, Jr., in the Western District.

Nov. T. "William Gillespie, Hervey George and Thomas Peery are by the Court recommended to the Executive of this Commonwealth as suitable persons to execute the office of Sheriff of this county, by votes of all the Justices present, given viva voce in open court."

1845

Jan. T. Archibald Hedrick appointed constable in the place of Robert Montague, resigned, in the Eastern District.

Feb. T. William Gillespie qualified as sheriff of the county and the following deputy sheriffs were appointed: Thomas H. Gillespie, Reese B. Gillespie, John W. Gillespie, Robert Barns, George P. George, Joseph N. Nash and Daniel H. Harman. William B. Aston qualified to practice law in this court.

April T. Samuel Cecil appointed guardian of Cecil heirs named: Samuel W., Nancy, J., Julia A., Witten A., and Russell F. Cecil.

Peter H. Dills and Waddy T. Currin appointed deputies for William Gillespie, sheriff of this county.

Certain persons appointed as Commissioners to superintend the approaching elections in this county, at the various precincts as follows:

At Court House: William Cox, Samuel Cecil, Hervey G. Peery, Thomas S. Carnahan, and John Wynn.

At Peter Dills: James C. Davidson, Stephen Gose, Gordon C. Thorn, James M. Compton, and Mark R. Bogle.

At Burks Garden: George Spracher, Ambrose Hall, Thomas Peery, John Thompson and James S. Vail.

At Charles Tiffany's: Erastus G. Harman, Howard Bane, Charles F. Tiffany, Henry P. McDowell and John Harry.

At Shadrach White's: Shadrach White, William Brown, Chapman A. Spotts, William Blankenship and Samuel Cecil.

At the Mouth of the Slate: Joseph Looney, Elijah Vance, Richard Ratcliff, Benjamine Cox and Martin Gibson.

William Cox reported the amount raised by this county for the construction of the Cumberland Gap and Price's Turnpike $6462.22 and that all had been raised but $175.00 which amt. Cox was directed to borrow.

The cost of the Cumberland Gap and Price's Turnpike through this county was certified to be $16,155.33-1/3 of which the county has paid two-fifths of the entire cost.

Alexander McClanahan elected Constable in the place of Martin Gibson, resigned.

Apr. T. Hamilton R. Bogle appointed a constable in the Eastern district in place of John M. Witten, resigned

"Ezekial Holly, a free man of color, having been registered by the Clerk of this court as the law requires, to-wit; the said Ezekial Holly, who was registered on this day and numbered 4, is twenty nine years of age, of a clear yellow color, 5 feet 10-3/4 inches in stature, born free, and has no particular marks, stout built; wherefore the court doth certify that the said register has been duly made."

"William Holly, a free man of color, who has been registered by the Clerk of this court as the Law requires, to-wit: the said

William Holly, who was registered on this day and numbered 5 is twenty seven years of age, of a clear yellow color, five feet and nine ¾ inches in stature, born free, and has the following marks, sears, etc., to-wit: A small scar under the left eye, and a scar on the third finger of the left hand, and stout built; whereupon the Court doth certify that said register has been duly made."

July T. Isaac Chapman qualified as deputy for George W. G. Browne, Clerk of the county.

"Ordered that the County be laid off into nine districts and that one constable be appointed in each district, except in the fifth district in the Western Battalion in which there shall be two." Then follows the ten constables elected: David B. Greever, Peter Honaker, John B. Harman, Waddy T. Currin, John W. Gillespie, Milton W. Thompson, Hamilton R. Bogle, Samuel Cecil, Jr., Daniel H. Harman and Isom Collins.

Archibald Maloney, a Revolutionary pensioner died on the 21st day of February, 1840, which was certified by the court on motion of his widow, Rachel Maloney.

"Kiah Harman come into court and resigned his office of Escheator."

"Moses Hankins, James Hankins, Hugh S. Bailey, Milton Hankins and William Anderson came into court and agreed to construct fences for Ebenezer Brewster which was made necessary to be built on account of the construction of a public road from said Brewster's to said Anderson's mill." This is now known as Graybeal's Mill at Maxwell.

John B. George appointed a deputy for William Gillespie, Sheriff.

Thomas Peery appointed constable in place of Waddy T. Currain, resigned.

Geo. F. Holmes admitted to practice law in this court.

Aug. T. Kiah Harman, under commission of the Governor of the Commonwealth, qualified as Surveyor of the County for the term of seven years.

Henry D. Harman appointed deputy surveyor for the county.

David Muncy, a Methodist Minister, authorized to celebrate the rites of matrimony.

Joseph Moore appointed Commmissioner of the Revenue for the Eastern District and William B. Young for the Western District.

Jefferson Matney appointed constable in the Western District in place of Samuel W. Cecil resigned.

1846

Jan. T. Samuel W. Higginbotham appointed constable in the Western district in place of Stephen Henderson, resigned.

Wm. E. Neel is authorized to celebrate the rites of matrimony, as it has been represented to this court that no ordained minister of the Gospel is convenient on the Clear Fork in this county.

Feb. T. Peter Honaker qualified as deputy for Harvey George, Sheriff of this county.

Apr. T. James W. M. Witten, David B. Greever, John B. Harman and Samuel W. Higginbotham qualified as deputies for Harvey George, Sheriff of the county.

May T. Stirling F. Watts qualified to practice law in this court.

Under the Act releasing the right of the Commonwealth's interest in the Cumberland Gap road, the same was officially recognized by the court.

Daniel H. Harman appointed Deputy for Harvey George, Sheriff of this county.

Jessee Harper's additional evidence of claim as a Revolutionary soldier.

July T. Samuel W. Austin qualified as Deputy for Kiah Harman, Surveyor of the county.

Sept. T. William McDonald elected by the Justices present for Commissioner of the Revenue for the Eastern District and Chapman A. Spotts elected as Commissioner of the Revenue for the Western District.

Dec. T. John H. Peery appointed constable in the place of Thomas Peery, resigned, in the Eastern Battalion of this county.

John C. Gillespie appointed constable in the place of Jefferson Matney, resigned.

1847

Jan. T. "Ordered that Joseph Hankins be appointed Surveyor of the highway on Precinct No. 43 from Henry Pattinson's to Moses Hankins' bars."

Feb. T. Hervey George commissioned by the Governor, qualified as Sheriff of the county.

William O. George appointed deputy for Hervey George, Sheriff; also Daniel H. Harman, John B. Harman, Hamilton R. Bogle, Samuel W. Higginbotham, David B. Greever and Peter Dills qualified as deputy Sheriffs.

June T. Constables elected by the acting Justices present were as follows: David B. Greever, Alexander Mahood, Peter C. Honaker, Samuel P. Davidson, John B. Harman, Waddy T. Currin, Henry Gillespie, James W. Morton, Samuel W. Higginbotham, Rees Steel, James Thompson, John Allen, John A. Brown, Jefferson Matney, Hamilton R. Bogle, John M. Witten, Daniel H. Harman and David Matney.

Archibald Maloney, a Revolutionary pensioner, died on Feb. 21st, 1840, was duly certified.

John H. Peery elected a constable and assigned to the 4th district in the Eastern Battalion.

Peter C. Honaker qualified as constable.

July T. George Frederick Holmes, having complied with the requirements of the Act of Congress of the United States .... is admitted as a citizen of the United States, having renounced allegiance to Queen Victoria.

Alexander Mahood qualified as a constable.

Sept. T. "Herrmann Leopold Moss, heretofore a subject of Leopold the 1st, Grand Duke of the Grand Duchy of Baden, Germany, this day appeared personally in Court and presented an authenticated copy from the Records of the Court of Pleas and Quarter Sessions of the County of Guilford in the State of North Carolina, under the seal of that court, showing that at the February term 1844, of said Court of Pleas and Quarter Sessions for said County of Guilford, he the said Herrmann Leopold Moss, on his oath declared his intention to become a citizen of the United States, and renounced and abjured allegiance and fidelity to every foreign Prince, Potentate, State or Sovereignty whatever and particularly to the said Grand Duke of the Grand Duchy of Baden, in Germany; and that he would support the Constitution of the United States."

"And it appearing to this Court that the said Herrmann Leopold Moss, has resided for at least five years last past, continuously in the United States, and at least one year in this Commonwealth.......... It is therefore declared by this Court that the said Herrmann Leopold Moss, having complied with the requirements of the Act of Congress .... he is admitted a citizen of the United States."

John Thomas, Jesse R. Justice, James M. Compton, Robert C. Graham, William Brown, Bartlett Rose, John Breeding and Archibald Thompson qualified as Justices of the Peace for this county.

Thirty-seven Justices noted present at this term, who were summoned to take action on the application of Mathews, a free man of Color, late a slave and the property of Elijah King and emancipated by his last will, for leave to stay within the Commonwealth. The Justices elected unanimously the said permission be given, upon the proof that the said Mathews "is a person of good character, peaceable, orderly and industrious and not addicted to drunkenness, gaming or any other vice." He was not only allowed to remain in the Commonwealth but permitted to reside in this county. The population of the county might be greatly reduced if only those who can prove such a character as Mathews, were permitted to reside therein.

Addison Crockett was elected Commissioner of the Revenue for the Eeastern district, and James W. Thompson for the Western district.

"The church near here having been destroyed by fire, it is ordered that the Court House may be used as a place of public worship till the 1st day of January next.

Oct. T. Shadrach White qualified as a Justice of the Peace

Martha Elizabeth Hawkins, John R. Hawkins and William F. Hawkins, orphans of ——————— Hawkins, made choice of James W. M. Witten as their guardian.

1848

Feb. T. Thomas Peery qualified as Sheriff of the county.

Mar. T. Calvin M. McCarty, Hamilton R. Bogle, William E. Peery and Joseph N. Nash qualified as deputies for Thomas Peery, Sheriff.

Charles F. Tiffany elected Overseer of the Poor.

Martin Gibson elected constable in the place of Daniel Matney.

John McVaughlin a Revolutionary pensioner died February 17th, 1848, leaving his widow, Judith, was certified by the court.

Daniel H. Harman qualified as deputy Sheriff.

Waddy T. Currin and Hervey G. Dillion qualified as deputy Sheriffs.

Apr. T. Peter C. Honaker is appointed deputy Sheriff for Thomas Peery, Sheriff.

May T. Samuel W. Cecil qualified to practice law in this court.

June T. Casper, a free man of color, who had been emancipated by the last will of Adam Harman, was duly registered as the law requires.

James Barrett, a native of Ireland, declared his intention to become a citizen of the United States and renounced all allegiance to any foreign Prince, Potentate, State or Sovereignty and particularly to Queen Victoria, queen of the United Kingdom of Great Brittain and Ireland.

Gilbert Peery elected constable in the place of John M. Peery, resigned.

Aug. T. Reuben C. Fudge was granted leave to make the brick for paving the streets of Jeffersonville on the public ground, north of the jail.

Sept. T. William R. Bane elected Commissioner of the Revenue for the Eastern district and Reese B. Gillespie for the Western district.

Nov. T. Rees T. Bowen, Ephriam G. Repass, Thomas J. Higginbotham, William M. Gillespie, James W. M. Witten, Addison A. Spotts, Archibald Thompson, Hamilton R. Bogle, Addison Crockett, David Peery, Charles F. Tiffany, James M. Compton and James Davis elected School Commissioners in this county for the ensuing year.

1849

Feb. T. Thomas Peery qualified as Sheriff of this county; Daniel H. Harman, Hamilton R. Bogle, James W. M. Witten, Calvin M. McCarty and Joseph N. Nash qualified as his deputies.

Mar. T. Susannah King emancipated several slaves who were duly registered.

May T. James H. Harman and John B. Harman appointed constables.

"James Bourne, a native of England, this day declared on oath it is his bone fida intention to become a citizen of the United States and to renounce forever all allegiance and fidelity to any foreign

Prince, or Potentate, State or Sovereignty whatever, and particularly to Victoria, Queen of the United Kingdom of Great Brittain and Ireland."

June T. Ordered that the county subscribe to the stock of the Tazewell Court House and Fancy Gap turnpike, etc.

Casper, a free man of color, who was emancipated by Adam Harman, by his will, having shown his good character, was admitted to reside in the county.

John B. Harman, Daniel C. Harman, Henry Gillespie, Alexander Mahood, Stephen S. Taylor, Andrew Baldwin, John Allen, William Anderson, George W. Deskins, Daniel H. Harman, Martin Gibson, John Brown, Ephriam G. Repass, Samuel P. Davidson, Peter C. Honaker, Harvey P. Witten, Samuel W. Higginbotham and Resin R. Steel, were elected constables of this county.

On account of the destitution of persons to celebrate the rites of matrimony in some parts of the county, George Gibson and Thomas P. Lambert are authorized to perform said rites.

Aug. T. Rees B. Gillespie appointed deputy for George W. G. Browne Clerk of this court.

Madison S. Crockett qualified to practice law in this court

John B. Harman qualified as deputy for Thomas Peery, Sheriff

Sept. T. Elias G. W. Harman and James H. Peery were elected Commissioners of the Revenue for the county.

"Ordered that the Sheriff summon all the Justices of the County to attend here on the first day of the next term, to take into consideration the application of Henry, Amy, Cosby Ann, Elizabeth, Ellan & Louisa, free persons of color, late slaves, the property of Susannah King, dec'd. & emancipated by her last will & testament, for leave to remain in the Commonwealth."

Joseph C. Brown was elected School Commissioner in the place of William M. Gillespie, resigned.

Oct. T. Martin Gibson qualified as deputy for Thomas Peery, Sheriff.

Nov. T. Upon application of Alexander St. Clair, a road was ordered to be viewed from his mill to the Court House.

1850

Feb. T. William Thompson qualified as Sheriff of the county, and Hamilton R. Bogle, John W. Gillespie, John B. Harman and Joseph N. Nash qualified as his deputies.

Noah B. Bruce qualified as constable.

Mar. T. James T. Bane, Ephriam G. Repass, Gustavus R. Crockett and George W. Payne qualified as deputies for William Thompson Sheriff.

Re-assessment of lands ordered and Charles H. Greever and Archibald Thompson were elected assessors.

Daniel H. Harman qualified as deputy Sheriff.

Reuben C. Fudge, Addison A. Spotts and John A. Kelly applied for permission to erect gates on the new road from Tazewell Court House to St. Clair mill, which was allowed.

May T. Henry Bowen's will probated. Rees T. and Henry E. Bowen, Executors.

June T. Charles Mitchell authorized to celebrate the rites of matrimony, on account of the destitution of preachers in some parts of the county.

"Ordered that the Sheriff collect from each tithable .81¼c for the purpose of defraying the expense of the county, and .43¾c for the support of the poor and 25c on the amount of revenue paid by each tax payer in the county, for the construction of the Fancy Gap Road."

Aug. T. Henry Gillespie and Samuel C. Crockett elected Commissioners of the Revenue for the county.

1851

Apr. T. Hamilton R. Bogle, John B. Harman and Daniel H. Harman qualified as deputies for William Thompson, Sheriff.

Ordered an election be held to take the sense of the voters on making a subscription to the Raleigh and North Carolina road.

May T. James H. Gilmore qualified to practice law in this county.

S. Dolsbery, a pensioner, died Aug. 2, 1850. He left no widow nor children.

Archibald T. Hedrick elected a constable.

Robert Barnes, Joseph N. Nash and Henry A. Yost qualified as deputies for William Thompson, Sheriff.

Ordered that the sense of the voters be taken on the proposition to subscribe $4,000 to the stock of the Tazewell Court House and Saltville Turnpike and $1,000 to the Raleigh and North Carolina Turnpike, according to the provision of the law.

July T. Isaac N. Naff authorized to celebrate the rites of matrimony.

At this term the following constables were elected: Samuel P. Davidson, Peter C. Honaker, Archibald T. Hedrick, Alexander Mahood, John B. Harman, Hervey E. Dillion, Noah Bruce, Daniel H. Gillespie, John Allen, Harvey P. Witten, William B. Goodwin, Samuel W. Higginbotham, Rees Steel, George W. Deskins, William Anderson, Ephriam G. Repass, Jefferson Matney, Frederick Stiltner, George W. Payne and Daniel H. Harman.

Robert Gillespie qualified as deputy for William Thompson, Sheriff.

Oct. T. James C. Davidson elected a director of the Raleigh and North Carolina Turnpike Company.

William J. Crutchfield qualified as deputy sheriff.

Alexander Mahood qualified to practice law in this court.

Dec. T. William H. Maxwell qualified to practice law in this court.

1852

Feb. T. Edwin H. Harman, an infant above the age of fourteen years nominated Henry B. Harman to be his guardian; and the Court appointed said Henry B. Harman guardian of Elvira, Martha Ann, Olivia, Robert, Howard Bane, and Charles Creigh Harman, infant orphans of Erastus G. Harman, deceased; and said guardian executed bond in the penalty of $20,000, conditioned according to law.

June T. Kiah Harman qualified as Surveyor of the county for a term of six years from the 1st day of July next.

July T. Henry D. Harman, Hez. A. Harman and Thomas Davis are by Kiah Harman, Surveyor of this county, appointed his deputies.

Samuel C. Graham, who has been duly elected Clerk of this Court for the term of six years from and after the 1st day of July, instant, qualified as such Clerk.

William B. Harman elected Commissioner of the Revenue.

On motion of John W. Gillespie, Sheriff of this county, John Allen qualified as his deputy.

Sept. T. John B. George chosen by a vote of the Justices present, to be the Presiding Justice. The said Justices directed that they be classified into seven classes for the performances of their duties, and assigned certain Justices to hold the monthly terms of the Court, alternating the Justices and designating four for each term of the Court.

Ordered an election held for electing Justices and Constables in the several districts.

"Ordered that Louisa Cousins, James C. Cousins and Charley Earley (or Easley), free persons of color be allowed to register in the Clerk's Office of this Court and that the Clerk certify the same."

Dec. T. Charles Taylor and Robert H. Taylor qualified as deputy sheriffs.

William Terry admitted to practice law in this court.

John D. Vincil authorized to celebrate the rites of matrimony.

CHAPTER XII.

JUSTICES OF THE PEACE FOR TAZEWELL COUNTY FROM 1800 TO 1852.

David Ward, Henry Bowen and David Hanson, formerly Justices of Russell County; and George Peery, Robert Wallace, William Neel and Samuel Walker, formerly Justices of Wythe County, by operation of law, became the County Court of the newly formed County of Tazewell, because of their residence in that part of the territory of said counties respectively, which was embraced within the lines of the new county. Justices thereafter qualified as follows:

Oct. 1800: Joseph Davidson, Thomas Witten, John Thompson, Hezekiah Whitt, Thomas Gillespie, Hezekiah Harman, Henry Harman, Jr.

Nov. 1809: John Cecil, and John Laird, Isaac Brown, (Dec.) William Taylor.

Jan. 1810: John Wynn.

Apr. 1814: Peter Gose, Thomas Harrison and Ambrose Hall

Jan. 1816: William Smith *Feb. 1816:* John B. George

Sept. 1820: William Gillespie, Harvey George, Thomas Peery, William Williams.

Oct. 1820: John Davidson. *Nov. 1820:* William Thompson, Junr.

Dec. 1820: Philip Lambert, James C. Davidson

Jan. :1821: James S. Witten, William Barnes

Apr. 1822: Ephriam Dunbar.

Feb. 1832: George W. Messick, Samuel P. Davidson, William Cox.

Apr. 1832: Hugh Tiffany, Jr.

July 1832: William T. Moore, Samuel Witten.

Apr. 1834: Bird Lockhart

May 1834: Cornelius White

Dec. 1834: John W. Read, Joseph Looney

Sept. 1835: C. A. Spotts.

Mar. 1837: Erastus G. Harman, Alexander Harrison, James C. Spotts, Thomas S. Carnahan, Hervey G. Peery.

Mar. 1839: Edward Collins.

June 1841: George R. C. Floyd, James S. Vail, Charles H. Greever.

Sept. 1841: William E. Higginbotham, John J. Greever, Gordon C. Thorn, James H. Moore.

Dec. 1841: Joseph H. Wynn

Sept. 1847: John Thomas, Jesse R. Justice, James M. Compton, William McDonald, Henry H. Harman, Charles Taylor, Granville Jones, Edward R. Baylor, Robert C. Graham, Isaac M. Benham, Archibald Thompson, Thomas J. Higginbotham, William Brown, Shadrach White, Thomas Davis, Bartlett Rose, Elias C. Harman, Elijah Vance, John Breeding, Thomas K. Lambert.

CHAPTER XIII.

SUPERIOR COURT OF LAW; ORDERS FROM MAY 1809 TO JUNE 1831.

1809

May Term of the Superior Court of Law.

"At a Superior Court of Law appointed by law to be holden at Tazewell Court House on the first Monday after the fourth Monday in April.

Present, the Honorable William Brockenbrough one of the Judges of the General Court allotted to the thirteenth Judicial Circuit.

"Ordered that the appointment of John Crockett, Clerk of the County Court of Tazewell to the Office of the Clerk of the Superior Court of said County be confirmed ...." and said Crockett entered into bond in the sum of ten thousand dollars with Henry Bowen, Hezekiah Harman, William Taylor, James Peery, Thomas Peery and David French his sureties, conditioned according to law"

Henley Chapman and James Thompson, gentlemen, qualified to practice law in this court

Ordered that James Thompson, Gentleman, Attorney at Law, be appointed to prosecute on behalf of the Commonwealth in this Court"

The first Grand Jury Empanelled:

"William Taylor, Foreman, John Laird, James Witten, William Ward, William Thompson, James Moore, James Peery, Robert Doak, Joseph Moore, Thomas Peery, William Brooks, Isaac Brown, David Peery, Audley Maxwell, James Maxwell, William Witten, Andrew Peery, David Ward, William Peery and Hezekiah Harman."

"William Cecil and William Neel who were summoned hear this day as Grand Jurors, were solemnly called but came not, therefore it is considered by the Court that for their said contempt they make their fine, with his Excellency, John Tyler, Esq. Governor or Chief Magistrate of the Commonwealth, and his successor, by the payment of eight Dollars each, to the use of the Commonwealth, unless sufficient cause of their inability to attend, be shown at this or the next Court."

"At a Superior Court of Law Continued and held for Tazewell on 2nd day of May, 1809 (See p. 3, Order Book)

"Ordered that John Crockett, Clerk of the Superior Court of Tazewell County be allowed fifteen dollars for his services on behalf of the Commonwealth during this term, and that the same be certified to the Auditor of Public Accounts."

"Ordered that James Thompson, Prosecutor for the Commonwealth in this Court be allowed for two days attendance during this term the sum of ten dollars. . . ."

"Ordered that Henry Bowen, Sheriff of the County, be allowed ten Dollars for his services on behalf of the Commonwealth during this term. . . ."

"Ordered that this Court adjourn until the first day of the next term."   "W. BROCKENBROUGH"

1809

Oct. Term Second Grand Jury Empaneled:

"Hezekiah Harman, Foreman, Thomas Witten, Nathaniel Young, David Harrison, James Maxwell, John Peery, David, Whitley, Thomas Peery, Sr., George Steel, David Robinson, Jacob Francisco, Abednego White, Philip Gose, Ambrose Hall, John Lasley, David Young, Abram Davis, John Thompson, John Davis, (Carpenter) Daniel Waggoner."

William Neel and William Cecil appeared in Court and gave their excuse for not appearing as Grand Jurors at the first term and the fines were remitted.

Andrew McHenry qualified to practice law in this court.

1810

Sept. T. Names of Grand Jurors at this term: William Taylor, Joseph Davidson, John Lasley, Isaac Brown, John Peery, John Wynn, William Hall, Howard Bane, Hezekiah Harman, James Maxwell, Sr., John Bailey, Samuel Shannon, Samuel C. Witten, Mose Workman, Lewis Vencel, Bird Lockhart, Ambrose Hall, John Davis (Big), Henry Bowen, Thomas Gillespie, Philip Gose, John Cecil, John Laird and Oliver Wynn.

David Hanson, Sheriff of the County.

A defendant who was charged with offering Sheriff one dollar to summon certain persons on the Jury to try him, and was being questioned by the Court as to the truth of the charge, said he had a troublesome set of people to deal with and he only wanted good men to serve on the Jury that tried him, and further said that he had seen some juries in Tazewell that he did not consider good ones, and further said he intended no contempt of Court by his said acts. He admitted saying to the Sheriff "that I would not begrudge him a dollar if he would summon such men as he suggested." The Judge not being fully satisfied with the explanation fined him $10.00.

Hon. Peter Johnson was designated to hold the next Court.

1811

Apr. T. Present, Hon. Peter Johnston, one of the Judges of the General Court allotted to the 13th Judicial Circuit.

On Grand Jury: Reese Bowen, Peter Gose, Charles Young, Hugh Wilson, Moses Higginbotham, Robert Higginbotham, Isaac Johnston, William Dills and John Griffith, together with several others who served on the Grand Jury at the last term of this Court.

Sept. T. Names of Grand Jurors: David Ward, Foreman, John Ward, Wm. Taylor, Joseph Davidson, John Thompson, Hugh Wilson, Isaac Brown, John Bailey, Hezekiah Harman, Elias Harman, William Harman, James Moore, Thomas Peery, John Lasley, Samuel Lusk, Thomas Allen, Reese Bowen, George Rineheart, Henry Bowen, John Cecil and William Ward.

William Smith qualified to practice law in this court. Lewis Amiss qualified to practice law in this court.

Names of the petit Jury at this term: Absolem Young, Henry Harman, John Stobaugh, Robert Ward, Joseph Hankins, Thomas Cassaday, Thomas Harrison, Reese Thompson, Moses Higginbotham, Martin Peery, John Davis and Charles Young.

1812

Apr. T. Names of Petit jurors: Richard Brooks, Thomas Owens, John Davis (little), David Peery, Buse Harman, Samuel Peery, George Peery, Henry Harman, James Maxwell, Jr., Lewis Vincel, Moses Hankins and William Davis.

Joseph Moore qualified as deputy for John Crockett, Clerk of the Court.

Sept. T. "Ordered that William Hall, Sheriff of the County, be allowed ten dollars for his public services for the preceeding six months."

1813

Sept. T. Hon. Peter Randolph, presiding.

"Ordered that the following officers be paid the several amounts for their services, viz: John Crockett for last twelve months, $30.00, Wm. Smith, Atto. for the Commonwealth, for two days service at this term, $10.00; William Hall, Sheriff, for services the preceeding twelve months, $20,00 and that John B. George, jailer, be allowed for his services during the preceeding year, $20,00."

1816

April T. Present, Hon. Peter Johnston, Presiding.
Alexander Smith qualified to practice law in this court.
Ordered that Alexander Smith, Gent. be appointed prosecutor on behalf of the Commonwealth in this court.

1817

April T. James Campbell qualified to practice law in this court.
Special July Term. Benjamine Estill, Gent. appointed to prosecute for the Commonwealth.
Charles C. Johnston qualified to practice law in this court

1818

Sept. T. David McComas qualified to practice law in this court. A Venireman was fined $30.00 for having a conversation with a person charged with felony, after being summoned on the venire for the trial of said person, the amount later reduced to $5.00.
John Peery, Sheriff of the County now.

1820

March T. Jacob T. Fishback appointed deputy Clerk to this court.
Joseph Davidson, Sheriff of this County.

1821

April T. James E. Brown qualified to practice law in this court.
Sept. T. Thomas Witten, Sheriff, allowed compensation for his services.

1822

Sept. T. William Smith and Henry J. Fisher qualified to practice law in this court.

1823

April T. Silas M. Stilwell appointed deputy Clerk for this court.

1824

Mar. T. John H. Fulton and Harold Smith qualified to practice law in this court.

Aug. T. John Thompson serves as Sheriff at this term.

1826

Aug. T. David McComas appeared as Prosecuting Attorney, etc. Hezekiah Whitt appears as Sheriff at this term.

1828

Apr. T. Thomas Gillespie appears as Sheriff of the courts. Robert Gillespie deputy for Thomas Gillespie, Sheriff.

1829

Feb. T. William W. King and Albert G. Pendleton qualified to practice law in this court.

1830

Feb. T. Hezekiah Harman, Sheriff of this County, etc.

1831

June T. Joseph Draper, Charles C. Johnston, David McComas, Thomas O'Neil, Charles E. Harrison, Geo. W. Hopkins, A. G. Pendleton, James F. Pendleton and Joseph Stras, qualified to practice law in this court.

Charles E. Harrison appointed to prosecute in this court on behalf of the Commonwealth.

From an examination of the records of Order Book No. 1, for the Superior Court of Law and Chancery from 1809 to 1831, it appears that no special public matters are noted, as most of such matters have been previously chronicled from the records of the County Court.

CHAPTER XIV.

A Few Genealogies Shown in First Chancery Order Book—1832 to 1855.

1832

April T. This Term began in 1st Law Order Book.
Hon. B. Estill, Judge Presiding.
"At a Circuit Superior Court of Law & Chancery," etc.

1834

April T. Mathias Harman Jr.   Complt
        vs.   Amended Bill p. 12 Cont. p. 17.
Mathias Harman, Senr and Wm. McGuire

Sept. T. Samuel Laird   Complt.
    vs.   page 25
Harman's Representative   Deft.

1835

James Peery & wife
    vs.   Leave to file Bill. Decree pp 60-61
Harman's Heirs

James Peery and Nancy his wife & James P. Harman
    vs.   Decree pp. 60-61
Jane Harman, widow of Mathias Harman, decd

"The defendants Jane, the widow & Rebecca, Matilda, Margaret, Lavisy and Daniel C. Harman, children and heirs of the said Mathias Harman decd. severally filed their answers and James M., Mathias B., and John B. Harman infant children of the said Mathias Harman, deceased filed their answers, by" etc.

Commissioners were appointed to lay off Dower and make partition etc. of slaves etc.

1836

Hezekiah Harman et al   Complts
vs.
Christina Harman   Deft

Sent to Wythe County for trial as the Judge had been interested in the case. Later remanded to Greenbrier County.

1841

Mathias Harman vs. Harman & McGuire—Dismissed Memo: For Genealogy of Tazewell Records: Chy.

- Margaret Day & als vs. Adam Waggoner & als 1844, Chy. O. B. p. 166—See for several pages of heirs at law of *Jacob Waggoner Senr., dec'd*. A deed dated December 25th, 1828, from Jacob Waggoner Senior to Gideon Wright is set aside, and the lands partitioned to numerous persons. Jacob Waggoner died March 15th, 1830, leaving as his heirs at law the following: John Martin and Susanah his wife, who was his sister of the half blood; Margaret Day, his sister of the whole blood; Joshua Day, Peter Day, Travis Day and Rebecca his wife of Fannin, the children of Hames Day and ————, his wife, decd, his sister of the whole blood; Christina, the wife of Thomas Walker; Robert Neel and Nancy his wife, Rhoda Lambert, Adam Waggoner, Jacob Waggoner, Philip Lambert and Sally his wife, Robert Neel and Rebecca his wife, Gideon Wright and Nelly his wife, Randolph Holbrook and Mary, his wife, Hampton Foster and Jemima, his wife, children and heirs of Daniel Waggoner, deceased, who was his brother of the whole blood, Elias Waggoner, ———— Stafford and Margaret his wife, Adam Waggoner, Elizabeth Waggoner and Hiram Waggoner, children and heirs of George Waggoner, decd. who was his brother of the full blood, the unknown heirs of David Waggoner, deceased, who was his brother of the full blood; ———— Dun and Christina, his wife who was sister of the full blood; ———— Pence and Nancy his wife who was his sister of the full blood; ———— Stobach and ————, his wife, who was sister of the whole blood; and the three last mentioned sisters of the said Jacob Waggoner Senr. and their husbands towit: ———— Dunn and Christina his wife; ———— Pence and Nancy, his wife; and ———— Stobach and ————, his wife having removed from the County to parts unknown many years prior to his death etc., they are allowed seven years in which to assert their claim to their part of the estate.

1848

James Peery   Complainant
     vs.   In Cancery—Partition
Peery's heirs & als   Defts.
For a list of heirs at law, see p. 251

Noah Bruce & Wife   Complt.
     vs.   In Chancery—Partition
James Whitley's widow & others   Defts.
See page 253 for list of heirs.

1849

Polly Brown   Complainant
     vs.   Chy. O. B. p. 268
William Brown & Als.   Defendants.
Partition of lands among a long list of heirs etc.

1854

(William Williams died in 1853.)

Moses Asberry had instituted a chy. suit vs. him, which, on page 359, Chy. O. B. seems to have been revived vs. Julius C. Williams. The latter, we suppose, was the son of Wm. Williams.

1855

William Williams heirs among whom his estate was divided:
Mara A., Titus V., Marcus A., Cyrus, Patrick, and Margaret Williams, infants, and Louisa B. Williams.

CHAPTER XV.

GENEALOGY OF TAZEWELL FAMILIES AS SHOWN BY WILLS—WILL BOOKS NUMBERS 1, 2 AND 3.

From 1800 to 1852.

JAMES WALL. Will probated Sept. 2nd, 1800. Will Book No. 1, p. 1. Devises his property to his wife, Catherine, his sons, James, David and John; and to his daughters, Barbara, Peggy, Ruth, Nelly, Mary and Lydia.

JOHN DESKINS. Will probated Aug. 13th, 1801. Will B. No. 1, p. 4. Devises his property to his wife, Mary.

BENJAMINE ONEY. Will probated Aug. 13th, 1801. Book 1, p. 5. Devises his property to his sons, Richard, Joseph, William, and Edward; to his sons-in law, Stapleton and Obadiah Pain.

ROBERT EVANS. Will probated Feb 11th, 1802. W. B. No. 1, p. 10. Devises his property to his wife, Mary; his sons, James, Thomas, William, Robert, David and Moses; to his daughters, Jereta Outhocess, Martha Ommer and Dorothy Blead.

ROBERT BELCHEE. Will probated May 13th, 1802. W. B. No. 1, p. 12. Devises his property to his wife, Mary; to his daughters, Elizabeth and Pheby; to his sons, Robert, David, Thomas, Richard, Joshua and Joseph. Thomas Gillespie and Henry Bowen Executors.

ROBERT BARNS. Will probated June 10th, 1802. W. B. No. 1, p. 15. Devises his property to his wife, Grace; his sons William and John; his son-in-law, John Goodwin. (William and John both under 21 years of age). Charles Young and Hugh Wilson, Executors.

ROBERT WHITLEY. Will probated July 15th, 1802. W. B. No. 1, p. 16. Devises his property to his wife, Jane; his granddaughter, Nancy and grand-son, William; to his daughters, Mary Wynne, Jane Brooks, Sarah Wynne; to his son, David. David Whitley and Josiah Wynne, his son-in-law, Executors.

MARY DESKINS. Will probated Sept 16th, 1802. W. B. No. 1, p. 21. Devises to her three sons, John, Smith and Stephen.

WILLIAM GENT. Will probated Nov. 15th, 1804. W. B. No. 1, p. 34. Devises his property to his sons, Kuziah, Mark, Jushua, William and Josiah; to his daughter Eleanor.

WILLIAM WYNNE, SR. Will probated July 26th 1808. W. B. 1, p. 42. Devises his property to his wife, Phillis; to his daughters, Ruth Washburn, Orphey Edward, Sally Janes; to his son John Wynne, and to Hugh Currin; to his sons of his first wife, viz: William, Josiah, Elkanah, Oliver and Harman; to his sons, Samuel, Robert, Harry, Peter, Miner and James, children of his 2nd wife; to his daughters Mary, Pheby, Margaret, Elizabeth, Martha, Anna and Nancy.

MARTHA KING. Will probated Feb., 1810. W. B. 1, p. 53. Devised to her sons, Elijah and Isaac; to her daughters Susanah King, Nancy McMillen, and to her grandchildren, Martha, Jane, Robert, Nancy and John McMillen and to her sister, Agnes Thompson.

GINNEY WHITLEY, Widow of Robert Whitley. Will probated July, 1812. W. B. 1, p. 67. Devises to her son, David Whitley; to her daughters, Polly Wynn, Sally Wynn and Jinney Brooks; to her grand-children, Nancy and William Whitley.

ISAIAH WYNNE. Will probated Feb., 1813. W. B. 1, p. 70. Devises his property to his wife, Mary; to his sons William, Robert, Peter, Oliver, David, Harman, and Josiah; to his daughter Jenney.

Appointed his wife, his son Robert and his son-in-law, David Whitley his executors.

SIMON CARTER. Will probated April, 1814. W. B. No. 1, p. 72. Devises his property to his wife Catherine; to his sons, John, Daniel, Samuel and Joel. He states that he had previously made provision for his other children.

JAMES BROWN. Will probated Sept., 1814. W. B. No. 1, p. 73. Devises his property to his wife, Esther; to his son William; to his daughter Elizabeth McGuire; to the children of his deceased daughter Mary Claypool; to his sons John, Thomas, James; to his daughters, Margaret, Ann, Rebecca Shortridge, Sarah Oney, Katy. He mentions his son-in-law; Joseph McGuire and William McGuire.

JAMES P. THOMPSON. Will probated April, 1814. W. B. No. 1. p. 79. Devises his property to his wife, Margaret; to his son, Patton James and to his little daughter, Catherine Shelby Thompson.

THOMAS HARRISON. Will probated Aug., 1815. W. B. No. 1, p. 85. Devises his property to his wife, Anna D. To his first wife's children, viz: John, Elizabeth—now Edea, Mary Ervin and Hannah Asberry's heirs; and to his last wife's children, that is, Joseph, Thomas, James Samuel and Eleanor.

MARGARET WAGGONER. Will probated July 28th, 1818. W. B. 1, p. 93. Devises her property to her brothers, Adam and Jacob, and to her youngest sisters, Polly and Nancy.

PETER WYNN. Will probated Nov. 24th, 1818. W. B. No. 1, p. 93. Devises his property to "My sister Peggy Currins (?) Son William . . . and to my brother John Wynn."

HENRY WYNN. Will probated Nov. 26th, 1816. W. B. No. 1, p. 97. Devises his property to his mother, Philis Wynn, and to his sisters, Polly Peery, Peggy Curren, Anna Charles, Elizabeth, Nancy Wynn, and to his father-in-law, Samuel Witten. To his brother Miner Wynn on condition that he release the land in Burk's Garden devised to him by his father, William Wynn, deceased, to be sold and the value divided betwixed John, Samuel, Robert, Peter and James Wynn and himself at the time the said Miner should come to the age of 21.

ANDREW LOCKHART. Will probated January, 1816. W. B. 1, p. 98. Devises his property to his wife Mary, and to all his children equally, viz: Sarah McGuire, William Lockhart, James Lockhart, Polly McGuire, Jane Belcher and Daniel Lockhart.

DANIEL HARMAN, SR. Will probated Jan. 25th, 1820. W. B. 1, p. 116. Devises his property as follows: To his sons Mathias, William, Daniel, Henry, Adam, Buse and to his daughters, Pheby Davidson, Christina Harman, Rebecca Wright, Nancy Milam, Levicy Harman; to his son-in-law, Adam Harman.

THOMAS PERRY. Will probated June 27th, 1820. W. B. No. 1, p. 132. Devises his property as follows: "To my two eldest sons, Johnathan and James, and to William, Thomas, Joseph, Harvey; to my two eldest daughters, Polly Peery and Nancy Helms, and to daughters Rebecca Nelly and Parmilley."

ROBERT WYNN. Will probated Aug. 25th, 1818. W. B. No. 1, p. 135. Devises his property to his wife, Levina, to his sons Joseph and William, and to his daughter Phillis.

JAMES MAXWELL. Will probated March 27th, 1821. W. B. 1, p. 137. Devises his property as follows: "To his wife Jane, his sons William and Robert, and to his daughter Mary, and to her son Maxwell Campbell; and to his four other daughters, Elizabeth, Margaret, Jane and Nancy; to his sons, John and James.

JOHN MCENTOSH. Will probated March 27, 1821. W. B. 1, p. 136. Devised his property as follows: To his sons, John, George, and his son-in-law Thomas Brewster; and to his daughters, Elizabeth, Katherine, Peggy, Polly, Anny, Nancy, Sally and Rachel.

DUDLEY YOUNG. Will probated July 24th, 1821. W. B. 1, p. 147. Devised his property as follows: To Israel Young's wife, Levicie, and Charles Young's wife, Margaret. Also to his relations, Charles Young, Israel Young, Nathaniel Young and David Young.

JAMES THOMPSON. Will probated Aug. 28th, 1821. W. B. 1, p. 149. Devises his property as follows: To his sons, James Doak Thompson, George Washington Thompson, and to his sisters, Rachel Doak, and Lydia Doak, and to his brother William Thompson and to William Thompson, son of his said brother William; also to his brother Alexander Thompson. He gives a horse each to William Mitchell and Thomas Mitchell, and also a devise to James B. Thompson, the son of Archibald Thompson. He appointed his half-brother Archibald Thompson, one of his executors.

JAMES PERRY, SR. Will probated Nov. 27th, 1821. W. B. 1, p. 151. Devises his property as follows: "I give unto my living children, that is, Nancy Bandy, Samuel Peery, Hannah Peery and Michael Peery all the money I have on hand". To his son-in-law, John Crockett a rifle gun, to his grand-son Addison Crockett, his silver watch. He also names his three grand-children, John, Rufus and Robert Crockett.

GEORGE WAGONER. Will probated June 25th, 1822. W. B. 1, p. 165. Devises his property as follows: To his sons, Elias, Adam and Highram, his daughters Rebecca, Elizabeth and Peggy.

HEINRICH (HENRY) HARMAN, SR. Will dated Feb. 18th, 1804. Probated July 23rd, 1822. Will Book No. 1, p. 167. Devises his property as follows: "First to my son, Elias; second to each of the lawful heirs of my son Daniel, deceased; thirdly to my sons, Henry, Adam, George and Hezekiah, and to my sons-in-law William Neel (husband of Rhoda) and James Davis (husband of Louisa) . . . . Fourthly, to each of the children of my son Mathias, deceased. . . ." Appoints his sons Hezekiah and Elias as Executors.

ISOME BELCHER. Will probated Jan. 28th, 1823. W. B. 1, p. 181. Devises his property as follows: To his children, Phebe, Obadiah, John, James, Nancy, Isome, Micaga, Jude, Ase, Henry, Moses, James, Johnathan and Robert. John Davidson and Henry Bailey, Executors.

WILLIAM DILLS. Will dated April 24th, 1820. W. B. 1, p. 187. Devises his property as follows: To his daughter, Gressa Smith, to his son, Peter Dills, to his daughters, Susanna Thorn and Rebecca Suiter. To his children by his present wife, to-wit: Peggy, William, Lydia, Henry, John and Benjamin Robbins. Appointed his wife Rebecca as Executrix.

PATRICK KINDRICK. Will probated Oct. 1825. W. B. 1, p. 201. Devises his property as follows: To his sons, William P. and James Q; to his daughters, Polly Clark (Formerly Kindrick), Jane Brown (formerly Kindrick), Isabelle Scott (formerly Kindrick), Elizabeth Scott (formerly Kindrick), Lydia Kindrick, Nancy Kindrick; and to his wife Elizabeth Kindrick.

HENRY ASBERRY. Will probated November, 1826. W. B. No. 1, p. 209. Devises his property as follows: To his wife Martha Asberry, to his sons, William and Jesse, and to his daughters, Polly, Jinny, Betsy and Rebecca; and to his sons Moses, Aaron, James and Thomas.

MOSES HIGGINBOTHAM. Will probated November, 1826. W. B. 1, p. 211. Devises his property as follows: To his wife Betsy; To his sons Joseph, George, Charles, William, Thomas, Moses and Aaron; also to his daughters, Frances, Jane and Rachel.

DAVID WARD. Will probated June, 1827. W. B. No. 1, p. 221. Devises his property as follows: To his wife Eleanor Ward; to his sons Isaac, Hiram, Addison and Reese; to his daughters, Jane, Nancy, Phebe and Matilda Ward.

SOLOMON JONES. Will dated December 9th, 1827. W. B. No. 1, p. 227. Devises his property as follows: To his son Juble, who is to maintain testator and his wife, Sena Jones etc. to his sons, Lewis, Harvey and John; to his three daughters, Elizabeth, Rhody and Rebecca.

REES BOWEN. Will probated March, 1828. W. B. No. 1, p. 239. Devises his property as follows: To his wife Rebecca; to his daughters, Lilly, Elizabeth, Levicie; to his brother's son, Rees T. Bowen; to his sister's sons David Ward and Reese Ward; to his nephew

Rees B. Thompson; to his niece Lilly Heldridge. . . . Henry Bowen and John Ward, Executors.

WILLIAM SHANNON. Will probated May, 1828. W. B. No. 1, p. 242. Devises his property as follows: To his wife, Margaret Shannon; to his children, Thomas, Agnes and Elizabeth.

JOHN CUMPTON, SR. Will probated June, 1828. W. B. No. 1, p. 244. Devises his property as follows: To his wife, Eleanor; to his sons, Elihu, Joseph, William, Hiram, Hickman; to his daughters, Nancy Cartmal, Rebecca Shannon, Sally.

JOHN JUSTICE. Will probated January 25th, 1830. W. B. No. 1, p. 290. Devises his property as follows: To his wife Polly; to his sons, Henderson, Daniel, Jehu, Jesse and James; and to his daughters, Jane, Ann, Nancy, Sally, Elizabeth and Manervy.

GEORGE RHINEHART. Will probated March, 1830. W. B. 1, p. 294. Devises his property as follows: To his sons, Hugh T., and John N. Rhinehart, and to his wife Patsey.

JAMES WITTEN, SR. Will probated March, 1830. W. B. 1, p. 310. Devises his property as follows: To his wife Rebecca; to his sons, Samuel, William, Thomas and James; and to his daughters, Linna Cecil, Cynthia Quinn, Eleanor Quinn, Eliza Quinn and Matilda Thompson.

HANNAH HARRISON. Will probated June, 1830. W. B. No. 1, p. 311. Devises her property as follows: To her sons, Thomas, James, Joseph, Samuel, Audly (or Adley) and Alexander; and to her daughter, Nelly Thompson; and to her grand-daughter, Hanny Thompson; and to her grand-daughter, Hannah Harrison (Thomas Harrison's daughter) and to her daughter-in-law, Polly Harrison; and to the heirs of her daughter, Mary Gillespie, deceased.

WILLIAM PEERY, SR. Will probated August, 1830. W. B. No. 1, p. 314. Devises his property as follows: To his wife, Sally; to his sons, Robert, George, Thomas, and H. F. Peery; and to his daughters, Sophia, Emily, Cosby, Polly, Nancy, Olica and Cynthia.

GEORGE PERRY. Will probated November, 1831. W. B. No. 1, p. 323. Devises his property as follows: To his wife Martha; to his nine daughters, Rebecca Thompson, Polly Gibson, Nancy Muse, Martha G. Carroll, Peggy Hall, June Witten, Elizabeth Peery, Parmala Gibson, Attila Ann Rutledge; and to his sons, Andrew and Thomas. "The tract of land on which I live I intended for my son

Joseph, but in consequence of his having traded away his Claim to Jonathan Peery, I now bequeath the said tract of land to Jonathan Peery."

JAMES CARTER. Will probated February, 1831. Will Book 1, p. 324. Devises his property as follows: To his wife Elizabeth; to his daughters, Catherine French, Rebecca French and Nancy Carter.

JOHN LAIRD. Will probated May, 1831. Will Book 1, p. 327. Devises his property as follows: To his wife, Elizabeth, to his sons, Samuel and Cornelius; and to his daughters, Jane Witten, Letty Sayers, Polly Davis and Margaret Pratt. Appointed James F. Pendleton and Thomas Davis, his son-in-law, Executors.

MICHAEL STUMP. Will probated January, 1832. Will Book 1, p. 355. Devises his property as follows: To his wife, Polly; to his son Crockett, and to his daughter Catherine.

WILL BOOK No. 2.

HOWARD HAVEN. Will probated January, 1833. W. B. 2, p. 19. Devised his property as follows: To his wife Martha and to his children, John, Matilda Whitley, wife of David Whitley, and Nancy Bane, wife of Russell Bane.

HENRY BAILEY. Will probated June, 1834. Will Book No. 2, p. 33. Devises his property as follows: To his wife, Elizabeth; to his children, John P., Philip P., Elijah, James M. and William R.

MATHIAS FOX. Will probated August, 1834. Will Book 2, p. 36. Devised his property as follows: To his wife Barbary; to his children, David S., Peggy Ana, Barbary, Mathias, Malindy, Peter Elizabeth Gose, Sally Wynn—lately Baldwin. Peter Fox and Stephen Gose, Executors.

FRED COOK. Will probated, 1834. Will Book No. 2, p. 43. Devises his property as follows: To his children, George, Elizabeth Steel, Thomas, Nancy, Zachariah and William.

ISABELLA GOSE. Will probated May, 1835. Will Book No. 2 p. 52. Devises her property as follows: To her children, Betsy and Eveline, now in the State of Indiana, and remainder to her sister, Sallie Heniger, and to the mother of testatrix.

JEREMIAH LAMBERT. Will probated July, 1835, Will Book No 2, p. 54. Devises his property as follows: To his wife, Sally, and to his grand-daughter, Delila and Sally Lambert; his grand-son

William French, and the balance to be divided among his children, Levicy French, Nancy Stowers, and Sally Lambert, wife of his son Philip. Joseph Stras, Executor.

JOHN BAILEY (of Bluestone). Will probated March 30th, 1836. W. B. 2, p. 66. Devises his property as follows: To his children, Martha Harman, Rebecca McComas, Jonathan, George, Archibald, and Mastin; and to the children of his son James, viz: John Madison, Elizabeth Virginia and Henry Buren; to his daughter-in-law, Polly Bailey, formerly the wife of his son James.

SAMUEL PERRY. Will probated September, 1836. Will Book No. 2, p. 72. Devises his property as follows: To his children, James, Mariah Gillespie (wife of Thomas Gillespie). Testator then states: "I allow my three youngest daughters to have their part" etc. but he does not mention their names. He provides for his wife but does not give her name.

SHARTON SMITH. Will probated December, 1836. Will Book No. 2, p. 86. Devises his property as follows: To his grand-daughter Rebecca Micham.

WILLIAM McGUIRE. Will probated April, 1837. Will Book No. 2, p. 99. Devises his property as follows: "To my two daughters Nancy and Pricilla . . . to my grand-daughter, Mary McGuire, of John." To his sons John, Jashua, William, Daniel Johnson, (son-in-law) Squire McGuire, Hannah Johnson, Polly Wingo, Eleanor Huckaly (or Huckaby) Rachel Lewis.

DANIEL DAY. Will probated January, 1839. Will Book No. 2, p. 127. Devises his property as follows: To his wife, Christina, and to his daughters who are not married, viz: Lucy, Edy, Christina, Malinda and Isabella; to his son James and three other sons, whom he doesn't mention by name. He does not mention the number or names of his married daughters.

MICHAEL STUMP. Will probated March, 1839. Will Book 2, p. 147. Devises his property as follows: To his wife Anna and to his children, Christopher, Tazewell, Caty Burton, Peggy Franklin and Berry (or Benny).

JOHN HENINGER. Will probated May, 1839. Will Book No. 2, p. 148. Devises his property as follows: To his wife, Sally, and to his grand-son John, son of Henry, deceased; to his grand-son William Heninger, son of his son Joseph, deceased; to his son, Solomon, to his daughter Sally Lewis' son, William Lewis; and daughter Lewisa Lewis; to his sons, Shadrach, Philemon, and Christopher; his daughters, Anna and Caty Wilson; to his sons Charles, Nicholas, and William; and to his daughter Jane Wynn.

TILMAN CROCKETT. Will probated October, 1839. Will Book 2, p. 149. Devises his property as follows: To his wife, Araminta; to his three daughters by his first wife, viz: Ellenor Wilson, Hannah Owens and Dolly (?) Stump; and to his other children, Elizabeth Jane, John, and Lavisa Franklin.

RICHARD STEEL. Will probated February, 1840. Will Book 2, p. 158. Devises his property as follows: To his wife, Eleanor, to his children, Shadrack, Richard, and Harvey; to his grand-sons, Calvin and Marvin Steel; and to his grand-daughters, Ann Eliza, and Elizabeth Steel; to his daughter Nancy Huton (?) and her children; to his sons, Edmond, Thomas, and Westley; to his son-in-law George Steel, and to his daugters Sharlotty Steel, and Tony (?) Steel.

ARCHIBALD MALONY. Will probated April, 1840. Will Book No. 2, p. 162. Devises his property as follows: To his son John, and to his daughter Mary Pruett, and to his wife Rachel Malony.

ELLENER STEEL. Widow of Richard Steel. Will probated April, 1840. Will Book No. 2, page 169. Devises her property as follows: To her sons Richard, Shadrach, and Edmond; to her daughters Ann Eliza, and Elizabeth; and to her son Harvey.

JOHN C. CROCKETT. Will probated December, 1840. Will Book 2, p. 175. Devises his property as follows: "To Hannah Peery during her life," to his sons, Robert and Addison, to his daughter Maria, his son Samuel and his children, to his sons John and Rufus, and to his daughters Jeen, Margaret, and Julia.

WILLIAM BROOKS. Will probated January, 1841. Will Book 2, p. 177. Devises his property as follows: To his wife, Ann; to his daughter Polly, and to his sons, Richard, John, Thomas, William, and James; and to his daughters, "Margaret Kirk, Nancy Clyburn; heirs of Lowisa Asberry heirs of Sarah Todd and my grand-daughter Sarah Stephenson."

LOW BROWN. Will probated February, 1841. Will Book No. 2, p. 174. Devises his property as follows: "I give unto my three daughters, Cinthy, Jane, and Elizabeth." "Unto four of my sons, Joseph, Andrew, George, and Low; to my daugter Sarah; grand-son Henry McGrannaham, to sons **William and John,** daughters Polly and Martha.

DANIEL JUSTICE. Will probated December, 1833. Will Book No. 2, p. 219. Devises his property as follows: His oldest son, John, his daughter Anna Robinett, his sons Moses, George, Daniel, his daughter Elizabeth Compton, wife of Hickman Compton, and to his daughter Sally Justice, then to her son George Washington Thompson; and to his daughters Betsy Robinett, Nancy Robinett, and Caty Robinett.

JOHN TRACY. Will probated August, 1842. Will Book No. 2, p. 243. Devises his property as follows: To his wife Elizabeth; and to his children *Amen,* John, Sally and Winston.

WILLIAM HARMAN. Will probated November, 1843. Will Book No. 2, p. 266. Devises his property as follows: To his son John B., to his wife Anna, to his son Henry H., to his daughter Nancy Dills, wife of William Dills, Peggy Havin, wife of John D. Havin; to his sons James H., and William R., His daughters, Jane, Louisa, and Marietta Harman.

JOHN PERRY. Will probated August, 1844. Will Book No. 2, p. 277. Devises his property as follows: "To his grand-son Hiram P. Peery and Clarissa Steel, his daughter and to Reuben Steel.

WILLIAM WHITMAN. Will probated August, 1844. Will Book No. 2, p. 278. Devises his property as follows: To his wife Elleanor, and at her death to his brother John Whitman; to his niece, Elleanor Peery, the daughter of William Peery, and to his nephew, Whitman Peery, the son of James Peery.

DAVID WHITLEY. Will probated October, 1844. Will Book No. 2, p. 278. Devises his property as follows: To his wife, Peggy, and to his six daughters: Jane Maxwell, Polly Six, Peggy Moore, Mary Hendrick, Betsy Hendrick, and Cynthia Whitley; to his sons Andrew J., James, William and David R.

MARGARET DAILEY. Will probated November, 1844. Will Book No. 2, p. 289. Devises her property to her son, Issac Dailey.

WILLIAM HENIGER of Burk's Garden. Will probated January, 1845. Will Book No. 2, page 293. Devises his property as follows: To his wife Elizabeth, to his sons Isaac, Phillip, Thomas, and Samuel; and to his daughter Peggy Tolbert, to his two grandsons, Harvey and Thomas Heniger, sons of Abraham Heniger, dec'd.

SAMUEL FLUMMER of Bluestone, 76 years old. Will probated April, 1845. Will Book No. 2, page 300. Devises his property as follows: To his wife Elizabeth, to his son William, and to his sons-in-law: George B. Clark, David Tabor, Allen Justice, and Constantine Adams, who married his daughter Nancy, and to his son Solomon.

GIDEON WRIGHT. Will probated May, 1845. Will Book No. 2, p. 301. Devises his property as follows: To his wife, Eleanor, to his sons, Gideon, Harvey George, Daniel Harman, to his grandson Gideon H. Totten, to his daughters, Nancy, Eliza Jane, Elean Myrinda, Rebecca and Lucinda.

HEZ. HARMAN. Will probated July 3, 1845. Will Book No. 2, p. 302. Devises his property as follows: Directs that his Executor pay out of his estate $50.00 for the support of the Gospel in the way he has heretofore done; 2nd, to his wife, his son Kiah, his daughter Polly Davidson, his son Erastus G., his daughter Jane G. Harris, Martha B. Neel, Nancy N. Fudge, Rhoda N. Harman, and to his sons, Henry B., Elias G. W., and William W. He further directs that Henry and Ruth, two slaves, be liberated upon the death of the testator's wife; and directed that said slaves be well taken care of in their old age. "I allow my estate to give them a comfortable support in their old age, till death."

REUBEN BAILEY of Bluestone, being 75 years old. Will probated January, 1846. Will Book No. 2, p. 325. Devises his property as follows: To his wife Milley, to Barissa Waldron, daughter of Samuel Waldron by his daughter Sally, to his sons, William, Reuben and James; to his daughter Elizabeth Shrewsberry, and to his sons-in-law, Thomas White, Reuben Tanetson, David Mills, Samuel Waldron, Charles Cranforces and Shan Belsha.

ARCHIBALD THOMPSON. Will probated Sept., 1846. Will Book No. 2, p. 335. Devises his property as follows: To his sons William, John and James B., to his grand-son, George Erastus Thompson, his three grand-children: Marthy, Rebecca and Caroline Thompson, to his daughter-in-law, Margaret Thompson, to his daughters Jane C. Ward, Marthy D. Ward, Mary Thompson, Nancy Rutledge and Liddy Rutledge.

JAMES H. MOORE. Will probated December, 1846. Will Book No. 2, p. 259. Devises his property as follows: To his wife, Jane, and to his children: Mary Kezia, Samuel Lycurgess and Sara Christina.

JEREMIAH CLAYPOOL. Will probated December, 1846. Will Book No. 2, p. 361. Devises his property as follows: To his oldest son, Miles, to his wife, Charity. Mentions his grand-children Amanda Asburry and Eli C. Asburry; to his daughter, Elizabeth McGuire. He then mentions Ephriam Claypool and James Claypool "your brothers" to assist in the division of the estate, then to James Claypool, Senr. brother of testator. Testator then says: "Jeremiah B. Claypool shall have the lot where I live. . . ."

GEORGE SPRACHER. Will probated January, 1847. Will Book No. 2, p. 375. Devises his property as follows: To his wife Pheby, and to his children: Peter, Barbary Rhudy, John Spracher, Jemima Crabtree, Stephen Spracher, Jacob Spracher, Ann Goodman, Margaret Ritter, and Catherine Spracher.

ELIJAH KING. Will probated June, 1847. Will Book No. 2, p. 415. Devises his property as follows: To his wife, Polly. Then he emancipates all his slaves at the death of his wife.

JOSEPH PERRY. Will probated Sept., 1847. Will Book No. 2, p. 418. Devises his property to be equally divided among his children, but mentions only one by name—"my daughter Angeline." He mentions the fact that he is a brother of Henry Peery.

SAMUEL HANSHEW. Will probated Sept., 1847. Will Book 2, p. 428. Devises his property as follows: To his son John and "daughters, Elizabeth, Catherine, Gemima and Barbary." He mentions his wife also, but does not give her name.

JOSEPH MOORE. Will probated February, 1848. Will Book No. 2, p. 435. Devises his property as follows: To his wife Christina, to his daughters, Rhoda, Attillia, Cynthia, Nancy, Polly and Martha.

HENRY HARMAN (of Burk's Garden). Will probated February, 1848. Will Book No. 2, page ——. Devises his property as follows: To his wife, Polly, to his sons Henry J., and Adam; to his daughters, Christina, Nancy, Sally and Lewanne. He also mentions the fact that his brother Adam had willed to him certain property.

GABRIAL CRABTREE. Will probated August, 1848. Will Book No. 2, p. 465. Devises his property as follows: To his sons, Rees H., Thomas B., and Gabriel, and to his daughters, Polly and Catherine.

SUSANNAH KING. Will probated December, 1848. Will Book No. 2, p. 471. Frees all her slaves and divides her estate among them.

JOHN GOODWIN. Will probated May, 1849. Will Book No. 2, p. 481. Devises his property as follows: To his wife, Nancy, and to John Sayers and said Sayers children by his first wife, viz: Nancy, William, Susan, Alexander, Sally, John, David and Margaret; to Nancy, Elizabeth and Robert Goodwin, children of Robert Goodwin, deceased. Devised to his son Thomas Goodwin; to Samuel D. Goodwin, infant son of David Goodwin, deceased. To Grace Higginbotham, wife of Thomas Higginbotham, and to Sally Wilson, wife of Edward Wilson.

WILLIAM TAYLOR. Will probated March, 1849. Will Book No. 2, p. 491. Devises his property as follows: To his wife, Milly; to his children Latitia Sanders Harrison, Susan Taylor, John Taylor, Sally Buchanan McDonald, Matilda George Taylor, Stephen Sanders Taylor and Charles Taylor. Testator mentions the fact that he is a son of John Taylor.

WILLIAM JONES. Will probated January, 1850. Will Book No. 2, p. 513. Devises his property as follows: To his wife, Sally; to his son Minatree, and to his daughters, Dorthy and Reginna.

MATHIAS HARMAN. Will probated February, 1850. Will Book No. 2, p. 515. Devises his property as follows: To his wife Nancy; to his sons, Elias V., Daniel H., William B., and Mathias H.

JACOB HAGER. Will probated February, 1850. Will Book, 2, p. 516. Devises his property as follows: To his wife Sarah, to his son, Squire; to his daughter, Polly: "To all the rest of my heirs" not mentioned by name.

HENRY BOWEN. Will probated May, 1850. Will Book No. 2, p. 524. Devises his property as follows: To his daughters, Louisa and Ellen; to his sons Rees and Henry.

WILL BOOK No. 3.

LILES DOLSBURY. Will probated October, 1850. Will Book 3, page 7. Devises his property as follows: To his daughter, Catherine Reed; and to his grand-children, James Reed, Nancy W. Reed, Thomas Reed, Catherine Cook, Hysam Hyden. Col. Wm. Gillespie Executor.

JOHN THOMPSON. Will probated July, 1850. Will Book No. 3, p. 10. Devises his property as follows: To his wife, Polly; to his sons, Walter W., William, Henry B., Arch, John and James; To his daughters, Jane Peery, Levicie S. Witten and Peggy Ward.

WILLIAM DAVIS. Will probated July, 1850. Will Book No. 3, p. 12. Devises his property as follows; to his wife, Katherine; to his sons, James L., Joseph, William and Wilburn; to his daughters, Polly Ann Fletcher, Elizabeth Carter, Rebecca D. Stairns and Margaret Milem.

JAMES HARRISON. Will probated January, 1851. Will Book 3, p. 20. Devises his property as follows; to his wife, Polly; to his sons, James, John C., Thomas G., and Joseph; to his daughters, Elizabeth Taylor and Cosby Graham.

MAXWELL MARRS. Will probated October, 1851. Will Book 3, p. 30. Devises his property as follows: to his wife (name not mentioned); to his daughters, Jane, Betsy, Sally, Polly and Margaret; to his sons, Robert, Henry, William and John; to William Pruett.

JOSEPH DAVIDSON. Will probated October, 1851. Will Book 3, p. 32. Devises his property as follows; to his wife, Matilda; to his sons, John, Henry, Robert, William, James and Samuel; to his grand-sons, Joseph Davidson (son of Henry) Samuel Richardson, Joseph Davidson (son of William), and to John Havens; to his grand-daughters, Matilda, Hannah and Irene Richardson, children of his daughter Jane; to his daughter Nancy Sullender; and to Martha Bane.

ELIZABETH LAIRD. Will probated January, 1852. Will Book 3, p. 41. Devises her property as follows: to her daughters Margaret Pratt and Polly Davis; to her son Cornelius.

JONATHAN PEERY. Will probated June, 1852. Will Book 3, p. 60. Devises his property as follows; to his wife (name not given); to his son Richard; to his daughters, Jane, Margaret and Catherine; to his grand-son John Henry Owens, son of deceased daughter Margaret.

WILLIAM THOMPSON. Will probated Sept., 1852. Will Book 3, p. 77. Devises his property as follows; to his sons, Thomas, William, and Milton; to his daughters, Minerva, Peggy, Jane, Polly and Narcissa.

LETITIA FLOYD. Will probated March, 1853. Will Book 3, p. 89. Devises her property as follows; to her sons, George, John, Ben Rush, and William; to her daughters, Lavalette, Letitia and Nicketti.

JAS. W. SHANNON. Will probated October, 1852. Will Book 3, p. 90. Devises his property as follows; to his wife, Nancy, all land and money during her life; at her death to be divided equally among his children (names not given).

CHAPTER XVI.

GENEALOGY SHOWN BY DEEDS—DEED BOOK No. 1.
FROM 1800 TO 1809.

James Brown and Esther, his wife, of the County of Russell and State of Virginia, to John Stephenson of the County of Tazewell, Virginia, dated June 3rd, 1800; p. 1.

From Richard Pemberton and Mary Pemberton, his wife to Elijah King. Deed is dated 1800; p. 2.

Teste: JOHN WARD, Clerk.

A power of Attorney, From George Webb to William Stalman of N. C., Dated Feb. 20th, 1800; p. 3.

Deed dated June 4th, 1800 and recorded in D. B., No. 1, p. 4. From Samuel Ferguson and Mary his wife and William Peery and Sally his wife to David Ward, George Peery, Robert Wallace, William Neel, Henry Bowen, David Hanson and Samuel Walker, composing the Worshipful Court of Tazewell County and their Successors in office for the use of said County. "For and in Consideration of the public buildings for said County have granted bargained and sold . . . unto the said Court of Tazewell and their successors forever, a certain tract of parcel of land lying and being in the County of Tazewell on the waters of Clinch River, Containing twenty three acres and twenty eight square poles" etc. This is the land on which the public buildings still stand and on which the main business part of the town of Tazewell (formerly Jeffersonville) now stands. From this deed we also secure the names of the magistrates composing the first Court held for the County.

Samuel Young and Susanna his wife to Israel Young, 1800; p. 5.

Edley Maxwell and Ann his wife to Jeremiah Witten, 1800; p. 6.

Edley Maxwell and Ann his wife to Abraham Davis, 1800; p. 7.

Robert Belchee and Mary Belchee his wife to James Richardson, 1800; p. 8.

Andrew Thompson to James Thompson, 1799; p. 9.

John Ferguson and Margaret his wife of Wythe County, Va., to Samuel Ferguson Senr. of same county, 1800; p. 11.

Dudley Young to Charles Young and John Young, 1800; p. 12.

Mathias Harman and Lydia his wife of Fleming County, Kentucky to William George of Wythe County, Virginia. Lands joining Henry Harman and Thomas Peery and having been granted to Mathias Harman by patent, dated Oct. 12th, 1787. Deed Dated 1799; p. 13.

Daniel Trigg, Executor of the last will and testament of William Ingles to Daniel Harman, 1800; p. 14.

Lydia Thompson, widow and heir of William Thompson, decd, John Thompson and Levisa his wife, Archibald Thompson and Rebecka his wife, William Ward and Nancy his wife, late Nancy Thompson, Robert Doak and Rachel, his wife, late Rachel Thompson, Andrew Thompson and Rebecca his wife, James Thompson, John Mitchell and Ames his wife, late Ames Thompson, heirs and devisees of said William Thompson to James Sloan and Jane his wife late Jane Thompson, 1802; p. 15.

John Compton and Rebecka his wife, to John Powers, 1800; p. 17.

William Lewis to Robert Wallace, 1800; p. 18.

Andrew Todd and Elizabeth his wife, to James Lockhart, 1800; p. 19.

Same Grantors to John Goodwin. Same date; p. 20.

Benjamine Porter Mahoney, to Daniel Young, 1800; p. 21.

John Peery and Sarah his wife, to John Evans, 1800; p. 22.

James Richardson and Nancy his wife, to Moses Higginbotham, 1800; p. 24.

John Greenup and Elizabeth his wife, to John McIntosh, 1800; p. 25.

James Frugate to Stephen Deskins, 1800; p. 26.

George Peery of Bottertout County, Virginia to Joseph Davidson, 1800; p. 28.

William Hall and Mary his wife to James Justice, 1801; p. 29.

Daniel Justice and Elizabeth his wife to James Day, 1801; p. 30.

John Greenup Senr. and Elizabeth his wife to Thomas Greenup, 1801; p. 31.

William Clark and Jane his wife, to David Hanson, 1801; p. 32.

John Tollett and Peggy his wife to William Shannon, 1800; p. 33.

Robert Belchee and Mary his wife to John Edde, 1801; p. 34.

John Asberry and Keziah his wife to William Asberry, 1801; p. 35.

David Ward and Ellenor his wife, to Hugh Wilson, 1801; p. 37.

Aleanah Wynne to David Whitley, 1801; p. 39.

Henry Marrs and Elizabeth his wife, to Christopher Marrs, 1801; p. 40.

Obadiah Gent to Gideon Fowler, 1801; p. 41.

Abednego White, of Russell Co., Va., to John Ratliff, 1801; p. 42.

Philip Lambert to Jeman Carter, 1801; p. 43.

Joseph Hoge to Thomas and John Cartmill, 1801; p. 44.

James Jones and Rhoda, his wife, to John Brooks and Richard Brooks, 1801; p. 45.

Abraham Lusk of Lee County, to John Davis, 1801; p. 46.

William Cecil and Nancy his wife to Henry Marrs, 1801; p. 47.

William Hall and Mary Hall his wife to William Wynne, 1803; p. 48.

James Shannon to William Shannon, 1803; p. 49.

Andrew Thompson and Rebecka his wife, of Montgomery Co., Virginia, to Edward Corder, 1802; p. 50.

Henry Harman, Senr. and Nancy his wife, of Tazewell Co., Virginia to Low Brown of Montgomery Co., Va., conveys 175 acres in Wrights Valley. Deed dated Oct. 7th, 1800; p. 52.

Same Grantors to same Grantees for 100 acres in Wrights Valley, 1800; p. 54.

John Vincent Grant, to Henry Darter, 1801; p. 56.

Absalom Stafford and Nancy his wife, to Micajah Anderson Thorn, 1801, p. 57.

William Oney and Mary his wife to Hezekiah Oney, 1800; p. 58.

Abraham Davis and Nancy his wife, to Jeremiah Witten. Deed dated Sept. 10th, 1801. Recorded in D. B. No. 1, p. 59.

Jeremiah Witten and Sarah his wife, to Thomas Witten, Deed dated Sept. 10th, 1801. Recorded D. B. 1, p. 60.

Truman Canter and Cynthia his wife, to Lewis Milam, 1801; D. B. 1, p. 61.

William Dills and Rebecca his wife to Peter Dills, 1801; D. B. 1, p. 62.

William Belchee and Hanna his wife, to Daniel Young, 1801; D. B. 1, p. 64.

Daniel Young and Mary his wife, to William Belchee, 1801; D. B. 1, p. 65.

Christian Shull and Sarah his wife, to John Hacney, 1801; p. 66.

John Hacney and Jane his wife to Solomon Milam, 1801; p. 67.

Daniel McFarlane of Cumberland Co., Ky., to James McFarlane of Russell Co., Va., 1801; p. 69.

Lawrence Comer and Margaret, his wife, to Hezekiah Harman, 1801; p. 71.

William Griffitts Senr. and Mary his wife to John Griffitts, 1802; p. 73.

Thomas Godfrey and Susanna his wife to Samuel Lusk, 1802; p. 75.

William Peery and Sally his wife to Canfield Taylor and James Taylor of Rockbridge County, Va., 1802. For lot in the Town of Tazewell, p. 76.

Thomas Godfrey and Susanah his wife to Isaac Adkins, 1801; p. 77.

James Rice and Mary his wife to Jeremiah Lambert, 1801; D. B. 1, p. 78.

Henry Harman Senr. to Hezekiah Harman, 1801; D. B. 1, p. 80.

Henry Harman Senr. to George Rinehard, 1801; p. 81.

William Peery and Sally his wife to Peter Kinder of Wythe Co., Va., 1802; p. 82.

Harry Smith, Sally Smith and Peggy Smith, heirs of Henry Smith, dec'd, of Russell County, Va., to Jeremiah Claypool, 1802; p. 83.

William Peery and Sally his wife to Audley Campbell, 1802, p. 84.

John Ratliff and John Crockett, entered into a contract to continue a Salt well on said Ratliffs place which said Ratliff had begun for the purpose of manufacturing salt, 1801; p. 85.

James Day and Mary his wife to John Stobaugh, 1802; p. 86.

Thomas Witten and Nelly his wife to Ebenezer Bruster, 1802; p. 87.

John Evans to Archibald Thompson, 1802; p. 88.

Daniel Trig, Surviving Executor of the will of William Ingles to Daniel Harman, 1802; p. 89.

Daniel Trigg, surviving Executor of the will of William Ingles to Mathias Harman, Senr., 1802; p. 90.

Christian Shull and Sarah his wife, of Montgomery Co., Virginia to Lawrence Comer, 1801; p. 91.

Smith Deskins and Mary his wife, to John Deskins, 1802; p. 92.

Low Brown of Montgomery Co., Va., to George Rinehart, 1802; D. B. No. 1, p. 93. Signed L. W. Brown.

William Lesley to his son John Lesley, 1802; p. 94.

Stephen Deskins to Smith Deskins, 1802; D. B. 1, p. 95.

William Saxton and Henry Wainwright of Boston, Mass., by their attorney Erastus Granger, to Henry Harman, son to Mathias Harman Senr. for land lying on Dry Fork where said Henry Harman now lives, 1803; D. B. 1, p. 96.

Henry Harman, son to Mathias Harman and Sarah his wife, to Joseph White, 1804; D. B. 1, p. 97.

Henry Harman Junr. and Christina, his wife, to Mathias Harmans senr. and Daniel Harman Senr. Lands out of the 360,000 Acre Tract, granted March 28th, Sept., 1794, for Wilson Cary Nicholas, situated on Dick Creek of Dry Fork etc., 1803; p. 98.

Mathias Harman Senr. & Lydia his wife, of County of Tazewell to William George. Consideration $1600. Lands lying on Clinch River joining the lands of Hezekiah Harman, Samuel Ferguson, Daniel & Mathias Harman, 1802; D. B. 1, p. 99.

John Young and Elizabeth his wife to Charles Young, 1802; D. B. 1, p. 100.

William Irwin and Mary (Polly) his wife, to John Young, 1802; D. B. 1, p. 101.

Daniel Harman Senr. and Nancy his wife, to Hezekiah Harman, 1802; D. B. 1, p. 102.

John Stinson and Phebe his wife to Israel Young, 1802; p. 103.

James Maxwell and Jenny (Jane) his wife to Audley Campbell, 1802; p. 103.

James Evans of Tazewell County, Va., and William Evans of Shelby County, Kentucky, legatees to the Estate of Robert Evans, decd, to Moses Evans of Tazewell County, Virginia, for 205 acres on Kimberlands fork of Walkers Creek, 1802; D. B. 1, p. 105.

Andrew Thompson and Rebecah his wife of Montgomery County, Va., to William Ward, 1802; D. B. 1, p. 106.

Thomas Ferguson and Nancy his wife to Rees Gillespie, 1802; p. 107.

Israel Young and Levisy his wife to Nathaniel Young, 1802; p. 108.

Hezekiah Harman and Polly his wife to Henry Harman, Jr., 1802; p. 109.

Richard Pemberton and Mary his wife to William Lockhart, 1802; p. 110.

William Hall and Mary his wife to John Crow, of Montgomery Co., Virginia, 1802; D. B. 1, p. 111.

William Peery and Sally his wife to Abram Davis, 1803; p. 112.

William Peery and Sally his wife to Samuel Laird, 1803, p. 113.

William Peery, Sr. and Sally his wife to Samuel Walker, 1802; p. 114.

Samuel Ferguson and Mary his wife, to Hezekiah Harman, 1802; p. 115.

John Hancy and Jane his wife to Emanuel Scyson, 1803, p. 117.

John Edde and Elizabeth his wife to Robert Higginbotham, 1802; page 118.

Thimothy Roark and Sarah his wife to Thomas Bruster, 1803; p. 119.

Timothy Roark to William Cecil, 1803; D. B. No. 1, p. 122.

Andrew Thompson and Rebecca his wife of Montgomery County, Va., to John Mitchell, 1802; D. B. 2, p. 123.

John Miller Russell of Suffolk, Massachusetts, to Henry Harman, Junr., 1802; p. 124.

Henry Harman, Junr. and Christina his wife to Margaret Essex, 1803; p. 125.

Margaret Essex to Henry Harman, Junr., 1803; p. 126.

Thomas Bruster and Sarah his wife to Thomas Barret, 1803; p. 127.

John Compton Junr. and Ellenor his wife, to Frederick Cook, 1803; p. 128.

William Hall and Mary his wife, to Andrew Thompson of Wythe County, Virginia, 1803; p. 129.

William Hall and Mary his wife to Robert Sayers of Wythe County, Virginia; 1803; p. 130.

William Hall and Mary his wife to Thomas Shannon of Montgomery County, Virginia, 1803; p. 131.

William Saxton and Henry Wainwright of Boston, Massachusetts, by their Attorney Erastus Granger, to Isaac Dailey, 1803; p. 132.

William Saxton and Henry Wainwright of Boston, Massachusetts, by their Attorney, Erastus Granger, to Henry Harman Jr., son of Henry Harman, Sr., 1803; p. 133.

William Saxton and Henry Wainwright of Boston, Mass by their Attorney, Erastus Granger to Adam Harman and Mathias Harman, sons of Mathias Harman Senr., being part of the tract on which Mathias Harman Senr. now lives on the Dry Fork of Sandy River, 1803; p. 134.

Same Grantors to Thomas Harrisson, 1803; p. 135.

Same Grantors to Adam Harman and Mathias Harman, sons of Mathias Harman Senr., land on Dry Fork of Sandy, 1803; p. 136.

Hezekiah Harman and Polly his wife to John Perry (Blacksmith), 1803; p. 137.

Hezekiah Harman and Polly his wife to Samuel Ferguson, 1802; p. 139.

Lewis Milam and Molley his wife of Montgomery County, Virginia, to Aaron Fletcher, 1803; p. 140.

Andrew Thompson and Rebecka his wife of Montgomery County, Virginia to James Thompson, 1803; p. 141.

Thomas Ferguson of Knox County, Kentucky, and Nancy his wife to John Ward, 1803; p. 141. Conveys the right of Nancy as widow of John Bowen, decd, in consequence of Thomas Ferguson's interference with the said widow.

John Peery to Hezekiah Harman, 1803; p. 142.

Nancy Sullard, formerly Nancy Daniel, leased for ten years her Plantation to John Shifely, 1803; p. 143.

Joseph Patterson, of Wythe County, Virginia, Attorney in fact for John Walker of Rockbridge County, Virginia, to John Graham, for land on Plum Creek, 1803; p. 144.

Samuel Duff and Rebecka his wife of Russell County, Virginia, to Thomas Peery, 1803; p. 146.

Obadiah Gent to Henry Bowen, 1802; p. 147.

Jeremiah Claypool and Mary his wife to Jesse Young, 1803; p. 148.

Arch Haselrig of Wythe County, Virginia to Daniel Harman, son of Mathias Harman, decd., 1803; p. 149.

James Barrett of Montgomery County, Virginia, to Jesse Harper, 1803; p. 150.

Henry Harman Junr. and Christina his wife to John Peery, 1804; p. 151.

Larkin Kidd to Samuel Muncey, 1802; p. 152.

William Smith and Elizabeth his wife, to Benjamine Sloan, 1803; p. 153.

Zachariah Stanley and Sarah his wife of Montgomery County, Virginia, to Oliver Wynne, 1803; p. 154.

Archibald Haslerig of Wythe Co., Va., to Thomas Pickens, 1804; p. 156.

Arch. Heselrig to John Compton, 1803; p. 157.

Arch Haselrig to Jeremiah Witten, 1804; p. 158.

James Johnston, Attorney in fact for Daniel Johnston, Senr. of Knox County, Kentucky, to William Cecil, 1803; p. 159.

Daniel Young and Mary his wife to Nathaniel Young, 1804; p. 160.

Thomas Evans, Peter Outhouse and Geretta his wife, Michael Hammer and Mary Martha his wife, William Evans, Moses Evans, Robert Evans, late of Henry Co., Ky., legatees to the Estate of Robert Evans, decd., to James Evans, 1803; p. 161.

William Hall and Mary his wife to William Witten, 1804; p. 164.

Alexander Stuart of Monroe Co., Va., to Benjamine Hall and Pricilla his wife. Consideration is natural love and affection for said Pricilla, daughter of said Stuart, 1802; p. 165.

Same grantor to same grantee, p. 166.

Same grantor to same grantee, p. 167.

Daniel Harman Senr. and Nancy his wife, to Mathias Harman Senr. 1804;; p. 168.

James Brown and Esther his wife of Russell Co., Va., to Andrew McMillen of same County, 1804; p. 171.

David Lusk and Chloe his wife to John Lawson, 1804; p. 172.

Jeremiah Witten and Sarah his wife to Abraham Davis, 1804; p. 173.

John Evans to John Allen, 1804; p. 174.

William Lockhart Jr. and Jane his wife to Jeremiah Witten, 1804; p. 175.

Micajah A. Thorn and Susanna his wife to William George, 1804;; p. 176.

Wyett Daniel and Sarah his wife, to Obadiah Gent, 1804; p. 169.

John Graham of Floyd Co., Ky., to his son Thomas Witten Graham, 1804; Conveys one negro boy, p. 176.

Micajah A. Thorn and Susanna his wife to William George, 1804; p. 176.

Absalom Stafford and Nancy his wife, to William Burress, 1804; p. 177.

Henry Darter and Anne his wife, to John Crockett, 1804; p. 178.

Samuel Ferguson and Mary his wife to Thomas Harrison, 1804; p. 179.

Same Grantor to same Grantee, 1804; p. 180.

David Ward and Ellenor his wife to Arthur Blankenship, 1804; p. 181.

James Bristow and Elizabeth his wife to Ralph Blankenship of Russell County, Virginia, 1804; p. 182.

Elijah King to John Davis, 1804; p. 183.

Larkin Kidd to Oliver Wynne, 1803; p. 184.

Newett Drew and Sarah his wife to James Maxwell, 1804; p. 185.

John Hays and Rebecka his wife of Wilson Co. Tenn., to James Maxwell, relinquishes claim to land, 1801; p. 186.

John Stobaugh and Leah his wife to Philip Gose of Wythe County, Virginia, 1804; p. 187.

John Sansom (Lauson?) and Betsy his wife to Isaac Adkins, 1805; p. 188.

Robert Belshee of Lincoln Co., Ky., to Christian Trout, 1805; p. 189.

Alexander Boyd and Leah his wife of ———— Co., Tenn., to Robert and John Engledove of Wythe Co., Va., 1805; p. 190.

John Greenup and Elizabeth his wife, Joshua Dickerson and Susanna his wife, Philip Witten and Ruth his wife, Jeremiah Witten and Sarah his wife, Joshua Cecil and Keziah his wife, Thomas Witten and Ellenor his wife, William Cecil and Ann his wife, James Witten and Rebecka his wife, of Wythe County, Virginia to William Witten of said County. The above named being legatees of the Estate of Thomas Witten decd., dated 1794; p. 191-2.

William Smith and Elizabeth his wife to Hugh Wilson, 1804; p. 193.

James Moore and Nancy his wife to William Smith, 1805; p. 194.

Joseph Ward and Keziah Ward his wife, to John Ward, 1805; p. 195.

Joseph Oney and Rebecka his wife of the County of Montgomery to John Justice, 1805; p. 196.

Joseph Ward and Keziah his wife to John Ward, 1805; p. 197.

James Moore and Nancy his wife to William Smith, 1805; p. 199.

John Young and Elizabeth his wife to Israel Young, 1805; p. 200.

Thomas Harrisson Sr. and Hannah his wife to Thomas Harrisson, Junr., 1805; p. 201.

John Compton, Junr. and Ellenor Compton to Joshua Day, 1805; p. 202.

Allen Marlow and Jane his wife to John Young, 1805; p. 203.

John Ward and Nancy his wife to James Robertson, 1805; p. 204.

Same Grantors to Joseph Ward, 1805; p. 206.

Richard Muse of Wythe Co., Va., to Henry Shrader, 1803; p. 207.

William Asberry to Jared Bowling, 1805; p. 208.

William Witten and Letticie his wife to Rutherford Whitt and Joseph Oney, 1805; p. 209.

William Cecil and Nancy Cecil to Archibald Meloney, 1805; p. 210.

William Witten and Letticie his wife to John Laird, 1805; p. 211.

Samuel Laird and Elizabeth his wife to James and Cafley Taylor 1805; p. 212.

John Tollett and Margaret his wife to David Whitley, 1805; pp. 213-214-215.

Thomas Owens and Polly his wife to Henry Luster, 1805; p. 216.

William Smith and Elizabeth his wife to James Robinson, 1805; p. 217.

Robert Belshee to Christian Trout, 1805; p. 218.

Henry Banks of the City of Richmond to James Thompson, Power of Attorney, 1805; p. 219.

John Tollett and Margaret his wife to Thomas Pickens, 1805; p. 220.

Same Grantors to same Grantee, 1805; pp. 221-222.

William Witten and Letticie his wife to Samuel Laird, 1805; p. 223.

Same grantors to same Grantee, 1805; p. 224.

William Witten and Letticie his wife, John Greenup and Elizabeth his wife, to John Tollett, William Witten, James Witten, Jeremiah Witten, Thomas Greenup and Smith Deskins, Trustees in trust. Conveys four acres and a half, situate on Clinch River, including a small spring under the north bank of Clynch River, upon which to erect a church for the use and benefit of the members of the Methodist Episcopal Church in the United States of America etc. Said four and a half acres described by metes and bounds and comes out of a 121 acre survey made to John Greenup and Thomas Witten, decd., 1787, 1805; p. 225. This is the first deed made to Church property as shown by the Deed Books. Doubtless prior donations of lands for Church purposes were made and shown by the records of the older counties from which Tazewell was formed.

Smith Deskins and Margaret Deskins his wife, to John McIntosh, 1805; p. 227.

Andrew Davidson and Sally his wife to Joseph Clark, 1805; p. 228.

Lemaster Cooksey and Nancy his wife, to John Goodwyn, 1805; p. 229.

John Young and Elizabeth his wife to Walter Mattingly, 1805; p. 230.

Stephen Deskins and Annie his wife to John Deskins, 1805; p. 230.

P. Kendrick and Elizabeth his wife to John Deskins, 1805, p. 231.

William Brown of Montgomery Co., to John Lasley, 1805; p. 232.

William Brown and Mary his wife to Jacob Shull, deed of release, 1805; p. 233.

Jacob Shull and Mary his wife to William Brown, 1805; p. 235.

John Asberry and Kesiah his wife to Christian Trout, 1805; p. 235.

Andrew Heburn and Eunice his wife to William Smith, 1805; p. 236.

Christian Trout and Elizabeth his wife to Arthur Blankenship, 1805; p. 237.

Same Grantors to same Grantee, 1805; p. 239.

William Davidson and Polly his wife to David Lusk, 1805; p. 240.

James Sloan and Jane his wife to George Grubb, 1805; p. 241.

Robert Lasley of Floyd Co., Ky., to Lewis Milam, 1806; p. 241.

Low Brown of Montgomery Co., Va., to George Rhinehart, 1805; p. 242.

George Davidson and Jennie his wife and John Davidson to Joseph Moore, 1806; p. 243.

James Moore and Nancy his wife to John Davidson, 1806; p. 244.

Thomas Harrison and Hannah his wife to Jonathan Peery, 1806; p. 245.

Same Grantors to same Grantee, 1806; p. 246.

Justice of the Court, to-wit, David Ward, George Peery, William Neel, Robert Wallace, Henry Bowen, David Hanson, and Samuel Walker to Thomas Harrisson Senr. for lots in Jeffersonville, 1804; pp. 247-8.

Henry Patton and Martha his wife of Montgomery Co., Va., to Joseph Davidson and William George, 1806; p. 248.

In Deed Book No. 1, page 249, Henry Bowen and Thomas Witten, who are Commissioners for holding the election for President and Vice President of the United States, certified that at the election, held on the first Monday in November, 1804, that there were twenty four Electors on the Presidental Ticket, each one of whom received forty-nine votes in Tazewell County. The names of said Electors are given, among whom is General John Preston of Montgomery County. It will be seen from this record that a very small number of the voters of Tazewell County participated in this election, in which Thomas Jefferson was elected for the second time as President of the United States. The electors on this ticket received the solid vote of Tazewell County. William McKinley was an Elector on this ticket.

Thomas Owens and Mary his wife to Francis Starr, 1806; p. 250.

Daniel Harman and Nancy his wift to their son Mathias Harman, for land on Lincolnshire Branch, 1806; p. 251.

Alexander Stuart of Monroe Co., Va., (now W. Va.,) to Alexander Hutcheson of Augusta County, Virginia, 1806; p. 252.

Micajah Bailey and Naomi his wife to Archibald Bailey, 1806; p. 253.

William Taylor to Andrew Peery, 1805; p. 254.

Cornelius McGuire and Esther his wife of Floyd Co., Ky., to William George, 1805; p. 255.

William Oney to Zachariah Scaggs, 1806; p. 256.

Cawfield Taylor and James Taylor to William Taylor, 1806, p. 257.

Thomas Witten and Ellenor his wife to Samuel C. Witten and William Witten (brothers), 1806; p. 258.

George Peery and Martha his wife, William Davidson and Polly his wife, Low Brown and Jane' his wife, Joseph Davidson and Matilda his wife, Andrew Davidson and Sally his wife, John Burk and Peggy his wife George Davidson, and Jennie his wife, Jessee Farley and Betsy his wife and John Bailey, Legatees of John Davidson, deceased, of the counties of Montgomery and Tazewell, of the one part, and Joheph Moore of Tazewell Co., Va. of the other part. This deed conveys land on Bowyer's Branch of Bluestone and some of the head waters of East River, 1806; page 259-60.

William Taylor and Milley his wife, John Peery, Blacksmith, of Tazewell Co., Va., and James Taylor and Sarah his wife of Washington Co., Va., to Mathias Harman, Junr. of Tazewell Co., Va., 1806; p. 261-2.

James Peery, Senr. and Peggy his wife and John Peery (BS) to Solomon Peery, 1806; p. 263-4.

Above named legatees of John Davidson, conveyed to James Bailey, 1806; p. 264.

George Peery of Knox County, Tenn., to James Peery Junr., 1805; p. 266.

William Kidd to Larkin Kidd, 1806; p. 267.

Same Grantor to same Grantee, 1806; p. 268-9.

Solomon Peery and Sarah his wife to Henry Harman, Jr., 1806; p. 269-71.

John Borders and Caty his wife to Nehemiah Bonham of Wythe County, Virginia, 1805; p. 271-2.

Samuel Walker and Susannah his wife to Joseph Raburn, 1806; p. 273-4.

John Cartmill to James Bean of *Jiles* Co., Va., 1806; p. 273-4.

William Burris to Henry Stump, 1806; p. 274-5.

Isaac Bristow and Margaret his wife to John Athey of Washington County, Virginia, 1806; p. 276-7.

Daniel Trigg, surviving Executor of William Ingles of Montgomery County, Virginia, to John Grills, 1806; p. 278-9.

John Grills and Hannah his wife to James Witten, 1806; p. 279.

James Evans and Elizabeth his wife of Tazewell County, to George Harman of Wythe County, Virginia, 1806; p. 281. This deed conveys 350 acres lying in Tazewell Co., Va., on Kimberling's fork of Walker's Creek, and, being part of a tract of 580 acres granted to Robert Evans.

Alexander Orr and Margaret his wife of Wythe Co., Va., to James Evans, 1806; p. 283-4.

Moses Evans of Shelby Co., Ky., to Oliver Powers, 1806; p. 284-5.

Nehemiah Bonham and Rachel his wife of Wythe Co., Va., to Jacob Taller, 1806; p. 287-8.

William Clark and Jean his wife to John Wilson, 1806; p. 289.

James Evans and Elizabeth his wife to Solomon Jones, 1806; p. 291.

Micajah A. Thorn and Susanah his wife to Henry Hoppis of Wythe County, Va., 1806; p. 292. (Conveys 650 acres on head waters of Clinch where said Thorn now lives).

John Lain and Margaret his wife to William George, 1806; p. 293.

Hez. Harman and Polly his wife to Henry Harman and George Harman, sons of Daniel Harman, decd. Conveys 130 acres in Wright's Valley, 1807; p. 294. (Henry and George were evidently the sons of the Daniel Harman, son of Henry Harman, Sr., who was killed by the Indians in 1792).

Andrew Davidson of Palasky Co., Ky., to John Davidson, 1807; p. 295.

James Cartmill to William Wall, 1806; p. 296.

William Meguier to John Compton, 1807; p. 297-8.

Henry Bowen and Ella his wife to Berryman Porter, 1807; p. 299.

Henry Harman, Jr. and Christina his wife, to Evalina Dills, infant daughter of Rebecky Dills, 1807; p. 300.

Obadiah Gent to Henry Bowen, 1807; p. 301.

James Thompson, Atto. in fact for Henry Banks to Moses Workman, 1807; p. 302.

James Thompson, Atto. in fact etc. to William Witten, 1807; p. 303.

Micajah Anderson Thorn and Susannah his wife to William Hall, 1807; p. 305.

William Davidson and Phebe his wife to Hugh Tiffany of Monroe Co., Va., 1807; p. 306.

William Davis, Power of Atto. to Stephen S. Welch, 1810, p. 306.

James Cartmill and Margaret his wife to Samuel Flummer, 1806; p. 309.

Smith Deskins and Margaret his wife to Adam Harman and Mathias, his brother, 1806; p. 310.

Thomas Barrett and Polly (Mary) his wife to Adam and Mathias Harman, 1806; p. 311.

Thomas Barrett and Mary (Polly) his wife to Adam and Mathias Harman, 1806; p. 312.

John Greenup and Elizabeth his wife to Thomas Greenup, 1808; p. 313.

James Cartmill to John Compton, 1806; p. 314.

Gideon Foster to Obadiah Gent, 1806; p. 315.

William Lockhart and Rachel his wife to John Davis, 1807; p. 316.

John Davis and Peggy his wife and George Davidson and Jenny or (Jean) his wife to Samuel and William Witten, 1807; p. 317-18.

Same Grantors to same Grantee, 1807; p. 319.

Samuel C. Witten and Susannah his wife and William Witten and Nancy his wife to Thomas Witten, 1807; p. 321.

Samuel Walker and Susannah his wife, to Thomas Owens, 1807; p. 322-3. (Conveys 600 acres on North fork of Clinch, adjoining lands of Joseph Raeburn, Henry Harman, John Peery, William Neel, James Sloan, and David Peery. Consideration, 600 pounds).

William Peery and Sally his wife to John Trigg and William King, 1807; p. 224-5.

Members of the County Court to Gordon Cloyd and Joseph Moore. A lot in Jeffersonville, 1807; p. 226-7.

Richard Bailey Senr. to Eli Bailey, 1807; pp. 327-8.

Members of the County Court to John I Trigg and William King, 1807; p. 329. (Lot in Jeffersonville).

Susanah Aston of Madison County, Ky., (formerly the widow of Joseph Wray) and George Aston (her present husband) to Zechariah Belcher, relinquishes dower, 1806; p. 331.

John Grills and Hannah his wife to Daniel Justice Senr., 1807; p. 332.

Same Grantors to Mathias Fox, 1807; p. 333.

Howard Bane and Lettice his wife to George Webb, 1807; p. 334.

Same Grantors to John Nuckles, 1807; p. 335.

John and Thomas Cartmill to John Lasley, 1806; p. 336.

Robert Wallace and Nancy his wife to William Walls, 1807; p. 339.

William Hall and Mary his wife to Peter Gose, 1807; p. 340.

James Thompson of Washington Co., Va. to Samuel Shannon, 1807; p. 341.

George Kendrick of Russell County, Virginia to Daniel Horton, 1808; p. 343.

Richard Bailey Senr. and Elizabeth his wife to Hugh Tiffany of Monroe County, Virginia, 1807; p. 344.

Frederick Trent and Elizabeth his wife to Tyron Gibson, 1807; p. 245-6.

Hezekiah Whitt and Rachel his wife to John Davis, Junr., 1808; p. 347.

Samuel Ewing, Atto. for Francis Preston, to Andrew Shortridge, 1808; p. 348.

James Thompson to Philip Gose, 1807; p. 349.

Samuel Ewing etc. to James Harper, 1808; p. 350.

Rutherford Whitt and Hannah his wife and Joseph Oney and Susanah his wife to Ebenezer Bruster, 1807; p. 352.

John Bristow and Margaret his wife to David Robinson, 1808; p. 353-4.

John Laird and Elizabeth his wife to James Witten, 1808; p. 355.

William Ward of Wythe County, Virginia to Hezekiah Harman, 1808; p. 356.

Hezekiah Harman and Polly his wife to John Evans, 1808; p. 357.

Low Brown and Jane his wife of Montgomery County, Virginia, to Isaac Brown, 1808; p. 358.

Henry Harless and Charity his wife to George Justice, 1807; p. 359.

Thomas Witten and Ellenor his wife and John Evans to Archibald Thompson, 1807; p. 360.

Daniel Johnston and Rachel his wife to Daniel Horton, 1807; p. 361-2.

Abednego White and Elizabeth his wife of Russell County, Virginia and John Bristo and Ralph Blankenship to Richard Steele, 1808; p. 363.

John Tollett and Margaret his wife of Roan Co., Tenn., to David Whitley, 1807; p. 364.

Zachariah Elkins and Rachel his wife of Kanawha Co., Va., to Frederick Cook of Wolf Creek, Tazewell Co., Va., 1807; p. 366-7.

Andrew McMillin and Nancy his wife to James Brown, 1808; p. 368.

Mathias Harman, Senr. of Tazewell, Co., to Walter McCoy, 1808; p. 369.

Thomas Bruster and Sarah his wife to Ebenezer Bruster, 1807; p. 370.

Garland Hiat, Atto. in fact for John Moore, to Benjamine Porter, 1808; p. 371.

James Robertson and Sarah his wife to Andrew McMillin, 1808; p. 372.

Boundary Line between the Counties of Russell and Tazewell, reported by Commissioners, H. Bowen and David Hanson as follows: "Beginning at a Double chestnut and Maple at the head of Cove Creek at the former corner of Division between the said Counties Thence 23° w. 1440 poles to Jacob Franciscos Mill, Thence N 25° 30' W 560 poles including Daniel Hortons Dwelling house in Tazewell County to a White oak red oake and Two Sour woods thence North 39° W 1064 poles to the Mouth of Cole Creek where the commissioners thought advisable to stop their measurement at present".   Signed

"H. BOWEN
DAVID HANSON."

This certificate admitted to record June Term, 1808; p. 374.

Daniel Harman and Nancy his wife to Rebecka Wright, 1808; p. 375.

Daniel Harman and Nancy his wife to Solomon Milum, 1808; p. 376.

Zachariah Stanley to John Crockett, 1808; p. 377.

Hezekiah Whitt and Rachel his wife to James Whitt, 1808; p. 378-9

Hezekiah Whitt and Rachel his wife to Griffitt Whitt, 1808; p. 380.

Benjamine Porter to William Newton, 1808; p. 380.

Daniel Horton, Atto. for Daniel Johnston and Rachel Johnston to Travis Kendle, 1808; p. 383-4.

Same Grantors to Patrick Kendrick, 1808; p. 385.

James Maxwell Senr. to William George, 1808; p. 386.

William George and Jenny his wife to James Peery Sr., 1808; p. 387-8.

William Davidson Sr. to his children, Peggy Williams, Betsy, Polly, Millinde, Jenny and Joseph Davidson, 1808; p. 389.

Walter Mattingley to William Boling, 1808; p. 390.

Philip Gose to Peter Gose.

Tryon Gibson and Peggy his wife to John Brown, 1808; p. 392.

John Crow and Hannah his wife of Montgomery Co., Va., to Robert Sayers of Wythe Co., Va., 1806; p. 393.

John Peery to James Peery his son, 1808; p. 395.

John Grills of Washington Co., Va., to John Ingles, 1808; p. 397.

James Peery and Pheby his wife to Daniel Hensley of Kanawa Co., Va., 1808; p. 399.

Thomas Pickings and Sarah his wife to John Tollett, 1808; p. 402-3-4.

Mathias Harman and Lydia his wife to Thomas Bruster, 1808; p. 405.

Walter McCoy to Mathias Harman, 1808; p. 406.

William Garrison and Jane his wife to David Young, 1808; p. 407.

Jessee Young to Jeremiah Claypool, 1808; p. 408.

Hezekiah Oney and Barbara his wife to William Smith, 1808; p. 409.

James Thompson of Washington Co., Va., to Ambrose Hall, 1808; p. 413.

John Preston and Mary his wife of Montgomery Co., Va., to Francis Starr, 1806; p. 414-16.

William McGuyer of Floyd Co., Ky., to Thomas Cartmill, 1808; p. 416-17.

Same Grantor to Joseph Moore, 1808; p. 418.

Thomas Pickens to Joseph Moore, 1808; p. 419.

Same Grantor to same Grantee, 1808; p. 420.

Richard Brooks and Peggy his wife to John Brooks, 1808; p. 421-2.

Archibald Meloney and Esther his wife to John Meloney, 1808; p. 423.

John Vandyke and Charlotte his wife to James Vandyke, 1808; p. 424.

John Vandyke Senr. and Charlotte his wife, to John Vandyke Junr.

Same Grantors to Charles Vandyke, 1808; p. 426.

Samuel Hough of Loudon Co., Va., to Zechariah Stanley of Montgomery Co., Va., 1808, p. 428-9.

John Lasley and Martha his wife to Howard Bane, 1809; p. 430.

William Davidson Senr. and Phebe his wife to Hugh Tiffany, 1809; p. 431.

Thomas Harrison Junr. and Rebecka his wife to Robert Maxwell, 1809; p. 433.

Zechariah Stanley and Sarah his wife of Montgomery Co., Va., to William Day, 1809; p. 435.

John Peery, Blacksmith, to David Peery, his son, 1809; p. 436.

Thomas Belchey of Madison Co., K., Power of Atto. to Arthur Blankenship, 1808; p. 438.

John Mitchell to John King, 1809; p. 439.

Arthur Blankenship, Atto. etc. to Joseph McGuire, 1809; p. 440.

David Lusk and Chloe his wife to Hugh Tiffany, 1809; p. 441.

Alexander Wolcott of Connecticut to Margaret Douglas, conveys 22,600 acres of land on Sandy River, 1801; p. 422.

Arthur Blankenship, Atto. in fact to Thomas Belchey, to Joseph Joseph McGuire, 1809; p. 444.

John Preston and Mary R. his wife of Montgomery Co., Va., to Elizabeth Madison. Land lies on Nobusiness Creek a Branch of Walker's Creek etc., p. 445.

William Davidson, Senr. and Phebe his wife to James McGranahan of Monroe Co., Va., 1809; p. 447.

Robert Wallace and Nancy his wife to William Walls, 1807; p. 448.

Same Grantors to John Lesley, 1807; p. 449.

Samuel Ewing of Russell Co., Va., Atto. etc. for Francis Preston, to Patrick Kendrick, 1808; p. 450.

Same Grantor to Stephen Deskins, 1809; p. 451.

John Hankins Senr and Elizabeth his wife to Moses Hankins, 1809; p. 452. (Land in Baptist Valley).

Simon Crockett of Montgomery Co., Va., to Thomas Dailey, 1809; p. 453.

James Thompson to Andrew Messersmith, 1808; p. 454.

Travis Kendall and Susanah his wife to Patrick Kindrick, 1809; p. 455.

Thomas Cartmill and Nancy his wife to George Rinehart, 1809; p. 456.

Christopher Marrs and Mary his wife to Jonathan Peery, 1809; p. 457-8.

Have listed every deed in Deed Book No. 1.

Har—20

CHAPTER XVIII.

Showing all Deeds to Churches from 1800 to 1922.

1805. Deed Book No. 1, page 225.

William Witten and Letticie his wife, John Greenup and Elizabeth his wife, to John Tollett, William Witten, James Witten, Jermiah Witten, Thomas Greenup and Smith Deskins, Trustees in trust, Conveys four acres and a half, situate on Clinch River, including a small spring under the north bank of Clinch River, upon which to erect a church for the use and benefit of the members of the Methodist Episcopal Church in the United States of America ect. Said four and half acres described by metes and bounds, and comes out of a 121 acre survey made to John Greenup and Thomas Witten, decd. This is the first deed made to Church property as shown by the Deed Books. Doubtless prior donations of lands for Church purposes were made and shown by the records of the older counties from which Tazewell was formed.

1815. Deed Book No. 2, page 330.

Hez. Harman conveyed to Isaac Charles, Robert Wynne, Hez. Harman, Evans Peery, and Henry Wynne, Trustees of the Methodist Episcopal Church, "one acre around Bethel meeting house on the head of Clinch."

1815. D. B. No. 2, p.. 509.

John Lasley conveyed to Isaac Brown, William Brown, Samuel Flummer and Thomas Alin, Trustees of the Methodist Church, a half acre, "of the tract of land I now live on."

1831. D. B. No. 5, p. 243.

Samuel Sayers and Elizabeth, his wife, conveyed to James Meek, George Spraker, Philip Gose, Oliver Wynn and Samuel Sayers, Trustees of "The Burkes Garden Church." "To erect a house for Religious worship," one and a half acres "whereupon said meeting house now stands." No denomination is mentioned in this deed.

George Rudey and Catherine, his wife, conveys same land to same Trustees. See D. B. 5, p. 253.

1844. D. B. No. 8, page 285.

Hervey George and Sallie, his wife, Thomas Witten and Nancy, his wife, conveyed ten acres to Hervey George, James S. Witten, Samuel Witten, Zeno S. Sprinkle, William Brown, James Whitley and George W. G. Browne, Trustees, for the use of the Methodist Episcopal Church as a Camp Ground.

1859. D. B. No. 12, page 500.

John W. Johnston conveyed to Richard Vincent Wheelan, Bishop of Wheeling and his successors in office, a lot in the town of Jeffersonville on which the Catholic Church stands." This lot was subsequently conveyed to Trustees of the Christian Church, and later acquired for Tazewell High School and is now occupied by Tazewell High School Chapel.

1852. D. B. No. 10, page 352.

William Stump and Polly, his wife, to Jocab Burton, Adam Hedrick and Moses Kearns, Trustees for the use and occupancy of the "Methodist, Presbyterian, Lutheran and Baptist Churches, and such others as they may in their discretion permit to occupy, the same observing the rule that the appointment first made shall always have preference according to the above regulation." This is Concord Church situate about five miles east of the Court House.

1859. D. B. No. 12, p. 543.

John C. Bandy and W. P. Cecil to William Seabolt, J. J. Mays, William Pruett, R. W. Mars and H. W. Mars, Trustees of the Christian Church. The property is situate on Cavitts Creek near the residence of John C. Bandy and contains about three quarters of an acre. The Church house to be erected thereon is to be called Bullards Chapel.

1858. D. B. No. 12, p. 483.

Daniel P. Gregory and Mary J. Gregory, his wife, to Christopher Shawver, Daniel Gregary and Adam Britts, Trustees. "For the purpose of having a meeting house built on the land conveyed, free for the use of all denominations professing the Christian religion when not occupied by the Christian Church." The lot is situate on Clear Fork and contains about one and a half acres. This Church is now known as Chestnut Grove Church and is still used by the Christian Church of the neighborhood.

1873. D. B. No. 15, p. 521.

William Perry and Harrison Tabor to Hugh D. Dudley, Charles A. Hale, Granger Brown, Austin Mullin and John Tabor, Trustees, Conveys a certain lot near Falls Mills, containing one acre and twenty (20) poles, "for the purpose of erecting a house of religious worship thereon for the use of the Christian Church, the Methodist Episcopal Church South, and free for the use of other religious denominations except Mormons and Roman Catholics."

1823. D. B. No. 3, p. 337.

John Wynn and Levie, his wife conveyed to Isaac Quinn, James Witten, Samuel Witten, John Laird, Thomas Cecil, Thomas Peery, Jacob Helms, James Wynn and Hez. Harman, Trustees for the Methodist Episcopal Church, a certain lot containing one and a half acres and twelve square poles, "in the boundaries of said Wynn's lands on the Sulphur Spring ridge and near the east end thereof."

1828. D. B. No. 4, p. 236.

Betsy Higginbotham and Charles, her son, conveyed to David Young, William Higginbotham, James Higginbotham, Daniel Belche and David Allen, Trustees, a certain lot containing one acre adjoining the lands of Daniel Belche. The house to be used for school purposes and for a "meeting house."

1846. D. B. 12, p. 301.

Mark R. Bogle, Euell S. Murphy and Samuel H. Murphy, To Stephen Gose, Henry C. Kidd, Thomas Cook, Elijah Kidd and Isaac Repass, Trustees, Conveyed "a certain lot in the valley of Wolf Creek at the ford of the Green Valley branch, containing one acre." "For school and for meeting house." For Methodist, Lutheran, and presbyterian Churches, as a place of public worship and for other purposes. The trustees are to so arrange the hours of meetings of the several denominations "that no clashing in the appointments for the ministers shall interrupt the harmony of the neighborhood." This property is situate in Bland County.

1858. D. B. No. 12, p. 293.

William Redrick and Zillah C., his wife, conveyed to Stephen Gose, Wm. M. Neel, Archibald Barnett, Isaac Repass and James V. Pendleton, Trustees, a lot of land on Wolf Creek containing two acres for the benefit of the Methodist Church South and for the Lutheran Church. This property lies in Bland County.

1843. D. B. 8, p. 18.

John Eiler and Rebecca, his wife, and Samuel Carter, convey to Randal Holbrook, Joseph A. Moore, William R. Bane, William V. Shannon, John B. Harman, James H. Moore and George W. G. Browne, Trustees of the Methodist Episcopal Church for a school house and meeting house. All other orthodox preachers in good standing in their Church permitted to preach in said house so as their appointments do not interfere with those of the Methodists. Said land lies on the waters of Bluestone on the branch between said Eiler's house and Samuel Carter's on the turn pike road.

1844. D. B. 8, p. 287.

Birdine Deskins and Margaret, his wife, convey to Thomas Barnett, Sr., Charles Mitchell, James Deskins, Thomas Davis, Birdine Deskins, James Maxwell, Jr., Archibald Bruster, George Deskins, Jr., and Thomas Barrett, Trustees for the Methodist Episcopal Church, three-fourths of an acre of land. The description of this lot is as follows: "Lying in Tazewell County, Virginia, bounded as follows: 'Beginning on a small sugar tree on a line of a tract of land that formerly belonged to Bird Lochart, thence South one pole to the main road, thence with said road, north and east to the fork, being twenty poles, thence south 70° West, 18 poles to the beginning." We have not so far identified this property, but think it is located west of Maxwell on the hill.

1849. D. B. No. 9, p. 487.

Reese H. Crabtree conveyed to James B. Crabtree, Robert J. Stephenson, William Higginbotham, Richard Roberts, Solomon C. Turley, John Chiddix, Samuel C. and Thomas Turley, Trustees, a certain lot on the North bank of the Laurel Fork of Holston River, containing one acre, for the use of the Methodist Episcopal Church, South.

1849. Deed Book No. 9, page 490.

James C. Davidson and Julia H. Davidson, his wife, conveyed to Robert W. Davidson, John C. Carpenter, Peter C. Honaker, Alexander Suiter, Edward Wilson, John P. Lambert and James C. Davidson, Trustees, "a certain lot containing two acres lying on

Wolf Creek opposite the mouth of Terry's Spring branch on the west bank of Wolf Creek, for the use of the Methodist Episcopal Church, South." This property is in Bland County.

1848. Deed Book No. 9, page 508.

Andrew P. Moore and Nancy, his wife, conveyed to William T. Moore, Waddy T. Curren, Wesley Gibson, William G. W. Curren, Harden Nuckles, and Thomas G. Witten, Trustees, "a certain lot of land in Abbs Valley, Beginning on the line of said Andrew P. Moore and Waddy T. Curren, etc., "for the use of the members of the Methodist Episcopal Church, South."

1850. D. B. No. 10, p. 149.

William R. Bane and Nancy, his wife, conveyed to Charles F. Tiffany, William R. Bane, Howard Bane, William V. Shannon, Joseph A. Moore, Randolph Holbrook, Zechriah S. Witten, James Reynolds and John Harry, Trustees, a certain lot containing one and a half acres, for the use of the members of the Methodist Episcopal Church, South. Said lot Beginning at a stake near the turnpike road, thence Northward, 13 poles, ect. Only courses and distances given. We suppose this is the lot on which Ebenezer Church now stands.

1850. D. B. 10, p. 174.

Henry F. Peery and Caroline H. his wife, conveyed to George W. G. Browne, Rawley W. Witten, A. H. Spotts, and Granville Jones, Trustees, a certain lot in the town of Jeffersonville (described) for the use of the members of the Methodist Episcopal Church, South. It appears that a Church building was erected on this lot prior to the execution of the deed. This church was located on Main Street in the west end of Jeffersonville.

1851. D. B. 10, p. 306.

Francis Tabor and Mary (Polly), his wife, conveyed to Wm. G. W. Currin, Waddy P. Currin, James Mars, Jr., Moses Belcher, James Tabor, Francis Tabor, Harden Nuckles, Wesley Gibson and Richard Tabor, Trustees, a certain lot on the South side of Valley Ridge, containing two and three quarter acres, for the use of the members of the Methodist Episcopal Church, South.

1855. D. B. No. 11, p. 448.

William Blankenship conveyed to William Brown, Henry S. Bowen, John G. Taylor, Erastus B. Ward, Thomas Cecil, Meshich

Steele, and Resin R. Steele, Trustees, a certain lot containing three-eighths and four poles. Lots described by metes and bounds, Beginning on a line between Wm. Blankenship and Henry Steele and on the south edge of the turnpike. Said lot is conveyed for the use of the members of the Methodist Episcopal Church, South.

1855. D. B. 11, p. 501.

A. L. Jones, and Elizabeth, his wife, conveyed to C. A. Spotts, Elijah McGuire, Joseph C. Brown, Hugh S. Bailey, William Martin, John R. Brown, T. M. Scott, James M. Cecil and A. L. Jones, Trustees, a certain lot containing one and a half acres. Lots described; Beginning on the bank of the turnpike road near C. A. Spotts' and J. M. Cecil's lower line, etc. This is the lot on which Jones' Chapel now stands. Said meeting house to be erected on said lot "Shall be free for the use of all orthodox ministers to preach in when not occupied by the Methodists, provided further that the said meeting house shall not be used for political meetings or discussions, nor for public exhibitions or shows."

1859. D. B. 12, p. 504.

Robert Crockett and Eliza, his wife, conveyed to A. A. Spotts, John C. Hopkins, Henry B. Harman, Francis P. Spotts, John A. Kelly, E. R. Baylor, I. C. Fowler, James P. Kelly and Elias G. W. Harman, Trustees, "for the congregation of the Methodist Episcopal Church, South, at the Town of Jeffersonville." Said lot described as Beginning at the South East corner of the Trans-Alleghaney Bank lot and running along the Main Street fifty (50) feet, thence leaving said street and running a line paralel to the east line of said Bank lot, sixty five feet, thence running paralel in the Main Street to the said Bank lot line being fifty feet by sixty-five feet of the Southwest portion of the lot said Robert Crockett now lives on.

1859. D. B. 12, p. 591.

James Q. Kendrick conveyed to Shadrack Ratcliff, John M. Brown, Thomas Brown, Wm. P. Kendrick, George W. Lockhart, Richard H. Ratcliff and John G. Prater, Trustees, a certain lot containing one acre. Said lot is described as follows: "Beginning at a red oak at the mouth of a small hollow on the turnpike road, (the first hollow on the road east of Wm. P. Kendrick's dwelling house) thence fourteen poles Northwest to a stake, then South ten poles to the turnpike road and with said turnpike road to the beginning." For the use of the Members of the Methodist Episcopal Church, South. We suppose this is the lot on which Miles' Chapel stands.

1857. D. B. 13, p. 86.

Hervey George conveyed to Wm. O. George, Addison Crockett, Samuel Witten, Francis M. Peery, James W. Morton, James P. Harman and Thomas W. Witten, Trustees, in behalf of the denomination of Christians called Methodist Episcopalian, and more particularly called George's School House, etc. Said lot is near the residence of Wm. O. George, upon which the new church now stands.

1860. D. B. 13, p. 91.

Thomas J. Higginbotham and Nancy, his wife, conveyed to Robert Barnes, E. B. Ward, Z. Belcher, Thomas J. Higginbotham and Henry S. Bowen, Trustees, for the Methodist Episcopal Church, South, a certain lot containing ninety poles. Beginning at a white oak on the bank of the turnpike road, S. 58 W. 22 poles to the middle of said road, thence up the said road N. 27 E. 16½ poles to the bend of the road near the cattle scales S. 78 E. 12½ poles to the Beginning.

1860. D. B. 13, p. 164.

Hugh S. Bailey conveyed to Thomas S. Christian, William Altizer and Robert McGlothlin, "Trustees of a meeting house built on the land that said Bailey bought of Alexander Christian." Said lot contains one acre. Beginning at a white oak a corner of Hugh Bailey, on the east line, thence East thirteen poles to a chestnut oak, thence N. W. 13 poles to a poplar, thence 13 poles to a chestnut tree, thence S. 13 poles to the beginning."

1859. D. B. 14, p. 155.

A. A. Spotts and Harriet, his wife, conveyed to J. A. Kelly, J. P. Kelly, F. P. Spotts, J. C. Hopkins, E. R. Bogle, Isaac C. Fowler, H. B. Harman, E. G. W. Harman, and A. A. Spotts, Trustees for the Methodist Episcopal Church South, a lot "In the town of Jeffersonville on the back street near the junction of main street and said back Street in the west end of said town."

1871. D. B. No. 14, p. 504.

Isaac M. Daily and Margaret, his wife, conveyed to I. M. Dailey, A. F. Dailey, W. M. L. Hubble, John Yost, and Wyley W. Yost,

"Trustees of Daileys' Chapel for the use of the Methodist Episcopal Church, South," a lot in Baptist Valley on the east end of Isaac M. Dailey's farm.

1872. D. B. 15, p. 28.

Samuel Laird conveyed to Bird Elswick, J. A. Brown, James P. Brown, Chapman Elswick, F. N. Neikirk, Bazewell Elswick and George W. Brown, Trustees, for the Methodist Episcopal Church, South, a certain lot on the dividing ridge, near the line between the Counties of Tazewell and Buchanan, containing one and a half acres.

1855. D. B. 11, p. 526.

Joseph Stras, Sterling F. Watts, Samuel L. Graham, William P. Cecil, Wade D. Strother, John W. Johnston, F. P. Spotts, Wm. M. Gillespie and Wm. Cox, convey to Isaac N. Naff, Rufus Brittain and Washington Spotts on behalf of the Christians known as the New School Presbyterian Church at Jeffersonville. Said lot described as follows: Being in the N. E. quarter of the Town containing by estimation one-fourth acre and bounded on the South by the back St. of the Town and on the West by the lot, the title of which is in the name of the heirs of Lewis Smith, Decd., and on the N. and E. by the lands lately the property of Joseph and Thomas Harrison.

1859. D. B. 12, p. 473.

Nathaniel Dillion and Jane, his wife, conveyed to Wesley Gibson, Lewis K. Havens, Obadiah Belcher, Trustees, for the Methodist Church, South, a certain lot containing one acre, situate on the dividing ridge upon which the Church is now standing.

1883. D. B. 18, p. 494.

Susanah Wallace conveyed to "The Christian Church, Methodist Episcopal Church, South, and Missionary Baptist Church a certain lot near Springville, on which a church has been erected. Names of trustees as follows: R. B. Tabor, representing the Christian Church, Daniel Carter, representing the Missionary Baptist Church, and R. P. Harman, representing the Methodist Episcopal Church, South.

1889. D. B. 21, p. 474.

J. R. Sparks and Patsy, his wife, and John Lambert and Mary, his wife conveyed to Primitive Baptist and Christian Baptist Church of Baptist Valley, a certain lot, being a part of the original tract of James Hankins, deceased.

1888. D. B. 23, p. 576.

B. W. Stras and Hattie, his wife, conveyed to the State Mission Board of the Baptist General Association a certain lot in the Town of Jeffersonville.

1889. D. B. 24, p. 571.

Levi Hickman and Elizabeth, his wife, conveyed to Archibald White and R. J. Brown, Trustees of the Primitive Baptist Church for divine worship and also for a school house, a certain lot at the Forks of Big Creek. (A mile or so North of the Town of Richlands.)

1890. D. B. 25, p. 578.

Southwest Virginia Improvement Company conveyed to David Johnson, Alex Neal, James O. Fulton, Charles Cobbs, Beverly Williams, Nelson Holmes and John W. Winston, Trustees of the Colored Baptist Church, a certain lot in the Town of Pocahontas on the North side of the Railroad, etc.

1891. D. B. 32, p. 43.

Henry May and Rhoda, his wife, conveyed to Charter Mitchell, J. R. Sparks and J. N. Harman, Trustees of the Church of Christ (known as Primitive Baptist) a certain lot on the Dry Fork about one and a fourth miles westward from the Willow Bridge, etc., "other orthodox denominations to use said house when not occupied by said church."

1889. D. B. 32, p. 223.

The Southwest Virginia Improvement Company conveyed to George Dodds, L. T. Adkinson and F. H. Baker, Trustees, of the Baptist Church at Pocahontas, lots seventy-two (72) and seventy-three (73), as shown on the plan of said Town, etc.

1892. D. B. 33, p. 432.

J. N. Harman and Bettie, his wife, conveyed to Rees Bandy, George White and Charles Dingus, Trustees of the Missionary (colored) Baptist Church at Tazewell, Virginia, the Northern half of lot No. 17 as shown by the Stras and Fudge Plat of lots which is of record in Deed Book No. 23, p. 169, and being on West Side of Birch Avenue, (also known as Railroad Avenue, etc.

1897. D. B. 41, p. 125.

Elias J. Hale and M. C., his wife, conveyed to Thomas Leese, Julius Coales, and T. P. Wright, Trustees for the Graham Baptist Tabernacle, a certain lot in the Town of Graham, being lot No. 13 as appears on a plat of lots by Elias Hale.

1899. D. B. 44, p. 78.

N. C. Parsons conveyed to Thomas Leece, Julius Cole, and T. P. Wright, Trustees for the Graham Baptist Tabernacle, lots numbers eight, nine and ten, Block A., as shown on the plat of lots of Morton Harman & Co., recorded in the Clerk's Office in Deed Book No. 31, page 408.

1900. D. B. 44, p. 246.

John H. Greever and Lettice C., his wife, conveyed to Dr. James R. Crockett, Adison Cook and Miss Lettie A. Goodman, Trustees of the Baptist Church of Burkes Garden, a certain lot lying on the West side of the turnpike road, etc.

1905. D. B. 56, p. 345.

M. B. Linkous, Martha J. Linkous, E. J. Suthers and T. F. Suthers, her husband, M. M. Stevens and G. B. Stevens to J. W. Coleman, W. S. King and S. W. Garnett, Trustees of Graham Baptist Church, a certain lot therein described.

1906. D. B. 63, p. 206-7.

The Pocahontas Colieries Company conveyed to C. G. Betelle, John L. Belcher and J. M. Newton, Trustees of the Baptist Church of Boissevain, a certain lot containing .011 acres, (Described in a map attached recorded on page 209.)

1883. D. B. 24, p. 421.

Right Rev. J. J. Kain, Bishop of Wheeling, conveyed to George W. Gillespie, George W. Shawver, James W. Baker and James H. Wingo, Trustees, in behalf of the Christian Church at Tazewell Court House, a certain lot and church thereon, situated on the Eastern side of the street running South from the Virginia Hotel etc. (The Tazewell High School Chapel now stands on this lot.

1890. D. B. 30, p. 26.

Benjamine Dickinson and Catherine, his wife, conveyed to Oliver Harper, Augustus Higginbotham, and Reece Higginbotham,

Trustees of the Christian Church (colored) a certain lot on Mud Fork, (fully described). The church building to be used by other Protestant denominations when not occupied by the Christian Church.

1891. D. B. 32, p. 455.

Jessie J. Jennings and Sarah J., his wife, conveyed to Dexter B. Daniel, Robert W. Bowman and John W. Daniel, Trustees of Horsepen Christian Church, a certain lot therein described.

1892. D. B. No. 34, p. 47.

Graham Land and Improvement Company conveyed to C. P. McWane, C. W. McWane, O. A. Metcalf, Trustees of Graham Christian Church of the Town of Graham, lot number two in section sixteen, plan B., recorded in Deed Book No. 29, page 8.

1894. D. B. 37, p. 181.

Elizabeth Cole, William Cole and Rhoda, his wife, conveyed to D. W. Dudley, Patton G. Shrader, Samuel Crockett, B. Frank Riley, R. W. Pruette, Trustees for the Christian Church, a certain lot in Crocketts Cove on Grassy Spur.

1892. D. B. 38, p. 497.

J. N. Harman and Bettie, his wife, conveyed to C. A. Banks, Albert Crockett, and Stuart Crockett, Trustees of the Christian Church, (colored) of the Town of Tazewell, a certain lot lying on west side of Railroad Avenue about half way between the town of Tazewell and the railway station.

1897. D. B. 40, p. 286.

George Harman and Ressie, his wife, conveyed to Jacob Witten, Aaron Cecil and Harvy Baldwin, Trustees of the Christian Church, (colored) a certain lot at Tip Top, Virginia.

1898. D. B. 41, p. 180.

George W. St. Clair and Annie, his wife, conveyed to James W. Baker, H. W. Pobst, L. C. Wingo and R. B. Gillespie, Trustees of the Christian Church at Tazewell. The present Christian church is located on this lot.

1899. D. B. 43, p. 11.

John W. Gillespie and Margaret, his wife, conveyed to William F. Harman, R. B. George, and S. S. F. Harman, Trustees of Cavitts Creek Christian Church, a certain lot at the forks of the road, etc., being the lot on which the present church building stands. When the house is not occupied by said congregation it may be used by others.

1901. D. B. 45, p. 254.

Tazewell Court House Improvement Company conveyed to Charles Harman, Samuel Young and Miles Cecil, Trustees of King's Chapel Christian Church, (colored) a certain lot in the Town of Tazewell, being lot No. 10 in section 29, shown on map recorded in Deed Book No. 30, pages 12 and 13.

1902. D. B. 49, p. 37.

Rebecca C. Davis conveyed to W. C. Williams, J. B. Hurt, R. H. Ireson, R. K. Gillespie, R. M. Sparks and John Robinett, Trustees for the Christian and Methodist Church, South, at Pounding Mill, Virginia, a certain lot etc. This is the lot on which the present house of worship now stands.

1902. D. B. 49, p. 239.

M. F. Brown and A. A. Brown, his wife, conveyed to Powell Ellis, Ward Ratliff, and M. C. Osborne, Trustees of the Little Valley Christian Church, a certain lot upon the waters of Tumbling Creek, in Little Valley, etc. The house to be used by other denominations when not occupied by this congregation.

1905. D. B. 58, p. 46.

Thomas Brown and Mary, his wife, conveyed to G. B. Fuller, M. Murry, James Beavers, G. W. Deskins, N. Asberry and Joseph Rose, Trustees, a certain lot between the head waters of Dry Fork and Cavitts Creek adjoining the lands of Julia A. Graham and H. T. May, "To be dedicated to the Lord, in the name of the Second Advent Christian denomination, but the building to be used by other orthodox ministers." "The book of Mormon to be excluded as a text book."

1886. D. B. 41, p. 216.

John W. Beavers and Lucy, his wife, conveyed to Thomas R. Bandy, M. J. Beavers and J. H. Gillespie, Trustees for the Church of Christ, (Desciples) a certain lot on Dicks Creek."

1885. D. B. 20, p. 336.

H. C. Alderson and Mary C. his wife, conveyed to B. W. Stras, R. R. Henry, D. B. Baldwin, George W. Spotts, Thomas G. Witten,

W. E. Peery and A. F. Hargrave, Trustees of the Protestant Episcopal Church at Tazewell Court House, a certain lot etc. The Episcopal Church now standing on said lot.

1885. D. B. 21, p. 31.

Southwest Virginia Improvement Company conveyed to B. W. Stras, D. B. Baldwin, George Spotts, Edward Peery, William Ingles and John Izzard, Trustees for the benefit of the Protestant Episcopal Parish in the County of Tazewell, a certain lot in the Town of Pocahontas.

1888. D. B. 24, p. 22.

G. W. Doak and Rose A., his wife, conveyed to R. M. Lawson, C. J. Barnes, C. E. Brown and B. W. Stras, Trustees for the benefit of the Protestant Episcopal Parish in Tazewell County, a certain lot near the Town of Tazewell, adjoining the lands of A. J. May. A chapel was built on this lot which was used for some time but later abandoned.

1885. D. B. 33, p. 301.

Southwest Virginia Improvement Company conveyed to B. W. Stras, D. B. Baldwin, George Spotts, Edward Peery, William Ingles and John Izzard, Trustees, for the benefit of the Protestant Episcopal Parish in the County of Tazewell, a certain lot in the Town of Pocahontas.

1893. D. B. 35, p. 522.

C. A. Fudge and M. G., his wife, conveyed to J. H. Hampton, Wm. H. Goins and W. P. Whitley, Trustees of the Mount Pleasant Church for the use and benefit of the Protestant Church, all that certain lot situate on the ridge between Whitley and Lincolnshire branches, containing one-half acre.

1884. D. B. 19, p. 251.

H. C. Alderson and Mary C., his wife, conveyed to D. B. Baldwin, B. W. Stras, R. R. Henry, George W. Spotts, Thomas G. Witten, W. E. Peery and A. F. Hargrave, Trustees for the Protestant Episcopal Church at Tazewell Court House, a certain lot etc.

1903. D. B. 52, p. 116.

Clinch Valley Coal & Iron Company conveyed to B. W. Stras, John E. Jackson, Trustees of the Protestant Episcopal Church for Diocese of Southern Virginia, two certain lots in the town of Richlands.

1906. D. B. 59, p. 110.

J. W. Maxwell conveyed to W. W. Lawson, S. W. Lawson, W. L. Hoops, Rolley Puckett and J. E. Long, Trustees to the house of God, a certain lot at Maxwell's switch.

1881. D. B. 18, p. 107.

James E. Rhudy, Charles T. C. Rhudy and John C. Rhudy, conveyed to Trustees by a new deed confirming or perfecting a previous conveyance to the Lutheran Church in Burkes Garden, with privilege to be used by the Presbyterians and Methodists.

1889. D. B. 28, p. 49.

C. A. Fudge and M. G., his wife, conveyed to M. L. Peery, C. W. Greever and William L. Spracher, Trustees of the Evangelical Lutheran Church, a certain lot in the town of North Tazewell. This property now is owned by the Methodist Episcopal Church, South.

1902. D. B. 49, p. 360.

J. S. Moss and Barbara J., his wife, and J. A. Greever and Sallie B., his wife, conveyed to M. L. Peery, J. S. Moss, J. A. Greever and C. W. Greever, Trustees for the Evangelical Lutheran Church at the Town of Tazewell, a certain lot, (described), being the lot on which the Lutheran Church now stands.

1903. D. B. 51, p. 226.

Juston Young, Pleas Young, Julia F. Sanders and Allen Sanders conveyed to Thomas Peery, L. C. Cole and J. S. Karr, Trustees for the Graham Congregation of the Evangelical Lutheran Church at Graham.

1872. D. B. 16, p. 72.

Thomas G. Crockett and Nancy, his wife, and Rush F. Crockett, conveyed to Rush F. Crockett, George P. McQuire, David S. Fowler, L. S. Shrader and Henry H. Mars, Trustees, a certain lot on the right of the public road leading from the town of Jeffersonville, for the use of the Methodist Episcopal Church, South. Said lot is situate in Crocketts' Cove.

1877. D. B. 16, p. 310.

James L. Carroll conveyed to Beverly Warren, George Crockett and David Bell, Trustees of the Methodist Episcopal Church in the United States of America, a certain lot in the West end of Jeffersonville.

1878. D. B. 16, p. 397.

Malcolm McNeil and Mary E., his wife, conveyed to John B. Young, Thomas C. Christian, Ebenezer Bruster, Hugh S. Bailey and Malcolm McNeil, Trustees for the Methodist Episcopal Church South, a certain lot, "Beginning at the ford of Indian near Lochart's Chapel, containing one-half acre, running with the Bearwallow road and Indian Creek," etc.

1878. D. B. 16, p. 461.

Robert Steele and Julia A. his wife, conveyed to William C. Cecil, Rush F. Cecil, Robert M. Cecil, Samuel Steele and James H. Gillespie, Trustees for Steele's Chapel of the Methodist Episcopal Church, South, a certain lot containing one hundred poles, etc.

1878. D. B. 16, p. 599.

E. L. Whitley and Fanney A., his wife conveyed to W. P. Whitley, John W. Whitley, Andrew Hounshell, John W. Brown, and H. B. Harman, Trustees of Whitley's Chapel Methodist Episcopal Church, South, a certain lot containing one acre, lying about two miles Northwest of Jeffersonville, etc.

1883. D. B. 19, p. 54.

William Marrs and Louisa, his wife, conveyed to William Marrs, E. G. Brown, John W. Argabright, F. F. Brotherton, C. A. Deaton, J. H. Flummer and Nelson H. McClaugherty, Trustees of the Methodist Episcopal Church, South, a certain lot near Falls Mills, containing one-fourth of an acre, etc.

1883. D. B. 19, p. 121.

T. M. Bourne and Lucinda M., his wife, Annie Buchanan, Wm. P. Buchanan, Edward A. Buchanan, Stephen Bourne and Lula, his wife, conveyed to Wm. H. Kelly, Thomas M. Bourne, Thomas K. Hall, Felix Bourne, Gabriel Crabtree, Wm. Burton, David G. Yost, Trustees of the Methodist Episcopal Church, South, a certain lot on the dividing ridge between the waters of Clear Fork and Clinch River, on the East side of the Wytheville turnpike Road, etc.

1886. D. B. 20, p. 504.

Andrew L. Jones and Elizabeth, his wife, conveyed to M. R. Russell, John Russell, Jacob Jones, Saunders Wilson, J. M. Cochran, John Sword, and Richard Ferrell, Trustees of the Methodist Episcopal Church, a certain lot near the mouth of Indian Creek, Beginning at the road at J. M. McGuire's corner, etc.

1884. D. B. 21, p. 115.

J. Dickinson Sargent of Philadelphia conveyed to Robert Holly, Lee Bane, and George Preston, Trustees of the Methodist Church of America of the county of Tazewell, a certain lot in the town of Graham, etc.

1886. D. B. 21, p. 125.

Southwest Virginia Improvement Company conveyed to George W. Thomas, B. P. Maxey, C. M. Sherestz, Charles H. Witten, P. Y. Veeder, J. B. Saunders and G. B. Stevenson, Trustees of the Methodist Episcopal Church, South, a certain lot in the Town of Pocahontas.

1885. D. B. 23, p. 54.

William B. Morton and Margaret, his wife, conveyed to W. E. Bane, R. A. Hale, J. B. Higginbotham, Joseph Davidson, Calvin Harry, and Wm. B. Morton, Trustees for the Methodist Episcopal Church, South, at Graham, Virginia, a certain lot in the Town of Graham on the corner of Morton Street and Water Avenue, etc.

1889. D. B. 24, p. 520.

John M. Thompson and Eliza, his wife, conveyed to John A. Higginbotham, John M. Thompson, and A. J. Steele, Trustees of the Methodist Episcopal Church, South, a certain lot in the lower end of Thompson Valley, the place where George Bowling resides and adjoining the lands of Alex Dills, etc.

1889. D. B. 25, p. 356.

R. W. Witten conveyed to W. G. Bottimore, John C. St. Clair, W. W. Peery, John Peery and R. W. Witten, Trustees of the Methodist Episcopal Church, South, a certain lot on Clinch River near "Old Pisgah Church," containing one acre, etc.

1890. D. B. 30, p. 64.

Sallie Steele conveyed to James L. Carroll, J. B. Warren, C. C. Holly and M. Richards, Trustees of the Methodist Episcopal Church in the United States, a certain lot in the west end of the Town of Jeffersonville on Main Street, adjoining the Church lot conveyed from Samuel L. Carroll to Beverly Warren and others, Trustees, by deed dated June 27, 1887 and recorded in Deed Book No. 16, page 310.

1890. D. B. 32, p. 222.

Southwest Virginia Improvement Company conveyed to John A. Brown, Bascomb Sinkford, John Willoughby, Wm. E. Mitchell, Cheshire Froe, Trustees of the Colored Methodist Church of Pocahontas, a certain lot in the Town of Pocahontas, etc.

1890. D. B. 33, p. 299.

Patton J. Lockhart and Caroline, his wife, conveyed to George C. Bailey, Hugh Tabor, Theodore Arms, Wm. P. Brown and Patton J. Lockhart, Trustees of the Methodist Episcopal Church, South, at Mount Carmel Church in Baptist Valley, a certain lot on the North side of the public road, etc.

1893. D. B. 36, p. 101.

Clinch Valley Coal & Iron Company, conveyed to H. Wade Steele, James B. Crabtree, James F. Hurt, J. Muncey Ratcliff and A. C. Gardner, Trustees of the Methodist Episcopal Church at Richlands, two lots numbers nineteen (19) and twenty (20), etc.

1888. D. B. 36, p. 398.

Wm. A. Ward and Jennie Bell, his wife, and Wm. E. Baylor to James M. McGuire, James Peery, P. J. Lochart, Elijah McGuire and J. Marion McGuire, Trustees of the Methodist Episcopal Church, South, at Cedar Bluff, a certain lot in the Village of Mouth of Indian, etc.

1893. D. B. 36, p. 571.

T. H. Kinser and Mary, his wife, conveyed to James A. Harman, William Jones, M. T. Christian, G. S. Compton and H. M. Kiser, Trustees of the Methodist Episcopal Church, South, a certain lot on Clear Fork, on South side of said creek containing 2,658 feet, etc.

1894. D. B. 37, p. 263.

J. W. Tabor and Fannie, his wife, conveyed to I. H. Harry, W. C. Tabor, W. W. Saddler, George A. Butt and J. W. Tabor, Trustees of the Methodist Episcopal Church, South, at Falls Mills, a certain lot near the village of Falls Mills, etc.

1896. D. B. 38, p. 575.

C. A. Fudge and M. G., his wife, conveyed to W. P. Whitley, J. H. Whitley, C. H. Peery, W. I. Hall, H. G. Peery, Jr., C. A. Fudge, John F. Ireson, H. F. Peery and John C. Bailey, Trustees of the M. E. Church, South, a certain lot in the town of North Tazewell in exechange for old "Whitleys Chapel" lot, etc.

1896. D. B. 39, p. 181.

A. St. Clair and Mariah J. his wife, conveyed to Wm. Summers, C. A. Bane, J. B. Shannon, A. P. Tabor, Trustees of the M. E. Church, South, a certain lot on Bluestone upon which stands the Church building known as Ebenezer, etc.

1896. D. B. 39, p. 388.

James Bandy and Sallie, his wife, conveyed to M. M. Hankins, Wm. Bandy, S. F. Allison, Thomas G. Bruster, and Shadrack Creed, Trustees of the Methodist Episcopal Church, a certain lot containing one acre in west end of Baptist Valley at the forks of the road, etc.

1881. D. B. 40, p. 214.

Jessie J. Harris and Ardelia, his wife, conveyed to John M. Smith, George Harman, and J. J. Harris, Trustees of the Methodist Episcopal Church of Mud Fork Circuit, a certain lot on Mud Fork on which a church has already been erected.

1899. D. B. 43, p. 84.

Charles W. Butt and Celie V., his wife, conveyed to James Sluss, Sr., J. T. Billips, Edward Tiller, Gus Billips, Sr., Charles Harman and C. D. Butt, Trustees of the Carner's Chapel, M. E. Church, South, a certain lot lying on Mud Fork, etc.

1899. D. B. 43, p. 149.

M. L. Peery, C. W. Greever and Wm. L. Spracher, Trustees of the Evangelical Lutheran Church, conveyed to W. P. Whitley, J. H. Whitley, C. H. Peery, W. I. Hall, H. G. Peery, Jr., C. A. Fudge, J. F. Ireson, H. F. Peery and J. C. Bailey, Trustees of the Methodist Episcopal Church, South, at North Tazewell, Virginia.

1897. D. B. 48, p. 336.

Wm. A. Davis and W. P. Davis and Julia A., his wife, conveyed to W. A. Davis, Mark T. Lockhart, Bird J. Lockhart, Sparrell Steele, and J. W. Rimmer, Trustees of Davis Chapel of the M. E.

Church, South, at Davis Chapel, a certain lot adjoining the lands of J. F. Prater and others.

1897. D. B. 55, p. 290.

A. J. May and Mary M. May, his wife, conveyed to Bascomb Sinkford, Alexander Trigg, Robert Dickerson, Dennis Hogan and George Harman, Trustees of the Methodist Episcopal Church at Tip Top, a certain lot situate in the village of Tip Top, being lot No. 12 in Block 2, etc.

1888. D. B. 23, p. 390.

W. E. Bane and Emma G., his wife, conveyed to C. O. McCall, W. E. Bane, Samuel Graham, G. M. Hanson, and A. V. Shell, Trustees of the Presbyterian Church in the United States, at Graham, a certain lot in the town of Graham, etc.

1892. D. B. 34, p. 71.

Southwest Virginia Improvement Company conveyed to E. J. Ware, A. L. Hill and W. R. Graham, Trustees of the Presbyterian Church at Pocahontas, a certain lot in the Town of Pocahontas on the North side of Moore Street, etc.

1899. D. B. 53, p. 571.

Charles W. Butt and Celia V., his wife, conveyed to Jermiah Yates, Robert Buffalow, and George Boswell, "as Trustees of the Rye's Chapel, North of Mud Fork, according to usages of the Churches," a certain lot on Mud Fork on the road that leads from Abbs Valley to Clinch, and South of the Valley Ridge, etc., containing about half an acre.

1902. D. B. 47, p. 496.

J. H. Lester and E. W., his wife, conveyed to John G. Lester, George Lambert, Samuel Ward, and Robert Lester, Trustees of the Methodist Episcopal Church, South, at Lesters Chapel, a certain lot containing one half acre, situate in Wards Cove being a part of the land now owned and occupied by J. H. Lester.

1902. D. B. 48, p. 551.

D. Green conveyed to D. Green, Jackson Copenhaver, John Green, Balfour White and J. T. Lester, Trustees of the M. E. Church, South, at Green's Chapel, formerly Big Spring, a certain lot containing one fourth of an acre on the Fincastle Road about two miles East of Paint Lick, etc. It is provided that when the Church on this lot is not occupied by the M. E. Church, South, it may be occupied by other denominations.

1902. D. B. 49, p. 37.

Miss Rebecca C. Davis conveyed to W. C. Williams, J. B. Hurt, R. H. Ireson, R. K. Gillespie, R. M. Sparks, and John Robinett, Trustees for the joint and equal use of the M. E. Church, South, and the Christian Church, a certain lot in the Village of Pounding Mill on the North side of the County road as it approaches the Railroad station from the West, etc.

1904. D. B. 53, p. 38.

C. A. Fudge and M. G., his wife, conveyed to John B. Peery, John Watkins, O. B. Thompson, Rees Smith, and Fred Peery, Trustees of the M. E. Church, a certain lot in North Tazewell, Virginia, etc.

1904. D. B. 54, p. 298.

J. T. Dills conveyed to M. E. Church, South, a certain lot on the Divides of Bluestone and Clinch Rivers, containing a half acre for Church purposes.

1896. D. B. 58, p. 207.

James G. Higginbotham and Laura J., his wife, conveyed to H. W. Stowers, R. G. Shufflebarger, M. F. Neel, and James A. Harman, Trustees of the M. E. Church, South, a certain lot lying on Cove Creek near the ford thereof.

1906. D. B. 58, p. 365.

M. F. Wynn and Annie E. Wynn, his wife, conveyed to M. F. Wynn, W. R. Stowers, B. R. Moss, A. L. Davis, T. H. Short, John Fox, R. M. Lawson, George Moss, and John D. Greever, Trustees of the M. E. Church, South, a certain lot in Burkes Garden, adjoining the lands of M. F. Wynn, and John Fox, and the public school lot, etc.

1907. D. B. 60, p. 574.

J. W. Laird and J. R. Laird, executors of S. H. Laird, deceased, conveyed to A. M. Christian, J. W. Christian, G. H. Brown, J. T. Altizer and James B. Altizer, Trustees of ::Lairds Chapel" Church of the M. E. Church South, a certain lot, situate on the top of the

Dividing Ridge, bewean Dismal and Middle Creek, mostly on the Middle Creek side, etc.

1903. D. B. 52, p. 212.

Martha Thompson, Widow of G. O. Thompson, Mary Grace Thompson, Rebecca Elizabeth Thompson, Georgia Alice Thompson and Archibald Thompson, conveyed to Joseph G. Barnes, Samuel J. Thompson, D. W. Lynch and J. E. Buchanan, Trustees of the Thompson Valley Presbyterian Church, the Liberty Hill Presbyterian Church and the Cove Presbyterian Church, a certain lot in Thompson Valley containing three acres and being situate about fifty yards from the store of R. B. Peery & Company.

1914. D. B. 77, p. 146.

Jonas Sparks conveyed to Bethel Church of the Regular Baptist Denomination, a certain lot on Clinch River near Cliffield, containing one half acre.

1914. D. B. 76, p. 350.

Pocahontas Consolidated Collieries Company conveyed to J. G. Groseclose, J. W. Wilson and G. C. Cunningham, Jr., Trustees of the Boissevain M. E. Church, South, etc., a certain lot in the Town of Boissevain.

1910. D. B. 68, p. 522.

Miss Amy Mullin conveyed to G. M. Mullin, J. N. Harman and Thomas E. Tabor, Trustees for the Christian Church, at Christs Chapel, a certain lot at the foot of the Stoney Ridge, near Falls Mills on the waters of Bluestone River, on the county road leading from Falls Mills to Graham, etc.

1907. D. B. 72, p. 16.

George F. Brewster and Patsy, his wife, conveyed to D. W. Dudley, R. W. Pruette and B. F. Riley, Jr., Trustees of the Christian Church at Grassy Spur, a certain lot adjoining said Church lot, containing a half acre, to be used as a grave yard, etc.

1917. D. B. 83, p. 245.

George R. McCall and Exie, his wife, conveyed to L. D. Boyd, J. Sam Gillespie and George R. McCall, Trustees, a certain lot west of and near the Town of Raven, for the use of the M. E. Church, South, the Methodist Church and the Christian Church. The first story of the building to be used by said denominations and the second story to be used by I. O. O. F. Lodge No. 313, etc. Other denominations to use the house—the trustees in their discretion may permit same to be used by other religious denominations for the purpose of worship.

1908. D. B. 66, p. 318.

Rufus Smith and Poca H. his wife, conveyed to Floyd Houchins, T. C. Hughes, and Rufus Smith, Trustees for "The Church of God," a certain lot on the East side of Big Creek near the Town of Richlands, containing one-fourth of an acre, etc.

1910. D. B. 69, p. 275.

Florence Barnes and Rush Barnes, her husband, conveyed to Sam Young, Charlie Harman and Oscar Hedrick, Trustees of the Colored Christian Church at Tazewell, a certain strip of land adjoining the lot of the said colored Christian Church.

1912. D. B. 72, p. 441.

H. Millner and Mollie, his wife, conveyed to Harry Gross, H. J. Ferrimer and Norman Kwass, Trustees of Congregation Ahovas Chesad, a religious organization of the Town of Pocahontas, a certain lot in the Town of Pocahontas containing 1750 square feet &c.

1916. D. B. 81, 259.

H. Milner, (widower) conveyed to Norman Kwass, Harry Gross and H. J. Ferrimer, Trustees of Congregation Ahovas Chasad of which I am a member and which is composed of the Jewish people in the Town of Pocahontas, who adhere wholly to the Orthodox Jewish faith and customs, a certain lot in the town of Pocahontas, etc. It is further provided in said deed that this property is not to be used by the "Reformed Jewish Church."

1914. D. B. 79, p. 90.

Edward Foster and Julia, his wife, conveyed to George Douglas, William Myers and J. P. Jordan, Trustees, for the First Colored Baptist Church at Tazewell, two certain lots, etc.

1917. D. B. 83, p. 437.

Pocahontas Fuel Company conveyed to Ben Armstead, R. L. Jackson, J. T. Cheatham, T. W. Green and J. E. Woods, Trustees of the First Baptist Church, colored of Pocahontas, a certain lot, etc.

1917. D. B. 82, p. 528.

James A. C. Harman and Nettie, his wife, conveyed to S. W. Garnett, C. W. Matthews, and W. G. Neese, Trustees for the Graham Baptist Church of Graham, a certain lot in said town, etc.

1914. D. B. 76, p. 481.

V. Alice Buck and John A. Buck conveyed to W. L. Burton, W. P. Hagy and J. F. Dudley, Trustees of Graham Christian Church, a certain lot in the Town of Graham, being lot number 4 in section 24, etc.

1916. D. B. 80, p. 489.

Graham Land & Improvement Company conveyed to the Trustees of the M. E. Church, South, Graham Circuit, lot number four in Section twenty-nine, (29).

1911. D. B. 75, p. 21.

George Harman and Rissa, his wife, and others, conveyed to Isom Witten, Cecil Harman, William Witten, Charles Harman, Sheffie Harman, Oscar Thompson and William Anderson, Trustees of the Methodist Episcopal Church in the United States, a certain lot at Tip Top, etc.

1908. D. B. 64, p. 493.

J. R. G. Brown and C. M. Brown, his wife, conveyed to J. R. G. Brown, J. H. Peery, F. J. Brown, R. B. Conley, and J. R. Davidson, Trustees of the M. E. Church, South, a certain lot on the South side of Big Stony Ridge, etc.

1897. D. B. 67, p. 197.

O. M. Brown and Zarilda, his wife, conveyed to Samuel B. Ward, Joseph G. Barnes, Samuel J. Thompson, Henry Bowen and J. O. Brown, Trustees, Southern Presbyterian Church and the Methodist Episcopal Church, South in the "Cove" to be known as the "Cove Church," and being the lot on which the Church building now stands.

1910. D. B. 68, p. 565.

W. P. Hagy and Rhoda V. His wife, conveyed to George A. Reynolds, George P. Crockett and R. F. Alley, Trustees of the M. E. Church, South, a certain lot in West Graham being lot No. 15, in section 6.

1912. D. B. 72, p. 445.

W. P. Payne and T. J. Payne, his wife, conveyed to the Methodist Church, South, a certain lot on Indian Creek at the ford near the old Lochart Chapel, etc.

1915. D. B. 78, p. 469.

Faraday Coal and Coke Company conveyed to S. E. Marrs, A. R. Beavers and T. E. McCall, Trustees of the M. E. Church, South, a certain lot on Dicks Creek and near the mouth thereof.

1911. D. B. 72, p. 123.

Caleb Smith and Martha, his wife, conveyed to Richard White and Henry Smith, Trustees of the Primitive Baptist Church at Mount Olive.

1913. D. B. 75, p. 319.

W. A. Buchanan and Sallie J., his wife, conveyed to Felix Bourne, Sr., Thomas Burton, J. C. Bourne, W. A. Buchanan, and G. S. Gildersleeve, Trustees for the Mount Olivet M. E. Church, South, a certain lot on the Dividing Ridge between the waters of Clinch River and Clear Fork, etc.

1915. D. B. 81, p. 26.

Pocahontas Consolidated Collieries Company, and others, conveyed to G. H. Landon, B. W. Stras, S. N. Huffard and T. N. Williamson, Trustees of the Protestant Episcopal Church in Tazewell County, a certain lot in the town of Pocahontas, etc.

1915. D. B. 81, p. 384.

Pocahontas Consolidated Collieries Company, and others, conveyed to G. H. Landen, B. W. Stras, S. N. Huffard and T. N. Williamson, Trustees, Protestant Episcopal Church, a certain lot in the Town of Pocahontas, etc.

1908. D. B. 65, p. 335.

M. C. McCorkle and Rhoda, his wife, George W. Gillespie and Barbara, his wife, and J. N. Harman and Bettie, his wife, conveyed to W. P. Farmer, M. M. Hankins, and C. N. Donnahue, Trustees of Richlands Christian Church, a certain lot in the Town of Richlands, etc. The Trustees in their discretion are authorized to permit other ministers and congregations of other religious denominations to use the building for Divine worship when not occupied by said Christian Church, etc.

1908. D. B. 64, p. 99.

Graham Land and Improvement Company conveyed to Thomas Williamson, Robert Williamson, and Samuel N. Hufford, Trustees for the use of the Protestant Episcopal Church at Graham, two certain lots in the Town of Graham, designated as lots numbers 13 and 14, etc.

1910. D. B. 68, p. 232.

Same Grantor to same Grantees as above, conveyed lot number 48 in section 34, etc. Also a conveyance from Samuel Walton and Margaret C., his wife, and Jennie Y. Watson, to said Trustees, lot No. 47, section 34, etc.

1911. D. B. 70, p. 301.

B. R. Butt and Maggie A., his wife, to T. N. Williamson, R. B. Williamson and S. N. Hufford, Trustees of Saint Paul's Mission of the Protestant Episcopal Church of the Diocese of Southern Virginia, a certain lot at Yards, etc.

1912. D. B. 72, p. 186.

Trustees of Baptist State Mission Board conveyed to C. H. Reynolds, W. N. Surface and N. W. Kiser, Trustees of Tazewell Baptist Church, the lot in the town of Tazewell on which the Baptist Church now stands.

1909. D. B. 66, p. 19.

T. R. Smoot and Kate, his wife, conveyed to S. A. Witten, Robert Tarter, Frank Pyott, C. C. Brown and James McDowell, Trustees of the Tip Top Methodist Episcopal Church, South, a certain lot in the village of Tip Top.

1912. D. B. 73, p. 267.

H. P. Linkous and Mary J., his wife, conveyed to J. R. Linkous, J. B. Hankins and B. O'Quinn, Committee, a certain lot on Dry Fork, the lower story of the house erected thereon to be used by the people as a Union Church and the upper story as a Hall for the I. O. O. F. and Rebecca Star, etc.

1918. D. B. 85, p. 76.

G. W. Mays and Sarah E., his wife, J. W. Gentry and Bettie, his wife, conveyed to R. L. Jackson, Ben M. Armstead, John Cheatham, Thomas W. Green and James Woods, Trustees of the First

Baptist Church, colored, of Pocahontas, a certain lot situate in said Town.

1918. D. B. 85, p. 159.

E. E. Hale and Mary E., his wife, conveyed to W. M. Painter, W. L. Burton and J. F. Dudley, Trustees of Graham Christian Church, a certain lot in the Town of Graham, designated as lot 3 in section 24, etc.

1915. D. B. 86, p. 48.

H. Y. Brown and Mary, his wife, and J. O. Brown, and Nannie E., his wife, conveyed to W. J. Gillespie, J. O. Brown, Henry Copenhaver, S. J. Thompson, J. G. Barnes George Ward and C. O. Barnes, Trustees for the Presbyterian Church, and M. E. Church, South, a certain lot in Wards Cove. The house to be erected thereon to be used by other denominations also.

1918. D. B. 86, p. 183.

J. R. Swartz and N. P. Miller of Rockingham County, Virginia, conveyed to J. C. Lambert, W. J. Hinkle and J. M. J. Tilley, Trustees of the Holiness Pentecostal people, known as the Assembly of the Church of God of Laurel Creek, Tazewell County, a certain lot lying and being at the Mouth of Laurel Creek, a tributary of Indian Creek.

1919. D. B. 86, p. 312.

John A. Mathena and F. J., his wife, conveyed to J. A. Mathena, J. R. Puckett, W. H. Harman, and Mrs. Johnny Michen, Trustees for the Church of God, a certain lot on the waters of Mud Fork, etc.

1913. D. B. 86, p. 369.

Graham Land and Improvement Company conveyed to C. H. Green, J. C. Holley, C. L. Roberson, H. C. Brown and S. L. Trigg, Trustees for the M. E. Church, in the United States of America, a certain lot in the Town of Graham, designated as lot number 15, in section 36, etc.

1919. D. B. 86, p. 483.

W. B. Steele and Corrie, his wife, conveyed to C. H. Trayer, W. B. Greear, Charles McGuire, James McGuire, and Henry Phillips, Trustees of the Hebron Methodist Church, South, a certain lot on Pounding Mill Branch, and road, about three or four miles southeast of Pounding Mill Depot.

1920. D. B. 88, p. 60.

R. E. Baldwin and Lucy L., his wife, conveyed to G. B. Stevens, C. W. Matthews, and J. D. Whitescarver, Trustees of Graham Baptist Church, a certain lot in the Town of Graham and designated as Lot 11 in section 44.

1920. D. B. 88, p. 66.

Wm. M. Gillespie and Mary G., his wife, conveyed to E. K. Crockett, Gratt M. Bowen, T. M. Greear, J. H. Wilson and S. A. Witten, Trustees of the M. E. Church, South, at Wittens Mills, a certain lot at Wittens Mills on which is situated May's Chapel.

1920. D. B. 88, p. 151.

G. W. Rimmer and Ella, his wife, conveyed to J. L. Goss, John L. Lamie, W. J. Blankenship, W. A. Montgomery, W. H. Wright, and Vernie Hernandon, Trustees of the Church of God, a certain lot in the Town of Richlands.

1920. D. B. 88, p. 432.

J. P. Cameron and Olivia, his wife, conveyed to George P. Crockett, Lee J. Barbee, J. E. Baylor, G. M. Bayley and G. A. Reynolds, Trustees of the M. E. Church, South, a certain lot in the Town of Graham.

1920. D. B. 88, p. 433.

James A. C. Harman and Nettie E., his wife, conveyed to George P. Crockett and other trustees above mentioned, a certain lot in the Town of Graham.

1920. D. B. 90, p. 41.

B. D. Humphrey and Minnie, his wife, conveyed to James J. Fields, Reece Cordle and Mrs. Kate McDilda, Trustees of the Church of God, at Cedar Bluff, a certain lot in the "College Hill" Annex, designated as Lot No. 74, etc.

1921. D. B. 90, p. 219.

Pocahontas Fuel Company conveyed to E. J. Ellett, B. B. Scott and T. B. Breniger, Trustees of the Baptist Church at Pocahontas, a certain lot in Pocahontas, or rather an addition or confirmation of a previous conveyance to the said Church trustees, etc.

1921. D. B. 92, p. 10.

Wm. S. Taylor, George W. Taylor and Mattie, his wife, conveyed to Albert S. Caldwell, James M. Osborn and Robert L. Ellis, Trustees of the Church of Christ, (Christian Church) a certain lot on top of the Spur West of Matneys Branch in Poor Valley, etc.

1922. D. B. 92, p. 499.

Richlands Civic Betterment League Incorporated, conveyed to Trustees of the Funds of the Protestant Episcopal Church, ten lots in the Town of Richlands.

1921. D. B. 93, p. 4.

W. M. Hardy and Orie Hardy, his wife, conveyed to C. R. Havens, W. M. Leathco, and C. E. Goodwin, Trustees of the Church of God at Boissevain, a certain lot near the Town of Boissevain.

1922. D. B. 93, p. 46.

H. P. Brittian, W. T. Gillespie and S. L., his wife, conveyed to C. W. Matthews, G. B. Stevenson and John D. Whitescarver, Trustees of the Graham Baptist Church, a certain lot in the Town of Graham, being lot No. 19 in section 2.

1921. D. B. 93, p. 82.

Graham Land and Improvement Company, conveyed to S. M. Graham, V. L. Sexton, H. C. Calaway, E. G. White, and V. T. Strickler, Trustees of the Graham Presbyterian Church, a certain lot in the Town of Graham.

1922. D. B. 93, p. 112.

W. E. Hilt and Mattie T., his wife, conveyed to W. E. Taylor, W. A. Hilt, J. P. Holmes and George French, Trustees of Crabtrees Chapel Methodist Church, South, a certain lot in Poor Valley, etc.

1922. D. B. 93, p. 135.

M. J. Alexander and M. P., his wife, and L. J. Stump, conveyed to J. W. Owens, D. D. Baker, G. W. Rogers, George W. Gillespie, Jr., and J. W. Jones, Trustees of the Pocahontas Church of Christ (Christian Church) a certain lot in the Town of Pocahontas.

1922. D. B. 93, p. 259.

G. B. Stevens and Mollie M., his wife, conveyed to C. W. Matthews, G. B. Stevens, and John D. Whitescarver, Trustees of the Graham Baptist Church, a certain lot in the Town of Graham.

1921. D. B. 93, p. 582.

Raven Red Ash Coal Company conveyed to B. H. Hilton, Charles Green, and Walker Deel, Trustees of the Assembly of God Church at Red Ash, on Coal Creek, a certain lot to be "used solely for public religious worship by said denomination only." The trustees however in their discretion may permit the use of any building erected on said lot, by other religious denominations, etc.

Church Deeds are here listed covering the period from 1800 to 1922, that those who may write historical sketches of their denomination for vol. two of these ANNALS may have the complete record of all deeds to date.

PART II.

HISTORY

OF THE

SETTLEMENT AND INDIAN WARS

OF

TAZEWELL COUNTY

VIRGINIA

WITH

Statistical Tables and Illustrations

BY

GEO. W. L. BICKLEY, M. D.
COR. MEM. AMER. PH. SOC.; COR. MEM. WEST. ACAD. NAT. SCIENCES.;
SEC. JEFF. HIST. SOCIETY

"Who would not cherish the history of such men as our ancestors?"

Entered, according to Act of Congress, in the year 1852, by
GEO. W. BICKLEY,
In the Clerk's Office of the District Court of the United States
for the Western District of Virginia.

JEFFERSONVILLE (Now Tazewell).

CHAPTER I.
INTRODUCTION TO THE HISTORY OF TAZEWELL.

The local nature of this work precludes the necessity of entering into a lengthy introduction, yet a few remarks seem to be essential, to make the reader somewhat acquainted with the nature of the subject before him.

For many years, the county of Tazewell has enjoyed a very high reputation in Virginia and the surrounding states. Located in what was not many years ago the wilds of Virginia, immediately in the line of the great Indian road from the Ohio to the western settlements, we might reasonably calculate that many daring deeds and bloody massacres took place within its borders. And such seems to have been the case, for, perhaps none of the western counties afford such a number of either, as Tazewell.

The lands of the county are open and inviting to the emigrant, and it is essential only, that he should have a correct knowledge of the county, its history and its resources, to convince him that he will nowhere find a more desirable country than this. The people of the county themselves, need a spur to urge them on to greater exertion. The rapid growth of the county and its wealth show that it will compare with any in the state. To those who would spend a summer in the mountains, a more pleasant retreat from the cares and turmoils of business, could not be found. To the valetudinarian, the pure air, the fine scenery, the mineral water, the good society, all are inviting. To the capitalist the county opens a wide field of operations. Occupying a central position in the south-west, it may be looked upon as an average specimen of the surrounding country. The county has thus far made but small figure; the south-west has been overlooked; to advocate the claims of the latter and to perpetuate the history of the former, as well as to set the car of improvement in motion, is one of the objects of this work. The day is not far distant when Tazewell will be an important county; a slight glance at the maps of Virginia, Kentucky, Tennessee, and North Carolina will be sufficient to convince the most superficial, that in the course of things, a new state, at no very distant day, must be hewed out of the corners of the above states. If we but look at the staple productions, the character of the soil, the distance of market, the sameness of facilities, the climate and character of the population, the distance from the seats of government, and the oneness of interest, we cannot fail to see that the formation of a new state would redound to the interest of the people of the specified district.

It may be said that this new state would be cut off from any navigable stream as much as Switzerland in Europe. But, when we consider, in this age of "velocity," navigable streams have, and are daily becoming subservient to the speed and utility of the metal horse, whose dreadful stamp and wild scream is spreading life and energy in the veins of the honest yeomanry of the land, we shall all agree that his objection would not be valid.

I would ask, what advantages are now accruing to the people of the specified section from navigable streams? Do they not roll back upon us, daily, a tide of losses, by bringing us in competition with those who have their every advantage? Have the people of south-western Virginia, eastern Kentucky and Tennessee, and north-western North Carolina, ever been on a footing with others of their respective states?

Will their respective legislatures vote money to carry on internal improvements in these remote corners, so as to bring them on a footing with their more favored statesmen? Have they enabled them to sell their corn, wheat, tobacco and stock on as good terms as those nearer market? Have the states named, tried to put the "corner men" within thirty miles of market, as they might? No, we must travel thirty days with our stock, grain, etc., to market, which, when there, nets little more than half that received by our more favored brethren.

No country can equal ours, and why be poorer than the poorest? Let us urge upon our respective states the importance of placing us on an equal footing with others, or ask leave to help ourselves, by making us a separate and distanct commonwealth. Let us do this, and show the world that here is the garden-spot.

Too little has been said, by writers of Virginia history, upon south-western Virginia. Several works have been written purporting to be histories of Virginia, Kentucky, Tennessee and North Carolina, and all neglect their mountainous sections. The last works I have seen upon Virginia, are those of Howe and De Hass. Neither of these, do that justice to the south-west, which it so justly merits. The character of Mr. Howe's work precluded the possibility of saying much of any section. But, De Hass's work purports to be a **History of the Settlement and Indian Wars of Western Virginia.**" If he had called it a history of the settlement and Indian wars of **North-western** Virginia, he would certainly have been quite as near the thing. It is most undoubtedly a history of north-western Virginia, and as such is an honor to its author.

To write a history of Virginia which should do justice to every section, would be a task greater than could be performed by any one man; for, to use the words of one well versed in Virginia history "the half will never be told."

Local history is rather a new feature in literature, and must be written for the people of its locality. I write the history of a county and for the people of that county. After the history of every county shall be written, a condensed work of the whole will be called a History of the South-west.

CHAPTER II.

DISCOVERY AND SETTLEMENT.

1766.] It has been with much difficulty that I have been able to collect anything of importance, relating to this section, at the date indicated in the margin. Perhaps there is really little to record. What little I have gleaned from the obscured pages of the book of the past, has now become little more than mere tradition. For, situated as I am, in an isolated region, the advantages of a public library are denied me, and from a large private library little is to be found, throwing any light on this uncertain part of my work. The information here embodied, was received from the grandsons, sons, and even from the men themselves who were the principal actors in the drama to be recorded. Memory cannot survive the decay of the physical system, unimpaired; and hence, caution is necessary, in recording an event told us, even by the chief actors therein. With this fact before me, I have placed more reliance on an incident related to me by a son of a pioneer, than if related by the pioneer himself.

Whether the discoverers were allured to this section, by the exaggerated tale of some friendly Indians; the hope of finding some valuable mineral, with which to enrich themselves; or to find a region more abundantly stocked with game, from the peltry of which they would derive a profit, cannot now be easily determined. It is most likely that the latter supposition is the true cause; for, it is certain, that at the date indicated, hunting was considered a manly exercise, and one of which Virginians have ever been fond. They would brave every danger to enjoy the sport. Amusement was here combined with labor and profit; and hence, the hardy backwoodsman of Augusta frequently left home and all its endearments, and took upon himself the toil and fatigue, as well as the pleasures, of a trapper's life. The "trapper life" here led, differed, in many respects, from that followed by the north-western trapper, or **courceurs de bois,** who married among the Indians, assumed their dress, and remained out on an expedition, one, two, and even three or four years; while the backwoodsman returned regularly to his family, at the end of a few months, perhaps poorer, but equally as happy as the **courceurs de bois** or rangers of the wood.

The hunters usually went to the mountains in companies of eight or ten, having pack-horses, with which they brought home their peltry. The equipment, for a trip of this kind, consisted of a rifle, powder, ball, a hatchet or tomahawk, knife, and blanket. They also carried salt and provisions enough to last them two days or beyond the settlement, from which time the forest yielded a plentiful supply. Tobacco, and a clean shirt a-piece, generally made up the remainder of their stores, which was to serve them for months in the western wilds. Their dress was usually of heavy woolen, and the manufacture of their wives and daughters. The suit worn off had to last till their return; for, except the spare shirt, they carried but one suit.

Heavy buckskin moccasins and leggins were usually worn, with a hunting shirt, and a cap made of beaver or otter-skin. The hatchet was worn in a belt around the body, while hunting-knife was lodged in a sheath fastened to the strap of the shot-pouch. I know of no more formidable personage than a backwoodsman in full dress; expecially if you reflect upon the precision with which he deals the missiles of death, from his long black rifle, and his great power to endure the fatigue and hardships incident to a hunter's life.

Once upon the route, thus equipped and prepared, none were so happy or so free from the cares and vexations of civic life, as the Augusta backwoodsman, to whose homes even Washington, in after years, expected to be compelled to fly, to nourish and defend the last faint spark of republican liberty.

Pasturage for thier horses was to be found everywhere; and, game in such abundance, that plenty of good cheer were their companions from the time they left their homes, till their return. After having reached the game region, and were seated around the camp-fire, at night, their thoughts might revert from the incidents of the day and the anticipation of the morrow's scenes, and kindly hover over those left behind; but, if so, such thoughts invariably brought forth the soliloquizing ejaculation, "**Well now, if I had the old woman and babies here I should be fixed!**"

It will be recollected that, previous to this time, the French had mingled with the Indians, and given countenance to their acts, till the close of the war between France and England, in February, 1763. This peace did not, however, terminate the Indian war against the colonies. They were displeased with the provisions of the treaty, and commenced a war of merciless extermination against the western frontier settlements, which was waged till December, 1764, when it was brought to a close by what is usually known as Johnston's treaty.

The Shawanoes, who lived on the Wabash, Scioto, and Ohio rivers, soon after the completion of Johnston's treaty, became engaged in a war with the Cherokees, who lived in the upper parts of Alabama, Georgia, and the western part of North Carolina, and continued it till 1768, when the southern Indians, who were being pressed by the Shawanoes and Delawares, sued for, and obtained a peace, which restored quiet to the frontiers, till April, 1774.

The reader will bear in mind that this war, between the Shawanoes and Cherokees, was waging at the time of which we are writing (1776), and that the country, of which Tazewell now forms a part, lay between the contending nations, so that the hunter was in danger of falling into the hands of the predatory bands of either tribe. There was, however, little danger, for each nation was anxious to secure the sympathy of the whites. A few loads of powder were sufficient to have ransomed a man. But it appears that no company was molested, who were hunting within the present limits of Tazewell.

The first of these hunting companies visited this part of the Clinch valley in 1766; of their acts nothing is known. In the following year another company came out, in which were two men, named Butler and Carr. They were, also, in the first company.

1767]. When this second company was ready to start back, Butler and Carr concluded to stay and wait the arrival of a company expected out that fall. They built a small cabin, at a place now known as the Crab orchard, about three miles west of the present seat of justice. During the spring they opened a small field, and planted some corn, which they received from a band of Cherokees. In the fall, the expected company of hunters arrived, and were joined by Butler and Carr, who had, by this time, acquired a correct knowledge of the geographical features of the country. They hunted till spring, leaving Butler and Carr to spend another summer in the mountains. Having received, from the last company, a supply of ammunition, etc., they became settled in their resolution to make the wild backwoods their home, and, accordingly, began to improve around their camp, and open lands, on which to raise bread.

1768.] Early in the summer, about two hundred Cherokee warriors camped near them, to spend the summer and kill elk, which frequented a lick near, and on the present plantation of, Mr. Thomas Witten. These were, however, soon disturbed by the appearance of several hundred Shawanoes; men and women. The Shawanoes and Cherokees had long been deadly enemies, and it was not to be supposed that they could camp near each other, and hunt at the same lick, without a battle.

The Shawanoes, as a people, are overbearing: and they were not long in exhibiting this feature of their character. The Shawanoe chief sent a peremptory order to the Cherokees, to evacuate their position and seek a new hunting-ground. This was early in the day. The messenger was sent back to defy the Shawanoes, who soon began to prepare for battle.

The Cherokees retired to the top of Rich mountain and threw up a breastwork, which was finished before night. It consisted of a simple embankment, about three or four feet high, running east and west along the top of the mountain about eighty yards, and then turning off at right angles to the north or down the mountain side. The Shawanoes commenced the ascent of the mountain before night of the first day, but finding their enemies so strongly fortified, withdrew and posted themselves in a position to commence the attack early the following morning.

Long before day the fiendish yells of the warriors might be heard echoing over the rugged cliffs and deep valleys of the surrounding country. Day came, and for the space of half an hour, a deathlike stillness reigned on the mountain top and side. With the first rays of the rising sun, a shout ascended the skies as if all the wild animals in the woods had broke forth in their most terrifying notes. The sharp crack of rifles and the ringing of tomahawks against each other; the screams of women and children and the groans of the dying now filled the air for miles around.

Both parties were well armed and the contest nearly equal. The Shawanoes having most men, while the Cherokees had the advantage of their breastwork. Through the long day the battle raged with unabated vigor, and when night closed in, both parties built fires and camped on the ground. During the night the Cherokees sent to Butler and Carr for powder and lead, which they furnished. When the sun rose the following morning the battle was renewed with the same spirit in which it had been fought the previous day. In a few hours, however, the Shawanoes were compelled to retire. The loss on both sides was great, considering the numbers engaged. A large pit was opened and a common grave received those who had fallen in this last battle fought between red men in this section. Both parties left Virginia for their homes in the south and west, leaving Butler and Carr in possession of the Elk lick, which was the cause of dispute. My informant had this account from Carr, an eye-witness. the battle-ground, breastwork, and great grave are yet to be seen.

1769.] Carr separated from Butler and settled on a beautiful spot on one of the head branches of the Clinch river, two miles east of the present town of Jeffersonville. Peace being restored among the Indians, more hunters came out, who returned laden with peltries and giving such glowing descriptions of the country (which still perhaps failed to come up to its true description) that the desire to emigrate began to exhibit itself among the substantial men of worth.

1771.] In the spring of this year Thomas Witten and John Greenup moved out and settled at the Crab orchard, which Witten purchased of Butler. Absalom Looney settled in a beautiful valley now known as Abb's valley. Matthias Harman, and his brothers Jacob and Henry settled at Carr's place. John Craven settled in the Cove (see Map), Joseph Martin, John Henry, and James King settled in the Thompson valley, and John Bradshaw in the valley two miles west of Jeffersonville. The settlers, this year, found but little annoyance from the Indians, who were living peaceably at their homes in the west and south. The consequence was the settlers erected substantial houses and opened lands to put in corn, from which they reaped a plentiful supply, in the fall.

1772.] The following persons moved out, this year, and settled at the several places named. Capt. James Moore and John Pogue, in Abb's valley; William Wynn, at the Locust hill (the place that Carr settled), which he purchased from Harman. John Taylor, on the north fork of Clinch, and Jesse Evans, near him. Thomas Maxwell, Benjamin Joslin, James Ogleton, Peter and Jacob Harman, and Samuel Ferguson, on Bluestone creek. William Butler,* on the south branch of the north fork of Clinch, a short distance above Wynn's plantation; William Webb, about three miles east of Jeffersonville; Elisha Clary, near Butler; John Ridgel, on the clear fork of Wolf creek; Rees Bowen, at Maiden spring; David Ward, in the Cove, and William Garrison, at the foot of Morris's knob.

1773.] Thomas, John, and William Peery, settled where the town of Jeffersonville now stands; John Peery, jr., at the fork of Clinch, one mile and a half east of the county seat; Capt. Maffit, and Benjamin Thomas, settled about a mile above, and Chrisly Hensley, near them. Samuel Marrs settled in Thompson's valley; Thomas English, in Burk's garden (see description and remarks); James and Charles Scaggs, Richard Pemberton, and Johnson, settled in Baptist valley, five miles from where Jeffersonville

---

*Perhaps the same from whom Thomas Whitten purchased the Crab orchard, and the first settler.

now stands. Thomas Maston, William Patterson, and John Deskins, settled in the same valley, but farther west—Hines, Richard Oney, and Obadiah Paine, settled in Deskins valley, in the western part of the county.

1774-76.] The settlers who came in during the years of '74-5 and '6, generally pitched their tents near the one or other of the localities already mentioned. Even yet there is a preference manifested for the older settlements. This may be accounted for, from the fact that the first settlers generally chose the most desirable localities; the lands being now better improved, and society more advanced, still render these places more attractive than other parts of the county settled at a later period.

Cresop's war, as it is sometimes, though perhaps erroneously, called, broke out in 1774, which drove the settlers into neighborhoods where they might have the advantages of blockhouses, forts, and stations. The Revolution was soon resolved upon, and the frontiermen, having to combat the Indians, who had become allies to the British, were much from home. This tended, also, to draw still closer the families then settled in the county. Whatever contributed to the safety of one, conferred a like boon upon the rest. In speaking of the Indian wars, we shall see the utility of general rendezvous for families.

Our market at this time was in eastern Virginia, or the old settlements, and by the continued passage of the traders, a line of communication was kept open, over which was transmitted, with some dispatch, news of what was transpiring in the east. Even before the battle of Lexington, the subject of revolution had been talked over by the frontiermen, and we shall see, hereafter, how they conducted themselves during the war. After the declaration of war, emigration slackened, though a few, who either sympathized with the mother country, or felt no interest in the contest, moved out. Having now given such an outline of the settlement as will enable the reader to know the position in which the people were placed, during the first few years of the settlement, I shall proceed to a period somewhat later, that he may have an idea of the formation and outline geography of the county.

CHAPTER III.

FORMATION AND OUTLINE GEOGRAPHY.

By an act, passed December 19th, 1799, the county of Tazewell was formed of parts of Wythe and Russell. The following are the boundary lines: "Beginning on the Kanawha line, and running with the line which divides Montgomery and Wythe counties, to where said line crosses the top of the Brushy mountain; thence along the top of the said mountain to its junction with Garden mountain; thence along the top of the said mountain to the Church (perhaps Clinch) mountain; thence along the top of said mountain to the top of Cove creek, a branch of the Maiden-spring fork of Clinch river; thence a straight line to Mann's gap, in Kent's ridge; thence north 45° west, to the line which divides the state of Kentucky from that of Virginia; thence along said line to the Kanawah line, and with said line to the place of beginning."*

By an act of the Virginia legislature, passed February 3d, 1835, the line which had hitherto divided Russell and Tazewell counties was altered from Mann's gap, in Kent's ridge, so as to run north 45°, 45' west, to the distance of 974 poles, which portion was afterward ceded to Tazewell. An act of the General Assembly, passed February 4th, 1828, altered the eastern boundary line, in consequence of the formation of the county of Giles; and, again, in 1837, in consequence of the formation of the county of Mercer; which, however, owing to an omission in the act of Assembly, was not defined till April, 1848.

The subjoined Map exhibits the lines as they now stand; which owing to a want of facilities, is not offered as being in every respect correct, but near enough to convey a good general idea of the shape and geographical features of the county.

Tazewell county was named, not in honor of Littleton W. Tazewell, as is generally supposed, but received its name somewhat in the following manner. Simon Cotterel, who was the representative from Russell in 1799, having been authorized to apply for the formation of a new county, drew up a bill, and proposed it on the 18th of December, 1799, but met with the most violent opposition from Mr. Tazewell, a member from Norfolk county, and a relative of L. W. Tazewell then in Congress. Cotterel rose in his seat, and begged the gentleman to withhold his remarks till his bill was matured, to which he assented. Cotterel erased the proposed name and inserted that of Tazewell, and the next day (19th), presented his bill thus amended. Tazewell was silenced; the bill passed, receiving Tazewell's vote. To this stratagem the county is indebted for its name.

The county is bounded on the north by the State of Kentucky, Logan and Wyoming counties, Virginia; on the east by Mercer and Giles; on the south by Wythe and Smyth, and on the west by Russell. It has a super-

---

* Virginia Statutes, from 1792 to 1806; Vol. II, chap. 27, sec. 1, page 217.

ficial area of about 1,920,000 square acres, or 3000 square miles, and is traversed by numerous ranges of the Alleghany and Cumberland mountains. Clinch, one of the principal mountains, passes through it in an easterly and westerly direction, about forty miles. This mountain was named, as will be seen in the chapter on mountains, in consequence of the Clinch river. Rich mountain passes through the county about twenty miles; it is a branch of the Clinch. Garden and Brushy mountains are in the southern part of the county, the latter being the county line; they run parallel with Clinch mountain. Paint Lick and Deskin's mountains are also parallel and north of the Rich mountain. They are parts of the same range with East river and Elk-horn, being separated by the Clinch river, in the valley in which stands the town of Jeffersonville. There are no other mountains deserving of notice, at this place, except the Great Flat Top, in the north-east corner of the county.

The county is traversed by many streams; some of considerable size; the principal of which are Clinch river, Bluestone, La Visee, Dry, and Tug forks of Sandy river and their branches. The Clinch river rises from three springs; the first on the "divides," about ten miles east of the town of Jeffersonville; the second in the valley between Elk-horn and Rich mountains; the third in Thompson's valley, about eight miles south-east of the county seat. The two first unite about one and a half miles east of Jeffersonville, and flow, in a westerly direction, about twenty-five miles, and unite with the Maiden-spring fork, and thence flow through Russell, Scott, Lee, and a part of Tennessee, and, after receiving the Powell river, empty into the Tennessee about sixty miles above Kingston.

Bluestone creek rises in the eastern part of the county; flows in a north easterly direction, and empties into the Great Kanawha. The different branches (see Map) of the Sandy river, rising in this county, flow in a northerly direction and empty into the Ohio. The county is well watered. The climate and soil are treated of, in other places, under appropriate heads (which see); as also, the manners, customs, etc. Jeffersonville is the county seat.

CHAPTER IV.

CLIMATE.

WINTER IN TAZEWELL.

Owing to its elevation, the climate, in winter, is more severe than in the surrounding counties. Snow appears generally before the commencement of the first winter month. The inhabitants, at this season, are much exposed in feeding and caring for their stock. Ice is seldom seen over six inches thick, and attains that thickness only a few times in the course of the winter. Less snow falls than would be supposed, from the latitude and elevation of the country. It lies but a short time, and is generally succeeded by rain, which is plentiful at this season. The water-courses are usually high during the winter, though seldom impassable, except for a short time immediately after long rainy spells. The reflection of light from the mountains, when covered with snow, renders a sunny day remarkably light: and to this circumstance is owing the absence of that gloomy appearance so often seen in level countries during the winter; except indeed, when snow is falling, at which time the mountains are obscured and a death-like shadow is cast over everything. During the winter season the country presents a business air to be seen at few other seasons of the year. This is owing to the return of the drovers, who supply the people with the almighty dollar, the influence of which is felt everywhere. Its plentiful presence seems to instil life, energy, and action into those ordinarily lethargic and idle. Contracts, based upon the credit system, are now discharged and pledged faith redeemed.

During the middle of winter comes Christmas, with all its joys and pleasures. It is here celebrated as in England four hundred years ago. The young people commence the dance, which is kept up for several weeks. The figures are mostly the variety of reels. The violin, triangle, and tambourrine, constitute the band.

Dancing is an amusement greatly loved by the people of Tazewell and in which they excel. The intimacy and good cheer existing at these gatherings (in which even the older people sometimes participate), will doubtless account for the general good feeling which exists among the people of the county, and which is proverbial.

The new year steals in amid all their hilarity, and is welcomed with hearty good-will. The end of winter puts a stop to all these amusements, and the people return to the plow, the loom, and the anvil.

SPRING.

Spring, which succeeds the cold and amusements, is the most beautiful season imaginable. At the earliest dawn of spring, the sap begins to flow in the sugar-maple (**Acer saccharinum**), and then begins the process of sugar-making. This is effected by boring auger holes in the body of the tree, and introducing part of an alder stalk, or something of the kind, to serve as a conductor for the sap, which falls in a trough, and is conveyed in pails thence to the kettles, where it is boiled into sugar. The water is evaporated while the saccharine principle remains. It is a dark, compact sugar, which might be improved by slightly altering the mode of manufacture.

The following remarks are taken from a work published by the American Tract Society: "The sugar maple is a beautiful tree, reaching the height of seventy or eighty feet, the body straight, for a long distance free from limbs, and three or four feet in diameter at the base. It grows in colder climates, between latitudes 42 and 48, and on the Alleghanies to their

THE SUGAR CAMP.

southern termination, extending westward beyond lake Superior. The wood is nearly equal to hickory, for fuel, and is used for building, for ships, and various manufactures. When tapped, as the winter gives place to spring, a tree, in a few weeks, will produce five or six pailsful of sap, which is sweet and pleasant as a drink, and when boiled down will make about half as many pounds of sugar. The manufacturer, selecting a spot central among his trees, erects a temporary shelter, suspends his kettles over a smart fire, and at the close of a day or two will have fifty or a hundred pounds of sugar, which is equal to the common west India sugar, and when refined equals the finest in flavor and beauty.

"When the sap has been boiled to a sirup and is turning to molasses, then to candy, and then graining into sugar, its flavor is delightful, especially when the candy is cooled on the snow. On this occasion the manufacturer expects his wife, children, and friends, if near, to enjoy the scene." The person in the engraving on this page is represented as blowing the candy or wax, to ascertain how far the boiling has advanced. 41,341 pounds are annually manufactured in Tazewell county.

When the sugar-making season is over, spring has fairly begun; though few trees exhibit full grown leaves, those of the maple and buckeye, or horse-chestnut (Aesculus glabra), being earliest. The soft green foilage of these trees, the few spring flowers, the verdant meadows, the sweet warbling of forest birds, and general activity of the animal kingdom, make this the paradisian era of the year. By the first of June, nothing can exceed the beauty of this mountain region; the hill sides are variegated with a profusion of flowers; sweet odors stimulate the olfactories at the inhalation of every breath, and these

"Pleasant breezes, and slight showers,
And the sweet odor of flowers,"

produce a carelessness, and happy contentedness, known to few other than oriental lands.

SUMMER.

This does not differ much, in appearance, from spring; yet materially in its effects. The grains are now nearly ready for harvesting, except corn, which is not gathered till fall. The summers are warm for a country so elevated, yet not so warm as the surrounding counties; there is, too, less rain at this season. But little traveling is done, and business dull; the farmers being closely engaged at home. About the fourth of July the harvest begins, and continues several weeks. This ended, the farmers begin to gather their cattle for the drovers, who carry from the county, annually, about 7,000 head, starting usually in the latter part of August and beginning of September. At times, the roads may be seen lined with cattle for miles, many of them passing through the county, from Kentucky and Tennessee, on their way to the eastern markets. The labors of the farm slacken till frost appears.

AUTUMN.

Fall is remarkable for the great beauty of the decaying foilage. Numerous plants are now in full bloom, and with the varied colors of the forest, present a sight of loveliness rarely seen. The nights become cooler, till fire is required, and soon in the month of October frost appears. Snow sometimes falls in this month, but most generally, not till November.

Soon after the appearance of frost, in October, the Indian summer sets in—a season as beautiful as its name. The air is pleasant, and a smoky haze fills the atmosphere.

This season, of all others, would be preferred for a perpetual climate. It lasts from ten days to three weeks. Many beautiful Indian love-tales are connected with this season, but are better suited to the pages of a magazine than this place. The seasons of Tazewell are objectionable only for one thing, viz: sudden changes, as mentioned under the head of Meteorology.

CHAPTER V.

METEOROLOGY.

Important as this subject is to the farmer, little attention has been paid to it. Few, I am persuaded, have appreciated its importance; and until our farmers avail themselves of the important laws, and consequent deductions which it has brought to light, we need not expect to see our land producing their proportionate amount of sustenance.

Meteorology, is the scientific designation of that science which treats of the atmosphere, and its varied phenomena. It is an essential part of a farmer's education, and without a knowledge of its principles, he must act upon the rude systems which have been conjured up by the wild superstitions of his fathers, in whose maxims he sees all science.

The every-day experience of any farmer will satisfy him that light, heat, air, temperature, etc., play an important part in the vegetable, as well as in the animal worlds.*

The following remarks are based upon the observations of two winters and a summer. I have, also, availed myself of some of the current opinions which exist among the more learned farmers of the county. From the nature of the country—mountainous and much elevated, as mentioned in another place—almost every variety of climate, from 36° to 50° N. Latitude, is to be found in certain localities of the county. The climate of Quebec and Charleston alike exist; the former on the mountain-peaks, and the latter in the deepest valleys. Owing to this fact it is difficult to give correct meteorological information unless observations have been made at different places.

I give the result at Jeffersonville, as being probably near the mean of the county.

The mean temperature for Winter months is 30° Fahr.
The mean temperature for Spring months is 52° Fahr.
The mean temperature for Summer months is 73° Fahr.
The mean temperature for Fall months is 61° Fahr.
The fall of rain in the Winter months is $27\frac{1}{4}$ inches.
The fall of rain in the Spring months is $16\frac{5}{8}$ inches.
The fall of rain in the Summer months is $8\frac{1}{4}$ inches.
The fall of rain in the Fall months is $6\frac{3}{4}$ inches.

Thus we have 54° as the mean temperature, and $58\frac{7}{8}$ inches of rain during the year; which gives to each season $14\frac{3}{4}$ inches, and to each day 0.1599 inches, or about 1 1-6 of an inch.

Snow falls in the valleys from the first of November to the first of April, and on the mountain tops, a little sooner and later. Its early fall, in autumn, destroys large quantities of timber, the leaves of which catch the snow till the weight becomes insupportable. The branches, and sometimes the body, giving way, fill the roads with fragments, rendering them impassable.

The winds vary very much, with the direction of the valleys, and it is often difficult to determine their real course; every valley seeming to draw a current through it. West, N. W. and east winds, prevail; though southerly winds sometimes blow for a short time. Northerly winds usually produce fair weather, while Easterly winds bring rain. Much rain is required for the soil, hence, vegetation shoots with the greatest rapidity during the wet season of spring.

The general temperature seems to be higher than it formerly was, there being less snow, and ice, during the winters, as well as less rain, than during the first years of settlement. This no doubt, is owing to the loss of timber on the cleared lands; it is the only way in which we can account for this change of climate. This explanation has the sanction of Baron Von Humboldt (see his Cosmos), than whom no man was a better judge, or closer observer of this department of nature.

The dry season, in the beginning of summer, sometimes does much mischief, not only to vegetation, but to man's health. The effects of light upon the soil, are nowhere more perceptible than here. The number of rays of light, falling at right angles on the south sides of the mountains during a greater part of the year, seems to have quite exhausted the soil, especially near the summits. On the north sides of the mountains, even from the tops, the soil is of the finest quality, and very productive. From this we should conclude, that to preserve and foster the productive energy of the soil, it requires shading. Changes of temperature are very sudden, the thermometer sometimes sinking rapidly from 70° to 20° Fahr., remaining so a few hours, and then rising as rapidly again, to 60° to 70°. This irregularity constitutes an objection to the climate, which, it is to be hoped, will be removed when the lands are entirely cleared up.

It is certainly a great pity, that meteorological investigations have not been instituted in this country; and it is still more unfortunate, that the farming community should have paid so little attention to a subject which so seriously affects their dearest interests.

"If a small portion of the talent and public patronage of this country could be turned to the study of vegetable and animal physiology, in their connection with farm economy, and to chemistry, entomology, agricultural geology, and meteorology, unquestionably, the average of our wheat, corn and cotton crops, would soon be doubled."*

The farmers of this region have long believed that a plain English education, i. e., to read, write, and cipher, was all sufficient for a farmer, and hence science has been discarded as useless. The truth is, we need a scientific farmer's school, founded upon Socrates' idea of useful knowledge—to teach that, which would admit of application. We have too many schools where the mere theory of life and its means are taught.

---

*Lee—Patent Office Report, Part II, 1849.

CHAPTER VI.

DESCRIPTIVE GEOGRAPHY.

MOUNTAINS.

The principal mountains of Tazewell are Clinch, Rich, East River, Brushy, Garden, Paint Lick, Deskins and Flat Top. They have an elevation, above the valleys, of about eighteen hundred feet, and about three thousand above the level of the sea. For remarks upon their geological formation I would refer the reader to the Transactions of the Jeffersonville Historical Society. The general course of these mountains is N. 67° E.

Clinch mountain, which receives its name from Clinch river, extends through the entire length of the county. It has several gaps, through which wagon-roads pass.

Rich mountain, so called from the character of its soil, is a branch or spur of Clinch mountain, running parallel to its entire length.

East River mountain, so called from a stream of that name flowing along near its base, begins a few miles east of Jeffersonville, and runs parallel to the Rich mountain to the county line on the east.

Brushy mountain, receiving its name from the brushy character of its growth on the south side, runs in the same direction as the Clinch, and forms the southern boundary line of the county.

Paint Lick mountain is a continuation of the House and Barn mountain in Russell county, and is separated from it by the Maiden Spring fork, of Clinch river. There was once a great elk and deer lick, near its western end, and there are many paintings (still visable), supposed to have been executed by the Shawanoe Indians, or perhaps, by the Cherokees. The paintings represent birds, women, Indian warriors, etc. From these paintings, the lick was named, which was soon applied to the mountain. It rises near the western county line, and runs in the general direction to near Jeffersonville: it here sinks, to admit the passage of another fork of Clinch river, and again rises, forming Elkhorn mountain.

Deskins' mountain, so called from an early settler, runs parallel, and near the Paint lick, for about the same distance.

The Great Flat Top, rises from a spur of the Cumberland mountains, which traverse the county. It is in the northeast corner of the county, and on it, corner Tazewell, Mercer, and Wyoming counties. It receives its name from a large level area on its summit.

To notice the remaining small mountains and great ridges, would occupy too much space. The northern part of the county is much cut up with them and renders it almost valueless for farming purposes. For grazing, however, it cannot be excelled.

VALLEYS.

The principal valleys, are the Clinch, Abb's, Poor, Baptist, Thompson's, and Deskins'. They are not so wide as those of the adjoining counties, yet sufficiently broad, to afford room for some beautiful farms.

Clinch valley, through which flows the north fork of Clinch river, and from which it was named, is the most important, and perhaps, contains the best lands in the county. In it is located the seat of justice, and through it passes the Fincastle and Cumberland Gap turnpike.

Abb's valley, so called from Absalom Looney, the first white settler, is a narrow, but beautiful and fertile valley, under which runs a creek of considerable size, its entire length of about twelve miles—it is much celebrated, in consequence of the horrible massacres which were perpetrated in it.

Poor valley, is between Clinch and Brushy mountains: it is narrow, and the lands poorer, than most of the surrounding country; yet in point of mineral wealth, it is one of the richest valleys in the county. It is several hundred feet lower than the adjoining valleys.

Thompson's valley, between Rich and Clinch mountains, is one of the most beautiful in the county. The lands are good and in a high state of cultivation. It is from two to three miles wide, and was so called from a large family residing in it, and who were among the earliest settlers.

Baptist valley, was so named from the number of persons belonging to the Baptist denomination of Christians, who settled in it. It is a valley of some importance, the Tazewell C. H. and Kentucky turnpike passing through its entire length.

Deskin's valley, between a range of hills, and Deskins' mountain, received its name from an early settler. There are some fine farms in it, though the valley is small.

RIVERS AND CREEKS.

Clinch is the principal, and Sandy, the most important in the county. The latter heads in the county, and is navigable to the county line, for flat-boats. East river, Tug, and Bluestone creek, are considerable streams.

Clinch river heads in this county, and receives its name from an incident which occurred on it in 1767. A hunter named Castle, left Augusta and went to what is now Russell county, to hunt with a party of friendly Indians, who were living on it. This tribe made frequent visits to the settlement, carrying off horses, and such other stock as they could get hold of. A man named Harman, who was robbed of some things, and believing Castle to be the instigator to these acts, applied to a Mr. Buchanan, a justice of Augusta, for a writ to arrest Castle and bring him to trial. The writ was issued, and a party raised to arrest him, among whom, was a lame man named Clinch. The party went to Castle's camp, and attempted to arrest him, but the Indians joined Castle, and Harman's party was forced to retreat across the river.

In the hurry of the moment, Clinch got behind, and while fording the river was shot by an Indian, who rushed forward to secure his scalp, but was shot by one of Harman's party. The vulgar tradition is, that an Indian was pursuing a white man, who clenched, and drowned the Indian in the stream.

I had the former statement, however, from a grandson of the magistrate who issued the warrant for Castle's apprehension.

As before stated, the river rises in the county, east of Jeffersonville, running in a westerly direction, and receiving numerous small streams, till it reaches what is known as New Garden, in Russell county. It is then joined by the Maiden Spring fork, which rises in Thompson's valley, flows a short distance, sinks several miles and rises again near what is known as Maiden Spring, owned by Col. Rees T. Bowen, and one of the loveliest places in Tazewell. This spring is named also, from an incident which happened to Rees Bowen, the earliest settler near it, and grandfather of its present owner.

When Mr. Bowen first saw the spring, he discovered a fine young female deer, feeding on the moss within the orifice from which gushes the spring. He shot it, and when he went to get his deer, saw a pair of elk horns standing on their points, and leaning against the rocks. Mr. Bowen, was a very large and tall man, yet he had no difficulty in walking upright under the horns. He chose this place for his home, and the spring and river, have since been known as Maiden Spring and Fork.

The Sandy river has several branches heading in this county, the most important of which, are the La Visee, Dry, and Tug Forks.

La Visee, has many branches in Tazewell, and is navigable for flat-boats, to the county line. The first white man who ascended it, was a Frenchman, who found a well-executed design, or painting upon a peeled poplar; hence its name—"la", translated, meaning the, and "visee," meaning a design, aim or representation. It is sometimes called Louisa fork, from Louisa C. H., Kentucky, near its junction with the Tug river.

The Dry fork, heads about six miles N. W. from Jeffersonville, and flows into the Tug river. So named, because the waters on it get very low during the summer.

The Tug river, is named from an incident which took place in 1756. "Maj. Andrew Lewis was appointed to command this expedition (one ordered by Gov. Dinwiddie, to march against the Shawanoes on the Ohio), and directed to proceed against the Shawnee villages, near the mouth of the Great Kanawaha. Maj. Lewis led his men, through great peril and suffering, within a few miles of the Ohio, when a messenger, ordering a return of the expedition, reached him. The whole party suffered intensely during this march, and once were reduced to the necessity of cutting their buffalo-skins into tugs, and eating them; hence the name Tug River."* The river is in the northern part of the county, and abounds in fine fish. It is too much obstructed by falls, to be navigable at any stage of water.

East river, so called from the direction which it flows, is a small stream, emptying into the Kanawha.

---

* DeHass's History of Western Virginia, pages 202-3.

Bluestone creek or river, also, flows east, and is remarkable for the clear blue color of its waters; hence its name. In addition to these rivers (which are but large creeks), there are quite a number of creeks, only a few of which will here be noticed.

Great Indian Creek, rises in what is known, as the Sinking waters, and flows southerly, into Clinch river, sixteen miles west of Jeffersonville. A man named Ray, was killed on it, by some Indians. At its head is a spring, said to possess the property of petrifying nuts, twigs, etc., some of which are in my possession.

Cove Creek, rises in the Cove, and meanders under ground through it, coming out at Maiden Spring, numerous openings from the surface enable stock to get water from it.

Wolf creek, rises in Burk's Garden, flows into the Kanawha (here called New River), and was named from an encounter with a wolf on its margin.

There are hundreds of others, each one of which, by its name, perpetuates some traditional incident; but I have not space to notice them.

DESCRIPTION OF PARTICULAR LOCALITIES.

COVE.

This is a large area of nearly level land, containing about fifteen square miles, and situated at the west end of Thompson's valley, between Clinch

COVE AND MAIDEN SPRING FARMS.

and Short mountains, which was evidently, at one time, connected with the Rich mountain. The waters seem to have accumulated, and forced a way through that spot now known as Maiden Spring. The land is very fertile, well timbered and watered, and the surrounding farms in fine order. Add to it the adjoining lands and residence of Maj. H. S. Bowen and Col. Rees T. Bowen, and I know of no place or section in Tazewell county, of the same extent, so desirable. The society is good, and the inhabitants very hospitable. I hesitate not to call this the garden-spot of Tazewell county. It was settled in 1772, by John Craven, who was followed, the next year, by Rees Bowen, David Ward, and William Garrison. The latter, however, settled on its very edge. The descendants of these men are still living in the Cove. The Wards, Bowens, Gillespies, Barneses, and Youngs, constitute a major part of its population. The scenery from here is fine, and the climate warmer, than other parts of the county.

RICHLANDS.

This locality is in the western part of the county, on Clinch river, and is noted for its fine lands. It is a pretty place, and in every sense of the word, desirable.

BLUESTONE.

Here is to be found another fine farming country; the people moral and prosperous, and blessed with "peace and plenty." It is in the eastern part of the county, on Bluestone river. The Fincastle turnpike passes through it. The settlement contains a division of the Sons of Temperance, which speaks much for its population.

BURK'S GARDEN.

The following description of Burk's garden, was written by Thomas G. Harrison, a gentlemen of Jeffersonville, and published in the Jeffersonville Democrat, in September 1850, which, polished in novel style as it is, is in the main correct.

"Burk's garden, in Tazewell county, Virginia, considered in its geological and geographical character, abounds with a beauty perhaps unparalleled by any other scope of land, of equal area, on the American continent. It is about ten miles in length, from east to west, and five in breadth, from north to south; entirely surrounded by lofty mountains, save a narrow pass, through which flows Wolf creek, a small, rippling rivulet, which derives its name from the number of wolves caught in traps, and otherwise exterminated on its margin.

"Seventy years ago, a man named Burk ascended the Garden mountain on the south side, and from its summit beheld, for the first time ever civilized man did, this enchanting vale, rich in the exuberance of nature's virgin dress. According to a well-authenticated tradition, Burk descended the mountain late in the evening, accompanied by his dogs and gun, and erected his camp near a tinkling fountain; breaking, for the first time, the primeval solitude that had reigned in this dell since creation's birth, the undisturbed genius of the woods. At every stroke of his ax in the gnarled oak and smooth poplar, echo, aroused from her lair, answered loud, and flew shrinking back into her covered recess, as if mad at the rude invasion. The branching antlered buck, and screaming panther, stalked around his camp with an air of curiosity, as if wondering what his presence could mean, yet proud of their native freedom, and unconscious of their deadly foe. What a beautiful prospect was spread out before Burk on that solitary evening. Flowers of every hue and odor, and bright speckled trout, flirting the crystal waters with their glittering fins, and anon skimming the surface of the pearly rill birds of gaudy plumage and silvery sound, apparently sporting in an ecstasy of glee at the idea of having for an auditor, a fair visaged biped of stately step and comely form; and perchance they poured from their mellow throats a thousand varied choruses of harping melodies, soothing and charming the wrapped sense of the astounded Burk, until he fancied himself in a very Jehosaphat, or an elysium, in which every fleeting zephyr was freighted with a tuneful intelligence, whispering happiness, or, as Milton would say

"It seemed a fit haunt for the gods,"

As, in truth, it was a real haunt for the wild gods of Columbia—the red men of the forest. Two Indian tribes, the Cherokees and Shawanoes, frequented south-western Virginia, at the time Burk explored these wilds. He was an excellent hunter and pioneer, of the Daniel Boone style; and buffalo, elk and deer, were quite numerous, at this period, in Burk's garden (I under stand that buffalo were scarce. B.)—for wild pea-vine, and blue-grass, grew four or five feet high, from mountain to mountain—making it a perfect paradise for the grazing species."

In 1848, the legislature of Virginia granted a charter for the construction of a road, called Fancy gap and Tazewell C. H. turnpike, which will pass through the interior of the garden, and which, when completed, will add greatly to its importance."

I have not space for the insertion of the whole article, and hence have been compelled to partially mutilate it. There is some dispute about Burk having discovered the garden; some contending that it was discovered by Morris Griffy, a stepson of Burk. The garden is located in the south-east part of the county, about sixteen miles from Jeffersonville. It was evidently at one time, nothing more than a pond, which eventually, forced its way through Wolf creek pass. The soil is certainly alluvial. I beg to differ with Mr. H. about its being the most desirable part of the county, for two reasons, first, its climate is too cold to mature corn well, and secondly, it is hard of access. It is 900 feet higher than Jeffersonville, or 1000 feet above the bed of Clinch river. Its winters are four weeks longer than those of the country around the C. H., and six weeks longer than those of the Cove. Small grain and grass do exceedingly well upon its soil.

COUNTRY AROUND JEFFERSONVILLE.

The lands here are well improved, and will compare favorably with any in the county. There are many fine farms near the town, among which may be mentioned those of Thos. Peery, Esq., John Wynn, Esq., Col. John B. George, Kiah Harman, Henry, Elias, G. W., and William Harman, Joseph, and Thomas G. Harrison, A. A. Spotts, Hervey G. Peery, Esq., and Dr. H. F. Peery.... 50,000 acres of these lands, are worth from forty to fifty dollars an acre, and little could be purchased for even that sum.

These farms are well stocked, and laid down in fine grasses, among which may be mentioned, blue-grass, long English, timothy, and clover. The dwellings are good, and an air of ease, and opulence, is everywhere seen. The water is an excellent quality of blue limestone.

CLEAR FORK SETTLEMENT.

This is in the eastern part of the county, on the creek of that name. It has the reputation of being a fine farming country, and a place every way desirable. When Tazewell county shall be generally as well improved, as the places which have been mentioned, it may well be called a **Mountain Garden.**

JEFFERSONVILLE.

(See Frontispiece).

Jeffersonville is the seat of justice or capital of the county, and is situated on an elevated plain in Clinch valley, about one mile from the river. It is centrally situated in the county, if regarded from east to west, but not so from north to south, being within ten miles of the southern line, and upward of forty from its northern boundary. The surrounding scenery is indeed beautiful. Immediately south of the town rises Wolf creek knob, or **the Peak,** the summit of which, in winter, is frequently covered with snow, while verdant grass is seen lower down the mountain side, in beautiful contrast with the dreariness of the snow-mantled top. In summer it is beautifully decorated with laurel and ivy blossoms; great quantities of these shrubs growing near its summit.

To the east are seen the three abrupt and rocky heads of East River mountain; to the west, like ends of Paint Lick and Deskins' mountains, which, however, are somewhat obscured by large hills. To get a good view a hill north of the town must be ascended; from this hill the view on the opposite page was taken.

In this view, the high peak to the left represents Morris's knob. The other two to the right, are the ends of Paint Lick and Deskins' mountains. In the distance are seen mountains in Russell county. North of the town a pleasant succession of hills rise, which give a beautiful aspect to the country, especially when the forests are covered with foliage.

The town contains about eighty houses, and numbers over three hundred inhabitants. Few villages anywhere in south-western Virginia, have a neater appearance, or present a more business-like scene. The streets are laid out at right angles, the principal ones running east and west. The main street is well paved and partially McAdamized; it will soon be completed. The houses are usually well built, and painted white. A better site might have been selected for its location, but the land could not be purchased. The most objectionable feature to its present location is the difficulty of getting water. A single spring supplies most of the town with water, which is hauled in barrels. Considering the danger of the town in case of fire, it is a little strange why water has not been brought into the town by pipes from a spring of purest water three or four hundred feet above the town on the side of the mountain. The cost of doing so would not probably exceed $1,000.

SCENERY WEST FROM JEFFERSONVILLE.

Jeffersonville was founded in June, 1800, and named from Thomas Jefferson. The name really signifying Jefferson's village.

The following is a business directory of the town:

NORTHWESTERN BRANCH BANK.—Main St., E. C. H.

Officers.—President, John W. Johnston; Cashier, Isaac M. Benham; Clerk, Rees B. Gillespie.

Directory.—John C. McDonald, John B. George, Kiah Harman, Geo. W. G. Browne, S. F. Watts, Samuel Graham, Isaac E. Chapman.—Capital $100,000.

Discount day, Friday.

JEFFERSONVILLE SAVINGS BANK.—Main St., nearly opposite Court House.

Officers.—Cashier or Treasurer, Addison A. Spotts; Secretary, William O. Yost.

Directory.—Thomas Peery, Rees T. Bowen, A. A. Spotts, Granville Jones, William Cox, William O. Yost, John C. Hopkins.—Capital, by limitation, $100,000.

Discount day, Saturday.

UNION HOTEL.—Main St., one door west of the C. H. Proprietors, R. W. & T. Witten.

VIRGINIA HOUSE.—Main St., three doors east of the C. H. Proprietors, McCarty & Bosang.

POST OFFICE.—Opposite C. H. P. M., A. A. Spotts. Deputies, Witten and Chapman.

MAIL ARRIVALS.

Northern mail, via Wytheville, Tuesdays and Fridays.
Northern mail, via Fincastle, Tuesdays and Saturdays.
Southern mail, via Broadford, Wednesdays.
Western mail, via Lebanon, Mondays and Saturdays.
Western mail, via Richlands, Wednesdays.

MAIL DEPARTURES.

Northern mail, via Wytheville, Wednesdays and Saturdays.
Northern mail, via Fincastle, Mondays and Saturdays.
Southern mail, via Broadford, Wednesdays.
Western mail, via Lebanon, Tuesdays and Saturdays.
Western mail, via Richlands, Thursdays.

PHYSICIANS.

H. F. Peery.   Office, west end Main St.
R. W. Witten.   Office, Union Hotel.
Jas. R. Doak.   Office Main St., West C. H.
G. W. L. Bickley.   Office, Union Hotel.
Jno. M. Estill.   Office, Main St.
Thos. G. Witten.   Office, Main St. opposite Va. House.

LAWYERS.

Joseph Stras.   Office, Main Street.
John A. Kelly.   Office, Main Street.
John W. Johnston.   Office, Main Street.
Wade D. Strother.   Office, Main Street.
Wm. Henry Maxwell.   Office, Court-House room.
Sterling F. Watts.   Office, Main Street.

CLERK SUPERIOR AND COUNTY COURTS.

G. W. G. Browne.   Office, C. H.

JAILER.

William J. Crutchfield.

PRINTING OFFICE.

S. W. Advocate.   Geo. Fred. Holmes, Editor.

MERCHANTS.

Witten & Chapman, Main Street, Groceries and Dry Goods.
A. J. Dunn, Main Street, Groceries and Dry Goods.
F. P. & W. Spotts, Main Street, Groceries and Dry Goods.
W. W. Dunn & Bros., Main Street, Groceries and Dry Goods.
John C. McDonald, Main Street, Groceries and Dry Goods.
St. Clair & Hopkins, Main Street, Groceries and Dry Goods.
W. Page & Co., Main Street, Jewelers.
A. McPhatridge, Main Street, Tinware.
W. O. & H. A. Yost, Main Street, Saddlery.
William Cox, Back Street, Saddlery.
Eldred R. Baylor, Main Street, Clothing Store.
P. Ingoldsby, Main Street, Clothing Store.
W. O. Yost, Back Street, Tannery.
W. Cox, Back Street, Tannery.
G. G. Hickman, Court Alley, Boots and Shoes.
Tho Witten, Back Street, Tannery.
W. J. Crutchfield, Jail Building, Boots and Shoes.

BLACKSMITHS.

Granville Jones, Main Street.
S. G. Huddle, Main Street.

CHURCHES.

Methodist, Main Street, Rev. G. W. G. Browne, Pastor.
Presbyterian, Main Street, Rev. Mr. Naff, Pastor.
Catholic, Near Main Street,——————, Priest.

Masonic Lodge, Main Street, Tuesdays.
Floyd Lodge, 84, I. O. O. F., Main Street, Wednesdays.
B. U. (H. F.) C. A. Circle, Jail Buildings Saturdays.
Sons Temperance—Hall, Main Street, Fridays.
Jeffersonville Hist. Society—Library Room, Main Street, Quarterly.

There are several industrial establishments, which are not noticed.

LIBERTY HILL.

Situated on the Fincastle and Cumberland Gap turnpike, eight miles west of Jeffersonville, is a flourishing little village, and would soon grow to importance if it was located as to afford building-ground: but situated in a narrow valley, between high hills, there is little room for expansion. It has one hotel, three stores, and several industrial establishments. Notwithstanding its proximity to Jeffersonville, it has considerable trade.

It was founded in 182–, and named from a church used by all denominations of Christians. "Hill" was added to distinguish it from Liberty in Bedford county, Va. It is well supplied with water, and is a pleasant place.

CHAPTER VII.

SOIL AND PRODUCTIONS.

There are three kinds of land in Tazewell, which will be noticed in order. It is generally known that it is the celebrated blue-grass soil, strongly impregnated with lime, and very productive. It is a clay loam, very tanacious in its nature, and easily resuscitated. But to the description of the different kinds.

1st. The bottom lands, generally limestone, soil stiff, and very productive. The soil of the bottom lands may be regarded as slightly alluvial, for it is generally deposited from the hill-side and water during the wet seasons of winter and spring.

Few rocks appearing above the surface renders it easy to cultivate, and enables the farmer to do so with most advantage.

Corn is mostly grown on the bottom lands, because it is easier to plow. It makes fine meadows.

2d. The hill, or upland. This is to be found on the base of mountains, and over small hills. This class of land is quite as valuable as the bottom lands; it is generally laid down in meadow grasses. It is somewhat disfigured by rocks, occasionally near the surface, or jutting through the soil. They really injure the land less than one used to rockless lands would suppose. The soil near them is richer than it is in a few yards from them; hence, the grass is ranker, and produces as much to a given area as if no rocks appeared. Experiment has tested this.

Very many acres of this upland is destitute of rocks, and then nothing can exceed, in agricultural beauty, the soft, luxuriant blue-grass with which it is covered.

The 3d class, or mountain land, is generally used for pasturage. It is found on the mountains, above an elevation of 600 feet. It is equally as rich as either the first or second classes, but is too cold to mature grains, unless it be rye. It is also too steep for cultivation, or even for growing grass, had it to be mowed. The stock, however, succeed in climbing the mountain-sides for it, and during the summer keep fat. It was formerly but little valued; it now bears a good price.

There is a strange phenomenon here (as in other mountain countries), effecting the difference of lands found on north and south hill-sides. The cause, or explanation, has been given under the head of Meteorology. The soil on the north sides of the mountains and hills is a dark, loose loam, and extremely rich; the rocks (though few) are the finest quality of limestone. On the south, they are essentially different in kind and quality, being flint and clay slate, often pulverized so as not much to impede the plow. It will require some geological speculations to account for this difference in rock, and to such works I refer the reader. The growth on the south sides, above

600 feet, is shrubby, and generally oak and chestnut; and the land does not produce, by any means, as well as the valley or north side lands. The south side land, below 600 feet, was formerly but little valued, being gritty, but it is now looked on as the finest wheat land.

I remarked that the soil of the land in Tazewell was "Tenacious;" I mean by this that it wears well. A field on the Crab-orchard farm, cleared in 1775, upward of seventy-five years ago, has not had a year's rest, and now produces equally as well as any land in the county. With anything like care, the farmer here can never impoverish his lands.

I have never known a judge of land to examine those of Tazewell without passing the highest encomiums upon them, and I hope I shall not be accused of partiality when I say—I have seen lands in most of the states and territories, and have found none, anywhere, more deserving enomiums than those of Tazewell county, Virginia. To the farmer it will be gratifying to know, that our lands, though broken, do not wash.

[List of Plants and Trees are Omitted.]

The botanist will find many plants not generally supposed to grow in mountainous districts; while the medical gentleman will agree with me, that nature seems to have made this county the home of the most important medicinal plants in her materia medica. The following remarks, I quote from an address to the public, by the author, prefacing the constitution and by-laws of the Jeffersonville Historical Society, and published in 1851.

"The Botany of western Virginia is not surpassed by that of any other section in the temperate zones. 'This region,' as Torrey says, 'may be called a garden of medicinal plants.''

Ornamental, as well as medicinal plants, are here scattered with a profuse hand. To every disease of this region, nature seems to have furnished a remedy. If in any country botany can be studied with advantage, it is here; for flowers of the same class, genera, and species, are blooming for several months. Those in the valleys first, and those found upon the ascent of the mountains, later. Many have been the pleasant days which I have spent in botanical rambles on these mountains, where from frost till frost flowers are ever found.

CHAPTER VIII

LIVE STOCK

I have not space to treat this subject at that length, which its importance demands, nor is it necessary to go into details, as the people of Tazewell seem awake to their interest, which is closely connected with this subject' When the stock markets of the east are dull, business is seriously affected in this county; the export of stock, constituting a principal source of wealth (see Commerce). The live stock of the county, is valued at 517,330 dollars, and it probably greatly exceeds that sum. My calculations are based upon the census returns for June 1850, since which time, a year and a half has passed, and, of course, has proportionally increased, so that if their valuation was now stated to be 600,000 dollars I should perhaps be within the bounds of truth. There is no subject more interesting to a majority of farmers, but want of space compels me to leave its perfect elucidation to others better qualified for the task.

HORSES.

Tazewell has long been celebrated for its fine horses. The principal breeds in the county, are the Tamoleon, Yorick, Packalet, Cooper, and Trueblue.

The **Tamoleons** are celebrated for their riding qualities, and when crossed with the cultivator, are, perhaps, equal to any in the United States. They are very docile, and easily kept in good order. They are sorrel, with flax mane and tail, and with the exceptions of a few defects about the head, are fine specimens of the species.

The **Yorick** breed, are generally black, rather small, well muscled, fiery and make excellent saddle-horses. They are remarkable for having sprung from Yorick, the bitter foe of the Indians (see History of Moore Family—Book, III).

The **Packalet** was introduced into Tazewell from Botetourt county, Va. Most of the fine grays, seen in our county, are of this stock. They are fine harness horses, and are not much inferior to others, if used under the saddle.

The **Coopers** and **Trueblues** are, also, quite numerous, and with many are favorite breeds.

If we except the Arabians, no people are fonder of fine horses, than those of Tazewell. Boys, from an early age, manifest great partiality for them. They are generally good judges of a horse, and have them well used. From the character of the country, the labors of a horse are slavish. They bear a good price, first class horses selling from one hundred and fifty, to one hundred and sixty dollars, and second class selling from one hundred, to one hundred and twenty-five dollars. There are upward of 5,000 in the county:

about 200 are annually driven south and east. Much money is made by buying and selling in the county; but those who drive them off, generally lose, prices being too high, at home, to admit of speculation, when driven to a distance.

MULES.

There are but few in the county, though their culture is beginning to engage public attention. Our climate and pastures seem every way calculated to produce as fine mules, as any part of Kentucky. They require little or no feeding, and will, therefore, yield greater profits than horses, which require more or less grain, during the entire winter. It seems difficult to convince the older farmers, that they are as able to perform the labors of the farm as the horse. Time will, however, convince them that this objection is futile. They should be raised for exportation, as they require as little care as cattle, and yield much greater profits.

CATTLE.

There is nowhere to be found, a country better adapted to grazing cattle than this county. The grass is said to be superior, both in abundance and quality, by all stock dealers. About 7,000 head are annually driven to market; but on which, like all other live stock, great losses are sometimes sustained. This could not be otherwise, while markets are at such a distance.

The improved, are the **long and short horned Durham** and **Devon.** A majority of the cattle in the county are, however, of the unimproved, **or** native stock, which are less, and do not bear so good a price as the improved.

Three year old steers, are worth from twelve to sixteen dollars, according to the scarcity, and the reported demand in market. There are somewhere in the neighborhood or 1800 in the county. A part of those driven from the county, are bought up in Kentucky and Tennessee during the fall, wintered and kept till September, when they are taken to market.

SHEEP.

There are only about 20,000 head of sheep in the county, and these suffered to run at large on the mountains, without shepherds, subject to the mercy of the wolves and dogs. It is no unusual thing for great numbers to be killed in the spring. The owners pay but little attention to them, and do not even make them as profitable as they might be made.

There are few improved flocks: but the small, unimproved, are here a superior sheep. About 25,000 pounds of wool are annually taken, and a a major part exported. It is to be regretted, that our farmers have paid so little attention to wool growing. I am well convinced, that the same amount of capital invested in sheep, that is invested in cattle, would pay a much better profit. No county in the state is better adapted to the rearing of sheep, than this—a poor sheep being seldom seen.

HOGS.

There are 21,000 in the county, though not over 500 are annually driven to market. 10,000 pounds are baconed, a portion of which is sold to the adjoining counties of Washington and Smyth. Hogs do not seem to thrive so well here as formerly, owing, no doubt, to the uncertainty, and sometimes scarcity of the chestnut and acorn crops. The markets are in Eastern Virginia. There are not goats sufficient to require notice.

CHAPTER IX.

COMMERCE OF TAZEWELL.

Considering the population of Tazewell, its commerce is rather extensive. To give a correct idea of its growth I shall be compelled to turn back from the present to an early period. It has been elsewhere stated, that during the first years of settlement, all goods were brought from the east on packhorses. The goods then imported were pottery, and hardware, consisting of axes, knives and forks, pocket-knives, hammers, saws, chisels, ect. Neither groceries nor dry goods, found a place on the list of importations. After the peace of 1783, the list was enlarged. Hitherto almost everything had been paid for in peltries, a currency much easier acquired by the frontiermen, and much less liable to depreciation, than the continental money then in circulation.

There being at this time, no roads over which wagons could pass, of course the task of importation was tedious, and sometimes uncertain. From all appearances, none thought it scarcely creditable, that in the short space of half a century, so great a change would have been made. An incident related to me by Mr. Samuel Witten, seems to the point:—

James Witten, one of the early settlers, whose keen judgment had led him to expect that this county was, at some future time, destined to be the seat of a free, happy, and independent people, one day at a house-raising jocosely inquired of his comrades, what they would think, if in twenty-five years, wagons actually came into the county, and passed along the very valley in which they were at work? The rest of the company laughed at the idea, nor could the old man persuade them, that such a thing would take place even in fifty years. Yet, in a few years—much less than twenty-five, the road was made, and wagons passed over the very spot predicted by Mr. Witten, to the no small wonder of the older people, and terror of the children.

The road, however, was not what would now be expected by the name. From this time, the roads continued to improve, and the importation of goods to increase. They were then wagoned from Philadelphia, one wagon-load generally supplying the whole county. About the year 1800, a sack of coffee, for the first, time was brought into the county. It was kept by Mr. Graham, the merchant, a year and a half, and sent back as being altogether unsaleable. Yet the sons and daughters of these very people, now consume not far from 50,000 pounds in a single twelve-month.

The opening of the Fincastle and Cumberland Gap turnpike in 183-, furnished another market to the merchant; goods were now purchased in the northern cities, and shipped to Lynchburg, and were thence brought to the county by wagons. About fifteen days is the usual time which elapses from the day of loading in Lynchburg, to the time of arrival in Jeffersonville. Freight is about two dollars and fifty cents per cwt. There is now brought into the county annually, dry goods and groceries to the amount of one hundred and twenty-five thousand dollars. The percentage on goods sold here is considerable, owing partly to the freight, and to the credit system which prevails.

Feathers, beeswax, ginseng, hides, tallow, butter, and wool, are usually bought by the merchants, or bartered for goods. We have no market for wheat, corn, potatoes, oats, hay, buckwheat, or barley.

Cattle are driven to the north-eastern part of the state, and sold to speculators, who fatten and dispose of them in Baltimore, and the nothern cities. Hogs are usually driven to the east and south-east part of the state. Horses are driven south and east—generally into North Carolina. Much of the live stock is bought on credit, and paid for upon the return of the drovers. This accounts for the credit system of the county. The merchants have claims upon the people of the county, for upward of one hundred and forty thousand dollars, but this is a small sum, when we consider that the stock trade alone, brings to the county every year upward of one hundred and ten thousand dollars.

As soon as the Virginia and Tennessee railroad has been completed to Wythville (which will be during the year 1852), this over-balancing will be in favor of the farmer, in place of the merchant. The percentage on importations will not be so great, and the expense of exporting will likewise be lessened. The grains will find a market, and many farmers will buy most of their necessaries themselves. Instead of driving cattle to the N. E. counties of Virginia, they will, most likely, be driven to Saltville, slaughtered, pickled up, and sent to a different market. It is to be greatly lamented that efficient steps have not been taken to get a branch from the main road extending into Tazewell county. Could the central road pass us and go to the mouth of Big Sandy river, as it should, we should also find a market for our coal, which is exhaustless, and of the finest qualiry.

There is at no time over twenty thousand dollars, in active circulation in the county. Large amounts of small bills, issues of the Tennessee, Kentucky, Washington City, and North Carolina banks, are to be seen; and though it is a violation of the laws, to receive or pass them, no attention is paid to it, either by the people or the commonwealth.

HOME MANUFACTURES.

Linsey, jeans, tow-linen, flax-thread, hose, and carpets, are the principal home manufactures of this county: the value of which, according to the census report, is twenty-five thousand four hundred dollars. I have no data from which to estimate the amount of either, but am satisfied that jeans linsey, stand first in valuation. Tow-linen, which sells for about ten cents per yard, does not cost the Tazewell manufacturer far short of thirty cents. A like statement might be made about the whole list.

These articles are manufactured at the houses of the farmers, their planations supplying all the material, except cotton, which is imported from North Carolina, spun and put up in bales. Wool is carded by machines in the county, and spun by hand. The weaving is done on the common hand-loom. House furniture, of nearly all kinds, is manufactured in the county. Saddles, boots, shoes, iron-work, etc., is also done here. Lumber of the finest quality, may here be had, for the trouble of cutting it.

When speaking of the loss attending home manufactures I have been more than once told, that "this kind of work is done by women when they could do nothing else." To such, I again say, if I have made a correct statement, they had better cease labor. Beside, I have yet to find a woman who can do nothing else but weave and spin. Why send our children to school, if their mothers have time to educate them? We should at least save tuition fee. Let the education of our youths be intrusted to women, and I venture to affirm, that they will become as learned and pious, as under the instruction of men. Woman is eminently qualified to instill christianity in the plastic minds of children; and her very nature fits her to enter into the sympathies of childhood, when men disregard them. It is time that the yardstick, tapestring, and rule, be transferred into their hands, and the masculine part of the race betake themselves to pursuits more manly, and better calculated to develop the talents God has given them.

I would not be called an advocate for petticoat government, but I would make woman my equal and restore to her, her natural rights. I would have her share, in common with man, the business transactions of life, and thus afford her fields of labor in which to develop her god-like faculties. To see a feminine, soft-handed man measuring lace, while a rosy-cheeked girl is chopping wood to make him a fire, induces me to think man has forgotten from whence he sprung.

CHAPTER X.

EDUCATION.

The following article is the substance of a report made by Mr. Rufus Brittain, a competent teacher of this county, to the Jeffersonville Historical Society. It is so true that no apology is needed here for inserting it. I presume that few will be found who will dissent from his opinions. Yet, I fear, few there are, as ready to act as Mr. Brittain. A thousand reasons might be adduced for properly educating the children of this county, and from signs now becoming visible, it is to be hoped that many years will not elapse before Tazewell will be ranked foremost in this best of causes. To properly educate the children of the county between the ages of six and twenty years, we need upward of seventy schoolhouses. We have now about fifteen, which are better suited for barns than seats of learning.

The increased interest now manifesting itself for the cause of popular education, is mostly among the younger persons. The present generation must pass away before we can expect a general diffusion of knowledge.

Mr. Brittain says:

"This cause, so important to the best interest of every well-regulated community, has not heretofore, in this section, received that attention it deserves: and as a natural consequence of this neglect, we find the county sadly deficient in the means of training up the children of her citizens for stations of honor and usefulness.

"By the returns of the last census, it is found that out of 3,317 persons in the county over twenty-one years of age, 1,490 are unable to read and write. This is indeed a deplorable picture of the intelligence of our county, and might well cause every intelligent man in it to blush with shame, were it not that we find some excuse for this ignorance when we consider the situation of the greater portion of our population, scattered as it is over a wide extent of country, and laboring under great disadvantages for maintaining schools.

"The early settlers of this region had many difficulties to encounter in their efforts to procure homes for themselves and their children, and too frequently education appears to have been of but secondary importance in their estimation. Yet primary schools of some sort seem to have been maintained from an early date after its settlement, in those neighborhoods where children were sufficiently numerous to make up a school, and parents were able and willing to support a teacher. Instances, also, have not been wanting where families not situated so as to unite conveniently with others, yet appreciating the advantages of a good school, have employed teachers to instruct their children at home, and thus afforded them privileges of which the children of their less enlightened neighbors were deprived. But of later years, since portions of the county have become more densely populated, and in various ways much improved, the cause of education here has not kept pace with that improvement, for even in those parts of the county best able to maintain schools, no permanent provision has been made for their continuance: and in those schools that generally have been best supported, long intervals between sessions so frequently occur, that pupils forget much of what they had acquired during their attendance; and thus the little time spent by many in schools is spent under the greatest disadvantage for the proper development of their intellectual faculties. Teachers, as might be supposed, under these circumstances, together with the fact that their compensation is usually very moderate, are often incompetent for the task they have assumed, both as respects talents and acquired qualifications. And though under these circumstances good teachers are sometimes obtained, yet most generally in such cases the office is only assumed as an available stepping-stone to some other and more profitable pursuit. Indeed, it would be unreasonable to expect persons to prepare themselves for the proper discharge of the onerous duties of a primary school-teacher, unless they hoped to receive some adequate reward for their services.

"Now in consideration of the state of our schools, and the deplorable ignorance in which the children of our county are in danger of growing up, it must be evident to all who think properly on this subject, that we need to adopt and carry out some effcient school system, by means of which, our schools shall be made more permanent, and sufficient inducements be held out to command and retain the services of competent and well qualified teachers: and that the means of a good primary education be brought within the reach of every child in the community, and for those who desire it and excel in the branches taught in primary schools, that opportunities be afforded to acquire a knowledge of the higher branches of a good English and scientific education.

"These important objects, our schools, as now conducted, fail to accomplish, and the state school-fund for the education of indigent children, is in a great measure wasted, as by its regulations, it must depend chiefly on the schools as they now exist.

"But the legislature of the state has provided a Free School System, which if adopted and carried out with proper energy and in an enlightened manner, these noble objects, in a great measure, might be attained. In order to its adoption the law requires a vote in its favor of two-thirds of the legal votes of the adopting district or county. Such a vote, we fear, could not be obtained here, until some effort is made to enlighten our citizens on the subject of education and school systems; and show them the advantages that would accrue to themselves and their children by having the latter furnished with the proper means of moral and intellectual culture. There would also be a variety of difficulties to encounter in the execution of this Free School System. In some portions of the county the population is quite sparse, and a sufficient number of children could not be included within a convenient school district. This difficulty, however, has no remedy under our present method of keeping up the schools, unless families thus isolated are able to employ teachers to instruct their children at home.

But if schools were established in these thinly-settled districts, by taking in boundaries large enough to furnish a sufficient number of children to each, and some efforts made to overcome the inconvenience of a distant school, by conveying the children to and from school in such manner as could best be provided: the mere fact of a good school being kept up, would be a new induceement for persons to emigrate to those districts, and in a few years the population would so much increase that a school could be made up within convenient bounds. This system, also, being chiefly dependent on funds raised for its support by taxation, might meet with great opposition from those who have a higher appreciation of the value of money than they have of intelligence; and again, others who are possessed of large amounts of taxable property and few or no children to send to school, may think it oppressive, unless convinced that it is the duty of every state or community to educate, or furnish the means to educate, the children of its citizens. In a republican government like ours, the permanence of which evidently depends on the virtue and intelligence of its citizens, it might be deemed unnecessary to demonstrate the importance of every child being properly instructed and furnished with the means of acquiring that knowledge which will fit him to perform the duties incumbent on a citizen of a free and enlightened country. Yet there are too many who are slow to perceive or acknowledge the importance of good schools, and the necessity of being at some trouble and expense to keep them up. Hence all patriotic and intelligent members of the community who have tasted the blessing of an education, or felt the want of one, should co-operate with each other, and use their influence for the improvement of our schools, and the increase of the virtue and intelligence of our citizens."

CHAPTER XI.

SLAVERY IN TAZEWELL.

Did my limits admit it, I should enter into a lengthy detail of this institution as it exists in this county. This institution has long been denounced by the northern presses, and generally, greatly misrepresented. It has been contended that the slaves of the south are barbarously treated, ill-fed, poorly clothed, worked hard, and kept in ignorance. These assertions are not true, and the every-day experience of any southern man will bear me out in the declaration. True it is, that a few masters are tyrannical, but these are altogether exceptions, and should not be looked on as a necessary feature of the institution. These calumnies have been heaped upon us by men, many of whom, have seen but few or no slaves, and are consequently ignorant of the real state of slavery in the south.

They have been borne with a patience, which at once portrays the magnanimity, and patriotic devotedness of southern men to the Union. A few irascible politicians have cried out dissolution and secession, but the feeling has never been general in the south, nor is it likely to be, if the general government continues to carry out the designs of the constitution. There are, it is known, many highly intellectual and virtuous citizens of the nothern states, as well as many respectable presses, who discountenance this abuse. It is generally the rabble, and foreigners, who keep up the excitement.

The insulting and degrading course of northern and western fanatics, has been the cause of introducing stricter discipline among the slaves. The ardent desires of abolitionists are thus rendered still more hopeless. Anti-slavery societies have, in a few instances, sent missionaries, under the guise of Christianity, to decoy off our slaves; and have sometimes been the means of causing the slaves to shed the blood of their masters, for which they will have to account in the day of general reckoning up. Were the people of the free states to come among us, and examine slavery as it really exists, they would no longer contenance the depredations of their fellow citizens; which, if not stopped, must ultimately result in a dissolution of the bonds of union, sealed by the blood of our fathers. Then civil war, and a total and merciless extermination of the African race, with all its dire consequences, would inevitably follow. Southern character has been mistaken by northern men; let them inform themselves and assist us in our labors to make this nation, as it should be, the seat of freedom, industry, and religion. The slavery of the south, is infinitely preferable to the degrading, antirepublican slavery and bondage, and poverty, and misery of the north. Show me so great a slave as the northern factory girl. Show me in the kitchen, or negro hut of the southern planter, the misery, and poverty, and hunger, which is to be met with among the poor widows, and orphans, and **free** negroes of the north! Show me that southern master, who has ever refused his servant bread: for every one shown, I will show ten beggars in the streets of any northern city. But it is not my purpose to write a defense of this institution; I am, however, to record facts, and such are these.

The first slaves brought to this county, were purchased by the early settlers, with ginseng. They have increased, and others have been brought from the eastern part of the state. This species of property has not, however, been found so valuable here, as in the cotton lands of the south. Hence it has been less sought after.

There were on the first of June, 1850, eleven hundred and sixteen colored persons in the county, of whom fifty-six were free negroes, leaving ten hundred and sixty slaves, worth about five hundred and thirty thousand dollars.

They are well clothed, have often as good houses as their masters, work no harder, and have the same fare. They are generally trusty, and jealous of their honor. They are acquainted with the leading movements in the political world, are moral, and many read; few write, and their reading is mostly confined to the Bible. They converse well; have much tact and judgment, and often conduct the farming operations. They are generous, kind, and seem much devoted to their masters. Such are the slaves of Tazewell county.

And yet abolition societies send out men to persuade them to leave their homes of peace and plenty, where want and care are unknown, and make their way to **free states,** where they are really less respected, and where hunger, cold and nakedness ever await them. To the northern fanatics I would say, as the great Master said: "Why beholdest thou the mote that is in thy brother's eye, but considerest not the beam that is in thine own eye?"

CHAPTER XII.

AGRICULTURE.

As I am writing for the information of the people of the county, most of whom are farmers, I trust I shall be forgiven if I am apparently verbose on this most interesting of subjects. The historian, I believe, is an annalist, with the privilege of giving his own opinion upon matters of which he writes. Of this latter license I shall avail myself, and hope I shall not entirely fail to interest.

Since by the labors of the husbandman we all live, either directly or indirectly, and upon the productive energy of the soil does not only our own existence but that of every animated creature upon the face of the earth depend, I shall not be accused of a stretch of the imagination, if I say, that mankind could better afford to give up every art and science than that of tilling the soil. Nor is it in the power of any man to picture the distresses which would follow a single failure of the earth to "bring forth." Scarcely a man will be found who would deny the above inferences; yet it will be equally as hard to find one who seems to appreciate the great necessity of renovating the soil, and bestowing agricultural educations upon her people.

I care not how viewed, whether in a political, religious, civil, useful, or physical light, all other arts are subservient to this; and none so worthy of our attention. I verily believe that the very existence and perpetuation of our Republic depends upon the successful cultivation of the soil. There is a moralizing influence attending the labors of the farmer, to be found nowhere else. No occupation that has yet appeared or been followed among men, seems so well calculated to develop the mind, or foster the principles of virtue as this. In order to the successful cultivation of the ground, a general knowledge of many of the arts and sciences is necessary. To develop the physical powers, and insure a healthy body, and a consequent healthy mind, agriculture seems peculiarly adapted.

Under a false idea that honor was alone attached to the so-called "learned professions," the occupation of "farmer" has been too much neglected; but agriculture stretches out her collatteral arms, and embraces the labors of even these, which she appropriates to her legal domain. Astronomy and chemistry are her tools, while botany, or vegetable physiology is her offspring, to whose growth she yearly adds her treasures. Meteorology is her handmaid. Political economy is proud to obey her, while commerce and navigation, without her fostering hand, would sicken and pine in their infancy.

This false idea should be exploded. We need educated farmers who would seek to place the soil in such a state as to make it produce to its utmost extent. There are, perhaps, fewer scientific men engaged in this occupation than in any other; yet no occupation requires so many. European countries have lately turned their attention to this subject through sheer necessity. The attention which our government is now paying to the subject, leads me to look for an entire revolution in agricultural matters in less than fifty years.

The agencies and improvements now acting, will tend to bring about this state of things. The proximity to each other, induced by the rail-car, will cement more closely the interest of the farming community of this extended land, and open up inducements hitherto unknown, especially in the isolated region of Tazewell. The press, sending forth its sheets from Maine to California, before they are fairly dry, and the astonishing workings of the telegraph are now exhibiting their influence upon the machinery of civil society, and in no country more perceptibly than in the Untited States.

Give us railroads, and let the press make known the claims of southwestern Virginia, and the "gee up" of the New England plowboy will soon be heard upon our mountain sides. Our mountaineers will soon be seen trading in Richmond, Baltimore, Philadelphia, New York, and Boston. Our neglected fields will bloom under the hands of scientific agriculturists, till wagons will no more be seen passing westward with men to build up new states on the ruins of those they have left.

I now proceed to point out briefly the history and peculiarities of agriculture in Tazewell. Among the early settlers, and even in the present day, a sufficiency of provisions alone seems to be sought after. Large quantities of land—too large for the force employed—are cultivated, and this very system of having too much land in a farm, has retarded the agricultural advancement of the county of Tazewell more than any other one cause. By endeavoring to cultivate so much land, it has been imperfectly worked, and hence the soil does not yield to the husbandman her proper stores.

The manner, too, of cultivation, is similar to that practiced by the early settlers. And I hope I shall be pardoned for saying that the people of Tazewell who cultivate the soil, work, less than most any other similar community to be found in the United States. This may be owing to the want of proper markets, which will not be much improved till our farmers turn their attention to internal improvements, and no longer vote against the construction of railroads and turnpikes.

Most of the cereals do well in Tazewell. I have in my possession a stalk of corn, grown on common upland, sixteen feet nine inches high; four stalks grew in a hill; it was planted in May, and cut up in September. Irrigating the lands is much neglected. Wheat does exceedingly well in this county, especially those kinds known as Mediterranean, walker, and white chaff: but as no market is afforded for its sale, more is not grown than is consumed, there being only 28,220 bushels reported on the census books for 1850. (See table.)

The county is more remarkable for its production of grasses than anything else. Though tobacco does very well, fortunately, its culture has been discarded, the county not producing 1,000 pounds per annum.

The exceedingly fine grasses of the county have made it decidedly a grazing county, and much celebrated for fine stock. Bluegrass (**Poa pretensis**) is the principal native (?) grass: though timothy, herd, and most others do well. In no country does clover succeed better. The grasses have received much of the farmer's attention, and with the increasing interest shown in improving the live-stock, it would seem that the county is destined to take a prominent stand among the stock-raising counties in the state. There are some farms in the county well improved, but they are too few.

CHAPTER XIII.

CHURCH HISTORY—JUDICIARY.

No portion of my labors, if properly investigated, would be more interesting than this: yet the paucity of material afforded me, makes it quite difficult to give anything like a correct and full church history of this section The principal denominations in the county are Methodists, Baptists, Presbyterians, and Roman Catholics; each of whom will be noticed.

The first sermon preached in the county was in 1794, by Rev. Mr. Cobbler, appointed to the New River circuit, by the Baltimore conference. This sermon may be regarded as the budding of Methodism in Tazewell county. The seeds sown by this good man fell upon a genial soil, and he had the satisfaction of seeing Jeremiah Witten and Mrs, Sarah Witten, William Witten and his lady, John and Sarah Peery, Elizabeth Greenup, Samuel Forguson, Isabella Forguson, and two colored persons, flock around the Christian standard, determined that Christ should not be forgotten, even in the mountain-gorges of the wild "backwoods."

Thomas Peery gave them a piece of land, and in 1797 they built a meetinghouse about one mile west of Jeffersonville.

Between 1794-7, meetings were generally held at the house of Samuel Forguson, near the present seat of justice. Before 1794, prayer-meeting was the only form of worship practiced: this seems to have been coexistent with the earliest settlement. The march of Methodism has been steadily onward; they have, at present, seven churches in regular fellowship.

The first Baptists in the county, were the Scaggs and Hankins. The first sermon preached to them, was by Rev. Simon Cotterel from Russel county, in 1796. Their first meetings were held in private houses, in the Hankins' settlement. The Baptists seem not to have made as rapid progress as the Methodists; as they have now only two regular churches in the county. I have been unable to learn the number of communicants, but understand that it is greater than would be supposed from the number of churches.

The first Presbyterians in the county were William Perry, Samuel Walker, and his wife. Prof. Doak preached the first sermon to them, somewhere about 1798. He was soon followed by Rev. Mr. Crawford, from Washington county. The first church organized was in the Cove, in 1833, which was placed in charge of Rev. Dugald McIntyre, assisted by Rev. Mr. McEwin. This church, from some cause, was suffered to go down, and the Presbyterians were without a regular church till the summer of 1851, when a church was organized at Jeffersonville, and placed in charge of Rev. Mr. Naff. They have one church, and about twenty communicants.

At what time the first Roman Catholics appeared in the county, is not known. Edward Fox, a priest who resided at Wythville, preached the first sermon to them in a union church at Jeffersonville, in 1842. He continued to preach, at intervals, till the close of the controversy between him, and President Collins of Emory and Henry College. Having been beaten from every position, he quit Wytheville, and consequently the Tazewell catholics were left without a priest. Bishop Whelan coming to this section of the state, took occasion to visit his flock in Tazewell; the Methodists opened their pulpit for him, and in acknowledgment of their kindness, one of his first sentences was not only to insult them, but the house of God. He remarked, he **"felt embarrassed because he was preaching in an unconsecrated house."** President Collins, who had firmly opposed the spread of this doctrine in south-western Virginia, being in the neighborhood, heard of the occurrence and replied to him in a few days. Notwithstanding this, Catholicism began to spread, and preparations were made for building a cathedral, which is now in course of construction.

JUDICIARY.

The formation of the county, necessarily caused some derangement in the courts. The magistrates who had been acting under the authority of Wythe county, however, met in May, 1800, and held the first court at the present residence of Col. John B. George. John Ward was elected clerk, and Major Maxwell made sheriff. In the following month the election for county officers came off, and the court was opened at Harvey G. Peery's house. In June the county seat was fixed upon, and Judge Brockenborough held the first circuit court in a court-house built of buckeye logs, for which the county paid ten dollars. Peter Johnson was now appointed to fill the station of resident judge: James Thompson was the first commonwealth's attorney. The Buckeye C. H. was soon converted into a workshop, and a plain frame-house substituted. The court-house is now a substantial brick building. Court days, Wednesday after the fourth Monday of each month.

In connection with this subject, it may be remarked, that a trial for murder has never taken place in this county, and fewer lawsuits, according to the population, occur in our courts than any county in the state.

CHAPTER XIV.

LITERARY AND BENEVOLENT INSTITUTIONS—NEWSPAPERS.

The Jeffersonville Historical Society, is the only literary institution in the county. It was founded August 14th, 1851, through the exertions of H. F. Peery, M. D., and the author. The movement was warmly supported by John Wynn, Thos. Peery, Rees T. Bowen, William Cox, H. R. Bogle, William Barnes, William Henry Maxwell, and other leading gentlemen in the county, who seem to be fully awakened to the necessity of exciting in the community a spirit of literary culture. The following remarks are taken from the Richmond Examiner of 16th January, 1852:

"The recent excitement of railroad subjects in southwestern Virginia, seems to have been the means of calling public attention to the subject of literary culture in this section of the state. The citizens of Tazewell, one of the most isolated counties of the commonwealth, are taking a prominent stand in this cause. The establishment of the Jeffersonville Historical Society, in a wild, mountainous country, would seem to indicate something more of its citizens, as patrons of literature, than has heretofore been supposed to exist. The society numbers already about seventy members, many of whom occupy positions not only of high civil trust, but prominent situations in the literary world.

"One principal object of this society seems to be, to preserve the history of the settlement and Indian wars of the southwestern part of Virginia—to develop its resources, and scatter knowledge among the people. A cabinet, in which will be found specimens from the mineral, vegetable, and animal kingdoms, is attached to the institution. Also, a library containing the principal works which could assist in researches either upon the Indians, who at a former period inhabited this section, their manners and customs, or upon the natural history of the county. The society receives papers upon most subjects which throw light upon the best means of promoting the interests of this section of the state. * * * * *

"Whether this society may be able to effect any good, cannot be answered till more time has been allowed for the development of its labors. Certain it is, however, that if the society publish their reports, as they most likely will, and they are read by the people of south-western Virginia, some good must be done." * * * * * * *

There is a moral influence attending the existence of such associations, which cannot be otherwise than sanitary. The very fact of the existence of such an institution, will incite the surrounding community to prepare themselves to share in its labors. This society embraces most of the prominent farmers in the county, and is likely to stretch its arms out over the respectable of all classes, and indirectly, if not directly, they will become laborers in the association, and thus interested in its prosperity.

Say ten gentlemen are asked to furnish a report upon the natural history of the black perch; ten more upon the culture of the grape-vine; ten more upon the amount of iron ore, and extent of coal-fields; ten more upon the kinds of roads best adapted to our hill country; ten more upon some subject in geology, or mechanices, or agriculture, or botany, or any other subject coming within the range of the institution. What will be the effect? why this—the gentlemen will procure the works which treat of the respective subjects on which they are required to report, and study them. It is readily seen that in a few years, they will become, more or less, familiar with the principal sciences; and as the acquisition of knowledge engenders a want of more, in a few years we shall have a reading population, who will begin to act upon some efficient means of educating the rising generation. Nor is this all, the annual exhibitions or fairs will incite a more lively interest in excelling in agriculture, mechanics, etc. This is too apparent to need elucidation.

A desire to excite this society to a sense of the important work before them and to furnish an index to Tazewell has resulted in this history.

The most important **benevolent** institution is that of the **Independent Order of Oddfellows,** a lodge of whom, was established at Jeffersonville, by G. M., Jas. McCabe, 6th December, 1850. The lodge numbers about forty-five members, and is designated as Floyd Lodge No. 84.

The **Sons of Temperance** have a division, being the one hundred and fifth in the state, which numbers some eighty or ninety members. There is also a division of the "Sons" at Bluestone, and another at Liberty Hill. The former of the three, was established at Jeffersonville in 1848; the second at Bluestone, was established in the summer of 1850; that at Liberty Hill, in 1851. These three divisions have done much good in reforming the people.

A Circle of the Brotherhood of the Union, encircled in the H. F., was established at Jeffersonville 4th July, 1850, and is known as Independence Circle, B. U. (H. F.) C. A. 131-4. This institution numbers about twenty members, and is calculated to do much good in the cause of reform. In the summer of 1850, a lodge of Masons was also established at this place. So there are four secret societies existing in this town, and if their designs be carried out, much good may be expected in the way of social progress.

Their influence is plainly perceivable at Jeffersonville. Few villages or places in the United States present so much good feeling and brotherly love—so much sound morality, and so extensively diffused, or so little suffering. There is less backbiting, wrangling, and ill-will among the people of Jeffersonville, than any village to be found in the state; nor is it a bad feature in the character of our people.

NEWSPAPERS.

At the opening of the presidential campaign in 1847, there was not a single democratic press in south-western Virginia. The citizens of Tazewell being mostly democratic, felt the necessity of some organ through which to utter their sentiments, and called loudly for a press. Finally, Dr. H. F. Peery was prevailed on to purchase a second-hand press, then laying idle at

Abingdon. He commenced the publication of the "Jeffersonville Democrat" in August, 1847, and with so much ability and zeal did the worthy editor handle his pen, that the influence of the "Democrat" was felt, to a greater or less degree, throughout south-western Virginia. A new field of labor seemed opened, and the citizens of the county seem to fully appreciate the advantages of a press, and fostered its existence with great care. A spirit of inquiry was stirred up among the people. Education received an impetus; morality and religion began to look up, and when professional duties compelled the editor to relinquish his task, in August, 1850, there was a general murmur of complaint at the fall of the press. So urgent were the appeals of the community to the editor to again divide his labors, that he was compelled to make preparations to start the paper again. While engaged at this, he had an offer from the present editor, which was accepted, and Mr. George F. Holmes, a gentleman of ability, and formerly professor in one of the Virginia institutions of learning, became the proprietor, and in August, 1851, commenced editing the "South-Western Advocate." The paper has a circulation of about three hundred and fifty copies, and with proper caution, might be placed on a firm basis. Among the pioneer editors of south-western Virginia, few will be found to possess the tact which so eminently characterized the editor of the old "Democrat."

CHAPTER XV.

MINERALS AND NATURAL CURIOSITIES.

The minerals of this county are both numerous and important. Silver, iron, lead, arsenic, sulphur, salt, niter, gypsum, and large quantities of coal being found. I have several times been asked to examine what was thought to be gold; but have generally found it to be pyrites of iron, and sometimes sulphur.

Some attempt has been made to work a silver mine in Poor valley, about seven miles from Jeffersonville, but it was undertaken by persons unacquainted with mining, and, of course, under such circumstances, we could look for no important results.

There is also silver, but to what extent I cannot say, on a string of ridges north of Clinch river.

Iron is so abundant that it is hard to find a section destitute of it. The best specimen I ever saw, was lately placed in the cabinet of the Jeffersonville Historical Society, by Mr. Rufus Brittain. Ore, of this county, was worked at an early day, by a man named Johnson, which was pronounced to be of a good quality. The ore is, generally, specular and magnetic oxides, and would admit of being worked to advantage.

The mineral wealth of the county, will likely not be known, till there is a greater demand for it. As soon as our lands are impoverished, gypsum will be taken from the earth and scattered over them. And when the demand is sufficient, we shall manufacture large quantities of sulphur. Many saline springs exist, from which salt will be manufactured at no distant day. There is, within four miles of Jeffersonville, on the lands of Mr. Thomas Witten, every indication of a good salt stream. The county has already produced much niter.

Coal exists everywhere, though wood is so plenty that it has not been used as fuel to any extent; hence, no search has been made for it. Bituminous, and, probably, cannel coal, exist in great quantity. The nearest to Jeffersonville, that has yet been discovered, is on the lands of G. W. G. Browne, in Poor valley, about four and a half miles from Jeffersonville. It is generally thought that coal does not exist on the head branches of Clinch river, but I imagine the supposition has no foundation. It has been found below, and in every direction around, and no doubt, exists generally through the county. When shall we have an outlet for this coal?

NATURAL CURIOSITIES.

There are, in the county, many natural curiosities, such as caves, precipices, bone caverns, etc. A cave, running under Rich mountain, has excited some curiosity. I am informed, by Mr. Thompson, who has explored it, that it is one of the most magnificent caves in the country, as yet known. The ceiling, in some places, being so high, that the best torch light will not discover it; nor will a stone, thrown from the hand, reach it. A fine stream flows through it, in which fish are said to exist. It is nearly destitute of those rugged cliffs, usually to be found in such places.

During winter, vast numbers of bats (**Oreillard insectivora**) are to be seen; some, fastening themselves to the ceiling, are seized on by others, and these again by others, till they sometimes form lengthy bunches, resembling a swarm of bees after they have pitched. On placing the flame of a candle near them, they set up a piteous cry, which is generally plaintive enough to divert the destroyer's hand. It would be an endless task, to give a description of half the caves to be found in the county. There is much sameness about them. They are, frequently, the receptacle of vast numbers of human bones, of an extraordinary size, and thought to be those of an extinct race, formerly inhabiting this region.

Stalacities* are usually found in these caves, many of which are beautiful. It is said that a cave, near Liberty Hill, exhibits the prints of human feet, in the solid rock: this may, or may not be true, for I have never had bravery enough to take pleasure in examining caverns. If they are really to be seen, I think they may be accounted for, by supposing that some miner, in search of niter, had entered and left his tracks upon the mould usually to be found in such places. The abundance of iron existing in some kinds of clay, seems to keep the lapidifying, or rock-making process, constantly progressing, so that what were mere tracks in the clay, sixty years ago, may now be impressions in solid rock. In confirmation, I beg to mention the following incident, related to me by Mr. William Thompson, a worthy citizen of the county. In 1805, Mr. Thompson killed a snake, which was thrown in a hollow, or bottom, on a large, exposed stratum of rock. Heavy rains caused the submersion of the rock, and when the water dried up, it was found that the rock was covered several inches in clay. In 1813, or eight years after, the clay was washed off by heavy rains, and behold, there was the serpent, which had become a part of the rock, as may be seen to this day. I ask, if some of our scientific gentlemen had seen this snake, without knowing the circumstances, would they not most likely have pronounced it an antediluvian work? That this conclusion of the present progress of lapidification is true, I offer another example. There are, in the northern part of the county, rocks bearing the impressions of buffalo tracks, too plain to be mistaken.

Petrifactions constitute no small share of our natural curiosities. I have elsewhere referred to a spring, in the northern part of the county, having the property of petrifying. In the western part of the county, about eighteen miles from Jeffersonville, is a location where great quantities of petrified turtles, snakes, lizards, etc., etc., are found. On the road leading to Abingdon, at what is known as Thompson's Gap, petrified or fossil ducks, frogs, and a variety of other reptiles were found, when grading the road across the mountain. Fossill remains are so abundant that it is useless to

---

*From **stalazo**, to drop. Water, holding lime in solution, drops regularly at one place, and deposits the lime in long rods, often hollow; these are called stalactites.

attempt to describe them. At Maiden Spring, on the lands of the Messrs. Bowens, are limestone rocks containing great quantities of fishes. I have in my possession the major part of a fish much resembling a dolphin, which is pure flint of hardest texture.

While searching for Indian paintings on Paint Lick mountain, in company with Col. Rees T. Bowen, we discovered a thin stratum of Medina sandstone, composed almost entirely of fossil fucoids. The larger and less solid parts of the stems are not so well preserved. We traced the stratum about one and a half miles, along the mountain, and know not how much farther it may extend. I suppose the stratum to be about two hundred feet below the surface, with an inclination of 60°. It can be reached only by entering the clefts of the mountain. Myself and the Col. were fatigued, and accidentally sat down to rest near a cleft from which a few fragments of the rock had broken, and rolled down the mountain side. The discovery of a small piece, led us into the search; specimens of this rock may be seen in the cabinet of the Historical Society. As I have been often asked to account for this collection of fucoids, perhaps the most remarkable in the world, I beg to offer the following remarks, premising, that as I am not writing for the information of geologists in particular, I shall avoid technicalities:

Fucoides Harlani is only one species of the family **Algea**. It occurs almost invariably in, and is, therefore, a type of, Medina sandstone. The stratum here referred to, is found upon the ridge of the Alleghany or Appalachian chain of mountains during their whole course, and even further than these extend. It is to be found in New York, Pennsylvania, Virginia, N. Carolina, Georgia, and many other sections remote from this chain of mountains.

Let us suppose that at a remote period, the surface of the earth was nearly level, and, as is most likely true, the sea covered the continent, and that the **Focoides Harlani**, which is a native of the sea (hence its common name, seaweed), was beaten down by the force of the waves, or dying, became specifically too heavy to keep upon the surface. It was then deposited on the bottom of the sea, and other matter depositing itself over this, it became lapidified; and upon the lapidification of other strata, in the course of a long series of years, the Fucoides Harlani became an under stratum; and hence we find it now deep in the bowels of the earth. Then, the same convulsion of nature which caused the upheaving of the mountains, raised this stratum to its present elevated position, which is about 1400 feet above the bed of the Clinch river.

CHAPTER XVI.

WATERS.

The waters of Tazewell are both numerous, and of fine quality. White, blue, red, salt, sweet and warm sulphur springs; chalybeate, iodureted, carbonated, alum, lime, and freestone springs are abundant. Perhaps no county in the state exhibits such a variety of waters as this; yet so little has been done to inform the valetudinarian of our mineral waters, that they are almost a useless appendage to our county. In truth, mineral waters are so common, that it excites no interest to speak of them. Only a few of our springs have been analyzed, a circumstance to be regretted.

The Tazewell White Sulphur springs, now owned by Thos. H. Gillespie, are four miles west of Jeffersonville. Those wishing to spend a season in retirement, can find no more suitable place than at the Tazewell White Sulphur. When I say **retirement,** I do not mean that they will see no one else, or never hear the enlivening ring of the violin, for a considerable number are to be found here every season; the dance is assumed at the pleasure of the company; in fact, most amusements usually found at watering-places, are here offered to the visitor. But the visitors are mostly ladies and gentlemen from the adjoining counties, who are seeking to restore lost health, rather than to find pleasure. The little expense, the good fare, the beauty of the mountain scenery, the purity and salubrity of the air, the excellent quality of the water, and conveniences of the establishment, render it at once attractive to the valetudinarian.

Six miles east of Jeffersonville, are Taylor's springs. Here, as at the Holston springs, are a variety of waters; six kinds, clearly different, rise from as many springs within a few feet of each other.

There is a spring in Baptist valley, about eighteen miles west of the C. H., belonging to Mr. Spotts, somewhat impregnated with alum. When I examined this spring, it had but a short time before been cleaned out, and had rather an earthy taste—the water is strongly tinctured with iron, a circumstance which has led some to question the existence of alum in it at all. There is, however, a small quantity of alum, yet not enough to render the springs notable.

A spring, said to contain iodine, rises upon the lands of Mr. Crockett, near Jeffersonville.

A sweet spring, without any trace of sulphur, but containing much iron, breaks out from the south side of Clinch mountains, in the Poor valley; but as few know even its location, its medicinal properties have not been properly tested. It is known to be highly cathartic, and my guide to its location, declares it cured him of dropsy when the physicians failed. It was a very cold day in winter, and the snow falling fast, when I visited it, so my observations were imperfect.

Springs slightly salty are so common, that no attention has been paid to them. Their existence might yet prove to be the index to the existence of vast quantities of salt.

I am informed by Mr. Wynn, that a warm spring gushes from the base of Round mountain, in the south-east corner of the county, and that on the summit of the mountain, there is a spot the temperature of which is so high, that snow never lies on it half an hour after its fall, and generally melts while falling.

That kind of water used for culinary and ordinary purposes, is more important, however, to the people of the county, than any other; I mean the common blue limestone. This kind of water is used in all parts of the county, except that which is drained by the Sandy river. This blue limestone water has only one objection: it is rather hard, and is thought by some, to operate to the injury of both the digestive and urinary organs. (See further remarks upon this opinion, in the chapter on General Health.)

The springs usually have a temperature of 45° to 50° Fahr., during the summer, and about the same in winter. The average for a summer and a winter month was 49° Fahr. Except in a few instances, the occurrence of heavy rains, seems to affect the amount of water discharged, slightly. I think that the quantity of lime in our water is, perhaps, less than in some other sections in the south-west. To the taste, no water can excel ours; it is true that when persons formerly in the habit of using freestone water, commence using ours, it proves pleasantly aperient; this is owing to the presence of magnesia.

HEALTH OF TAZEWELL.

This county is not at present so healthy as one would suppose from its character in other respects. This, I imagine, may be easily accounted for. One of the most prominent causes of disease in any mountain country, where disease prevails, will be found to be the want of comfortable buildings. Some are too close—others too open—others want light, and others are too damp. The country being incapable of producing malaria, is, of course, exempt from miasmatic diseases. The only disease worth of particular notice, is what is known among our physicians as typhoid fever, but which will most generally answer to some form of pneumonia. It seems to be generated entirely from exposure, and does not assume a serious form except in inclement seasons.

Here is to be met with a greater variety of diseases than I have anywhere seen. The quality of the water may account for the numerous cases arising from derangement of the digestive apparatus. I know that my position will be disputed by those who have cherished, from their cradles, the idea that no waters are so healthy as those of the mountains; yet, this should not prevent me from stating my opinions, and the reasons why I entertain them.

There are living in the town of Jeffersonville, five physicians, who get a reasonable amount of practice; and, so far I have conversed with them, they all declare, that if the diseases arising from the digestive apparatus be discarded, that there will not remain sufficient practice for two of the five. Now what should impair the digestion in this region more than any other, if it be not the water?

That this county, naturally, is superlatively healthy, no one will doubt; and as soon as a little more attention is paid to the laws of life, and the quality of our mountain water, we may expect to see a decided improvement. It is high time that my brethren of the grade-glass and mortar, were investigating this subject.

CHAPTER XVII.

MANNERS AND CUSTOMS

Under such a general head, I could say but little for the information of my readers, I shall therefore, introduce several subjects, properly belonging to this place. And I must ask such of the sons and daughters of the noble people whose habits form a theme for my pen, who are either vain or proud, to forgive me for exhibiting their fathers and mothers, in such a light as I necessarily must. I too, am of these people, and hope I am as sensitive of my ancestors, as the vainest or the proudest.

The people of all mountain-countries have some customs peculiarly their own. The same pastoral simplicity which characterizes the people of the Scotch highlands, the mountainous regions of Europe, and the hill country of ancient Judea, may be here clearly traced. The same industry, love for stock, determination to be free, hatred of oppression, pure sentiment, etc., are found here.

DRESS OF THE EARLY SETTLERS.

That worn by the men, has already been described; that worn by the women, is well described by Dr. Doddridge, in the words, "linsey coats and bedgowns," which he says "were the universal dress of women in early times," and further suggested "that they would make a strange figure at the present day."

The garments made in Augusta, Botetourt, and other older settlements,, had worn out, and a different material was brought into use. The weed now known among us as wild nettle (**Urtica dioica**), then furnished the material which served to clothe the persons of our sires and dames. It was cut down while yet green, and treated much in the same manner in which flax is now treated. The fibrous bark, with the exception of the shortness of the fibers, seemed to be adapted to the same uses. When this flax, if 1 may so term it, was prepared, it was mixed with buffalo hair and woven into a substantial cloth, in which the men and women were clothed. It is a true maxim, "necessity is the mother of invention."

HOUSE FURNITURE.

"The furniture for the table, for several years after the settlement of this county, consisted of a few pewter dishes, plates, and spoons; but mostly of wooden bowls, trenchers, and noggins. If these last were scarce, gourds and hardshelled squashes, made up the deficiency. Iron pots, knives and forks, were brought from the east, with the salt and iron, on pack-horses."

"These articles of furniture corresponded very well with the articles of diet. 'Hog and hominy,' were proverbial for the dish of which they were the component parts. Johnny-cake and pone were, at the first settlement of the country, the only forms of bread in use for breakfast and dinner. At supper, milk and mush was the standing dish. When milk was not plenty, which was often the case, owing to the scarcity of cattle, or the want of proper pasture for them, the substantial dish of hominy had to supply the place of them; mush was frequently eaten with sweetened water, molasses, bears' oil, or the gravy of fried meat."

"In our whole display of furniture, the delft, china, and silver, were unknown. It did not then, as now, require contributions from the four quarters of the globe, to furnish the breakfast table, viz: the silver from Mexico; the coffee from the West Indies; the tea from China; and the delft and porcelain from Europe or Asia. Yet, a homely fare, and unsightly cabins and furniture, produced a hardy race, who planted the first footsteps of civilization in the immense regions of the west. Inured to hardships, bravery and labor from their early youth, they sustained with manly fortitude the fatigue of the chase, the campaign and scout, and with strong arms 'turned the wilderness into fruitful fields,' and have left to their descendants the rich inheritance of an immense empire, blessed with peace, and wealth, and prosperity."*

THE WEDDING.

A wedding is thus described by Dr. Doddridge, and from what I have seen and can learn, a more faithful picture could not be drawn of a pioneer wedding:

"For a long time after the first settlement of this country, the inhabitants in general married young. There was no distinction of rank, and very little of fortune. On these accounts, the first impression of love, resulted in marriage, and a family establishment cost but little labor, and nothing else.

"A description of a wedding, from beginning to end, will serve to show the manners of our forefathers, and mark the grade of civilization which has succeeded to their rude state of society, in the course of a few years.

"In the first years of the settlement of a country, a wedding engaged the attention of a whole neighborhood; and the frolic was anticipated by old and young, with eager expectation. This is not to be wondered at, when it is told that a wedding was almost the only gathering which was not accompanied with the labor of reaping, log-rolling, building a cabin, or planning some scout or campaign. On the morning of the wedding-day, the groom and his attendants, assembled at the house of his father, for the purpose of reaching the home of his bride by noon, which was the usual time for celebrating the nuptials; and which, for certain reasons, must take place before dinner.

"Let the reader imagine an assemblage of people, without a store, tailor, or mantua-maker, within a hundred miles; and an assemblage of horses,

---

* Doddridge.

without a blacksmith or saddler within an equal distance. The gentlemen dressed in shoe-packs, moccasins, leather breeches, leggins, linsey hunting shirts, and all home-made. The ladies dressed in linsey petticoats, and linsey or linen bedgowns, coarse shoes, stockings, handkerchiefs, and buckskin gloves, if any. If there were any buckles, rings, buttons or ruffles, they were the relics of olden times; family pieces from parents or grandparents. The horses were caparisoned with old saddles, old bridles or halters, and pack-saddles, with a bag or blanket thrown over them: a rope or string as often constituted the girth as a piece of leather.

"The march, in double file, was often interrupted by the narrowness of our mountain paths, as they were called, for we had no roads; and these difficulties were often increased, sometimes by the good, and sometimes by the ill-will of neighbors, by falling trees, and tying grape-vines across the way. Sometimes an ambuscade was formed by the wayside, and an unexpected discharge of several guns took place, so as to cover the wedding company with smoke. Let the reader imagine the scene which followed this discharge; the sudden spring of the horses, the shrieks of the girls, and the chivalrous bustle of their partners to save them from falling. Sometimes, in spite of all that could be done to prevent it, some were thrown to the ground. If a wrist, elbow, or ankle, happened to be sprained, it was tied up with a handkerchief, and little more was said or thought about it.

"The ceremony of the marriage preceded the dinner, which was a substantial backwoods' feast of beef, pork, fowls, and sometimes venison and bear meat, roasted and boiled, with plenty of potatoes, cabbage, and other vegetables. During the dinner, the greatest hilarity always prevailed; although the table might be a large slab of timber, hewed out with a broad-axe, supported by four sticks, set in auger-holes; and the furniture, some old pewter dishes and plates; the rest, wooden bowls and trenchers: a few pewter spoons, much battered about the edges, were to be seen at some tables. The rest were made of horn. If knives were scarce, the deficiency was made up by the scalping knives, which were carried in sheaths, suspended to the belt of the hunting-shirt. Every man carried one of them.

"After dinner the dancing commenced, and generally lasted till the next morning. The figures of the dances were three and four handed reels, or square sets and jigs. The commencement was always a square form, which was followed by what was called jigging it off; that is two of the four would single out for a jig, and were followed by the remaining couple. The jigs were often accompanied with what was called cutting out; that is, when either of the parties became tired of the dance, on intimation, the place was supplied by some one of the company, without any interruption to the dance. In this way the dance was often continued till the musician was heartily tired of his situation. Toward the latter part of the night, if any of the company, through weariness, attempted to conceal themselves, for the purpose of sleeping, they were hunted up, paraded on the floor, and the fiddler ordered to play 'hang out till to-morrow morning.'

"About nine or ten o'clock, a deputation of young ladies stole off the bride, and put her to bed. In doing this, it frequently happened that they had to ascend a ladder, instead of a pair of stairs, leading from the dining and ballroom to the **loft**,* the floor of which was made of clap-boards, lying loose. This ascent, one might think, would put the bride and her attendants to the blush; but the foot of the ladder was commonly behind the door, which was purposely opened for the occasion, and its rounds, at the inner ends, were well hung with hunting-shirts, dresses, and other articles of clothing. The candles, being on the opposite side of the house, the exit of the bride was noticed but by few.

"This done, a deputation of young men, in like manner, stole off the groom, and placed him snugly by the side of his bride. The dance still continued; and if seats happened to be scarce, as was often the case, every young man, when not engaged in the dance, was obliged to offer his lap, as a seat for one of the girls; and the offer was sure to be accepted. In the midst of this hilarity, the bride and groom were not forgotten. Pretty late in the night, some one would remind the company that the new couple must stand in need of some refreshment: black Betty, which was the name of the bottle, was called for, and sent up the ladder; but sometimes, black Betty did not go alone. I have many times seen as much bread, beef, pork, and cabbage sent along, as would afford a good meal for half a dozen hungry men. The young couple were compelled to eat and drink, more or less, of whatever was offered.

"But to return. It often happened that some neighbors or relations, not being asked to the wedding, took offense; and the mode of revenge, adopted by them on such occasions, was that of cutting off the manes, foretops, and tails of the horses of the wedding company.

"On returning to the in-fare, the order of procession, and the race for black Betty, was the same as before. The feasting and dancing often lasted several days, at the end of which, the whole company were so exhausted with loss of sleep, that many days' rest were requisite to fit them to return to their ordinary labors."

I have quoted this account, written by Dr. Dodridge, because nothing could be more correct, and it was beyond my power to tell an original tale so well.

HUNTING.

This constituted one of the greatest amusements, and, in some instances, one of the chief employments of the early settlers. The various intrigues of a skillful hunter—such as mimicking a turkey, owl, wolf, deer, etc.—were soon learned, and the eye was taught to catch, at a glance, the faintest impression left upon the earth by any animal. Marks, which would be, by any but a hunter, overlooked, were easily detected. The times, and ground on which deer, elk, etc., fed, were soon learned, and then the important lesson of preventing spells or enchantments by enemies, were studied; for it is a singular fact that all hunters are, more or less, superstitious. Frequently, on leaving home, the wife would throw the ax at her husband, to give him good luck. If he chanced to fail to kill game, his gun was enchanted or spelled, and some old woman shot in effigy—then a silver bullet would be

---

*I have emphasized this word, because, even now, the second stories of some of our most costly mansions are termed "lofts" by the older persons.

run with a needle through it, and shot at her picture. To remove these spells, they would sometimes unbreech their rifles, and lay them in a clear running stream for a certain number of days. If this failed, they would borrow patching from some other hunter, which transferred all the bad luck to the lender, etc.

Game was plenty at the time this county was first settled by the whites, and accordingly, the woods furnished most of the meat. Considerable bear still exists in various parts of the county. Deer are scarce, and elk and buffalo extinct. The elk and buffalo were generally killed at the licks whither they repaired to salt themselves; and even yet, deer licks are watched with profit to the hunter.

Animals were hunted there not merely for their meat, but for their skins and furs. These served to pay for powder, lead, or anything else, being nominally the currency of the country.

MANNERS AND CUSTOMS.

Neither was hunting, the mere pastime, devoid of skill, which it now is. The hunter might be considered somewhat of a meteorologist; he paid particular attention to the winds, rains, snows, and frosts; for almost every change altered the location of game. He knew the cardinal points by the thick bark and moss on the north side of a tree, so that during the darkest and most gloomy night he knew which was the north, and so his home or camp. The natural habits of the deer were well studied; and hence he knew at what times they fed, etc. If, in hunting, he found a deer at feed, he stopped, and though he might be open to it, did not seek to obscure himself, but waited till it raised its head and looked at him. He remained motionless till the deer, satisfied that nothing moving was in sight, again commenced feeding. He then began to advance, if he had the wind of it, and if not he retreated and came up another way, so as to place the deer between himself and the wind. As long as the deer's head was down he continued to advance till he saw it shake the tail. In a moment he was the same motionless object, till it again put down its head. In this way, he would soon approach to within sixty yards, when his unerring rifle did the work of death. It is a curious fact that deer never put their heads to the ground, or raise it, without shaking the tail before so doing.

The quantity of game will be apparent when it is known that Mr. Ebenezer Brewster killed, during his life, upward of twelve hundred bears in this county. He died in the summer of 1850, and this statement occurred in an obituary notice.

CHAPTER XVIII.

SCENERY—DIAL ROCK

Dial Rock is one of the three heads of East River mountain, and is about three miles east of Jeffersonville. How it came by its name cannot be accurately determined; though tradition tells that there is, on the rock, a natural sun-dial. I shall not deny its existence, but must own that I was unable to find it when I visited the rock. These rocks are elevated in the air to about the height of fifteen hundred feet above the valley of Clinch river, which flows gently along near the base of the mountain. The ascent to the foot of the cliffs is gentle, and may be easily rode over by such as care more for themselves than their horses. Nothing remarkable exists, to

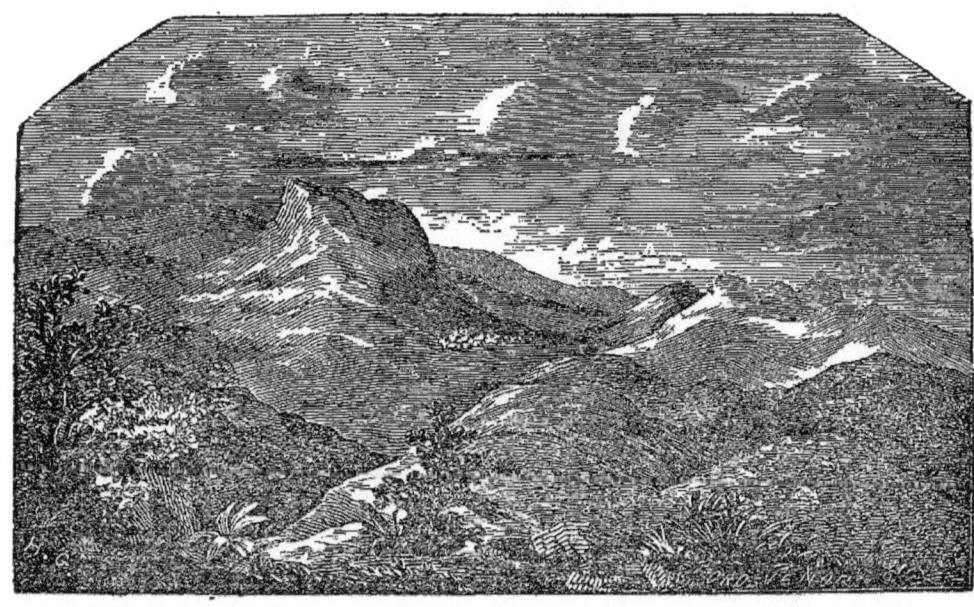

SCENERY FROM DIAL ROCK.

attract particular attention, till the base of the naked cliffs is reached. These cliffs are from one hundred and fifty to two hundred and fifty feet above the common level of the summit of the mountain; and seem as if some internal commotion had started them from the bowels of the earth to awe and affright the eye that should dare look from their tops.

The first rock to the west being reached, the ascent is begun by climbing its steep and rugged sides, which, owing to the clefts is easily done. When this is done, the eye is involuntatily turned to the east, when a still more naked rock appears, towering still higher in the air, and looking still more sublime and awful. Passing on over the top of the first rock, the visitor soon finds himself upon the very brink of a cleft about ten feet wide, the sides of which are perpendicular, and not far from one hundred feet deep. This must be passed, or the second rock cannot be gained. Turning now to the left or north, he finds that he may descend to the bottom of this gulf, by means of other irregular clefts breaking into it. This descent begun, and the visitor begins to feel the wild grandeur of the scene around him. Huge rocks, lying on thin scales so loosely that seemingly the slightest blow would sever the props that uphold them, and let them down with a crash, from which nothing could escape, and caverns of all shapes and sizes, filled with darkness impenetrable, seem to stand gaping for the victims of the rocks above, should they give way.

Descending into one of these dark pits, over loose rocks of immense size, from the hollows of which you expect, every moment, to see the head of a rattlesnake hissing and bidding defiance to your further progress, you find yourself soon at the bottom of the first cleft in the mountain; and then the painful and tedious ascent of the second rock begins, after which the visitor imagines all farther troubles are comparatively light. A few yards to the eastward, after the top or summit is gained, will dispel this fond hope, and instead of affording an easy passage, opens to view another cleft still more grand and awful. Here is seen the same wild confusion of rocks (themselves mountains), thrown together, as if nature had, at this place, collected the rubbish of her materials, in mountain-making. This defile must be passed before the third rock can be scaled; the task of which having been accomplished, the visitor finds that on and on, to the east, the cliffs rise higher and higher, and he eagerly hunts a passage of the defile that he may gain the most elevated of this beautiful yet terrific array of rocky monuments. Soon it is found, the third and fourth rocks are passed, and he finds himself, tired and thirsty, upon the summit of the fifth. A basin of clear, ice-cold water invites him to quench his thirst, and proceed to the sixth rock, from the top of which he casts his eye down the beautiful Clinch valley, when lo! beauty indescribable presents itself. Mountains rise above mountains, in endless succession, till far in the smoky distance his vision ceases to distinguish the faint outline of the Cumberland and the Tennessee mountains. Looking to the north, he sees the great Flat-Top, from which others gradually fade into indistinctness, and imagination seems to say, there, there is the valley of the beautiful Ohio—the garden of commerce and industry. To the west rises Morris's Knob, the highest point of Rich mountain, its summit kissing the very clouds, and seeming to bid defiance to the storms of heaven. To the right, rise Paint Lick and Deskins' mountains, and nearly behind them, the rocky peaks of House and Barn mountains, in Russell county. Far in the distance are seen ranges of Clinch mountain and its various spurs. To the left is seen Wolf Creek knob, a continuation of Rich mountain. Close at hand, the rocky sides and top of Elk-horn, and far in the distance, ridges of the Alleghany range. From this beautiful scene the eye is directed down to the valley beneath, when a disposition to shrink back is felt. The visitor now sees himself standing on the pinnacle of Dial Rock, overhanging the valley, fifteen hundred feet below him. The scene, in the distance, is beautiful beyond description. The scene around him is sublime beyond conception. It is beyond the power of the wildest imagination to picture half of its grandeur.

It is here I felt the disposition to bring the infidel, and ask him, "Is there a God?" The works of nature speak more than ten thousand printed volumes, and though innate, their eloquence is adapted to the comprehension of every tongue.

I have taken the scenery from Dial Rock, as being suited to my purpose, not because there is no view so fine, but because it is well known by persons who have visited the county. Very many such views are to be had. To appreciate the above, and the following, they must be seen.

A DAY IN THE MOUNTAINS.

The dawn of day found me on my feet, in the piazza of a friend (with whom I had stopped the previous night, in a beautiful valley, surrounded by lofty mountains), gazing eastward, to watch a rising sun in this region of beauty. The brilliant stars shone brightly in the western sky, while those in the east were growing dim and faint amid the gray beams of light which were shooting up from the hidden sun, and resembling the flitting lights of the icy north made permanent. As the sky became more lighted, the rough outline of the huge mountains became visible, and cast their long shadows far down the valley in which I stood. The bright rays shooting from the morning sun, now fell upon the boughs of the forest-trees which towered above the mountains, giving to the pearly dew-drops suspended from the smaller twigs, the appearance of so many diamonds hung as ornaments on the leafless branches.

> "I know of a drop where the diamond now shines,
>   Now the blue of the sapphire it gives;
> It trembles—it changes—the azure resigns,
>   And the tint of the ruby now lives.
> Anon the deep emerald dwells in its gleam
>   'Till the breath of the south-wind goes by;
> When it quivers again, and the flash of its beam
>   Pours the topaz-flame swift on the eye.
> Look, look on yon grass-blade all freshly impearl'd,
>   There are all of your jewels in one:
> You'll find every wealth-purchased gem in the world
>   In the dew-drop that's kissed by the sun."—E. COOK.

A part of the disc of the sun was now seen slowly rising above the summit. At this instant, the scene was beautiful beyond description; the whole top of the mountain seemed in a blaze—a moment and its beauty was lost. Aurora rose brightly above the mountains, casting her gentle beams upon the valley below. In this were many cottages, from the chimneys of which, soft columns of smoke were seen ascending in the clear, still atmosphere, presenting a scene worthy of the most refined pencil-work. Horses, cattle, and sheep, might be seen scattered over the rich meadows, while the merry notes of the cartman, and the deep-toned bay of the fox-hound, and the shrill ring of the huntsman's horn, were heard echoing in a thousand variations, among the glens and gorges of the surrounding mountains. The tender emotions excited by the loveliness of this scene, and their deep impressions were such, as to defy the atheistical reasonings of either Thomas Paine, or of my own insensible heart. Deity was stamped upon everything.

Breakfast being over, I soon found myself upon the road, intending to visit a distant part of the county. But now, the wind had risen, and a mistiness was spreading itself over the mountain-tops. As I rode on, the heavy murmur of the winds in the timber on the mountains, convinced me that there would soon be a change of weather. None but those who have either been at sea and heard an approaching storm, or have listened to the roar of the mountain-blast, can have anything like a correct idea of this awful sound. Soon a vapory cloud was seen enveloping the mountain-summits, and in four hours it was raining in torrents. The little rippling rivulet, was now converted into the roaring mountain-torrent: how different the scene from what it was a few hours before!

Soon the wind changed to the N. E., and it became colder; presently it was in the north, and the white flakes of snow were falling thick and fast. This continued for several hours, when the wind changed to the west and it was clear. The sun was now nearing the western horizon, and casting back his bright beams upon the snow-capped mountains, which looked indescribably grand and imposing. Not a single dark spot was to be seen, but everywhere the same unsullied white mantle was thrown over them, till they looked like vast monuments reared in the air emblematic of purity. Any attempt to describe a mountain in this State, known here as the "Budding Frost," must fall far short of correctly portraying the scene. Nothing but painting, executed in the highest style of art, can give the remotest idea of the original. I have seen something as grand, but nothing as beautiful as a mountain in this state.

In a short time the sun was seen sinking behind the western mountains, and here again was such a view, as would fix the attention of the most unobserving, and on which the artist would dwell with pleasure. The rays of light falling through the sunny crystals on the hill-tops, looked like so many brilliant pearls. A single streak of cloud shot out from behind the mountains, crimsoned with the setting sun, while its edge, or border, seemed belted with electricity itself. Though this scene was viewed from the town of Jeffersonville, where from the bustle of business, few stop to contemplate scenery, I observed crowds gazing with intense interest, and admiring the gorgeousness of a setting sun in a mountain-country.

APPENDIX.

APPENDIX.

TABLES.

TABLE REFERRING TO POPULATION.*

Persons over 100 years of age in county, June 1, 1850	1
Persons over 90 years of age in county, June 1, 1850	4
Persons over 80 years of age in county, June 1, 1850	18
Persons over 70 years of age in county, June 1, 1850	40
Persons over 60 years of age in county, June 1, 1850	126
Persons over 50 years of age in county, June 1, 1850	214
Persons over 40 years of age in county, June 1, 1850	543
Persons over 30 years of age in county, June 1, 1850	955
Persons over 20 years of age in county, June 1, 1850	1410
Persons over 10 years of age in county, June 1, 1850	2231
Persons under 10 years of age in county, June 1, 1850	3330
Slaves in the county	1060
Total, including 56 free negroes	9932

MISCELLANEOUS TABLE.

No. of blind persons in the county	8
No. of deaf and dumb	13
No. of idiots	24
No. of paupers	24
No. over 20 years of age who can neither read nor write	1490
No. of children attending school	694
State tax on county	$ 2000
County tax	$ 786
County receives from public fund for school purposes	$ 546
County cost of supporting paupers	$ 605

TABLE SHOWING THE WEALTH OF THE COUNTY.

Value of lands	$3,189,080.00
Value of farming utensils	$ 36,390.00
Value of live stock	$ 517,330.00
Value of agricultural productions	$ 226,579.95
Value of mechanical productions	$ 7,000.00
Value of slave property	$ 530,000.00
Value of stock in trade	$ 85,000.00
Total wealth of the county	$4,581,379.95

*The above table has been compiled from the census books for the year 1850. It is the opinion of Mr. William O. Yost, the gentlemanly marshall of the county, that there was, at the time he took the census, very near 11,000 persons in the county. It was his duty, however, to report only such as were in the county on the first of June of that year.

TABLE SHOWING NUMBER ENGAGED IN PROFESSIONS, TRADES.

No. of physicians in the county	10
No. of lawyers in the county	8
No. of teachers in the county	36
No. of merchants in the county	22
No. of clerks in the county	9
No. of saddlers in the county	10
No. of painters in the county	1
No. of printers in the county	2
No. of hatters in the county	2
No. of shoemakers in the county	10
No. of brick-masons in the county	7
No. of carpenters in the county	41
No. of millers in the county	9
No. of wagon-makers in the county	11
No. of blacksmiths in the county	21
No. of tanners in the county	6
No. of cabinet makers in the county	18
No. of gunsmiths in the county	2
No. of tailors in the county	8
No. of coopers in the county	2
No. of tavern keepers in the county	3
No. of barber in the county	1
No. of tinner in the county	1
No. of watchmaker in the county	1
No. of farmers in the county	1922

TABLE LIVE STOCK—KINDS AND VALUE.*

Specified Kinds.	Number	Value.
Horses	5,150	$ 309,000.00
Mules and asses	127	$ 8,890.00
Milch cows	4,576	$ 54,840.00
Working oxen	117	$ 2,340.00
Other cattle	10,260	$ 102,600.00
Sheep	19,530	$ 19,530.00
Swine	20,130	$ 20,130.00
Total value of live stock		$ 517,330.00

TABLE SHOWING VALUE OF LANDS.

Kinds etc.	Amount of each.	Value.
Improved land	58,110 acres	$ 696,320.00
Unimproved	220,530 acres	$ 441,060.00
Unentered or in large surveys	1,641,360 acres	$2,051,700.00
Farming implements†	value	$ 36,390.00
Total am't of land	1,920,000 acres	$3,225,470.00

*There were slaughtered in the county, during the year 1850, animals to the amount of $38,062.
†I have added the value of farming implements in this table, for want of a more convenient place.

TABLE SHOWING THE PRODUCTIONS OF THE COUNTY AND VALUE*

Name of Articles.	Amount Raised.	Cash Value.
Indian corn	244,430 bush.	$ 97,772.00
Oats	124,710 bush.	$ 31,177.75
Wheat	28,020 bush.	$ 21,020.00
Rye	4,110 bush.	$ 2,055.00
Irish potatoes	2,279 bush.	$ 1,139.50
Sweet potatoes	772 bush.	$ 386.00
Buckwheat	3,108 bush.	$ 1,864.80
Hay	1,824 tons	$ 18,240.00
Grass seed	48 bush.	$ 192.00
Flax	19,350 lbs.	$ 1,935.00
Maple sugar	41,244 lbs.	$ 4,134.40
Beeswax and honey	12,248 lbs.	$ 1,837.20
Tobacco	300 lbs.	$ 30.00
Butter	102,287 lbs.	$ 10,228.70
Cheese	6,006 lbs.	$ 600.60
Wool	25,360 lbs.	$ 7,608.00
Flax seed	910 bush.	$ 919.00
Value of home manufactures		$ 25,400.00
Total value		$ 226,579.95

*Calculated from the census book. It is highly probable that the actual production is considerably greater than is shown by the table.

BOOK III.

INDIAN WARS.

CHAPTER I.

INTRODUCTION TO INDIAN WARS OF TAZEWELL.

[Only a small part of this Introduction is copied.]

From what has been said, it is evident that the name of south-western Virginia, three hundred and twenty years ago, was XUALA; and that it was peopled by a hardy race, whose chief subsistence was the game abounding in their dense mountain-forests, and the fishes swimming in their clear mountain streams. De Biedma says, "They were a hospitable race," though poor. He tells us, as also other early writers, that those people living south of the Hiwassee, or Tennessee river, lived in log-houses, daubed with clay, and very comfortable during the winter months; but that during the summer they usually reposed in the open air, by fire, or in thickets, and that much of their time was spent in hunting. And further, it is stated, that those of Xuala were, in addition to the chase, fond of manly exercises and war.

To supply the place of iron instruments of a warlike nature, sharp stones, slings, bows and arrows, and clubs were made and used. The inhabitants of all the continent, and especially of the country south of the Potomac, lived in towns, each of which was furnished with a temple, a burial-place, and a mound, on which stood the house of the Cacique, or chief. We are informed by De Biedma, Hacklyt, De Tonty, La Salle, and others, that this was a general custom, and gave rise to those mounds which are now regarded as burial-places, and which are sometimes opened by the whites, who expect to find in them treasures of value.

This mound building leads to some important conclusions, and reminds us strongly of the Egyptian custom of building pyramids.* It is highly probable that the sizes of these mounds are an index to the power of the princes who had them built.

The town built by the Xualan, differed a little from that of the more southern Indians, for they seem to have built a town which was at once a town and a fort. The species of fort needed by the natives of Xuala, differed from what would now be needed by a people who had to defend themselves against the arms and engines of the nineteenth century. The traces of many of these forts are now to be seen in south-western Virginia. These cannot be Cherokee forts, though they captured the Xualans, and hence became masters of the country, for they do not build forts in the same manner; beside, the trees growing on some of them, prove, beyond doubt, that they have been evacuated three hundred years. That they were towns

---

* Might not the natives have been originally from Egypt, having been driven thence after embracing the religion of the Hebrews?

as well as forts, is proved by the existence of many fragments of earthenware, etc., found on or around them, and from their shape and general location, they were certainly forts.

They were circular, varying in size from three hundred to six hundred feet in diameter. An embankment of earth was thrown up five or six feet, and, perhaps, this mounted by palisades. A few of these towns or forts, were built of stone, and sometimes trenches surrounded them. A stone fort, of great size, stood in Abb's valley, in Tazewell county, Virginia, and has but lately been removed. A large sassafras, which stood near the center of the walls, might, if proper observation had been made, have given some important chronological information, but which, alas! as is too often the case, has been swept off, as if desirous to obliterate the last vestige of the race of red-men.

The remains of a remarkable fort are to be seen on the lands of Mr. Crockett, near Jeffersonville, having evident traces of trenches, and something like a drawbridge. This fort has been evacuated, judging from the timber on it, over two hundred years.

The roads left by the Indians is another source of information, of which few writers have availed themselves. I beg to refer the reader to a report of a company sent out by the French colony in Louisiana, to search for roads. It is to be found in what is usually called Bienville's report, previously referred to.

The principal Indian trails in Tazewell, led through the Clinch Valley, but after the whites began to settle, and the Indians had removed west, their trails all led from the Ohio river. These were probably made by animals, in the first instance; afterward used by the Indians in their visits to their native hills, and have since become roads under the improving hands of the white man.

One of these trails led up the Indian ridge till opposite the trace fork of Tug river; it then crossed over to that branch, and keeping into the lowest gaps of the hills, led into Abb's valley settlement. Another, now much used by the whites, left the ridge and struck Tug river at the mouth of Clearfork creek; thence up it, till it fell over on a branch emptying into the dry fork of Tug river. It then wound up that stream to its head, and passed through Roark's Gap. This led into the Baptist valley settlement. Another came up the La Visee fork of Sandy river, leading into the settlements in the western part of the county. Those trails which passed through the county, always crossed the mountains at the very lowest gap. At these places they have built small monuments of loose stones, piled up with great exactness on each other. Most of these have suffered from the cupidity of the whites. This custom of building stone pillars, reminds us of the custom so common among the Jews at an early period, of marking places where covenants had been made, by piling up stones.

To recapitulate—the south-western portion of Virginia was visited in 1540, by Hernando De Soto, who found the country occupied by the Xualans. These were afterward conquered by the Cherokees, in whose possession the English found the country. The Cherokees were driven out and the country taken possession of by the whites. The country has been claimed by four civilized governments, viz: England, France, Spain, and its present owners. The quantity of game seems to have made the country desirable to the Indians, while its pure water, beautiful scenery, and rich soil seem to have captivated the whites:

There is still remaining another vestige of the Indians, which, if closely observed, might throw some light upon this obscure subject. I refer to the vast collections of bones, or human skeletons, some of immense size, deposited in almost every cavern in this section. It is to be earnestly hoped that some one will be curious enough, or be enough interested to examine this trace of Indian existence in ancient Xuala. Time is passing so rapidly, and laying its blighting finger upon material things with such destroying effect, that there does not remain a day for suspended action. "Now or never," must be the watchword of the historian.

CHAPTER II.

HISTORY OF THE SHAWANOES.

[Is omitted.]

CHAPTER III.

DEFENSIVE POSITION OF TAZEWELL DURING THE FRONTIER WAR.

In order to appreciate the true situation of the frontiermen during the long wars which so devastated the settlements, it is essentially necessary that the reader should know the exact position which they occupied, and how much depended upon their own exertions. For this purpose has this chapter been set apart.

Previous to 1776, the settlers were engaged in erecting suitable houses to protect their families from the inclemencies of the weather, as well as to render them more secure from the attacks of the indians. Their lands had to be opened, and consequently, they were much in the forest. As there was an abundance of game, and few domestic animals, their meat was taken mostly from the forest; this likewise took them from home. They were few, and to raise a house, or roll the logs from a field, required the major part of a settlement. This likewise left their families exposed; yet such work was usually executed during the winter months, when the Indians did not visit the settlements. To give further protection to the families of the settlers, in every neighborhood block-houses were, as soon as convenient, erected, to which the families could repair in times of necessity.

After 1776, forts and stations were built, as it became necessary for many of the settlers to join the army. In these forts, and particularly at the stations, a few men were left to defend them. But the extent of country to be defended was so great, and the stations so few, that there was, in reality, but little safety afforded to the families of the settlers.

De Hass has given correct descriptions of block-houses, forts, and stations, to which I beg to refer the reader. There was a fort erected by William Wynn, a strict old Quaker, and one of the best of men, on Wynn's branch; another at Crab orchard, by Thomas Witten, and one at Maiden Spring, by Rees Bowen—two men whose names will be cherished in the memories of the people of Tazewell for ages to come.

There was a station on Linking Shear branch, containing a few men under the command of Capt. John Preston, of Montgomery; another on Bluestone creek, in command of Capt. Robert Crockett of Wythe county, and another at the present site of the White Sulphur springs, in command of Capt. James Taylor of Montgomery. It is also said, that there was a station in Burk's Garden; I imagine, however, that it was not constructed by order of the Government.

The following persons, citizens of the county, were posted in these forts and stations, viz:

Bailey, John	Burgess, Edward
Bailey, James	Belcher, Robert
Belcher, Joseph	Brewster, Thomas
Chaffin, Christopher	Maxwell, John
Connelly, James	Maxwell, Thomas
Crockett, John	Marrs————(?)
Cotterel, John	Peery, James
Evans, John, Sr.	Pruett, John
Evans, John, Jr.	Thompson, Archibald
Gilbert, Joseph	Witten, James
Godfrey, Absalom	Wynn, Oliver
Hall, William	Wright, Michael
Lusk, David	Ward, John
Lusk, Samuel	Ward, William
Lusley, Robert	Wright, Hezekiah.
Martin, James	

These men were to hold themselves in readiness to act as circumstances might demand. To make them more efficient, spies were employed to hang upon the great trails leading into the settlements from the Ohio. Upon discovering the least sign of Indians, they hurried into the settlements and warned the people to hasten to the forts or stations, as the case might be. They received extra wages for their services, for they were both laborious and important, and also fraught with danger. For such an office the very best men were chosen; for it will be readily seen, that a single faithless spy, might have permitted the Indians to pass unobserved, and committed much havoc among the people, before they could have prepared for defense. But it does not appear that any "spy" failed to give the alarm when possible so to do. They always went two together, and frequently remained out several weeks upon a scout. Great caution was necessary to prevent the Indians from discovering them, hence their beds were usually of leaves, in some thicket commanding a view of the war-path. Wet or dry, day or night, these men were ever on the lookout. The following persons were chosen from the preceding list, to act as spies, viz:

Burgess, Edward	Martin, James
Bailey, James	Maxwell, John
Bailey, John	Wynn, Oliver
Crockett, John	Witten, James

The last of whom, was one of the most sagacious and successful spies to be found anywhere on the frontier. His name is yet as familiar with the people as if he had lived and occupied a place among them but a day ago.*

Such as were too old to bear arms in the government service, usually guarded the women, children, and slaves, while cultivating the farms. Tazewell had but a small population at this time, yet from the number engaged in the regular service, we should be led to think otherwise. The following table will convey a good idea of their dispersion over the country, their families, in the meantime, exposed to the horrors of the tomahawk and scalping-knife.

Names.	Where Engaged.	Where Killed.	Wounded.
Bowen, Rees	King's Mountain	King's Mt	
Bowling, Jarret			
Brown, Low	Clark's Ex. to Illinois		
Cartmill, James	Alamance		
Dolsberry, Lyles	Pt. Pleasant, etc		
Ferguson, Saml	Alamance		
Harrison, Thos	Brandywine, Germantown and Yorktown		
Harper, Jesse			
Lasly, John	Clark's Ex. to Illinois		
Maloney, Archer	Brandywine and Stony Point		
McGuire, Nealy	Clark's Ex. to Illinois		
Moore, Capt. James†	Alamance		
Peery, William	Alamance and Illinois Ex.		
Peery, Thomas	Alamance	Alamance	
Peery, John¶	Alamance		Alamance
Stratton, Solom	Clark's Ex. to Illinois		
Tomlinson, Isam	Brandywine, Germantown, etc.		

*James Witten was born January 7th, 1759, in the colony of Maryland, and emigrated to Tazewell with his father, Thomas Witten, in 1773. At this time, though only about fifteen years of age, he was much distinguished as a hunter and woodsman. He was brave and generous to a fault; and was remarkable for decided action even at this early age. He married in 1783, and became at once a conspicuous character in the border war, which had not yet ceased. From 1794 to '96, he was employed as a regular spy. When any duty requiring bravery, firmness, and prudence, had to be performed, James Witten was the man invariably chosen, as he possessed these qualities in an eminent degree. Many incidents of interest are related of him, which should be preserved.

The writer has seen a coat worn by the spy, James Witten. It is now in the possession of William Ed. Perry, a merchant in Tazewell, who is one of his descendants. It is in a splendid state of preservation.—Harman.

†Capt. James Moore was afterward killed by the Indians, in Abb's valley. See History of Moore Family.

¶This man actually received fifty-four saber cuts in this engagement. He was disabled and thrown upon the ground, and as Tarlton's troops passed, each man gave him a cut. His head and arms were literally cut to pieces, yet he recovered, and lived many years to enjoy the freedom which cost him so dearly.

It is a little strange that the frontiers should have furnished so many men for the army, when their absence so greatly exposed their families. But when we reflect that no people felt the horrors of war more sensibly than they did, and that no people are readier to serve the country in the day when aid is needed, than those of mountainous regions, we shall at once have an explanation to their desire, and consequent assistance, in bringing the war to a close. Beside, the people of Tazewell have ever been foremost in defending the country; showing at once that determination to be free, which so eminently characterizes the people of mountainous districts.*

The reader, by consulting the Map, and learning that during the Indian wars the population did not much exceed five hundred, will see at once that Tazewell county afforded an open field for the depredations of the Indians.

---

*The following list of persons who served in the war of 1812-14, will corroborate the above statement, viz,

Asbury, William	Higginbotham, James	Tabor, Daniel
Bowen, Col. Henry	Higginbotham, Wm.	Thompson, Henry B.
Barns, William	King, Isaac	Vandyke, Charles
Belcher, James	Lusk, David	Vandyke, John
Bostic, Isaac	Peery, Capt. Thomas	Witten, William
Brooks, James	Peery, Jonathan	Wynn, Peter E.
Bainheart, George	Peery, Solomon	Ward, Alexander
Davidson, John	Robertson, David	Wilson, Hugh
Earley, Jeremiah	Stevenson, Matthew	Wynn, Samuel
Franklin, Pleasant	Smith, William	Walls, Joseph
Green, William	Shannon, John	Young, Nathaniel
Gose, Peter	Thompson, Rees B.	Young, Israel

Two companies offered their services to the government to engage in the Mexican war; they were not accepted, however, as a sufficiency of men had already been received. **James Wynn** and **Wesley Hubbard**, however, joined the Washington troops; with these exceptions, Tazewell may be said not to have participated in the war with Mexico.

CHAPTER IV.

THE EVANS FAMILY.

John, and Jesse Evans, his son, emigrated from Amherst county, Virginia, near Lynchburg, and settled in Tazewell in 1773. John settled at the Locust bottom; Jesse, at a place now owned by Mr. Buze Harman, about a mile distant from his father's place, and eight miles from the present seat of justice.*

In 1777 John Evans was taken prisoner, from the Locust bottom, by a band of Shawanoes, and marched off to the Indian towns in the west. From there, he was taken to some of the Canadian towns, from whence he either escaped or was exchanged, and made his way to Philadelphia. His son, hearing of his arrival at Philadelphia, went after him in the spring of '78, and brought him home. He was much exposed, and represented his sufferings as immense. This capitivity, exposure, and anxiety of mind, planted the seeds of consumption, and he fell a victim to its ravages in 1801.

In the summer of 1779, Jesse Evans left his house with six or eight hired men, for the purpose of executing some work at a distance from home. As they carried with them various farming implements, their guns were left at the house, where Mrs. Evans was engaged in weaving a piece of cloth. Her oldest daughter was filling quills for her; while the remaining four children were either at play in the garden, or gathering vegetables.

The garden was about sixty yards from the house, and as no sawmills were in existence at that day in this county, slab-boards were put up on the manner called "wattling" for palings. These were some six feet long, and made what is called a close fence. Eight or ten Indians, who lay concealed in a thicket near the garden, silently left their hiding-places, and made their way, unobserved, to the back of the garden; there removing a few boards, they bounded through and commenced the horrid work of killing and scalping the children. The first warning Mrs. Evans had was their screams and cries. She ran to the door, and beheld the sickening scene, with such feelings as only a **mother** can feel.

Mrs. Evans was a stout, athletic woman, and being inured to the hardships of the times, with her to will was to do. She saw plainly that on her exertions alone could one spark of hope be entertained for the life of her "first-born." An unnatural strength seemed to nerve her arm, and she

---

*As I have traced the history of this family beyond the limits of Tazewell county, it may not be improper to state my reasons for doing so. In the first place, every incident connected with their history is well worth the perusal, and hence, worthy the attention of the historian. Secondly, one of the largest and most respectable families in this county have sprung from them, to whom it must be interesting to have recorded the deeds of such worthy ancestors. The last, but not least, motive under which I act, is, that common justice to the memory of brave men requires me to give a sufficiency of their history to unfold their characters.

resolved to defend her surviving child to the last extremity. Rushing into the house she closed the door, which being too small left a crevice, through which in a few seconds an Indian introduced his gun, aiming to pry open the door, and finish the bloody work which had been so fearfully begun. Mrs. Evans had thrown herself against the door to prevent the entrance of the savages, but no sooner did she see the gun-barrel than she seized it, and drew it so far in as to make it an available lever in prying to the door. The Indians threw themselves against the door to force it open, but their efforts were unavailing. The heroic woman stood to her post, well knowing that her life depended upon her own exertions. The Indians now endeavored to wrest the gun from her; in this they likewise failed. Hitherto she had worked in silence; but as she saw no prospect of the Indians relinquishing their object, she began to call loudly for her husband, as if he really were near. It had the desired effect; they let go the gun, and hastily left the house, while Mrs Evans sat quietly down to await a second attack; but the Indians, who had perhaps seen Mr. Evans and his workmen leave the house, feared he might be near, and made off with all speed.

While Mrs. Evans was thus sitting and brooding over the melancholy death of her children, anxious to go to those in the garden, but fearing to leave her surviving one in the house, exposed to a second attack, a man named Goldsby stepped up to the door. Never did manna fall to the hungered Jew more opportunely; yet no sooner did he hear her woeful tale, than he turned his back upon her, and fled as if every tree and bush had been an Indian taking deadly aim at him. Such were his exertions to get to a place of greater safety, that he brought on hemorrhage of the lungs, from which he with much difficulty recovered.

Seeing herself thus left to the mercy of the savages, Mrs Evans took up the gun she had taken from them, and started, with her remaining daughter, to Major John Taylors, about two miles distant, where, tired and frenzied with grief, she arrived in safety. She had not been gone a great while when Mr. Evans returned, and not suspecting anything wrong, he took down a book, and was engaged in its perusal for some time, till finally he became impatient, and started to the garden, where he supposed Mrs Evans was gathering vegetables. What must have been his feelings when he reached the garden, to see four of his children murdered and scalped? Seeing nothing of his wife and eldest daughter, he supposed they had been taken prisoners; he therefore returned quickly to the house, seized his gun, and started for Major Taylor's, to get asisistance, and a company to follow on, and try, if possible, to retake them. Frantic with grief, he rushed into the house to tell his tale of woe, when he was caught in the arms of his brave wife. His joy, at finding them, was so great, that he could scarcely contain himself: he wept, then laughed, then thanked God it was no worse. As is common in such cases, in a new country, the neighbors flocked in to know the best or worst, and to offer such aid as lay in their power. They sympathized, as only frontiermen can sympathize, with the bereaved parents; but the thought of having to bury four children the next moring, was so shocking, and so dreadful to reflect on, that little peace was to be expected for them. Slowly the reluctant hours of night passed away, and a faint gleam of light became visible in the eastern sky. The joyous warblers were gayly flitting from branch to branch, and caroling their sweetest lays, while the sun rose above the mountain summit, shooting his bright beams on the sparkling dew-drops, which hung like so many diamonds from the green boughs of the mountain shrubbery, giving, altogether, an air of gorgeous beauty, which seemed to deny the truth of the evening's tale. The light clouds, swimming in the eastern atmosphere, brilliantly tinted with the rising sun,

> And the gentle murmur of the morning breeze,
> Singing nature's anthem to the forest trees,

seemed to say such horrid work could not be done by beings wearing human form. But alas! while nature teaches naught but love, men teach themselves lessons which call forth her sternest frowns.

A hasty breakfast was prepared, and the men set off to Mr. Evans's house to bury the murdered children. With a heart too full for utterance, the father led the way, as if afraid to look at those little forms for whose happiness he had toiled, and braved the dangers of a frontier life. But a day ago he had dandled them on his knee, and listened to their innocent prattle; they were now monuments of Indian barbarity.

Turning a hill, the fatal garden was instantly painted on the retina of the fond parent's eye, to be as quickly erased by the silent tears which overflowed their fountain, and came trickling down his weather-beaten face.

The party came up on the back of the house; on the front stood the milkhouse, over a spring of clear cold water, when lo! they beheld coming up, as it were, from the very depths of the grave, Mary, a little child only four years old, who had recovered from the stunning blow of the tomahawk, and had been in quest of water at the familiar old spring, around which, but a day before, she had sported in childish glee. The scalp that had been torn from the skull, was hanging hideously over her pale face, which was much besmeared with blood. She stretched out her little arms to meet her father, who rushed to her with all the wild joy of one whose heart beats warm with parental emotions: She had wandered about in the dark from the time she recovered, and it may be, that more than once tried to wake her little sisters, on whose heads the tomahawk had fallen with greater force. This poor, half-murdered little child lived, married, and raised a large family.

After this unfortunate affair, Mr. Evans became dissatisfied, and resolved to emigrate to Tennessee. He did so, and settled in a neighborhood near a fort about fifteen miles from Nashville. During the summer season, the frontiermen placed their families in forts, as well in Tennessee as in Virginia. In the summer of 1775 or '76 Mr. Evans took his two sons, Robert, a lad of fourteen, and Daniel, an elder son, together with five hired men, and set out to work a piece of corn about two miles from the fort. When they arrived at the field, they stacked their guns, and began their labors: they had not worked long, when they were fired upon by a party of about fifteen Indains. Fortunately, no one was killed; a ball entered Daniel's thigh, which disabled him. The white men started for their guns with all haste, but seeing that the Indains were likely to get to them as soon as themselves, all turned back but Mr. Evans and his son Robert, who pushed on to the stack. As Mr. Evans was in the act of getting hold of a gun, he was seized by a large Indian, who threw him to the ground, and had already unsheathed his scalping-knife and raised it to give the fatal blow, when Robert seized a gun, and placing it against the Indian's side as he lay upon his father, fired. The ball entered the Indian's heart; the knife fell harmless, and from under his writhing body, Mr. Evans sprung to his feet, and commenced a rapid firing upon the advancing Indians: Robert followed his example, and the Indians were soon brought to a halt. The men who had run off, seeing how affairs stood, turned back, and soon routed the Indians. Daniel was carried to the fort, where he lay for some time in consequence of the wound in his hip.

In the fall, about the time Daniel was getting well, flour became scarce in the fort, and as it could be purchased only at Nashville, a company of five were ordered to start after it. Companies ordered on such excursions were usually chosen by lot, and this time Jesse Evans was allotted to form one of the number. When the horses were ready, Daniel begged to take his father's place. The old man objected, but Daniel succeeded in drawing off his father's attention long enough to mount his horse; putting spurs to him, he was soon out of the old man's reach. About two hundred yards from the fort was a dense canebrake, through which led the Nashville trail. Daniel's maneuvering with his father, had thrown him some thirty yards in the rear; looking ahead, he saw quite a number of guns on either side of the trail. He hallooed to his companions to push through; they however turned about, and tried to gain the fort, but to no purpose, as they were killed to a man. Daniel made his way through, and by a circuitous route reached the fort unhurt. When he examined, he found three bullet-holes through his clothes, and two through his hat near his head. The people in the fort hearing the firing, and the groans, and screams of the dying, and yells of the Indians, rushing out, attacked the Indians. Among those who left the fort, was the boy Robert Evans. In a short time the Indians were scattered and concealed in different parts of the canebrake. A drive, as it is called, was instituted: this was effected by stretching themselves across the canebrake and forming a line which would scour its entire body, so that nothing could escape detection which might be lodged in the brake. In the course of the drive, Robert was separated from the main body, and got a considerable distance ahead. In passing a fallen tree, an Indian sprung from behind it and attempted to shoot him: but before the Indian could get his rifle leveled, Robert had hold of it, and in a second wrenched it from the Indian's grasp. The Indian rushed on Robert, who sprang back and snapped the gun at the Indian's breast. On came the enraged savage, who had by this time drawn his scalping-knife, to engage in one of those close combats so common in Indian warfare; but Robert dropped the gun, and drawing his tomahawk, sent its blade deep into the head of his savage antagonist; a spring in the air, a fall, a groan, and the Indian was dead.

Taking up the gun, Scalping-knife and tomahawk, he soon joined the main body, who were sent to bring forth the dead Indian from the canebrake, as a trophy of Robert's valor. This feat, and the death of the Indian whom he shot from his father, had made Robert a conspicuous character, and few expeditions were undertaken, in which he did not participate.

The appearance of about two hundred warriors in the settlement, caused Col. Crawford to raise a company to repel them. He succeeded in raising about one hundred men as volunteers, among whom, were the two Evans boys, Daniel and Robert. When they got to the Tennessee, they found the Indians camped on the opposite side. The men refused to ford the river, which was deep and rapid, before the appearance of daylight. But Col. Crawford saw the necessity of striking the enemy while asleep, accordingly he began to ask for volunteers to follow him over. The first that stepped out was Robert, then several others, among them Daniel, and finally fifty joined him. So small was Robert, and so rapid the stream, that Crawford and another man took him between them to keep the current from washing him off.

When the fifty had crossed, Col. Crawford organized, and made Daniel's fire the signal for the commencement of the battle. They cautiously approached and found the Indians sound asleep. When all were sufficiently near, Daniel leveled his gun at a very large Indian who had made a pillow of the root of a tree, and was wrapped in sweetest slumber, little dreaming, how near was the mortal end. He fired; the Indian rolled over and expired. In a second the camp was lighted up by the glare of the backwoods' rifle; the Indians sprung to their feet only to be shot down. Those who escaped took to the woods, and were no more heard of. Upward of fifty Indians were killed in much less time than it takes to tell the tale.

When Gen. Jackson commenced operations in the south, these boys, who were now able-bodied men, together with John, a younger brother, joined him, and were with him in all his battles. At New Orleans they figured conspicuously. Daniel and Robert had both married, previous to joining Jackson's army. In 1817, Robert died (a poor man), leaving four children. These General Jackson offered to educate, and insisted on the privilege, from the great intimacy which had existed between himself and Robert; but Daniel, who had married wealthy, thought that it would be allowing himself to be outdone by strangers, and accordingly took charge of them himself. Daniel died in 1835. At the last accounts, John, and old Mrs. Evans, their mother, were living.

CHAPTER V.

JAMES MOORE AND THE MOORE FAMILY.

JAMES MOORE TAKEN PRISONER.

In September, 1784, a party of Indians had entered the present limits of Tazewell, and dividing themselves into small parties to steal horses and to annoy the settlers, three had entered the Abb's valley settlement, in which resided Capt. James Moore and a brother-in-law named John Pogue—(this name is spelled Podge by the writer of the Moore narrative in Howe's History of Virginia). The Indians had been for a day or two lurking round, waiting, and looking for an opportunity to seize horses or murder the settlers. While they are thus waiting, we will turn to a scene in Captain Moore's cabin, and take a look at western life and become somewhat acquainted with the hero of this narrative.

The cabin stood in Abb's valley, near the present residence of William Moore, Esq., son of our hero. It was built of heavy logs, and for the age in which it was built and existed, exhibited some show of comfort. A ladder leading "up stairs" (or as the common name for that apartment of a building still prevalent in the country "loft"), or in other words where a second story would have been sought for, was placed behind the door, on the rounds of which, were hung various articles of clothing, the manufacture of the amiable lady of the house, who, though situated in the wild backwoods, showed that the lessons given by an Augusta mother to her daughter, had not been in vain. At the head of a bed occupying one corner of the room, stood several guns, which showed plainly that war was expected. On a shelf between two beds, were, among other things, a few scattered volumes, of English print, and among them the well-thumbed leaves of a **family Bible.** The old gentleman was conversing with his wife upon the condition of the meal, and was told by her that he would have to send to mill, which was about twelve miles distance from Capt. Moore's residence.

James, Jr., our hero, a lad of fourteen summers, was busily engaged in reading the tale of Valentine and Orson, the vivid characters of which, had taken complete possession of his young and active imagination. So engrossed was he with the history of these brothers, that he continued up, long after the remainder of the family had retired to rest. He had got to the most thrilling part of the narrative where Orson is depicted in his most hideous aspect, when the screaming of the geese reminded him it was bed-time.

He lay down, but his imagination had been carried to that degree of excitement which prevents sound slumber, and he frequently awoke, from imperfect naps, to be continually harassed by the imaginary form of Orson by his side, until sleep forsook his eyes and he suffered his imagination to take its own sway, and work up such demons, in the shape of hairy men, as it might see fit.

The breaking day called up the father, who was an early riser, to prepare for the labors of the season, and to get a bag of corn ready for the mill. As soon as breakfast was had, James, whose mind was still confused with the dread of imaginary hairy men, was sent by his father to get a horse on which to ride to the mill. He started to a waste plantation about two and a half miles distant. We will let Mr. Moore tell a portion himself, which I quote from the Rev. Mr. Brown's narrative inserted in Howe's History of Virginia.

"Notwithstanding this, I had not proceeded more than half the distance to the field, before a sudden dread, or panic, came on me. The appearance of the Indian who took me, was presented to my mind, although at the time I did not think of an Indian, but rather that some wild animal in human shape would devour me. Such was my alarm, that I went on trembling, frequently looking back, expecting to see it. Indeed I would have returned home, but for the fear that with such an excuse, my father would be displeased, and perhaps send me back. I therefore proceeded on till I came near the field, when suddenly three Indians sprung from behind a log, one of whom laid hold of me. Being much alarmed at the time with the apprehension of being devoured, and believing this to be the animal I had dreaded, I screamed with all my might. The Indian who had hold of me, laid his hand on my head, and, in the Indian language, told me to hush. Looking him in the face, and perceiving that it was an Indian, I felt greatly relieved, and spoke out aloud, 'it is an Indian, why need I fear,' and thought to myself, 'all that is in it, is, I will have to go to the Shawnee towns.'

"In this company, there were only three Indians, a father and son, and one other; the former bearing the name of 'Black Wolf,'' a middle aged man, of the sternest countenance I ever beheld, about six feet high, having a black beard. The others, I suppose, were about eighteen years of age, and all of the Shawnee tribe. I belonged to the Black Wolf who had captured me: we immediately proceeded to an old cabin, near which were the horses. Here we made a halt, and the old Wolf told me to catch the horses, and gave me some salt for that purpose. My object was to catch one and mount, and make my escape; but suspecting my intention, as often as I would get hold of a horse they would come running up, and thus scare him away. Finding that I could not get a horse for myself, I had no wish, and did not try to catch one for them, and so, after a few efforts, abandoned the attempt This, I suppose, was about one o'clock in the afternoon.* The Indians then went into a thicket, where were concealed their kettle and blankets, after which we immediately proceeded on our journey.

"In consequence of the high weeds, green briers, logs, and steep mountainous character of the country, the walking was very laborious, and we traveled that evening only about eight miles. The two younger Indians went before, myself next, and the old Wolf in the rear. If marks were made, he would carefully remove them with his tomahawk. I frequently broke bushes, which he discovered, and shook his tomahawk over my head to let me know the consequence if I did not disist. I would then scratch the

---

*They must have occupied much time in trying to catch the horses, or I am wrongly informed as to the time that James left home.—Bickley.

ground with my feet. This he also discovered, and made me desist, showing me how to set my feet flat, so as not to leave any marks. It then became necessary to cease my efforts to make a trail for others, as they were all immediately detected. In the evening, about sun-down, the old Wolf gave a tremendous war-whoop, and another next morning at sun-rise. These were repeated evening and morning during our whole journey. It was long, loud and shrill, and intended to signify that they had one prisoner. Their custom is to repeat it as frequent as the number of prisoners. It is different from their war-whoop when they have scalps, and in this way it can be known, as far as the whoop is heard, whether they have prisoners or scalps, and also the number.

"But to return; the night was rainy; we lay down in a laurel thicket, without food or fire. Previous to this, the old Wolf had searched me carefully, to see whether I had a knife. After this he tied one end of a leading halter very tightly around my neck, and wrapped the other end around his hand, so as to make it secure, as well as very difficult to get away without awaking him. Notwithstanding my situation was thus dreary, gloomy and distressing, I was not altogether prevented from sleep. Indeed, I suppose few persons were ever more resigned to their fate.

"The next morning we resumed our journey about daybreak, and continued down Tug creek about two miles, until we reached the main ridge of Tug mountain, along which we descended until we came to Maxwell's gap. At this place, the old Wolf went off and brought in a middle-sized Dutch oven, which had been secreted on their former expedition. The carriage of this was assigned to me. At first it was fastened to my back, but after suffering much, I threw it down, saying I would carry it no more. Upon this, the old Wolf placed down his bundle, and told me to carry it, but on finding that I could not lift it, I became more reconciled, took up the oven again,* and after some days filled it with leaves, and carried it with more ease. We continued on the same ridge the whole of that day, and encamped on it at night, In the evening there came on a rain, and the son of the Black Wolf pulled off my hat. This I resented, struck him, and took it from him. He then showed me by signs with it that he wished to protect his gun-lock from the rain. I then permitted him to have it, and after the rain he returned it.

"For three days we traveled without sustenance of any kind, save some water in which poplar bark had been steeped. On the fourth day we killed a buffalo, took out the paunch, cut it open, rinsed it a little in the water, cut it up, and put it into the kettle, with some pieces of the flesh, and made broth. Of this we drank heartly, without eating any of the meat. After night we made another kettle of broth, yet eat no meat. This is Indian policy after fasting.

"I traveled the whole route barefooted; the consequence of which was, that I had three stone bruises on each foot, and at this time my sufferings were very great. Frequently I would walk over rattlesnakes, but was not permitted to kill any, the Indians considering them their friends.

"Some few days after this, we killed a buffalo that was very fat, and dried as much of the meat as lasted for several days. After this, we killed

---

*There is some ambiguity in this part of the narrative.—**Bickley.**

deer and buffalo as our wants required, until we reached their towns, near what is now called Chillicothe, in Ohio, just twenty days from the time we set out. We crossed the Ohio between the mouths of Guyandotte and Big Sandy, on a raft made of dry logs, and tied together with grapevines. On the banks of the Sciota we remained one day. Here they made pictures to represent three Indians, and me, their prisoner. Near this place, the old Wolf went off and procured some bullets which he had secreted.

"When we came near the towns, the Indians painted themselves black, but did not paint me. This was an omen of my safety. I was not taken directly to the town, but to the residence of Wolf's half sister, to whom I was sold for an old horse. The reason why I was not taken directly to the town, was, I suppose, first, because it was a time of peace; secondly, that I might be saved from running the gauntlet, which was the case with prisoners taken in war. Shortly after I was sold, my mistress left me entirely alone, for several days, in her wigwam, leaving a kettle of hominy for me to eat. In this solitary situation I first began to pray, and call upon God for mercy and deliverance, and found great relief. Having cast my burden on the Lord, I would rise from my knees, and go off cheerfully. **I had been taught to pray. My father prayed in his family**; and I now found the benefit of the religious instructions I had received.

"On one occasion, while on our journey, I was sent some distance for water. Supposing that I was entirely out of view, I gave vent to my feelings, and wept abundantly. The old Indian, however, had watched me, and noticing the marks of tears on my cheeks, he shook his tomahawk over my head, to let me know I must not do so again. Their object in sending me off was, as I suppose, to see whether I would attempt to escape, as the situation appeared favorable for that purpose. After this, I was no longer fastened with a halter. In about two weeks after I was sold, my mistress sent me, with others, on a hunting excursion. In this we were very unsuccessful. The snow being knee deep, the blanket too short to cover me, and having very little other clothing, my suffering from hunger and cold were intense. Often, after having lain down, and drawn up my feet to get them under the blanket, I became so benumbed that it was with difficulty that I could straighten myself again. Early in the morning, the old Indian would build up a large fire, and make me and the young Indians plunge all over in cold water. This, I think, was a great benefit, as it prevented us from taking cold.

"When we returned from hunting, in the spring, the old man gave me up to Captain Elliot, a trader, from Detroit. But my mistress, on hearing this, became very angry, threatened Elliot, and got me back. Some time in April there was a dance at a town about two miles from where I resided. This I attended in company with the Indian to whom I belonged. Meeting with a French trader from Detroit, by the name of Batest Ariome, who took a fancy to me on account of my resemblance to one of his sons. he bought me for fifty dollars in Indian money.* Before leaving the dance, I met with a Mr. Sherlock, a trader from Kentucky, who had formerly been a prisoner to the same tribe of Indians, and who had rescued a lad by the

---

*This consisted of silver brooches, crosses, etc.

name of Moffit, who had been captured at the head of Clinch, and whose father was an intimate and particular friend of my father's.* I requested Mr. Sherlock to write to my father, through Mr. Moffit, informing him of my captivity, and that I had been purchased by a French trader, and was gone to Detroit. This letter, I have reason to believe, father received, and that it gave him the first information of what had become of me.

"Mr. and Mrs. Ariome were to me parents indeed. They treated me like one of their own sons. I ate at their table, and slept with their sons, in a good feather bed. They always gave me good counsel, and advised me (particularly Mrs. Ariome) not to abandon the idea of returning to my friends. I worked on the farm with her sons, and occasionally assisted him in his trading expeditions. We traded at different places, and sometimes went a considerable distance in the country.

"On one of these occasions, four young Indians began to boast of their bravery; and among other things, said that one Indian could whip four white men. This provoked me, and I told them that I could whip all four of them. They immediately attacked me, but Mr. Ariome, hearing the noise, came and took me away. This I considered a kind providence; for the Indians are very unskillful in boxing, and in this manner of fighting, I could easily have whipped all of them; but when they began to find themselves worsted, I expected them to attack me with clubs or some other weapon, and if so, had laid my plans to kill them all with a knife, which I concealed in my belt, mount a fleet horse, which was close at hand, and escape to Detroit.

"It was on one of these trading expeditions, that I first heard of the destruction of father's family. This I learned through a Shawnee Indian, with whom I had been acquainted when I lived with them, and who was one of the party on that occasion. I received this information some time in the summer after it occurred. In the following winter, I learned that my sister Polly had been purchased by Mr. Stogwell, an American by birth, but unfriendly to the American cause. He was a man of bad character—an unfeeling wretch—and treated my sister with great unkindness. At that time he resided a considerable distance from me. When I heard of my sister, I immediately prepared to go and see her; but as it was then in the dead of winter, and the journey would have been attended with great difficulties, on being told, by Mr. S., that he intended to remove to the neighborhood, where I resided in the following spring, I declined it. When I heard that Mr. Stogwell had removed, as was contemplated, I immediately went to see her. I found her in the most abject condition, almost naked, being clothed with only a few dirty and tattered rags, exhibiting to my mind, an obfect of pity indeed. It is impossible to describe my feelings on that occasion; sorrow and joy were both combined; and I have no doubt the feelings of my sister were similar to my own. On being advised, I applied to the commanding officer at Detroit, informing him of her treatment, with the hope of effecting her release. I went to Mr. Simon Girty, and to Col. McKee the superintendent of the Indians, who had Mr. Stogwell brought to trial to answer to the complaint brought against him. But I failed to procure

---

*Mr. Moffit had then removed to Kentucky, and was still living there.

her release. It was decided however, when an opportunity should occur for our returning to our friends, she should be released without remuneration. This was punctually performed, on application of Mr. Thomas Ivans,* who had come in search of his sister Martha, already alluded to, who had been purchased from the Indians by some family in the neighborhood, and was, at that time, with a Mr. Donaldson, a worthy and wealthy English farmer, and working for herself.

"All being now at liberty, we made preparations for our journey to our distant friends, and set out, I think, some time in the month of October, 1789; it being a little more than five years from the time of my captivity, and a little more than three years from the time of the captivity of my sister and Martha Ivins. A trading boat coming down the lakes, we obtained a passage, for myself and sister, to the Moravian towns, a distance of about two hundred miles, and on the route to Pittsburgh. There, according to appointment, we met with Mr. Ivins and his sister, the day after our arrival. He had, in the meantime, procured three horses, and we immediately set out for Pittsburgh. Fortunately for us, a party of friendly Indians, from these towns, were about starting on a hunting excursion, and accompanied us for a considerable distance on our route, which was through a wilderness, and the hunting-ground of an unfriendly tribe. On one of the nights, during our journey, we encamped near a large party of these hostile Indians. The next morning four or five of their warriors, painted red, came into our camp. This much alarmed us. They made many inquiries, but did not molest us, which might not have been the case, if we had not been in company with other Indians. After this, nothing occurred, worthy of notice, until we reached Pittsburgh. Probably we would have reached Rockbridge that fall, if Mr. Ivins had not, unfortunately, got his shoulder dislocated. In consequence of this, we remained until spring with an uncle of his, in the vicinity of Pittsburgh. Having expended nearly all his money in traveling, and with the physician, he left his sister and proceeded on with sister Polly and myself, to the house of our uncle, William McPhaethus, about ten miles south-west of Staunton, near the Middle river. He received, from uncle Joseph Moore, the administrator of father's estate, compensation for his services, and afterward returned and brought in his sister."

Mr. Moore finally returned to Tazewell county, and settled on the lands formerly occupied by his father. He raised a numerous and respectable family, one of whom still resides upon the place. Mr. Moore, the subject of this narrative, lived to an advanced age. He died in September, 1851, in the eighty-first year of his age.

MASSACRE OF CAPT. JAMES MOORE'S FAMILY.

In July, 1786, a party of forty-seven Indians, of the Shawanoes tribe, again entered Abb's valley. Capt. James Moore usually kept five or six loaded guns in his house, which was a strong log building, and hoped, by the assistance of his wife, who was very active in loading a gun, together with Simpson, a man who lived with him, to be able to repel the attack of of any small party of Indians. Relying on his prowess, he had not sought

---

*This name is spelled wrong, the orthography being Evans.

refuge in a fort, as many of the settlers had; a fact of which the Indians seem to have been aware, from their cutting out the tongues of his horses and cattle, and partially skinning them. It seems they were afraid to attack him openly, and sought rather to drive him to the fort, that they might sack his house.

On the morning of the attack, Capt. Moore, who had previously distinguished himself at Alamance, was at a lick bog, a short distance from his house, salting his horses, of which he had many. William Clark and an Irishman were reaping wheat in front of the house. Mrs. Moore and the family were engaged in the ordinary business of housework. A man, named Simpson, was sick up-stairs.

The two men, who were in the field, at work, saw the Indians coming, in full speed, down the hill, toward Captain Moore's, who had ere this discovered them, and started in a run for the house. He was, however, shot through the body, and died immediately. Two of his children, William and and Rebecca, who were returning from the spring, were killed about the same time. The Indians had now approached near the house, and were met by two fierce dogs, which fought manfully to protect the family of their master. After a severe contest, the fiercest one was killed, and the other subdued. I shall again use Mr. Brown's narrative, it being quite authentic.

"The two men who were reaping, hearing the alarm,* and seeing the house surrounded, fled, and alarmed the settlement. At that time, the nearest family was distant six miles. As soon as the alarm was given, Mrs. Moore and Martha Ivins (who was living in the family) barred the door, but this was of no avail. There was no man in the house, at this time, except John Simpson, the old Englishman, already alluded to, and he was in the loft, sick and in bed. There were five or six guns in the house, but having been shot off the evening before, they were then empty. It was intended to have loaded them after breakfast. Martha Ivins took two and went up stairs where Simpson was, and handing them to him, told him to shoot. He looked up, but had been shot in the head through a crack, and was then near his end. The Indians then proceeded to cut down the door, which they soon effected. During this time, Martha Ivins went to the far end of the house, lifted up a loose plank, and went under the floor, and requested Polly Moore (then eight years of age) who had the youngest child, called Margaret, in her arms (which was crying), to set the child down, and come under. Polly looked at the child, clasped it to her breast, and determined to share its fate. The Indians, having broken into the house, took Mrs. Moore and her children, viz: John, Jane, Polly, and Peggy prisoners, and having taken everything that suited them, they set it and the other buildings on fire, and went away. Martha Ivins remained under the floor a short time, and then came out and hid herself under a log that lay across a branch, not far from the house. The Indians, having tarried a short

---

*They saw the Indians before a gun was fired, and squatted in the grain till the Indians surrounded the house, and then started: Clark ran directly to Davidson's fort: the Irishman to a settlement creek, on Bluestone, about six miles distant. The Irishman got lost, and coming upon a drove of horses, frightened them. The horses, of course, ran home, and he followed.

time, with a view of catching horses, one of them walked across this log, sat down on the end of it, and began to fix his gunlock. Miss Ivins, supposing that she was discovered, and that he was preparing to shoot her, came out and gave herself up. At this he seemed much pleased. They then set out for their towns. Perceiving that John Moore was a boy, weak in body and mind, and unable to travel, they killed him the first day. The babe they took two or three days, but it being fretful, on account of a wound it had received, they dashed its brains out against a tree. They then moved on with haste to their towns. For some time, it was usual to tie, very securely, each of the prisoners at night, and for a warrior to lie beside each of them, with tomahawk in hand, so that in case of pursuit, the prisoners might be speedily dispatched. * * * * *

"Shortly after they reached the towns, Mrs. Moore and her daughter Jane were put to death, being burned and tortured at the stake. This lasted some time, during which she manifested the utmost Christian fortitude, and bore it without a murmur, at intervals conversing with her daughter Polly, and Martha Ivins, and expressing great anxiety for the moment to arrive, when her soul should wing its way to the bosom of its Savior. At length an old squaw, more humane than the rest, dispatched her with a tomahawk."

Polly Moore and Martha Evans eventually reached home, as described in the narrative of James Moore.

Several incidents, in this narrative, have been left out. When the Indians set fire to the house and started, they took from the stable the fine black horse **Yorick**. He was a horse of such a vicious nature, that no one could manage him but Simpson. The Indians had not proceeded far when one mounted him, but soon the horse had him on the ground, and was pawing him to death with his feet; for this purpose a few strokes were sufficient. Another mounted him and was served in like manner. Perfectly wild with rage, a very large Indian mounted him, swearing to ride him or kill him; a few plunges and the Indian was under the feet of the desperate horse, his teeth buried in his flesh, and uttering a scream as if he intended to avenge the death of his master; he had just dispatched the Indian, when another running up, stabbed him, and thus put an end to the conflict. "ALAS! POOR YORICK."

It is said that Mrs. Moore had her body stuck full of lightwood splinters which were fired, and she was thus tortured three days, before she died.

When Martha Evans and Polly Moore were among the French, they fared much worse than when among the Indians. The French had plenty, but were miserly, and seemed to care little for their wants. The Indians had little, but would divide that little to the last particle.

A song, in commemoration of the Moore captivity, is sung by some of the mountaineers to this day, but as it is devoid of poetical merit I omit its insertion. It may be seen in Howe's History of Virginia.

CHAPTER VI.

HARMAN AND PEMBERTON FIGHTS—BATTLE BETWEEN THE HARMANS AND SEVEN INDIANS.

In the fall of 1784[1] Henry Harman and his two sons, George and Matthias, and George Draper left the settlement, to engage in a bear hunt on Tug river. They were provided with pack-horses, independent of those used for riding, and on which were to be brought in the game. The country in which their hunt was to take place, was penetrated by the "war-path" leading to, and from the Ohio river; but as it was late in the season they did not expect to meet with Indians.

Arriving at the hunting-grounds in the early part of the evening, they stopped and built their camp; a work executed generally by the old man, who might be said to be particular in having it constructed to his own taste. George and Matthias loaded, and put their guns in order, and started to the woods, to look for sign, and perchance kill a buck for the evening's repast, while Draper busied himself in hobbling and caring for the horses.

In a short time, George returned with the startling intelligence of Indians! He had found a camp but a short distance from their own, in which the partly consumed sticks were still burning. They could not, of course, be at any considerable distance, and might now be concealed near them, watching their every movement. George, while at the camp, had made a rapid search for sign, and found a pair of leggins, which he showed the old man. Now old Mr. Harman, was a type of frontiermen, in some things, and particularly that remarkable self-possession, which is so often to be met with in new countries, where dangers are ever in the path of the settler. So taking a seat on the ground, he began to interrogate his son on the dimensions, appearances, etc., of the camp. When he had fully satisfied himself, he remarked, that "there must be from five to seven Indians," and that they must pack up and hurry back to the settlement, to prevent, if possible, the Indians from doing mischief; and, said he, **"if we fall in with them, we must fight them."**

Matthias was immediately called in, and the horses repacked. Mr. Harman and Draper, now began to load their guns, when the old man observing Draper laboring under what is known among hunters as the 'Buck Ague,' being that state of excitement, which causes excessive trembling, remarked to him, "My son, I fear you cannot fight."

The plan of march was now agreed upon, which was, that Mr. Harman and Draper should lead the way, the pack-horses follow them, and Matthias and George, bring up the rear. After they had started, Draper remarked to Mr. H., that he would get ahead, as he could see better than Mr. H., and that he would keep a sharp lookout. It is highly probable

---

[1]Nov. 12th, 1788, is the correct date, as shown by reliable documents.

that he was cogitating a plan of escape, as he had not gone far before he declared he saw the Indians, which proved not to be true. Proceeding a short distance further, he suddenly wheeled his horse about, at the same time crying out, "Yonder they are—behind that log:" as a liar is not to be believed, even when he speaks the truth, so Mr. Draper was not believed this time. Mr. Harman rode on, while a large dog, he had with him, ran up to the log and reared himself up on it, showing no signs of the presence of Indians. At this second, a sheet of fire and smoke from the Indians rifles, completely concealed the log from view, for Draper had really spoken the truth.

Before the smoke had cleared away, Mr. Harman and his sons were dismounted, while Draper had fled with all the speed of a swift horse. There were seven of the Indians, only four of whom had guns; the rest being armed with bows and arrows, tomahawks and scalping-knives. As soon as they fired, they rushed on Mr. Harman, who fell back to where his two sons stood ready to meet the Indians.

They immediately surrounded the three white men, who had formed a triangle, each man looking out, or, what would have been, with men enough a hollow square. The old gentleman bid Matthias to reserve his fire, while himself and George fired, wounding, as it would seem, two of the Indians. George was a lame man, from having had white swelling in his childhood, and after firing a few rounds, the Indians noticed his limping, and one who had fired at him, rushed upon him thinking him wounded. George saw the fatal tomahawk raised, and drawing back his gun, prepared to meet it. When the Indian had got within striking distance, George let down upon his head with the gun, which brought him to the ground; he soon recovered, and made at him again, half bent and head foremost, intending, no doubt, to trip him up. But as he got near enough, George sprang up and jumped across him, which brought the Indian to his knees. Feeling for his own knife, and not getting hold of it, he seized the Indian's and plunged it deep into his side. Matthias struck him on the head with a tomahawk, and finished the work with him.

Two Indians had attacked the old man with bows, and were maneuvering around him, to get a clear fire at his left breast. The Harmans, to a man, wore their bullet-pouches on the left side, and with this and his arm he so completely shielded his breast, that the Indians did not fire till they saw the old gentleman's gun nearly loaded again, when one fired on him, and struck his elbow near the joint, cutting one of the principal arteries. In a second more, the fearful string was heard to vibrate, and an arrow entered Mr. Harman's breast and lodged against a rib. He had by this time loaded the gun, and was raising it to his face to shoot one of the Indians, when the stream of blood from the wounded artery flew in the pan, and so soiled his gun that it was impossible to make it fire. Raising the gun, however, had the effect to drive back the Indians, who retreated to where the others stood with their guns empty.

Matthias, who had remained an almost inactive spectator, now asked permission to fire, which the old man granted. The Indian at whom he fired appeared to be the chief, and was standing under a large beech tree. At the report of the rifle, the Indian fell, throwing his tomahawk high among the limbs of the tree under which he stood.

Seeing two of their number lying dead upon the ground, and two more badly wounded, they immediately made off; passing by Draper, who had left his horse, and concealed himself behind a log.

As soon as the Indians retreated, the old man fell back on the ground exhausted and fainting from loss of blood. The wounded arm being tied up and his face washed in cold water, soon restored him. The first words he uttered were, "We've whipped, give me my pipe." This was furnished him, and he took a whiff, while the boys scalped one of the Indians.

When Draper saw the Indians pass him, he stealthily crept from his hiding-place, and pushed on for the settlement, where he reported the whole party murdered. The people assembled and started soon the following morning to bury them; but they had not gone far before they met Mr. H., and his sons, in too good condition to need burying.

Upon the tree, under which the chief was killed, is roughly carved an Indian, a bow, and a gun, commemorative of the fight. The arrows which were shot into Mr. Harman, are in possession of some of his descendants.

PEMBERTON'S FIGHT.

Richard Pemberton, the hero of this battle, lived in the Baptist valley, about five miles from Jeffersonville. In addition to a small farm around his cabin, he cultivated a field, now owned by William O. George, about one and a half miles from his dwelling.

On a Sabbath morning late in August, 1788, he started to his field accompanied by his wife and two children, to see that his fences were not down, and to repair any breach that might have been made. According to the custom of the times, Mr. Pemberton had taken with him his gun, which was his constant companion. After satisfying himself that his crops were safe, the little party started back. They had gone but a few hundred yards, however, when two Indians, armed with bows and arrows, knives, and tomahawks, came yelling toward them at full speed. In an instant the pioneer's gun was leveled and the trigger pulled; it missed fire, and in his hurry to spring the lock again, he broke it, and of course could not fire. Seeing him raise his gun to shoot, caused the Indians to halt, and commence firing arrows at him. Keeping himself between his wife and children and the Indians, he ordered them to get on as fast as possible and try to reach a house at which a Mr. Johnson lived, and where several men were living. This house was some half mile distant, but he hoped to reach it, and save those whom he held dearest—his wife and children. The Indians made every possible attack to separate him from his family, all of which proved vain. They would retreat to a respectful distance, and then come bounding back like so many furies from the regions of indescribable woe. When they came too near, he would raise his gun as if he was really reserving his fire, which would cause them to halt and surround him. But at every attack they shot their arrows into his breast, causing great pain.

For nearly an hour this running fight was kept up; still the blood-thirsty savages pressed on; at last, he was sufficiently near to Johnson's house to be heard, and he raised his powerful voice for succor; he was heard, but no sooner did the men at the house hear the cry of "Indians," than they took to their heels in an opposite direction. At last he arrived at the house, closely pursued by the Indians, and entering after his family, barred up the door, and began to make preparations for acting upon the offensive, when the Indians made a rapid retreat. Pemberton reached his own house the following day, where he resided many years, an eyesore to those who had so ingloriously fled from his assistance. Many arrow points which entered his breast, were never removed, and were carried to the end of life, as the best certificate of his bravery, and devotion to his family.

CHAPTER VII.

CAPTIVITY OF THE DAVIDSON FAMILY, AND OTHER MASSACRES.

To tell a tale of Indian barbarity, is at all times painful. Even where the hardy backwoodsman is the victim, our sympathies become aroused for those of our own race, and we ardently wish the tale could have been otherwise told. But I have only learned the extent of my synpathy, when mothers and children have been the suffering party, in a tale told me by a hoary-headed old man, whose breast would heave as though some uncommon emotion was interfering with the natural pulsations of his heart. To witness the pearly drops gathering in his eye, as memory called up the days of yore, and the trembling of his voice, as he recounted the many sufferings of the captive mother or daughter, have never failed to awaken the tenderest sympathies of my soul, and produce a desire to so tell the same tale, that others might be similarly affected. This though, cannot be done—the intonations of the voice cannot be written, nor would it be in proper taste to attempt to throw around a scene, intended for a historical collection, the enchanting colors of language. Beside, there are a variety of tastes to please, and the writer who can give universal satisfaction has yet to write. There is one distinguishing feature, however, which all admire, and I have made this the test by which I have tried my labors, viz: **simple truth.** It is my place to record the **fact**, which may, in course of time, become material for him who delights to dwell on the ideal.

Andrew Davidson left his house, on business of importance, which would keep him from home several days. His horse was ready saddled, and kissing his wife and children, bade them adieu for a season, promising to make all speed and return. Long and anxiously did the kind-hearted mother look at his retiring form. But as he passed from her sight, she turned again to her children, and silently wept over them, as if she felt the desolation of her situation. The family consisted of the three children of Mrs. Davidson, two girls and a boy, all small, and a bound boy and a girl, orphans, whose parents were Broomfields.

The bound children were between seven and ten, and, of course, were but little help to Mrs. Davidson. At the period of which I write, 1789-'90, the women of western Virginia willingly shared in the more laborious part of the household toil, and when their husbands were absent, performed such labors as were before performed by their husbands.

Several days had elapsed since the departure of her husband, when Mrs. Davidson found her doors suddenly darkened by the swarthy forms of several Indians, who, speaking English, told her she must go with them to their towns in the west.

There remained no alternative to her, though her situation was such as almost to prevent the possibility of her performing such a trip. She took up her youngest child, the Indians taking the others, and left the house to try the realities of Indian captivity, of which she had heard much said. They had not proceeded far when they relieved her of her burden; one of the Indians taking her child, and, unexpectedly to her, carried it on in safety.

The exertions and anxiety of mind undergone by Mrs. Davidson, was the cause of an addition of numbers to the captives. Two hours relaxation from the march, was sufficient rest, in the estimation of the Indians, and again they pushed on, one of the Indians carrying the stranger, which after a day's time, was drowned, on account of apparent or real indisposition.

The Indians who captured Mrs. Davidson, were more humane that she expected. They seemed to pity her, and showed every leniency that could be asked for, under the circumstances.

But, when they arrived at the Indian towns, quite a different fate awaited them. The two girl children were tied to trees, and shot before her eyes. The boy, her son, was given to an old squaw, who, in passing over a river, upset her canoe, and he was drowned. What became of the bound boy and girl was never known.

Mr. Davidson, two years after, it being a time of peace, went to the Shawanoe towns to look for his wife, who had been sold to a French gentleman. Mr. Davidson made inquires after her, but could learn nothing of her fate. An old Indian, who no doubt pitied him, told him that if any Indian in the town knew of her whereabouts, he could not be told, as they would have to refund the price paid for her in case she had to be given up. But, that if he(Mr. Davidson)would go home, that he would find out where his wife was, and inform him. Mr. Davidson returned, little thinking that the Indian would keep his promise.

In a short time after Mr. Davidson returned, the old Indian conveyed the necessary intelligence to him, and he set out a second time, but now toward Canada, whither he had been informed she was. When he had got into the Canada settlements, he stopped at the house of a wealthy French farmer, to get a meal's victuals, and to inquire the way to some place where he had heard she was.

He noticed a woman passing him, as he entered the house, but merely bowed to her and went in. Asking for his dinner, he seated himself, and was, perhaps, running over in his mind, the chances of finding his wife, when again the woman entered. She laid down her wood, and looked at the stranger steadily for a moment, when she turned to her mistress, and said: **I know that man,**" "Well, who is he?" said the French lady. **It is my husband!** Andrew Davidson, I am your wife." Mr. Davidson could scarcely believe his senses. When he last saw her, she was a fine, healthy-looking woman; her hair was black as coal; but now, her head was gray, and she looked many years older than she should have looked. Yet it was her, though he declared nothing but her voice seemed to say she was Rebecca Davidson.

Soon the French gentleman returned, and being a humane man, gave up Rebecca to her husband, also a considerable sum of money, and next morning sent them on their way rejoicing.

THE HENRY FAMILY MASSACRED.

In May, 1776, John Henry and his family fell victims to savage barbarity. Mr. Henry lived in Thompson's valley, on a plantation now owned by James S. Witten. The circumstances attending this melancholy occurrence, are not sufficiently clear. The simple fact of the massacre is beyond doubt. But the old gentleman who furnished me with the circumstances, showed such marked evidences of a decaying state of the mind, that I fear the tale is not altogether as authentic as we might desire. But impressions of this kind seem to be indelibly written upon memory's tablet, even when other incidents, of a different nature, are forgotten. More than once have I seen this exemplified in conversing with the witnesses to the incidents which have been given.

Mr. Henry had retired to rest with the blessing of a good conscience—the honest man's reward—resting upon his head. After passing a night of quiet rest, he arose and dressed himself to prepare for the labors of the coming day. His wife had also arisen, and was preparing to commence some culinary operation. The children—seven in number—were asleep, little dreaming how soon they were to be startled from the morning's slumber by the sharp crack of an Indian rifle.

The sun had already begun to cast the golden tints of a summer-morning upon the light clouds which floated in the western atmosphere; yet it was not light, and might best be illustrated by saying it was the gray of the morning, when Mr. Henry stepped to the door and unbolted it, with the intention, no doubt, of looking abroad, and yawning in the open air. Stepping in the door, he stretched himself up to inhale the sweet odors of the morning breeze, when a party of Indians, who lay near, fired a gun, and he fell on his face in the yard. He wore on the waistbands of his pantaloons, a large metal button, which must have served as a target to the Indian's gun, as the ball passed directly through it, and into Mr. Henry's body.

The savages rushed forward, no longer fearing the stout arm of Henry, and were soon among the sleeping babes, who had, as yet, scarcely waked from their slumbers. While the Indians were in the house, engaged in their horrible work, Henry rose to his feet, and started for Mr. Martin's, his nearest neighbor. He had seen the Indians pass him, and enter his house, and knowing his inability to assist his wife and children, he thought only of personal safety. Though bleeding, and feeling that his end was nigh, he pressed on for Martin's house, hoping to save Martin's family, if nothing more.

Martin had likewise risen early, intending to start to what is now known as Smyth county, with his family. He had started, and was on the road when he met Henry on his hands and knees, crawling on as if determined to warn others of the presence of the Indians. But, poor man, he was now too weak to act the part of a messenger. Martin learned the circumstance, and placing Henry on a horse, so altered his course as to avoid passing Henry's house, and hurried on to the Cove, about seven miles distant. Here he left Henry, and proceeded to his destination. In a few hours Henry breathed his last, and was buried on the present plantation of William Barnes, Esq. A company was soon collected and preparations made to follow the Indians, whom it was supposed, had carried off the rest of the family. But when they arrived at the fatal spot, the family, consisting of a wife and six children, were found murdered, scalped, and piled up after the manner of a log heap, on a ridge a short distance from the house. One child was not to be found, a little boy, whom it was supposed had been carried off. A large hole was opened, which became a common grave for the mother and her unoffending children.

The identical spot on which Henry was buried, could not be marked for a number of years—a few years ago, a grave was opened near the supposed place, which accidentally proved to be the very spot on which Henry was buried, which was known from the presence of boards or puncheons, which had been substituted for a coffin, and the identical button through which the fatal ball passed. The button is now in possession of some one in this county.

DEATH OF GILBERT

In the latter part of the summer of 1792,* Maj. Robert Crockett of Wythe county, was informed that a considerable band of Indians had been seen in the settlement on the Clinch, endeavoring to steal horses, but had not at that time succeeded. He immediately raised a company of forty, and went in pursuit of them, thinking it likely that he should fall in with them as they were leaving the settlement with their booty.

He found their trail, over which they had but a short time passed, and having no doubt of the route which they would take, concluded that it would be an easy matter to come up with them that night. Being short of provisions, he stopped and ordered the men to separate in pairs, and try to kill a few deer. They were to hunt but two hours when the march was to be resumed.

Joseph Gilbert, and Samuel Lusk, acting as spies, were ordered to keep on and carefully note every sign, and in case they found the Indians, to return and give information. These two men were noted spies, and had often served together. They continued on the trail for about an hour, when they came upon a lick at which the Indians, who were also in need of provisions, lay concealed, waiting for the deer or elk which frequented it.

The Indians fired, missing Gilbert but wounding Lusk in the hand. Gilbert turned to run, and had made off a few yards, when Lusk called to him to return and save him, if possible. The affectionate tone in which this appeal was uttered, fired the manly heart of Gilbert, who turned about and shot the nearest Indian, who fell upon the spot. The Indians closed in upon him as he stood over the body of Lusk, who had fainted from the loss of blood, but dropping his gun, he drew his heavy hunting-knife, and fell to

---

*I say, that this circumstance took place in the latter part of the summer, not because I was so informed, but from circumstances equally conclusive. The date furnished me was simply 1792, but it will be seen that the Indians were engaged in catching the young of the otter (Lutra vulgaris), which do not bring forth their young, till latee in the summer.—(See Goldsmith and American Zoologist).

upon the naked bodies of his enemies with such spirit, that the Indians no longer dared to approach within reach of his arm. Keeping out of his reach, they began to hurl their tomahawks at him with such force and accuracy, that he soon lay dead on the earth by the side of his now reviving companion. The wounded hand of Lusk was immediately cared for by the Indians, who after scalping Gilbert, commenced a rapid march for the Ohio. The firing was too far off to give Maj. Crockett any warning of what was going on; but when the two hours had expired, he took up the line of march and followed on after his spies. When they arrived at the lick, they found the body of Gilbert, and pushed on with all possible speed, after burying him near the bank of the creek which now bears his name, but could not come up with the Indians.

The Indians told Lusk, whom they took prisoner, and who returned in a short time, that if Maj. Crockett had not stopped to hunt, he must have cut them to pieces, as they were, but a few moments before they came to the lick, engaged in catching young otters, their arms in the meantime lying on a little knoll several rods from them.

MURDER OF WILLIAM WHITLEY.

William Whitley lived in Baptist valley, and had been out on a bear hunt. He came home, and finding that a choice dog was gone, started the following morning to look for him. The day passed off and he did not return. His family became uneasy, and a company started out to hunt for him. They had not gone far, however, when they met a man named Scaggs, who had passed a murdered man at the mouth of Dick's Creek. The company pushed on and identified the man to be Whitley. He was dreadfully mutilated—his bowels torn out and stretched upon the bushes, his heart in one place, and liver in another. A hole was opened, and the fragments gathered up and interred. This happened in 1786.

MOFFIT'S CHILDREN CAPTURED.

Capt. Moffit lived near Clinch river, on the plantation now owned by Kiah Harman. Two of his children were attending to a sugar camp, when they were captured and taken off to the Indians towns in the west. Whether the boys ever got back is unknown, as Captain Moffit soon afterward moved to Kentucky, where some of his descendants still reside.

MASSACRE OF THE ROARK FAMILY.

James Roark lived at the gap of the dividing ridge, between the waters of the Clinch and Sandy rivers, through which passed the Dry Fork road, and which has since been known as Roark's Gap. Early in 1789, a band of Shawanoe Indians left their homes in the west, and ascending the Dry fork, fell upon the defenseless family of Mr. Roark, and killed his wife and several children. Two sons and Mr. Roark were from home, and it may be, thus saved their own lives, as the Indians were rather numerous to have been beaten off by them, even if they had been at home.

This is the only instance that I have met with, of the Indians visiting the settlements of Tazewell before the winter had clearly broken. There was a heavy snow upon the ground at this time.

From this time forward, the Roarks became the deadly enemies of the Indians, and sought them, even beyond the limits of the county. Mr. Roark and one of his sons (John), were afterward killed in a battle, fought at what was then known as the Station bottom, within the present limits of Floyd county, Kentucky.

RAY'S FAMILY KILLED.

I have been unable to learn anything of the particulars of this ocurrence, more than the bare fact, that Joseph Ray and his family were killed by the Indians, on Indian Creek, in 1788 or '9. It is from this circumstance that Indian Creek has taken its name.

DANIEL HARMAN KILLED.

Daniel Harman left his house, on the head of Clinch, on a fine morning in the fall of 1791, for the purpose of killing a deer. Where he went, for that purpose, is not known, but having done so, he started for home with the deer fastened to the cantle of his saddle. Harman was a great hunter, and owned a choice rifle, remarkable for the beauty of its finish, and the superior structure of its triggers, which were, as usual, of the double kind. So strong was the spring of these, that when sprung, the noise might be heard for a considerable distance. He was riding a large horse, fleet, and spirited, and had got within a mile of home, and was passing through a bottom, near the present residence, and on the lands of Mr. William O. George, when suddenly a party of Indians sprang from behind a log, and fired on him. He was unhurt, and putting spurs to his horse, away he went through the heavy timber, forgetting all other danger, in his precarious situation. On he went, but his horse, passing too near a tree, struck the rider's knee, breaking his leg, and throwing him from his horse. In a few minutes the savages were upon him, and with their tomahawks, soon put an end to his sufferings. The horse continued his flight till he got to the house, at which were several of the neighbors, who immediately went to look after Harman. Passing near the Indians, they heard the click of Harman's well-known trigger. A panic struck the men, and running in zigzag lines, they made a rapid retreat, leaving the Indians to silently retrace their steps from the settlement.

DIALS AND THOMAS KILLED.

On the 11th of April, 1786, Matthias Harman and Benjamin Thomas, returning from a spying expedition, stopped at John Peery's where lived a man, named Dials, who kept liquor for sale. The three (Harman, Thomas, and Dials) were soon under its influence, and the two who had just returned from the woods, being hungry, asked Mrs. Dials for dinner, which she promised to furnish if they would get some wood with which to cook it. Dials and Thomas started for that purpose, leaving Harman at the house. When they got to the mouth of the lane, which was about two hundred yards from the house, they were fired upon by a party of six or seven Indians. Three of the balls entered Dial's body, who fled toward the house, and a warrior after him. The Indian pressed him so close, that in catching at him, he succeeded in drawing Dial's shirt from his pantaloons. The Indian, finding that there were men at the house, gave up the chase and joined his companions at the mouth of the lane. Dials fell against the chimney corner and died in a few hours.

When the Indians fired, it seems that only one attempted to shoot Thomas, and he was so close that Thomas struck up his gun as he fired, and the ball entered an oak high above his head. He was, however, knocked down with a war-club, by another Indian, scalped, and left for dead. Harman, who was getting boozy enough to feel brave, ran out, mounted his horse and pursued the Indians a short distance, challenging them to stop and fight. This they declined, and made off as rapidly as possible.

Thomas was left on the battle-ground till next morning, when William Wynn found him, and took him to his fort, where he survived seven days. It seems a little strange that a wounded man should be left out all night; but he was supposed to be dead, and it was not necessary to disturb him till assistance could be got to bury him; and this could not be done sooner than the following day. Within the sound of one's voice, several hundred might now be collected on the spot in a few hours, but this is the year of our Lord 1852.

CAPTURE AND MASSACRE OF THE ENGLISH FAMILY.

In the spring of 1787, a small company of Shawanoe Indians entered Burk's Garden, through Wolf creek Gap, and attacked the family of Thomas English, who, at the time, resided upon the plantation now owned by John Thompson. Mr. English being absent, the Indians easily succeeded in taking Mrs. English and her children prisoners. Not long after the Indians had left the house, Mr. English returned, and, as he was passionately devoted to his family, made every possible exertion to get a company to go in pursuit of the Indians. His movements were so rapid, that by sunset, the same day, he and his party were fairly in pursuit. Night came on; but still the frantic husband and his brave companions pushed on; They came up with the Indians at about eleven o'clock at night. One of the men, named Thomas Maxwell, had on a white hunting-shirt, which English desired him to pull off; telling him that he would become a mark for the Indians rifles. He refused to do so, and declared his willingness to die. As soon as the Indians found that the whites were in pursuit, they quickened their pace. English, who had been a prisoner among them, and speaking their language, bantered them to stop and fight him; all to no purpose, however, for as soon as they entered Maxwell's Gap they charged the Indians, who fired in return, upon the whites, doing no injury, however, to any except to Maxwell, whose white hunting-shirt had furnished a target amid the surrounding darkness. Hence the name of the gap in which this scene transpired.

The Indians, finding themselves pressed, killed one child, scalped another, and also Mrs. English.

Mrs. English and her mangled child were brought back to William Wynn's fort, where they received such attendance as was necessary. The child died the next day, but Mrs. English recovered, and raised a small family afterward.

JOHN DAVIDSON KILLED.

At what precise time this occurrence took place I have not been able to learn. It is supposed to have occurred sometime in 1789–'90. Mr. Davidson was on his way home from a trip to Rockingham county, whither he had been on business, and had got as far back as to where John D. Peery now lives when he was killed by a band of Indians. The circumstances of his murder, were told to some prisoners who had been taken from this county, and who were then among the Indians. It seems that Mr. Davidson had stopped at an old cabin to feed his horse and rest himself, when the Indians fired on him. The Indians say, a white man was with them, and that they found in his saddlebags a considerable sum of specie.

A few days after his son, Col. Davidson, became uneasy on account of his absence, and raising a small company went in search of him. Luckily, when they got to the cabin, they found a hatband, which, being of peculiar structure, was recognized as that worn by Mr. Davidson. After considerable search, his body was found stripped of clothing, and somewhat disfigured by birds.

As the Indians had been too long gone to be overtaken, Mr. Davidson was taken home and buried.

SKIRMISH AT THE ISLANDS OF GUYANDOTTE.

The Indians, in visiting the frontier settlements, had several objects in view; among which horse-stealing was an important one. It is true, that the Indians rarely failed to kill the whites when suitable opportunities were offered, but at the same time, it must be acknowledged that a fine horse was valued nearly as much as a scalp. And it was not unusual that the Indians spared the life of a few persons to get a drove of horses for the Canada markets. Companies starting on a horse-stealing expedition, were usually larger and better provided with provisions than the predatory bands which killed, or carried into captivity, the first settlers or their families.

Such a company made a descent upon the settlement of Bluestone, and on the head of Clinch in 1790, and after collecting about eighty horses, started for their towns in the west. A hunter came upon their camp on the first night, which was but a short distance from the settlement, and hastened to give the alarm at the forts and stations. A large company from Bluestone, and another from the head of Clinch, were ready to go in pursuit by twelve o'clock the next day. They made forced marches, and came up with them about one o'clock at night, at what is called the Islands of Guyandotte. Some of the whites were for attacking them immediately, and others wished to wait till morning, when they might see. While thus in parley, the Indians in the meantime apparently preparing for some movement, a horse neighed; in a moment a fire was opened upon them, but to no effect. The Indians raised a yell, secured a few of the horses and fled, leaving a good breakfast, and several dozen pairs of moccasins to be taken home as trophies by the whites. The breakfast of bears' meat and turkey, was consumed by the whites, whose appetites were too keen to suffer themselves to enter into speculation as to the probable nicety of their runaway cooks.

CHAPTER VIII.

MOTIVES FOR WAR ON THE PART OF THE INDIANS.

It is a melancholy fact, which cannot be denied, that almost every American—every man, who has any idea of the principles of abstract justice—must, and generally does, acknowledge that the Indians have been badly treated, and have ever had sufficient cause for making war upon the whites Though the whites may not have made the first assault directly, yet they did indirectly. They came to their shores from countries where nations fought for conquest; and conquest was the avowed object of all the expeditions of discovery, from the time of the **Genoese** navigator to that of Raleigh.

Yes, they came as friends, but claimed the privilege of taking from the poor native, everything which he possessed if found valuable. A few valueless beads were given to the simple native in exchange for fortunes that princes might envy. The whites made settlements upon the lands of these people, and even tried to subject them to the chains of bondage; and when opposed by these **natural republicans**—fired by a patriotic love of country, home, and the graves of their ancestors—war! war to the knife, was opened upon them.

These people possessed sagacity enough to see, that a final obliteration of their race must be the result, and accordingly took such steps as their savage nature suggested, to prevent the catastrophe.

They waged a cruel war—which was returned with as much or more cruelty by the whites. The Indians waged a war for home—for wives—children—the tombs of their fathers, and their hunting-grounds. The cruel manner in which the whites were sometimes killed, did not justify a Christian people to wage a similar war, and butcher their victims in a like manner.

In most atrocities, in early warfare, by the Indians, the cause came indirectly from the whites, who kept their wigwams in a state of riot by intoxicating liquors, of the excitement of which, the Indian as well as the white-man was fond; and when under its terrifying influence the Indian committed a depredation, the white-man was sure to repay it with a vengeance calculated to inflame the already over-excited resentment of the injured and insulted child of nature. All acknowledged that before the year 1492, the Indians owned every foot of land from the North Sea, to Cape Horn, and from the Atlantic to the Pacific Ocean; and that now, they do not own a foot which can be called their own. It will be said that the lands were purchased from the Indians: I answer by asking, What equivalent did they receive? they did not receive the value of a grain of wheat to the acre. Would the sale be a valid one in an American court of justice? No, the truth is, that the principle on which this land was bought, was to blind the eyes of the world, and did not show any desire on the part of our government, or the governments of Great Britain or Spain, to give the ignorant red-man a fair valuation of his lands. The sum required to do this, was forty-eight billions of dollars, or forty-eight thousand millions—a sum greater than all Europe was ever able to pay. For the ten or twenty millions paid the Indians, the whites have received seven fold from them in the shape of exchanges for valueless beads, etc.

It is said by a wise philosopher, that "intellect is universal in its application, it may become the handmaid of any of the faculties." In this instance it seems to have been the instrument by which the base passion of avarice sought satiation And so the Indians now feel: in illustration I may be excused for here introducing a speech delivered at Fort Wayne in 1803, by an Indian chief, perhaps Laulewasikaw, the notorious prophet and brother to Tecumseh, the Tippecanoe warrior.

"The Master of Life," said he, "who was himself an Indian, made the Shawanoes before any other of the human race; and they sprang from his brain; he gave them all the knowledge he himself possessed, and placed them upon the great island, and all the other red people descended from the Shawanoes. He made the French and English out of his breast, the Dutch out of his feet, and the Long-knives (Virginians) out of his hands. All these inferior races of men he made white and placed them beyond the stinking lake (Atlantic Ocean). The Shawanoes continued for many ages to be masters of the continent, using the knowledge they had received from the Great Spirit in such a manner as to be pleasing to Him, and to secure their own happiness. In a great length of time, however, they became corrupt, and the Master of Life told them he would take away from them the knowledge which they possessed, and give it to the white people, to be restored when, by a return to good principles they should deserve it. Many ages after that, they saw something white approaching **their shores;** at first they took it for a great bird, but they soon found it to be a monstrous canoe, filled with those who had got the knowledge which belonged to the Shawanoes. After these white people landed, **they were not content with having the knowledge which belonged to the Shawanoes, but they usurped their lands also:** they pretended indeed to have purchased these lands; but the very goods they gave for them, were more the property of the Indians than the white people, because the knowledge which enabled them to manufacture these goods, actually blonged to the Shawanoes: but these things will soon have an end. The Master of Life is about to restore to the Shawanoes both their knowledge and their rights, and he will trample the Long-knives under his feet."*

Tecumseh said to Gen. Harrison that, "the Americans had driven the Indians from the sea-coast, and would soon push them into the lakes," and that he as one was, "resolutely determined to take a stand, and prevent, if possible, the farther encroachment of the whites upon the Indian lands."†

It was this idea of knowledge and Christianity, being the instruments of torture and oppression, that drew from the lips of the St. Domingo chief, **Hautey,** the memorable remark which has portrayed so much truth in so

---

*Life of Tecumseh. †Dawson.

‡Las Casas, in an article describing the cruelties of his countrymen in the New World, and quoted by Prescott in his conquest of Mexico.

few words. Having fled from St. Domingo to escape the oppression of the Spaniards, he was captured and ordered to be burned alive; this order was given by the governor of Cuba, Velasquez. When urged at the stake to embrace Christianity, he inquired if the white men would go to heaven? on being answered in the affirmative, he replied, "then I will not be a Christian; for I would not go again to a place where I must find men so cruel."‡

Were I sent forth to find men true and brave, I know of none to whom I should go sooner than to the Indians. Were their deeds of heroism emblazoned upon the page of unfading history, a brighter light could not be cast upon the works of God.

I have been induced to make these remarks to mitigate, in a measure, the feelings that must have been harrowed up, by the perusal of the massacres contained in the last few chapters. I may be accused of being overpartial to the Indians; but I cannot persuade myself that such is the case, or that I have said one word too much for them, nay rather do I feel my inability to do justice to the lords of the American forest, with whom, the proudest of the proud, might seek an alliance.

The day of trial to the poor Indian has not yet passed, the whites are yearly encroaching upon the territory set apart for their residence by the general government. Lawless men, who seek only self aggrandizement, are daily insinuating themselves among the Indians, and selling to them intoxicating liquors—destroying not only life, but domestic peace, and fitting the poor savages for the commission of deeds which will bring vengeance upon their heads.

If this custom is not arrested, we may expect to see the Indians contininue to dwindle away before the now powerful, but ungrateful offspring of their guests, driven hither by oppression, but a few hundred years ago. That all deplore this fact, who suffer themselves to reflect for a moment, none will deny. We seldom meet with an individual who is so dishonest as to claim that justice has been done the Indians even by historians.

With pleasure we recount the deeds of the heroes of past ages—each striving to color them highest—but amid all our labors, few wield the pen to perpetuate the deeds of heroism acted by the many brave warriors who have figured among the American Indians. Why is this? Ah! the answer is plain—it requires much labor, and does not pay so well as those labors which are bestowed on a familiar theme. Hannibals or Napoleons may not have led their hosts of red-men to the battle-fields in the forests of America; but men with the patriotism of a Washington, have fallen battling for their homes. How many must be the daring feats which have been performed by these brave people; and how pure were those emotions which actuated the Indian father to leave his home, and all its endearments, to repel the advancing foe! How devoted must have been that Indian mother to the land in which reposed the bones of her boy? for it has not yet been proved, that civilization and love are inseparable.

It may be, that the obliteration of the Indian race, was but the working of an allwise Providence, and if so, then none will complain. But that they might have been civilized, and brought to an understanding of the truth of Christianity, is proved beyond a doubt, by the present condition of the Chickasaw and Choctaw tribes. In college, the Indian boy has not been found deficient; nor can I subscribe to the opinion, sometimes expressed, that they are an inferior race of men. Circumstances have conduced to make them such—but instances have not been wanting, where the unfavorable conditions have been removed, of great depth of mind, and general vivacity of intellectual powers, having been exhibited by the North American Savages.

It is a remarkable fact, that most of the tribes or fragments of tribes of North American Indians are but little more advanced than they were centuries ago. The Indians of the west, still hunt with the bow and arrow, and make war with the lance and shield. Their religion, manners and sustoms, have undergone little change for three hundred years. The same vague superstitions—the same stupid ignorance—the same mutual dissensions which have ever been the barriers to their prosperity, yet exist—a few tribes, originally settled east of the Mississippi river, have become somewhat civilized, and Christianized; but the greater portion of the western Indians are still savages. The labors of Christian missionaries have been too confined and cramped, to accomplish what we could have wished to see.

But surely, the Christian denominations, if not the general government will take some steps to reclaim this lost people. The more we learn of them, the more we find to admire. Then how noble would be the labor of a life among them, that their full history might now be saved, and not perish, as it will most likely, without exertions, in less than two centuries, when not one representative of these once powerful people will exist, to remind us of their ancestors—our benefactors.

Who is he that would not contribute something to the cause of education —one of the first steps to civilization—among the poor ignorant savages of the western wilds? Surely, if such a man lives, he will not let his existence be known.

The day is coming when the western wilds must be converted into happy homes, and if the red-man who now occupies them is not first taught to fill the injunction laid upon Adam, he must go the way of his ancestors and be no more known among the nations of the earth.''

Keeping in view the purpose of the author of these Annals to chronicle only such matters as are directly related to Tazewell County, we have omitted from the republication of Bickley's History, the following: The Preface, Outline History of Virginia, Table of Contents and the greater part of Introduction to Indian Wars. We have also omitted to copy the authors concluding "Note" and the chapters on Birds, Animals and Plants. Bickley's list of the Members of the Legislature has not been copied because a complete list appears elsewhere in Part One.—Harman.

ILLUSTRATIONS

JEFFERSONVILLE (Frontispiece)	336
THE SUGAR CAMP	349
COVE AND MAIDEN SPRING FARMS	356
SCENERY WEST FROM JEFFERSONVILLE	360
DIAL ROCK	396

Index to Tazewell County, Virginia - Vol. #1

ABB,	24	REUBEN Q.	67	. MARTHA	161
ABBS,	310	APP,	24	. MOSES	77
ADAMS,CONSTANCE	89	ARENHART,LOUISA	117	. PATSE	94
. CONSTANTINE	281	ARENHEART,LUCINDA	106	. SMITH	162
. JAMES	69	ARGABRIGHT,JOHN W.	320	. TABITHA	118
. NANCY FLUMMER	281	ARIOME,	423	. THOMAS H.	103
. WILLIAM	95	ARMS,SUSAN	139	. WILLIAM	123,413
ADKINS,DAVIDSON	106	THEODORE	322	ASTON,GEORGE	301
. EDWARD	219-220	ARMSTEAD,BEN	327	. SUSANAH	301
. ISAAC	50,74,289,294	BEN M.	330	. WILLIAM B.	250
. POLLY	87	ARMSTRONG,THOMAS	23	ATHEY,JOHN	298
ADKINSON,L.T.	314	ARNHART,SUSANNA	68	ATKINS,ANDERSON	117
AKERLING,SAMUEL	19	ASBERRY,AARON	275	. ANNALIZA	117
ALBERT,JAMES	166	. ANN	53	. DAVID P.	242
ALCORN,ROBETY	20	. BETSY	275	. DAVIDSON	243
ALDERSON,H.C.	317-318	. CHARLOTTE	152	. LARKIN	80
. MARY	317	. GEORGE	79,171	. LEGCY	80
. MARY C.	318	. HANAH	100	. PETER	127
ALDRIC,THOMAS	141	. HANER	134	. REBECA	72
ALDRIDGE,THOMAS	141	. HANNAH HARRISON	273	. ROBERT T.	142
ALEXANDER,JOHN	206	. HENRY	173,184,275	AUSTIN,SAMUEL W.	128,253
. M.J.	333	. JAMES	57,275	BAGLEY,MARGARET	50
. M.P.	333	. JESSE	275	BAILEY,ALEXANDER	167
ALFORD,RUSSELL	137	. JINNY	275	. ARCHIBALD	67,174,278
ALIN,THOMAS	306	. JOHN	54,288,296	.	298
ALIZER,MARY	85	. KESIAH	296	. BETSEY	57
ALLEN,DAVID	308	. KEZIAH	288	. CLAY	72
. ELIZABETH	101	. LOUISE BROOKS	246	. DILLY	61
. EUNICE	53	. LOWISA	279	. DODRIGGE	56
. JAMES	130	. MARTHA	275	. EDWARD B.	207
. JOHN	80,254,259,293	. MARY ANN	67	. ELI	300
. MADISON	162	. MOSES	270,275	. ELIJAH	277
. ROBERT	64,233	. N.	317	. ELIZABETH	61,72,277
. SALLY	49	. NELLY	51	.	281,301
. SALLY D.	96	. POLLY	86,275	. ELIZABETH VIRGINIA	278
. THOMAS	265	. REBECCA	275	. GEORGE	278
. WILLIAM	122	. TABA	52	. GEORGE C.	322
ALLEY,ASA	121	. THOMAS	99,275	. HENRY	82,187,207,212
R.F.	328	. WILLIAM	52,134,180,275	.	219,275,277
ALLIN,DAVID	58	.	288,295	. HENRY BUREN	278
ALLISON,S.F.	323	. WITT	56	. HUGH S.	252,311-312
ALLTIZAR,WILLIAM	109	ASBERY,GEORGE	62	.	320
ALLTIZER,KATY	105	. JEAN	66	. ISAAC	108
ALSOP,NATHANIEL	96	. NANCY	124	. JAMES	99,278,281,298
ALTISER,JOHN	116	. POLLY	66	.	411
ALTIZER,ANNA	102	. THOMAS	66	. JAMES M.	277
. J.T.	325	ASBURRY,AMANDA	282	. JESSE	167
. LILLY	113	. ELI C.	282	. JOHN	82,99,212,264-265
. RILEY	134	. POLLY	54	.	278,298,411
. SALLY	129	ASBURY,AARON	77	. JOHN C.	323
. THOMAS	151	. ALBERT P.	162	. JOHN MADISON	278
. WILLIAM	312	. ARCHIBALD	75	. JOHN P.	215,218,277
AMISS,LEWIS	185	. BETSY	73	. JOHN W.	145
ANDERSON,	230	. CHARLOTTE	96	. JONATHAN	278
. JAMES	15	. DARCEY	123	. MARTHA	51,278
. JOHN	26	. ELIZA	118	. MASTIN	102,278
. LOUISA J.B.	121	. ELIZABETH H.	130	. MICAJAH	93,298
. NANCY	130	. JACOB	104	. MILLEY	281
. NANCY S.	106	. JAMES	104,145	. NANCY	87,97,101,103
. WILLIAM	101,216,252	. JANE	96	. NAOMI	298
.	259,328	. JERUSA	98	. OMY	82
ANDREWS,ADAM	20	. MALINDA	107	. PEGGY	97

Index to Tazewell County, Virginia - Vol. #1

Name	Page
. PHILIP P.	277
. POLLEY	55,82
. POLLY	74,99,278
. POLLY F.	82
. REBECCA	278
. REBECKAH	82
. REBEKAH	67
. REUBEN	87-88,281
. RHODA	60
. RICHARD	69,300-301
. SALLY	71,91,281
. SARAH	48
. WILLIAM	53,68,281
. WILLIAM M.	277
BAILLEY,SALLY	95
BAILY,JOHN	72
BAINEY,JENE	70
BAINHEART,GEORGE	413
BAIRD,LUCY	73
BAKER,ANDREW	22,147
. D.D.	333
. F.H.	314
. GEORGE	12
. HUMPHREY	12,18,20
. JAMES W.	315-316
. MARIA T.	152
. NARCISA	158
BALDWIN,ANDREW	93
. D.B.	317-318
. HARVY	316
. LUCY L.	332
. R.E.	332
. SALLY FOX	277
. WESLEY	163
. WILLIAM M.	157
BALER,PETER	79
BALL,BENJAMIN	68
. GREEN	120
. PETER	149,157
BALLARD,REBECCA	79
BALLINGER,ISAAC	24
BALLY,ELLIE	101
BALY,JOHN	98
BANDY,ELLEN	112
. JAMES	323
. JOHN C.	108,307
. NANCY PERRY	274
. POLLEY	71
. REES	314
. SALLIE	323
. THOMAS	117,161,165
. THOMAS R.	317
. WILLIAM	323
BANE,C.A.	323
. EMMA G.	324
. HOWARD	104,184,251,264
.	301,304,310
. JAMES	244
. JAMES T.	243,246-247
.	258
. JESSE	163
. LEE	321
. LETTICE	301
. MARGARET H.	105
. MARTHA DAVIDSON	284
. MARTHA L.	159
. NANCY	91,310
. NANCY HAVEN	277
. RUSSELL	277
. SALLY	84
. W.E.	321,324
. WILLIAM R.	93,256
.	309-310
BANKS,C.A.	316
HENRY	295,300
BARBEE,LEE J.	332
BARBOUR,JAMES	37
BARNES,	357
. C.J.	318
. C.O.	331
. FLORENCE	327
. J.G.	331
. JOHN	191,203
. JOSEPH G.	326,328
. MARIAN	116
. ROBERT	258,312
. RUSH	327
. WILLIAM	208,236,242
.	261,382,433
BARNET,ANNA	85
. ARCHABLE	64
. JAMES	73
. MARRY	125
. NELLY	106
BARNETT,ARCHIBALD	148
.	308
. CATHERINE	129
. JAMES	148
. JOHN H.	144
. JOSEPH	90
. LARISSA J.	144
. MARGARET BRUSTER	144
. MARY	137
. POLLEY	71
. POLLY	137,161
. RACHEL	151
. ROBERT H.	144
. SUSAN	108,139
. SUSANAH E.	163
. THOMAS	309
BARNS,GRACE	271
. JOHN	62,189,192,271
. MARY B.	122
. MATILDA	116
. NANCY W.	130
. ROBERT	171,175,250,271
. SUSAN	102
. WILLIAM	41,66,201-202
.	212,235,248,271,413
BARR,GEORGE	119
BARRET,THOMAS	291
BARRETT,ELIZABETH M.	144
. JAMES	256,293
. MARY	300
. NANCY	62
. POLLY	300
. ROBERT	71
. SALLY	97
. THOMAS	300,309
BARROTT,REBECCA M.	124
THOMAS	124
BARRUM,JOHN J.	85
BARTLETT,HENRY	97
BARTRUM,JOHN	51
BATEMAN,ELIZABETH	143
BATES,CHARLES	52
JESSE	130
BATTON,HENRY	19
BAUGH,ABRAM	80
BAUNNON,JESSE	78
BAYAN,REBECCA	76
BAYLEY,DAVID	83
. G.M.	332
. GEORDEN	105
. WILLIAM	66
BAYLOR,E.R.	311
. EDWARD R.	262
. ELDRED R.	362
. J.E.	332
. JOHN G.	144
. WILLIAM E.	322
BEAN,ELIZABETH P.	112
JAMES	19,298
BEARD,WILLIAM	21
BEAVERS,A.R.	329
. ADAM	243-244
. ALEXANDER	151,153
. AMIABLE	76
. ANDREW	115
. ARMENDY	116
. ELEXANDER	76
. JAMES	317
. JANE	141
. JOHN	69
. JOHN W.	317
. KATHARINE	116
. LUCY	317
. LYDIA	116,132
. M.J.	317
. MATTHIAS H.	134
. MOSES	64,208
. NANCY	98
. POLLY	69
. REBECCA	148,151
. ROBERT	151,163
. SALLY	116
. THOMAS	147
. WILLIAM	81
BECKELHEIMER,ABRAM	166
BECKEM,CHARLES	214
BECKLEHIMER,FRANCES	82
BEDNERS,ADAM	113
BEEL,M.F.	325
BEEMER,GUSTAVUS A.	115
BEEN,JESSEY	165
BEEVERS,NANCY	64

Index to Tazewell County, Virginia - Vol. #1

POLLY	64	. HARVEY	137	JOSEPH	23
BELCHA, PHEBE	68	. HENRY	109	BLACKWELL, BETSEY	56
BELCHE, DANIEL	308	. ISAAC	143	NANCY	57
. JOSEPH	214	. ISOM	82	BLAGG, JOHN	11,21
. PEGGEY	51	. JANE	89	BLAIR,	13
BELCHEE, HANNA	289	. JOHN	72	BLAKENSHIP, WILLIAM	251
. MARY	286-287	. JUDY	88	BLANENSHIP, JOHN	78
. ROBERT	286-287,294	. LEWIS	93,115	BLANGY, ISAAC	24
. WILLIAM	289	. MILLEY	88	BLANKENSHIP, ARTHUR	294
BELCHER, ANDREW	151	. NANCY	68,152	.	297,304
. ASE	275	. OBADIAH	150,155	. BECA	135
. BARTLEY	102	. POLLY	80	. BETSY	54,97
. BENJAMIN	111	. RHODA	127	. CHARLOTE	117
. DAVID	271	. ROBERT	96	. CLINTON	156
. ELIZABETH	151,271	. TOBIAS	126	. CONDLY	141
. HENRY	97,275	BELSHEY, SAMUEL	172	. CONLEY	158
. ISOME	275	BENGOT, JOSHUA	157	. CONLY	150
. JAMES	275,413	BENHAM, ISAAC	248	. DANIEL	115
. JANE LOCKHART	273	. ISAAC M.	246,360	. EDWARD	109
. JESSE	58,68	. TEMPERANCE	87	. ELEANOR	114
. JOHN 57,60,178,180,183		BENJAM, ISAAC M.	262	. ELENDER G.	98
.	185,188,275	BENOURS, CATY	86	. ELI	54
. JOHN L.	315	BENTON, JOHN	24	. ELIJAH	97
. JOHNATHAN	275	TITUS	24	. ELIZABETH	135
. JOSEPH	271,411	BERRY, WILLIAM	50	. EVELINE	142
. JOSHUA	271	BETELLE, C.G.	315	. HENRY	61
. JUDE	275	BETS, JOHN	23	. HEZEKIAH	57,105
. LIZABETH	70	BEUS, WILLIAM	19	. HIRAM	142
. MARTHA	108,151	BEVERLY, HANNAH	56	. JANE	94
. MARY	271	BEVERS, JAMES W.	147	. JOHN	147
. MARY ANN	97	WILLIAM	57	. JOHN M.	135
. MICAGA	275	BICKLEY,	6,420-421,443	. JONATHAN E.	121
. MOSES	102,275,310	G.W.L.	361	. JOSEPH	114
. NANCY	70,275	BILETER, EDWARD	85	. KIAH	118
. OBADIAH	313	BILITER, CHARLES	105	. LAIRSINDA	147
. OBEDIAH	275	BILLE, WILLIAM WALKER	149	. LUCY	53
. PHEBE	56,275	BILLIPS, ELIZABETH	105	. LUSINDA	79
. PHEBY	271	. GUS	323	. MAHALA	93
. RICHARD	271	. HARRIET	157	. MAHALEY	93
. ROBERT 70,271,275,411		. J.T.	323	. MARTHA	99,128
. SALLY BROWN	246	. JAMESON RICHARD	57	. MARY	125
. THOMAS	271	. REBECCA	93	. MILLY	54
. WILLIAM	105	BILLUPS, HEZEKIAH	127	. MOLLEY	51
. Z.	312	. JANE	115	. NANCY	109,151
. ZECHARIAH	301	. JOHN	126	. NATHAN	127
BELCHEY, THOMAS	304	. MARTHA	137	. OBADIAH	132
BELCHY, EMILY	134	BIRCHFIELD, NOAH	155	. PEGGY	142,150
BELL, DAVID	140,320	BIRD,	7,11	. POLLY	130,149,155
. ISAAC	82	BIRK, THOMAS	108	. PRESBY	106
. JAMES	153	BISHOP, CATHERINE	78	. PURLINA	164,166
. JENNIE	322	. DAVID	50,103	. RACHEL	49,137
. JOHN	12	. ELIZABETH	128,162	. RALPH	294,302
. SAMUEL	153	. GEORGE	114	. RAWLEY	97
. THOMAS	209	. JOHN	86	. REBECCAH	119
. WILLIAM	22	. JOSEPH	143	. RUTH	108
BELSHA, SHAN	281	. LARKIN	73,78	. SALLY	114
BELSHE, DAVID	51	. MARY	124,145	. STEPHEN	49
. JOHN	193	. MARY JANE	109	. TOLBERT	68
. RICHARD	80,89	. REBECCA	77	. W.J.	332
BELSHEE, ROBERT	295	. RUTH	94	. WILLIAM	53,70,117
BELSHER, ANDERSON	126	BLACK WOLF,	420	.	310-311
. ELIZA	152	BLACK, JOHN	18	. WILLIS	138

Index to Tazewell County, Virginia - Vol. #1

BLANKNSHIP,ELIZABETH 135	JAMES 109	. VIRGINIA 166
BLANKSHIP,NATHN 127	BOSTICK,ANNE 66	BOWNE,GEORGE W.G. 122
BLEAD,DOROTHY EVANS 271	. JAMES 89,98	BOX,BENJAMIN 251
BLEDSOE,ANTHONY 12,22	. JANE 68	BOYD,ALEXANDER 294
BOGLE,DUNN 213	. SARAH 58	. EDWARD 217
. E.R. 312	BOSWELL,GEORGE 324	. L.D. 326
. H.R. 382	BOTTIMORE,W.G. 321	. LEAH 294
. HAMILTON R. 113,249	BOUGH,MICHAEL 156	. ROBERT C. 139
. 251-252,254-258	BOURNE,FELIX 320,329	. SUSANNA 66
. JOHN 108,143	. J.C. 329	. SUSANNAH 68
. MARGARET 144	. JAMES 256	BOYL,JOHN 69
. MARK 213	. LUCINDA M. 320	POLLY 69
. MARK R. 158,251,308	. LULA 320	BRADSHAW,JOHN 344
. POLLY 213	. STEPHEN 320	BRECKINRIDGE,
. RACHEL 213	. T.M. 320	. ALEXANDER 23
. RACHEL ANN 158	BOWAN,REBECKAH 86	. GEORGE 23
BOIL,ELIZABETH 145	BOWEN, 387	. ROBERT 23
BOILES,JOHN 71	. ELIZABETH 64,275	BREEDEN,SYNDESTY 121
BOILS,WILLIAM 64	. ELLA 298	BREEDING,ALFRED H. 138
BOLAND,ELEANER 123	. ELLEN 283	. JOHN 255,262
. JAMES B. 139	. ELLEN E. 112	. NANCY 142
. JANE 123	. GRATT M. 332	. PRISCILLA 138
. JARRAT 86	. H. 302	. STACY 138
. JICY 145	. H.S. 357	BRENIGER,T.B. 332
. JORDAN E. 104	. HENRY 39,42,168-170	BREWSTER,EBB 238
. JOSEPH 170	. 178-183,185-186,191	. EBENEZER 173,252,395
. LAVICA 138	. 193,235,242-244,258	. ELIZABETH 94
. LYNSA 68	. 261,263-265,271,276	. GEORGE F. 326
. POLLEY H. 83	. 283,286,292,297-298	. JAMES 165,247
BOLEN,GEORGE W. 121	. 300,328,413	. PATSY 326
. HENRY H. 98	. HENRY E. 258	. REBECCA 99
. HIRAM 70	. HENRY S. 310,312	. REKATA J. 154
. JARED W. 92	. HENRYAM 211	. THOMAS 171,198,203,274
BOLIN,DAVID 121	. JEAN C. 58	. 411
. HENRY 53	. JOHN 170,292	. WILLIAM 93
. JARED 234	. LEVICIE 49,275	BRIGHT,GEORGE 18
BOLING,BALAM 59	. LEVICY 70	TOBIAS 18
. CATHERINE 130	. LEVISA 170	BRISON,AMANDA E. 159
. ELIZABETH 51	. LEVISE S. 61	BRISTO,JOHN 302
. JARRED 110	. LILLY 66,275	BRISTOW,ELIZABETH 294
. JORDAN W. 138	. LOUISA 283	. ISAAC 170,298
. LINDSAY B. 139	. MARY 150,155	. JAMES 294
. LINNEY 100	. MARY JANE 156	. JOHN 301
. NANCY 57	. NANCY 292	. MARGARET 298,301
. WILLIAM 51,303	. REBECCA 275	BRITTAIN,RUFUS 160,313
BOLLAND,ELIZABETH 114	. REES 79,172,175,177	372,385
. JANE 114	. 275,283,344,355,357	BRITTIAN,H.P. 333
. JANE G. 104	. 410,412	BRITTS,ADAM 307
BOLLEN,JANEY 48	. REES T. 99,256,258,275	BRNET, 195
BOLLING,MELINDA 133	. 355,357,360,382,387	BROADHEAD, 230
BONHAM,HEZEKIAH 208	. REESE 265	BROCKENBOROUGH, 381
. NEH. 50	. THOMAS 208	BROCKENBROUGH,W. 264
. NEHEMIAH 50,52-53,55	BOWERS,PATTERSON 150,155	WILLIAM 263
. 71,79,209-210,298	BOWLAND,POLLY 49	BRONE,GEORGE W. 137
. RACHEL 298	BOWLES,EDWARD A. 137	BROOKE,ROBERT 37
BOONE, 7,26-28	BOWLING,GEORGE 321	BROOKS,ANGELINE 142
. DANIEL 27-28,358	. HENRY P. 130	. ANN 279
. SQUIRE 28	. JARED 295	. ANNA 246
BORDERS,CATY 298	. JARRET 412	. BETSEY 49
JOHN 298	. SARAH 145	. ELENOR 164
BOSANG, 361	BOWMAN,DANIEL 85	. ELIZABETH 246
BOSTIC,ISAAC 413	. ROBERT W. 316	. ELIZABETH JANE 139

Index to Tazewell County, Virginia - Vol. #1

. JAMES   66,246,279,413
. JANE   64,145
. JANE WHITLEY   271
. JINNEY WHITLEY   272
. JOHN   67,75,246,279,288
.   304
. JOHN B.   160
. LEVICIE   68
. LEVICY   66
. LOUISE   246
. MARGARET   79,246,279
. NANCY   53,79,246,279
. PEGGY   304
. POLLY   246,279
. RICHARD   100,176,178
.   181,246,265,279,288
.   304
. ROBERT   110
. SALLY   100,135,246
. SARAH   51
. THOMAS   98,246,279
. THOMAS J.   145
. WILLIAM 89,123,171,173
.   184,245-246,263,279
BROOMFIELD,   431
BROTHERTON,F.F.   320
BROWN,   420,425
. A.A.   317
. ABIGAIL   85
. ADMUEL   19
. ANDREW   208-210,279
. ANDREW D.   246
. ANDREW L.   140
. ANN   85,272
. BATHSHEBA   118
. BETSEY   68
. C.C.   330
. C.E.   318
. C.M.   328
. CATY   67
. CINTHY   279
. CORNELIAS   58
. COSBY T.   100
. CYNTHIA   76,246
. E.G.   320
. ELENOR   113
. ELIZABETH 113,156,246
.   272,279
. ESTHER   272,286,293
. F.J.   328
. G.H.   325
. GEORGE   198,203,279
. GEORGE B.   246
. GEORGE D.   86
. GEORGE W.   313
. GEORGE W.G.   112,114
.   235
. GRANGER   308
. H.C.   331
. H.Y.   331
. HENRY   19
. ISAAC   49,175,180-182

.   187,198,212,246,261
.   263-265,302,306
. J.A.   313
. J.O.   328,331
. J.R.G.   328
. JACOB   18,92
. JAMEES   168
. JAMES   130,171,272,286
.   293,302
. JAMES A.   148
. JAMES E.   201,265
. JAMES M.   150
. JAMES P.   313
. JAMES W.   155
. JANE   91,246,279,302
. JANE A.   124
. JANE PEERY   298
. JEREMIAH   135
. JOHN   49,188,192,197
.   203,246,257,272,280
.   303
. JOHN A.   114,254,322
. JOHN M.   113,162
. JOHN N.   311
. JOHN R.   139,311
. JOHN W.   320
. JOSEPH   68,78,246,279
. JOSEPH C.   257,311
. JULIA A.W.   144
. KATY   272
. L.W.   290
. LARRISSA   81
. LOW   68,97,220-221
.   245-246,279,288,290
.   297-298,302,412
. LYDIA ANNIS   105
. LYDIA E.   163
. M.F.   317
. M.I.   151
. MARGARET   49,272
. MARIAH   99
. MARTHA   246,280
. MARY   94,272,296,317
.   331
. NANCY   113
. NANNIE E.   331
. O.M.   328
. POLLY   48,94,246,270
.   280
. POLLY A.   150
. R.J.   314
. REBECAH   52
. REBECCA   163,272
. RHODA   147
. SALLY   72,103,246
. SARA   128
. SARAH   58,272,279
. THOMAS   57,187-188,198
.   210,213,272,311,317
. WILLIAM   67,85,180-181
.   185-186,233,246,251
.   255,262,270,272,280

.   296,306-307,310
. WILLIAM B.   151
. WILLIAM P.   322
. WILLIAM W.   143,174
. ZARILDA   328
BROWNE,G.W.G.   361-362
.   385
. GEORGE   122
. GEORGE W.G   128
. GEORGE W.G.   102,108
.   111,115-117,119-120
.   121,123,125-127,131
.   132-133,135-138,140
.   141-145,147-150,152
.   153-155,159,161,167
.   235,241-242,248,252
.   257,307,309-310,360
. W.G.   237
BROWNING,HARIET   130
   RICHARD   52
BRUCE,H. ADDINGTON   27
. JAMES   71
. JOHN G.   158
. JOSHUA   79
. JOSHUAY   71
. JOSIAH   75
. NOAH   259,270
. NOAH B.   258
BRUGOT,DILLA   149
BRUMFIELD,POLLY   53
   SALLY   61
BRUSTER,ANDREW   163
. ARCHIBALD   82,309
. BENJAMIN   158
. BIRD   132
. BIRD L.   144
. DNANCY   145
. EBENESER   124
. EBENEZER   289,301-302
.   320
. HANNAH   59
. ISBEL   61
. JAMES   162
. JEAMES   64
. MARGARET   144
. MELINDA   149
. NANCY   55,103
. POLLY   121
. REBECCA   163
. SALLY   52
. SARAH   291,302
. THOMAS   59,64,178,291
.   302-303
. THOMAS G.   323
. THOMINAS   159
. WILLIAM   141
. ZILPHA   49
BRYAN,WILLIAM   12
BRYANS,WILLIAM   22
BUCHANAN,   354
. ALEXANDER   23
. ANN C.   102

Index to Tazewell County, Virginia - Vol. #1

. ANNIE	320	BUTT,B.R.	330	CARROLL,JAMES L.	320-321
. ARCHIBALD T.	144	. C.D.	323	. MARTHA G. PERRY	276
. EDWARD A.	320	. CELIA V.	324	. SAMUEL L.	322
. GEORGE W.	156	. CELIE V.	323	CARTER,	26
. HENRY	123	. CHARLES W.	323-324	. ADALINE	95
. J.E.	326	. GEORGE A.	322	. BETSEY	91,111
. JOHN	12,21-22,161	. MAGGIE A.	330	. CATHERINE	272,277
. NICHOLAS	23	BYARS,WILLIAM	38	. CEINCON	90
. ROBERT	23	BYLES,PAULINA	159	. CELIA	137
. SALLIE J.	329	BYRCHFIELD,NOAH	150	. CHARERIE	82
. W.A.	329	BYRD,	11-12,21	. CHARLES	24
. WILLIAM H.	129	CABELL,WILLIAM H.	37	. CYNTHIA	288
. WILLIAM P.	320	CAFFEE,CHARLE	101	. DALE	215
BUCHANNON,JAMES	92	CALAWAY,H.C.	333	. DANIEL	145,272,313
NANCY	92	CALFEE,JAMES	130,145,149	. DELILA	164
BUCHANON,POLLY	99		154,159-160	. DICKSON	129
BUCK,JOHN A.	328	CALHOUN,	17	. ELIZABETH	277
V. ALICE	328	. EZEKIEL	17-19	. ELIZABETH DAVIS	284
BUENTY,MATILDA	110	. GEORGE	18	. JAMES	277
BUFFALOW,ROBERT	324	. HAMES	17	. JEMAN	288
BULLY,ANDREW JACKSON	119	. JAMES	17-18	. JOEL	272
BURCHAM,IREDELL	128	. PATRICK	17-18	. JOHN	56,97,272
RUTH	136	. WILLIAM	17-18	. LETITIA ANN	126
BURCHET,MARY	82	CALLAWAY,RICHARD	28	. MARINDA	109
BURCHFIED,CHARITOTY	138	CALVERT,ELIZA ANN	166	. MATILDA	115,145
BURCHFIELD,CHARITY	138	CALWELL,SAMUEL	68	. NANCY	109,115,277
JOHN HENRY	137	CAMERON,DUNCAN	234,236	. POLLY	80,99
BURD,	12	. J.P.	332	. RANDOLPH	145
BUREN,JOHN J.	91-92	. JACOB	122	. REBECCA	78,277
BURGE,JOHN	133	. OLIVIA	332	. SALLY	92
BURGESS,EDWARD	411	CAMPBELL,ARTHUR	15-16,23	. SAMUEL	115,272,309
JOHN	48	.	38	. SIMON	272
BURK,	357-358	. AUDLEY	289-290	. SMITH	131
. JAMES	19,117,139	. C.	127	. THOMAS	38
. JOHN	298	. COLEMAN	127	. TRUMAN	288
. PEGGY	298	. DAVID	38,41	. WILLIAM	57
BURKE,ISAIAH J.	157	. EDWARD	38	. WILSON	130
WILLIAM	95	. JAMES	18-19,191,265	CARTMAL,	
BURKET,JACOB	156	. JAMES M.	172,176	NANCY CUMPTON	276
BURRASS,SOPHRINIA	133	. JOHN	23,175	CARTMILL,ELIZABETH	50
THOMAS	165	. MARY MAXWELL	274	. JAMES	298,300,412
BURRESS,DANIEL	80	. MAXWELL	274	. JENNY	53
WILLIAM	294	. ROBERT	23	. JOHN	172,177,288,298
BURRIS,THOMAS	179	. WILLIAM	190,231	.	301
WILLIAM	298	CANADA,RACHEL	163,165	. MARGARET	300
BURRISS,THOMAS	183	CANNEN,WILLIAM	88	. NANCY	305
BURTON,ANNE	106	CANTER,CYNTHIA	288	. SALLY	50
. CATY STUMP	278	TRUMAN	288	. THOMAS	48,177,288,301
. ELIAS	133	CAPERTON,ALLEN T.	39	.	304-305
. FIELDING	55	CARDWELL,ALBERT S.	333	CARVER,BETSEY	56
. JACOB	90	CARLOCK,CONRAD	20	. JAMES	163,165
. JOCAB	307	. DAVID	20	. MARY ANN	165
. SALLY	111	. FREDERICK	20	. MILY	101
. THOMAS	329	. GEORGE	20	. ROBIN	74
. W.L.	328,331	CARNAHAN,THOMAS S.	136	CASEY,SIMPSON	125
. WILLIAM	320		239,251,261	CASSADAY,THOMAS	68,193
BURUM,JOHN I.	87	CARPENTER,EMILY	162		265
. JOHN J.	215	JOHN C.	309	CASSADY,THOMAS	213-215
. JOYCE N.T.	84	CARR,	343-344	CASSELL,MARY	111
BUTCHER,JACOB	56	JOHN G.	127	CASSIDAY,BETSEY	77
BUTLER,	206,343-344	CARRANE,WILLIAM G.W.	90	THOMAS	188-189
WILLIAM	344	CARREL,JAMES P.	54	CASSIDY,THOMAS	186

Index to Tazewell County, Virginia - Vol. #1

CASTLE,	354-355	. WITTEN A.	148,251	. JOHN	105
JACOB	18,20-21	CECILL,DERINDA	71	. LAVISA	112
CATLET,THOMAS K.	214	. GEORGE	84	. LEVICA	147
CAVITTS,	317	. JOHN	175	. LILLY	161,165
CAWAN,DAVID	86	. LINNY	52	. LOUISEY	136
CECEL,RACHES	60	. ZACHARIAH	71	. M.T.	322
CECELL,ELIZABETH	71	CERAL,COSBY J.	123	. MASTEON	70
CECIL,	186	CERRIL,SAMUEL	70	. MASTIN	243-244,246
. AARON	316	CHAFFIN,CHRISTOPHER	193	. MOSES	64,234
. ANN	294	.	411	. NANCY	147
. BETSEY	52	. POLLY	62	. REBECCA	144
. CATHERINE M.	152	. RUTH	70	. RUTH	65
. DORIND C.	106	. THOMAS	54	. RUTHY	150,155
. ELIZABETH JANE	138	CHAFIN,BETSEY	56	. SAUSANIAH	136
. GEORGE	91	PEGGY	86	. SUSANAH	163
. GRANVILLE G.	144	CHALKLEY,	26	. SYNDIA	162
. J.	251	LYMAN	7	. THOMAS	85,102,137
. JAMES	170-171	CHALMERS,FANNY	152	. THOMAS C.	320
. JAMES M.	311	CHAMBERS,	199	. THOMAS S.	312
. JEREMIAH	144	. BENJAMIN	196	. WILLIAM	12,129
. JOHN	39-40,54,99	. THOMAS	181	CHRUM,HENRY	240
.	172-173,179-182,185	CHAMP,ELKANAH	115	PRISCILLA McGUIRE	240
.	188,193,208,211,214	CHAPEL,NANCY	99	CHURCH,THOMAS	158
.	217,233,236,248,261	CHAPMAN,	361-362	CIPERS,JOHN G.	129
.	264-265	. AUGUSTUS A.	39	CISEL,ANN ELIZA	68
. JOSHUA	49	. HENLEY	40,263	CISIL,HENRY W.	68
. JULIA A.	251	. HENLY	175	CLAFEE,JAMES	167
. JULIA ANN	139	. ISAAC	252	CLAINE,MICHAEL	18
. LINNA WITTEN	276	. ISAAC E.	360	CLARK,	412
. LOUISA M.	105	. JOHN	180,209	. BETSEY	61
. MARGARET	117	. M.	217	. DANIEL	61
. MARY	149,157	CHAPPELL,JAMES	104	. ELIZABETH	65
. MARY B.	162	SILAS	104	. FEDRICK	64
. MILES	317	CHAPPLE,GEORGE	100	. GEORGE B.	85,281
. MILLY	56	CHARLES,ANNA WYNN	273	. GEORGE ROGERS	221
. NANCY	57,223-225,228	. CATHERANER	126	. JANE	287
.	240,251,288,295	. ELIZABETH	158	. JEAN	298
. NANCY JANE	130	. G.W.	150	. JOSEPH	208,296
. PEGGY	93	. ISAAC	306	. JOSEPH M.	190
. PHILIP	68	. JAMES	57,59,64,67,70	. MARY	52
. RACHEL L.	136	.	73,75-77,80-81,85,88	. POLLY KINDRICK	275
. REBECCA	94	.	90,92,97,99,102,108	. REBECCA	425
. ROBERT M.	320	.	110,113,117,119	. WILLIAM	53,176,178,287
. RUSH F.	320	. JOHN	84	.	298,425
. RUSSELL F.	251	. LIDEY	154	. WILLIAM L.	156
. SALLY	61	CHARSTE,MARTE	150	CLARY,ELISHA	344
. SAMUEL	62,114,179,208	CHEATHAM,J.T.	327	CLAUGHTON,R.A.	143
.	210,214-215,248,251	JOHN	330	RICHARD A.	141
.	252	CHIDDIC,WILLIAM	97	CLAY,WILLIAM	102
. SAMUEL W.	139,144,251	CHIDDIX,JOHN	309	CLAYPOLE,JOSEPH	61
.	253,256	CHILDERS,FLEMMON	85	. MILES	106
. SARAH ANN	113	MARY ANN	129	. REBECCA	68
. THOMAS	54,308,310	CHISWELL,	22	CLAYPOOL,AMY	114
. W.P.	307	CHRISTIAN,A.M.	325	. CHARITY	282
. WILLIAM	171,173,192	. ADISON	144	. ELIZABETH	94,282
.	223-226,228-229,240	. ALEXANDER	140,312	. EPHRAIM	282
.	244,249,263-264,288	. ANTHONY	140	. HARVEY	113
.	291,293-295	. DANIEL	90,144,147,233	. JAMES	282
. WILLIAM C.	320	. DAVID	69	. JEREMIAH	282,289,292
. WILLIAM P.	248,313	. ELIJA	196	.	303
. WILLIAM S.	106	. ISRAEL	12,21	. JEREMIAH B.	282
. WITTEN	133,241,243,246	. J.W.	325	. JOHN W.	135

Index to Tazewell County, Virginia - Vol. #1

. MARY	292
. MARY BROWN	272
. MILES	282
. PHEBE	49
. SABINA	151
CLAYPOOLE, JEREMIAH	187
CLAYTON, MARY E.	153
SAMUEL A.	153
CLAYTOR, JAMES H.	160
. MARY E.	153
. SAMUEL A.	153
CLEAR, JAMES	116
CLERK, WILLIAM	106
CLEVENGER, JAMES	158
POLLY	78
CLEVINGER, LEVI	151
SUSANNAH	58
CLIBORNE, JAMES A.	142
CLINCH,	354-355
CLINE, HERENTEN	151
. JOHN	98,160
. MIKEL	118
. MITCHELL	119
. POLLY	98
CLOUD, PETER	23
CLOYD,	231
GORDON	300
CLYBURN, LENNEL	53
NANCY BROOKS	246,279
COALES, JULIUS	315
COBBLER,	380
COBBS, CHARLES	314
COBURN, LIZABETH	48
COCHRALL, SALLY	49
COCHRAN, J.M.	321
COCKE, WILLIAM	28
COLDWELL, ELIZABETH	148
JAMES	61
COLE, AUGUSTUS	112
. ELIZABETH	316
. JULIUS	315
. L.C.	319
. RHODA	316
. TIMOTHY	14,20
. WILLIAM	316
COLEMAN, ANN	81
. BETSEY	90
. CHARLOTTE	129
. HANNAH	93
. J.W.	315
. JAMES	161
. JANE	72
. JOHN	68
. PETER	119
. WILLIAM	88
COLLINS,	381
. EDWARD	243-244,262
. GEORGE	22
. HANNAH	54
. ISOM	252
. LOUISA	138
. LUCINDA	167
. MARGARET	150
. MARGRET	155
. RANDAL	103
. WILLIAM	142,163,165
COMB, SHADRACK	114
COMBS, LUISA	131
COMER, LAWRENCE	289-290
MARGARET	289
COMPTON, ANNA	87
. BENJAMIN W.	117
. CORNELIUS	109
. ELENOR	68
. ELISHA	89
. ELIZABETH	162
. ELIZABETH ROBINETT	280
. ELLENOR	291,295
. G.S.	322
. HIRAM	61
. HIRAM C.	136
. HUGH A.	105
. JAMES	114
. JAMES M.	118,251
.	255-256,262
. JOHN	51,173,184,287
.	291,293,295,298,300
. JOHN M.	239
. JOSEPH	95
. NANCY	48,119
. REBECCA	110
. REBECKA	287
. SARAH	68
. SQUIRE M.	93
. STEPHEN	111
. WILLIAM W.	68,119,212
CONALLY, PEGGY	95
CONLEY, JAMES	50,179,182
. JOHN	20
. LAYER	97
. R.B.	328
. ROBERT	145
CONNELLY, JAMES	411
CONTREL, JOHN	21
COOK, ADISON	315
. ALEXANDER	64
. ANDERSON	116
. CATHERINE	283
. ELIZABETH	95,277
. FRED	277
. FREDERICK	51,179
.	188-189,198,203,291
.	302
. GEORGE	247,277
. GORGE	247
. HARVILEY	107
. JOHN	239
. JOHN AUGUSTUS	70,203
. MARY	70
. NANCY	106,277
. THOMAS	277,308
. WILLIAM	150,157,277
. ZACHARIAH	277
COOKSEY,	182
. LEMASTER	296
. NANCY	296
COOPER, DEBBE	124
. FRANCIS	24
. LEWIS	118
. WILLIAM	130
COPENHAVER, HENRY	331
JACKSON	324
CORBIT, PEGGY	59
CORDELE, ISAM S.	139
CORDELL, JOSEPH	144
CORDER, EDWARD	288
. JOHN	69
. POLLY	64
CORDILL, SUSANNAH	98
CORDLE, REECE	332
COREL, ELIZABETH	83
JOSHUA	210
CORELL, JOSHUA	79
MARY ANN	160
CORLL, REBECAH	89
CORNET, HARVEY GEORGE	189
CORNWALLIS,	194,196,199
CORNWELL, WILLIAM	136
CORPLEY, MARY ANN	143
CORREL, BURDINE H.	73
CORRELL, MARY	92
COTHAN, MARY	94
COTTEREL, JOHN	411
SIMON	346,380
COTTON, BETSEY	58
COUDON, JAMES	12
COUNCE, MARTIN	20
COUSINS, JAMES C.	260
LOUISA	260
COVE, JAMES	20
COWAN, ANDREW	24
COWDEN, AMOS	145
COX, BENJAMIN	111,243-244
. JOHN	22
. WILLIAM	215,218,220
.	235,238,241,251,261
.	313,360,362,382
CRABTREE, CATHERINE	282
. ELIZABETH ANN	121
. GABRIAL	282
. GABRIEL	282,320
. JAMES	24
. JAMES B.	309,322
. JEMIMA SPRACHER	282
. MARTHA	107
. POLLY	282
. REES	113
. REES H.	282
. REESE	241
. REESE H.	309
. SARAH ANN	148
. THOMAS	82,86
. THOMAS B.	282
CRAFFORD, OLIVER	64
CRAIG,	20
. CHARLES	199

Index to Tazewell County, Virginia - Vol. #1

. JOHN	11,21
. SAMUEL	196,199
CRANFORCES,CHARLES	281
CRAVEN,JOHN	344,357
CRAWFORD,	380,418
. CHRISTOPHER Q.	98
. JAMES M.	112
CRAYS,CHARLES	196
CREED,ELIZABETH	151
SHADRACK	323
CRESOP,	345
CRESSWELL,JOHN Y.	104
CRESWELL,ELIZABETH	85
. HENRY	188
. JOHN Y.	249
. JOHNY	249
CRISMOND,JOHN M.	114
CRISWELL,HENRY	189
CROCKEETT,JOHN	107
CROCKETT,	17,88,388,408
.	435
. ADDISON	42,209-210,220
.	234,236,241,247-248
.	249,255-256,274,279
.	312
. ALBERT	316
. ARAMINTA	279
. DOLLY	279
. E.K.	332
. ELEANOR	69
. ELIZA	311
. ELIZABETH	154
. ELIZABETH JANE	279
. ELLENOR	279
. FRANSIS	76
. GEORGE	320
. GEORGE P.	328,332
. GUSTAVUS R.	140,258
. HANNAH	73,279
. HANNAH PEERY	279
. HUGH	22
. JAMES R.	315
. JANE	76
. JEEN	279
. JOHN	48,54-55,57,59-61
	66,68-69-70,72,74,77
.	83,85-86,88-91,95,99
.	101,169,174,178,190
.	191-192,197,210,213
.	216-219,221,233,237
.	242,247,263-265,274
.	279,289,294,303,411
. JOHN C.	279
. JOSEPH	19,22
. JULIA	279
. JULIA A.	123
. LAVISA	279
. MADISON S.	257
. MARGARET	279
. MARGARET E.	118
. MARIA	65,279
. MARIA LETITIA	150,155
. MARY	156
. NANCY	319
. POLLY	75,77
. ROBERT	22,161,274,279
.	311,410,434
. ROBERT G.	156
. RUFUS	274,279
. RUFUS K.	108
. RUSH F.	319
. SAMUEL	279,316
. SAMUEL C.	258
. SIMON	305
. STUART	316
. THOMAS G.	319
. THOMPSON A.	136
. TILLMAN	210
. TILMAN	208,279
. VIRGINIA	150,155
. WALTER	38,222,224
.	226-229
CROEL,REBECCA ANN	113
CRON,JOHN	59
CROSS,MARTHA	119
CROUCH,L.W.	148
CROW,ELECY	107
. HANNAH	303
. JOHN	57,59,291,303
CRUM,HENRY	240
PRISCILLA McGUIRE	240
CRUNK,JOHN	14
CRUTCHFIELD,W.J.	362
WILLIAM J.	259,361
CUBB,	24
CUMMINGS,GEORGE	53
.	194-195
. JANE	110
. JOHN	59
. NANCY	115
. WILLIAM C.	88
CUMMINS,JANE	49
CUMPTON,ELEANOR	276
. ELIHU	276
. HICKMAN	55,276
. HIRAM	276
. JOHN	276
. JOSEPH	276
. NANCY	119,276
. REBECAH	57
. REBECCA	276
. SALLY	276
. WILLIAM	276
CUNDIFF,JULIA	163,165
CUNNINGHAM,G.C.	326
CUPPENHEFFER,JANE	131
CURDE,NANCY	114
CUREL,JOSHUA	208
CUREN,CATHERINE T.	107
CURL,LUVICEY	116
. MARGARET	116
. WILLIAM	54
CURLE,HENERY	106
CURREN,PEGGY WYNN	273
. WADDY T.	109,310
. WILLIAM G.W.	310
CURRIN,HUGH	51,272
. PEGGY WYNN	273
. WADDY T.	244,251-252
.	254,256
DABNEY,CHARLES	196
DAILE,SAMUEL C.	135
DAILEY,ISAAC	71,170,280
.	292
. ISAAC M.	313
. JAMES T.	134
. MADISON	144
. MARGARET	280
. MARGRET	58
. REBECCA	92
. SALLY	59
. SAMUEL	51
. THOMAS	58,305
DAILY,A.F.	312
. ISAAC M.	312
. MARGARET	312
DALTON,ALLEN	103
DALY,ELNOR	106
DANDRIDGE,	
. ALEXANDER -	
.	SPOTTSWOOD 28
DANEL,REBECCA	48
DANIEL,DEXTER B.	316
. JOHN W.	316
. NANCY	49,292
. SARAH	294
. WYETT	294
DANIELS,GEORGE	150,155
MANVILLE	150,155
DANOY,IRENE	127
DARRSET,HENRY	101
DARTER,ANNE	294
HENRY	288,294
DAUGHERTY,THOMPSON	86
WILLIAM H.	161
DAUGHTRY,JOSIAH B.	75
DAVAS,THOMAS	81
DAVIDSON,	10,425
. ANDREW	172-173,177,296
.	298,431-432
. BETSY	303
. CALEB	68
. GEORGE	50,172,177
.	179-180,297-298,300
. HENRY	186-187,190-191
.	208-209,234,284
. HENRY P.	212,214-215
.	217
. J.R.	328
. JAMES	208,284
. JAMES C.	41,199,201
.	209,211,233,251,259
.	261,309
. JANE	284
. JANE G.	69
. JEAN	300

Index to Tazewell County, Virginia - Vol. #1

- JENNIE 297-298
- JENNY 300,303
- JOHN 62,172,174,177
- 190,193,197,200,211
- 212-213,240,261,275
- 284,297-298,413,438
- JOSEPH 168,171-172,179
- 185,189,192-193,196
- 197-199,211-212,261
- 264-265,284,287,297
- 298,303,321
- JULIA ANN 93
- JULIA H. 309
- MARTHA 284
- MATILDA 284,298
- MATILDA J. 163
- MATILDA P. 104
- MATILDA S. 165
- MATTEY 53
- MILLINDE 303
- NANCY 127,284
- PEGGY 303
- PHEBE 300,304-305
- PHEBY HARMAN 273
- POLLY 53,99,297-298
- . 303
- POLLY HARMAN 281
- REBECCA 432
- ROBERT 73,284
- ROBERT W. 309
- SALLY 296,298
- SAMUEL 284
- SAMUEL P. 213,218,220
- 254,257,259,261
- TABITHA WITTEN 247
- WILLIAM 51,191,210,284
- 297-298,300,303-304
- 305
- WILLIAM G. 101

DAVIS, 196,199,205
- A.L. 325
- ABRAHAM 173,176,286
- 288,291,293
- ABRAM 264
- AZARIAH 28
- CATY 51,57
- DORINDA 162
- ELEANOR 51
- ELENDA 101
- ELIZA 75
- ELIZABETH 48,148-149
- 155,284
- JAMES 20,23,256,274
- JAMES C. 201
- JAMES L. 284
- JESSE 98
- JOEL 90
- JOHN 18,176,180,184
- 264-265,288,294,300
- 301
- JONATHAN 177
- JOSEPH 284

- JULIA A. 323
- KATHERINE 284
- KISSY 158
- LOUISA HARMAN 274
- MARGARET 284
- MARTHA JANE 121
- MORGAN 132
- MOSES 67,113
- NANCY 288
- PEGGY 300
- POLLEY 51
- POLLY ANN 284
- POLLY LAIRD 277,284
- PRESLY 49
- REBECCA C. 317,325
- REBECCA D. 284
- REES 112
- REESE 144
- ROBERT 23
- RUTH 69
- SIMON 76
- SQUIRE 147
- THOMAS 110,210,213,242
- 248,259,262,277,309
- W.P. 323
- WILBURN 284
- WILLIAM 23,57,156,173
- 188,204,265,284,300
- WILLIAM A. 323

DAWSON, 441
- HELEN 115
- JOHN 60

DAY,BETSEY 55
- CHRISTENA 60
- CHRISTINA 278
- DANIEL 50,278
- EDY 99,103,278
- ELIZABETH 84
- HAMES 269
- ISABELLA 278
- JAMES 97,198,203,278
- 287,289
- JANE 131
- JOHN 176-177,179,182
- 231
- JOSHUA 115,175,184,215
- 269,295
- LAVINIA 115
- LUCINDA 100
- LUCY 278
- MALINDA 278
- MARGARET 269
- MARGARET MARTIN 269
- MARTHA 89,91
- MARY 81,289
- PEGGY 88
- PETER 52,269
- POLLY 68,128
- REBECCA 51,97-98,269
- RHODA 77,105
- SOLOMON W. 115
- TRAVIS 269

- WILLIAM 73,181,185
- 187-189,304
DAYLEY,CHARLES 59
DEAL,JOSHUA 108
- RICHARD 102
- SINTHY 108
DEAN,NANCY E. 150,155
DEATON,C.A. 320
- MARIA E. 157
DEAVOR,WILLIAM 154
DEBAIS,HENRY 194
DEEL,CATHARNE 117
- CONLEY 132
- ELIZABETH 122
- JOSHUA 138
- THOMAS 112
- WALKER 334
DEESKINS,STEPHEN 204
DEIGS,THOMAS 21
DESKINS, 354,359,397
- ANNIE 296
- BERDINE 113
- BIRDINE 309
- CATHERINE 112,139
- CHRISTENER 94
- CHRISTOPHER 139
- DANIEL 53
- ELIZABETH 82
- G.W. 317
- GEORGE 112,309
- GEORGE W. 123,249,257
- 259
- HARVEY 129,210
- HENRY 121
- HERVEY 41,203,209
- JACOB 120
- JAMES 109,125,309
- JEFFERSON 93
- JOHN 58,109,189,192
- 271,290,296,345
- LILLE 147
- LILLY 76
- LUCINDA 108
- MARGARET 145,296,300
- 309
- MARY 271,290
- MARY JANE 139
- MUNCY 105
- NANCY 99
- POLLY 64,96
- REBECCA 89
- SALLY 49
- SARAH 50
- SMITH 96,173,271,290
- 296,300,306
- STEPHEN 48,184,210,214
- 271,287,290,296,305
- WASHINGTON 109
- WILLIAM 67,89
DEVOR,JAMES 213
- MARGARET 213
DIALS, 436-437

Index to Tazewell County, Virginia - Vol. #1

. ANDREW	180	DOAK,	380	. REES B.	66
. POLLEY	180	. G.W.	318	. SAMUEL	292
DICKENSON,JAMES C.	149	. JAMES	196	DUMBAR,EPHRAIM	57
DICKERSON,HENRY	38	. JAMES R.	361	DUN,CHRISTINA	269
. JOSHUA	294	. JENNY	51	DUNBAR,EPHRAIM	204,207
. ROBERT	324	. LYDIA THOMPSON	274		211,261
. SUSANNA	294	. MARY	125	DUNBARR,EPHRAM	59
DICKESON,WILLIAM	73	. RACHEL THOMPSON	274	DUNCAN,CHAPMAN	131
DICKINSON,BENJAMINE	315	.	287	LANDON	70
. CATHERINE	315	. ROBERT	49,263,287	DUNN,A.J.	362
. J.	321	. ROSE A.	318	. JOHN	213
DIE,JANE	141	. SENIA	83	. MARY	213
DIEL,RACHEL	97	DOAKE,ELIZABETH	64	. THOMAS	213
DILION,SAMUEL W.	153	DODD,RICHARD	21	. W.W.	362
TEMPY	153	DODDRIDGE,	391-392,394	. WILLIAM W.	152
DILL,JOHN	19	DODDS,GEORGE	314	DYER,COLVIN F.	118
PETER	19	DOKE,LYDIA	73	DYSART,JAMES	24
DILLION,CHRISTOPHER	60	POLLY	96	DeBIEDMA,	407
. ELIZABETH	68	DOLLY	157	DeHASS,	340,355,410
. HERVEY E.	259	DOLSBERRY,LYLES	412	DeSOTE,HERNANDO	408
. HERVEY G.	256	DOLSBERY,S.	258	DeTONTY,	407
. JANE	313	DOLSBURY,CATHERINE	283	EAKINS,GEORGE	59
. JESSE	82	LILES	283	EARLEY,CHARLEY	260
. MARTHA	72	DOLTON,ALLEN	145	JEREMIAH	413
. MASTEN	91	. REBECCA	93	EARLY,MORDECAI	19
. NATHANIEL	313	. WILLIAM	87	EARNHART,POLLY	78
. POLLY	69	DONAHY,JOHN	18	EARNHEART,JOSH	87
. REBECCA	93,137	DONALDSON,	424	EASLEY,CHARLEY	260
. ROLIN	61	DONALSON,	230	ECHE,D.C.	72
. SAMUEL	62	DONELSON,	9	EDDE,ELIZABETH	291
DILLS,ALEX	321	DONNAHUE,C.N.	329	JOHN	287,291
. BENJAMINE ROBBINS	275	DOSSON,JOSEPH H.	108	EDEA,	
. EILLIAM	280	DOUGHERTY,GILES	96	ELIZABETH HARRISON	273
. ELIZABETH	82	. HENRY	24	EDMANSON,	229
. EVALINA	298	. ISAAC K.	152	EDMONDS,PRESTON	90
. GRESSA	275	. J.B.	76	EDMONSON,ANDREW	58
. HENRY	217,275	. JOHN	75	EDWARD,ORPHEY WYNNE	272
. HENRY W.	93,249	. JOHN S.	120	EHEART,ABRAHAM	172
. J.T.	325	. MICHAEL	229	EILER,JOHN	309
. JAMES	99	DOUGLAS,GEORGE	327	REBECCA	309
. JOHN	275	. JAMES	28	EKIN,GEORGE	119
. LYDIA	86,275	. MARGARET	304	ELETT,ELIJAH	96
. MARGARET	96	DOWNING,JOHN	19	ELKINS,ARCHABALD	57
. MARY	50	DRAKE,CELIA	124	. DICEY	51
. NANCY HARMAN	280	. GEORGE	97	. HANNAH	75
. PEGGY	275	. JOSEPH	25	. RACHEL	302
. PETER	50,175-176,184	. MARGARET	94	. ZACHARIAH	302
.	207,243,251,254,275	. MARY	80	ELLETT,E.J.	332
.	288	. RACHEL	86	ELLIOT,	422
. PETER H.	141,251	. ROBERT M.	139	JOHN	164
. REBECCA	48,73,275,288	. SAMUEL	96	ELLIS,POWELL	317
. REBECKY	298	DRAPER,	20,428-429	ROBERT L.	333
. REBEKAH	68	. GEORGE	18,427	ELPHISTONE,FREDERICK	21
. SUSANNA	275	. JOHN	12	ELSWICK,BASIL	151
. WILLIAM	51,97,173,208	. JOSEPH	203,235,267	. BAZEWELL	313
.	215,217-218,265,275	DREW,NEWETT	294	. BIRD	313
.	288	SARAH	294	. CHAPMAN	313
. WILLIAM P.	148	DUDLEY,D.W.	316,326	. ELIZA J.	159
DINGUS,CHARLES	314	. HUGH D.	308	. HENDERSON	143
DINWIDDIE,	355	. J.F.	328,331	. ISAAC	164
DOACK,ROBERT	23	DUFF,ELIZABETH I.	110	. JOHN	160
WILLIAM	23	. REBECKA	292	. JOHN W.	128

Index to Tazewell County, Virginia - Vol. #1

. JOSIAH	162	
. LUSY	160	
. NANCY	124	
. SAREY	128	
. WILLIAM	108-109	
. WINNY GIVEN	160	
EMSHWILER, ISAAC	145	
ENGLEDOVE, JOHN	294	
ROBERT	294	
ENGLISH,	9,20,438	
. MATTHEW	18	
. THOMAS	18,344,437	
. WILLIAM	14,18	
EPPERHEART, HENRY	60	
ERVIN, MARY HARRISON	273	
ERWIN,	202	
ESLWICK, JOHN W.	128	
ESSEX, MARGARET	291	
ESTEP, WILLIAM	128	
ESTEPT, SAMSON	127	
ESTESS, LUCINDA	103	
URIAH	103	
ESTHAM, FRANCIS	19	
ESTILL, B.	268	
. BENJAMINE	265	
. JOHN M.	361	
EVANS,	415	
. DANIEL	416-418	
. DAVID	271	
. DOROTHY	271	
. ELIZABETH	298	
. JAMES	271,290,293,298	
. JANE T.	133	
. JERETA	271	
. JESSE	221,344,414,417	
. JOHN	194-196,287,289	
.	293,301-302,411,414	
.	418	
. MARK	19	
. MARTHA	271,424,426	
. MARY	271,416	
. MOSES	271,290,293,298	
. PETER	21	
. ROBERT	271,290,293,298	
.	416-418	
. SAMP	21	
. THOMAS	271,293,424	
. URIAH	19	
. WILLIAM	271,290,293	
EWING, SAMUEL	301,305	
FANNAN, JANE	52	
FANNON, ACLES	70	
DAVID	180	
FARLEY, BETSY	298	
JESSEE	298	
FARMER, W.P.	329	
FARRAR, JACOB	104	
FERABY, ISAAC	160	
FERGERSON, GREENVILLE	145	
FERGUSON,	169	
. HENRY	21	
. JOHN	286	
. MARGARET	286	
. MARY	286,291,294	
. NANCY	292	
. SAMUEL	168,170,173,286	
.	290-292,294,344,412	
. THOMAS	48,172,175,292	
. WILLIAM	176,291	
FERRELL, RICHARD	321	
FERRIMER, H.J.	327	
FICKLE, BETSY	213	
. MARY	213	
. THOMAS	213	
FIELDS, ELIZABETH	147	
. JAMES J.	332	
. MARTHA	144	
. SAMUEL	132	
. TILMAN	159	
. WESLEY	93	
FILES, HENRY	112	
FISHBACK, JACOB T.	265	
FISHER, HENRY J.	267	
FITZGEREL, WILLIAM	24	
FLEMING, DAVID	216	
FLEMMER, WILLIAM	79	
FLETCHER, AARON	292	
. ARON	184	
. DANIEL	81	
. ELIZABETH	82	
. MILAM	72	
. POLLY	106	
. POLLY ANN DAVIS	284	
. RACHEL	163,165	
. RHODA	154	
. WILLIAM	184	
FLOYD, BEN RUSH	285	
. BENJAMIN R.	237	
. GEORGE	285	
. GEORGE R.C.	245,248	
.	262	
. JOHN	38,285	
. JOHN B.	235,244	
.	246-247	
. JOHN BUCHANAN	38	
. LAVALETTE	285	
. LETITIA	285	
. NICKETTI	285	
. NICKETTI B.	131	
. WILLIAM	285	
FLUMMER, ELENOR	77	
. ELIZABETH	85,281	
. ELLEANOR	75	
. J.H.	320	
. NANCY	89,281	
. SAMUEL	281,300,306	
. SOLOMON	281	
. WILLIAM	281	
FOGLESON, CHRISLEY	83	
FOLIO, THOMAS DUNN	106	
FOLLEN, PATTEY	57	
FOLLING, SARAH	58	
FOREMAN, JOHN	20	
FORESTER, JOHN	107	
FORGERSON, MARY ANN	100	
FORGUSON, ISABELLA	380	
SAMUEL	380	
FORTNER, HARDY	80	
. NANCY	57	
. SALLY	74	
. TEMPERANCE	68	
. VIOLET	103	
FOSTER, EDWARD	327	
. GIDEON	300	
. HAMPTON	68,269	
. JEMIMA	269	
. JOHN	213	
. JULIA	327	
FOWLER, DAVID S.	319	
. GIDEON	288	
. I.C.	311	
. ISAAC C.	312	
. ROBERT	24	
. THOMAS	220	
FOX, BARBARY	277	
. D.T.	107	
. DAVID S.	277	
. EDWARD	380	
. ELIZABETH	277	
. JOHN	325	
. KATHERINE	93	
. MALINDY	277	
. MARGARET	122	
. MATHIAS	137,277,301	
. PEGGY ANA	277	
. PETER	76,277	
. SALLY	88,90,277	
FRANCISCO, CATY	57	
. JACOB	264,302	
. JAMES	113	
. NANCY	76	
. PEGGY	53	
FRANKLIN, LAODICIAN	75	
. LAVISA CROCKETT	279	
. PEGGY STUMP	278	
. PLEASANT	112,413	
. THOMAS	75,77	
. THOMAS H.	119	
. TILMAN	110	
. WILLIAM	155	
FREEMAN, JAMES M.	116	
FRENCH, ANDREW L.	97	
. CATHERINE CARTER	277	
. CHARLES	78	
. DAVID	263	
. ELIZABETH	166	
. EZEKIEL	82	
. GEORGE	333	
. ISAAC	77	
. JAMES	88	
. JAMES S.	147	
. JOHN B.	133	
. LEVICY LAMBERT	278	
. REBECCA CARTER	277	
. WILLIAM	278	
FROE, CHRESHIRE	322	

Index to Tazewell County, Virginia - Vol. #1

FRUGATE, JAMES 287	. HENRY P. 41,65,187,197	. DANIEL H. 142,259
FUDGE, 314	. 209	. ELENDER 96
. C.A. 318-319,323,325	. HERVEY 42-43,196,198	. EMILY 152
. M.G. 318-319,323,325	. 200-201,203,217,235	. EMMERINE V. 115
. NANCY N. HARMAN 281	. 238,247-248,250,253	. GEORGE W. 315,329,333
. REUBEN C. 243-244,256	. 254,307,312	. HENRY 70,96,198,203
. 258	. JANE M. 127	. 208,254,257-258
. REUBEN S. 90	. JENNY 185,303	. HENRY H. 97
FUGATE, FRANCIS 24	. JOHN 185	. J. SAM 326
FULCHER, LEVI F. 164	. JOHN B. 38,40-41	. J.H. 317
FULK, RALPH 52	. 186-189,198,207,212	. JAMES H. 320
FULKS, PRISCELLA 51	. 215,248-249,252,260	. JAMES M. 110
FULLER, G.B. 317	. 261,265,359-360,381	. JOHN 54,110,188,193
STEPHEN 106	. LAURA J. 147	. 207,212,214
FULTON, ANDREW S. 242	. MARTHA C. 76	. JOHN B. 119,198,207
. JAMES O. 314	. MARY A. 81	. 215,217,236
. JOHN H. 41,267	. PATTON 194	. JOHN C. 136,253
. WILLIAM M. 214	. POLLY 215	. JOHN W. 250,252,257
FURGISON, ELIZABETH 143	. R.B. 316	. 259,316
GAMBLE, JOSIAH 23	. SALLIE 307	. LEVISA B. 123
GARDNER, A.C. 322	. THOMAS I. 198-199	. LISEY 89
GARLOCK, CONRAD 20	. 208-209,212-213,215	. LORENZO D. 215,236
. DAVID 20	. THOMAS J. 41,237	. LOUISE 138
. FREDERIC 20	. WILIAM 125	. MARGARET 79,107,162
. GEORGE 20	. WILLIAM 169,171-172	. 316
GARNETT, S.W. 315,328	. 174,177,287,290,293	. MARGRET 87,112
GARRATSON, REUBEN 82	. 294,297-298,303	. MARIA 112
GARRETSON, WILLIAM 94	. WILLIAM O. 123,254,312	. MARIA T. 153
GARRISON, JANE 303	. 429,436	. MARIAH PERRY 278
. PAUL 18	GIBBIT, JOHN 59	. MARY A. 140
. WILLIAM 171,184,303	GIBSON, CHARLES C. 71	. MARY F. 159
. 344,357	. ELIZABETH 150,155	. MARY G. 332
GARRISSON, WILLIAM 54,170	. GEORGE 142,147,149,155	. MARY HARRISON 276
GARWOOD, NOAH 20	. 158,160,164,166,257	. NANCY 118
OBADIAH 20	. JANE 155	. NANCY W. 145
GATES, ELIZABETH 103	. JOEL 97	. R.B. 316
. JOHN H. 136	. MARTIN 246,249,251,255	. R.K. 317,325
. POLLY 110	. 257	. REES 49,173,291
. RICHARD 113	. PARMALA PERRY 276	. REES B. 71,115,204,257
. WILLIAM H. 166	. PEGGY 303	. 360
GELASPY, LEUEECE 54	. POLLY PERRY 276	. REESE B. 247,249-250
GENDER, GEORGE 23	. PRUDENCE 138	. 256
JASPER 23	. SARAH 132	. ROBART 68
GENEANS, NANCY 86	. THOMAS 107	. ROBERT 41-42,188-189
GENEBENED, ESTER 87	. TYRON 175,301,303	. 191,203,208-210,214
GENT, ELEANOR 272	. WASLEY 310	. 215,217,240,259,267
. JOSIAH 272	. WESLEY 107,152,310,313	. S.L. 333
. JUSHUA 272	. WILLIAM 60	. SARAH ANN 102,123
. KUZIAH 272	GILBERT, 435	. THOMAS 85,96,168
. MARK 49,272	. JOHN 57	. 170-171,184,192-193
. OBADIAH 171,288,292	. JOSEPH 411,434	. 208-209,211,213-214
. 294,300	GILDERSLEEVE, G.S. 329	. 215,261,264,267,271
. PHEBE 135	GILES, WILLIAM B. 38	. 278
. POLLY 93	GILFIN, SALLY 122	. THOMAS H. 43,237,241
. RANSOM 161	GILL, JOSEPH 130	. 243,246,248-250,388
. SALLY 98	GILLASPEY, JAMES 52	. THOMAS J. 244
. WILLIAM 49,272	POLLEY 52	. THOMAS R. 145
GENTRY, BETTIE 330	GILLENWATER, JOSEPH 140	. THOMAS S. 242
J.W. 330	GILLESPIE, 357	. W.J. 331
GEORGE, GEORGE P. 248-249	. BARBARA 329	. W.T. 333
. HARVEY 43,208,211-212	. CALVIN 130	. WILLIAM 41,76,87
. 217,253,261	. CROCKETT P. 148	. 179-181,183,185,187

Index to Tazewell County, Virginia - Vol. #1

. 188-189,191,193,197	
. 198,200-201,212,214	
. 215,219,242,250-251	
. 252,257,261,283	
. WILLIAM B.	145
. WILLIAM L.D.	141
. WILLIAM M.	233,248-249
. 256,313,332	
. ZERILDA	140
GILLESPY,THOMAS	171
GILMER,THOMAS WALKER	38
GILMORE,JAMES H.	258
GILPIN,WILLIAM	156
GILUSPIE,NANCY	118
GININGS,ALAMANDA	89
GINNINGS,MILES	96
GIPSON,ALEXANDER	101
. ANDREW P.	104
. HENRY	108
. JOHN	64
. NATTEN	101
. REBECCEY	132
. SAMUEL T.	107
. TILDA	112
GIRFFITTS,JOHN	289
. MARY	289
. WILLIAM	289
GIRTY,SIMON	423
GISON,THOMAS	48
GIVEN,WINNY	160
GLANDON,MARY ANN	140
STEPHEN	140
GODFREY,ABSALOM	411
. ABSOLUM	55
. JULINA	97
. PEGGY S.	98
. SUSANNA	289
. THOMAS	289
GOFF,MARY ANN SUSAN	141
GOINS,WILLIAM H.	318
GOLDMAN,HENRY	20
. JACOB	19-20
. JOHN	19
GOLDSBY,	415
GOLDSMITH,	434
GOLINS,WILKINSON	113
GOLLEHEN,PETER	51
GOODEN,DAVID	217
GOODMAN,ANN SPRACHER	282
. DAVID	217
. ISAAC	131
. JOSEPH	131
. LETTIE A.	315
GOODSON,THOMAS	22
GOODWIN,BETSEY	69
. C.E.	333
. DAVID	105,234,283
. ELIZABETH	139,283
. GRACEY	86
. ISABELLA	110
. JOHN	176,271,283,287
. LOUISA M.	148

. LUCY	70
. NANCY	283
. PEGGY	80
. ROBERT	283
. SALLY	106,283
. SAMUEL D.	283
. THOMAS	283
. WILLIAM B.	259
GOODWYN,JOHN	296
GOOLDY,CLARINDA	166
GOSE,ANNE	62
. BARBARA	154
. BETSY	277
. CATHERINE	84
. CHRISTOPHER	83
. DAVID	110,216,242-243
. ELIZABETH	88
. ELIZABETH FOX	277
. EVELINE	277
. GRIZILDA	116
. ISABELLA	277
. JOHN H.	83
. MALINDA	133
. PEGGY	65
. PETER	62,75,182-183
. 187,192-193,208,211	
. 212,221,233,238,261	
. 265,301,303,413	
. PHILIP	264,294,301,303
.	306
. SARAH	106
. STEPHEN	193,251,277
.	308
. THERESSA	79
GOSS,J.L.	332
GRAHAM,	369
. AARON	143
. COSBY HARRISON	284
. JOHN	49,292,294
. JULIA A.	317
. REBECCA WITTEN	247
. ROBERT C.	126,255,262
. S.L.	157,163,165
. S.M.	333
. SAMUEL	118,324,360
. SAMUEL C.	259
. SAMUEL L.	154,160,165
.	313
. THOMAS WITTEN	294
. W.R.	324
. WILLIAM L.	137
GRANGER,ERASTUS	290,292
GRANT,JOHN VINCENT	288
GRAY,	229-230
JOHN G.	209
GRAYBEAL,	252
GRAYSON,THOMAS	12
GREEAR,T.M.	332
W.B.	331
GREEN,	219,231
. C.H.	331
. CHARLES	334

. D.	324
. DESKINS	73,99
. ELEANOR	145
. GEORGE	66
. HENRY	145
. JAMES	81
. JOHN	129,324
. MARY	105
. NANCY	164
. POLEY	64
. POLLY	66
. REES B.	145
. ROBERT	9
. T.W.	327
. THOMAS W.	330
. WILLIAM	58,413
GREENE,FANNY	144
NELSON	81
GREENUP,ELIZABETH	287
. 294,296,300,306,380	
. JOHN	52,287,294,296
.	300,306,344
. POLLY	52
. THOMAS	172-173,178,287
.	296,300,306
GREENUPS,JOHN	171
GREER,DAVID	202
GREEVER,C.W.	319,323
. CHARLES	215,236
. CHARLES H.	43,104,236
. 238-239,241,243,245	
.	258,262
. DAVID B.	245-246,249
.	252-254
. J.A.	319
. J.J.	131,155-156,164
. JOHN D.	325
. JOHN H.	262,315
. JOHN J.	246
. LETTICE C.	315
. PHILIP	68
. PHILLIP	70
. SALLIE B.	319
GREGARY,DANIEL P.	307
MARY J.	307
GREGORY,FRANCIS R.	235
. JOHN MUNFORD	38
. MARTHA T.	159
. MARY C.	138
GRENUP,SUSANNA	48
GRIEVER,JOHN	111
GRIFETHS,GEORGE	98
MARGARET	98
GRIFFEY,NANCY	68
GRIFFITES,WILLIAM	107
GRIFFITH,ABEL	49
. JOHN	265
. MARGARET	142
GRIFFITHS,METHYSELAH	19
GRIFFITS,MARGRET	52
. MARTIN	161
. SARAH J.	164

Index to Tazewell County, Virginia - Vol. #1

. WILLIAM	164
GRIFFITT,JAMES	54
MARY	50
GRIFFITTS,ALETHIA	73
. CATHERINE	64,113
. EVANS	70
. JAMES	141
. JOCAB	74
. MARGARET	139
. NANCY	66
. PHEBE	58
. RHODY	120
. SUSANNAH	62
. WILLIAM	57,184,186-187
GRIFFY,JAMES	73
MORRIS	358
GRIFITTS,RACHEL	99
GRILLS,CHRISTENA	159
. ELIZABETH	123
. ELIZABETH JANE	149
. HANNAH	298,301
. JOHN	39,72,171,298,301
.	303
GROSE,HARVEY	129
WILLIAM	112
GROSECLOSE,J.G.	326
GROSS,CATY	83
. HARRY	327
. MARY	151
. RALEIGH	103
. THOMAS	151
. TISHE	129
GRUAN,DAVID B.	107
GRUBB,GEORGE	80,297
JOSEPH D.	156
GRYMES,WILLIAM	12,21
GULLION,HUGH	24
GUTHRIE,JAMES G.	82
HACKLYT,	407
HACNEY,JANE	289
JOHN	289
HAGAR,JEREMIAH	164
POLLY	91
HAGER,ALEM	72
. CATY	66,68
. ELIZABETH	50
. JACOB	174,283
. JAMES	71
. JEREMIAH	87
. POLLY	283
. RUSSELL	133
. SARAH	283
. SQUIRE	80,283
. THURSZA	55
HAGEY,JOHN	103
HAGY,DANIEL	116
. POLLY	112
. RHODA V.	328
. W.P.	328
HALE,CHARLES A.	308
. CONROD P.	130
. E.E.	331

. ELIAS	140
. ELIAS J.	315
. ELIZABETH	138
. JOHN E.	157
. M.C.	315
. MARY E.	331
. R.A.	321
HALL,AMBROSE	172,176
.	178-179,186,188,193
.	197,211-212,233,244
.	245-246,248,251,261
.	264,304
. AMBRUS	50,182
. BENJAMIN	293
. DAVID	240
. GEORGE	217
. GEORGE P.	234,236
. ISHAM	142
. JAMES	62
. JANE	116
. JOHN	181
. JULIETT	67
. MARGARET	104
. MARY	287-288,291,293
.	301
. NANCY	48
. NEBBA	122
. PEGGY PERRY	276
. POLLY	76
. PRICILLA STUART	293
. RECCA	110
. THOMAS	244
. THOMAS K.	320
. W.I.	323
. WILLIAM	168,171
.	185-187,194-195,197
.	234,264-265,287-288
.	291,293,300-301,411
HAMILTON,ISAIAH	20
. JOHN	174
. WILLIAM	20
HAMMER,MARY MARTHA	293
MICHAEL	293
HAMMOND,NATHAN	28
HAMPTON,J.H.	318
HANCHOS,BARBARA	90
HANCY,JANE	291
JOHN	291
HAND,	199
HANKINS,	380
. ABEL	101
. CARTER	122
. CHARLOTTE	103
. CYNTHIA	147
. ELIZABETH	76,305
. HALEY	78
. J.B.	330
. JAMES	247,252,314
. JOHN	204,211,305
. JOSEPH	58,204,253,265
. LUCY	104
. M.M.	323,329

. MILTON	113,252
. MOSES	211,252-253,265
.	305
. NANCY	122
. PATTY	111
. POLLY	151
. RACHEL	72
. REBECCA	76
. ROBERT	98,105
. SALLY	57
. SUSAN	105
. WILLIAM	103,134
HANLOW,WILLIAM	18
HANNON,AUGUST EDWARD	75
EDWARD	77
HANSHEA,ELIZABETH	81
HANSHEW,BARBARY	282
. CATHERINE	282
. ELIZABETH	282
. GEMIMA	282
. JOHN	282
. SAMUEL	282
HANSLEY,	21
HANSON,D.	184
. DAVID	168-169,173,180
.	182-186,261,264,286
.	287,297,302
. G.M.	324
HARCKRIDER,REBECCA	129
HARDY,ORIE	333
W.M.	333
HARGRAVE,A.F.	318
HARKRIDER,JOHN	76,123
. LIZABETH	70
. NANCY	102
HARLESS,CHARITY	302
. HENRY	302
. PHILLIP	66,68
HARMAM,ENRY	174
HARMAN,	5,354-355,412
.	428-429,437,443
. ADAM	19-20,47,59,65
.	179,183,185,197,236
.	250,256-257,273-274
.	282,292,300
. ANNA	280
. BETTIE	314,316,329
. BUSE	216,237,265,273
. BUZE	414
. CAMPBELL	217
. CASPER	257
. CECIL	328
. CHARLES	317,323,328
. CHARLES CREIGH	259
. CHARLIE	327
. CHRISTEN	85
. CHRISTINA	128,239,247
.	269,273,282,290-291
.	293,298
. CHRISTINER	135
. DANIEL	14,47,109,124
.	137,173,176,183,188

15

Index to Tazewell County, Virginia - Vol. #1

- 197,203,216,218,234
- 240,247,250,273-274
- 287,289-290,292-293
- 297-298,303,436
- DANIEL C. 87,243
- 245-246,257,268
- DANIEL H. 249-250
- 252-256,258-259,283
- E.G.W. 312
- EDWIN H. 259
- ELEANOR 51
- ELIAS 116,172,175-178
- 186,199,265,274,359
- ELIAS C. 262
- ELIAS G.W. 244,257,281
- 311
- ELIAS V. 283
- ELIZA 167
- ELIZA JANE 247
- ELIZABETH 57,59
- ELVIRA 259
- ERASTUS G. 209,213
- 215-216,219,238,242
- 245,248,259,261,281
- ERASTUS GRANGER 84,207
- 211
- G.W. 359
- GEORGE 209,274,298,316
- 323-324,328,427-428
- GRANGER 198
- H.B. 312,320
- HEINRICH 274
- HENRY 14,47,50-51,68
- 112,125,168,171-172
- 173-175,178,181,184
- 186,193,197-198,203
- 207,212,239-241,248
- 261,265,273-274,281
- 282,287-293,298,300
- 344,359,427
- HENRY A. 135
- HENRY B. 233,237,239
- 243,245,259,281,311
- HENRY D. 138,252,259
- HENRY H. 262,266
- HENRY J. 282
- HENRY M. 136
- HESECIA 48
- HEZ 178,242
- HEZ. 201,281,298,306
- 308
- HEZ. A. 259
- HEZEKIAH 168,170-171
- 174-176,178,182,191
- 193,197-198,200,209
- 211-214,216-218,233
- 237-238,242-245,247
- 261,263-265,267,269
- 274,289-292,301
- HOWARD BANE 259
- J. NEWTON 6
- J.N. 314,316,326,329

- JACOB 344
- JAMES A. 322,325
- JAMES A.C. 328,332
- JAMES H. 256,280
- JAMES M. 268
- JAMES P. 237,268,312
- JANE 142,237,268,280
- JANE G. 281
- JESSE 293
- JOHN 237
- JOHN B. 247,249
- 252-254,256-259,280
- 309
- JOHN C. 245
- JOHN P. 156
- KIAH 198,203,216,237
- 239-240,247,252-253
- 259,281,359-360,435
- LAVICY 236
- LAVISA 59
- LAVISY 268
- LETTITIA 212
- LEVICY 273
- LOUISA 156,274,280
- LWEANNE 282
- LYDIA 287,290,303
- MALVINA 68,102
- MARGARET 268
- MARGARET L. 142
- MARGARET P. 112
- MARIAH 118
- MARIETTA 280
- MARINDA JANE 107
- MARTHA 85
- MARTHA ANN 259
- MARTHA B. 281
- MARTHA BAILEY 278
- MARTHA P. 131
- MATHIAS 71,216,237-238
- 268-269,273-274,283
- 287,290,292-293,297
- 298,300,302-303,427
- 428,436
- MATHIAS B. 237,268
- MATHIAS H. 283
- MATILDA 107,136,268
- MATTHIAS 344
- MORTON 315
- NANCY 47,65,90,97,112
- 207,273,280,282-283
- 288,290,293,297,303
- NANCY B. 97,107
- NANCY JANE 141
- NANCY N. 281
- NETTIE 328
- NETTIE E. 332
- OLIVA 259
- PEGGY 99,280
- PEGGY ANN 105
- PETER 344
- PHEBE 64,176
- PHEBY 273

- POLLY 51,73,213
- 281-282,291-292,298
- 301
- POLLY BROWN 246
- REBECCA 102,141,268
- 273
- RESSIE 316
- RHODA 99,136,274
- RHODA N. 281
- RISSA 328
- ROBERT 99,259
- RODA 54
- RUTH 281
- S.S.F. 316
- SALLY 282
- SANDY 234
- SARAH 290
- SHEFFIE 328
- SOPHEA 71
- SUSAN 72
- VALENTINE 14,24,28
- W.H. 331
- WILLIAM 149,180,214
- 216,236,265,273,280
- 359
- WILLIAM B. 133,259,283
- WILLIAM F. 168,316
- WILLIAM M. 130
- WILLIAM R. 150,155,280
- WILLIAM W. 132,248,281
- HARMON,ADAM 18
- BUSE 57
- GEORGE 18
- JACOB 18
- JANE 87
- LOVES 109
- PHEBE 51
- SARILDA 136
- VALENTINE 18,20
- HARNAN,POLLY 94
- HARPER,ASA 73
- GEORGE 164
- JAMES 103,301
- JANE E. 163
- JESSE 412
- JESSEE 250,253
- LEONARD 57,117
- MARISSA 121
- OLIVER 315
- PATTON 102
- POLLY 166
- RACHEL 120
- WILLIAM 94
- HARRIS,A.N. 118
- ABRAHAM 56
- ARDELIA 323
- ELIJAH 145
- J.J. 323
- JAMES 20,87
- JANE G. HARMAN 281
- JESSIE J. 323
- RETSEY N. 110

Index to Tazewell County, Virginia - Vol. #1

HARRISON, 441
. ADLEY 276
. ALEXANDER 43,68,103
. 209,234,239,261,276
. ANNA D. 273
. AUDLY 276
. BENJAMIN 37
. CHARLES 214
. CHARLES E. 267
. COSBY 284
. DAVID 264
. EDMUND 208
. EDWARD 241
. ELEANOR 273
. ELIZA 104
. ELIZABETH 273,284
. GUY 217,233
. GUY T. 210,215
. HANNAH 90,273,276,297
. JAMES 181,215,238-239
. 273,276,284
. JOHN 273
. JOHN C. 110,239,243
. 284
. JOSEPH 273,276,284,313
. 359
. LATITIA SANDERS 283
. MARGARET 102
. MARY 273,276
. NELLY 276
. POLLY 276,284
. REBECKA 304
. ROBERT 217
. ROBERT G. 238
. SAMUEL 273,276
. SARAH ANN 121
. THOMAS 40,48,174,177
. 192,233,261,265,273
. 276,294,297,304,313
. 412
. THOMAS C. 284
. THOMAS G. 357,359
HARRISSON,ALEXANDER 193
. 203
. CLERICA 141
. COZBI 118
. EDMON 76
. EDMOND 101
. ELEANOR 156
. ELIZABETH 84
. GEORGE T. 129
. GUY 209,214
. GUY T. 145
. HANNAH 295
. HENRY 154
. JAMES 52,130,213
. JOHN 207
. JOSEPH 49,162
. JULIAN ANN V. 119
. LEVISA 100
. NANCY 81
. RUFUS K. 138

. THOMAS 174-175,179,185
. 188,197,212,292,295
. 297
. WILLIAM 81
HARROD,JAMES 28
HARRY,ADELINE 115
. CALVIN 321
. I.H. 322
. JOHN 251,310
HARSON,GEORGE 104
. JAMES 86
. JOSEPH 111
HART, 28
. CHARLES 18
. SIMON 18
HARTLEY,THOMAS 202
HARTWELL,ANDREW 94
HARVEY,HARRIET 149
HASBURY,JAMES 147
HASELRIG,ARCH 292
HASLERIG,ARCHIBALD 293
HASTLEY,THOMAS 202
HATCH,ELIZABETH 98
. RYNDA 133
. SUSAN 124
HAUTEY, 441
HAVEN,HOWARD 277
. JOHN 277,284
. MARTHA 104,277
. MATILDA 85,277
. NANCY 277
HAVENS,ABIGAIL 119
. C.R. 333
. ELIJAH 95
. ELIZA 128
. HOWARD 136
. JOHN D. 105
. LEWIS K. 313
. MARY 99
. NANCY 93
. RHODICEN 140
. SARAH 90
HAVIN,JOHN D. 280
   PEGGY HARMAN 280
HAVINS,ELEANOR 159
   HOWARD 53,92
HAWES,DICEY 97
HAWKINS,JOHN R. 255
. MARTHA ELIZABETH 255
. WILLIAM F. 255
HAWRY,JAMES 111
HAWS,MILTON 75
HAYES,JAMES 23
HAYS,JOHN 294
   REBECKA 294
HAYTER,JAMES E. 135
HAYWOOD,SAMUEL 77
HEARN,WILLIAM 58
HEBURN,ANDREW 296
   EUNICE 296
HEDRIC,SUSANNAH 103
HEDRICK,ABIGAL 73

. ADAM 112,307
. ANGELINE 121
. ARCHIBALD 250
. ARCHIBALD T. 258-259
. BARBARA 90
. ELIZABETH M. 156
. GRANVILLE H. 145
. HENRY 99
. MARIETA 145
. OSCAR 327
. PHEBE CLARA 123
. WILLIAM 156
HELDRIDGE,LILLY 276
HELDRITH,LILLEY 62
HELLEMDOLLAR,NANCY 84
HELMANDOLLAR,JANE 92
. JOHN 116
. LIVY 159
HELMINDOLLAR,
   ELIZABETH 112
HELMS,CAROLINE 130
. JACOB 308
. MARY ANN 114
. NANCY PERRY 273
HELTON,ASA 106
HENDERSON, 27-28
. ARTHUR M. 193
. GRANVILLE 187
. RICHARD 27
. SAMUEL 28
HENDRICK,
. BETSY WHITLEY 280
. MARY WHITLEY 280
HENDRICKSON,MARK 117
HENIGAR,MATILDA 156
HENIGER,ABRAHAM 280
. ELIZABETH 280
. HARVEY 280
. ISAAC 280
. PEGGY 280
. PHILLIP 280
. SALLIE 277
. SAMUEL 280
. THOMAS 280
. WILLIAM 280
HENINGER,ANNA 279
. CATY 279
. CHARLES 279
. CHRISTOPHER 279
. HENRY 278
. JANE 279
. JOHN 278
. JOSEPH 278
. NICHOLAS 279
. PHILEMON 279
. REES 156
. SALLY 278
. SHADRACH 279
. SOLOMON 278
. WILLIAM 278-279
HENKEL,NICY 112
. POLLY 58,101

17

Index to Tazewell County, Virginia - Vol. #1

. WILLIAM   101,104-105
.   108,112-113,116,122
.   129,131,137
HENKELL,DICY   129
   WILLIAM   125
HENKLE,RANDLE   61
. SOPHIA   52
. WILLIAM   86,93
HENNEGAR,HENRY   59
HENNEGER,CATHERINE   76
. POLLY   80
. WILLIAM   208
HENNIGER,WILLIAM   210
HENNING,   30
HENRY,JOHN   344,433-434
. PATRICK   37
. R.R.   317
HENSHAW,JOHN   107
HENSLEY,CHRISLY   344
   DANIEL   303
HERBERT,WILLIAM   23-24
HERKIMER,   194
HERMAN,ERASTUS G.   251
   HEZEKIAH   172,212
HERNANDON,VERNIE   332
HERVEY,JOSHUA   66
HERVY,JOSHUA   68
HESELRIG,ARCH   293
HEYWARD,   9,11-12
HIAT,GARLAND   302
HICKMAN,ELIZABETH   139
.   314
. G.G.   362
. GEORGE G.   152
. LEVI   314
. MARGET   125
. MICHAL   101
. RUTH   120
HICKS,JOSEPH   174
. R.H.   154
. RHODA   52
. WILLIAM   116
HICTENRIDGE,MARGARET   111
HIGGENBOTHAM,JOSEPH   61
HIGGINBITHAM,
   SAMUEL W.   248
HIGGINBOTHAM,AARON   275
. AUGUSTUS   315
. BETSY   275,308
. CHARLES   54,79,275,308
. CHARLES G.   135
. CLARISSA   98
. ELEANOR LETITIA   144
. FANNY   54,59
. FRANCES   275
. GEORGE   70,275
. GRACE   283
. J.B.   321
. JAMES   110,308,413
. JAMES G.   325
. JANE   96,275
. JINNEY   69

. JOHN A.   321
. JOSEPH   275
. LAURA J.   325
. LILLY   96
. LOUISA   145
. MARGARET   104,134
. MOSES   265,275,287
. NANCY   312
. POLLY E.   104
. RACHEL   83,275
. REECE   315
. ROBERT   173,265
. SALINA J.   145
. SAMUEL M.   106
. SAMUEL W.   248-249
.   253-254,257,259
. THOMAS   86,275,283
. THOMAS J.   256,262,312
. TOBERT   291
. WILLIAM   179-180
.   189-190,275,308-309
.   413
. WILLIAM E.   92,247,262
. WILLIAM K.   51
HIGGINBOTHEM,MARY   53
HILL,A.L.   324
HILT,MATTIE T.   333
   W.E.   333
HILTON,B.H.   334
HINES,   345
HINKLE,MARY   135
. NANCY   93
. SUSANNAH   162
. W.J.   331
. WILLIAM   94,98
HITE,ISAAC   28
HIX,BUSANNAH   58
. JOSEPH   12,68
. LEVINA   58
. LUCINDA   118
. SALLY   59
HOBBS,ELENDER   124
   JAMES   50
HOGAN,DENNIS   324
HOGE,J.H.   153,162
. JOHN H.   103
. JOSEPH   288
HOILMAN,JOHN H.   153
HOLBROOK,COLBY   97
. ISAAC   82,111
. MARY   269
. RANDAL   309
. RANDOLPH   269,310
. VERTIN   103
HOLBROOKS,LOUISA   165
HOLEBROOK,RANDLE   90-91
HOLICE,JAMES   23
HOLLEY,EDMOND   126
   J.C.   331
HOLLY,C.C.   321
. EZEKIAL   251
. ROBERT   321

. WILLIAM   141,251-252
HOLMES,GEORGE F. 252,384
. GEORGE FRED   362
. GEORGE FREDERICK   254
. J.P.   333
. NELSON   314
. WILLIAM T.   163,165
HONAKER,ANDREW J.   133
. ELIZA JANE   133
. MARGARET   167
. PETER   249,252-253
. PETER C.   254,256-257
.   259,309
HOOFACRE,MICHAEL   23
HOOFMAN,WADE   87
HOOK,MICHAEL   20
HOOLBROOK,LOUISA   162
HOOPACK,GEORGE   14
HOOPAUGH,GEORGE   14
HOOPS,NANCY A.   152
. W.L.   319
. WILLIAM   152
HOOVER,ABRAHAM   24
. FELTY   24
. JOHN   24
HOPES,ROBERT   202
   SAMUEL   23
HOPKINS,   362
. GEORGE W.   216,267
. J.C.   312
. JOHN C.   123,311,360
. POLLY   149,157
HOPPIS,HENRY   298
HORD,JOSEPH   12
HORTON,DANIEL 92,180-182
.   185,187,241,243,301
.   302
. DANIEL W.   113
. JOHN   128
. LEVI   208
. LEWIS   69,207-208,210
.   213-215,217
. ROBERT   73
HOUCHINS,FLOYD   327
HOUGH,SAMUEL   304
HOUNCAL,JOHN   23
HOUNSHELL,ANDREW   320
HOWARD,EBENEZAR S.   159
HOWE,   340,419-420,426
   DANIEL   231-232
HOWELL,JOHN   76
   NANCY   113
HOWRY,WILLIAM   140
HUBBARD,WESLEY   413
HUBBLE,W.M.L.   312
HUCKABY,
   ELEANOR McGUIRE   278
HUCKALY,
   ELEANOR McGUIRE   278
HUCKLEY,
. ELLEN McGUIRE   240
. JOHUA   240

Index to Tazewell County, Virginia - Vol. #1

. JOSHUA	240	. JESSIE J.	316	. JUBEL	209-210
HUDDLE,S.G.	362	. SARAH J.	316	. JUBLE	275
HUEFF,HARRISON I.	111	JENT,JANE	129	. LEWIS	275
HUFFARD,S.N.	329	JEMIMA	79	. LOCKEY	68
HUFFORD,SAMUEL N.	330	JESEY,DAVID	150	. LORTHY	131
HUGHES,T.C.	327	JEWEL,DANIEL	132	. MARGARET	113
HUMPHREY,B.D.	332	JOB,ISAAC	12	. MARY	48
. DAVID T.	145	JOHNSON,	344,385,429-430	. MINATREE	283
. MINNIE	332	. DANIEL	129,278	. POLLY	108
HUMPHREYS,BERY	75	. DAVID	314	. RACHEL	137
HURST,CAMPBELL	106	. ELLEN	145	. REBECCA	275
. GEORGE W.	139,150	. GEORGE W.	143	. REGINNA	283
. JAMES M.	155	. HANNAH McGUIRE	278	. REJINA	90
HURT,GARLAND	92	. HUGH	104	. RHODA	83,288
. J.B.	317,325	. ISAAC	139	. RHODY	275
. JAMES F.	322	. JACKSON	98	. RUTHA	106
. JOHN M.	117	. JACOB	128	. SALLY	283
. LOUISA M.	161	. JOSEPH	38	. SENA	275
. WILLIAM D.	128	. LEVICY	142	. SOLOMON	275,298
HUSK,JAMES	52	. MAHALA	109	. WILLIAM	53,283,322
MARGARET	94	. MARY JANE	160	JONSON,DANIEL	70
HUSTON,JAMES	21	. PETER	265,381	JORDAN,J.P.	327
HUTCHENSON,JOHN	210	. RINDA	117	JOSLIN,BENJAMIN	344
HUTCHESON,ALEXANDER	298	. SARAH	105	JUSTICE,ALLEN	75,77,281
HUTON,NANCY STEEL	279	. WILLIAM C.	143	. ANN	276
HYDEN,HIRAM H.	130	JOHNSTON,	342	. ANNA	280
HYSAM	283	. CHARLES C.	193,265,267	. DANIEL	186,276,280,287
INGLES,	12,22-23,26	. CORNELIUS	190,208-209	.	301
. JOHN	16,19,24,303	. DANIEL	240,293,302-303	. ELIZABETH	55,71,276
. THOMAS	16,19	. ELIZABETH	78	.	287
. WILLIAM	19,287,289-290	. HANNAH McGUIRE	240	. GEORGE	48,280,302
.	298,318	. HUGH	98,103,214	. HENDERSON	276
INGLIS,	8	. ISAAC	94,265	. JAMES	276,287
INGOLDSBY,P.	362	. JAMES	293	. JANE	276
INGRAM,HIRAM	234	. JOHN E.	307	. JEHU	276
IRESON,JOHN F.	323	. JOHN W.	43,61,131,145	. JESSE	276
R.H.	317,325	.	243,249,313,360-361	. JESSE R.	255,262
IRWIN,MARY POLLY	290	. MARY	56	. JOAB	149,155
WILLIAM	290	. NEELY	57	. JOHN	179,236,276,280
ISAAC,ELISHA	18	. PETER	265	.	295
IVANS,MARTHA	424	. RACHEL	302-303	. MANERVY	276
THOMAS	424	. SARAH	103	. MOSES	48,280
IVINS,	426	. SQUIRE	64	. NANCY	276
MARTHA	425-426	. WILLIAM	77	. POLLY	141,150,276
IZZARD,JOHN	318	JONES,A.L.	311	. SALLY	75,276
JACKSON,	418	. ABIGAIL	127	. WILLIAM R.	149,155
. ELENDER	73	. ANDREW L.	321	. WILLIAM W.	142,150
. JAMES	82	. ARMINDA	101	KAIN,J.J.	315
. JANE	161	. CHRISTENA	112	KAINE,HENRY S.	235
. JOHN E.	318	. DORTHY	283	KANE,	26
. LUCINDA	151	. ELIZABETH	54,80,93,275	KARR,J.S.	319
. R.L.	327,330	.	311,321	KEARNS,MOSES	307
. SMITH	85	. GEORGE W.	235	KEEN,ELIZABETH	139
. WILLIAM	70	. GRANVILLE	262,310,360	. JEFFERSON	167
JACSON,IZE	132	.	362	. JOHN	139
JAMES I,	10	. HARVEY	275	. JOHN P.	158
JANES,SALLY WYNNE	272	. J.W.	333	. JONAS	161
JEFFEREY,WILLIAM	177	. JACOB	321	. JUDITH A.	161
JEFFERSON,PETER	22	. JAMES	178,182,288	. MARY	151
THOMAS	37,297,360	. JOHN	51,112,189,275	. MATHIAS	85
JENKINS,ABRAHAM	159	. JOSEPH	129	. RHODA	142
JENNINGS,ELIZABETH	100	. JUBAL	69	. RHODY	150

Index to Tazewell County, Virginia - Vol. #1

. SARAH 139,150,155	. ISABELLE 275	. 197,209,211-212,216
KELLEY, EDWARD 52	. JAMES Q. 275	. 261,263-264,277,295
KELLY, EDWARD 49-50,52	. JEAN 67	. 301,308
. GEORGE 156	. LUCINDA M. 149	. LETTAY 62
. J.A. 312	. LYDIA 275	. LETTY 277
. J.P. 312	. NANCY 275	. MALVINA JANE 143
. JAMES P. 311	. PATRICK 275	. MARGARET 277,284
. JOHN A. 249,258,311	. POLLY 64,275	. PEGGY 69
. 361	. WILLIAM P. 275	. POLLY 277,284
. WILLIAM H. 320	KINDSER, FRANKLIN 150	. S.H. 325
KENDALL,	KING WILLIAM 4TH, 229	. SAMUEL 43,214,218,237
. ELIZABETH BROWN 246	KING WILLIAM, 45	. 241,243,245,268,277
. JANE BROWN 246	KING, AMY 257	. 291,295-296,313
. SUSANAH 305	. COSBY ANN 257	LAM, JOSIAH 150,155
. TRAVIS 305	. DORCAS 126	LAMB, SAMUEL 15
KENDLE, LEWIS 214	. ELIJAH 173,175,255,272	LAMBERT, CLARASSA 149
TRAVIS 188-189,303	. 282,286,294	. DELILA 277
KENDRICK, ELIZABETH 296	. ELIZABETH 257	. GARRET P. 132
. GEORGE 301	. ELLAN 257	. GEORGE 324
. ISABELLA 72-73	. HENRY 257	. GORDON 249
. JAMES Q. 82,116,311	. ISAAC 73,272,413	. HENRY MARTHA 160
. LYDIA 82	. JAMES 344	. HIRAM D. 154
. LYDIA J. 141	. JOHN 304	. ISAAC 80
. MARY E. 136	. LOUISA 257	. ISAAC W. 167
. NANCY 93	. MARTHA 272	. J.C. 331
. P. 296	. NANCY 272	. JEMIMA 84
. PATRICK 303,305	. POLLY 282	. JEREMIAH 91,177,179
. W.P. 73	. REBECCA 136	. 213,236,241,243,246
. W.S. 72	. SUSANNAH 256-257,272	. 277,289
. WILLIAM P. 311	. 283	. JOHN 56,74,183,211,313
. WILLIAM T. 153	. THOMAS S. 104	. JOHN P. 309
KENNEDY, RANSOM 100	. W.S. 315	. JOSEPH P. 192,210
KENT, 346	. WILLIAM 120,300-301	. LEVICY 278
JACOB 22	. WILLIAM R. 165-166	. LOUISEY 112
KERR, MOSES E. 101,124	. WILLIAM W. 267	. MARTHA 101
217	KINNAMAN, MARGARET 137	. MARTHREW 118
KESKY, BETSEY 64	KINSER, DAVID 159	. MARY 130,313
KID, ELIAS 50	. MARY 322	. MARY M. 150,157
KIDD, ELIJAH 55,177,308	. T.H. 322	. MILTON 236
. ELISHA 84	KIRK, DELILA 92	. NANCY 60,134,163,165
. GEORGE 80	. MARGARET BROOKS 246	. 278
. HENRY C. 308	. 279	. PHILIP 120,186,191,193
. JULIA 137	KISER, H.M. 322	. 197-198,201,208-209
. LARKIN 173,293,298	N.W. 330	. 211,233,261,269,278
. LARKIN S. 54	KITTZ, JOHN 154	. 288
. RINDA 86	KNEEL, CATY 86	. REBECCA 83
. WILLIAM 133,171,298	. JAMES 86	. REBECKAH 82
KIMBERLING, 298	. LINCY 96	. RHODA 269
MICHAEL 22	KNOT, PATTY 50	. RICHARD 56-57,66
KIMBROUGH, ISABELLA 62	KNUCKLES, JENNY 67	. SALLY 57,59,269
KINDER, JACOB 23	WILLIAM 67	. 277-278
. JESSE 118	KWASS, NORMAN 327	. SAMUEL 82
. LUCINDA 167	LAIN, JOHN 298	. SARAH 151
. MELINDA 148	MARGARET 298	. SELAH 163
. PETER 19,289	LAIRD, CORNELIUS 277,284	. SOLOMON 91
. REES T. 159	. ELIZABETH 277,284,295	. STEPHEN 149,177
. TEELY 159	. 301	. THOMAS K. 118,151,153
KINDLE, JESSE 91	. J.R. 325	. 262
. MAY H. 86	. J.W. 325	. THOMAS P. 257
. SUSANAH H. 92	. JANE 277	. WILLIAM T. 137
KINDRICK, ELIZABETH 73	. JOHN 177,179,181-182	LAMIE, ANDREW 15
. 275	. 184,186,191-193,195	. JOHN L. 332

Index to Tazewell County, Virginia - Vol. #1

. SAMUEL	15	. ROBERT	324	. JANE	273,293
LAMME,SAMUEL	15	. SUSANNA	111	. JOHN	248
LAMMIE,SAMUEL	15	. THOMAS	94	. JOHN M.	243,246
LANDENHAVN,NANCY	112	. TIMOTHY	117	. MARK T.	323
LANDON,G.H.	329	. WILLIAM	94,114,143	. MARKE T.	99
LANE,JOHN	18	LEWIS,	10,13	. MARTHA	128
. SAMUEL	85	. ANDREW	12,355	. MARY	135,273
. SARY	128	. BENJAMIN	241	. MILLEY	143
LANGHRY,JOHN	177	. GRANVILLE	245	. MILTON L.	234
LANWELL,WILLIAM	70	. HARMAN	126	. NANCY	104,114
LARCH,MATHIAS	20	. JAMES J.	163	. PATTON J.	144,322
LARD,JINNEY	58	. JAMES M.	118	. POLLY	273
JOHN	176	. JOHN	80,158	. RACHEL	64,300
LARID,JOHN	217	. LEWISA	279	. REBECHA	100
LASLEY,JOHN	186,264-265	. LOUISA	158	. SALLY	59
.	296,301,304,306	. NICHOLAS	14	. SARAH	273
. MARTHA	304	. PHEBY	48	. SARH ANN	121
. ROBERT	297	. RACHEL McGUIRE	240,278	. WILLIAM	273,291,293
. RUTH	56	. SALLY HENINGER	278	.	300
LASLY,JOHN	412	. WILLIAM	278,287	LOCKHEART,JAMES	173
LATHAM,ROBERT	248	. ZACHARIAH	9	. JOHN M.	70
LAUGHRY,JOHN	177	LEWISES,JOHN	158	. MILTON	99
LAUSON,BETSY	294	LINAM,ANDREW	20	. SCYNTHIA	117
JOHN	294	LINCUS,WILLIAM P.	162	LOGAN,JAMES V.	119
LAWSON,JOHN	293	LINDIMOED,ELIZABETH	113	. JOHN B.	133-135
. MARY JANE	152	LINKOUS,H.P.	330	.	142-143,145
. MATILDA	134	. J.R.	330	LONG,J.E.	319
. PLEASANT M.	134	. M.B.	315	WILLIAM	195
. R.M.	318,325	. MARTHA J.	315	LOONEY,ABSALOM	344,354
. S.W.	319	. MARY J.	330	. CATHERINE	143
. W.W.	319	LINN,VIRGINIA	120	. ELIZABETH	128,166
LAYNE,BENJAMIN	118	LINSEN,ELIZABETH	84	. HENRY	166
LAZEWEL,WILLIAM	58	LIRM,ELIZABETH	160	. JOSEPH	115,119,121,124
LEARD,MARY	81	LITTLE,THOMAS	53	.	129,132,138,143,151
LEATHCO,W.M.	333	LITTS,JOHN	102	.	158,162,243,251,261
LEDFORD,	19	LITZ,ELIZABETH S.	156	. MARY	158
LEE,	195,204,352	. JOHN	216	. ROBERT	243
. ELIZABETH	96	. PETER	208,216	. SALLY	128
. HENRY	37	LOCHARD,ASEBY	163	. THOMAS	18
LEECE,THOMAS	315	BIRD W.P.	163	LOONY,ELIZABETH	164
LEEPER,WILLIAM	20	LOCHART,	320	. HENRY	164
LEESE,THOMAS	315	. BIRD	163	. JOHN	160
LEFTWICH,WILLIAM	23	. MILTON	163	. JOSEPH	108,111,114
LEFTWICK,ISAAC	216	. P.J.	322	. SYNTHA	160
LEINDAMOOD, POLLY	145	LOCKART,CHARITY	49	LORTON,ISRAEL	18-19
LEOPOLD 1ST,	254	. DANIEL	49	LOUTHAN,FRANCIS	156
LESLEY,JOHN	179,290,305	. RACHEL	49	LOUTHEN,HENRY	100
WILLIAM	290	LOCKERD,BIRD	48	LOUTHER,JOHN	100
LESTER,BRESEY	105	LOCKHARD,BIRD	135	LOUTHIAN,JOHN	105
. CATHARINE	147	LOCKHART,	320	LOVE,	17
. CINTHA	114	. ANDREW	273	PHILIP	12,22
. E.W.	324	. BIRD	96,163,234,241	LOVELADY,THOMAS	23
. ELIHU	107	.	244,261,264	LOW,BENNYON	124
. HARVEY	78	. BIRD J.	323	. CALVIN	108
. J.H.	324	. CAROLINE	322	. LUTHER	112
. J.T.	324	. DANIEL	89,273	. STEPHEN	62
. JAMES C.	135	. ELIJAH	145	LOWDER,DAVID	156
. JOHN G.	324	. ELIZABETH	82	. ELIZABETH	112
. JOHN V.	151	. EMANUEL	83	. NANCY	97
. MARTHA	120,132	. GEORGE W.	113,311	. SARAH ANN	137
. PALUY	156	. JAMES	49,100,171,177	LUKE,CHLOE	304
. POLLY	121,154	.	273,287	. DAVID	304

Index to Tazewell County, Virginia - Vol. #1

Name	Page
. SUSANNA	68
LUKIS, JOHN	21
LURSTER, HANNAH	101
LUSK,	435
. ABRAHAM	288
. ABSOLUM	61
. BENJAMIN	87,124
. CHARLES	55
. CHLOE	293
. DAVID	233,293,297,411
.	413
. ELI	61
. ELIZABETH	67,83
. FLOYD	149
. JOHN C.	64
. NANCY	79
. PEGGY	74
. POLLY	51,74
. RUTH	69
. SAMUEL	48,177,180-181
.	183,187,190,265,289
.	411,434
. SUSANNAH	66
. WILLIAM	51
LUSLEY, ROBERT	411
LUSTER, ABERH.	143
. HENRY	295
. ISAAC	109
. JAMES	98
. JOHN	239,242
. LINSEY	112
. MICHAEL	128
. PATSEY	77
. POLLY	64,109
. RUTH	143
. RUTHY	51
. SARAH	109
. SOPHIA	115
. THOMAS	108
. WILLIAM	51,154
LUTTRELL,	28
LYNCH, D.W.	326
LYON, HUMBERSTON	18
. HUMBERTSON	20
. STEVEN	20
. WILLIAM	75
LYTHE, JOHN	28
LaSALLE,	407
MADISON,	21
ELIZABETH	305
MAEEIL, EDWARD	158
MAEEL, EDWAR	158
MAFFIT,	344
MAHONEY, ARCHIBALD	295
BENJAMINE PORTER	287
MAHOOD, ALEXANDER	254,257
.	259
. JAMES	214,216
. POLLY C.	164
MAHOON, ANGELINE	131
CYNTHIA ANN	131
MAIES, JAMES	20
MALONEY, ARCHER	412
. ARCHIBALD	205-206,244
.	252,254
. JOHN	244
. MARY	50,244
. RACHEL	244,252
MALONY, ARCHIBALD	279
. JOHN	279
. MARY	279
. RACHEL	279
MALORY, JAMES	96
MALOY, ABEL	100
DABNEY C.	104
MANN,	44,346
MARCUM, ELIZAY	142
MARES, WILLIAM	100
MARION,	219
MARLOW, ALLEN	295
JANE	295
MARRISSON, EPHRAM	71
MARRS,	411
. BETSY	284
. CHRISTOPHER	174,288
.	305
. ELIZABETH	159,288
. HENRY	170-171,284,288
. HENRY H.	152
. JAMES	55,230-231
. JANE	110,284
. JOHN	284
. JOHN B.	122
. LOUISA	320
. LOUISA JANE	158
. MARGART	284
. MARY	305
. MAXWELL	284
. NANCY	105
. OLIVA	109
. POLLY	284
. REBECCA	75
. ROBERT	284
. S.E.	329
. SALLY	284
. SAMUEL	153,344
. SARAH M.	163
. THOMAS	127
. WILLIAM	284,320
MARS, H.W.	307
. HENRY H.	319
. JAMES	163,310
. JOHN	104
. MAXWELL	64
. R.W.	307
. SARAH	67
. WESLEY W.	167
MARSHAL, JAMES	138
WILLIAM	151
MARSHALL, MARY	159
MARTAIN, BETSEY	73
MARTIN,	24,433
. BARBARY ANN	143
. BROOKS	127
. ELIZABETH	162
. ELIZABETH SUSAN	116
. JAMES	411
. JAMES A.	145
. JOHN	269
. JOSEPH	27,344
. LOUISA	141
. MARGARET	269
. MARY	137
. MATILDA	129
. NANCY	82
. ROBERT	162
. SUSANNAH	269
. WILLIAM	311
MASON, JOHN	19
. JOHN Y.	36
. MARY	52
MASTIN, THOMAS	221
	223-224,226-229
MASTON, THOMAS	345
MATENEE, ELIZABETH	82
MATENLE, NANCY	106
MATENLEE, ABIGALE	85
. CHARLES	85
. MARGRET	85
MATENLER, CHARLES	78
WILLIAM	85
MATHENA, F.J.	331
JOHN A.	331
MATHENY, JAMES	93
JOHN	99
MATHEWS, C.W.	334
. RICHARD P.	239
. THOMAS	145
MATINGLEE, JEAN	70
MATINLEE, CHARITY	85
MATNEY, DANIEL	255
. DAVID	254
. JEFFERSON	123,243
.	245-246,248-249,253
.	254,259
. JINNEY	73
. NANCY	119
. PRICEY	151
. WALTER	128,147
MATTHEWS, C.W.	328
	332-333
MATTINGLEY, BROOKS	193
MATTINGLY, MARY	61
WALTER	296,303
MAXEY, B.P.	321
MAXFEEL, NANCY	48
MAXWELL,	381,421
. ANNA	286
. AUDLEY	263
. CAMPBELL	69
. EDLEY	91,171,173,192
.	286
. EDLEY C.	99
. ELIZABETH	50,274
. ELIZABETH JANE	154
. J.W.	319

Index to Tazewell County, Virginia - Vol. #1

. JAMES 24,168,175-176	MILAM,ADAM 48	. CORNELIA 107
. 221,223-224,226-227	. ANDREW 115	. JOHN 287,291,304
. 228-229,263-265,273	. CHARITY 153	. LYDIA 100,151
. 274,290,294,303,309	. CHRISTENA 50	. MALINDA 145
. JANE 75,77,273-274,290	. CHRISTINAA 115	. OWEN 151
. JANE W. 105	. EDWARD 184	. SUSANNAH 82
. JANE WHITLEY 280	. ELIZABETH 88	. THOMAS 51,274
. JEAN 51	. HENRY 115	. THOMAS HARVEY 81
. JENNY 64,290	. JAMES 53,184,186,215	. WILLIAM 274
. JOHN 51,172,179,274	. JANE 115	. WILLIAM E. 322
. 411	. JOHN 58,197	MITCHEM,NANCY 132
. MARGARET 113,274	. LEVISEY 69	THOMAS 135
. MARY 274	. LEWIS 103,184,188,288	MITCHUM,ELIJAH 122
. NANCY 274	. 292,297	. SARY 120
. PEGGY 71	. MARGARET 126	. SUSY 120
. REBEAH 53	. MARTHA 143	. ZIBA 56
. ROBERT 53,274,304	. MOLLEY 292	MNANCY 291
. SALLY 84,109	. NANCY 97	MOBER,JOHN 196
. SUSANNAH 151	. NANCY HARMAN 47,273	MOFFIT, 423,435
. THOMAS 344,411,437	. POLLY 105	MOLLERY,DANIEL A. 152
. WILLIAM 49-50,184,274	. SOLOMON 47,289	MOLLOY,NANCY W. 92
. WILLIAM H. 259	MILEM,MARGARET DAVIS 284	MONCY,JANE 166
. WILLIAM HENRY 361,382	MILES, 312	MONETTE, 8,13
. WILLIAM M. 92	MILLAR,PATSEY 68	MONROE,JAMES 37,175
. WILLIAM P. 129	MILLARD,EMBLY 49	MONTAGUE,ROBERT 250
MAY,A.J. 318,324	MILLER,ELLIN 79	ROBERT R. 116
. H.T. 317	. HANNAH 78	MONTGOMERY, 17
. HENRY 136,314	. HENRY W. 114	. ALEXANDER 24
. MARY M. 324	. JAMES 20	. JAMES 18,23
. RHODA 314	. JANE 83	. JOHN 23-24,75,221
MAYS,G.W. 330	. JOHN 20	. ROBERT 23
. J.J. 307	. MELINDA 119	. SAMUEL 20
. SARAH E. 330	. N.P. 331	. W.A. 332
MEADOWS,FLOYD G. 123	. PATSEY 69	. WILLIAM 89
. LARKIN 113	. ROBERT 20	MONUTS,SARAH 147
. POLLY 81	. SAMUEL A. 132	MOODY,SAMUEL 22
. SAMUEL 164	. WILLIAM 20	MOONEY,JOSHUA S. 97
MEARIWEATHER, 195	MILLNER,H. 327	MOORE, 425
MEDOWS,LUCINDA 75	MOLLIE 327	. ANDREW P. 115,310
MEEK,ELIZA JANE 100	MILLS,DAVID 87,281	. ATTILLIA 282
. JAMES 208,215-216,220	HUGH 21	. CHRISTINA 282
. 235,240,306	MILNER,H. 327	. CYNTHIA 282
MEGUIER,WILLIAM 298	MILTON, 358	. ELIZA JANE 161
MELONEY,ARCHIBALD 295	MILUM,SOLOMON 303	. ELIZABETH 103
. 304	MINAR,ARCHIBALD 154	. ENOS 177
. ESTHER 304	MINTER,VIRGINIA B. 135	. ISAAC A. 140
. JOHN 304	MIRES,JACOB 20	. J. 56
MELONY,ARCHIBALD 72	MITCHAM,JEDEDIAH 59	. JAMES 124,171,263,265
MENTOSH,RACHEL 57	MITCHEL,CHARLES 97	. 295,297,344,412,419
MERIWEATHER, 195	. CHARTER 122	. 420,424,426
MERIWETHER,DAVID 22	. JAMES 132	. JAMES H. 93,247,262
THOMAS 22	. JOHN 57	. 281,309
MESSERSMITH,ANDREW 305	. LAVILA 134	. JANE 161,281,425-426
MESSICK,GEORGE W. 82,215	. LYDIA 134	. JANE S. 93
. 218,261	. MARTHA 131	. JEPHTA F. 179
METCALF,O.A. 316	. NANCY 58,94	. JOHN 302,425-426
MICHAM,REBECCA 278	. PERMILLA 65	. JOHN S. 97,167
MICHEL,MOSES 124	. REBECCAH 57	. JOSEPH 47,53-54,56,59
MICHELL,POLLY 103	MITCHELL,	. 75,169,173-174,178
MICHEN,JOHNNY 331	. AMES THOMPSON 287	. 241,252,263,282,297
MICHIE,THOMAS J. 207	. CHARLES 258,309	. 298,300,304,424
MICHUM,FRANCIS 115	. CHARTER 314	. JOSEPH A. 90,309-310

23

Index to Tazewell County, Virginia - Vol. #1

. LAVENA W. 157
. MARGARET 425
. MARTHA 282
. MARTHA P. 90
. MARY KEZIA 282
. MARY R. 157
. NANCY 282,295,297,310
. PATSEY P. 69
. PEGGY 425
. PEGGY WHITLEY 280
. POLLEY B. 83
. POLLY 282,423-426
. POLLY B. 85
. REBECCA 425
. RHODA 140
. SAMA 69
. SAMUEL LYCURGESS 282
. SARAH CHRISTINA 282
. SUSAN 75-76
. SUSANNAH 51
. THODA 282
. WILLIAM 28,94,419,425
. WILLIAM T. 84,91,122
. 218,261,310
MOORS,FRANCILLO M. 122
MOR,JAMES 48
MORAN,CHARLOTTE 165
MORE,AMANDA M. 135
ANDREW 132
MORGAN, 204-205
. JOHN 23
. NANCY 51
. SAMUEL 50
. THOMAS 49
MORON,CHARLOTTE 162
MORRIS, 359,397
ROBERT 242
MORROW, 169
MORTON,JAMES W. 254,312
. MARGARET 321
. RHODA J. 140
. WILLIAM B. 321
. WILLIAM T. 151
MOSER,ADREN 18
MOSS,B.R. 325
. BARBARA J. 319
. GEORGE 325
. HERRMAN LEOPOLD 255
. HERRMANN LEOPOLD 254
. J.S. 319
MREED,SARAH 163
MULINGBURG, 195
MULLENS,WILLIAM 163
MULLIN,AMY 326
. AUSTIN 308
. G.M. 326
MULLINS,BENJAMIN 122
. DORCAS 132
. MARGARET 158
. POLLY 90
. THOMAS 150,153,155,158
. 163,165-167

. THOMAS M. 141-142
. WILLIAM 117,165
MUNCEY,SAMUEL 293
W. 59
MUNCY,DAVID 252
. ELENOR 113
. ELIZABETH 48
. JANE 167
. JUDGEZA 102
. MARGARET 109
. MOSES 137
. THOMAS 141
MURPHY,EUELL S. 308
. HERNDON 166
. JOHN 157
. SAMUEL H. 308
. ZILLA 156
MURRY,LAWRENCE 185
M. 317
MUSE,NANCY PERRY 276
RICHARD 295
MUSTARD,ELISHA 234
MYARS,CATHERINA 90
LEONARD 145
MYERS,ANTHONY 141
. EMELY 164
. GRANVILLE H.B. 118
. JACOB 131
. JAMES T. 158
. JEFFERSON I. 117
. LOUISA 126
. MARY 84,92
. WILLIAM 327
McADAM,SAMUEL 23
McAFEE,GEORGE 22
WILLIAM 24
McBROOM,HENRY 173
. POLLY 48
. WILLIAM 175
McBROWN,JAMES 134
McCABE,JAMES 383
McCALL,C.O. 324
. EXIE 326
. GEORGE R. 326
. T.E. 329
McCAMANT,SAMUEL 42
McCANTOSH,GEORGE 61
. REBECAH 59
. SALLY 58
McCARTHY,JAMES 23
McCARTY, 361
CALVIN M. 255-256
McCENVILLE,JOHN 121
McCLAA,JOHN T. 109
McCLANAHAN,ALEXANDER 251
McCLANNAHAN,
ALEXANDER 138
McCLAUGHERTY,
NELSON H. 320
McCLURE,JOHN 178
McCOMAS,DAVID 41-42,265
. 267

. JAMES 67
. REBECCA BAILEY 278
McCOMMAS,DAVID 193
JAMES 197
McCORKLE,M.C. 329
RHODA 329
McCORMICK,SAMUEL 118
McCOY,SAMUEL 48
WALTER 302-303
McCRERY,JAMES 94
McDANIEL,JACOB 103
McDILDA,KATE 332
McDONALD,AMY 145
. CYRUS 157
. EDWARD 176
. GORDON 110
. JOHN C. 360,362
. LEWIS W. 110
. MARY JANE 115
. SALLY BUCHANAN 283
. WILLIAM 203,207-208
. 253,262
McDOWELL,HENRY P. 167
. 213,236,241,251
. JAMES 38,330
. MATILDA 167
McENTOSH,ANNY 274
. ELIZABETH 274
. GEORGE 274
. JOHN 274
. KATHERINE 274
. NANCY 48,274
. PEGGY 274
. POLLY 274
. RACHEL 274
. SALLY 274
McEWIN, 380
McFARLAND,JOHN 19
McFARLANE,DANIEL 289
. JAMES 289
. JOHN D. 209
. NANCY 74
McFARLIN,ROBERT 20
McFARLON,MARTHA 48
McGAUGHEY,WILLIAM 23
McGHEE,WILLIAM 23
McGLACHIN,PATRICK 76
McGLOTHLIN,MARY 111
ROBERT 113,312
McGRANAHAN,
. CYNTHIA BROWN 246
. JAMES 305
. JAMES P. 76
McGRANNAHAM,HENRY 280
McGRANNAHAN,ANNE 64
McGUIRE,
. ANALIZA 151
. ANDREW 76
. CAROLINE S. 144
. CHARLES 331
. COLENIUS 79
. CORNELIUS 73,298

Index to Tazewell County, Virginia - Vol. #1

. COSBY J. 163
. EDLEY 68
. ELEANOR 278
. ELENER D. 113
. ELIJAH 94,311,322
. ELISHA 96,234
. ELIZABETH 128
. ELIZABETH BROWN 272
. ELIZABETH CLAYPOOL 282
. ELLEN 240
. ESTER 73
. ESTHER 298
. HANNAH 240,278
. HARVEY W. 162
. J. MARION 322
. J.M. 321
. JAMES 331
. JAMES M. 322
. JASHUA 278
. JEAMES 68
. JEMIMA L. 139
. JOHN 94,124,151,240
. 278
. JOSEPH 65,272,304
. JOSHUA 61,72,240
. LINNEY S. 144
. LOUISA M. 117
. LOUISA S. 117
. LOURINDA 136
. MARY 49,278
. MATILDA 116
. NANCY 96,240,278
. NEALY 412
. NELINDA 121
. POLLY 61,98,240,278
. POLLY LOCKHART 273
. PRICILLA 278
. PRISCILLA 240
. RACHEL 240,278
. SALLY 70,116
. SARAH LOCKHART 273
. SKILLEN 80
. SQUIRE 278
. VIRGINIA 139
. WESLEY 145
. WILLIAM 49,77-78,81-82
. 85,88,94,98-99,102
. 105-106,109,113-114
. 117,120,124,128,130
. 136,139,144,147,152
. 162,165,212,240-241
. 268,272,278
McGUYER,JOHN 90
   WILLIAM 90,197,304
McHENRY,ANDREW 264
McINTOSH, 229-230
   JOHN 171,287,296
McINTYRE,DUGAL 88,95
   101,380
McKEE, 423
McKINLEY,WILLIAM 297
McKINNEY,JOSEPH 72

McKINSEY,SOPHIA 58
McKINTOSH,ELIZABETH 58
McLAUGHLIN,JACOB 65
   JOHN 232-233
McMEANES,ANNY 98
McMEANS,EDWARD 159
. ELIHU 66
. ELIJAH 162
. PBENE 105
McMILLAN,ANDREW 38
McMILLEN,ANDREW 293,302
. JANE 75,272
. JOHN 272
. MARTHA 80,272
. NANCY 89,272,302
. NANCY KING 272
. ROBERT 272
McMULLEN,ELIZA 140
   ROBERT 80
McMULLIN,BENJAMIN 137
   JAMES H. 145
McMURTRY,JOSEPH 22
McNEEL,JAMES 133
McNEELY,JAMES 58
McNEIL,JAMES 92,215,233
. 242-243
. MALCOLM 320
. MARY E. 320
McNEILL,JAMES 236
McPHAETHUS,WILLIAM 424
McPHATRIDGE,A. 362
McQUIRE,GEORGE P. 319
McTOSH,ANNE 48
McVAUGHLIN,JOHN 255
   JUDITH 255
McVEINSTER,JANE 70
McWANE,C.P. 316
   C.W. 316
NAFF, 362,380
. ISAAC B. 153
. ISAAC N. 160,163,259
. 313
NASH,JOHN T. 160
. JOSEPH 250
. JOSEPH N. 248,250
. 255-258
. MARGARET D. 145
NEAL,ALEX 314
. JOHN M. 85
. WILLIAM 39
NEALEY,JAMES 12
NEALLY,JAMES 21
NEEL,ANNA 86
. AUGUSTUS 123
. DAVID L. 149
. DAVID S. 157
. ELEANOR 133
. ELIAS H. 182,187,193
. 197
. ELIZA JANE 153
. ELIZABETH 68
. ELLENDER 190

. ESTHER 80
. HENRY P. 148
. J.W. 154
. JOHN M. 199
. JOHN W. 167
. LARKIN K. 86
. MADDISON A. 154
. MARTHA 72
. MARTHA B. HARMAN 281
. NANCY 95,269
. REBECCA 269
. RHODA HARMAN 274
. ROBER 55
. ROBERT 77,269
. TILLY 55
. WILLIAM 168-169,172
. 175-176,178-179,182
. 184-185,199,261,263
. 264,274,286,297,300
. WILLIAM E. 133,137,148
. 150,154,157-158,163
. 164-165,249,253
. WILLIAM N. 308
NEELE,JINNY 51
NEELEY,JAMES 12,22
NEELY,MARGARET 91
NEESE,W.G. 328
NEIKIRK,F.N. 313
NEIL,JAMES 92
NEILLEY,JAMES 12
NEILLY,JAMES 21
NELSON,I. 99
. ISAAC 75
. JAMES P. 84,92
. SINTHY 54
. THOMAS 37
NELY,RACHEL 109
NEWBERRY,ALLEN 213
. BETSY 213
. SAMUEL 69,75
NEWELL,JAMES 12
NEWLANE,RUFUS G. 131
NEWPORT,RICHARD 21
NEWTON,ELIZABETH 164
. J.M. 315
. SUSANNAH 156
. WILLIAM 49,303
NICEWONDER,ELIZABETH 136
NICHOLAS,WILSON CARY 38
. 290
NIELY,SAMUEL 19
NOBLE,ERASMUS 12
NORRIS,ROBERT 20
NORWD,ELIJAH 73
NUCKLES,EDY 91
. ELIJAH 99
. HARDEN 91,99,310
. JENNEY 60
. JINCEY 57
. JOHN 151
. MILLY 68
. PATSEY 68

Index to Tazewell County, Virginia - Vol. #1

Name	Page(s)
. RHODA	48
NUNNELEY, JOHN	65
NUTTER, WILLIAM	83
ODAIR, JOHN	133
ODANIEL, THOMAS	82
ODANOLD, MARTHA	153
ODARE, JOHN	176
ODEAR, WILLIAM	127
ODELL, RUTH	112
ODLE, FRANCINA	126
. JOHN	110
. WILLIAM	126
ODONALD, RUTH	65
ODONNELL, ISAAC	74
OGLE, BENJAMIN	18
OGLETON, JAMES	344
OMMER, MARTHA EVANS	271
ONEEL, THOMAS	183, 188, 190, 193
ONEIL, JAMES	94
THOMAS	195, 267
ONEILL, THOMAS	197
ONEY, BARBARA	303
. BENJAMIN	49
. BENJAMINE	271
. EDWARD	271
. HEZEKIAH	179, 288, 303
. ISAAC	100
. JAMES	105, 208
. JOSEPH	51, 179, 223-229, 271, 295, 301
. KATHARINE	135
. MALINDA	113
. MARY	99, 288
. NANCY	49, 128
. POLLY	70
. REBECCA	54
. REBECKA	295
. RICHARD	173, 194, 197, 271, 345
. SALLY	122
. SARAH	139
. SARAH BROWN	272
. SQUIRE	61
. SUSANAH	301
. WILLIAM	58, 129, 271, 288, 298
. WILLIAM PATTON	128
ONY, ELISHA	163
RICHARD	184
OQUINN, B.	330
ORR, ALEXANDER	298
MARGARET	298
OSBEN, MAHALA	127
OSBORN, JAMES M.	333
OSBORNE, CYRENA	166
M.C.	317
OSBOURNE, DAVID JESSE	142
RUEL	121
OSBUN, HANAH	117
OSHLYM, DAVID JESEY	150
OUREY, JOHN	95
OUTHOCESS, JERETA EVANS	271
OUTHOUSE, GRETTA	293
PETER	293
OVERTON, JOHN	204
OWENS, ANTHONY	140
. BOYD	166
. CHRISTENER	85
. ELIZABETH	145
. HANNAH CROCKETT	279
. J.W.	333
. JAMES	110
. JOHN HENRY	284
. MARGARET PEERY	284
. MARY	297
. POLLY	295
. THOMAS	73, 265, 295, 297, 300
OWRY, GEORGE	90
PACK, GREENVILLE	147
. HARDEN	150
. HARDIN	155
PAGE, ALEXANDER	12
. JOHN	37, 47
. W.	362
PAIGN, JAMES	142
PAIN, DAVID	98, 106, 126
. OBADIAH	271
. STAPLETON	271
PAINE, OBADIAH	345
PAINTER, CHARLES	116
. SARAH	162
. W.M.	331
PANE, DAVID	77
WILLIAM	88
PARKER, JAMES	137
PARR, SUSAN	147
PARRIS, SARAH ANN ELIZA	81
PARSONS, N.C.	315
PATE, JEREMIAH	20
PATRIC, MINURVEY	132
NANCY	132
PATTEN, HENRY	230
. JANE	108
. JOHN	162
PATTERSON,	17, 231
. ERWIN	19
. HARVEY H.	124
. HENRY	71
. JAMES R.	164
. JANE	109, 124
. JOSEPH	292
. NANCY	131
. THOMAS P.	134
. WILLIAM	84, 131, 345
PATTINSON, HENRY	253
PATTON,	10, 17, 231
. A.	101-102, 105
. ARTHUR	104
. AUSTIN	88
. HENRY	297
. JAMES	9, 13, 16-17, 20
.	272
. JOHN MERCER	38
. MARTHA	297
. WILLIAM	185
PAULEY, JONATHAN	66, 68
.	101
. SKIDMORE	93
PAYNE, ANDREW	105
. CLEARY	101
. DAVID	97, 101-103, 105-107, 112, 114, 116, 118, 120, 122, 125, 127, 132-133, 135, 137-138, 141, 143, 145, 147-148, 149-150, 153-154, 161, 165, 234
. ELIS	150
. ELIZABETH	122, 130, 133
. G.W.	162, 165
. GEORGE W.	116, 122, 160, 258-259
. JAMES	122
. LEAH	97
. LINA	83
. SIMAEN	116
. SIMEON	166-167
. T.J.	329
. W.P.	329
. WILLIAM	74
PEAKE,	22
PEEREY, JAMES	24
PEERY, ANDREW	39, 175, 177, 180, 263, 298
. ANGELINE B.	133
. ARCHIBALD	55
. ATTILLIA	65
. C.H.	323
. CAROLINE H.	310
. CATEY	51
. CATHERINE	104, 284
. CLARISSA	74
. COSBY	85, 276
. CYNTHIA	276
. CYNTHIE	64
. DAVID	51, 175, 177, 179, 184, 188, 193, 197, 256, 263, 265, 300, 304
. EDWARD	318
. EDWARD T.	74, 210
. ELEANOR	69
. ELIZABETH	67, 80, 233
. ELIZABETH H.	108
. ELIZABETH PERRY	276
. ELLEANOR	280
. ELLEN	108
. EMILY	276
. EVANS	188, 306
. FRANCIS M.	312
. FRED	325
. G.	171-172
. GEORGE	53, 168-170

Index to Tazewell County, Virginia - Vol. #1

.	174-175,180,182-183	. MARY	233	. JAMES	68-69
.	189,203,261,265,276	. MARY J.	167	. JAMES F.	277
.	286-287,297-298	. MATHIAS H.	159	. JAMES P.	214
. GILBERT	256	. MATILDA	84,91	. JAMES V.	308
. GILBERT M.	147	. MAYANNA	80	PENDLETON,	44
. H.F.	276,323,359,361	. MICHAEL	274	. A.G.	267
.	382-383	. NANCY	55,97,233,268	. ALBERT G.	39,214-215
. H.G.	323	.	276	.	244
. HANNAH	274,279	. NANCY H.	118	. FRANK S.	217
. HARRIET T.	107	. OLIVA	276	. JAMES F.	216-217,267
. HARVEY G.	43,71,217	. OLIVIA	90	. JOSEPH	101
.	236-237,381	. OLIVY	55	PENNINGTON,HIRAM	79
. HARVEY GEORGE	191	. PAMELA	67	PERDEW,BETSEY	60
. HENRY F.	310	. PATSEY	54	PERDUE,CINTHA	82
. HENRY T.	145	. PEGGY	50,84,298	PERRY,ANDREW	276
. HERVEY G.	234,239,261	. PERMILIA	60	. ANGELINE	282
.	359	. PHEBY	303	. ATTILA ANN	276
. HIRAM	56	. POLLEY	51	. CLARISSA	280
. HIRAM P.	280	. POLLY	48,53,118,276	. ELIZABETH	276
. J.H.	328	. POLLY AMANDA	122	. GEORGE	55,276
. JAMEES	208	. POLLY PERRY	273	. HARVEY	273
. JAMES	48,65,172,174	. POLLY WYNN	273	. HENRY	282
.	177,179,181-182,188	. R.B.	326	. HERVEY G.	251
.	192,198-201,212,233	. REBECCA	62,80	. JAMES	273-274,278
.	263,268,270,280,298	. RICHARD	284	. JANE	276
.	303,322,411	. ROBERT	187,276	. JANE H.	159
. JAMES H.	257	. SALLY	73,233,276,286	. JOHN	53-56,58-61,66-68
. JAMES M.	91	.	289,291,300	.	69,71,74,77,83-84,86
. JANE	108,121,233,284	. SAMUEL	265,274	.	87,89-91,95,101,106
.	298	. SARAH	97,287,298,380	.	111,117,171,280,292
. JANE THOMPSON	284	. SARAH ELIZABETH	160	. JOHNATHAN	273
. JESSE	131	. SOLOMON	50,298,413	. JOSEPH	273,277,282
. JINNEY	58	. SOPHIA	70,276	. MARIAH	278
. JOHN	71-72,80,168	. THOMAS	40-41,51,62,118	. MARTHA	276
.	170-171,173,181,185	.	172,174,180-182,186	. MARTHA G.	276
.	187,189,192,197,207	.	188,200,211-212,233	. MATTY	60
.	264-265,287,293,298	.	238,246,250-253,255	. NANCY	273-274,276
.	300,303-304,321,344	.	256-257,261,263-264	. NELLY	273
.	380,412,436	.	265,276,287,292,308	. OLIVA	88
. JOHN B.	325	.	319,344,359-360,380	. PARMALA	276
. JOHN D.	138,245,438	.	382,412-413	. PARMILLEY	273
. JOHN H.	253-254	. W.E.	318	. PEGGY	276
. JOHN M.	256	. W.W.	321	. POLLY	141,273,276
. JONATHAN	67,237,277	. WHITMAN	280	. REBECCA	273,276
.	284,297,305,413	. WILLIAM	85,168,170,172	. REBECKA	48
. JOSEPH	65	.	180,185,187,192,197	. SALLY	67
. JOSEPH D.	40,186	.	203,208,210,214-215	. SAMUEL	278
. JOSHUA	60,188	.	217,233,263,276,280	. THOMAS	273,276
. JULIA	233	.	286,289,291,300,344	. WILLIAM	273,308,380
. JULIA A.	148	.	412	. WILLIAM EDWARD	412
. LETITIA	136	. WILLIAM A.	107	PERSELL,QUINTON	99
. LOUISA	110	. WILLIAM E.	152,255	PETERS,CHRISTIAN	82
. M.L.	319,323	PEFFER,SAMUEL	12	WILLIAM	73
. MARGARET	87,110,284	PELL,SAMUEL F.	194	PETERSON,JANE	49
. MARGARET R.	167	PEMBERTON,	427,430	PHELAN,	9,12
. MARGARETT	111	. MARY	286,291	PHILIPS,CHARLES	108
. MARIA	85	. RICHARD	173,286,291	PHILLIPS,HENRY	331
. MARIA LOUISA	99	.	344,429	PHIPPS,ELIZABETH	111
. MARTAIN	65	PENCE,NANCY	269	PHIPS,WILLIAM	23
. MARTHA	110,233,298	PENDLETON,ALBERT G.	219	PICKENS,	231
. MARTHA BROWN	246	.	249,267	. PHEBY	48
. MARTIN	265	. EDMUND	14	. THOMAS	293,296,304

Index to Tazewell County, Virginia - Vol. #1

PICKINGS, SARAH	303	. MARY MALONEY	244	. MARY	87
THOMAS	303	. SALLY	104	QUICKSEL, AARON	109
PIKE, NANCY	137	PREWITT, HENRY	208	. DANIEL	113
PIPER, JAMES H.	42-43	PRICE, 235,241,243,251		. ELIZABETH	163
PLEASANT, CHARLES	56	. AUGUSTINE	19	QUICKSELL, THOMAS	129
PLEASANTS, JAMES	38	. JOHN C.	236	QUINN, ABIGAIL	71
POAGE, ROBERT	24	. MICHAEL	19	. CYNTHIA WITTEN	276
POBST, H.W.	316	. WILLIAM	52	. ELEANOR WITTEN	276
PODGE, JOHN	419	PRINCE, BENJAMIN	68	. ELIZA WITTEN	276
POFF, GEORGE	144	. DAVID	151	. ISAAC 52-53,58-62	
POGUE, JOHN	344,419	. JULIA	137	. 64-65,68,71,73,76,82	
PONTIAC,	16	. WILLIAM	127	. 193,197,308	
PORTER, BENJAMINE 302-303		PRION, JOSEPH	229	. JAMES	73
. BERRYMAN	298	PRITCHETT, ROBERT	49	. WILLIAM M.P.	71
. JAMES	62	PROPHET, EDWARD	139	RABURN, JOSEPH	298
. PATRICK	23	PRUET, ARCHABALD	94	RADER, ELIZABETH	102
POSTON, FIELDEN	86	. ARCHABLE	131	. MARTHA G.	123
POTTERS, PEGGY	97	. BENJAMIN	50	. MARY	96
POWELL, 8,23-25,27		. JOHN	124,132	. THOMAS P.	234
. JOHN M.	74	. SALLY	98	. WYRINDA	123
. THOMAS	86	PRUETT, ALEXANDER	121	RAEBURN, JOSEPH	300
POWER, JAMES	60	. ELIJAH	134	RAINEY, JENE	70
. JOHN	184	. ELIZABETH	121	RAKES, SARIAH	133
. NANCEY	60	. HENRY	184,203	RAMY, BENJAMIN	49
. REBECCA	56	. HERIVY H.	139	RANDOLPH, BEVERLEY	37
POWERS, JOHN 171,176,178		. JOHN	48,411	. EDMOND	37
. 185-186,287		. JOSEPH	58,145	. PETER	265
. OLIVER	298	. LETITIA	108	. PEYTON	37
PRATER, DORCAS	120	. LURANY	144	. THOMAS MANN	38,204
. ELIZABETH	109	. LYDIA	116	RATCLIFF, J. MUNCEY	322
. GEORGE	98	. MARY MALONY	279	. JOHN	176
. J.F.	324	. MOSES	85,139	. JOHN M.	162
. JAMES	58	. PELINA	101	. NELLY	67
. JOHN	52	. RACHEL	134	. PATSEY	162
. JOHN G.	311	. REBECCA	111	. RICHARD	94,251
. NANCY	77	. RUBIN	61	. RICHARD H.	311
. SARAH	99	. SARY	134	. SHADRACK	311
PRATT, MARGARET LAIRD 277		. WILLIAM 105,284,307		RATLEF, ELIJAH	82
.	284	PRUETTE, R.W. 316,326		SHADRACH	82
. NATHANIEL	69	PRUIT, SALLY	61	RATLIFF,	73
PRESCOTT,	441	PRUITT, JOHN	174	. ABEDNEGO	129
PRESLEY, ELIZABETH	143	PUCKET, JOHN	136	. ABIGAIL	138
WILLIAM	138	RACHEL	76	. BERSHEBA	70
PRESTICE, NANCY	79	PUCKETT, HENRY	103	. BURRELL	131
PRESTON, FRANCIS	40,301	. J.R.	331	. ENIS	98
.	305	. JOHN	111	. JOHN 114,179,181,187	
. GEORGE	321	. JOSHUA	116	.	288-289
. JAMES C.	197	. MARTHA JANE	163	. LEATHEA	57
. JAMES P.	38-39	. MARY	131	. LUCINDA	147
. JOHN 297,304-305,410		. ROLLEY	319	. LYDIA	94
. MARY	304	. SALEY	131	. MATILDA	114
. MARY R.	305	. WILLIAM	116	. MESHACK	147
. MOSES	159	PUSEY, WILLIAM ALLEN	26	. NANCY	94,128
. WILLIAM 21,222,224		PYOTT, FRANK	330	. PETER	114
. 226-229,231		QUEEN MARY,	45	. POLLY	54,70
PREWATT, EASTER	97	QUEEN VICTORIA,	254	. RACHEL	105
PREWET, JOHN	93	. 256-257		. REBECCA	86
PREWETT, ALEXANDER 89,91		QUICKSALL, ELIZABETH	236	. REUBEN	105
. BENJAMIN	244	. J.	87	. RICHARD	111
. ELIZABETH	113	. JOHN	236	. SARAH	129
. JOHN 113,229,232		. JONATHAN 76,78-79,81		. SPARREL	128
. LETISHA	90	. 87,209,236		. WARD	317

28

Index to Tazewell County, Virginia - Vol. #1

Name	Page
. WILLIAM	158,162
RATLIFFE,SILAS	128
RAY,	356
. JOSEPH	11,24,436
. PRISCILLA	122
READ,JOHN W.	261
READER,SUSANNA	71
REDRICK,WILLIAM	308
ZILLAH	308
REED,	20,24
. CATHERINE DOLSBURY	283
. JACKSON	162,165
. JAMES	283
. NANCY	134,163,165
. NANCY W.	283
. THOMAS	283
. USALE	107
REEDY,	26
REEVES,GEORGE	22
REMINE,JERNACY	81
REMINES,JAMES H.	120
RENTFRO,GEORGE	18
. PETER	18
. TINKER	18
REPASS,EPHRAIM G.	256
.	257-259
. FRANCES	163
. ISAAC	123,308
. JAMES A.	148
. MARTHA	154
. MARTHA J.	130
. MARY ANN	165
. MARYAN	163
REYNOLDS,C.H.	330
. G.A.	332
. GEORGE A.	328
. JAMES	310
RHINEHART,GEORGE	276,297
. HUGH T.	276
. JOHN N.	276
. PATSEY	276
RHUDY,	
. BARBARY SPRACHER	282
. CATHERINE	156
. CHARLES T.C.	319
. JACOB	156
. JAMES E.	319
. JOHN C.	319
. JULIA ANN	156
. S.	149
. STEPHEN	131
RICE,JAMES	289
MARY	289
RICHA,JOHN	58
RICHARDS,JOHN	22
. M.	321
. POLLY	108
RICHARDSON,ACIL	73
. ANCEL	71,84-85,88
. ANCIL	69,74,76,78,81
.	87
. HANNAH	284
. IRENE	284
. JAMES	286-287
. JANE DAVIDSON	284
. JOHN	166
. MATILDA	284
. NANCY	287
. RUBEN	157
. SAMUEL	284
. WILLIAM	52
RICHEY,WILLIAM	20
RICHISON,CHRISTOPHER	139
RIDGEL,JOHN	344
RIFE,LEWIS	155
RIGHT,POLLY	59
RILEY,B. FRANK	316
. B.F.	326
. GEORGE W.	166
RIMMER,ELLA	332
. G.W.	332
. J.W.	323
RINDHEART,GEORGE	265
RINEHARD,GEORGE	289
RINEHART,BETSEY	69
. GEORGE	68,179-181,183
.	187,290,305
. JANE	82
. MATILDA	102
. PATSEY	88
. POLLY	62
RINEHEART,HUGH T.	97
RITTER,ADAM	104
. GEORGE S.	156
. JULIA ANN E.	148
. LUCRETIA	100
. MARGARET SPRACHER	282
. NANCY	70
. PETER	131
. PHEBE	131
. SALLY	156
ROARK,	408,436
. ELIZABETH	115
. JAMES	435
. JOHN	436
. SARA	49
. SARAH	291
. TIMOTHY	171,173,291
ROBBINS,BENJAMIN C.	67
ROBERSON,C.L.	331
ROBERTS,DICY	122
. ISAAC	132
. ISAIAH	119
. R.C.	121
. RICHARD	208,309
ROBERTSON,DAVID	413
. JAMES	73,202,295,302
. PEGGY	49
. POLLY	49
. SARAH	302
. WYNDHAM	38,240
ROBESON,WILLIAM	133
ROBINETT,ADDISON	106,161
. ANNA JUSTICE	280
. BETSY	280
. CATY	280
. DANIEL	213
. ELIZABETH	154,280
. HIRAM	112
. JOHN	317,325
. MICHAEL	213
. NANCY	280
. PARIS	162
. SAMUEL	163
ROBINS,ISAAC	73
ROBINSON,	19
. DAVID	264,301
. GEORGE	18
. JAMES	17,21,295
. JOHN	17
. THOMAS	17
. WILLIAM	21-22
ROBNET,MARGET	150
ROBNETT,REBECCA M.	133
SOPHIA	143
RODGERS,THOMAS	24
ROGERS,G.W.	333
. GILBERT R.	83
. SAMUEL	154
. WILLIAM I.C.	113
ROMANS,JACOB	101
ROSE,ANNA	145
. ARMSTRONG	135
. BARTLETT	255,262
. DELIAH	134
. EDWARD S.	134
. ELIZABETH	114
. JOHN	138
. JOSEPH	149,317
. LEWIS	144
. MARGARET	144
. MARY	153
. SOLOMON	137
. TABITH	116
ROSS,ALEXANDER	49
DAVID	14
RUD,JAMES M.	114
SARAH	114
RUDD,ARCHIBALD	152,159
. JOSEPH	114
. MARTHA	114
. NANCY	145
. PATIENT	130
RUDEY,CATHERINE	306
GEORGE	306
RUDY,DAVID	93
ELIZABETH	93
RUFF,LEWIS	150
RUHAR,JOHN A.	107
RUNION,CHARITY	97
. MARTHA	115
. NANCY	115
RUNNIEN,MILLY ANN	127
RUNNION,ISAAC Q.	137
POLLY	157
RUNYAN,ANNE	55

Index to Tazewell County, Virginia - Vol. #1

. BENJAMIN 51	. THOMAS W. 109	. 287-288
. CHARITY 51	. WILLIAM 19,21,23,62	. WILLIAM V. 137,140,143
. HENRY 54	. 283	. 145,155,157,166-167
RUNYON,ELIZABETH K. 99	SCAGGS, 380,435	. 309-310
. NANCY 48	. CHARLES 344	SHARP,JOHN D. 41
. SALLY 66	. HANNAH 61	SHAWVER,CHRISTOPHER 307
RUSEL,MARTHA 132	. JAMES 51,344	GEORGE W. 315
RUSSELL,JOHN 321	. JOHN 217	SHEFFEY,DANIEL 39,173
. JOHN MILLER 291	. ZACHARIAH 298	JAMES W. 238
. M.R. 321	SCHERER,JACOB 111	SHELL,A.V. 324
. MILENDA J. 166	SCISN,CHARLES 67	SHELTON,JOHN 194-195
. PEGGY 56	SCOTO,SALLY 117	SHEPHERD,JAMES 138
. TABITHA A. 166	SCOTT,B.B. 332	SHEPLEY,HANER 70
. WILLIAM 38	. BEZA 109	SHERER,JACOB 93,100
RUTHERFORD,	. ELEXANDER 95	SHERESTZ,C.M. 321
. JANE ELLEN 153	. ELIZABETH KINDRICK 275	SHERLOCK, 422-423
. JOHN 38	. ISABELLE KINDRICK 275	SHIELDS,JOHN 48
RUTHLEDGE,JAMES 80	. JOSEPH 14	SHIFELY,JOHN 292
RUTLEDGE,	. RANDOLPH 72	SHILLING,MAHALA 167
. ATTILA ANN PERRY 276	. T.M. 311	SHIPLER,MARY 85
. LIDDY THOMPSON 281	. THOMAS M. 130	SHIVELY,JOHN 48
. NANCY THOMPSON 281	SCRIVENER,DAVID 194,196	SHOEMAKER,HAMILTON 20
. ROBERT F. 86	199-200	SHORT,JOSEPH 143
. THOMAS 65	SCYSON,EMANUEL 291	T.H. 325
SADDLER,W.W. 322	SEABOLT,WILLIAM 116,307	SHORTRIDGE,ANDREW 301
SAMPLES,	SEATT,JAMES 73	. BOON 124
. MANDA MALVINIA 139	SELLARS,SAMUEL C. 49	. GEORGE 51
. STEPHEN G. 148	SENTON,JOHN 197	. HOWARD 166
SANDERS,ALLEN 319	SEVIER,VALENTINE 19	. MARTHA 124
. DAVID 189	SEXTON,JOHN 131	. PERLINA 114
. ELIZABETH 68	V.L. 333	. REBECCA BROWN 272
. JULIA F. 319	SHANNAN,JANEY 48	. ROBERT 52,143,236
. MARY 82	NANCY 48	SHRADER,BARBARA 58
. NANCY 82	SHANNON, 100	. CHARLOTIE 140
. RACHEL 118	. AGNES 276	. DANIEL 145
. REBECKAH 61	. AGNES C. 116	. HENRY 184,295
SANFLEY,ADELIA M.C. 144	. CORNELIUS 64,188	. JENNSY 90
SANSOM,BETSY 294	. CYNTHIA B. 124	. L.S. 319
JOHN 294	. ELIZABETH 114,160,276	. LUCINDA 152
SAULYERS,JACOB F. 163	. ELLY 53	. MILDRED 82
SAUNDERS,J.B. 321	. EMELY 167	. PATTON G. 316
SAWYERS,ALEXANDER 184	. FLOYD P. 115	SHREDAR,DAVID 48
. JOHN 164	. GEORGE 126	SHREWSBERRY,
. ORLENA 164	. J.B. 323	ELIZABETH BAILEY 281
SAXTON,WILLIAM 290,292	. JAMES 288	SHUFFLEBARGER,PEGGY 70
SAYERS,ALEXANDER 20-21	. JAMES W. 119,285	R.G. 325
. 233,283	. JENNY 61	SHULL,CHRISTIAN 289-290
. AUGUSTUS B. 124	. JOHN 53,57,183,186-187	. JACOB 296
. DAVID 283	. 192,413	. MARY 296
. DIANA 152	. MARGARET 276	. SARAH 289-290
. ELIZABETH 306	. MARIA 157	SIMMERMAN,AHEART 98
. JOHN 69,283	. NANCY 95,285	SIMPSON, 424-425
. JOHN T. 129	. POWELL 167	JOHN 83,425
. LETTY LAIRD 277	. REBECCA 89	SINCENTAFFY,ELIZABETH 91
. MARGARET 283	. REBECCA CUMPTON 276	MARY 99
. MOSES S. 123	. SAMUEL 264,301	SINCLAIR,CHARLES 19
. NANCY 80,283	. THOMAS 276,291	SINKFORD,BASCOMB 322,324
. ROBERT 80,291,303	. VIRGINIA 126	SINNEY,POLLY 101
. SALLY 283	. WILLIAM 41,72,83,85,88	SINSENTAFFY,JACOB 84
. SAMUEL 88,306	. 90,93,95,97,99,103	SIPERS,ELLEMSA 100
. SAMUEL D. 69	. 105,108-110,115,127	SIPIRS,SALLY 104
. SUSAN 147,283	. 129,179-181,185,276	SISEMORE,ELIZABETH 122

Index to Tazewell County, Virginia - Vol. #1

SISSON, BALDWIN L. 81	. POCA H. 327	. F.P. 312-313,362
SIX, JOHN 110	. POLLY 52,54	. FRANCIS P. 311
. MARGARET 153	. REBECCA 62	. GEORGE 318
. POLLY WHITLEY 280	. REES 325	. GEORGE W. 317-318
SIZEMORE, JOHN 131-132	. ROBERT 89	. HARRIET 312
. 134,140,143,149	. RUFUS 327	. JAMES C. 42-43,91,216
. OWEN 134	. SALLY 289	. 218,220,237,239,242
. TOBIAS 134	. SHARTON 278	. 243,248,261
SKAGGS, HENRY 12	. SHORTER 154,193	. W. 362
JAMES 18	. VENA 56	. WASHINGTON 313
SKINS, THERSSA 85	. WILLIAM 38,66,96	SPRACHER, ANN 131,282
SLADE, WILBUR 149	. 172-173,177-178,180	. BARBARY 282
SLATER, JAMES 51	. 182,185,187-190,207	. CATHERINE 282
SLAUGHTER, THOMAS 28	. 219,261,265,267,293	. CATHERINE W. 156
SLAUTER, LUCY 67	. 294-296,303,413	. GEORGE 131,246,251,282
SLOAN, BENJAMINE 293	. WILLIAM B. 112	. JACOB 282
. JAMES 171,287,297,300	SMOOT, KATE 330	. JEMIMA 113,282
. JANE 297	T.R. 330	. JOHN 282
. JANE THOMPSON 287	SMYTH, 433	. MARGARET 131,282
SLUSS, HENRY 90	. ASHVILLE H. 124	. PETER 282
. JAMES 323	. JOHN 12	. PHEBY 282
. JUNE 166	. JOSIAH 82	. STEPHEN 282
SMALL, BARNET 23	SMYTHE, 10	. WILLIAM L. 319,323
SMITH, 10,13,219	. FRANKLIN 166	SPRAKER, GEORGE 306
. ABRAHAM 157	. HAROLD 207	SPRATT, JOHN 102,121
. ALEXANDER 265	. WILLIAM 174	SPRECKER, BARBARA 93
. ANDERSON 89	SNIDER, ELIZA 101	. JACOB 100
. BRITTAIN 175	. JACOB 97	. JOHN 93
. CALEB 329	. WILLIAM 90	SPRINKLE, ELIJAH 82
. DANIEL 23	SOCRATES, 352	. LUCINDA 81
. ELEANOR JANE 91	SOLSBERRY, PHILIP 57	. TIM 112
. ELIZABETH 126,293-295	SOUTH, WOODWARD 69	. ZENO S. 307
. FRANCES 121	SOWERS, MARTIAN 122	SQUITNER, TILDA 122
. FRANCIS 39-40,172	SPARKS, J.R. 313-314	SRADER, JAMES 81
. FRANKLIN 164	. JONAS 151,326	. MARIAH 87
. GEORGE WILLIAM 37,186	. JOSHUA W. 147	. SARAH 72
. GRESSA DILLS 275	. PATSY 313	. WILLIAM 87
. HANNAH 153	. R.M. 317,325	STACY, CLINTON 142
. HAROLD 267	SPEED, 7	. MATILDA 124
. HARRIET 147	SPEER, 26	. SHADRACK 115
. HARRY 289	SPENCE, ABNER 135	. SILBY 101
. HENRY 181,238,289,329	. ALCE 124	. SUEL 138
. JACOB 126	. BARTLETT 163	. WILLIAM 119
. JAMES 131	. CATHERINE 145	STAFFORD, ABSALOM 288,294
. JAMES Q. 135	. ELIZABETH 161	. JOHN 48
. JANE 89	. JAMES 164,167	. MARGARET 269
. JOANA 59	. JAMES R. 152	. NANCY 288,294
. JOHN 9,11,17-18,21,23	. JOSHUA 149	STAIRNS,
. 51,54,142,179	. MARTHA 131	REBECCA D. DAVIS 284
. JOHN M. 323	. MARY 136	STALEY, DAVID 105
. JONATHAN 110	. WILLIAM 161	STALKNER, SAMUEL 18
. JOSEPH 52	SPENSE, BENJAMIN 117	STALMAN, WILLIAM 286
. JULIAN 115	JOHN 122	STALNAKER, 21
. LEVY 12	SPERES, WILLIAM 148	. ADAM 20
. LEWIS 313	SPOTTS, 388	. GEORGE 20
. MARGRET 89	. A.A. 311-312,359,361	. JACOB 20
. MARTHA 329	. A.H. 310	. SAMUEL 20
. MARY E. 97	. ADDISON A. 107,256,258	STAMMIX, 194
. MARY JANE 138,145	. 360	STANLEY, DELILAH 121
. NANCY 75	. C.A. 261,311	. SARAH 293,304
. PEGGY 289	. CHAPMAN A. 118,239,245	. ZACHARIAH 293,303
. PHILIP 18	. 248-249,251,253	. ZECHARIAH 304

Index to Tazewell County, Virginia - Vol. #1

Name	Page
STANLICK, SAMUEL	20
STAR, REBECCA	330
STARLING, JOHN	161
STARR, FRANCIS	297,304
JAMES	51
STASY, ELIZABETH	105
STAUNTON, JOHN	21
STCLAIR,	362
. A.	323
. ALEXANDER	257
. ANNIE	316
. GEORGE W.	316
. JOHN C.	321
. MARIAH J.	323
STEAL, GEORGE	180
STEEL, ANN ELIZA	279
. CALVIN	279
. CAROLINE	154
. CHARLOTTE	98
. CLARISSA PERRY	280
. DAVID	60
. EDMOND	105,279
. ELEANOR	279
. ELI	139
. ELIZABETH	75,78,150
.	157,279
. ELIZABETH COOK	277
. ELLENER	279
. ESTER	213
. GEORGE	75,180,214,246
.	264,279
. GEORGE W	139
. HARVEY	66,279
. JAMES	130,213
. JEREMIAH W.	128
. JOHN	70
. JULIA F.	151
. MARGARET	73
. MARINDA	164
. MARVIN	279
. MARY ANN	139
. MESHARK	109
. NANCY	73,279
. OWRY	95
. RACH	99
. RALPH	50
. REES	254,259
. RESIN R.	257
. REUBEN	74,280
. RICHARD	124,279,302
. ROBERT	139,201
. ROSINDA	162
. SAMUEL	86
. SARAH	120
. SHADERICK	94
. SHADRACH	128
. SHADRACK	279
. SHARLOTTY	279
. THOMAS	81,279
. TONY	279
. WESTLEY	279
STEELE, A.J.	321
. CORRIE	331
. DANIEL	213
. GEORGE	236,249
. H. WADE	322
. HENRY	311
. JOHN	136
. JOHN W.	98
. JULIA A.	320
. MESHICH	310-311
. MONTIVILLE	151
. RESIN R.	311
. ROBERT	320
. SALLIE	321
. SAMUEL	98,320
. SPARRELL	323
. W.B.	331
. WILLIAM	94
STEPHENS,	194
STEPHENSON, ANN ELIZA	106
. DAVID	68
. ELIZABETH BROOKS	246
. ELIZABETH C.	162
. GEORGE	79
. HANNAH	57
. HENRY	139
. HIRAM	106
. JAMES	99,113
. JANE	143
. JOHN	70,98,286
. JOHN M.	128
. MALINDA	129
. MARY	103,139
. MATHEW	49
. ROBERT J.	121,309
. SARAH	279
. THOMAS	147
. WILLIAM W.	117
STEPHENSTON, WILLIAM	93
STERLING, FREDERICK	18
STERN, FREDERICK	12,20
STEVENS, G.B.	315,332,334
. M.M.	315
. MOLLIE M.	334
STEVENSON, ANNA	134
. G.B.	321,333
. JAMES	163
. JANE	134
. JOHN	135
. MATTHEW	413
. WILLIAM	163
STEWARD, ABRAM	105
. ELIZABETH	147
. GEORGE	160
. SANDERS	107
STEWART, ROBERT	121
STILL, ABRAHAM	69,72
STILNER, MATHEW	121
STILTENER,	
. CHRISTOPHER	119
. ELIAS	119
. MAHALA	119
STILTNER, CHARLES	143
. FREDERICK	138,161,259
. MELINDA	128
. NANCY	132
. POLLY	161
. RACHEL	151
. SARAH	138
STILWELL, S.M.	72-73
. SILAS M.	267
. SILAS M.	207
. SILAS MORRE	209
STIM,	24
STINSON, JOHN	86,290
. PHEBE	290
. WILLIAM	151
STOBACH,	269
STOBAUGH, JOHN	176,265
.	289,294
. LEAH	294
STOBOUGH, PATSY	82
. PEGGY	95
. RACHEL	50
STOGWELL,	423
STOKES, JAMES	170
MARY	48
STONE, URIAH	24
STOWERS, ANDREW	84,105
.	167
. CHARLOTTE	118
. CHRISTINA	154
. ELIZABETH	93
. FRANKEY	56
. H.W.	325
. HICKMAN	111
. JOHN W.	165
. JULY A.	153
. LARKIN	60
. NANCY LAMBERT	278
. SARAH	133
. SIMMS	133
. W.	163
. W.R.	325
. WILLIAM F.	167
STPENSON, JOHN	98
STRAS,	314
. B.W.	314,317-318,329
. HATTIE	314
. JOSEPH	144,217,221,236
.	243,267,278,313,361
STRATON, CATHERINE	116
STRATTEN, WILLIAM	161
STRATTON, CHARLES	192
. ELIZABETH	145
. ISAAC	194,200,204-205
. ISAAC N.	154
. JINNEY	54
. SOLOMON	96,412
. TABITHA	145
. THOMAS	51
STRICKLER, V.T.	333
STRIDE, JOHN	20
STROTHER, WADE D.	249,313
.	361

Index to Tazewell County, Virginia - Vol. #1

STROUD, JOHN 18	. JENNY 107	. CANFIELD 289
STUART, ALEXANDER 293,298	. REBECCA 74	. CAWFIELD 298
. PHEBEY 50	SWARDER, PERMILIA 98	. CHARLES 84,215,217
. PRICILLA 293	SWARTZ, J.R. 331	. 238-239,245-246,249
STUMP, ANN 111	SWEN, EARLS G. 37	. 260,262,283
. ANNA 278	SWORD, JOHN 321	. CHARLES C. 112
. BARKLEY 90	SWRADER, HENRY 103	. ELIZABETH 159
. BENNY 278	TABB, 196	. ELIZABETH HARRISON 284
. BERRY 278	TABER, AMY 103	. FRANCES 123
. CATHERINE 90,140	. ANY 82	. GEORGE W. 333
. CATY 278	. FRANCIS 82	. JAMES 289,295,298
. CHRISTOPHER 278	. HARRISSON 115	. JANE 69,71
. CISY 150	. ISAAC P. 160	. JOHN 283,344,411,415
. CORNELIAS 58	. JAMES 103	. JOHN G. 310
. CROCKETT 125	. JESSE 81	. LETITIA S. 103
. DOLLY CROCKETT 279	. JOHN 154	. LYDIA 148
. ELENOR 64	. MARTHA L. 127	. MATILDA GEORGE 283
. ELIZABETH 111,117	. NANCY 102	. MATTIE 333
. ELLENDER 190	. NANCY PRINCE 160	. MILLEY 298
. HENRY 61,190,298	. RICHARD 82	. MILLY 283
. HERVY 56	. SALLY 57,59,102	. PHEBE 103
. JACOB 95	. WILLIAM 97,126	. POLLY 132
. L.J. 333	TABLER,	. ROBERT H. 260
. LETITIA 118	CHRISTOPHER A. 241	. SALLY 50
. LEVISEY 126	TABOR, A.P. 323	. SALLY B. 110
. LUCINDA 154	. BAZEL 197	. SARAH 298
. MARGARET 75,77	. CHARLES 149	. STEPHEN SANDERS 283
. MARY B. 158	. DANIEL 413	. SUSAN 283
. MICHAEL 75,77,85,278	. DAVID 281	. W. 201
. PEGGY 278	. ELIZABETH C. 140	. W.E. 333
. POLLY 95,307	. FANNIE 322	. WILLIAM 50,170,179,181
. RHODA 87	. FRANCIS 310	. 183-184,186-187,189
. SARIAH 133	. HARRISON 308	. 192-193,197-200,203
. SUSANNA 48	. HUGH 322	. 211-212,216,235,237
. TAZEWELL 84,278	. J.W. 322	. 238-239,261,263-264
. VICY 155	. JAMES 310	. 265,283,298
. WILLIAM 91,134,164,307	. JOHN 308	. WILLIAM S. 333
STUTLER, JOHN 24	. MARGARET 149	TAZEWELL,
SUITER, ALEXANDER 84,309	. MARY 97,310	. LITTLETON W. 346
. CATY 192	. POLLY 310	. LITTLETON WALLER 38
. GRAYILLA 74	. R.B. 313	TECUMSEH, 441
. JAMES 192	. RICHARD 310	TEEL, PETER 110
. LUCINDA J. 148	. SALATHA A. 167	TERRY, 310
. REBECCA DILLS 275	. THOMAS E. 326	. POLLEY 84
SUITOR, POLLY 89	. W.C. 322	. THOMAS 95
SULLARD, NANCY DANIEL 292	. WILLIAM 80	. WILLIAM 260
SULLENDER,	TABOUR, STEVEN 159	. WILMARTH 103
NANCY DAVIDSON 284	TAFFER, ELIZABETH 92	TESEN, MASTON 122
SUMMERFIELD, FRANCIS 19	TAFFY, MARY SINCEN 99	TEVIS, JOHN 203
SUMMERS, WILLIAM 159,323	TAILER, POLLY 108	THOMAS, 437
SURFACE, W.N. 330	TAINEY, EASTER 105	. BENJAMIN 344,436
SUTEN, EVALINA DILLS 80	TALLER, JACOB 298	. GEORGE W. 321
SUTER, CATY 190	TANETSON, REUBEN 281	. HAYNES 154
. JAMES 190	TARLTON, 412	. HENRY 91
. JANE 69	TARTER, ROBERT 330	. JOHN 19,255,262
. REBECCA 80	TATE, BENJAMIN 141	. NANCY 110
. WILLIAM 48	. JAMES C. 235-236	THOMIS, ELI 124
SUTHERS, E.J. 315	. JOHN 24	THOMPSON, 344,354,356
. JOHN H. 100,112	. NANCY 24	. 385,433
. T.F. 315	. THOMAS M. 43	. AGNES 272
SUTOR, SALLY 101	TAYLOR, 388	. ALEXANDER 274
SWADER, HENRY 99	. CAFLEY 295	. ALEXANDER H. 128

Index to Tazewell County, Virginia - Vol. #1

- ALEXANDRIA G.   96
- AMES   287
- ANDREW   171,173,286-288
-                          290-292
- ARCH   284
- ARCHIBALD   66,172-174
-      179,182,186,198,208
-      210,215,255-256,258
-      262,274,281,287,289
-                  302,326,411
- ASA   159
- CAROLINE   281
- CATHERINE SHELBY   272
- ELIZA   131,321
- ELIZABETH   73
- G.O.   326
- GEORGE   136,153,193,198
-                             208
- GEORGE ERASTUS   281
- GEORGE P.   241,243,246
- GEORGE T.   107
- GEORGE W.   99
- GEORGE WASHINGTON   274
- GEORGIA ALICE   326
- HANNY   276
- HENRY B.   284,413
- JAMES   16,39-40,100,168
-      170-171,173,176,182
-      188,190,197,230,254
-      263-264,274,284,286
-      287,292,295,300-301
-                     304-305,381
- JAMES B.   148,274,281
- JAMES C.   123
- JAMES D.   100
- JAMES DOAK   274
- JAMES P.   180,272
- JAMES W.   255
- JANE   113,129,284,287
- JANE C.   281
- JENNEY   53,61
- JOHN   21,79,81,133,168
-      171-172,179,182,193
-      198,208-209,212,250
-      251,261,264-265,267
-                  281,284,287
- JOHN M.   321
- LEVICIE S.   284
- LEVICY   64
- LEVISA   287
- LIDDY   281
- LOUISA   137,154
- LOUISA B.   135
- LYDIA   86,274,287
- MARGARET   107,272,281
- MARTHA   156,326
- MARTHY   281
- MARTHY D.   281
- MARY   148,281
- MARY E.   157
- MARY GRACE   326
- MARY JANE   161
- MARY S.   145
- MATILDA WITTEN   276
- MATTY D.   62
- MILTON   243,246,284
- MILTON W.   249,252
- MINERVA   102,284
- NANCY   80,107,281,287
- NARCISSA   121,284
- NELLY HARRISON   276
- O.B.   325
- OSCAR   328
- PEGGY   284
- POLLY   49,66,284
- RACHEL   49,274,287
- REBECAH P.   135
- REBECCA   281,287
-                        290-291
- REBECCA ELIZABETH   326
- REBECCA P.   144
- REBECCA PERRY   276
- REBECKA   287-288,292
- REES   179,181
- REES B.   40,198,276,413
- REESE   265
- S.J.   331
- SAMUEL   136
- SAMUEL H.   59
- SAMUEL J.   326,328
- STEPHEN   102
- SYMS   78
- THOMAS   284
- TRYE D.   80
- WALTER W.   121,284
- WILLIAM   21,54,71,107
-      179,187,189,198,201
-      211-212,230,236,242
-      248,257-259,261,263
-      274,281,284,287,386
- THORN,GORDON C.   116,248
-                        251,262
- MARINDA   88
- MICAJAH A.   189,293-294
-                             298
- MICAJAH ANDERSON   288
-                             300
- SUSANAH   298
- SUSANNA   189-190
-                        293-294
- SUSANNA DILLS   275
- SUSANNAH   300
- WILLIAM B.   214-215
- THORNTON,JAMES   102
- TICKLE,BENJAMIN   72
- TIFFANEY,MARY ANN   71
- TIFFANY,CHARLES   65,243
-                             251
- CHARLES F.   161,240,251
-                     255-256,310
- HUGH   218-219,229,233
-                  261,300-301,304
- MARY T.   107
- TILLER,EDWARD   323
- IRA   109
- PATSEY   77
- TILLEY,J.M.J.   331
- TODD,ANDREW   287
- BETSEY   49
- ELIZABETH   287
- GEORGE   51
- JOHN   28
- NANCY   53
- SALLY BROOKS   246
- SARAH   279
- TOLBERT,
-   PEGGY HENIGER   280
- TOLER,JAMES   58
- ZACHARIAH   53
- TOLLET,JOHN   171
- TOLLETT,JOHN   48,173,178
-      287,295-296,302-303
-                             306
- MARGARET   295-296,302
- PEGGY   287
- TOMBLIN,ROBIT   82
- TOMBLINSON,ALEXANDER   83
- ISAM   53
- TOMLINSON,DELANY   80
- ELIZABETH   68
- ISAM   412
- TOMSON,POLEY   122
- TOSH,TASKER   19
- THOMAS   19
- TOTTEN,DRUSILLA   149
- GIDEON H.   281
- HESTER AN   94
- JANE   155
- JOSEPH H.   89
- LOUISA   94
- MARINDA   115
- NANCY   126
- POLLY   58
- RUFUS   155
- TOTTON,AMOS   108,120
- HARVY   101
- TOWN,JOHN   194
- TRACY,ELIZABETH   280
- JOHN   280
- SALLY   280
- WINSTON   280
- TRAYER,C.H.   331
- TRENT,CHLOE   65
- ELIZABETH   301
- FREDERICK   301
- LINNEY   69
- POLLY   56
- TRIG,DANIEL   289
- TRIGG,ABRAHAM   38
- ALEXANDER   324
- DANIEL   287,290,298
- FLEMING   180
- JOHN   300
- JOHN I.   301
- S.L.   331
- STEPHEN   14

Index to Tazewell County, Virginia - Vol. #1

TRILLAMAN, ELIZABETH 105	. HENRY 147	. ALEXANDER 177
TROTTEN, LEVINA 57	. J.D. 165	. BENJAMIN S. 150,157
TROUT, CHRISTIAN 294-297	. JN. O.D. 166	. CHRISPY ANOS 70
ELIZABETH 297	. JOHN 147	. CHRISTINA 269
TUBLEY, THOMAS 159	. LEWIS 265	. COUNCIL 97
TURLEY, DAVID 114	. MARGARET 92	. JOHN 292
. LEVISA 110	. MARY 109	. ROBERT 168
. MARY H. 164	. PHILIP H. 111	. SAMUEL 24,168-170,174
. SAMUEL C. 309	. PHILLIP 51	. 176,178-180,261,286
. SOLOMON C. 309	. POLLY 54	. 291,297-298,300,380
. THOMAS 309	VINCELL, ANNY 64	. SUSANNAH 298,300
TURNER, SUSANNA 81	. HENRY 64,86	. THOMAS 14,16,22-23,269
TURY, DELILE 106	. JOHN 62	. THOMAS S. 71
TYLER, JOHN 37-38,182,185	. PEGGY 129	WALL, BARBARA 271
263	VINCIL, ELEANOR H. 119	. CATHERINE 271
UNDERWOOD, JESSE 152	. JOHN D. 166,260	. DAVID 271
UPHRES, BERRY 76	. SARAH AN 110	. JAMES 271
VAIL, JAMES S. 102,245	VINCILL, PHILIP 81	. JOHN 271
248,250-251,262	VINSANT, NANCY 86	. LYDIA 271
VALT, JOSEPH J. 161	VOSS, EPHRAIM 19	. MARY 271
VANCE, ELIJAH 161,243-244	WADDLE, ANN 213	. MILLY 58
. 251,262	. JAMES 213	. NANCY 58
. JAMES H. 159	. ROBERT 62	. NELLY 271
. JOHN 20,120	. WILLIAM 142	. PEGGY 271
. MARY 106	WADE, DAVID 220	. RUTH 271
. SARAH 144	WAGGONER, ADAM 269,273	. WILLIAM 174,298
. WILLIAM H. 129	. CHRISTIANA 71	WALLACE, JOHN 141
VANCOURT, PHILI[194	. DANIEL 264,269	. NANCY 301,305
VANDIKE, CATHERINE 129	. DAVID 176,269	. ROBERT 168-169,175-176
. 140	. DAVID N. 157	. 178,261,286-287,297
. ELIZABETH 151	. ELEANOR 91	. 301,305
. JAMES 51,181	. ELIAS 269	. SUSANNAH 313
. JOHN 94,98	. ELIZABETH 269	WALLEN, 27
. JOSEPH 85	. ELONOR 60	JOHN 25
. NANCY 85,127,140	. GEORGE 269	WALLER, BENJAMIN 9
. SARAH 98	. HIRAM 269	WILLIAM 9
VANDIKES, NANCY 61	. JACOB 214,269,273	WALLICE, JOHN 159
SALLY 61	. JEMIMA 68	WALLIS, JOHN 104,111,148
VANDYKE, CHARLES 304,413	. MARGARET 273	POLLY ANN 161
. CHARLOTTE 304	. NANCEY 77	WALLS, JOSEPH 413
. ISRAEL 69	. NANCY 273	. NANCY 66,68
. JAMES 304	. POLLY 273	. POLLY 51
. JOHN 304,413	. POLLY H. 90-91	. WILLIAM 176,301,305
. MILTON 102	. REBECKAH 55	WALTON, MARGARET C. 330
VANSELL, EDWARD 12	WAGONER, ADAM 274	SAMUEL 330
VAUGHAN, 9	. ELIAS 274	WARD, ADDISON 275
VAUN, WILLIAM 131	. ELIZABETH 274	. ALEX 191
VAUSE, 21-22	. GEORGE 274	. ALEXANDER 61,110,188
VAUX, 12	. HIGHRAM 274	. 413
VEEDER, P.Y. 321	. JACOB 71	. CAROLINE 158
VENCEL, LEWIS 264	. PEGGY 274	. D. 49,184
VENCIL, ELIZABETH 139	. REBECCA 274	. DAVID 39-40,49,51,53
. JANE R. 112	WAINWRIGHT, HENRY 290,292	. 168-174,184,187-188
. JOHN D. 148	WALDEN, ZACHARIAH 127	. 261,263,265,275,286
. WILLIAM 209	WALDERN, ELIZABETH 82	. 288,294,297,344,357
VENCILL, ANN ELIZA 111	WALDON, SAMUEL 95	. E.B. 312
VENIREMAN, A. 265	WALDRON, BARISSA 281	. ELEANER 162
VESS, MARY 144	. CALVIN 136	. ELEANOR 275
VESTER, ABNER H. 122	. RICE 148	. ELLENOR 288,294
VICTORIA, QUEEN 254	. SALLY BAILEY 281	. ERASTUS B. 310
256-257	. SAMUEL 281	. GEORGE 331
VINCEL, ADAM 59	WALKER, 22,305	. HARVEY 83

Index to Tazewell County, Virginia - Vol. #1

Name	Page
. HENY	89
. HIRAM	275
. HIRAM D.	214
. ISAAC	275
. JANE	68,80,275
. JANE C. THOMPSON	281
. JENNIE BELL	322
. JENNY	68
. JOHN	40-41,47,168
.	172-173,176,178,182
.	207,265,276,286,292
.	295,381,411
. JOSEPH	295
. KEZIAH	295
. LEVISA	66
. LOUISA	92
. LYDIA	79
. MARTHY D. THOMPSON	281
. MATILDA	275
. MILTON	62,198,203
. NANCY	75,275,295
. NANCY T.	104
. NANCY THOMPSON	287
. PEGGY THOMPSON	284
. PHEBE	275
. POLLY	49
. RACHEL	107
. REBECCA JANE	152
. REBECCA T.	88
. REBECKAH B.	104
. REES	64
. REESE	275
. ROBERT	58,188,265
. SAMUEL	324
. SAMUEL B.	328
. SMITH	80
. THOMAS	68
. VIRGINIA	161
. WILLIAM	22,151,179,187
.	263,265,287,290,301
.	411
. WILLIAM A.	322
WARE,E.J.	324
WARREN,BEVERLY	320,322
J.B.	321
WASHBURN,RUTH WYNNE	272
WASHINGTON,	413
WATERFORD,ADAM	191
ADOM	55
WATKINS,JOHN	325
WATSON,EADY	142
. JENNIE Y.	330
. JOAB	52
. JOHN W.C.	239
WATT,JN T.	100
WATTS,CLARISSA T.	102
. S.F.	360
. STARLING F.	127
. STERLING F.	313
. STERLING W.	361
. STIRLING F.	253
. WILLIAM I.	97,108
WAYE,	196
WAYNE,	196,199
WEAVER,J.I.	109
WEBB,ANNA	132
. ELIZABETH	113
. GEORGE	60,174,286,301
. JACOB	241,243
. MARY	98
. NANCY	147
. POLLY	78
. SUSANNA	87
. WILLIAM	344
WEEB,SRILDA	127
WEIMER,HANNAH	166
WELCH,STEPHEN S.	300
WELLE,JOSEPH	58
WHEELAN,R.V.	157
RICHARD VINCENT	307
WHELAN,	381
WHIT,MILBURN	78
WHITAKER,MARY ANN	119
THOMAS	159
WHITE,ABEDNEGO	57,264
.	288,302
. ARCHIBALD	314
. BALFOUR	324
. BETSEY	60
. BRYANT	18
. CORNELIUS	234,261
. E.G.	333
. ELIZABETH	302
. GEORGE	314
. JACOB	90
. JAMES	74,106
. JOSEPH	290
. NANCY	66,96
. PETER	153
. RICHARD	329
. SHADRACH	213,243,251
.	255,262
. SHADRACK	173
. THOMAS	281
. WILLIAM	113
. WILLIAM G.	107
WHITEN,REBECCA G.	118
WHITESCARVER,J.D.	332
JOHN D.	333-334
WHITLEY,ANDREW J.	280
. BETSY	280
. CYNTHIA	126,280
. DAVID	85,264,271-272
.	277,280,288,295,302
. DAVID R.	280
. E.L.	320
. ELIZABETH	112
. FANNEY A.	320
. GINNEY	272
. J.H.	323
. JAMES	270,280,307
. JAMES M.	94
. JANE	69,271,280
. JINNEY	272
. JOHN W.	320
. MALINDA	117
. MARGARET	97
. MARY	271,280
. MATILDA B.	129
. MATILDA HAVEN	277
. NANCY	99,119,271-272
. PAUL	48
. PEGGY	280
. POLLY	272,280
. POLLY B.	145
. ROBERT	271-272
. SALLY	272
. SARAH	271
. W.P.	318,320,323
. WESLEY P.	167
. WILLIAM	83,271-272,280
.	435
WHITMAN,	
. ELIZABETH JANE	127
. ELIZABETH P.	118
. ELLEANOR	280
. JAMES P.	112
. JOHN	280
. WILLIAM	215,280
WHITMON,JOHN	80
WHITSEL,	231
WHITT,AUDLEY	153
. CINTHY	104
. ELIZABETH	132,147,163
. EMMA	128
. GRIFFITT	303
. HANA	124
. HANNAH	301
. HENRY	101
. HEZEIKAH	213
. HEZEKIAH	168,171,198
.	208-209,212-213,250
.	261,267,301,303
. JAMES	303
. JAMES G.	147
. JAMES M.	98
. JEREMIAH	121
. JOHN BUNYON	116
. JONATHAN	78,94
. LENA	98
. MARCUS A.P.	93
. NANCY	124
. NOAH	116
. OLIVIA	109
. POLLY	89,92
. RACHEL	113,301,303
. REBECCA	69
. REBECKAH	52
. REUBEN A.	116
. RICHARD	69,79
. RODDY	124
. RUTHERFORD	295,301
. SHORNE	81
. THOMAS	121
. TIMOTHY	93
. WILLIAM	121

Index to Tazewell County, Virginia - Vol. #1

Name	Page
WHITTEN, ELEANOR C.	70
. SAMUEL	48
. SAMUEL K.	118
. WILLIAM	48
WHITTLE, S.D.	36
WIEMER, HANNAH	165
WILCOX,	204
WILDS, SALY	127
WILEE, RICHARD	148
WILEY, JOHN	69
ROBERT	52
WILLIAMS, AVEY	53
. BEVERLY	314
. CATHERINE	57
. CYRUS	270
. E.D.	210
. EVAN D.	73
. EVIN D.	208
. FELEX	103
. HARRIOT	71
. ISABELLA	85
. JOHN	186
. JOHN C.	69, 215
. JOHN W.	37
. JONATHAN	54
. JULIUS C.	270
. LOUISA B.	270
. MALVINA	82
. MARA A.	270
. MARCUS A.	270
. MARGARET	270
. NANCY	80
. PATRICK	270
. PEGGY DAVIDSON	303
. POLLY A.	65
. RACHEL	56
. REBEA	71
. SARAH	116
. SUSAN	135
. TITUS V.	270
. W.C.	317, 325
. WILLIALM	217
. WILLIAM	79, 172, 174, 177
.	179, 194, 197, 200-201
.	211-212, 261, 270
. WILLIAM G.	102, 247-248
WILLIAMSON, R.B.	330
. ROBERT	330
. T.N.	329-330
. THOMAS	330
WILLKEY, JAMES	20
WILLOUGHBY, JOHN	322
WILLS, SARAH	151
WILLSON, MARGARET	118
WILSHIRE, NATHANIEL	19
WILSON, ANNA HENINGER	279
. ARON	84
. AUDLEY H.	126
. BENJAMIN	160
. CATY HENINGER	279
. DANIEL C.	123
. EDWARD	106, 283, 309
. ELEANOR	69
. ELIZABETH M.	138
. ELLENOR CROCKETT	279
. HENRY	86
. HERVEY	112
. HUGH	172, 175, 177-178
.	265, 271, 288, 294, 413
. J.H.	332
. J.W.	326
. JAMES	67, 69, 79, 124, 198
.	203, 209, 217
. JAMES B.	234
. JESSE	176
. JOHN	76, 89, 180, 185
.	187-188, 192, 197, 203
.	210, 298
. JULEY	89
. LEAR LUCINDA	160
. NANCY	123
. NANCY ELIZABETH	145
. RACHAEL	139
. SALLY GOODWIN	283
. SAUNDERS	321
. THOMAS	19, 283
. WILLIAM	64, 99
WILTSHIRE, JOHN	21
WINGO, ELIZABETH	105
. JAMES H.	315
. JANE	85
. L.C.	316
. POLLY	129
. POLLY McGUIRE	240, 278
. RACHO	102
. SQUIRE	85
. WILLIAM	49, 240
WINNE, PHEBY	51
WINSTON, JOHN W.	314
ROBERT	140
WISE, HERVEY	128
WIT, JESSE	108
WITEN, HARVEY P.	118
WITTEN,	361-362
. CHARLES H.	321
. CINTHEA	58
. CYNTHIA	276
. ELEANOR	215, 276
. ELEANOR T.	107
. ELEANOR W.	123
. ELENOR	73
. ELIZA	71, 276
. ELIZABETH	247
. ELIZABETH M.	119
. ELIZABETH P.	126
. ELLENOR	294, 298, 302
. HARVEY P.	257, 259
. HIRAM	58, 186-188, 208
.	247
. ISOM	328
. JACOB	316
. JAMES	62, 64, 163, 169
.	171-174, 179, 212, 236
.	246, 248, 263, 276, 294
.	296, 298, 301, 306, 308
.	369, 411-412
. JAMES R.	165
. JAMES S.	201-203, 247
.	261, 307, 433
. JAMES W.	255
. JAMES W.M.	42-43, 219
.	233, 253, 256
. JANE LAIRD	277
. JANE PERRY	276
. JEREMIAH	173, 184, 286
.	288, 293-294, 296, 306
.	380
. JOHN	188, 197-198, 247
. JOHN M.	104, 245-246
.	249, 251, 254
. JULIA ANN	131
. KENAH	51
. LETTICE	295
. LETTICIE	296, 306
. LEVICIE S.	-
.	THOMPSON 284
. LINNA	276
. LINNEY	247
. LINNY	54
. MARGARET M.	130
. MARTHA J.	127
. MARY	49
. MATILDA	71, 276
. NANCY	78, 300, 307
. NELLY	289
. PHILIP	294
. POLLY G.	72
. R.W.	321, 361
. RAWLEY W.	119, 310
. REBECCA	247, 276
. REBECCA JANE	110
. REBECCA W.	116
. REBECKA	49, 294
. RUTH	294
. S.A.	330, 332
. SAMUEL	51, 172, 177-179
.	218, 220, 233-234, 238
.	248, 261, 273, 276, 300
.	307-308, 312, 369
. SAMUEL C.	186, 247, 264
.	298
. SARAH	288, 293, 380
. SUSANNAH	51
. SUSANNAH R.	159
. T.	361
. TABITHA	62, 247
. THOMAS	39, 168, 171
.	185-186, 189, 192-193
.	197-200, 203, 207-208
.	211-212, 221-229, 236
.	247-248, 250, 261, 264
.	265, 276, 288-289, 294
.	296-298, 300, 302, 307
.	343-344, 362, 385, 410
.	412
. THOMAS G.	88, 310

Index to Tazewell County, Virginia - Vol. #1

.	317-318,361	
. THOMAS W.	156,312	
. WILLIAM	171,173	
.	185-186,215,236,244	
.	247,263,276,293-294	
.	295-296,298,300,306	
.	328,380,413	
. WILLIAM H.	244	
. ZACHARIAH S.	107	
. ZECHRIAH S.	310	
WITTON,JAMES	169	
. WILLIAM	68	
WOLCOTT,ALEXANDER	304	
WOLF,ELKENAH	82	
. HANNAH	120	
. MARIE	143	
. MARY	135	
. NANCY	130	
WOLFE,MATILDA	161	
WOLFORD,ELIZABETH	50	
. GEORGE	64	
. NANCY	109	
. POLLY	86	
WOLTZ,SAMUEL	151	
WOOD,	231	
. JAMES	37	
. SAMUEL	28	
WOODRIDGE,JOHN I.	72	
WOODS,J.E.	327	
. JAMES	330	
. SAMUEL	22	
WOOLDRIDGE,SALLY	117	
WOOLMAN,JACOB	18	
WOOSLEY,HEZEKIAH	94	
. MAHALA	86	
WORKMAN,ELEANOR	70	
. JAMES	213	
. MALVINA	68	
. MARINDA	95	
. MOSE	264	
. MOSES	67,125,300	
. OBADIAH	83	
. POLLEY	83	
. RACHEL	213	
. SLRANTLE	127	
. THOMAS	50	
WORKMON,SALLY	55	
WORTMON,MOSES	48	
WRAY,JOSEPH	301	
. SUSANAH	301	
WRIGHT,	288	
. DANIEL H.	131	
. DANIEL HARMAN	281	
. ELEAN MYRINDA	281	
. ELEANOR	281	
. ELIZA	145	
. ELIZA JANE	281	
. GEORGE	281	
. GIDEON	60,269,281	
. HARVEY	281	
. HEZEKIAH	411	
. LUCINDA	281	

. MICHAEL	411	
. NANCY	57,136,281	
. NELLY	269	
. REBECCA	108,281	
. REBECCA HARMAN	273	
. REBECKA	303	
. T.P.	315	
. W.H.	332	
WYNN,	389	
. ANNA	273	
. ANNE	57	
. ANNIE E.	325	
. ELIZABETH	273	
. HENRY	273	
. JAMES	70,273,308,413	
. JANE	79	
. JANE HENINGER	279	
. JOHN	189-190,199-200	
.	207,211-212,219,238	
.	251,261,264,273,308	
.	359,382	
. JOSEPH	247,273	
. JOSEPH H.	245-247,262	
. LAVINIA	233	
. LEVIE	308	
. LEVINA	273	
. M.F.	325	
. MAGDALEN	62	
. MARTHA	109	
. MARY	101	
. MINER	273	
. MINOR	217,237,245	
. MORGAN	246,249	
. NANCY	273	
. NANCY C.	148	
. OLIVER	264,306,411	
. PEGGY	273	
. PETER	273	
. PETER E.	92,413	
. PHILIS	273	
. PHILLIS	273	
. PHYLIS	233	
. POLLY	273	
. POLLY WHITLEY	272	
. ROBERT	58,233,273	
. SALLY FOX	277	
. SALLY WHITLEY	272	
. SAMUEL	59,273,413	
. WILLIAM	233,273,344	
.	410,437-438	
. WILLIAM P.	105,246	
WYNNE,ALEANAH	288	
. ANNA	272	
. DAVID	272	
. ELIZABETH	272	
. ELKANAH	272	
. HARMAN	272	
. HARRY	272	
. HENRY	306	
. ISAIAH	272	
. JAMES	272	
. JENNEY	272	

. JOHN	55,180-184,234	
.	236,272	
. JOSEPH H.	241,243-244	
. JOSIAH	171,271-272	
. MARGARET	272	
. MARTHA	272	
. MARY	272	
. MARY WHITLEY	271	
. MINER	272	
. NANCY	272	
. OLIVER	272,293	
. ORPHEY	272	
. PEGGY	51	
. PETER	272	
. PHEBY	272	
. PHILLIS	272	
. ROBERT	56,88,90,272	
.	306	
. RUTH	272	
. SALLY	272	
. SAMUEL	272	
. SARAH WHITLEY	271	
. WILLIAM	24,171,173,272	
.	288	
. WILLIAM P.	236,242-243	
YATES,HIRAM	114	
. JAMES	114	
. JEREMIAH	324	
. JOHN	124	
. SALLY	142	
. WILLIAM	158	
YATS,WILLIAM	158	
YOCT,ADDELINE	72	
YOSE,POLLY	90	
YOST,DAVID G.	120,320	
. EUPHINIA	116	
. H.A.	362	
. HENRY	87	
. HENRY A.	258	
. JOHN	111,117,312	
. JULIA	159	
. W.O.	362	
. WILLIAM O.	127,360	
. WYLEY W.	312	
YOUNG,	357	
. ABSOLEM	265	
. ABSOLUM	61	
. CHARLES	56,175,178,184	
.	239,265,271,274,286	
.	290	
. CHARLOTTE	61	
. CINTHA	104	
. DANIEL	56,287,289,293	
. DAVID	48,54,57-59	
.	61-62,64-68,70,73,75	
.	79-80,83,86,88-89,92	
.	95-97,100,102,104,106	
.	107,110,112,114-115	
.	118,120,123,129-130	
.	135,138-139,145,152	
.	160-161,163-164,181	
.	183-184,264,274,303	

Index to Tazewell County, Virginia - Vol. #1

- . 308
- . DRURY 52
- . DUDLEY 204,274,286
- . ELIZABETH 112,290
- . 295-296
- . FANNY 92
- . HUGH 70,203
- . ISAAC 145
- . ISRAEL 274,286,290-291
- . 295,413
- . JACOB 23
- . JANE 110
- . JESSE 292
- . JESSEE 303
- . JOHN 89,156,171,239
- . 241-243,286,290,295
- . 296

- . JOHN B. 320
- . JUSTON 319
- . LEVICIE 274
- . LEVISY 291
- . LUCY 96
- . MARGARET 95,274
- . MARTHA 92
- . MARY 289,293
- . MARY ANN 114
- . MARY M. 161
- . MILLY 61
- . NANCY 96
- . NATHANIEL 49,152,264
- . 274,291,293,413
- . PLEAS 319
- . REBECCA 110
- . REBECCA EVELINE 139

- . RICHARD 97
- . ROBERT 66,197,203
- . SAM 184,327
- . SAMUEL 48,58,286,317
- . SAMUEL W. 96
- . SUSANNA 286
- . SUSANNAH 75
- . WILLIAM 92
- . WILLIAM A. 92,133
- . WILLIAM B. 118,243-244
- . 246,249,252
- . WILLIAM H. 248
- ZINN,GARRETT 19

www.ingramcontent.com/pod-product-compliance
Lightning Source LLC
Chambersburg PA
CBHW020633300426
44112CB00007B/101